AF700952

Exploring Roguelike Games

Also by the author

Bug Voyage (2017)
Someone Set Us Up The Rom, Part 1 (2017)
Someone Set Us Up The Rom, Part 2 (2017)
21 Unexpected Games to Love for the Atari VCS (2018)
Extended Play (fanzine) (2018)
Memories of Arcadia (2019)
8 Bit Obituaries (2019)
Level Up! A JRPG Creator's Handbook (2019)

Exploring Roguelike Games

John Harris

CRC Press
Taylor & Francis Group
Boca Raton London New York

CRC Press is an imprint of the
Taylor & Francis Group, an **informa** business

First edition published 2021
by CRC Press
6000 Broken Sound Parkway NW, Suite 300, Boca Raton, FL 33487-2742

and by CRC Press
2 Park Square, Milton Park, Abingdon, Oxon, OX14 4RN

© 2021 Taylor & Francis Group, LLC

CRC Press is an imprint of Taylor & Francis Group, LLC

Reasonable efforts have been made to publish reliable data and information, but the author and publisher cannot assume responsibility for the validity of all materials or the consequences of their use. The authors and publishers have attempted to trace the copyright holders of all material reproduced in this publication and apologize to copyright holders if permission to publish in this form has not been obtained. If any copyright material has not been acknowledged please write and let us know so we may rectify in any future reprint.

Except as permitted under U.S. Copyright Law, no part of this book may be reprinted, reproduced, transmitted, or utilized in any form by any electronic, mechanical, or other means, now known or hereafter invented, including photocopying, microfilming, and recording, or in any information storage or retrieval system, without written permission from the publishers.

For permission to photocopy or use material electronically from this work, access www.copyright.com or contact the Copyright Clearance Center, Inc. (CCC), 222 Rosewood Drive, Danvers, MA 01923, 978-750-8400. For works that are not available on CCC please contact mpkbookspermissions@tandf.co.uk

Trademark notice: Product or corporate names may be trademarks or registered trademarks, and are used only for identification and explanation without intent to infringe.

Library of Congress Cataloging-in-Publication Data
A catalog record for this book has been requested

ISBN: 978-0-367-51372-6 (hbk)
ISBN: 978-0-367-48259-6 (pbk)
ISBN: 978-1-003-05357-6 (ebk)

Typeset in Minion Pro
by Apex CoVantage, LLC

Thanks to:

Simon Carless, former publisher and editor of GameSetWatch

Matt Matthews, friend and mathematician

Glenn Wichmann, Andrew Doull, Darren Gray, Pasi "paxed" Kallinen, Tarn Adams, Rodain Joubert, Rich Carlson, Robin Bandy, Daniel Ploog, Greg Johnson, Jeff Lait, Anna Anthropy, Dr. Julia Griffin and everyone who has ever taken up a parenthesis in battle

And Zeno Rogue, for corrections to a previous edition

—

In memory of:

Robert Pietkivitch, creator of XRogue

Noah Morgan, creator of Larn

Izchak Miller, major contributor to NetHack

Phosphorous, artist and illustrator of the first two Strange Adventures in Infinite Space games

They may each have passed but once, but their work will kill players forever

Contents

Section II Theory

Section III NetHack

Section VI Mystery Dungeon

Section VII Various Roguelikes

Section VV Miscellaneous

Notes on the Text

These chapters were written over a long period, with some sizable gaps mixed in. They cover a wide array of aspects of roguelike gaming, sometimes talking to experts, sometimes to novices and sometimes to developers. I've tried to arrange the pieces here in an order so that one can get started reading from the beginning, but this isn't really a book intended to be read start to finish.

Taking my lead from Martin Gardner and his legendary *Mathematical Games* column from *Scientific American* magazine, I went over subjects more-or-less randomly, and so should you read the material here you think you'll find more interesting. There are hundreds of pages, so there should be something here, somewhere! Once you're more conversant with the genre and have played a few (many of the games named here are open source, and most are either free or of very low cost), come back and maybe you'll be more interested in the obscurer topics.

(On Martin Garner and *Mathematical Games*: seriously, you should look that up, or seek out the huge compilation *The Colossal Book of Mathematics*. It is terrific.)

When the writing of these pieces began, the usage of *he* and *him* as the default pronouns in English was still prevalent. I have not engaged in much wholesale changing of them for this edition, but if they were written today, I would use *they* and *them* instead. Languages are supposed to change over time, and it is right that they be adjusted to reflect current norms.

About the Author

John Harris has been bumping around the internet for over 20 years. In addition to writing the columns @Play and Pixel Journeys for GameSetWatch and developer interviews for Gamasutra, he's spoken at Roguelike Celebration. John Harris has a MA in English Literature from Georgia Southern University.

1

An Introduction to Some Rogues

August 2006 Before we kick off this collection of essays on the niche-but-awesome genre of roguelike games, it should help to define what is meant by that term.

Roguelikes are dungeon-exploration computer games, patterned after their classic namesake Rogue and set in a randomly generated world. They are known for their tremendous difficulty, unpredictability, permanent character death and the large number of methods they use to inflict that death. They were most popular in college computer labs in the '80s, and while they didn't achieve widespread success at the time, the genre nevertheless persists, and prospers to this day, and its dedicated cadre of devotees will argue night and day that these are the greatest computer games ever made.

Just in case it isn't obvious by now: I am one of them.

1.1 "Is That a Computer Game or Bad ASCII Art?"

From one perspective, the roguelikes are throwbacks. Here is a class of games, not really mainstream but not obscure either, that has largely resisted modernization. While it might be difficult for someone looking at Colossal Cave to connect it with being of the same kind as, say, Telltale's A Wolf Among Us games, your major roguelikes, by and large, look similar to how they always have.

Although all of the major roguelike games (excepting perhaps the newest one, Brogue) have bit-mapped graphic modes now, they also retain their classic ASCII modes, and many other computer roguelikes use an ordinary text console window as their sole display. NetHack has inspired a number of attempts to give it fairly modern graphics (including one, Vulture, that is somehow sold on Steam), yet possibly the most played form of the game even now, 20 years after it came into being, is on public telnet servers with hundreds of players, not much different in appearance from Rogue itself back upon its release in 1980.

But while there is an air of the Neanderthal surrounding these games, they've survived for so long because, even after all that time, they're still so startlingly modern. Since Rogue was created, the grand parade of computer games is supposed to have advanced in every respect. Their graphics now approach the point where they are indistinguishable from reality. So it is damning indeed that many of them are not more interesting to play than an old terminal game that has barely changed in 36 years.

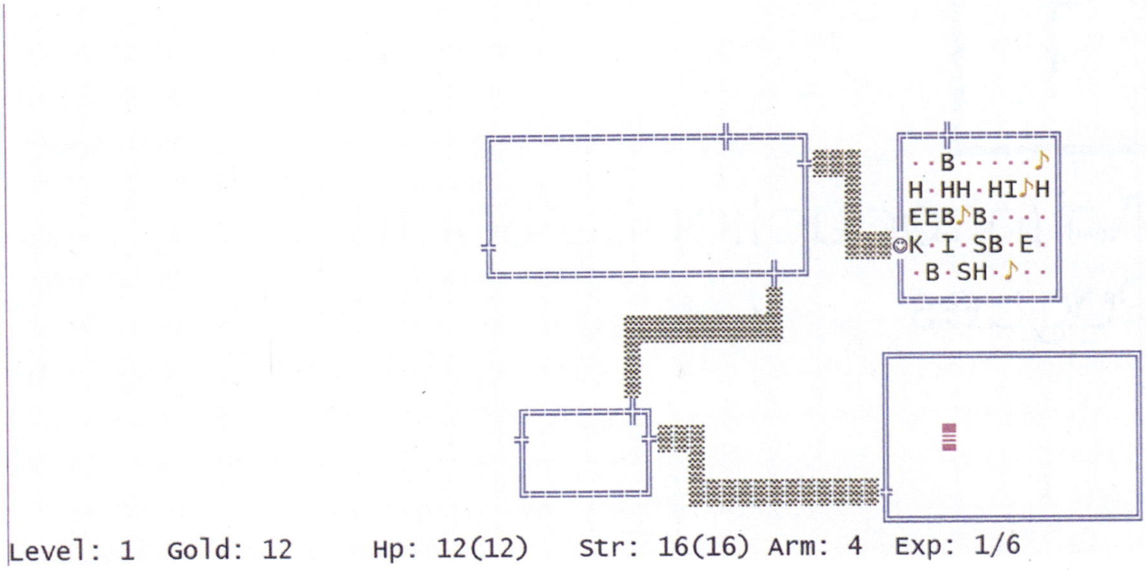

Figure 1.1

Rogue Clone IV, win32 version.

1.2 "But It Helped Me Last Time!"

Perhaps the biggest factor for roguelike longevity is that they are randomly created each game. Every play, the dungeon levels are generated anew, so the player must again explore the mazes in order to make progress. But these days this isn't as innovative as it once was, as a good number of other games have featured random dungeons since then. Many of them were directly inspired by Rogue or one of its descendants. Diablo, one of the biggest software success stories to date, remains quite popular. And yet in almost all cases, those games reveal only a glimmer of understanding of what makes Rogue so interesting.

Instead of just random dungeons, another defining feature of many roguelikes is that the items generated during the game are also randomly selected, and their appearance is scrambled each game. That is to say, when you find an unknown potion lying on the floor of the dungeon, you don't know at first what it will do when you drink it. One game it might heal you, the next it may rob your character of sight making you easy prey for wandering monsters.

That by itself isn't so interesting, but what is is that the appearance of the various items in the game is consistent within that character's life, so all orange potions will be the same type, and the same goes for all cloudy ones, milky ones and even plaid ones. The game's interface recognizes this too, so that if you drink a blue-green potion and get healed, all blue-green potions will be automatically renamed "potions of healing." Some of these items are less obvious in their effects (What the hell is "makes you feel warm all over" supposed to mean?), so for them the game will ask the player what he thinks the item is and will then use that name until the player can find a better one. Discovering items through experimentation, in this way, is an important process in many roguelikes, and its lack is what prevents Diablo, for all its admirable traits, from being as good.

1.3 Part Hack and Slash, Part Scientific Method

All the potions and scrolls in Rogue, and most of its descendants, work that way. The player drinks or reads the item, it is used up, and its effect upon the world is described as well as the player's character can see. But there is usually one type of item, the Scroll of Identify, that will infallibly name an object. Since some items are so subtle in their workings that the player is unlikely to ever figure out their use through trial and error, Identify scrolls are valuable treasures. But the player can only ID things he's carrying at the time the scroll is read, and he can only pick which item is to be ID'd, not pick the effect. If you're dying to discover which potion is extra healing, only chance can bring that knowledge to you.

There are other types of random items in Rogue too, which are even more difficult to figure out. Rings have subtle effects that are very challenging to discover through observation, and wands are dangerous to play around with. Even in a winning game it is unlikely that the player will see all the items that can be generated, let alone figure out what they all do. While there are plenty of other things to like about Rogue and its descendants, in the end it is this need to discover the game world anew every time that makes them fascinating. In a roguelike, the monsters are just one facet of a dangerous game world ready to do you in on a moment's notice, and sometimes the beasties are less likely to end a game than the player's stuff itself.

In the coming pages we'll be investigating many of the most interesting aspects of this venerable and challenging genre. We'll take a look at the most popular games, and many lesser-known ones too. We'll do that and much more, so let's get started! I'll be your tour guide: the guy waiting by the downstairs, whistling for his dog.

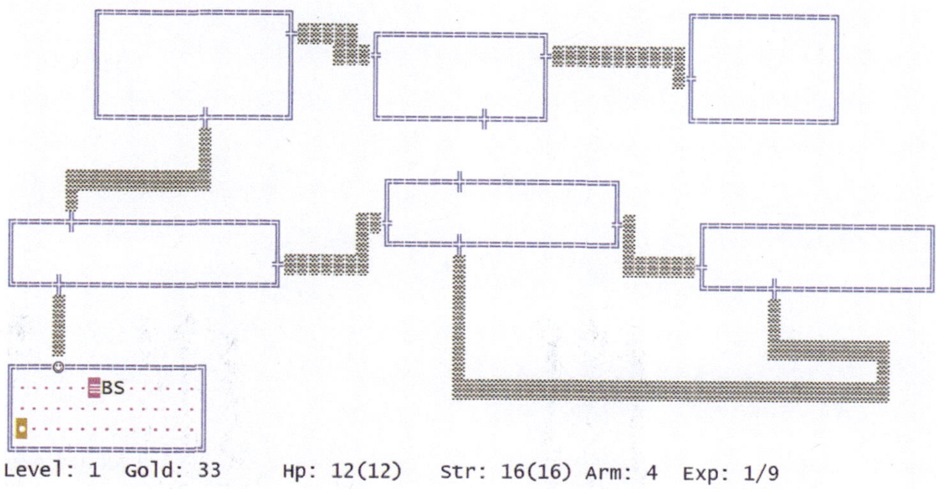

Figure 1.2

Section I
Basics

2

What the Hell Does Q Do Again?

August 2006 Let's start out by talking about something very basic, yet of vital importance to those getting involved with these games—hopefully including some of you. Whenever I've attempted to explain them, by far the most frequent barrier I've encountered in transferring my own enthusiasm to other people is not, as one may think, the graphics, the difficulty or permanent death. Almost every time, the primary reason initiates find to categorize roguelikes as Other-People-Things is the control scheme. So let's talk about how to get started controlling the original roguelike: Rogue.

If you'd like to play along at home, the modern port of Rogue, Rogue Clone IV, is probably the foremost DOS/Windows version. Debian Linux users can get Rogue itself from the package bsdgames-nonfree. ClassicRogue (www.oryxdesignlab.com/games) is a port with a couple of extra features and both Windows and Linux binaries. You can also get Rogue for Java (www.hexatron.com/rogue/), the Sega Dreamcast (http://dreamcast.dcemu.co.uk/roguedc.php) and even the Infocom zMachine (https://ifdb.tads.org/viewgame?id=oao0sdbcgitastyz).

As noted last time, roguelike games haven't changed much in their presentation since the days of playing on dumb terminals in college computer labs. There were no mice or joysticks on those systems. Many of 'em didn't have a numeric keypad, and some had no cursor keys.

What they did have, I'm sorry to say, was vi.

2.1 Behold the Wonders of vi

vi is a well-known and popular Unix text editor, in which lots of different keys do many different things. Unix computer terminals at the time of Rogue's creation did not customarily have dedicated cursor keys, so substitutes had to be found, namely the HJKL sequence, which was basically the WASD of the age. I know I'm gonna catch it from some people for dissing it, and it's certainly great for some things, but I don't think anyone can claim it's easy to pick up. Back in the days when lab students were the primary players of computer games, it could be counted on that many players would know vi, so it was natural to use its cursor movement system as the basis for Rogue's interface. Its legacy persists in several important games to this day, including venerable NetHack, although it and all the other major roguelike games now tend to default to using a number pad for movement.

(*June 2020*: There is now another excellent compilation of old versions of Rogue available for free download called Rogue Collection, at https://github.com/mikeyk730/Rogue-Collection)

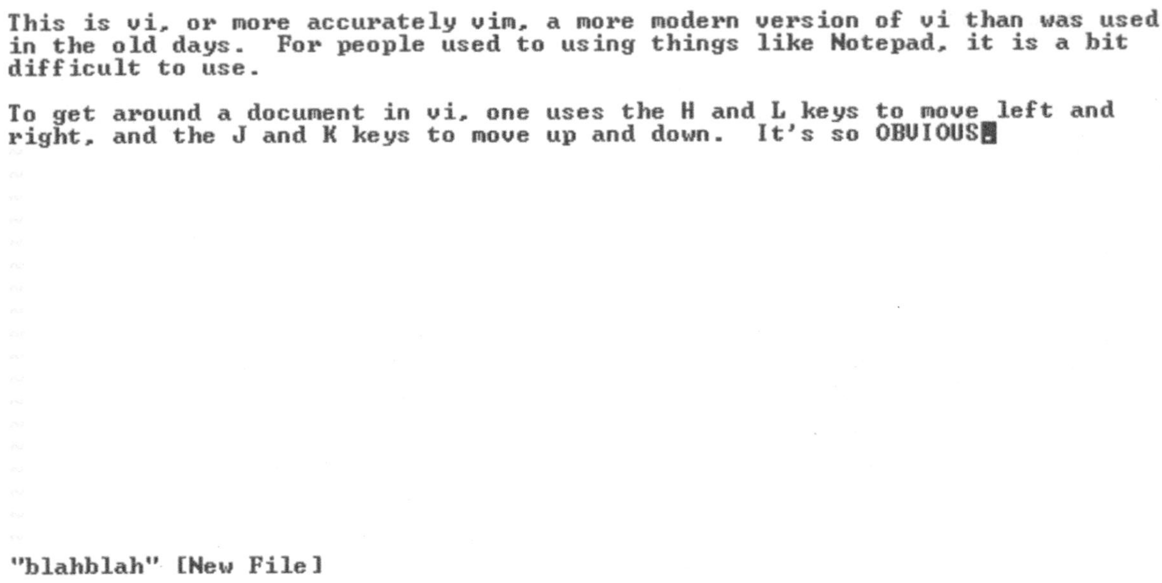

Figure 2.1

vim, a work-alike descendant of vi.

Also like vi, there are special keypresses for everything, and it is not a trivial matter to learn them all. And again, just like with vi, it does turn out to be an excellent interface when you know the keys. Many people still use and even swear by vi's descendants. If you want to read a scroll, you don't fumble around with icons and menus, you just press R, then the letter of the scroll in your inventory.

This is probably the thing that prevents most people from learning these games today. While most computer games take pains to simplify their interfaces as much as possible, to an initiate it may seem like Rogue and its progeny go out of their way to make things hard for the player. In NetHack, some keys do as many as four different things: pressing P (p)ays your bill in a shop, holding Shift and pressing P lets you (p)ut on an accessory such as a ring or an amulet, holding Ctrl and hitting P displays (p)revious pages of the message buffer, and Alt-P (p)rays to the gods for aid. It is true that these keys are all listed out, twice, in the game's help files, but who wants to run to Help every time he wants to have a meal or open a chest?

2.2 News (or Rather, Keys) You Can Use

Since most of these games are based, to some degree, on Rogue, the commands of that game tend to have precedence over any new ones introduced, so learning those will take a player quite far. Learn Rogue's keys, and the whole genre opens up to you. And the commands Rogue has tend to follow a logic that makes them easy to remember: press W to (w)ield something, press E to (e)at and so on.

Here, then, as a tutorial intended to get you playing these games instead of just reading about them, are the important keys of Rogue. All you need to win that game are on this list, and a few others besides. Other games will almost certainly have more than this, but these are usually the most commonly used commands in those games too, so you can generally learn the others as you go along.

> Movement: HJKL and YUBN (or number pad)
> H and L go left and right, while J and K are for up and down. Y, U, B and N are used to travel diagonally if possible. But take my advice and stick with the numpad.
> (Matt Matthews of Curmudgeon Gamer informs me that using J and K as up and down keys also works in Gmail! vi's roots are set deep indeed . . .)
> Combat: same as movement

In most roguelikes, you attack a monster by merely attempting to walk into it. This is more than just a convenience. When a character is confused, that state of mind is represented by randomizing some of his moves, which could result in unintended attacks under this system.

> (Shift-period): Travel downstairs
< (Shift-comma): Travel upstairs

When standing over a staircase, these are the commands used to go to the next/previous dungeon level. In Rogue the upstairs and downstairs are on the same spot, but in most other games they are usually located in different rooms on the level. NetHack uses these keys as a general way to indicate down and up as directions.

, (comma): Pick something up off the floor

Your character will automatically pick a thing up when moving into its space, but there are times when this doesn't happen, like when that feature is turned off or your inventory is full when you moved there. Pressing comma is an explicit request to grab loot at your feet.

. (period): Rest a turn
S: Search for things

These two commands are almost identical in apparent function. Both will pass exactly one turn, and neither will usually print any message on the screen. The only difference between them is that the period key will increase the chance that you'll regain some hit points that turn, and the S key will silently check all eight spaces around your character for hidden doors or traps. There's no guarantee that you'll find anything hidden even if it is there to find, so S is usually pressed several times in a row to reduce the chance that something has been missed.

Space bar: Clear [more] prompts

When a message appears that's longer than the width of the screen, press Space to see the rest. Simple.

Esc: Cancel a command

If you hit a key that you suspect you'll regret, so long as you haven't specified an inventory item yet you can usually abort the command without penalty. Just press Escape.

Shift-S: Save the game
Shift-Q: Quit the game

These are both Shifted commands to reduce the chance that they're hit accidentally, and they both usually ask if you're sure. Remember, if you quit, you can't go back to your last save! Saving the game in a roguelike always ends the current session, and restoring it later (usually by entering your saved character at the name prompt) will delete the save file.

I: Inventory

This is a very important command to remember. It not only prints out all the objects your character is carrying, but the letters assigned to each of them, which are used in all object request prompts. Most commands that require an item to act upon will offer a list of appropriate items if you press a particular key (either asterisk or "?," depending), and there is nothing wrong with relying upon this feature, but if you happen to remember the letter you can just press it and save a step. Asking for a list of your inventory never spends a turn: it is a "free action."

D: Drop (an item)

The Drop command asks you for an inventory letter, then drops the object you picked. Good for dumping useless or bad stuff.

C: Call (an item)

If you think you know what an item is, you don't have to wait for the game to name it for you. You can name it yourself with the Call command.

Shift-D: Discoveries

This lists everything you've conclusively learned the identity of, or Called, in your current game. It is worth noting that, in NetHack, this command is mapped to the backslash key instead.

Q: Quaff (that is to say, drink, applies to potion)
R: Read (a scroll)

These commands use up the object specified. After use the object is gone, leaving behind only its effects upon either you or the rest of the world.

W: Wield (an item, usually weapons)
Shift-W: Wear (armor)
Shift-T: Take off (armor)
Shift-P: Put on (rings)
Shift-R: Remove (rings)

In a console RPG all these would probably be grouped into a single Equip command, but there are reasons to keep them separate. For example, you can actually wield any object in your inventory, not just weapons. This can be useful depending on what game you're playing. Since you can wear up to two rings, the ring commands will ask you which hand is to be (un)adorned.

T: Throw (an item, usually missile weapons)
Z: Zap (a wand)

These commands ask for a direction to throw or zap in as well as the object to throw or zap. You can throw anything, but since most thrown objects carry a risk of being destroyed it's best to only throw things like darts. Note that arrows do more damage when "thrown" if you're wielding a bow, and bolts do much more damage if you're wielding a crossbow. Zapping a wand will expend some of its power, and if the wand is out of magic nothing will happen (or, if it's the infamous Wand of Nothing).

Ctrl-P: Previous message

Sometimes messages get accidentally flipped past before you can read them. Holding Ctrl and pressing P repeatedly will flip back through the last few displayed. Note that some versions of Rogue may use different keys for this, such as F4.

Either * or ? (asterisk or question-mark): List appropriate things from an inventory prompt

Pressing this (varies between games but usually one of the two) at any prompt that requests an inventory item will give you a list of things carried that are obviously relevant. If you press it after a (r)ead command, you'll get a list of scrolls, but after a (q)uaff command the game will list potions instead.

The asterisk list is sometimes presented automatically, without you having to ask. Sometimes, the list is misleading. Several items in Rogue may be used in ways that aren't obvious at first, and the item prompts will not give away the secret. If you want to, say, throw an item that is not commonly thought of as suitable for throwing, you can specify its inventory letter even if it's not listed on the asterisk list. This isn't used all that often, but is very helpful in specific circumstances.

(*January 2016*: By the way, if you still have trouble learning all these keys, you might be interested in Atari ST Rogue, an official version of the game with a greatly simplified control scheme. See Chapter 70 later in this book.)

3

A View of the Field

November 2006 This time out we are going to cover the state of the roguelike genre today, covering as many of the most notable games as we can at one time. I'm restricting this discussion to a fairly conservative definition of roguelike (I'm not even going to touch upon Mysterious Dungeon here), so surely, this won't take too long. How many can there be?

There are the "big three" games, the ones with their own Usenet groups that still have decent traffic, which are NetHack, Angband and ADOM, and their variants. Then there are up-and-comers Dungeon Crawl and Dwarf Fortress, the older games Larn and Omega, and the lost roguelikes that are finally beginning to emerge from obscurity. These are by no means all of the roguelike games there are to see, but this does include many of the more interesting ones.

NetHack I mention a fair bit. It is the most popular roguelike of them all, and has been for some years now. The logic of its world defies belief: a player can take a potion, dip it into a fountain to dilute it into water, then drop it on a co-aligned altar and pray to turn it into holy water. Then he can dip another item into that potion to bless it, or instead dip a pile of other potions of water into it at once to make lots more holy water in a single go. Or, instead of diluting a potion, he could throw it at a monster to attack it with its vapor, mix it with other potions or dip other items into it. Rumor has it the player can even *drink* them.

NetHack is an open source game, and because of this there has arisen a number of outside source forks, or variants, over the years. Most of the time they die out rapidly, such as with NetHack—("NetHack dash-dash"), or the "Japanized" versions JNetHack and NetHack Brass, or the insufferably geeky NetHack: The Next Generation, but sometimes they turn out to have staying power. The foremost NetHack variant is SLASH'EM, a frightening game that contains many more things than even NetHack, which was derived from the earlier variant SLASH. There are lots of variants at the moment under active development, with names like dNetHack, UnNetHack and GruntHack, which help to fill the often considerable time between official releases. There is also a thriving community of NetHack patch authors, some of their work almost counting as variants in themselves, and some of them in the past have had their additions to the game incorporated into the core release by the DevTeam, which is about as close to immortality you can get in the roguelike sphere without actually writing one from scratch.

Angband has long been NetHack's primary competition, almost like a nemesis. NetHack was derived from Hack, which was originally something of a clone of Rogue, while Angband traces is lineage back through Moria, another early roguelike of roughly equivalent antiquity. While NetHack's focus is on

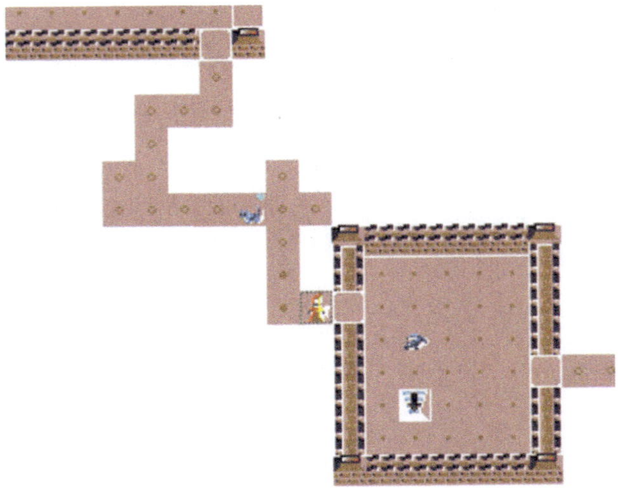

Figure 3.1

NetHack.

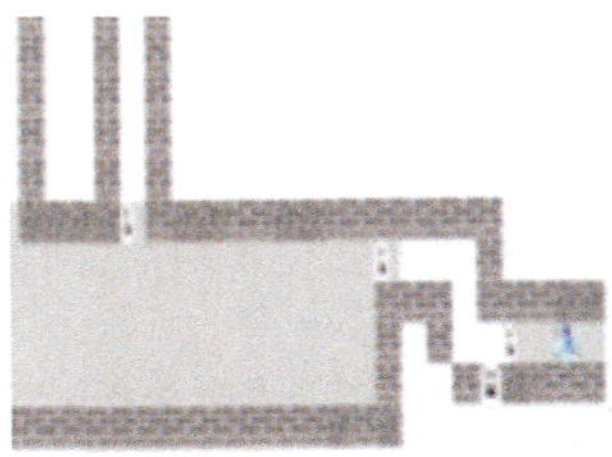

Figure 3.2

Angband.

strategic power acquisition, item discovery and overcoming varied situations (not all of which involve monsters), what Angband is mostly about is killing. It has less game flexibility but ultimately is a deeper tactical game than NetHack. Angband probably has more monsters and individual items than NetHack (and some of its variants definitely do), but they also do not tend to be as interesting, to me at least. Angband is a much larger game in terms of raw acreage, with its hundred levels each several screens in size, but since it lacks NetHack's tremendous depth of play there is generally less a player can do at any given moment. Angband is understood by many to be less dependent upon spoilers in order to play it well, and indeed its awesome "monster memory" feature allows players to generate their own personal spoilers as they play, taking automatic notes on monster hit points, attacks and resistances that can be kept between games.

While Angband's item discovery is but a shadow of NetHack's, or even Rogue's, it does take one of Rogue's features to heart far more than NetHack does. One of the more heart-stopping occasions in Rogue is when the player stumbles upon a zoo, a single room containing far more than the usual allotment of both monsters and treasure. A good zoo can make a player's game but is likely to break it first. While NetHack has zoos, and several other themed monster lairs besides, they are nothing like Angband's vaults, large rooms secreted away from the main system of tunnels that contain extremely dangerous monsters and unique foes. Vaults have a high probability of containing artifacts, the most potent objects in the game, but challenging the monsters for them is not a matter to be taken lightly.

While NetHack has a handful of variants it is still generally understood that the original is still the "real" game. Meanwhile, some of Angband's variants, called *'Bands* due to their propensity to change the first syllable of their parent game's name, are almost as popular as the original. There are dozens of variants of Angband out there, including versions with Lovecraftian monsters, versions with joke monsters, versions with randomized artifacts and even versions with an overworld map to explore and multiple dungeons to find on it.

There used to be a bit in this book about the most popular Angband variant being ToME, aka Troubles of Middle Earth, but some years after it was rewritten, redesigned and its name changed to Tales of Maj'Eyal (its acronym, cunningly, remaining the same). Whether it should continue to be considered one of the major roguelikes is a matter of personal taste.

(How many variants of Angband have there been? Look and see: www.thangorodrim.net/variants.html.)

3.1 Cats vs. Dogs, Joel vs. Mike, NetHack vs. Angband

The quickest instructive way I can think of to illustrate the differences between NetHack and Angband is to describe how they handle shops.

In Angband, a shop is a place on the surface level. Although the shop's walls take up a good amount of space on the town map, the contents of that space do not matter to the game. When the player walks into its entryway he is given a menu listing its contents. He can pick objects to buy off of that menu, haggle over prices and sell stuff he's found in the dungeon. Shops have a limited inventory—never anything truly powerful—but are restocked periodically, so the player can often use them to make up for basic deficiencies in his equipment.

In NetHack, a shop is a room in the dungeon. Like any other room, it has a door and walls. Unlike those other rooms, it has a shopkeeper standing at the door, and the shop's inventory litters most of the floor. Anything on the ground in the shop is considered to belong to the shopkeeper, and if the player picks something up he is told its price. If the player is carrying unpaid objects, the shopkeeper stands in front of the doorway until it is either dropped or paid for. To sell things the player simply drops an item, but the sale price can vary depending on the gold in the merchant's pocket.

Players can steal from shops in NetHack, but instead of it being pass/fail based off a roll of virtual dice, what players must do is figure out how to get objects out of the room past the shopkeeper. Most means of doing this will cause the shopkeeper to call the "Keystone Kops" out after the player. (I am not kidding about their name—NetHack has a number of weird things like that.) It will also make the shopkeeper angry, and they are formidable opponents to all but high-level characters, but ultimately they are still monsters just like any other, and by killing a shopkeeper the player can freely loot the store's inventory and any money the poor guy was carrying. Shops can stock almost any item in the game, but there are not many guaranteed shops, and they never restock with goods other than what the player sells to them, so they are less of a fallback source of basic supplies and more of an additional source of random treasure, albeit one with strings attached.

The third major roguelike, ADOM, is a bit of a departure from the others. For one thing, it has no ancestor game. While the lines of NetHack and Angband are known and storied, ADOM was created outright by its author, Thomas Biskup. He was obviously inspired by other roguelikes, but it also has features that are new and unique.

While NetHack and Angband are both open source games, and thus ultimately have no secrets from the eyes of a determined-enough player, ADOM's source is closed. Thomas Biskup now even maintains a commercialized, graphical version of the game, on Steam no less, although the original free ASCII version still exists. Because it's closed source there are also no variants of ADOM floating around, a state which has doomed a number of other once-famous roguelikes to obscurity. ADOM continues to chug along, though.

ADOM has aspects of Angband in play, but it more obviously takes after NetHack in its features. It has NetHack's variety of environment and monster, but includes Angband's level-dependent item creation, and

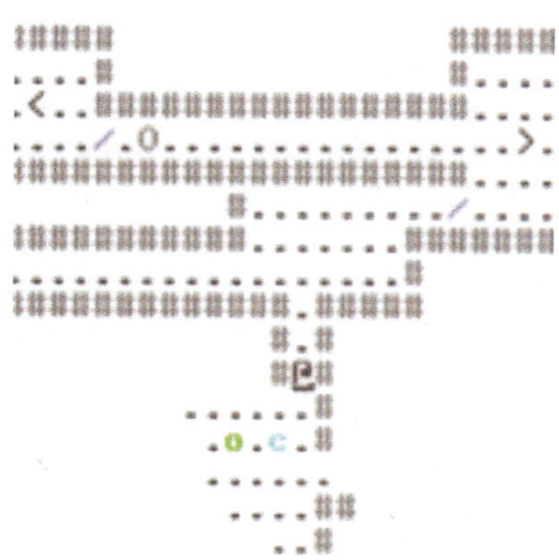

Figure 3.3

ADOM.

it has a monster memory. There is also a fair bit more of the traditional RPG in ADOM, as the game has a more overt, percentage-based skill system (akin somewhat to the pen-and-paper game Runequest), a great variety in races and classes, and a good number of quests. Some of ADOM's ideas are quite nifty and inventive (anyone who's played around with cellular automata will recognize the growth pattern of dungeon plants), but there is also a sense of unevenness there, perhaps unavoidably so, due to the game being the product of just one mind. ADOM is also known for having the player undergo periodic mutations as time passes and the effects of chaos prevalent in the world warp his body. Some of the mutations are helpful, but some are incredibly harsh. A player who mutates too much will lose the game, giving ADOM a time limit, although the pendulum is a bit further away from the player's neck than in Rogue.

ADOM's quest structure means that players effectively have an itinerary while playing, a set of places they either have to go at certain times/levels or else miss out on meeting/helping/killing various people. Alignment is also very important, in that it can change depending on a player's actions, and it determines which quests he can perform. The game also has a good number of objects that must be collected from its various dungeons in order to win the game. (Or, Really Win the game, or Really REALLY Win the game—there are multiple tiered "endings.") This sometimes leads to cases where the player does not know what options are available to him, or what he needs to do next, unless he is already spoiled. Like NetHack, players interested in someday winning are recommended to peruse the game's voluminous wiki.

Two other roguelikes that deserve an honorable mention here:

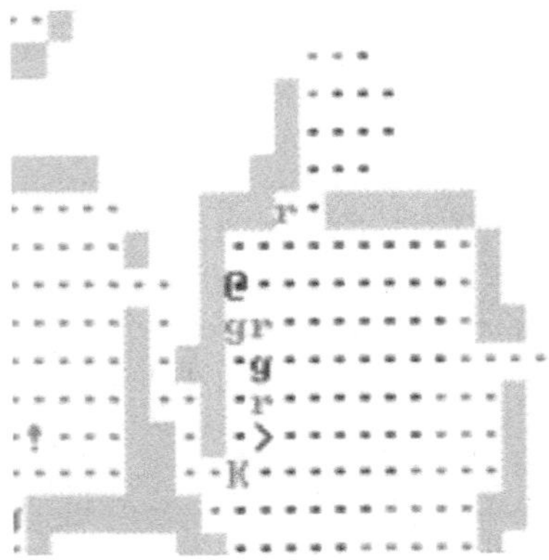

(Linley's) Dungeon Crawl is a relative newcomer to the field, being "only" 24 years old at this point, and it continues to see development. It seems to stick a smidgen closer to Rogue in its design than the likes of NetHack, but it also has a good number of classes and races to try out. Dungeon Crawl is exceptionally difficult even by roguelike standards, with players hounded by hordes of foes almost from the first turn, so a fair amount of persistence and/or luck seems to be necessary to get a game beyond the first levels.

More recently, the official variant Dungeon Crawl Stone Soup has taken over its place among the "major roguelikes." It has certainly changed a lot over the years, and it continues to change rapidly.

Dungeon Crawl is relatively new, but overnight indie gaming success Dwarf Fortress is an infant by comparison. Most of the attention paid to DF focuses (rightfully) on its interesting Fortress Mode, but it also contains an Adventurer Mode that is nominally a roguelike. Games from both modes take place in the same randomly generated world, created on the program's first run, and it's possible to have an adventurer explore a player fortress, and visit kingdoms which fortresses know only through trade and diplomacy. Further, in the event a Fortress game is lost, the map is saved and made available for play in a Reclaim Fortress mode, which also has roguelike similarities. While these modes are interesting, they do not have the varied item discovery play of Rogue and its kin. Some players may not even notice the game has a built-in roguelike.

Some other games:

Larn, ULarn and XLarn make up another roguelike branch that hasn't seen too much development lately. They were notable for having a time limit and for having some seriously powerful weapons, like the appropriately named lance of death. The game Omega is of moderate age for a roguelike and was the first roguelike to contain a significant "overworld," a landscape outside of the dungeons. The science-fiction game Alphaman has item discovery, and an interesting sense of humor, but even now I do not know much else about it.

There exists a Usenet group, rec.games.roguelike.misc, that is devoted to miscellaneous roguelikes that do not have their own group. In the days before ADOM got its own listing it was commonly discussed there, and Dungeon Crawl is a frequent source of conversation now. Also discussed there are a number of new roguelikes, many of which got their start as part of the 7-Day Roguelike Project. Some of these games are quite ingenious twists on the roguelike theme, among them ChessRogue (the foes are enemy pieces and after capturing enough of them the player's king gains new types of moves) and astoundingly prolific roguelike developer Jeff Lait's POWDER, Letter Hunt, Jacob's Matrix, Smart Kobolds and many other interesting games.

More recently there's Brian Walker's Brogue, an interesting game that we talk about later, which is intended as a kind of update of Rogue, but without many distractions common to RPGs, such as experience points and levels.

Finally, but significantly, there are the lost roguelikes, games that were not open sourced during their heyday and were too tied to one or another operating system to be run on modern machines. In particular, this includes the major Rogue variants Super-Rogue, UltraRogue, XRogue and Advanced Rogue, which were recovered from obscurity by the noble efforts of the Roguelike Restoration Project, although the source rescued by that abandoned project is now, again, starting to age.

Note: according to a defunct website, the author of Larn passed away some time ago. That's how old roguelikes are as a class of computer game: *developer mortality* has begun to take its toll.

But! What about Binding of Isaac?! What about Spelunky?! What about Enter the Gungeon?! Etc.

Back when most of these chapters were first written, none of those games existed. The term "*roguelike*" has never had an official meaning, but in the early days of the genre it had a specific meaning: terminal- and turn-based roleplaying games with randomized worlds and items, tricky monsters and permadeath. In the years since, the meaning has become muddied somewhat. These chapters generally take the tack that "roguelike" should continue to refer to games of that strain, that a different word should apply to games that adopt some of its conventions (randomization and permadeath) while abandoning others (turn basis). I personally now use *roguelite* for these other games; a ton of various games on Steam still use roguelike, as a marketing term.

I do refer to ToeJam & Earl as a roguelike later on. Back when I first did that, it was a novel usage. Now, it probably should be called a roguelite.

4

Tips for Travel in Gridland

February 2007 While there are around a half-dozen major roguelikes, and dozens of minor ones, there are a good number of attributes they all share. They almost all focus on exploration of a regular grid with spaces blocked by walls and doors, and with opposing characters who also travel through the grid through mostly the same mechanism as the player. Sometimes either side may find objects with which to aid them in their goal, or they may have innate abilities that help them, but they all tend to follow the pattern laid down in that ancient game, Rogue.

Because of this, there is a basic body of information that can help players play any roguelike they may find. So here I present a travel guide, a document that may aid you in your journey no matter where you might end up, whether it be the Dungeons of Doom, the Mazes of Morgoth or the Caverns of Chaos, any alliterative complex of rooms, items and monsters you might find—in short, any place worth being.

Remember: always find out the dollar-to-zorkmid exchange rate before embarking.

4.1 About Diagonals

There are some interesting consequences of moving around a grid-based game world. Most roguelikes allow players to move diagonally at the same cost as orthogonally, and some even allow for free movement through diagonal gaps in walls. But monsters can do the same thing and are usually a lot more comfortable with the idea than a human player might be.

An example of this is in order. Many games have crinkled passages, with sharp edges that don't actually need to be traveled through. This is very common in NetHack but applies to most roguelikes.

Note that this NetHack corridor (see facing page) looks as if it's a zig-zag, but in fact, you can just go straight down it diagonally. While these passages are most common in that game, this is a property of all the major dungeons other than Rogue's and Brogue's, which do not allow for diagonal movement in corridors.

Since the monsters take frequent advantage of this, it is not uncommon to get struck when turning a corner if one doesn't cut across it.

In the scene pictured from Dungeon Crawl, the player is escaping from a small horde of monsters. When he takes the corner, however, instead of cutting it like he should, he goes into the corner space. As a result, the rat gets a free attack when the player tries to move out of the corner. If the monster was something nasty, like an ogre, and the player were low on hit points, that could be a fatal mistake.

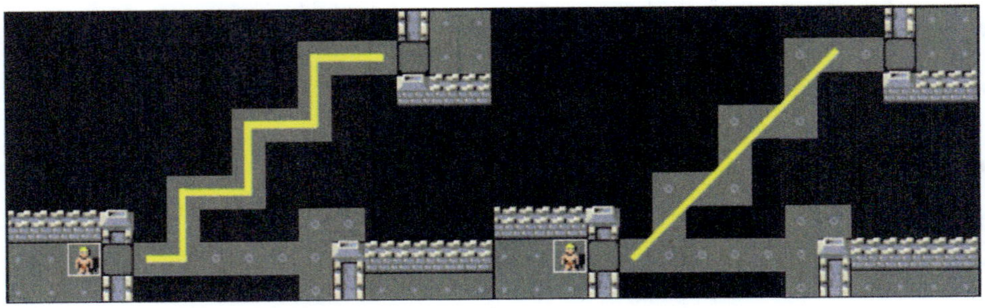

Figure 4.1

Left: Player moves through corners, wasting move and food. If he were being chased, he'd be jackal chow.

Right: Player moves diagonally through corridor, getting through in half the time and keeping ahead of pursuers.

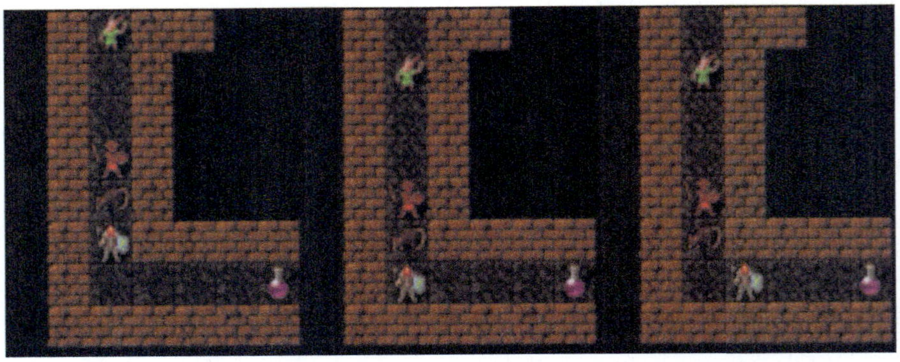

Figure 4.2

Left: In this situation, the dwarf at the bottom of this queue of monsters is trying to pass the corner without getting gnawed.

Middle: Here, he moved straight down, into the corner. When he moves right, the rat will get a free attack!

Right: Here, he moved diagonally down and right, cutting the corner, getting him there in one turn and staying ahead of the rat.

4.2 About Doors

One of the most underutilized terrain features to be found in a roguelike dungeon is the lowly door. Even for experienced players, it can be difficult to get over the impression that they are an obstacle to be overcome, instead of a resource to be utilized.

First you should know how to get through locked doors. Games in which doors can be locked, especially NetHack and ADOM, typically provide some way to get by them without needing a key. These games do it by providing a 'k'ick command for breaking them down, usually setting off any traps in the process. It also destroys the door, which makes it impossible to use tactically.

Doors are a problem because they block player exploration and fleeing, but they're an advantage because one can close them to block the approach of an enemy. If the enemy is intelligent this won't help much, since he'll just open it again, but for monsters with no hands it is an impassable barrier. And if you can lock that door, with a key or a locking spell, it will deter most humanoid opponents as well.

NetHack has some idiosyncrasies regarding doors that should be mentioned. Unlike the other games, an open door in NetHack is not tactically the same as an empty space. In one of its holdovers from Rogue, neither players nor monsters can move into or out of door spaces diagonally, but attacks can be made diagonally both to and from those spaces.

4.3 Dealing with Missile Users and Spellcasters

Here's another little problem. The dwarf character shown in Figure 4.3 is in a bit of a pickle in that they want to go forward, but that will put them in a wide-open area, where the centaur can hit wherever they go.

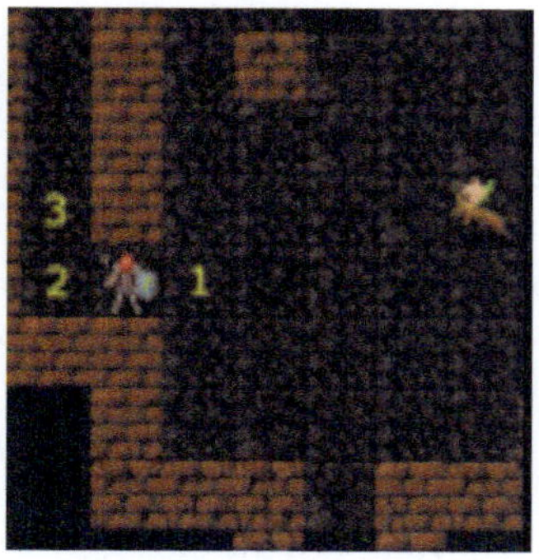

Figure 4.3

Centaurs are annoying opponents who can fire multiple arrows per turn. The dwarf's first impulse might be to move to Point 1 to close the distance, or even stay put and fire his own arrows, but they would just end up a pincushion. If they move to Point 2, they would be a little better off, but the centaur can just move and keep the dwarf in line. Moving to Point 3, and back a step from there, will block the centaur's shots and force the centaur to approach, almost to melee range . . . and dwarfs like melee.

It can be very difficult to survive a situation like this if the player doesn't have some means of distance attack themself, and even then, centaurs are strong and fast, so players are usually at a disadvantage here.

The proper solution to these kinds of situations is to get behind a corner as soon as possible. Missile-firers and spellcasters cannot attack what they can't see, so by getting yourself out of line-of-sight, one forces the enemy to close the distance. Once the monster has gotten close enough to see the player again, it's either in melee range or close enough that the player can reach it in one turn, and in many cases strong distance-attack monsters are pitifully weak up close. Even if it's not weak, at the very least the player has a chance of destroying the threat now, instead of just getting hit by it over and over.

Another tactic that sometimes works is to get another monster between you and the foe. In ADOM in particular, missile users will not fire if there is another monster between it and the player, even if it's weak sauce, so it'll fall back to generic monster behavior: approaching the player, even though it'll be in greater danger in that position. Once it's a space away, the player may then kill the nearby monster, then quickly approach and slay the archer.

This tactic does not work in NetHack, for its monsters have no love for one another, but another trick, again the result of having Rogue as a direct ancestor, does. Just like the player, NetHack monsters can only fire missiles, zap wands or breathe whatever in the eight compass-point directions, so a tricky player can almost always safely maneuver closer to an archer or wand user by making canny use of diagonal movement, to ensure that each turn he is either adjacent (for smacking purposes), or a safe knight's-move away from the foe.

It is interesting to note that this aspect of NetHack's universe is surely intentional, because some monsters are known to take advantage of it. Try getting a unicorn lined up for a shot in a room some time and you'll see what I mean.

4.4 Dealing with Wand Users

Wands are a subclass of missile weapons that are special because they are much stronger, including causing instant death in some cases, or can sometimes produce unusual effects, but usually with limited uses.

The textbook example of roguelike unfairness is when a NetHack gnome, a weak monster in plentiful numbers early in the dungeon, through some divine prank finds a "wand of death." While it seems these specific tools are never generated right in the hands of a gnome, it is possible that he found such a wand lying on the dungeon floor. Since a player cannot ordinarily see the possessions of monsters, and certainly can't without being in the space next to it, he'll have no prior clue that that monster, out of thousands, has suddenly become an opponent worthy of respect until the fatal zap.

In most games the only thing a player can really do is use missile tactics to lure the monster close then melee him; in some games this means he'll only use hand-to-hand attacks, while in the others it'll at least cause him to spend some of his turns trying to whack you. But, once again, Rogue and NetHack have a weird complication here. Attack ray wands in those games have the special property of being reflective, bouncing off of walls, potentially to hit the creature that fired it, meaning, provided you survive, the enemy has a chance of killing himself with the beam intended for you.

4.5 About Speed

There are two ways that speed is handled by roguelike games: player-centric and world-centric.

Player-centric speed was what Rogue used, and some roguelikes go through a period early in their development where they use it because it's simpler to implement. Under this scheme, all monster actions occur relative to moves the player makes. A fast monster might get an extra turn every other move the player makes, or even two moves to the player's one, while a slow monster sometimes loses turns. This way, all monster speeds must match up to multiples of the player's speed, which makes effects like Haste spells or speed potions very predictable. There was a trick in Rogue, which still works sometimes even in games that use more complex speed systems, where if the player drinks a potion of haste he can kill almost any monster safely, by getting into a flee-hit-flee-hit pattern. That way, the monster's turn would always be wasted in chasing the player, while the player could both run and hit on his turns.

More recently, the vogue has been world-centric schemes, where there is what amounts to an invisible universe-clock according to which both the player and monsters get their turns scheduled. This way, an actor's speed is measured in ticks, after every so many of which he gets an action. Under this system there can be monsters who are only slightly faster or slower than the players, and sometimes some randomization is even thrown in to make it harder to abuse.

4.6 Escape, Regeneration and Loops

Roguelikes present a random, hostile world in which time is rarely on the player's side. In general, turns wasted will come back to haunt the player, by attracting monsters, depleting food or just from plain old opportunity cost. But there are still times when the player may want to see some time pass.

It is a convention of roguelike games that characters heal much more rapidly than they would in real life, or even in a Dungeons & Dragons realm. With the exception of ADOM (which has notoriously slow healing rates unless the player takes measures), the passage of a couple hundred turns is all a body needs to go from death's doorstep to prime condition. Even this can be sped up by using the Rest key (usually period) instead of moving around or doing something, or by putting on a ring of regeneration. Yet in most of these games, monsters heal nowhere near as quickly as players, if at all.

The safest place, often, to pass healing time is on a different dungeon level. If you can get to the stairs with at least one space between you and a monster, you can escape any foe in most games. Even if monsters are adjacent to you when you take the stairs, certain species don't follow. Time generally does not pass for

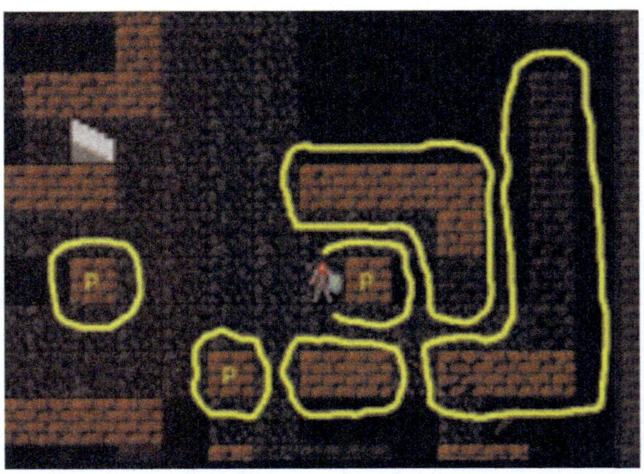

Figure 4.4

Loops are a dwarf's most valued friends. When running from tough opponents like ogres, instead of scrambling in fear halfway across the dungeon, possibly attracting more unwanted attention along the way, it is best to find a loop and let the ogre chase you around it. Hit the ogre to inflict damage until low on hit points, then run around the loop until HP is at safe levels again. Smaller loops, like "pillars" (marked with a P here), are best because the less ground you cover, the less likely another monster will find you.

monsters when you're off the level, but some, like Dungeon Crawl, try to fake time spent by those monsters when you re-enter the floor.

Finally, occasional games, Rogue itself chief among them, reach a point eventually where the player simply cannot hope to kill the monsters. There are occasions, in these games, when it comes time to hang up one's sword and just sprint for the goal. The end of games of Rogue, especially PC Rogue, is most times just such a mad rush for the Amulet, and then a hasty retreat: exit, screaming all the way, stage up.

Remember: he who fights and runs away, lives to flee another day.

5

Brought to You Today by the Letter "Q"

July 2008 Usually, when I talk about roguelike games here, it's in the context of being a kind of old-school Dungeons & Dragons simulator. This is an awesome thing all to itself, for reasons covered later on. Yet there are other attributes of the games that differ from D&D, or indeed any other RPG, either pen-and-paper or computer.

One of the most entertaining of these, if one has followed the evolution of the genre far enough, turns out to be a direct result of one of roguelike gaming's major limitations. While some have moved on to using simple graphics to represent the dungeon and its inhabitants, most classical roguelikes still at least have the option of using ASCII characters to represent the playing field. And the method of representation is one of the aspects of the genre that tie it back to Rogue: line-drawing characters for walls, an at-sign for the player and letters for the monsters.

Letters for the monsters. Oh, the troubles that spring from this simple idea.

5.1 First Problem: There Are Only 26 Letters

One of the many tiny, sparkling shards of awesomeness embedded in Rogue's thick hide is how it turns the limitation on monsters into a theme. The first level of rogue has a handful of monsters: bats, jackals, snakes, hobgoblins and kobolds. Every level after the first introduces one new monster until dragons enter the game on level 22. I submit that it is no coincidence that the Amulet of Yendor appears on level 26.

But Rogue, for its coolnesses, is still a fairly short and simple game. Most games these days want to offer more opponents than just 26. And so the great bestiary proliferation began.

Now those games that offer more than 26 monsters have to come up with some way to represent the new monsters. There are three ways this is done. The oldest, going back to the lost roguelikes, is to treat uppercase and lowercase monsters as different species. Nearly all of them do this now, but it still limits the opponent types to 52. The second was is to use different colors to distinguish between monsters, and this is also pretty common. A DOS-style terminal is capable of displaying 16 different colors, although one of them is black. 15 * 52 is 780 beasties, which sounds like a lot, although for other reasons we'll get to shortly still isn't enough.

The final idea was to allow a few symbols in there to add a few more creatures to the mix. NetHack uses @ symbols to represent humans and ampersands (&) for demons, along with a few others. In that game colons are lizards, semi-colons are sea monsters, and apostrophes are golems. We are not quite sure what system was used for assigning these; the secretive DevTeam hasn't said anything about it, although there is certainly

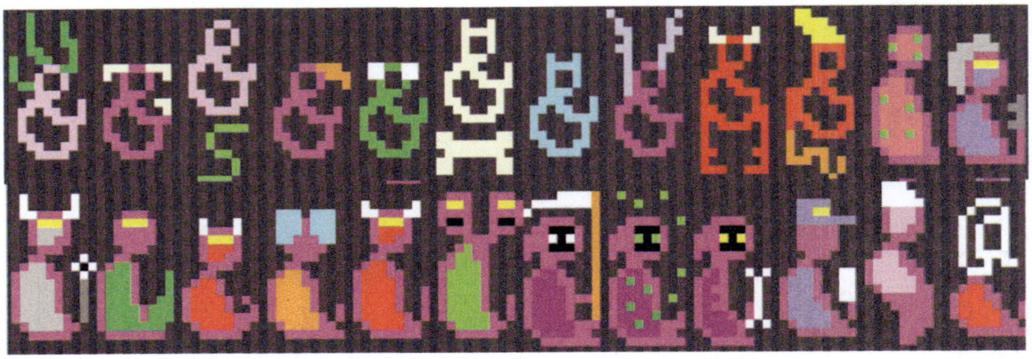

Figure 5.1

Geoduck tileset, demons. (The ampersand demons above come from the Geoduck Tileset, a clever NetHack modification that makes monster graphics tiles into appropriately customized ASCII versions. This is a fair-use section of a larger work, used only for informational purposes. It's at: www.olywa.net/cook/nhack.html.)

a chance that there is some pattern at work. Fiendishly, both NetHack and Angband dual-purpose some of the symbols used as game terrain to represent hidden monsters. NetHack ghosts are represented in-game by spaces, and Angband trappers use the same character as the floor. Mimics in both games may use the same characters as object types lying on the floor.

There are other letter-like symbols that could be used, if one is willing to poach characters from other languages. The basic ASCII alphabet doesn't have any of those, but extended ASCII and Unicode support them. This isn't as helpful as one might suppose, however; the advantage to ASCII is its universality, and furthermore, the primary advantage of using letters is that monsters are more easily recognizable by using the first letter of their name to represent the foe. Most players speak English, and there just aren't many monsters iconic enough for inclusion that use diacritical marks on their first letters.

All these options are still not enough for some games. NetHack, in particular, has a scheme whereby monster letters (upper- and lower-case considered separately) indicate a general monster type, and color depicts species. A comment in the source code notes the pattern behind these: monsters with an elemental affinity are to use an appropriate color (red for fire, white for ice), and leader or royal monsters are purple.

Yet under this system there are some monsters that appear identical on an ASCII display. The most troublesome result of this, in NetHack, happens near the end of the game, when the player reaches the elemental plane of Earth. Upon entry, the first two monsters the player meets are always another reincarnation of the Wizard of Yendor and an elflord, both represented by a purple "@." The elflord is a middle-level foe, not dangerous to a player who has literally been to hell and back, but the Wizard could be quite a pest.

5.2 Second Problem: Finding Monsters for the Less-Common Letters

Fitting all the monsters into 26 letters isn't exactly easy, but worse is finding monsters for the less-common letters of the alphabet.

ADOM is maybe the game least burdened by these considerations. While it does try to conform the monsters into families represented by particular letters, there are many letters that don't obviously match family names. Grues are x'es, while humans are generally @. Barbarians are K, bugbears are g, bears are N, golems are Y, sea monsters seem to be A and so on.

I've been thinking a bit about this problem myself, regarding NetHack, and I started compiling a list of monsters that begin with different letters. A few letters are easy. It turns out there is an abundance of G monsters: gnome, griffin, gargoyle, gremlin, gorgon, golem. V, a fairly uncommon letter, has more monsters than one might expect: vampire, vrock and vortex.

A few letters are troublesome, in particular: J, K, Q, X, Y and Z. It is entirely because of the letter Y that the Yeti appears in so many roguelike games. The difficulty of finding good monsters for K, Q and Y, ultimately, was responsible for the beginnings of what's kind of a roguelike tradition: the inclusion of weird monsters in order to fill out the whole alphabet.

I'll elaborate. The first versions of Rogue borrowed much of the opposition from Dungeons & Dragons. Later revisions switched out some of those monsters for a more idiosyncratic set. The rumor is that this was

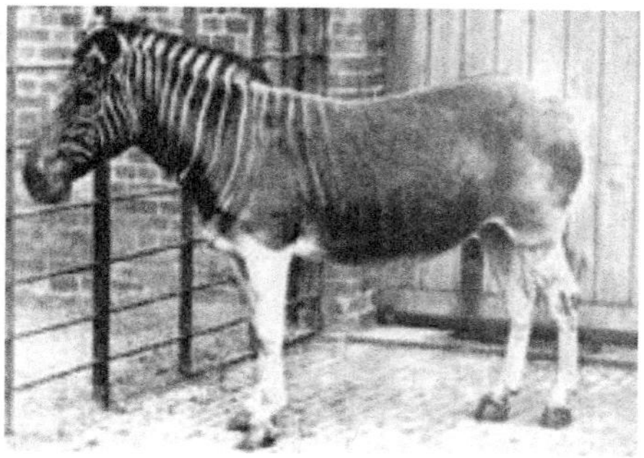

Figure 5.2

Quagga, an extinct subspecies of zebra. (Used under principle of fair use, https://en.wikipedia.org/wiki/Quagga#/media/File:Quagga_photo.jpg.)

done in order to foil Rog-O-Matic, the early Rogue-playing borg (game-playing AI), but to me it seems at least possible that it was also to distance the game from D&D around the time Rogue was being sold commercially by Epyx.

When the monsters were changed, they had to find new monsters for some of the hard-to-fill letters. This was the point that Lewis Carroll's Jabberwock became a Rogue monster, as did the Quagga, an extinct relative of the zebra, the Kestral, a type of falcon one might not expect to find underground, and my personal favorite, the *Xeroc*, replacing mimics. (If you don't get the joke, think about that name for a moment, in relation to copying things.)

NetHack's lowercase-Z monster is Zruty, a creature that appears to come from Slavic folklore. It is the only lowercase-Z monster in that game. But that's nothing . . . the first reaction that some people have upon finding out that Quantum Mechanics and Keystone Kops are NetHack foes is disbelief, and the second is annoyance, but view it in the context of the difficulty of finding good Q and K monsters and it seems almost inevitable.

Not even Angband is immune to this. One of that game's trademarks is a race of very-low-level humanoids called Yeeks, which actually originated in Angband's predecessor game Moria. Yeeks are something of an unofficial mascot for the games, as a race of monsters that are comically weak. Rumor has it, they're called Yeeks because that's the sound they make when stepped on. Yeeks have a kind of popularity in Angband culture; the basic game includes the King and Prince of the Yeeks (Boldor and Orfax) as unique monsters, and variants add the Yeekish Queen and President.

Some recent variants even make Yeeks a playable race. Being so weak, they gain experience levels rapidly, but unfortunately they must live with a -5 to Luck. Because, if you were born a Yeek, the laws of chance must not have been on your side.

Here are the monsters of Rogue, NetHack and Angband, sorted by letter:

Letter	Rogue V4	Rogue V5	NetHack l-case	NetHack u-case	Angband l-case	Angband u-case
A	Giant Ant	Aquator	Insect	Angel	Ant	Angel
B	Bat	Bat	Blob	Bat	Bat	Bird
C	Centaur	Centaur	Cockatrice	Centaur	Centipede	Canine
D	Dragon	Dragon	Dog	Dragon	Minor Dragon	Major Dragon
E	Floating Eye	Emu	Eye	Elemental	Eye	Elemental
F	Violet Fungi	Venus Flytrap	Feline	Fungus	Feline	Dragon Fly
G	Gnome	Griffon	Gremlin	Gnome	Golem	Ghost
H	Hobgoblin	Hobgoblin	Humanoid	Giant	Humanoid	Chimera
I	Invisible Stalker	Ice Monster	Imp	(invisible creature)	Icky Thing	Insect
J	Jackal	Jabberwock	Jelly	Jabberwock	Jelly	Snake
K	Kobold	Kestral	Kobold	Keystone Kop	Kobold	Killer Beetle
L	Leprechaun	Leprechaun	Leprechaun	Lich	Louse	Lich
M	Mimic	Medusa	Mimic	Mummy	Mold	Hydra
N	Nymph	Nymph	Nymph	Naga	Naga	(unused)
O	Orc	Orc	Orc	Ogre	Orc	Ogre

(Continued)

(Continued)

Letter	Rogue V4	Rogue V5	NetHack l-case	NetHack u-case	Angband l-case	Angband u-case
P	Purple Worm	Phantom	Piercer	Pudding	Lesser Person	Major Person
Q	Quasit	Quagga	Quadruped	Quantum Mechanic	Quadruped	Quylthulg
R	Rust Monster	Rattlesnake	Rat	Rust Monster	Rodent	Reptile
S	Snake	Snake	Spider	Snake	Skeleton	Spider
T	Troll	Troll	Trapper	Troll	Town Resident	Troll
U	Umber Hulk	Black Unicorn	Unicorn	Umber Hulk	Lesser Demon	Greater Demon
V	Vampire	Vampire	Vortex	Vampire	Vortex	Vampire
W	Wraith	Wraith	Worm	Wraith	Worm	Wraith
X	Xorn	Xeroc	Xan & Bugs	Xorn	(unused)	Xorn
Y	Yeti	Yeti	Light	Yeti	Yeek	Yeti
Z	Zombie	Zombie	Zruty	Zombie	Zombie	Hound

Others:

NetHack: commercial-at: Human or Elf, space: Ghost, colon: Lizard, semi-colon: Sea Monster, apostrophe: Golem, Ampersand: Demon
Angband: period: Lurker, comma: Plant Monster, dollar-sign: Creeping Coins, various symbols: Mimic

5.3 Sources

Angband monster spoilers: www.thangorodrim.net/spoilers/monsters0.html
NetHack Wiki: http://nethackwiki.com/
The Rogue Vede-Mecum: formerly at www.monmouth.com/~colonel/rvm.html, now at https://web.archive.org/web/20170115060237/http://userpages.monmouth.com/~colonel/rvm.html

6

Check and Mate

November 2010 While this book concerns roguelike design issues, it may be of use to players trying to figure out how best to make progress in these games. It may also be helpful in playing other games that strive to provide a roguelike kind of feel, those that are about providing an environment in which interesting situations can arise spontaneously and randomly, instead of all being pre-made by a level designer. It's about the nature of fairness, and some perhaps unintuitive aspects of that concept in conjunction with roguelikes. . . .

If a game has pre-made levels, then unfair situations can simply be made never to occur. In a game that generates situations algorithmically, a lot more care must be given, generally, to the rules of the world, and, specifically, the items and monsters within it, so as to ensure that the game is fair to the player regardless of what situations may occur.

Player fairness might seem at first to be a laughable thing for roguelikes to worry about. Is this not the genre that contains NetHack, of that legendary player mortality rate? But in fact NetHack is an almost ludicrously fair game; the fact that 10+ game winning streaks are possible, covering all the races and roles, proves that. When you look closely at it, nearly all causes of death come down to player ignorance or carelessness.

Now both of these sources of mortality, ignorance and carelessness, are substantial. Ignorance of the full breadth of NetHack's rules is understandable considering just how complex the game is; I have read and studied spoilers for over a decade, and have read a bit of the source code too, and I still run into new things occasionally. And perfect care requires a style of play unappealing to many players, again, including myself. But all the same, it is still possible to win the great majority of games of NetHack.

NetHack is so fair that, to a sufficiently knowledgeable player, the game may actually be a bit too easy. But one doesn't have to take fairness to NetHack's extremes to still recognize it as a concern. All well-designed roguelikes adhere to a certain type of fairness involving something I call critical moments. Understanding them is vital in designing not only good roguelikes, but all kinds of randomly generated games that use permanent death.

6.1 Permadeath Defined

A reminder is in order as to what constitutes "permadeath." Games that use it are those that allow the player to catastrophically fail, losing the game, without recourse to continuing play other than starting over. You might be able to "save" in these games, but upon resuming play the save data is rendered unusable. Saves could be considered analogous to temporarily holding one's place in a game rather than creating a checkpoint from which repeated resumption is possible. Sometimes I call saving under a permadeath system a "bookmark save." A more intuitive name these days might be "suspend saves," which mobile console games often provide for times of low battery.

One fact about games with permadeath is that they must be designed in a much more rigorous manner than games that allow multiple resumptions from a save file. In typical games that provide for saving, generally a player finds a save point right before a boss. When fighting the boss, it generally has a pattern or weak point that is difficult to figure out, possibly meaning the player's character dies. Although often (clumsily) called "a game over," the player then resumes from the save point and tries again, using the information observed from the prior attempt to try to do better this time. This may be repeated many times, until the player is at last successful, the boss is defeated, and the player may move on.

Most games made these days use a system like this. In fact, they have long been designed with the understanding that such a system will be in place. The result is that games are often not designed in such a way that players will be fairly able to complete a leg of the quest on one attempt. These games are expected to be played in many goes, with more information on difficult sections gained on each failed attempt. They don't even try to give the player enough information to be honestly capable of finishing a tough part upon seeing it the first time. There are often hints, sure, but there is really no effort expended in testing to ensuring bosses are fairly completeable without prior knowledge.

(Since I first wrote this, I have discovered that even Infocom text adventures did this in places. For example, if you try to finish The Hitchhiker's Guide to The Galaxy's infamous Babel Fish puzzle only using clues the game gives you, the machine will always run out of fish before you can get one, making the game unwinnable. You have to restore to a previous save and use the information gained on the first attempt in order to successfully solve the puzzle.)

Permadeath games do not have this luxury. Thus it is that much of what players hate about permadeath in games is, truthfully, just as much due to lax design in other games. I observe that, in games that use sparsely placed save points, the further apart the saves are, the more the implications of the play structure come to resemble those of permanent death. If it takes only a minute to get to a boss after a save, the stakes aren't as high as if it takes half an hour. In fact, a permadeath system could be considered analogous to a game with a single save point, right at the start.

But I digress.

6.2 Critical Moments

The best way to explain critical moments, I think, is to present them as a series of hypothetical situations. We'll use Rogue as our example game. Take this situation:

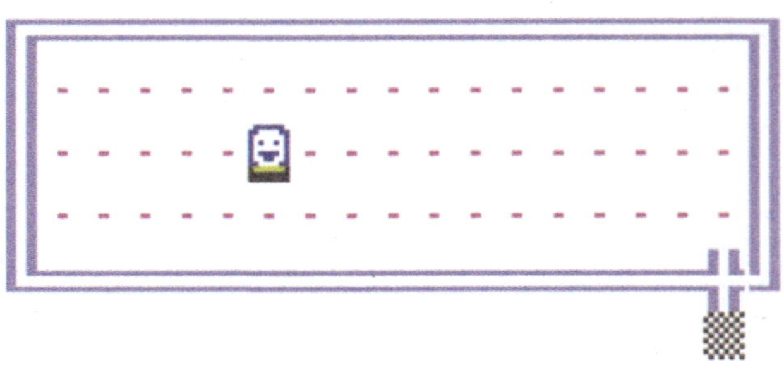

Here, the player has just come down the staircase into a new level. In this case the player seems to be relatively safe. They can move in any of eight directions. There is nothing nearby that can cause them harm. Immediately speaking, it doesn't matter much what the player does here. They are free to take whatever actions they feel necessary to secure the character's long-term survival. This is because this is not a critical moment.

Now, let's look at this situation:

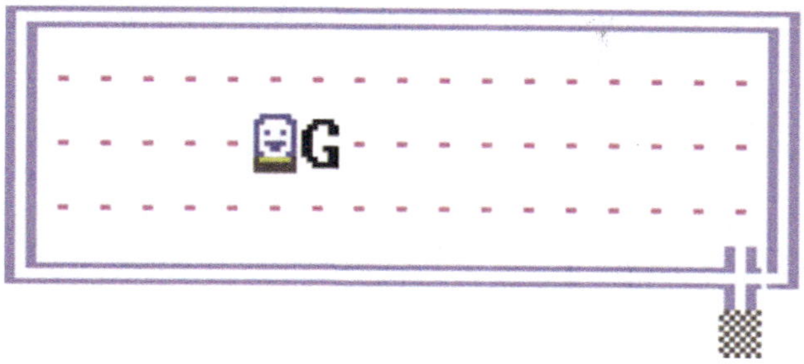

Figure 6.1

Rogue, encountering a Griffin

The situation pictured in Figure 6.1 is dire, although very unlikely early in the game. Griffins are among the strongest monsters in Rogue. If the player is low-level, then a single hit from a griffin could wipe him out. For the sake of argument let's assume this is the case. That then makes this a critical moment: if the player doesn't take the right action this turn, the game could end immediately. The right choice must be made to survive.

(*Note*: in some versions of Rogue, griffins can move double-speed. I'm ignoring this behavior for this example. Also note, earlier versions of Rogue used G to instead mean gnome, which are much easier to defeat than griffins.)

We might borrow a term from chess here and say he is "in check," which is appealing not just for the danger of the situation but because a roguelike character's movement options mirror those of a chess king. Like when a king is in check, the player must take immediate action to continue play. Note that, unlike chess, there is randomness in Rogue. If the player's character makes a mistake he may die, or instead the monster might miss on its attack, or it might do less damage than the player has hit points. Most situations in Rogue are like this, but what is important to this discussion is the fact the character *might* die.

So, if the player chooses to attack the Griffin, well, then if he's low-level he'll probably not kill the monster immediately. It'll then get its turn to counter-attack, which is perilous for him. Since we need to prevent those monster attacks, or at least postpone them, that's a bad move. If the player moves to another space adjacent to the Griffin then it can still hit for its turn, so that's also bad.

6.3 Fleeing

So, the choices here are either to move away from the griffin, or to use some other option. In the former case the griffin will certainly move another space forward, putting the player in danger again but postponing the fatal attack by one turn. That could be either a good or bad thing:

- Good
  - The player will have had an extra turn to heal from prior damage;
  - the monster might be naturally slower than him;
  - the player might come across the stairs out offering escape (true in Rogue but not always in NetHack or Crawl, where adjacent intelligent monsters can follow down stairs); and
  - the player might be able to continue retreating in a loop, possibly allowing healing up to full.

- Bad
  - The monster might be faster than the player, meaning on some of those running-away turns the monster might get a free attack;
  - the direction the player is running towards may be a dead-end, meaning the player won't be able to evade forever, and eventually his back will be to the wall, and he'll have to flee around the monster, or maybe even fight through; and
  - another monster might arrive from out of sight in the direction he's fleeing. Even if it's a weak monster, when it gets up to the player he'll have to spend a turn killing it, which will give the griffin a try at cleaning his clock.

In these "bad" cases, if the player has no other escape items then he has actually made a critical error in letting the griffin get this close, an issue we'll get to later. Item use is the other solution to this situation. Well-designed roguelikes provide a number of these items, one-use, multi-use, infinite use and equipable. If he doesn't have any of these he'll have to resort to fleeing, and the possibility of any of the bad things listed above.

6.4 Items

The point here is that the end of a game always comes down to such a critical moment, whether it is recognized as such by the player or not. The most devious moments are those that don't look dangerous.

- If
    - all critical moments in a game are recognizable and avoidable,
    - the player has complete knowledge of the game rules,
    - and is playing with sufficient care,
- Then
    - the player can always survive.

An entirely fair game is bound to always provide such situations. On the other hand, it bears no responsibility to warn of check, and so the player doesn't always know when he must take a particular move to survive. Also note, no non-trivial roguelike is entirely fair. Even marvin occasionally loses at NetHack. The point is, these circumstances are much less common than you'd think.

The player may have to improve his state sufficiently to increase his powers of survival, through increases in power, mobility or vision, to proceed. Doing so "pushes back" the criticality of situations. If the player has gained many hit points, then he will probably be able to survive a single hit by that griffin above. If he can move quickly (potion of speed) or slow the threatening opponent (wand of slow monster) he could escape, or use "hit and run" tactics to kill the monster. If he can see an extra space in passages or darkness, he might be able to see the griffin coming before it gets adjacent.

But there are also tools that don't offer a complete escape, or an escape with conditions or drawbacks, or a random chance of failure. To look at a more complex situation: if the player has a scroll of teleportation then he can probably escape from the griffin. But teleport scrolls are random in operation. They move the player to a random other in-room spot on the level. That may be adjacent to a monster just as dangerous as the griffin; it may in fact be one of the other spaces adjacent to the very griffin causing the trouble! It might seem that this makes the scroll a bad choice, but practically it is just a small risk. That is part of what makes the decision to use the scroll an interesting choice. In this case the player would probably want to use a surer escape item to get away from, or even neutralize, the griffin, but if no other choice is available the teleport scroll is still there as a last-ditch option.

6.5 The First Law of Roguelikes

To return to the game, let's consider this situation now:

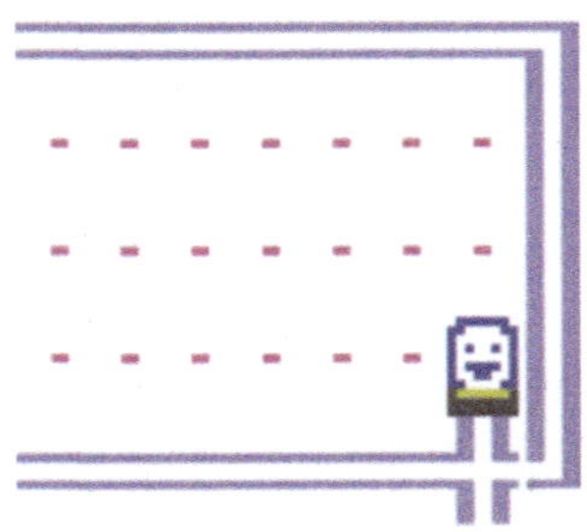

Figure 6.2

Rogue, standing before a door, what lies beyond it?

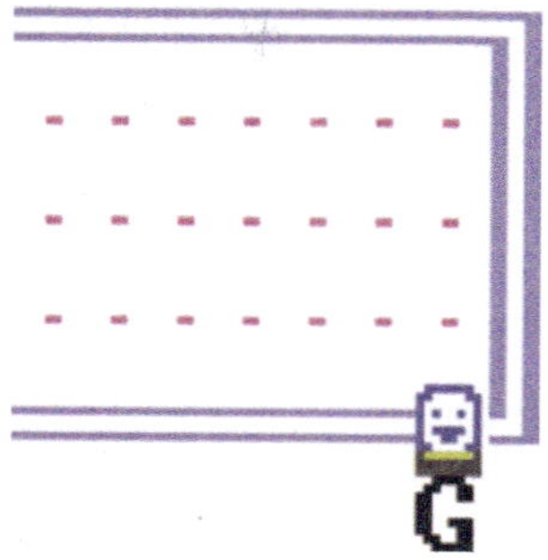

Figure 6.3

Rogue, surprise!

This is one of those cases where the player doesn't know if a situation is critical. Rogue doesn't let you see beyond doors until you step into them.

Although unlikely at a given moment, the strongest monster that can be generated on this level could be on the other side. One of the less fair things about Rogue (and many other roguelikes as well) is that, in a case like this where you blunder into an enemy, it'll get the first attack on you 50% of the time, and before you even know it's there. If that attack is strong enough to kill then your game is over solely because you did something you must do, frequently, just to play the game.

It's not likely for that to happen, but as I've said elsewhere, success in roguelikes comes from not playing dangerously if you can help it. If you survive in a situation 49 times out of 50, but keep encountering that situation, eventually the dice will roll against you. Even if you just roll once, that's still a 1-in-50 chance of losing, and slim chances come up sometimes. Thus, the player is advised not to enter doors at all if he can help it.

The trouble is, he can't help it. Players are constantly entering doors throughout these games. All the means of leaving rooms in Rogue either involve doorways or expending a resource of some type.

What's more, on the other side of doors are dark passages, twisty tunnels that the player can't see more than one space down, which in game terms is the same kind of danger as entering a doorway. Doors are entered only a relative few times each level, but every step taken down a passage might be its own critical moment!

If you were to extend the player's sight range in passages the situation is eased a bit, since the player can wait upon seeing an approaching monster and thus get in the first hit. But, assuming monsters have the same vision range as the player, even being able to see two or more spaces away in a dark corridor doesn't much lessen the criticality of monster meetings in passages. You might not be in danger of an attack this round, but the enemy still blocks that passage and forces you to move away. Unless the player has an escape item or some such, it merely postpones the inevitable.

When the player enters a new dungeon level, there is a small chance that he'll begin adjacent to a powerful monster forcing him to flee immediately. And, if the only good direction to flee is a dead-end, it's even possible that the "critical moment" was the turn before entering the new dungeon level, which the player has absolutely no chance of knowing ahead of time.

Certainly in these cases, the player is screwed. A situation nearly identical to the one pictured below occurred to me while I was taking screenshots for this column:

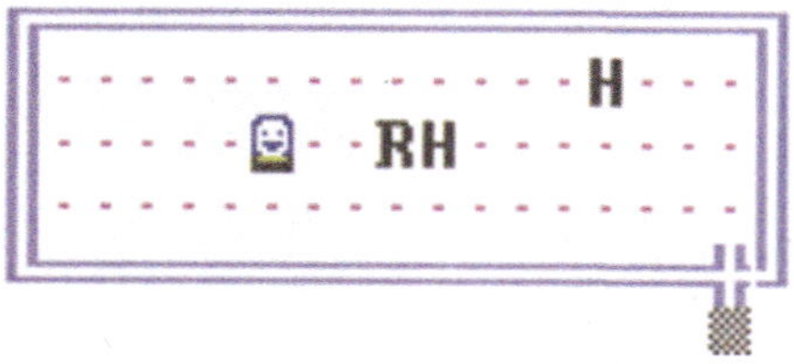

Figure 6.4

Rogue: rattlesnakes and hobgoblins

This happened when I came down the stairs from level 2! The game happened to send in the strongest monster that could appear on the level and two hobgoblins, and all of them stood between me and the only exit. Situations like this do occur in Rogue sometimes, though they are rare. I probably could have survived it with a scroll of scare monster, but with that item you can survive nearly anything. In this case the critical moment was the staircase on the previous level, and I had no way of knowing slithery death was waiting on the next floor.

Situations like these bring us to an important design dictum, so important we might call it the First Law of Roguelike Design:

Provided reasonable play, the player's character should not be killed or suffer great permanent harm in one attack.

"Reasonable" here means playing in the way intended as "normal" by the developer. If the player can survive, but only by playing in an annoying way, such as, say, from searching every space to ward against the possibility of an instant death trap, that is bad design. It also means that, if the player has a temporary condition that makes death more likely, he has no assurance of survival. Being low in hit points means you shouldn't go exploring dangerous tunnels.

"Permanent harm" here means types other than straight hit point damage, such as substantial strength drain. Those instances have the potential to stack up, so the character might be subject to multiple unavoidable such drains in a game, making him rapidly unplayable. Minor permanent harm may be okay though, depending on prevalence and the possibility of remedy.

The Rogue analogy is getting rattlesnake-bitten enough that your strength drains to extremely low levels. Strength drain cannot kill by itself in Rogue, but it is possible for it to get so low that the character is impossible to play unless he uses a potion of restore strength, which are not guaranteed items. How much harm is too great? It depends on the extent of the damage and how many turns it takes to get out of the zone in question. The rattlesnake floors in Rogue don't really last that long. The vampire floors later, depending on version*, could be hazardous but are the last floors of the game. The drain floors in Super Famicom Shiren are more dangerous, relatively speaking, but are only two levels out of 30.

The strictness of the law is less if the game's sight rules were changed to always look at least two spaces away, although it still applies in the case of changing dungeon levels. Still, this might be an interesting avenue for design exploration by inventive developers.

6.6 Situational Danger and Improving State

For illustration purposes I've overstated the danger a bit. If Rogue threw griffins at the player from the start it wouldn't be a very fun game. Fortunately, most monsters aren't able to kill in one hit. No monster in the game has such an "instakill" attack. Some might do so much damage as to deplete the player's health in one attack but only if he is very low-leveled. Thus, part of the necessary process of the game is improving your statistics to make dangerous areas survivable.

There exists one popular roguelike game, however, which is famous, or infamous, for its instadeaths: NetHack. And yet, NetHack is also known among experienced players for fairness. It might even be too fair. How are these two reputations reconciled? Let's look at some of its instadeath monsters and observe how they obey the stated law of design.

6.7 Cockatrices

Cockatrices can appear fairly early, before the player has had a chance to improve his state much. By one measure they are the deadliest monster in the game, the source of more unique death causes than any other monster.

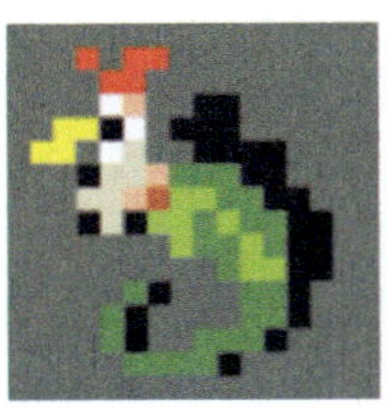

Figure 6.5

A cockatrice

* Rogue's vampires drain maximum hit points. It seems that Rogue Clone IV's vampires drain maximum strength instead, so be aware if you're playing that version.

However: In melee, cockatrices can only turn the player to stone if he hits without a weapon and isn't wearing gloves. In other cases, the player "hears the cockatrice hissing," which either has no effect or begins a gradual petrifaction process. This can be halted by eating a dead lizard or an acidic monster, both of which are common at low levels and both types are among the few corpses in the game that never rot. It is extremely unlikely the player won't have at least one melee weapon when he sees his first cockatrice: the only role that doesn't begin with one is the Tourist, they're frequent finds on the dungeon floor, and many intelligent monsters are generated with one that you could take.

Perhaps paradoxically, once the cockatrice has shuffled off its mortal coil it becomes more deadly to you, because it is awfully tempting to pick one up (when wearing gloves, of course) and start whacking monsters with it, turning them to stone. This is avoidable, simply, by not doing that. If you do, and are carrying so much that you are in burdened state, you are taking a grave risk since falling into a pit trap may cause you to land on the corpse, and pit traps are hidden features.

There are two genuinely treacherous instadeaths associated with cockatrices. The first: if you aren't wearing gloves and are blind, and step on a corpse, you are instantly turned to stone the moment you feel it at your feet. Fortunately, a cockatrice is dead usually because you killed it, and if you're blind you probably killed it in melee so you've probably heard its hissing. In those cases, you probably shouldn't walk around until your blindness has worn off.

The second case is when an enemy picks up a dead cockatrice and whacks you with it. This is legitimately terrifying, but surprisingly rare. Only intelligent humanoid enemies wearing gloves can use this trick. In practice this is almost exclusively soldiers, who you won't even see until the midgame. And again, they don't try to kill cockatrices themselves to use this trick; it only happens when you kill one yourself and they get to the body.

6.7.1 Medusa

Medusa petrifies your character immediately if you enter her presence while sighted. She always appears in each game and always stands on the downstairs of her level. But she always appears on one of two specific special levels, and once you know she's there she's not so bad. Blindfolds (or, in a pinch, towels that you can wrap around your head) usually can be found by the time you get to her. Barring those, you can just dig down through the floor on her level to bypass her until it's time to ascend with the Amulet, by which time you'll have had around 30 levels to scour for items and at least two wishes to boot.

In older versions of NetHack Medusa was much more treacherous. She could be generated in a normal room on an otherwise-ordinary level. That was certainly a case of her breaking the rules.

6.7.2 High-Level Magic Users

Some monsters in NetHack are able to cast spells, and if they're higher than a certain level one of those spells is Touch of Death. These foes generally appear late, but they are one of the most significant roadblocks in the game, the primary reason magic resistance, which provides an infallible defense against Touch of Death, is so important an element in the ascension kit. There are two major NetHack balance variants, Sporkhack and UnNetHack, and both take measures to reduce the essentialness of magic resistance. This spell doesn't break our rule only because by this time the player has probably had the chance to gain magic resistance. Yet note that if he hasn't this is a possible source of danger, perhaps the last really great danger of the game: the only guaranteed wishes (which can be used to gain an item that grants magic resistance) are in the Castle, and the courtyard of the Castle usually contains liches, who are capable of using Touch of Death. If you don't have magic resistance by this point, then it's advisable to genocide them if possible.

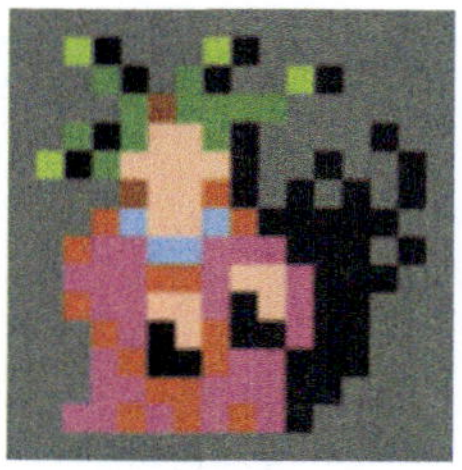

Figure 6.6

Medusa

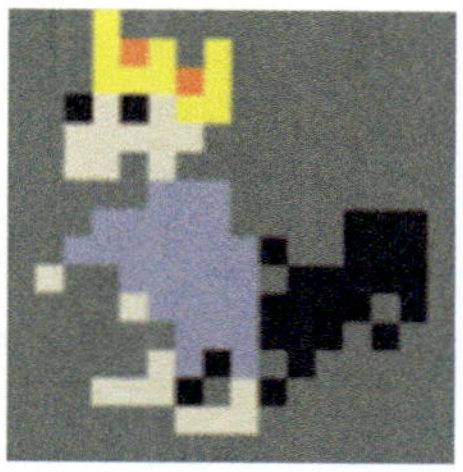

Figure 6.7

An archlich

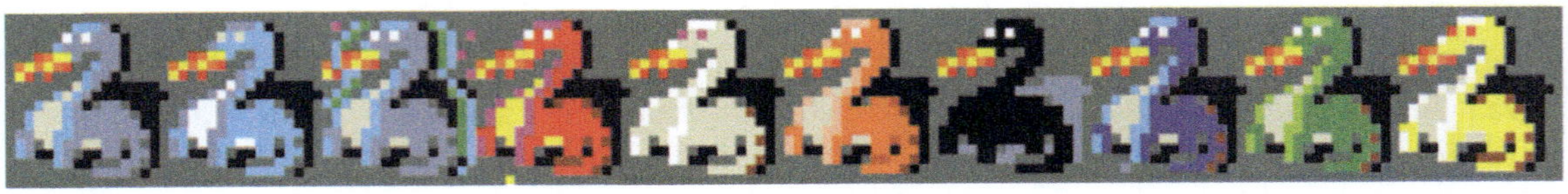

Figure 6.8

Dragons

6.8 Ray Users

Black dragons have a disintegration attack and might come into view lined up for a shot. If it chooses to breathe right off there's not much the player can do to avoid the attack. If he's wearing armor, however, that will get disintegrated first. That will put them in a lot of trouble, and vulnerable to a second blast, but at least they will still be alive. This is a reason why black dragons are sometimes a genocide target, which wipes them out of the rest of game. It's important to note that this case turns up surprisingly rarely, although at least one of these dragons usually turns up each game. They are mid-game enemies, and usually the player has a means of detecting them from afar by the time they enter generation.

More dangerous is the canonical NetHack screw-monster, the gnome that found a wand of death on the dungeon floor. While rare in individual games, every NetHack player encounters one eventually. The only perfect defense against a wand of death is magic resistance, which is hard to come by for most classes in the early levels. This is one of the few things in NetHack that can defeat even perfect play. Fortunately, random death wands are as rare as wands of wishing.

Almost as dangerous early on are strong attack wands such as fire, cold or lightning. Those are not typically instant kills, but they are powerful, magic resistance isn't entirely effective, and even the appropriate elemental resistances aren't perfect. In worse cases, the player may actually be forced to rely on one of NetHack's "quirks," the fact that wands can only be fired in cardinal or diagonal directions. Against a demonstrated wand user, the player can usually use the same tricks unicorns use, attempting to move to a knight's-move away so as to move into melee in the next turn.

There are a number of subtle aspects of Rogue's design that, while not immediately evident, combine to make a playable game. It is random, but not too random. Later on, we'll look at a more complete system of roguelike design rules.

Section II
Theory

7

The Berlin Interpretation

December 2009 In Chapter 60 on Dungeon Hack in this book, I noted that it doesn't quite fit up to all of the most common definition of a roguelike. While it has random dungeons, hack-and-slash gameplay and even items that must be identified, it is a first-person game.

And it doesn't even have an Ultima Underworld kind of first-personness, but the same kind of discrete, right-angled rotation, corridor-centered perspective and step-based movement used in the Wizardry games, which were many years old by that point. And it was a real-time game, too!

For me the game is obviously roguelike enough to be covered here, since we're more concerned with what it is that makes roguelikes fun to play than adherence to a laundry list of similarities. But for those who are interested in such classification, we have the Berlin Interpretation.

Developed at the International Roguelike Development Conference, starting from a document over at the website Temple of the Roguelike, the Berlin Interpretation is a set of feature descriptions that encapsulate what a lot of people consider when they think of roguelikes. It covers both graphical and gameplay elements, and has the added advantage of not being posed as a mere checklist. They recognize that some games that are probably roguelike do not meet the exact description presented by the list, and so it is divided into High and Low value factors.

We're going to take the list through several unusual cases we cover later on: ToeJam & Earl, Shiren the Wanderer (SNES version) and Dungeon Hack. We'll also compare NetHack, Dungeon Crawl and Diablo as controls. Let's have a look!

The original text of the Berlin Interpretation can be found at RogueBasin, at: http://www.roguebasin.com/index.php?title=Berlin_Interpretation.

To fold together how roguelike each of these games is, we rate them on a scale from 1 to 5. At the end we add the scores together and compare them to each other. Please note that this system is essentially arbitrary and probably counter to the intended use of the system. I'm just using it to give us a value to compare. This methodology probably wouldn't stand close observation. For example, I myself have a problem with ASCII graphics being given any kind of priority. So there you go.

(*December 2015*: Roguelike developer Darren Grey wrote an essay against the Berlin Interpretation, at: www.gamesofgrey.com/blog/?p=403.)

7.1 High Value Factors

7.1.1 Random Environment Generation

The game world is randomly generated in a way that increases replayability. Appearance and placement of items is random. Appearance of monsters is fixed; but their placement is random. Fixed content (plots or puzzles or vaults) removes randomness.

Dungeon Hack: 5, levels are surprisingly chaotic,
TJ&E: 4, levels are fairly complicated but more same-ish until later on
Shiren: 4, levels have more pizazz but some levels are actually static, not changing between games or drawn from a pool of possibilities
NetHack: 4, its level generator is aging a bit. Several major levels in NetHack are pre-made, although their contents are changed each game
Dungeon Crawl: 5, the best generator of those presented here
Diablo: 3, good generator visually, but less varied than the others due to a comparative lack of game-play-relevant dungeon features

7.2 Permadeath

You are not expected to win the game with your first character. You start over from the first level when you die. It is possible to save games, but the save file is deleted upon loading. The random environment makes this enjoyable rather than punishing.

Dungeon Hack: 2, offers permadeath as a custom option, but unless it's on for everything it doesn't make much difference
TJ&E: 4, has a system of lives, but the game is hard enough that many are lost at higher levels, and there are no continues, so it works out the same
Shiren: 4, the between-trip continuity options work slightly against it
NetHack: 5, good ol' permadeath. Note that NetHack contains Discover Mode, which lets players revive after death endlessly, but a Discover win doesn't count as a win to either the community or the high score list.
Dungeon Crawl: 5, it has full permadeath
Diablo: 2, Diablo 2 introduced permadeath in the form of Hardcore Mode

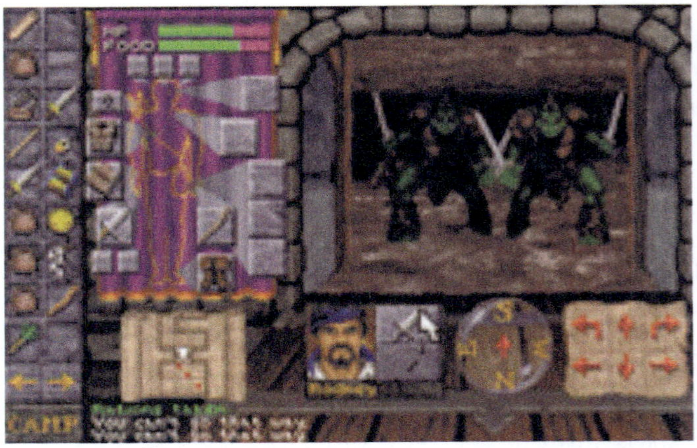

Figure 7.1

DreamForge's Dungeon Hack.

7.2.1 Turn-Based

Each command corresponds to a single action/movement. The game is not sensitive to time; you can take your time to choose your action.

Dungeon Hack: 2, game is a mix of turn-based and real time. Real time wins, generally.
TJ&E: 1, not turn-based at all
Shiren: 5
NetHack: 5
Dungeon Crawl: 5
Diablo: 1

7.2.2 Grid-Based

The world is represented by a uniform grid of tiles. Monsters (and the player) take up one tile, regardless of size.

Dungeon Hack: 4, at first the game doesn't look it, but really it's the same as most roguelikes, just first person instead of overhead view
TJ&E: 1
Shiren: 5
NetHack: 5
Dungeon Crawl: 5
Diablo: 1

7.2.3 Non-Modal

Movement, battle and other actions take place in the same mode. Every action should be available at any point of the game. Violations to this are ADOM's overworld or Angband's and Crawl's shops.

Dungeon Hack: 5
TJ&E: 4, due to the ability to order things at mailboxes, which is admittedly a very minor exception
Shiren: 5
NetHack: 5
Dungeon Crawl: 4, due to shops
Diablo: 4, due to shops

(It seems unfair to punish games for not including a signature feature of Hack, but it's in the description.)

7.2.4 Complexity

The game has enough complexity to allow several solutions to common goals. This is obtained by providing enough item/monster and item/item interactions and is strongly connected to having just one mode.

Dungeon Hack: 2, each class typically has only one solution to a given kind of problem, but often different classes have their own solution to special cases. This is against the spirit of the document, though.
TJ&E: 4, it offers a lesser variety of solution than other games, but still offers many ways through different situations depending on presents on-hand
Shiren: 5

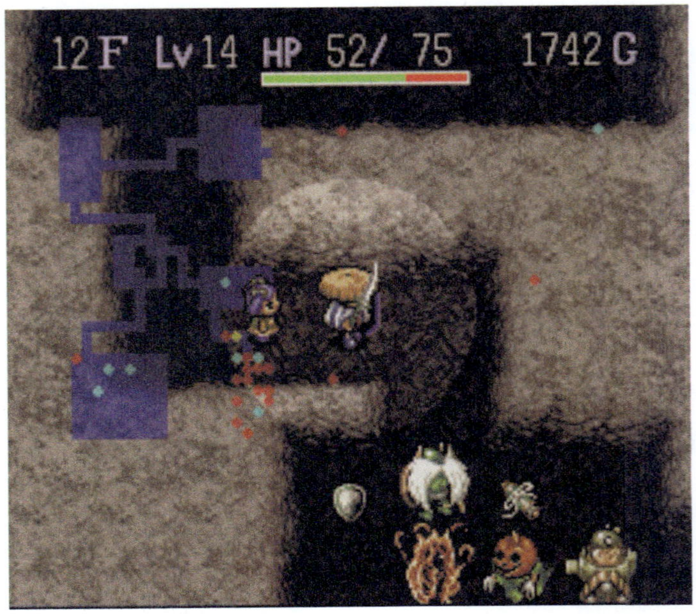

Figure 7.2

Mystery Dungeon: Shiren the Wanderer.

NetHack: 5, and more, it is NetHack's great strength
Dungeon Crawl: 4, solutions are less universal than in other games
Diablo: 1, most solutions come down to killing things with either swords or spells

7.2.5 Resource Management

You have to manage your limited resources (e.g. food, healing potions) and find uses for the resources you receive.

Dungeon Hack: 3, most resources have only one use, but it does make the player rely on them
TJ&E: 4
Shiren: 5
NetHack: 4, NetHack doesn't hold the player's feet to the fire as much as predecessors Hack and Rogue
Dungeon Crawl: 5
Diablo: 1, its shops break item scarcity

7.2.6 Hack'n'slash

Even though there can be much more to the game, killing lots of monsters is a very important part of a roguelike. The game is player-vs-world: there are no monster/monster relations (like enmities, or diplomacy).

All except TJ&E: 5
TJ&E: 1, the players can only fight monsters using certain presents, and further receive no experience for it. ToeJam & Earl is unusually pacifistic for a game in this genre.

7.2.7 Exploration and Discovery

The game requires careful exploration of the dungeon levels and discovery of the usage of unidentified items. This has to be done anew every time the player starts a new game.

Dungeon Hack: 5, surprisingly, the dungeon has a lot of character, there are several important features generated, and the items are much like in Rogue
TJ&E: 4, held back a little from presents being the only kind of item
Shiren: 5

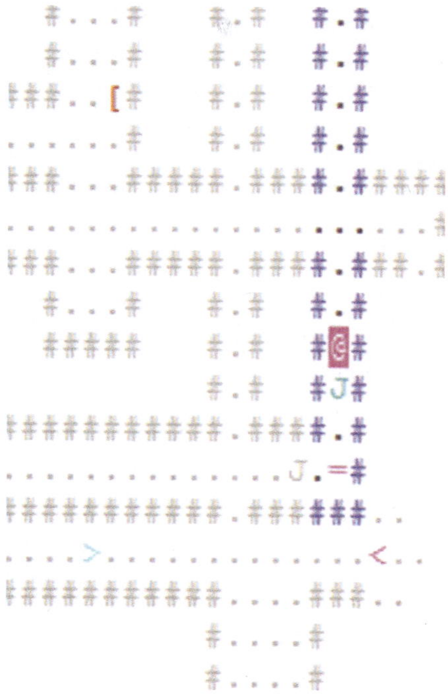

Figure 7.3

Dungeon Crawl Stone Soup (ASCII mode).

NetHack: 5
Dungeon Crawl: 5
Diablo: 2, item ID is faked—they cannot be used before identification, and that just becomes an extra step you have to perform before using or selling. Dungeons do have some important random features scattered about.

7.3 Low Value Factors

7.3.1 Single Player Character

The player controls a single character. The game is player-centric, the world is viewed through that one character, and that character's death is the end of the game.

Dungeon Hack: 5
TJ&E: 5 in single-player, 4 in two-player mode, the game's two-player mode is a big part of its appeal actually, but it does fall outside the realm of the document. Even in two-player mode the game is still very roguelike-ish, just with a second player played by a second person. Still, many games are played in one-player mode.
Shiren: 5
NetHack: 5
Dungeon Crawl: 5
Diablo: 5 in single-player, 2 outside of it. It beefs up monsters in multiplayer games necessitating teamwork, which might be good game design but isn't roguelike so much. Diablo is so strongly focused on multiplayer that I'm rating it as 3 in the aggregate scores.

7.3.2 Monsters Are Similar to Players

Rules that apply to the player apply to monsters as well. They have inventories and equipment, use items, cast spells, etc.

Dungeon Hack: 2, no inventories, limited abilities
TJ&E: 1, enemies are very limited compared to players
Shiren: 3, monsters have no inventory but move much like player
NetHack: 5, intelligent monsters are extremely flexible
Dungeon Crawl: 4, monsters use weapons and armor but only a small number of magic items
Diablo: 1, monsters are simply enemy obstacles, different types have unique abilities but they're nowhere near as flexible as a player character

7.3.3 Tactical Challenge

You have to learn about the tactics before you can make any significant progress. This process repeats itself, i.e. early game knowledge is not enough to beat the late game. (Due to random environments and permanent death, roguelikes are challenging to new players.) The game's focus is on providing tactical challenges (as opposed to strategically working on the big picture, or solving puzzles).

Dungeon Hack: 1, tactically light
TJ&E: 3, getting around opponents through evasion is challenging and fun, and evading danger is a big aspect of any good roguelike. There is little actual combat, though.
Shiren: 5, arguably the game's strongest feature, there are many dangerous situations that can only be escaped through clever use of the tools at hand
NetHack: 4, after the mid-game, many characters can bulldoze through most situations
Dungeon Crawl: 5, tactical combat is a focus of the game
Diablo: 3, focuses on the bad parts of hack-and-slash but still pretty good

7.3.4 ASCII Display

The traditional display for roguelikes is to represent the tiled world by ASCII characters.
(I don't place a lot of stock in this one myself.)

Dungeon Hack: 1
TJ&E: 1
Shiren: 1
NetHack: 5, has an ASCII mode available
Dungeon Crawl: 5
Diablo: 1

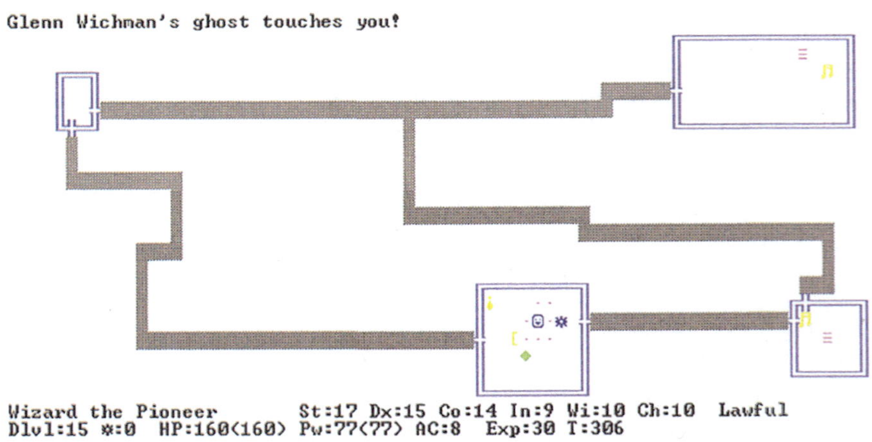

Figure 7.4

NetHack (Rogue level).

7.3.5 Dungeons

Roguelikes contain dungeons, such as levels composed of rooms and corridors.

Dungeon Hack: 5, actually has excellent dungeons, its level builder is among the best
TJ&E: 1, its weird land-and-space levels may be dungeon-like, but they aren't dungeons
Shiren: 3, many of its early areas are outdoors. If that sounds petty, well, it is, but it's a rather petty criterion.
NetHack: 5
Dungeon Crawl: 5
Diablo: 5, Diablo 2 introduced non-dungeon play environments

7.3.6 Numbers

The numbers used to describe the character (hit points, attributes, etc.) are deliberately shown.

Dungeon Hack: 5, HP bar can be switched to numbers and the PC, as a D&D 2E character, flaunts its statistics
TJ&E: 1, only score is visible numerically
Shiren: 5
NetHack: 5
Dungeon Crawl: 5
Diablo: 5, it places a strong emphasis on increasing your stats however you can, usually through equipment

Totals, counting low value factors for half:

NetHack & Dungeon Crawl (tie): 57.5
Shiren Super Famicom: 54
Dungeon Hack: 42.5
TJ&E: 33
Diablo: 29

The maximum score is 60, and the minimum is 12. These scores seem to me to be fairly consistent with the rogue-likeness of each of these games. Most games that, subjectively, have nothing to do with roguelikes would probably score in the low 20s at most, with lots of them coming in at 12. Rogue itself would probably get a 56 or 57, the only thing it is lacking being monster similarity to the player (monsters there don't have inventories).

The Berlin Interpretation seems to objectively be a good measure, but I wonder. Is it possible to devise a game that seems roguelike subjectively but purposely fails most of its tests? Spelunky might be a good game to hold up against it as an edge case.

8

Roguelikes and OD&D

May 2008 As you may have figured out by now, roguelikes are one of my favorite types of computer games. It's not that I hate other kinds of games, or even other RPGs. But roguelikes, good ones at least, provide essential gaming nutrients unavailable nearly anywhere else. They're games of skill instead of patience, which is rare for CRPGs. They are difficult but, once one knows how to play, often fair. And they are set in a world of wonder and amazement balanced by great danger.

The possibilities there seem endless. You could play Rogue a hundred times and not experience two games that are similar to each other. You could play NetHack or ADOM for years and still encounter a new aspect of the game from time to time. Dungeon Crawl is more than just a game: it is dozens of games, each class and race playing surprisingly differently from the others. Just being a roguelike doesn't make a game good, of course, but the best are among the greatest games ever made.

I believe that, someday, eventually, the tide will turn in the public perception of roguelike games, or at least the core ideas that drive them. This is not due to any magical quality bestowed by turn-based movement or grid-based game worlds, which are a superficial determination of roguelikeness but do not get to what makes them interesting. No, one plays a roguelike to explore an unknown world, relying on uncertain resources, figuring the rules out along the way and learning the underlying logic of the game. And of course, when people start talking about procedural content generation, they are unknowingly calling upon the ancient monster-deities of the Dungeons of Doom.

But these ideas did not originate with roguelikes. It must be remembered that approximately half of what makes roguelikes interesting as computer games was invented years before, in a pen-and-paper game created back when teletype machines roamed the earth.

8.1 That Roguelike Feeling

The soul of the roguelike, as I've mentioned before, was born in Dungeons & Dragons. But not a version one could recognize from reading any of the recent editions, 4e, 3.5 or 3rd. Neither can they be seen in 2nd Edition AD&D, which is largely where it was abandoned. But it didn't originate from 1st edition either, or the "classic" books edited by Holmes, Moldvay or Cook. To find their source, whence sprung the ideas in their purest form, one must go back to Original Dungeons & Dragons, a game that the internet is now calling "OD&D."

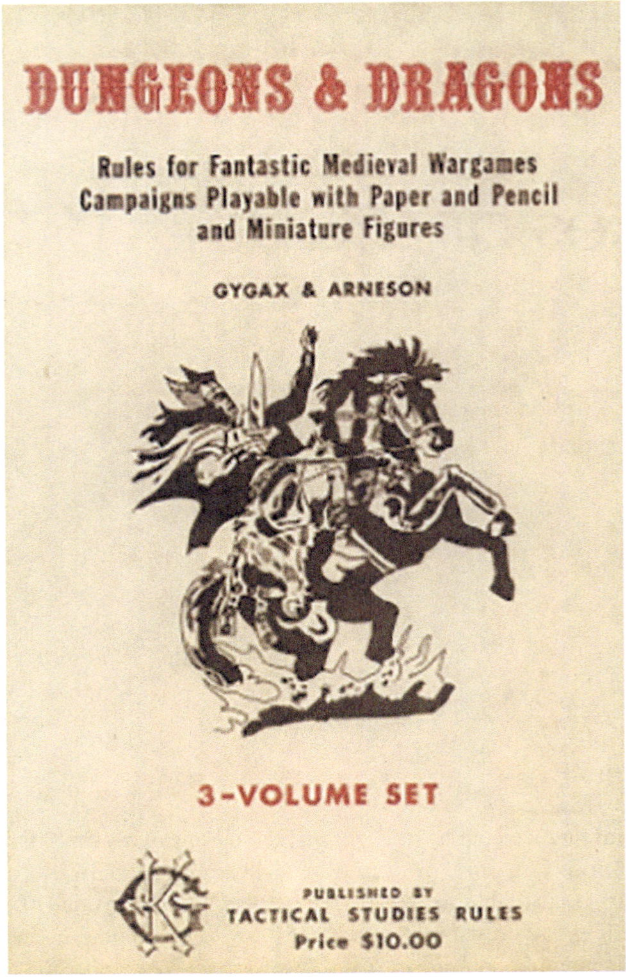

Figure 8.1

Cover to Dungeons & Dragons "0E" White Box release. (Image borrowed from Wikipedia, copyright by Hasbro. Used under principle of fair use, https://en.wikipedia.org/wiki/Dungeons_%26_Dragons_(1974)#/media/File:D&d_Box1st.jpg.)

It is a style of game that, in the aftermath of the death of Gary Gygax but before then too, has become reexamined in recent months on sites throughout the internet. Tried, and found to be awesome.

Given that many of its players are still alive, it is somewhat shocking just how much about it must be rediscovered. It is sometimes forgotten that that game, originally, had a strong, explicit setting, one that will seem familiar to any roguelike player. The word "Dungeon" in the title of the game refers to what is now termed a megadungeon. It is not just the place where the orcs terrorizing town are hiding out, or where the drow base their assaults on the surface world, or where the mind flayers sit and brood.

It is where all these things happen but is much more than any of those things. It is a huge space, stretching far down into the earth, its depths unplumbed, its age and origin beyond mortal knowledge. It is an archetypal setting, a meta-place.

It is a world, as in underworld, to itself. While it makes more internal sense than those thrown-together roguelike worlds, still, its reasons for being are not really logical ones:

- Why does that dragon guard the pile of gold?
- Where do all these coins and magic items come from?
- Why was all the bad magic stuff made? Did anyone really think a *sword -1, cursed* would be useful enough to craft?

The game provided answers, of a sort, to these questions. Respectively: dragons like treasure; deceased adventurers; and they were made by insane, prankster wizards.

8.2 Seriously, Prankster Wizards

With respect to the memory of Gary Gygax, these are not good reasons. For D&D's origins, they didn't have to be good. This is because Dungeons & Dragons grew out of an earlier game Gygax worked on called Chainmail, a form of miniatures wargame concerning itself with medieval combat. Now, wargames are not quite games in the same sense as Monopoly or Bridge. The ethic here is not to win at all costs. It is to enact pretend battles and bring to them enough statistical rigor so that the participants can see the outcome as definitive.

The goal of a wargame is to play the game itself and see which side *should* win. The fun is had in the playing and fighting more than success, and certainly not to gain power and see one's character as some variation on the theme of badass. There are enough things that can instantly kill any old-school D&D character, regardless of level, that the term "healthy paranoia" takes on a special aptness. Characters die often but are quick to roll up and largely interchangeable, which is good, because the more work you put into making one the worse you'll feel when he kicks the bucket.

Need I even remind you of the similarities here to a certain familiar type of computer game?

One might take this, also, to explain why roguelikes don't have stories to speak of. OD&D characters usually adventured without a motivation more complex than amassing treasure.

But this isn't really true of either game; narrative, after all, is inescapable. The things that happen to the character may be random strings of events, without reason, but human beings tend to perceive these strings as narrative.

8.3 "Storytelling" in Roguelikes

Important events that make the game easier or harder get remembered and the rest of the game is viewed in their light. Finding a two-handed sword makes all monsters easier to kill. Finding a ring of slow digestion means hunger becomes much less of a problem, while wearing a ring of regeneration makes death from wounds less dangerous but starvation much more likely. A character might find an amulet vs. poison, then ironically die to poison despite it. It might be coincidence that strings these things together, but if there's enough random stuff going on, coincidences tend to happen.

The result of these things is that it's typically much more interesting to hear either an OD&D or a roguelike player talk about a favorite adventure than a player of more recent D&D, or those of modern CRPGs. The stories that so-so fantasy writers come up with do not usually compare with the experiences of a sufficiently deep roguelike. There can be no goth-posing in a world where the monsters have so much over the players. No one is trying to tell a story during an OD&D game, and thus, the stories that do come have no affectation.

Don't believe me? Don't take my word for it. Check out the Shiren threads at NeoGAF and Gamespite. Dip into the archives of rec.games.roguelike.nethack and rec.games.roguelike.adom, searching those groups for the term "YASD." People have more fun dying in roguelike games than most folk have winning "traditional" CRPGs.

This is the same reason people obsess over The Sims, really. Human minds search for patterns in series of random events, recognizing them as narratives, and in attempting to explain them subconsciously attribute thought processes to the actors. This is the root of superstition, some would say of religion too, and it's why roguelikes don't lack for stories. What they lack are *pre-written* stories.

9

Storytelling, Bah!

April 2007 For a while now we've talked about all kinds of roguelikes, including many of the major ones and a few niche cases. These are games that can attract incredibly loyal fans, not loyal, perhaps, in the dress-up-at-DragonCon style, but fans who can nudge the system of an intrinsically chaotic game like NetHack to the degree that they can maintain incredible winning streaks.

Hmm, I said nudge there. That seems oddly appropriate; the game genre that roguelikes most resemble, in one sense, is pinball. Traditional RPGs are games in which the world is laid out beforehand, every encounter planned out. Other than the very earliest of these games, there is generally a way out of any situation you can get in. This is, in fact, more or less game design law these days throughout the industry. If the player is not dead or inescapably falling towards it (like, seconds away), then there must be a way out. Although one or two may strive mightily, there is nothing to prove that a roguelike is winnable every time.

The need, in traditional computer games, to avoid inescapable situations produces certain subtle limits to their play. Most Lucasarts adventures are actually impossible to lose. Because of this, the player can mostly disregard that pesky danger sense. He won't die, he won't get a puzzle into an unsolvable state, and he won't be able to lose an item he needs to win. If an item is needed to win, but can be lost, then if there is an infinite source of them somewhere in the game (like, say, the clown in the first year of Grim Fandango telling you he'll provide as many worm balloons as you want) it's a pretty sure bet it's important somehow.

The fourth case of the original Phoenix Wright has a place where Detective Gumshoe offers you a choice of three different tools to use in searching for clues. Only one provides the necessary clue. Because of this, it's always possible to go back and try a different item if you picked incorrectly. . . .

Can always go back? Wait a second! That doesn't sound like it's a real choice at all! And in fact, Phoenix Wright, traditional adventure games, and many other games too like console RPGs suffer from an absence of player choice. They may be able to roam around, but that rarely matters to the game. They may need to solve puzzles to proceed, but it's more of a choice between solving it and moving on, and not solving and being stuck. They may (in Phoenix Wright) lose a case because they've been penalized too many times, but running out of points is the only resource in the game, and the play doesn't change in any other way from losing them.

It seems to me, and feel free to debate me on this, that when you reduce the fractions all the way down these games end up being nothing more than sophisticated versions of a "next page" prompt. If games ultimately are about the choices a player makes and their consequences, then these cannot properly be called games.

Now, it should be said that the common definition of "game" is a little different from this and that even under a strict definition this is not always true. There are some computer games that tell a story with branching outcomes, and the player's decisions, ultimately, determine which branch is followed. There are even games that make the "decision" a game mechanic: Ogre Battle is notorious for its "Chaos Frame" game system, where a score is kept of a number of variables, with more points usually assigned to more difficult practices (like not over-leveling your characters), and the characters who join and the ending are determined by the score.

And there are interesting things happening with Chris Crawford's Storytron, which is an algorithmic storytelling engine. In fact, if you take a roguelike as being a tool for the player to create his own adventure story, then Storytron starts to look a little (but just a little) familiar.

This is why roguelike games are especially important now. As games move further into being "interactive stories," with increasing de-emphasis on "interactive," games are becoming less and less game-like. And as games increasingly take movies as their model instead of board games, puzzles, pinball and so forth, this problem will only get worse.

10

Pushing the Silver Boulder

January 2016 Roguelike players are, I've previously said somewhere, "awash in a sea of random numbers." Well that is the case with good roguelike games anyway. Note, that's a game that's good at being a roguelike. There are other kinds of good games, but if you're not going to use randomness effectively then why bother?

The best ones can throw unexpected events at the player, even after many games, so that the game is interesting even after months or years of dedicated play, yet there is a lot of room for skill to help the player overcome the many weird and chaotic situations that arise.

But as I write this description of roguelikes, I'm reminded of a certain other kind of game. A kind of game that's even more skill-based, and yet is even more random than roguelikes are! It's a kind of game also played for high score, and exceedingly skillful play is as thrilling to watch as a NetHack Pacifist, or a Crawl all-rune win, while being much shorter.

What kind of miracle game could this be? If you haven't guessed yet, it's pinball!

10.1 Ever Since I Was a Young Boy, I've Played the Silver Ball

Video games first became popular in arcades, and a lot of what made them popular was derived from pinball. My reading suggests that the first video game to use the "lives" system, where you have a certain number of ships/characters/cars/pac-people/whatevers, was Space Invaders, but pinball tables had been using "lives," as in balls, for years before. The idea of earning extra lives, too, comes from there. But pinball is an intrinsically arcade kind of thing, while roleplaying games may be the least arcade-like of all game styles. The most iconic arcade RPGs are games like Gauntlet, which is really more of an overhead-view shooter with an emphasis on crowd control, and Tower of Druaga, which, while interesting in its way, is esoteric enough that it never got an arcade release in the US, and anyway still very far from being a pure RPG experience.

In point of connection with roguelikes, too, there are some design similarities. Some pingames contain something called a progressive jackpot, which is a difficult-to-achieve award that builds from game to game until it's won. In theme this reminds one of NetHack's bones files, or Larn's taxes, in that it's an aspect of play in which previous games leak into and affect the current game. Other pinball games play around with the form of play in other ways: the table Junk Yard has a special mode that starts if a game happens to be running at midnight! And roguelike games ask you to develop a score, and purport to measure skill, in much the same way that pinball games do. If one were to ever make a genuine roleplaying game work in an arcade setting, whatever that would mean, it would probably end up looking a lot like a roguelike.

But once you get beyond the initial similarities, one is left with a whole ton of differences that must be reconciled between the two genres.

10.2 A Little History of Pinball

The first thing we must do is separate the game of pinball into two subgenres, the old electro-mechanical, or EM machines, and the later computerized games. The later games made a strong resurgence in arcades in the '90s, as multimedia features, high-powered licenses and deep rulesets resulted in the best-selling pinball machines of all time, such as Bally/William's popular tables The Addams Family and Attack From Mars. Many of the best machines of the era were made by Bally/Williams, but they're still being made to this day by Stern Electronics, making games with licenses as diverse as Monopoly, Ripley's Believe It Or Not, The Lord Of The Rings and Game Of Thrones.

Even modern pinball tables are built off of principles discovered during the EM days, the era of mechanical bells and clacking score counters, and one could consider that to be a purer form of pinball than the current period, which steals as many ideas from video games as video games originally stole from pinball. The case for similarity gets a lot easier once we get to the later era of pinball tables, which have complex rulesets and game states to explore that start to almost feel like a dungeon themselves, and that is the era I'm talking about. But a case can be made for EM games too, and one could argue they offer a purer pinball experience.

So, starting with the late '80s and early '90s, a new breed of pinball machine arose that went beyond just bouncing the ball around but asks the players to complete more complex kinds of tasks during the game. Some of these tasks take the form of modes, special periods where certain shots are more valuable than others, or when special targets or other opportunities might open up. A special kind of mode common to most machines is a multiball, when the game puts more than one ball on the table at once and makes huge score awards called jackpots available, and which you keep playing until all but one of the balls are lost. There are also shots that "build" as you shoot them, sometimes topping out at an extra ball and sometimes offering "things" to "collect" by hitting certain shots at the right time, like Mansion Rooms or Door Panels. If you manage to accomplish these tasks well enough, then really skillful players can start something called a wizard mode.

Let me express my hope that all of you out there get the chance to experience a good wizard mode at least once in your life. They're like drugs. If you've never played one, you have no idea.

10.3 Basics of Pinball

I'm assuming you know what pinball is generally ("You hit that ball at things, right?"), but knowing some terminology may help:

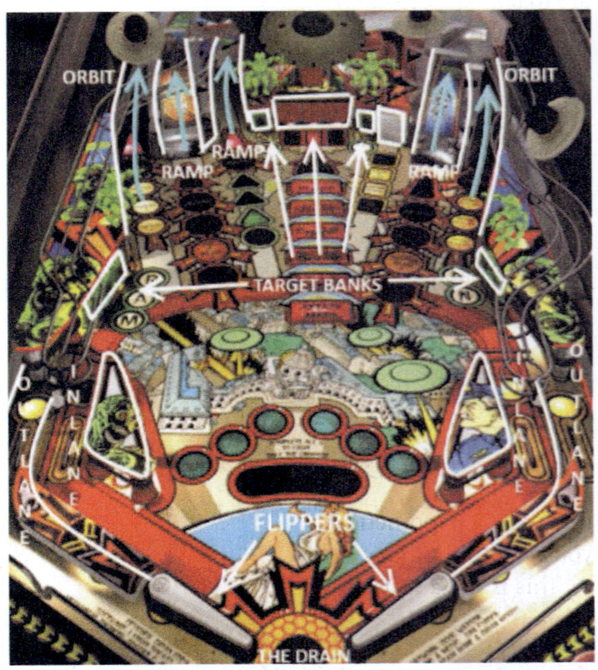

Figure 10.1

Attack From Mars, screenshotted from Farsight Studio's Pinball Arcade.

The table pictured is the popular Attack From Mars, designed by Brian Eddy (Bally/Williams, 1995). It's a relatively open table, with lots of space in the middle of the board for making unobstructed shots.

Pinball in a nutshell is about make good shots while keeping control of the ball. Success involves risk management. Made shots are safe and worth lots of points; missed shots cause wild bounces and put the ball in danger of going down the drain or outlanes. Different players will find different shots easy and hard, and the shots themselves cause different bounce angles when missed, so each player has to tackle the game in their own way and adapt to the game as it develops.

- Flippers: These are your primary way of controlling the ball. You can also nudge the table. It's not cheating if you're careful with it, but if you nudge too hard and too often the game will declare "tilt," and the game will lock the flippers and cause you to lose the ball as a penalty. That always hurts.
- The Drain: If the ball falls down here, you lose it—stop this from happening!
- Inlanes: These helpful routes deliver the ball to the flippers and slow it down for you.
- Outlanes: If the ball gets out to here, though, it gets routed straight to the drain.
- Slingshots: If the ball strikes the front of these, it's propelled away fast, towards the outlanes.
- Ramps: These distant shots, if made, are worth big points and return the ball safely to the inlanes.
- Orbits: These lanes are a bit riskier to shoot for, but still fairly safe to hit.
- Target Banks: Important shots, but rebounds may be dangerous; take care!
- Scoop: A hole that holds the ball, awards some value, then shoots it back out towards a flipper.

Older machines, especially EM ones, tend to have weirder boards than this and may not even put the expected two flippers at the bottom, or may arrange them in strange ways. The older the machine, the stranger its layout may be. Newer tables tend to have an open middle with targets sprinkled around the sides and top.

10.4 Williams Mutual: Invest in Our Portfolio of Bumpers and Ramps

As I said, pinball is about risk management. To score points you have to take shots, but each shot carries the risk of the ball draining. If you send it accurately to major targets (ramps and scoops especially), not only will you be rewarded with points and possibly other features like bonus modes and extra balls, but the game will return the ball in some way that's easy to handle. Trickier shots, like to target banks, cause the ball to carom off of them, so you'll have to be prepared for the consequences of its rebound. Missed shots are worst of all; those are the ones that tend to bounce around the board randomly. Sometimes when this happens the ball may hit the slingshots, which may send it to the outlanes and out of play, or it may go directly down between the flippers. Pinball aficionados call this SDTM, or "Straight Down The Middle."

I've said before about the best roguelikes: the longer the game goes without winning, the more likely you are to lose. Success at pinball requires taking this idea to heart. You're going to lose the ball eventually, so to prolong the time until that happens you try to minimize risk as much as you can.

Think about it statistically. If every shot you make has a 30% chance of draining before you regain control of the ball, you'll only get to attempt two shots before your odds of survival dip below 50/50. If every shot has a 25% chance of draining, you'll be able to get three shots. Drop the odds to 20% and you'll be able to attempt four shots, and so on. Every additional percent of safety increases your chances significantly. This is why your better tables will specifically include rules (combinations matching shots with consequences) to encourage riskier play for greater rewards; the game Attack From Mars, the one pictured above, particularly values that central target bank, the one that sends balls directly down the table when hit squarely.

All by itself this is a point of deep connection between roguelike-styled gameplay and pinball, in the management of risk. A deeper comparison of these games requires examining the process of human decision making and implementing, at the core of which is a mysterious thing that I call the point of impulse, which sounds like something out of physics, but it's really not, or at least not directly. I should explain. . . .

10.5 The Point of Impulse, Described and Examined

Let's take a hypothetical situation. Say you're driving a car down the road, trying to decide where in town you want to eat today as you go because most of the restaurants here suck. ("Write what you know!")

This is not a situation that is all that dissimilar to playing a real-time (that is, not turn-based) computer game. You have to coordinate a number of tasks at once, some of which through long practice have faded to semi-consciousness. Really, all the tasks you actually perform while driving are analogues, representative actions, relationships between the controls you manipulate (the steering wheel, the gas pedal, brakes, gear shifts) and the car's motion. You've internalized them, however, so that you don't think about them. The way it feels to you, pulling with your hand causes the car to steer, as if directly, and you don't think about the process you're initiating by turning the steering wheel.

But more than this, when you're driving, what does it feel like? Do you think of it in terms of: watch for the turn/ it's not there look for possible accidents/ if not where should I eat/ time to look for turn/ it's not there look for possible accidents/ if not . . ., like a computer program might? If you do, it's not consciously. Instead, riding there in the driver's seat, you are in a state of reactive openness, watching for things that might draw you out of that state. Driving by a possible place to eat could be one such thing. If a cat runs in front of your car, that is another thing. If an oncoming car looks like it might be out of control, that is something else. These out-of-the-ordinary events make it through your brain's expectations filter in a way that a commercial coming in over the radio, or a bird flying overhead, does not.

When you do spot something important or interesting, that is a point of impulse. It is the twitch of twitch games. It is an intrinsically exciting moment: your brain, having recognized some important stimulus, swings into action. If it's something expected, like approaching somewhere with good food, then it's already moving on to executing the necessary reactions: looking around to make sure other traffic doesn't pose an obstacle, flipping on the turn signal, applying the breaks and preparing to turn the wheel. If it's something unexpected, then it's recognizing this and simultaneously working to figure out what this means for your safety and applying general measures to ensure it, which in this case frequently means reducing speed.

When playing a computer game, part of the enjoyment comes from these points of impulse, which break us out of the ordinary flow of our lives. Even if the game is turn-based this is true; both the time between turns and time in ordinary, non-critical times are analogous to the time spent just driving, watching for unusual events and thinking about where you want to go. Even in a real-time game, though, there are those moments of waiting, where you're trying to determine what you want to do overall. Hyper-fast action games, like many classic arcade games, are almost a continuous stream of impulse points. Too many impulses in a short time are tiring, and cause attention to lag, which tends to pose a limit to the length of twitchy games. The cycle between those two processes, between thinking and reacting, amounts to a basic action loop for the human mind.

10.6 From Dendrite to Finger Muscle

Impulses operate best, feel best when you can limit the number of possible reactions, when you know what range of actions is appropriate. Every option you must weigh, once an action becomes imperative to perform, increases reaction time and reduces immediacy.

Of course roguelike dungeon exploration games are not real time, and you often have dozens of possible actions at each moment. You can walk in one of eight directions; you can rest a turn or search for secret passages; you can put on or take off armor, or wield a different weapon; you can eat a food ration, read a scroll or drink a potion; you can zap a wand, or throw a missile, or drop an item; and so on. But most of these acts are not strictly relevant to the matter at hand, and that helps you play. They might be important to your long-term success, to, say, wear the best armor you've got or drink a potion of strength, and that matters for strategy. Those are actions inspired by your consideration of what would be best throughout the course of the game.

But they aren't good moves at the critical point. If you're fighting a troll then matters have come to a head, the oncoming car is swerving wildly, and even if, in time terms, you can spend hours thinking about what to do, when it comes time to actually do something there's not really a lot of different actions that matter. You might fight him; you might run from him; you might drink a potion of healing; you might use an escape. Changing armor or weapon, eating, moving in a frivolous direction or dropping most things won't help your situation. Only a few things might positively affect your state, and your brain usually does a good job of filtering out the irrelevant actions.

When you're not fighting you're planning your route, which is something more important in these games than most. If you're in a largely linear action game, or even a linear RPG, there's really no choice of where to go, so the act amounts to looking for the first signs of a good way to go then going that way. You don't know, in a roguelike, which way is best, other than the general direction of down for the most part, which is more of a suggestion at a given moment than a direct imperative.

Contrast this to a pinball table. They greatly limit the number of possible actions available at once: you can press or release the left or right flipper buttons, or you can nudge the table, and that's it. The table itself is largely the same throughout the game; there aren't any dark corridors to check or unseen levels to advance to, although the purposes of those shots may change.

But the moments of impulse are still there. Instead of being when you encounter some dangerous monster, they are when the ball is approaching, or in contact with, the flippers. And while it may not seem like it, the implications of those moments, and the details of how you react to them (the timing of the press) correspond roughly with your choice of action in a roguelike. The effective results of those actions send the ball away; if it was a good response, the ball will go somewhere useful in a controlled fashion. If it wasn't, it'll hit something rubber and bounce.

10.7 Vector A + Vector B + Vector C -> Outlane

The basic skill of pinball is ball control, which is an attempt to limit the randomness in the system. If the ball approaches the flippers through an inlane or from the habitrail coming down off a ramp, it sets you up to propel the ball as well as you can expect. If then you shoot another ramp, then you'll again get the ball back in a safe manner. If you can cycle that, you're usually doing great.

Hitting the same shot over and over again, depending on the machine, might be very good or just a holding pattern. Eventually, depending on your knowledge of the rules, you might want to make another shot. Most good shots in pinball are designed so that hitting them limits the chaos of the ball bouncing around the table. Chaos is your worst enemy, the car swerving drunkenly in the opposite lane. An undirected ball has a good chance of hitting the slingshots and being sent spinning around even more randomly, or of approaching the flippers at a bad angle, forcing you to improvise and do what you can to reduce the kinetic energy in the ball—this could be to hold a flipper down to just deflect it, or attempt to cradle it in the raised flipper to arrest its movement, or attempt a "drop catch," where you release the flipper just as the ball strikes it and cause it to stop dead. You might even try to just make a shot, for if you hit a ramp you'll immediately defuse the situation—after going up the ramp, the ball will be returned to you in a controlled manner, problem solved. But that's risky, because shooting on the fly like that is harder to aim, and if you miss the shot, the ball will have more kinetic energy and be moving even faster.

If you don't get the ball under control, what will very likely happen is the ball will pass the flippers and you'll lose it, or it will get sent flying horizontally with enough energy to hit an outlane and become lost, or it will hit a slingshot, increasing the likelihood of the other two things happening.

The roguelike analogy to a wildly careening pinball is fighting multiple opponents at once, especially if they have special abilities that work well together. Then you are likely to die unless you work to make the system less unpredictable. Plowing through the enemies is like trying to make a ramp shot even though the ball is coming at an awkward angle. Instead: pull back, raise a flipper; find a doorway, deflect the ball; reduce the incoming blows to one a turn, cradle the ball. Then maybe you can turn the situation around.

Once you're used to basically manipulating the ball, you can start to focus on the particular set of modes and objectives that pinball table offers you. You can discover these during play, or you can go on the internet and find where people have written them all out for you. If you've spent any time with NetHack then this process is already beginning to sound familiar, and indeed, usually after digesting a game's rulesheet I find that I start playing much better than before.

Once you've got down the basics and know the rules, then in a sense the ball becomes like part of the apparatus of the table, part of the controls between you and the game. Like the steering wheel and gas pedal of the car, or like the controller or keyboard of the computer. Unlike those things, however, on a pinball table, the manipulation of the ball can never be taken completely for granted. There are situations where the ball is probably unsaveable no matter what you do, but once you figure out what the game's rewards are and how to go about achieving them, you may be able to make up for that randomness by earning special features like extra balls, kickbacks, ball saver posts and even free games.

Free games. That's a kind of reward that most roguelikes, to this date, are unable to match.

—

While there is no substitute for a real pinball table (for reasons that are too complicated to explain here, but are related to the physics and frame rate of video recreations), you can play a decent approximation of many classic tables, including Attack From Mars, in Farsight Studio's Pinball Arcade, available for many platforms. Zen Studios' Pinball FX 3 also hosts recreations of many classic machines, including Attack From Mars.

11

I Never Meta Rogue I Didn't Like

December 2006 One of the interesting ideas that that vanishing class of amusement machine, the pinball table, brought over to the scene from its less-reputable kin, the slot machine, is that some aspect of the game could carry over between plays. Although modern pinball games, which take almost as much inspiration in their design from video games as video games took from pinball back in the late '70s and early '80s, tend to downplay this kind of thing, it used to be that progressive jackpots were a common feature on pingames.

A progressive jackpot is an award that builds, not during just a single game, but over many, and when someone earns it it resets to a minimum value. This could be considered bad because the traditional concept of a score is of a measure of a player's skill, and this upsets that notion by potentially giving different scores to two jackpot-earning players who have had identical games, simply because one of them played when the pot was at a larger value than the other. It also seems nonsensical in that, unlike with gambling devices, the points awarded by a pinball machine are wholly arbitrary in nature. While a slot machine cannot dispense money indefinitely and thus progressive jackpots allow for a good balance between income and outlay, a pinball machine can mint points indefinitely.

But what progressive jackpots provide best is a sense of continuity between games. By introducing variables into the game that are not at a default or random state at the beginning of play, a sense is introduced that the game goes on even after the final ball is lost. Further, it draws in other players: if you play ten games and build the progressive jackpot up to a high value then walk away from the table, it will still be at that level when the next player comes along, and he could earn the whole thing. In that way, different players may contribute to a game in interesting ways, producing a collaborative effect, a truly meta kind of game. There is no real reason to put this kind of feature into an automated amusement device like a pinball machine or a computer game program, but it is still an oddly compelling idea. It injects an aspect of the real world into the play.

This idea, in a form, is used in Will Wright's Spore, which doesn't have literal multiplayer but does have in-game opponents supplied from other players' installations of the game, but beyond that it is interesting that so few other games proudly feature outside influences. They seek to simulate a world completely removed, or as removed as possible, from the real one, so every game begins from a zero-state. But of course, stories that feature Final Dark Sources of Ultimate Peril Threatening Generic Fantasyland, at the end, do not stand up well if they recognize the existence of prior, or future, playthroughs. The game would be subtly suggesting the world doesn't need saving, silly user, you already saved it last time.

So . . . do roguelikes do this kind of thing? The answer, sometimes, is yes.

11.1 Remembering Dragons, Beloved Developers and the Whole Wide World

All the major roguelikes feature a high score table, which is an elementary example of the type. Beyond that, meta game features vary widely, and many don't have any at all. Angband and ADOM sort of do, in their monster memory feature, by which a player can have his character inherit the knowledge of opponents gained from a prior character and carry it into a new game. But this doesn't actually change the play; it simply makes more complete the automatically compiled, but ignorable, information collected during the current game. It is possible to play both these games, and win, without even realizing that monster memory exists, especially if the player takes notes on discovered monster strengths himself, which we can consider to be the traditional form of monster memory.

But there are games that genuinely change the world in response to events outside the current play. ADOM also contains the Bug-Infested Temple, a special region that can only be found once 100 characters have died on that installation of the game. The region contains considerable dangers, so it is ignorable, even if present, if the player doesn't feel up to the challenge, but it also contains some nice rewards, along with statues of various maintainers and bug-finders who have worked on ADOM. Still, the existence of the temple falls under the category of Easter Egg more than a true influence to later plays of the game, since the temple's presence is binary. It's either there or isn't without degrees in-between, and it doesn't otherwise change no matter what the player might do. It doesn't truly utilize information gathered during prior runs, it just counts them.

On the opposite end of the spectrum is Dwarf Fortress, which stretches the definition of roguelike a bit. Its Fortress mode is definitely not roguelike in nature, but its Adventurer mode does play much like a very idiosyncratic roguelike, one that discards item identification and much of the genre's Dungeons & Dragons roots and ruleset underpinnings. What makes it truly fascinating, however, is that the contents of the game world are influenced by all the games that have been previously generated in that "world."

On the first run of Dwarf Fortress, the program spends a large amount of time randomly creating a world for many games, not just the first one, to take place in. In addition to an overworld, and cities, mountains and such, the game also generates civilizations relating to the world, which adventurers can contact and even attack, and with which player fortresses may build relations or trade, or be attacked by. More interestingly, when a player loses a game, the details of their game are added to the game's record files of the world in a substantive manner: tales of any legend they (or their dwarves) created are added to the game's logs, fortresses become abandoned and filled with monsters, and some of the old traps that had been constructed (which in Dwarf Fortress may be quite complicated) will remain in place to harass adventurers, and the whole complex becomes an area to explore rather than defend. And in the sense of turning lemons into lemonade, it is also possible to reclaim fortresses lost in prior games in an entire game mode that, by itself, can only be played if the player has already lost a Fortress game.

11.2 Civic Improvement through Reincarnation

Shiren the Wanderer, the popular Japanese roguelike made for the Super Famicom, takes the same approach that the Fushigi no Dungeon games have taken from the beginning. While in a traditional roguelike each game is considered to focus on a different character, of a class and race either decided by the player or chosen randomly, who dies when he runs out of hit points and then is no more, Shiren's play metaphor is subtly different.

In that game, and the others in its series, there is one character who attempts to explore the dungeon (or dungeon-like area) over and over again, who doesn't die when he runs out of hit points but is instead mysteriously (since it is a Mysterious Dungeon after all) returned to the beginning of his quest should he run out of HP. In some games he also loses his items, or experience levels, or both, which is, in essence, the same fate that awaits a player of a more traditional roguelike. However, it also implies that it makes more sense that a player's actions in one game may influence the world in the next.

During Shiren's quest, he encounters a number of towns along the way. Unlike the game's random dungeon levels, towns are always static, although shops in town may have random contents. Also in the game are warehouses that can be stocked with objects. An object left in a warehouse will remain there even for later games. An item may be taken freely out of warehouses to assist the player on his journey, although, naturally, it will not be available for later, and will be lost if Shiren should run out of hit points.

There are also people in towns to interact with who may offer quests to the player. One example: there is a restaurant in one of the towns that, after a few visits, contains a restaurant startup that is trying to get off the ground. To do this, they need a chef to prepare their food, and they need money to pay him. It is unlikely that a player will have enough cash to give to the proprietors on his first visit, but the total given persists between games so it can be paid off in stages.

When the full amount is paid, which may take many games, then the player must find the chef on one of the earlier dungeon levels and bring him to the restaurant, giving him the meat of a specific monster (which must be obtained by the player's own devices or with the Staff of Bufoo provided by the chef) to seal the deal. Once the chef is brought to the restaurant, the game unlocks these very useful Staves of Bufoo to be randomly generated in dungeons for later games.

Through participating in quests like this, the player is effectively making progress in two games at once. The real objective of Shiren the Wanderer is to complete the "inner game," getting Shiren to the top of Table Mountain before running out of hit points, and beating the big monster there, but this is very difficult to do on the first try. The task can be brought to a more manageable level of challenge by playing the "outer game": building up warehouses, stockpiling resources over many inner-games to improve Shiren's chances on later plays; completing townsfolk quests, which can gain Shiren new objects which may appear in dungeons, and by befriending various helper characters who can assist Shiren on his trip.

Thus, the first game of Shiren the Wanderer can be a substantially more difficult experience than the one in which the player finally gets the guy through. Just about all the Fushigi no Dungeon games, from Torneko's Mysterious Dungeon on, make use of this play metaphor, sometimes to the degree, in fact, that the roguelike qualities of the game are muddied. One of the greater sins of the Pokémon Rescue Team games is that they put too much focus on that outer game, necessitating many short, boring plays of the inner game to make progress in it.

This brings us, as with so many roguelike discussions, to NetHack.

11.3 "Oh Darn, It's 'Kill the Hero Day' in the Dungeons of Doom"

The primary persistent aspect of NetHack is its special "bones" files, but to describe them well it is necessary to explain a little of the way the game operates internally.

When a player is exploring a given level of the dungeon, at that moment, none of the rest of the dungeon exists in memory. When a level is left for another one, a file is saved to disk containing the complete state of the level at the point it was exited. When a level is reentered, its state is read back in and the floor's state picks up where it had left off, although modified slightly to take into account time passed since the level was last seen and objects and monsters that may have migrated there in the time since it had been last visited.

This function, the ability to save a snapshot of a level at any time and load it back in as a level of the dungeon later on, is the core of NetHack's unique bones feature. When a player dies, as they frequently do in NetHack, there is a chance that a snapshot will be taken of the level and saved to the game's bones directory, for later use.

Whenever a new random dungeon level is called to be generated, there is a one-third chance that, if a bones exists from a prior game for that level, it will be loaded instead and the file will be deleted. On the spot where the player died will be his corpse (or a grave), a ghost with his name, and, usually, all his stuff, most of it now cursed (some objects will be changed in rare cases; ultra-important objects like the Amulet of Yendor cannot be found this way, and artifacts that already exist in the game will be found to be ordinary things).

The level is otherwise much as it had been at the fatal moment, meaning if the previous character had met his end due to a monster, that monster is probably still around somewhere. If that was an incredibly strong monster relative to that level then this sometimes results in another quick death, which itself might generate a bones level. Most experienced NetHack players have stories about a series of poor games, each brought to an early end due to a string of bad luck in generating and loading bones. If you ask one to tell you the story you might be pleasantly surprised, but it's more likely you'll just get a lot of cursing, followed by weeping.

There are other cool things about bones levels too, and here we progress from the realm of merely awesome to that of really absurdly, extremely, mind-spinningly awesome. If one is playing NetHack on a multi-user instillation, as was formerly done quite often, then bones levels can be shared between players. It is possible to find the remains of a player who almost won the game, collect a whole pack-load of cool stuff, take three steps, then get engulfed by Juiblex (who had been summoned by the prior player due to a sacrificing accident) and rapidly sickened to death.

Not that I was mad about it.

11.4 But Really, Why Is That So Cool?

It is because an increasingly popular way to play NetHack is on public servers like alt.org, which count as multi-user systems in the same way as in the old days, and so players encounter bones from players they'll never meet, playing in ways obscure to their own local clutch of hackers. Much like how Spore is a single player game that utilizes data produced by other players, so NetHack can make use of the still-warm corpses of past games to inject a good measure of excitement (in both good and bad ways) into each game. There even exists a well-regarded utility, Hearse, that a user can run periodically to send and receive bones files between systems, so even games on single-user systems need not miss out on all the "fun."

11.5 But Really Really, Why Is This So Cool?

Honestly, I can't say. It just seems to be that way.

Something else that's cool without it being obvious why is NetHack's mysterious time and date effects. Long before games like Animal Crossing and Pokémon offered special events for playing at special times, NetHack was playfully modifying the game based upon the current real-life phase of the moon. These effects are a bit obscure (full moons provide a minor luck bonus and new moons make cockatrices a bit more dangerous), but at least neither is likely to greatly bork one's game. Unlike. . . .

Sometime during NetHack's long development process the decision was made that players should be given a small Luck penalty on Friday the 13ths. On a full moon, players get default to starting with a +1 to Luck, meaning that random effects like fountain drinking tend to be slightly better and the player hits more often in combat. On a Friday the 13th, players start out with a base Luck of -1, which is worse than a +1 is good because prayer, that essential resource of the newbie, which can fix problems ranging from being low on hit points to starving to death to turning to stone to being strangled by a piece of cheap jewelry, never works if the player has negative Luck. This makes the game substantively harder on that day, hard enough to avoid playing unless one is looking for a challenge.

According to the time spoiler, NetHack also has a couple of time-of-day effects, but they are encountered much more rarely: undead creatures do double damage during the hour of midnight (but they are not huge damage doers anyway), it's harder to tame dogs on full-moon nights, and gremlins sometimes steal intrinsic properties of the player (like fire resistance or automatic teleportation) on successful attacks between 10 p.m. and 6 a.m. In fact, for all the fuss that some players have made about them, NetHack's time and date effects, aside than Friday the 13th, are actually rather subtle.

And this is not really such a bad thing. It is one thing for a game to be somewhat different depending upon the hour at which it is played, but it is quite another for it to be constantly different every hour of every day. NetHack is already a game that, sometimes, pushes the amount of knowledge a successful player needs to know to extremes. ("Why should I not eat these eggs I found on the floor?") To add a calendar to the spoilers that most every winning player must read might be—if this is possible—too much.

SECTION III
NetHack

12

Giant Eel Stories, Volume 1

September 2006 One of the best ways to learn about NetHack, possibly the most popular of all the roguelike games, is from reading YAAPs ("Yet Another Ascension Posts"), descriptions of victorious games on the newsgroup rec.games.roguelike.nethack.

It may be an unusual impulse to write up a detailed report of a computer game, roguelike or not. It may be even more unusual to be interested in reading it, but it cannot be denied that they are fascinating. It is the same impulse, I believe, that causes people to want to watch speed runs. Most of them are typical wins (especially the first time someone prevails in this game infamous for its difficulty), but some are of difficult challenge, or "conduct," games. Some, such as the tale of Nightshade in the next section, are written in the style of an actual story, with the player's character usually the protagonist.

In this first installment of Giant Eel Stories, we'll be looking at two classic victory posts of the past. Since many of you are probably not NetHack fanatics, I'll supply much of the necessary information needed to understand them, and understand why they're cool, including a brief glossary at the end of this article. All links are to the original post on Google Groups.

To give an account of a victorious game, it is necessary to describe things that happen during it, and the tactics the player used, so there are heavy spoilers to follow. Spoilers are much less dangerous to a roguelike game than a more typical RPG, since so many of them are randomly generated, but there are still some who want to figure out everything for themselves—although in NetHack's case that would probably take many years. If you are one of those noble individuals, you may not want to read on.

(Oh, and giant eels are a particularly dangerous aquatic monster from NetHack's bestiary. Just so you know.)

12.1 Nightshade, Chaotic Female Elven Wizard, March 20, 2002, played by nyra

One of the cooler features of NetHack is that characters can be polymorphed into the form of various other monsters in the game. When a character is polymorphed, he gains all the special abilities, and drawbacks, of that monster. Turn into a xorn and you can walk through walls, but you're too large to wear armor—and will in fact destroy any you were wearing beforehand.

The new body assumed by the character is usually chosen randomly from the monsters in the game, but there are two exceptions to this rule. If the character has picked up a means of polymorph control somewhere in the game, usually from a worn ring, then the game will instead ask the player what new form he wants to take. Rings of polymorph control, thus, are excellent finds. And if a player is wearing colored dragon scales or a suit of dragon scale mail, then he will always turn into the type of dragon matching the scales: red dragon scale mail means a red dragon. The dragon scales are protected from destruction in that case.

Other than possible armor loss, polymorph is usually not that bad an affliction. While changed, the player is actually given a buffer zone of safety. If a polymorphed player runs out of hit points he doesn't die but turns back into his normal self, just a few hits shy of his maximum—meaning that polymorph can actually be an excellent source of healing. Further, after a while characters will always turn back into their normal selves, more quickly if their new body was much greater in power compared to their real form.

This is how it usually works, but a recent version of NetHack introduced a new item: Amulets of Unchanging. A character wearing such an amulet is completely immune (and thus his armor is immune too) from polymorph effects. But more interestingly, an already polymorphed character wearing an Amulet of Unchanging is immune from changing back. Until the amulet is removed, the character will remain, for better or worse, in his new body. The change will never expire naturally over time, and the character can remain in a cool powerful state the rest of the game if he likes. But if the character runs out of hit points he won't turn back all healed up: he'll actually die.

Now the interesting thing about NetHack polymorph is that, in the long run, the most powerful monsters in the dungeon are player classes. There are many monsters with powerful abilities, but almost all of them are rather low on hit points compared to a player, even if he's of only moderate level, and many powerful monster forms can't wear some of the most important types of armor. So although many monsters have nifty special abilities that can come in handy in special cases, including a few that cannot be obtained any other way, a permanently polymorphed player is at a disadvantage in terms of general survivability.

But nyra was not dissuaded by this. After a traumatic, yet cool, experience in her youth, character Nightshade gained a strange aspiration for her life, even for elves: she wanted to be a black dragon. Black dragons, as far as polymorph forms go, are one of the better choices: they can fly, they have good armor class, they have more hit points than most monsters, female dragons can lay eggs and thus eventually gain an army of followers following them around, and best of all, they are the only monster in the game with a disintegration breath attack, which instantly kills, and very few monsters have disintegration-resistance.

You now know what you need to know to begin the Tale of Nightshade the Black Dragon. Have a look at the original post on Google Groups here:

http://groups.google.com/group/rec.games.roguelike.nethack/msg/8d5da2a4761b19a7

12.2 Ciompi259, Neutral Male Human Tourist, February 22, 2004, played by Robert R. Schneck

Another relatively recent addition to the game of NetHack, which has overall changed little since version 3.1 was released quite long ago, is the idea of tracked conducts.

To explain. The jeweled drinking halls of rec.games.roguelike.nethack are filled with a wide assortment of player, both newbies and old demigods alike. Some of these people have won the game many times. In fact, some are so good at the game that they actually win (make it through and ascend to demigod-status) more often than they lose (die or quit or escape—but usually die). A few players almost never lose, if the victory percentages on public NetHack server alt.org are anything to go by: the player named "Ascension" has won 12 out of the 13 games he's played there.

And for the most successful of these players, the game inevitably became rather dull, until they hit upon the idea of playing conduct games. That is, the player would decide on some aspects of NetHack's vast array of features to avoid using that game and see if he could still win. NetHack is a game in which things can be done in lots of ways, but very few things are actually required to be victorious. All a player really must do to win out is gain the three essential "key" objects (the Bell of Opening, the Candelabrum of Invocation and the Book of the Dead), use 'em properly and get the Amulet of Yendor, escape the dungeon with it, then figure out a way through the five final levels to offer it on the correct High Altar on the Astral Plane. Those things are required to win. Most others, it turns out, are not.

A fairly recent version of NetHack aided this elite pastime by tracking conducts, with the game itself keeping a record of which aspects of the game the character has not used. To get a list of these, the player need only start a game and quit on the first turn.

It may seem difficult to believe, even to a player with some experience with the game, but each of these has been done lots of times, and so have many combinations of them, although doing them all in one game is almost certainly impossible.

The two single challenges that are the trickiest are possibly Pacifist and Foodless. Pacifist is difficult because NetHack characters usually encounter thousands of hostile monsters during the game and the player himself cannot kill any of them, even accidentally. If the player manages to survive the monsters, one of the requirements to obtain the Bell of Opening is that the player must achieve experience level 14, and without the slaughter of monsters this is very difficult, although not impossible, to achieve.

It is Foodless, however, combined with certain other conducts, that is the subject of Robert Schneck's game. Novice players soon find out that, while it's nowhere near as bad as Rogue, it is still easy to run out of food on NetHack's early levels. Even when they learn about all the food options available to them they still often starve to death until they discover the game's panic button, Alt-P, the (p)ray command. A prayer to the gods in NetHack is always a request for aid, and if the player hasn't prayed too recently, his Luck isn't negative (not real-life luck but an invisible statistic tracked by the game), and isn't in an area warded from his influence, your deity will help you out of most predicaments you could be in if they're dire enough. Being weak from hunger (not just hungry) is one of those troubles. Although the player cannot pray for aid in the second half of the main dungeon, there are ways in NetHack to quickly get out of there to a region in which prayer works.

This method of subsistence cannot be used if the player is attempting a Foodless Atheist, who disavows all knowledge of the gods until the final sacrifice of the Amulet of Yendor is made on the Astral Plane. But there are other ways to avoid starving: a ring of slow digestion decreases a player's food consumption to very low levels, though it's still not enough to enable a player to avoid starving before winning the game. amulets of life saving, if worn at the moment a player expires, will bring him back to life and fill his stomach one time, then disintegrate. Players can polymorph into monsters that don't need to eat, but they will always turn back to normal unless they wear an amulet of unchanging, which unfortunately introduces food consumption even if the player has no mouth or stomach. A polymorph-controlled player can request to turn into his own race, which will turn him into "a new man" or "a new woman," also fills his stomach, and won't even count as a polymorph to the game. That wasn't enough for Robert Schneck's character, Ciompi259, however.

The number in that name is the number of times he had to try this before he was successful. His character's epic story, that of a winning Foodless Atheist true-Polyselfless Survivor, in which he survived entirely on a Ring of Slow Digestion and the very slight nutrition provided by potions of fruit juice and water, can be read here:

http://groups.google.com/group/rec.games.roguelike.nethack/msg/a987da11a8df6d6b

12.3 Glossary of rec.games.roguelike.nethack Terms

!oGL or !GL: Potion of Gain Level
?oCharging: Scroll of Charging
/WoW: Wand of Wishing
/WoD: Wand of Digging
"oR: Amulet of Reflection
Bag of Holding:
AC: Armor Class, the old Dungeons & Dragons concept. NetHack may be the last game in the world to still use armor class that starts at 10 and counts down, heading past zero into negative numbers as it improves.
PYEC: Platinum Yendorian Express Card, a special artifact that can charge items indefinitely. Only Tourists can use it to its full effect, and they can always find it in their Quest dungeon.
Buc, or Blessed, Uncursed or Cursed: Any item in NetHack can be any of these three statuses, with blessed items generally being better to have than cursed ones.
Mines, Sokoban, Vlad's Tower: Three branches leading off from the main dungeon, some of which it is unnecessary to visit. Sokoban is a recent addition, and has special rules.

Quest: A special dungeon branch that is different for each character class. The player must be at least level 14 to get beyond its first level.
AoY: Amulet of Yendor, the object sought in the game
VotD: Valley of the Dead, a level deep in the dungeon
VS: Vibrating square, an important spot very deep in the dungeon
Wizmode: Short for wizard mode, a special debug mode included in some compilations of the game. Wins in wizard mode don't count, and scores won't be added to the score list.
Levelport: Short for "level teleport," a version of teleportation that moves the player vertically, to other dungeon levels, instead of elsewhere on the current floor
Reverse genocide: A clever tactic to summon several of a specified type of monster
Stash: A place the player keeps spare objects so he doesn't have to carry them around the dungeon, adding to his burdened status
Bones: A level left behind from a prior game
Sacrificing: Offering fresh corpses of defeated monsters on an altar, in the hopes of receiving favor and some goodies from one's deity
Pet: A friendly monster that helps the player. Players begin with one—a cat, dog or horse—but it's possible to get more.
Artifact: Unique weapons with additional powers, some very strong and some less so
Unique: A monster there is only one of; if killed once they never appear again (with a notable exception)
Rodney: The nickname of the Wizard of Yendor, the player's arch-foe
Farming: Purposely creating an abundance of some monster, or infinite opportunities to kill one that revives (like riders), for player advantage. Considered an abuse by some.
Protection racket: A novel, though often foolhardy, strategy, through which a very low-level character can gain points of intrinsic armor class cheaply, although not without a fair bit of risk
Ascension run: When the player gains the Amulet of Yendor, like in Rogue, the game becomes a race back to the surface before death strikes. NetHack makes this harder by limiting the player's ability to teleport, teleporting him back levels randomly and sending in a certain powerful monster at intervals to harass him.
The Planes: The final levels of the game
Riders: Three exceptionally dangerous monsters on the last level who cannot be killed permanently
High Altars: The ultimate destinations. One of these three, chosen randomly, must be found to win the game.
YASD: Yet Another Stupid Death

12.4 Acknowledgments

Thanks to:

Joe "Jove" Bednorz, who found and linked to ascension posts in a newsgroup message

tg, for additional links

Roguelike Magazine, now sadly defunct, for general awesomeness, and for first coming up with the idea of a look at classic win posts

13

Giant Eel Stories, Volume 2

January 2007 In Giant Eel Stories, we examine the phenomenon of Usenet victory posts, in which players crow about games which were very interesting, often because of something that happened, or some conduct they upheld, or they won. This time we again focus on NetHack, although we may not in the future.

In this installment:

- We learn about a wizard who wasn't just content with killing a lot of monsters, but had to kill all the monsters . . .
- After that, we meet a Healer who won the game without killing anything at all, although it must be said a large horde of henchmen was seen following him through the dungeons . . .
- And we have a look at the story of the Priest who did not win, but will still be remembered probably for years to come for getting the highest score. And when I say that, I mean she *really* got the highest score . . . .

13.1 Edward, Chaotic Male Elven Wizard Extinctionist, Ascended, played by Matthew E. Bourland

Some of the more useful objects in NetHack are (the problematically named) scrolls of genocide, which can be used to wipe entire species of monster out of the game. While they don't work on everything, they do work on a lot of things, and they do an utterly thorough job. Once genocided, a class of monsters will be completely absent from play for the rest of the current game. It will be cleared out of the current level, will be wiped from existence from previously visited levels when they are seen, and will never be generated again.

But there is another kind of "genocide" in the game as well. Unlike most other roguelikes (and RPGs in general), generally speaking, there is only a limited number of each kind of monster existing in the game. Every time a monster is generated, a counter is incremented for that species, and once it hits 120, generally speaking, no more of that monster will be seen. In game terms, that monster is "extinct." When the game rolls to generate a new roaming monster on a level, if that monster is chosen it'll roll again, and again if necessary. Levels that come stocked with that monster already on it, even non-random levels, will, in most cases, be a bit emptier. Those monsters can still be added to the game via a small number of other ways, but they won't be roaming around levels, in general, anymore.

NetHack is not a small game, but neither is it very big, and there are hundreds of types of monsters for the generation code to choose from, so it is rare that a quarter of those limits are reached in a game if the player is really trying to win, even if he drags his feet along the way. The extinction check is mostly there to put an ultimate barrier to certain kinds of monster farming behavior (which it really isn't too good at since the worst kind of farming, that of black puddings, uses a method that ignores extinction).

Even so, there has in recent years been established an unofficial conduct called Extinctionist, and many players have accomplished it now. The linked-to story describes the first such game recorded. What an Extinctionist tries to do is completely eliminate as many kinds of monsters from the game as possible, either through genocide if it's available, or from just depleting all the kinds of monsters that can be produced.

People who play these games, it must be said, often find that by the end it is not just the monsters that are exhausted. Extinctionist games can last weeks, and it is not even terribly exciting play along the way. A character with sufficient mojo to cause the game to run out of Archons will not have much to fear from the rest of the bestiary either, and the tremendous amounts of loot that rapidly pile up during these games eventually make what few sources of danger that remain trivial to overcome.

But Extinctionist games are interesting not just as an example of some players' degree of obsession with NetHack. When NetHack starts to run out of monsters, what happens is, first, the few monsters that aren't yet extinct appear much more often, which are often the harder foes in the game by that time (like Archons), but their increased numbers run them out faster as well. But in the long run, after even the rarest foes are depleted, the way NetHack handles it is that monsters just stop appearing. (This is its own problem, since without monster corpses to eat, and once all the territory in the game has been explored, most players will eventually run out of food.)

Another consequence of Extinctionist games is that vast amounts of loot will eventually be generated during those runs. Some of the loot generated are things that the player can use to increase his stats, or damage done, or armor class, or be used to make other useful things. By properly utilizing all this stuff, Extinctionist characters can become super-strong, powerful to a degree far beyond the realm of mortals. We're talking people in a world with 1st edition D&D sensibilities having hit points enough to make Final Fantasy characters jealous, armor classes of -60 and better, and a few other, esoteric benefits that most players go their entire NetHack careers without seeing, like acquiring high levels of intrinsic damage bonuses from eating many rings of increase damage.

But such extents of power are overkill, of course, as NetHack characters wielded by players who are steeped enough in the game's lore that they can seriously attempt Extinctionist games are rarely in tremendous danger after the early levels of the game, unless they are playing one of the truly extreme conducts. Like Pacifist.

Have a look at the original post on Google Groups here:

> https://groups.google.com/forum/#!original/rec.games.roguelike.nethack/oZz7lbgdXu4/faB3h_oPFPMJ

13.2 Patito, Neutral Male Gnomish Healer Pacifist, Ascended, played by Andreas Dorn

In a game in which thousands of monsters die by the end of a game, it seems like Pacifist characters shouldn't even be possible, but they are, and the conduct has been done several times now (https://groups.google.com/forum/#!original/rec.games.roguelike.nethack/f8CGeQ6guYU/4vrbvcWUqeoJ).

Pacifism, in NetHack, means that the player cannot bring about the death of a monster by his own actions. It is okay to hit monsters (there is another conduct, regarding wielded weapons, for that), although it can be dangerous to do so since one might accidentally kill it in the process.

The problem with playing a Pacifist is that there are so many monsters who want to kill the player, and without being able to kill them in return it is extremely difficult to survive long enough to get to deeper levels. Plus, many of the objects the player needs, and really wants, are held by particular monsters. The solution to that is to have lots of pets, and strong ones, to take care of those monsters for you.

The problem with that is that pets are vulnerable in ways the player is not and can be instantly killed or permanently transformed very easily, in addition to facing most of the same dangers player characters have to deal with. Pacifist players usually must continually acquire new pets to make up for the ones lost to attrition.

Pets are not as capable as players for other reasons besides. When monsters are tamed, many of their non-melee abilities, like dragon breath and spellcasting, are lost, and they will never willingly attack a foe more than one experience level greater than it. Most of the baddies towards the end (particularly the Wizard of Yendor, who gets stronger and stronger) have so high a level that no pet will attack them unless special measures are taken to enhance their power. Because of this, Healers are probably the best choice for Pacifist games, not just for their thematic appropriateness but because their quest artifact, the Staff of Aesculapius, can drain levels from foes when they are struck with it, eventually getting them to the point where they can be finished off by a handy horde of friends.

Pets are the key to surviving a Pacifist game (that and figuring out how to raise one's experience level without combat), and Patito the Gnomish Healer was extremely skilled at their acquiring and maintenance. So great was his mojo in this regard that he even managed to tame . . . Pestilence.

That's Pestilence, the Horseman of the Apocalypse who hangs out on the Astral Plane, a unique monster who cannot be permanently killed but, apparently, can be tamed.

13.3 Zadir, Neutral Female Human Priest, Killed by Overexertion, played by legopowa

NetHack is a roguelike game, a roleplaying game and its own self-consistent, algorithmically generated world, but it is also a computer program, and computer programs, as we discovered during the Y2K problem, have limits (https://groups.google.com/forum/#!original/rec.games.roguelike.nethack/pXRdYJck7Go/nTZKPfi73b4J).

Destroying all the monsters in the dungeon is one such limit, and another is the range of the player's score. When computer games are stretched beyond the expected limits, sometimes strange behavior is seen. The old arcade phenomenon of scores that rolled over to zero after passing a maximum value is an example of this. Many of them used a kind of binary-coded-decimal system to represent the score both on-screen and in memory, as a way of saving a few extra processor cycles, but with the result that, once the player's score exceeded however many 9s were allotted on-screen, the score value would "roll over," back to zero.

Modern computer games use a C number type, in NetHack's case 31 bits long plus one bit to hold a positive sign, to store the player's score. Just like with a decimal record-keeping system, this variable can overflow, but that value is so vastly great that the player would have to earn . . . let me see . . . ah, 2,147,483,648 points to do so. That's over 2 billion points in a game in which most games score less than 1,000, victories tend to score between 2 and 8 million, and Extinctionist games are in the tens of millions. So, would you believe that—

Aw heck, who am I kidding? Of course you believe it. We've already established that some people can win as Pacifists in a game in which anyone sane kills monsters reflexively.

Further, legopowa's game was not something he did at home, away from prying eyes that might discover any cheating methods he might have used. He played his game in public, on alt.org's NetHack server. For a while, players had amused themselves there with setting higher and higher scores, trying to gain the coveted top spot on the list, while all the ordinary players (like myself) were sent into deep despair of ever hoping to topple them.

NetHack points are earned for reaching new dungeon levels, for collecting gold and artifacts, and for a variety of other little things, but in the end the thing that makes up most of the score is experience points. Not "gift" experience, such as from finding sources of free levels, but experience gained from killing monsters. Players gain the great majority of their points through killing monsters, and there is really no way around that. While a player, once he's reached the point where he can kill with impunity, can basically mint his points, it still takes an incredible amount of time to earn scores even of 100 million. For 2 billion, it would seem to require decades, certainly at least years.

Legopowa, using macros to automate his game, did it in a week.

The full details are in the post, and he explains it better than I could, but the final results of his game are these: first, he scored MAXINT-1 points, getting the highest possible score without overflowing the score counter and thus finally and eternally claiming the top spot on alt.org's scoreboard, and second, he proved without doubt that NetHack's scoring system is broken. It might seem to be rather an extreme length to go to to prove such a thing, but that is just the kind of game it is.

14

Thou Art Early, but We'll Admit Thee

October 2006 The venerable roguelike NetHack, the most popular of them all and possibly the deepest computer game ever made, is filled with a great many ways to die.

A popular spoiler some time ago was a listing of many of those ways, more than 60 of them, in which the game can end.

When a player in NetHack dies, the game prints an ASCII tombstone for him embossed with character name, cash on hand at game end and the cause of death. This information also goes into the score list to be ranked against other players. One of the joys of playing NetHack on a multi-user system, in fact, is noting some of the unusual deaths experienced by other players and thinking to yourself at least it wasn't me that time.

Now, it is fun to build onto the reputation of a game noted for mercilessness, to tell inverse fish stories about the times you died in an impressive manner. And NetHack indeed is not afraid to kill the player if he does something worth being killed for, or fails to protect himself from that death. The existence of cockatrices in the game is more than enough proof of that. But it can take a good amount of trial, and a whole lot of error, to learn all those situations, and some people regard this as one of the game's flaws.

For example, the first time a player encounters a giant eel may end the game, because they can wrap themselves around him and drag him into the water, killing him in two turns. Eels are an extremely dangerous opponent. But once the player knows about the danger, it turns out there's quite a lot he can do in this situation:

- He can just use a means of taking care of the eel from afar, and since they can't leave the water that's not too difficult.
- Or he might grease his armor, making it difficult for the eel to gain hold.
- Or he might wear an oilskin cloak, which is similarly slippery.
- Or he might wear an amulet of magical breathing, making drowning impossible.
- Or he might polymorph into a monster that doesn't need to breathe.
- Or he might bridge the water with ice using a wand of cold, since eels are harmless out of the water.
- Or he might teleport the eel with a wand, hopefully onto dry land.
- Or he might trap the eel in a small pool by pushing boulders into the spaces around him, creating land.
- Or, if he's levitating, he can stop, surprising the eel and making him lose his grip.
- Or he could just wear an amulet of life saving.

NetHack has many ways of killing players, but it also tends to have as many ways of surviving those deaths. On top of that, many of the "causes" in the game are actually caused by just one thing really: damage. Everything in NetHack that causes damage, even as little as one hit point of it, potentially has its own unique epitaph on the score list.

Because of these things, the game has a bit of a reputation among some players for being unnecessarily cruel to new players, but once you know (finally) everything there is to know they say it's actually somewhat easy. This may, indeed, be true, but keep in mind that most people take years to get to that state, of Knowing It All, and many of them have a lot of fun along the way as well, so long as they don't get too broken up about dying all the time.

Anyway, here are some of the more interesting (or at least entertaining) of the many causes of death in NetHack.

14.1 Death by Inches

> Player, fell onto a sink.

One of the more back-handedly useful effects in the game is levitation, gained from wearing the appropriate ring or boots, or drinking a certain type of potion. If gained by ring or boots the effect lasts until the item is removed, and if the item in question is cursed then that's an exceptionally bad state to be in. Levitating players cannot pick up anything off the floor or go down stairs, although they can sail over water and many traps.

But there are clever ways out of many problems in NetHack, and involuntary levitation is no different. One of the ways to stop levitating is to move onto the same space as a sink. (Think about it for a second . . . and yes, there are kitchen sinks in this dungeon. For NetHack, it was only a matter of time.)

Players who attempt to levitate over a sink crash to the floor, and in the process (ah-ha) they take a small amount of damage. If that damage should just happen to put a player's hit points to zero or lower then they die, and the reason for death reported and saved to the score file is "fell onto a sink." Not the most notable way for a player to go, but there are worse ways . . . .

> Player, killed by an unrefrigerated sip of juice.

One of the most potent traps in NetHack for early players is the fountains scattered throughout the dungeon. You can tell when a player becomes serious about winning the game when he decides he's had enough of being killed by water demons or water moccasins, having his stuff stolen by water nymphs, dying from system shock from failed polymorphs, or drowning in created pools, and finally determines to himself that he's going to stop drinking from those damn fountains.

One of the possible results from drinking from a fountain is tainted water ("Perhaps it is run-off from the nearby slime mold farm?"), and when drunk—you can probably guess where this is going—it does a small amount of damage. Like with sink falls, if that puts a player into a health deficit he dies, the reaper forgoing his customary scythe in favor of that unrefrigerated sip of juice.

> Player, killed by an electric chair.

Another source of random effects is thrones, which unlike fountains have enough possible good effects to make them worth the utilization risk. When a player sits on a throne the best possible result is a wish for an object. The worst result is a shock of electricity that does, you guessed it, damage.

14.2 Death by Logic

> Player, killed by a scroll of genocide.

We're starting to go now from random novelties to genuine sources of peril, but this one's still pretty obscure. Scrolls of genocide eliminate all of one type of monster in the game. Blessed scrolls do the same for one whole class of monster—classes are all those monsters represented by the same character on the display, for example all "h"s. But one of those characters that represent monsters is "@," which of course represents humans and elves, and the player is also an @. Thus reading a blessed scroll and specifying @ is a very quick way to perish yourself.

Ordinarily this is just kind of a joke, as it's pretty easy, you know, to just not type a @ when asked what you want to genocide, but there is one circumstance where it can be very perilous indeed. One of NetHack's many unique features is that some items have different effects in some circumstances, like when they are blessed or cursed for example. It so happens that scrolls, when read while the player is confused, have entirely different effects from when they're read when clear-minded. Sometimes these effects are better than the normal ones (especially scrolls of taming, which become much better), but a few are worse, and worst of them all are scrolls of genocide, which automatically kill the player when read while confused. They are the primary reason it is bad idea to ID scrolls by experimentation while confused.

Player, unwisely ate the body of Pestilence.

NetHack's epitaphs are usually straight-faced. Sometimes they might seem a little pithy (like "killed by elementary physics," which comes from damage taken from throwing objects into the air and not having something hard to wear on your head), but this is the only one that actually passes judgement on the player, at least in a way other than killing him.

On the Astral Plane at the end of the game there are three specific monsters who cannot be permanently slain (at least not normally—as with almost everything, There Are Ways), three of the riders of the apocalypse, Death, Pestilence and Famine. You can run them out of hit points, but that will leave their corpse on the ground and it is always just a matter of time before it becomes animate again and resumes its pursuit.

Some players, who might think themselves pretty clever, will off one of these regenerating opponents and realize that he's fought foes like that before. Trolls in NetHack are infamous for resuming the fight over and over again, coming back to life repeatedly, until some method of disposing of their corpse is found. The method of choice is usually eating the corpse, but doing this against those final opponents will always kill the player, regardless of almost all other circumstances. That'll learn 'em.

Player, petrified by a cockatrice.
Player, petrified by swallowing a cockatrice whole.
Player, petrified by touching a cockatrice corpse.
Player, petrified by trying to tin a cockatrice without gloves.

The lowly cockatrice is perhaps the most dangerous monster in the game. There are plenty of monsters with more hit points, who do more damage, have special attacks and are just bigger, but cockatrices instantly kill anyone who touches them with their bare skin and are thus very likely to kill players unwise in their dealings with them. Even Death up on Astral Plane has to succeed in an attack against a player to deliver an instakill, but a cockatrice can kill by being attacked.

- If the player attempts to fight a cockatrice without a weapon or wearing gloves and hits, he turns to stone.
- If the player hears a cockatrice's hissing, there's a chance he'll begin to turn to stone slowly. There are a few ways to stop that process, but if none of them are used he is petrified that way.
- If he attempts to pick up a dead one with his bare hands, that will also turn him to stone. (It can also be wielded, however. Applications for a wielded cockatrice corpse are left for you to imagine, but I will say that it can be, hm, useful.)
- If he's blinded and steps on the same space as a dead cockatrice without gloves on, then, since the player can only discover what's on a space by feel in that event, he'll become a very confused-looking statue indeed.

Player, killed by a collapsing drawbridge.

There aren't really that many drawbridges in the game. There are never any before the Quest (around level 12–15), and usually the player won't find one until the Castle, which is quite deep into the dungeon. There's always a drawbridge on the Castle level, but many times there won't be any others.

The problem with drawbridges is that, if you're standing on the space in front of one and it opens you get squished, full stop. If you're standing on one that closes or gets destroyed you'll meet a similar end, even if you can breathe water. There are so few drawbridges in the game that discovering these deaths by trial and error means the end of very good runs, so many NetHack players come to develop an irrational fear of drawbridges, even if the actual deaths themselves are rare.

14.3 Deadly Reading

> Player, committed suicide.

Sounds pretty prosaic, right? Several things a player can do in NetHack can cause direct death but have their own epitaphs, so what must players do to be considered to have explicitly committed suicide? The cause is fairly obscure.

First, get a cursed scroll of teleport, or read an uncursed one while confused. Teleport scrolls usually transport the player to another spot on the current level, but if they are read while it's cursed or he's confused the player will instead be transported to another dungeon level.

Then, obtain a means of teleport control. There aren't many ways to get this, the least risky way being to find the eponymous ring. Once worn it means, when you teleport, you get to pick where you go instead of getting sent to a random location. And if you get level-teleported, you get to pick, by entering a number, which level you go to.

Yes, you can go very deep into the dungeon instantly with just the ring and one scroll if you like, and almost reach the lowest level with but two scrolls. But consider for a moment: what does it mean to go to some numbered level of a dungeon? If you go to level "1," you are one level beneath the surface. If, on the other hand, you were in the basement of a tower and you took an elevator to the first floor, you'd then be on ground level. The riddle here is: where would be the zeroth floor?

The proper answer is "nowhere," and if, when asked what level to be magically teleported to, you answer "0," the answering prompt should be more than enough warning:

> Go to Nowhere. Are you sure? [ynq] (q)

If you say "y," the result is:

> You scream in agony as your body begins to warp . . . You cease to exist. Your possessions land on the floor with a thud.

Why this lurid fate is masked on the score list with "committed suicide" is anyone's guess.

> Player, teleported out of the dungeon and fell to his death.

If, to the above prompt, you answered a negative number (that is, some level above the surface):

You are now high above the clouds . . . Unfortunately, you don't know how to fly. You plummet a few thousand feet to your death.

If you're a monster who can fly the result is different:

> You are now high above the clouds . . . you fly down to the ground.

Your game still ends, mind, but it's by escaping, not death. There is not really a lot of difference between the two results, you just get 10% more points and the comforting knowledge that your character can now roam the earth as a vampire lord or whatever.

> Player, went to heaven prematurely.

There's yet another result if you teleport to level -10 or, uh, higher:

> You arrive in heaven. "Thou art early, but we'll admit thee."

There are a good number of other neat death causes, including a couple that aren't seen too much these days: "panic," meaning NetHack encountered a seriously faulty internal state and ended the game to avoid a likely crash; and "trickery," which means the game, upon inspecting a save or temporary level file, discovered that it failed its internal consistency checks and assumes the player is cheating by modifying them.

14.4 The Most Obscure Death

First, get a means of polymorph (a certain potion will do the trick) and a ring of polymorph control. It doesn't matter what you turn into, it just has to be something that can read.

You'll also need a scroll of genocide. The idea is to genocide your own species while polymorphed into another type of monster. This produces the ominous message:

> You feel dead inside.

Now, when you change back to normal, your game will end instantly. Of course you could remain a monster indefinitely with an amulet of unchanging. You would, indeed, have to do this to stay in the game.

But what you want to do is not keep playing. You want to quit instead, with Alt-Q, which provides one of the cooler messages in NetHack:

> Player, quit while already on Charon's boat.

Charon is, by some accounts, the boatman who ferries souls to the underworld. He is also a monster who has long been seen in NetHack's source code but has never been actually included in the game. It seems like he has been doomed forever, along with Cerberus, on the sidelines of the monster definition array, kept away from existence by a mere comment barrier, since the days of 3.1 and before.

There are other ways to get the Charon's boat epitaph, as noted in a Google Groups message from 2003: https://groups.google.com/forum/#!topic/rec.games.roguelike.nethack/W9G1p7lqIMU.

It seems that it's possible to abort some versions of NetHack in a way that causes it to automatically save, such as ending a telnet session or hitting Ctrl-C at a [more] prompt. If the player has been taken down to zero or lower hit points by his last action, but hasn't gotten the "You die . . ." message yet, then upon restoring the game the player will die immediately and the Charon's boat message will be given as the cause.

Interesting causes of death are part of what makes NetHack, NetHack. Even players who consider that they have no chance of winning can still at least strive for a memorable way to end their life. One of the awards at /dev/null's (now retired) yearly NetHack tournament is one for most causes of death encountered during the one-month contest period. You can also play the game to win, competing against legendary players like marvin, aka Christian Bressler, who once won 13 games in a row to walk away with the Best of 13 trophy.

15

I Believe It Not!

March 2007 Simultaneously among the most beloved, and most loathed, features of the popular roguelike game NetHack is its wide variety of jokes and anachronisms. Often, when people who dislike the game, but appreciate other roguelikes, discuss their dissatisfaction with the game, it's because it contains things like candy bars, quantum mechanics, credit cards, magic markers and fortune cookies within its vague fantasy setting.

There are those of us who dearly love all these kinds of things, and in case you haven't guessed I'm one of them. I find that far too many fantasy games, both the regular kind and roguelikes too at times, take themselves too seriously. The most popular computer roleplaying games you can find don't care a whit about subtlety or humor except on rare occasions.

Even The Legend of Zelda, in its Twilight Princess edition, gave us a strongly typed light-dark motif that, although they did try to overturn it during the course of the game, still seemed to buy into it more than discredit. Yet considering how the whimsical and joyous Wind Waker was the worst-selling console Zelda for a long while, it seems that most gamers are perfectly happy with this. I am disappointed in modern gaming for many reasons, but none so more as this.

You know the kind of games I mean. Games that throw around words like "darkness" as if they were going out of style—and the sooner that happens the better as far as I'm concerned. Yet it is enlightening, perhaps, to note that other than a weird little tacked-on prologue before the game, we don't even know why NetHack's long succession of @-signs are braving the dungeon. It likely isn't to save the world; the player's god wants the Amulet, but it isn't a pressing fight against the forces of evil. I've always seen it as more of a quest for glory kind of thing.

Of the other major games, Rogue's quest is important only so that Rodney can gain admittance to the local fighter's guild. (In light of that game's tremendous difficulty, I can only imagine that he'll be in scarce company.) Crawl players seek the Orb of Zot; we don't know why. Angbanders wanna slay Morgoth, the great foe of Tolkien's Middle Earth (Sauron's boss), but it doesn't seem like he's about to up and invade at the moment. ADOM, alone among the major roguelikes, puts the player in a world-saving (or conquering) role, and perhaps because of this it is ADOM's quest, which has far more storyline than the other roguelikes, that seems the most petty. To save the world is a noble thing, but come on, it's been saved millions of times by now. Can't the durn thing take care of itself for a moment?

Well I say, let the technicolor phantastic realm-kingdom in dire need of salvation take a running leap. This time, our focus is digressions. A listing of jokes in NetHack. Let's go!

15.1 Strange Objects

15.1.1 Sinks

Some time ago NetHack DevTeam member Janet Walz saw the multiplicity of things in the game, and asked herself what thing is there that it lacks? The answer was obvious: the kitchen sink.

Sinks can be drunk from, if you have a death wish or something (there are two different ways to get polymorphed that way, and polymorph can destroy armor). They can be kicked, which can summon succubuses or incubuses for a bit of fun, or black puddings for a bit of the opposite of fun. Or you can drop rings down them, usually wasting the ring but providing a significant hint to its function in the process.

Those results aren't funny? Well no, they aren't, but come on now. There are kitchen sinks in the dungeon!

15.1.2 Shirts

Back when Tourists were added to the game, they were intended as a challenge class. They begin with no melee weapon, get overcharged in shops, and their starting armor is a "+0 Hawaiian shirt," which offers no protection at all.

More recent versions have changed this somewhat; many players agree that the Tourist quest artifact, the Platinum Yendorian Express Card, which doesn't charge general merchandise but does wands, is among the best in the game. And that "useless" shirt, when coupled with other armor, can be a boon. Any armor piece can only accept so much enchantment, you see, before it becomes likely that it'll disintegrate. A player can wear a suit of armor, a cloak, a helmet, a shield and a pair of boots, and their combined pluses can be substantial, but once it reaches a given maximum it becomes dangerous to enchant any more.

A shirt, you see, is an extra layer of armor that goes under armor, and so while it has no defense value itself it can be safely enchanted to +4 or +5, and that can make a big difference. Shirts are very rare items to find randomly, so it is useful to begin the game with one.

A few versions after Hawaiian Shirts entered the game, the DevTeam added T-shirts, which are functionally the same except for one useless, yet interesting, feature: they can be read. And there are quite a good number of things that can be printed on them, like:

> "I explored the Dungeons of Doom and all I got was this lousy T-shirt!"

(By the way, Tourists themselves are not, strictly speaking, an anachronism. They are a reference to Twoflower from Terry Pratchett's Discworld books. In fact, the Tourist quest takes place in leading Discworld city Ankh-Morpork, and the Tourist quest leader is Twoflower himself.)

15.1.3 Graves

They are found randomly throughout the dungeon, sometimes appear on bones levels at the spot a previous player met his end, and there are dozens of them deep in the dungeon, in the Valley of the Dead. They can be looted, but they can also be read. A sample grave marker . . .

> "Something is engraved here on the headstone.—more—"
> "You read: 'Og friend. Og good dude. Og died. Og now food.'"

15.2 Fortunes

Fortune cookies are an essential part of NetHack's hint system, with the meaning of the word "fortune" here being based more on the Unix command-line toy than the confection offered by Chinese food places. There are hundreds of possible messages, divided into "true" and "false" based on their usefulness. Blessed cookies always provide true fortunes, and cursed cookies false. Many of the fortunes, further, are frequently fairly funny:

> "So when I die, the first thing I will see in heaven is a score list?"
> A wish? Okay, make me a fortune cookie!
> Let's face it: this time you're not going to win.
> Not all rumors are as misleading as this one.
> Segmentation fault (core dumped).
> Sorry, no fortune this time. Better luck next cookie!
> You swallowed the fortune!
> You choke on the fortune cookie.—More—

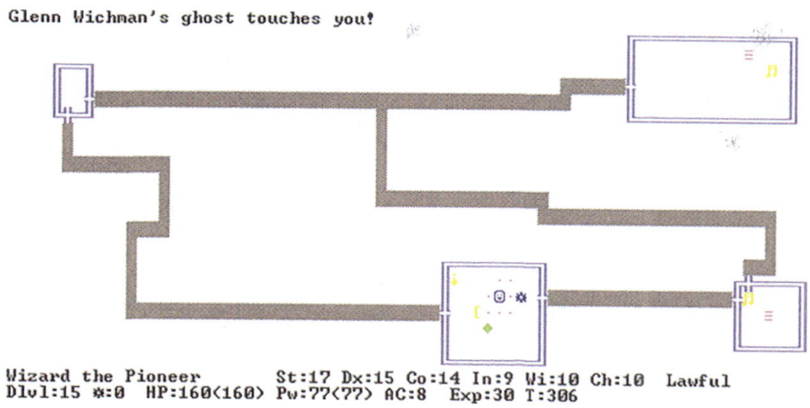

Figure 15.1

Nethack's rogue level

15.3 The Rogue Level

Never let it be said that NetHack has forgotten its roots. In addition to the game's many holdovers from its early history as a remake of Rogue, deep in the dungeon it contains the greatest homage of all: a complete level done in the style of Rogue, right down to borrowing its own idiosyncratic ASCII graphics. Even graphic versions of the game drop down to letters and line-drawing characters here, and it'll also make an effort to duplicate a version of Rogue produced for the platform the game is made for; the preceding picture is from the MS-DOS port. It also always contains a ghost named after one of Rogue's creators.

15.4 Cultural Borrowings

Perhaps the most awesome thing about NetHack, speaking as an English grad student? The game is loaded with cultural references! Most of the quest artifacts are taken from different fantasy series, from *Dying Earth* (Eyes of the Overworld) to Conan the Barbarian (the Heart of Ahriman). The Knight artifact is the Magic Mirror of Merlin, which goes all the way back to Edmund Spenser's *The Faerie Queene*, which was printed in 1596 for heaven's sake. Most of the other artifacts are borrowed similarly. Stormbringer comes from the Elric books. Grayswandir's from *Chronicles of Amber*. Vorpal Blade's from Lewis Carroll's "Jabberwocky." Sting and Orcrist, of course, are from *The Hobbit*. The artifact weapon Snickersnee is from Gilbert and Sullivan's "The Mikado," just about the last thing you'd expect a D&D-ish random dungeon game to borrow from. The gods worshipped by each character class are also cunningly chosen to be from a relevant world mythology (valkyries, for example, get Norse gods), with the exception of Tourists (Discworld gods) and priests (who get random deities chosen from the other sets).

Not only that: balrogs and hobbits are also from Tolkien, crysknives and long worms are from Dune, towels and their use from The Hitch-Hiker's Guide to the Galaxy, lots of things come from the Zork games and Adventure, and many of the named demons come from Christian tradition by way of early Dungeons & Dragons books, pre-obnoxious fundamentalist furor perpetuated by televangelists and rabble-rousing preachers.

All of this just scratches the surface. The game's built-in encyclopedia has a quote, from some work of literature, for most monsters in the game, as well as some of the more noted artifacts.

15.5 Coyotes

A recent version of the game introduced a new canine opponent, to go in alongside the domestic dog hierarchy (small dog, dog and large dog), jackals, wolves, winter wolves and hell hounds: the coyote. If you use the "What is" command, forward slash, to access the game's encyclopedia to get information on a coyote, the entry is:

> "This carnivore is known for its voracious appetite and inflated view of its own intelligence."

If that's not enough to convince you of the monster's esteemed inspiration, the forward-slash command adds an interesting extra bit of information to the What Is report, only for coyotes. . . .

"d a dog or other canine (coyote—Hard-Headipus Ravenus)"
"d a dog or other canine (coyote—Nemesis Riduclii)"
"d a dog or other canine (coyote—Road-Runnerus Digestus)"

15.6 Incidental Messages

If you somehow die on the very first turn: "Do not pass go. Do not collect 200 zorkmids."
If you have a pet pit viper or pit fiend, who falls victim to a pit trap: "The pit fiend falls into a pit! How pitiful. Isn't that the pits?"
If you are polymorphed into a metal eater and munch on a trident: "This trident is delicious! That was pure chewing satisfaction!"
If you're hallucinating the message is different: "This trident is delicious! Four out of five dentists agree."

Eating apples provides the report message "Core dumped." (Core dumps are what Unix/Linux programs do when they crash, they write the contents of their memory to a file, called a core.)

Finally, while I won't spoil it here, players who are really hungry or low on hit points, are playing a wizard or valkyrie or of elven race, and are familiar with the arcade game Gauntlet, are bound to be surprised eventually.

15.7 Hallucination Messages

That brings us to the large category of hallucination jokes, which the game contains so many of that at times it seems like the hallucination condition is there solely as an excuse to be funny. It is easy to overlook the fact that hallucination actually predates Hack, first being seen in later versions of Rogue.

The DevTeam did make the most of it, though. Almost anything the player does prompts a funny message when hallucinating, often with a pop culture joke or bit of hippie slang attached. (A personal favorite is "You feel that Odin is bummed.") There are so many of those, and they're scattered so thoroughly throughout the source code, that I won't even try to list them. I will offer extra points, however, to whoever can find the condition that causes the game to tell them "There's a tiger in your tank."

The actual effect of hallucination is that monsters (and items observed from a distance) appear to flip randomly through a set of possibilities, thus depriving you of knowledge of what type they are. In Rogue the random appearance was chosen from the monsters in the game, but NetHack will also pick from a list of monsters that don't actually exist, which cover a wide gamut of sources in games, books, TV, movies and comics. Favorites include giant pigmy, master lichen, grue, Y2K bug, rodent of unusual size, Smokey the bear, smurf, Klingon, Totoro, Dalek, teenage mutant ninja turtle, one-eyed one-horned flying purple people eater, and Morgoth from NetHack's distant cousin, Angband.

15.8 Shocking the Gods

Finally, a specific game event that most good players encounter eventually, but always comes as a surprise, and sometimes a rude one, the first time they see it. It is a kind of joke to do with the alarming tendency of NetHack characters, once they get a good 15 levels under their belt and a selection of all the useful equipment they can obtain in the game, of becoming unstoppable tanks.

While even advanced characters can be killed, and often are in the days running up to one's first victory, if the player really knows what he's doing, more than half of the game can become a foregone conclusion. A really knowledgeable NetHack character is in some danger at the beginning, a little bit danger maybe at the very end, and almost completely safe in between. Of the named demon lords that can accost the player later in the game, the great heavies of the old-school D&D world, only Demogorgon is a significant challenge by the time he might show up, and he makes an appearance in only a very small number of games. I've never run into him myself.

Of course ultimately, there's always a bigger fish. The dungeon of NetHack has a number of branches, but what is considered the "dungeon" is split into two major halves, the Dungeons of Doom, which go down to about level 25 or so, and Gehennom, which is the rest of the way. There are a number of significant differences between the two (like that Gehennom is a lot more frustrating to explore), but the foremost one is perhaps that prayer, NetHack's all-purpose escape valve for the almost-dead player, doesn't work in Gehennom. While there, all prayers get routed to Moloch, the game's antagonist deity. (See: fish, bigger.)

If alerted to a presence in his domain, there is a chance that what the thing does is fire a lightning bolt at the player's character, which instantly kills if it isn't resisted. But of course, by this time the player is likely to have gained shock resistance from one of several sources, and will pass through it unscathed, which gives Moloch an excuse to pull out the big guns, the wide-angle disintegration beam.

This beam cannot be reflected (like by a shield of reflection) and can destroy multiple inventory items at once. Magic resistance doesn't help either. However, it IS survivable, for one kind of monster in the game, black dragons, can confer the intrinsic state of disintegration-resistance if its flesh is consumed. The comment made by the Great God Moloch upon realizing he has been thwarted by a mortal is awesome to behold:

```
"I believe it not!"
```

16

How to Win at NetHack

May 2009 Please accept this hopelessly spoiler-tastic strategy guide for NetHack. The object here is to aid players who have played the game somewhat but always thought that winning was out of their league. It doesn't cover everything in the game, far from it, but with some practice it should get people up to the endgame.

Much of the information here has been checked against (and in some cases, gleaned from) the NetHack Wiki.

16.1 Recognize How Safe You Are at the Start of the Game

For most of the game, the difficulty of random monsters is determined by a simple formula:

Monster difficulty = (Player level + dungeon level) / 2

All monsters have such a difficulty rating. The program's internal name for this statistic is MONSTR.

The hardest random monster that can appear at a given time will have a MONSTR of this value + 1, and that happens rarely. So, while the player remains at experience level 1 and dungeon level 1, mostly it'll be monsters with a difficulty of 1 or less who can appear: grid bugs, jackals, kobold zombies, newts, sewer rats, foxes, lichen, goblins and kobolds. All of them a piece of cake.

If the player descends two levels, or gains two levels of experience, or one of each, MONSTR 2 monsters get added into the mix: shriekers, large kobolds, hobbits, gas spores, red molds, green molds, brown molds, acid blobs, yellow molds, gnome zombies, giant rats, geckos, coyotes, humans and bats.

Generic humans are not generated randomly; the four molds, acid blobs and gas spores only attack in retaliation; and the other monsters are only marginally more dangerous than a level 1 monster.

The lowest-difficulty random monsters that could potentially be troublesome are, ironically enough, the lowest-level pet types (kitten and little dog) and the two low-level lycanthropes (wererat and werejackal). All of these monsters are considered difficulty 3. The pets can be neutralized by throwing food at them; even if they won't eat the food, they'll often go peaceful from the consideration involved. The lycanthropes can be a problem, with their special lycanthropy-spread attack and summoning abilities. Gnomes also have a MONSTR of 3, and are sometimes generated with attack wands. Fortunately, difficulty 3 monsters usually only show up if the sum of player level plus dungeon level is 6 or more.

Difficulty 4 introduces dwarves (generated with considerable equipment); rothes and hill orcs (both of whom swarm); giant ants (swarm and are faster than most players); gnome lords (numerous in the Mines); and ponies (the toughest base pet type). This is where the monsters start to get really deadly. But so long as player level plus dungeon level is less than 8, the chances of running into one is small. If the player can find good-enough equipment before this point, his chances of survival shoot up greatly.

My point here is that NetHack characters are in almost no danger from monsters at the start of the game. He's better served by gaining equipment earlier on, which doesn't increase the difficulty of the monsters, than gaining levels. The better the equipment the player can find before the opposition ramps up, the better he'll do.

Notice that there is an exception to this rule. The Gnomish Mines start pre-stocked with a bunch of set opponents: gnomes and dwarves. The dwarves can be tough and will be there regardless of player level, so if you want to take the Mines right off having a little better level will probably help you, unless you plan on running the "protection racket," which is beyond the scope of this guide.

16.2 Do Not Give the Game Excuses to Kill You

Don't do dangerous things! By far, the most common of these is drinking from fountains. You might be able to drink from fountains 20 times safely, but all it takes is that 21st time summoning the water demon, water moccasin or water nymph to ruin your whole game. Water demons, in particular, are deadly. Some players drink from all the fountains they see in the hopes of lucking into an early wish. They are far more likely to get it out of a magic lamp in the Minetown shop than from a water demon and are much less likely to get killed in the process.

Also, don't drink from sinks, and don't kick sinks until you're able to handle black puddings. Don't dig up graves. Don't mess around unnecessarily. Don't anger shopkeepers, say, by trying to steal from shops in non-pet ways. And don't anger the guards in Minetown (from drying up a fountain or messing too much with locked doors in their sight).

A lot of the process of getting better at NetHack is discovering the stupid little things that can kill you, and not doing them. There aren't as many as you might think, and in large part avoiding them is common sense.

Here's a list of things to be careful of:

- Don't do things that do piddling damage to you if you're very low on hit points. Anything that can do at least one point of damage can potentially kill you in the right circumstances.
- Don't smack floating eyes. These will paralyze you, possibly for hundreds of turns, and leave you defenseless. Everyone dies to these babies in their first few games. Fortunately, they're slow and don't attack.
- Don't pray if it's been too soon since your last prayer. To tell for sure, try to sacrifice something; if you get a message that "You have a hopeful feeling," it's not safe to pray. If the message is "You have a feeling of reconciliation," then the offering's credit was just enough to eliminate your remaining prayer timeout.
- Don't pray if you have negative luck (luck is usually zero unless you've done things to change it; things which lower your luck are breaking mirrors, attacking peacefuls, carrying a cursed luckstone, playing on Friday the 13th, harming your pets in an irresponsible way and cheating in Sokoban. Prayers never work if your luck is negative. Luck gradually returns to zero over time unless you're carrying a luckstone.)
- Don't break wands of death.
- Don't teleport to level 0, or negative levels. These things may be funny to do once, but not in a game you care about losing.
- Don't genocide yourself.
- Don't wear amulets of unchanging while polymorphed unless you really know what you're doing. (Do you know what you're doing? No.)
- Don't wear-test amulets. They're the only item class that has a member that can quickly kill the player in normal use, the amulet of strangulation. It's best not to use-test things at all if you can help it, but amulets are especially important to be wary of.

16.3 Build the Essential Intrinsics as Soon as Possible

This starts to get into real strategy. The most important intrinsic in the early game is poison resistance, which safeguards strength and prevents all poison-related instadeaths. Until you get it, monsters with poisonous bites (spiders, killer bees, soldier ants and some snakes among them) have a chance of killing you outright with each attack, and so do spiked pit traps, a particularly cheap way to go. Unfortunately, poison resistance is not easy to gain without some luck. You can usually get it by eating the corpses of poisonous monsters or blobs. This is never instantly fatal, but poison monsters will still poison you, lowering strength (and thus carrying capacity), and blobs are usually acidic and do stomach acid damage, and that could be fatal if you're low on HP. When you gain poison resistance from eating, by the way, the given message is "You feel healthy!"

The easiest way to gain poison resistance is to start with it, by playing a Barbarian (one of the reasons they're the easiest class) or Healer (not recommended for beginners). Beyond that, if you can find a ring of poison resistance or amulet vs. poison, you can wear them long enough to gain intrinsic poison resistance through the eating poisonous monsters, and then discard the item.

Later on, the most important intrinsic is magic resistance, and it's one of the harder intrinsics to get. It can never be obtained naturally except through polymorph. The only ways to get magic resistance is by wearing a cloak of magic resistance, wearing gray dragon scales or gray dragon scale mail, by wielding the artifact Magicbane, or by holding a quest artifact that grants the property. Wizards begin with a cloak of magic resistance, and their first sacrifice gift, Magicbane, grants it when wielded.

Magic resistance is important because it prevents a wide range of troubles. They prevent teleport, level teleport and polymorph traps from working on the player, and they also protect against several monster spells, including the spell of destroy armor. Crucially, they're also the only reasonable way to survive death rays and the Touch of Death spell. Unlike other instadeath monsters, ToD-using monsters are usually capable of teleporting after the player, and so are very difficult to escape, and the worst monsters of the type, the lich family of opponents, are immune to death spells themselves. Because liches don't usually appear before the Castle, many players can do without magic resistance for a long time, but usually regret it if they don't obtain it by Gehennom.

Beyond those two things, the most important qualities to gain are:

- magic cancellation level 2 or 3 for protection against level drain and many other annoying monster attacks, best gained from a cloak of protection for the best defense, or an oilskin cloak, robe, plate mail or mithril armor for decent protection;
- a unicorn horn, which can nullify nearly all negative status effects without cost beyond using a few turns and can also serve as a means of restoring strength lost to poisonous corpses when trying to gain resistance;
- high-quality escapes to get away when all else fails, items like scrolls of teleportation, wands of teleportation (either zap yourself or the monster attacking you), wands of digging (aim ">" when asked for a direction), wands of sleep and death (be careful with them, however) and potions of full healing (uncursed extra and full healing potions also cure sickness).

16.4 Learn the Most Dangerous Monsters

- Soldier ants: on a game-by-game basis, they're the most lethal monsters in NetHack. They're poisonous, they sometimes appear in groups, they're too fast to run from and they get multiple attacks in melee. Don't count them out until you've got poison resistance and good AC.
- Mimics are one of the toughest monsters you'll find in the early levels. Fortunately, they appear almost exclusively in shops and are very slow. Still, treat them with respect.
- Hill orcs swarm and are generated with equipment. Mordor orcs and uruk-hai often get generated with poisoned arrows, another reason to go for poison resistance as soon as possible.
- Nymphs aren't very dangerous to your life, but their theft attacks are powerful even into the middle of the game. Have a pet kill these, or take care of them from a distance. Remember this: if she manages to steal from you and you want to get your item back, you can find her elsewhere on the same dungeon level. While tracking her down remember that she'll make effective use of the item(s) she stole.

- Chickatrices and cockatrices are the source of more instadeaths than any other monster in the game. Your pets won't touch these. Kill them from a distance! If you're forced into melee with one, be on the lookout for slowdown messages if you hear their hissing. And once they're dead, they can be even more lethal. Be careful around these guys.
- Purple worms are strong opponents, but once they engulf you, if you've found a wand of digging they're easy to kill. Many other wands do good damage to them when you're engulfed. However, they're lethal to pets, even ones with much higher level.
- Chameleons may turn into an unusually deadly monster. Eating a dead one causes you to polymorph. This is the only monster food effect that also affects pets, which could be either good or bad.
- Rust monsters will cause metal weapons you strike them with to degrade and can also harm metal armor. Disenchanters work similarly but aren't restricted to metal items and instead reduce an item's plus.
- No elemental is a slouch in battle, but air elementals are extremely quick so they get extra attacks, and can engulf the player. One thing that might help: if you're engulfed by a vortex-type monster like an air elemental, you can get expelled immediately by zapping a wand or spell of slow monster at it.
- Mind flayers and master mind flayers can drain intelligence and kill you if it gets too low, but their attacks also cause amnesia, one of the most annoying effects in the game. Amnesia (by mind flayer or scroll) causes you to forget item identifications and some level maps.
- Mumaks are rare and have no special abilities but can do extremely high damage relative to when they can appear in the game.
- Beware of all liches, for their touch of death spell and teleportation harassment. These are prime targets for genocide, followed by giant eels, mind flayers and mimics (for getting more loot out of shops).
- Medusa: learn to recognize her level and then don't approach unless blindfolded.
- Green slime is a late-appearing monster with a delayed instadeath sliming attack. Burn yourself, like with a wand of fire, to cure it. Prayer also can help.
- Black dragons are the only monster with a disintegration attack, which, if it hits, can only be survived by being disintegration-resistant—from eating a black dragon corpse or wearing its scales—or having reflection.
- Archons: the toughest random opponent in the game, who can blind and stun with a gaze.
- Demon lords and princes, immune to death rays in recent versions and perform teleport harassment.
- Demogorgon, who only appears rarely, but has a highly dangerous sickness attack.
- The Wizard of Yendor: touch of death spells, teleport harassment, and can't be killed permanently so can wear down the player over time; he is vulnerable to death wands and spells, however, and those are the recommended way of dealing with him.
- The riders, Death, Pestilence and Famine, are practically impossible to kill permanently, and each has a unique, highly dangerous attack.

Liches, the demon lords, some quest nemeses and the Wizard of Yendor all have an aggravating trick they like to pull. They all have both teleport-at-will and teleport control, and heal rapidly, so they can teleport away when they reach low hit points and renew the attack when they've recovered. It is very difficult (though not impossible) to kill one of these enemies through damage alone before they teleport away. There is a trick for dealing with them; when they teleport away, it's always to the upstairs of that level. If you move in and stand on the upstairs when they're attacking you, they'll generally be much easier to finally kill. Other ways to kill some quest nemeses and the Wizard are with a wand of death. Vorpal Blade and the Tsurugi of Muramasa also have a chance of instantly killing most of these monsters. And wielding a cockatrice corpse and hitting a monster with it can instantly kill almost any monster in the game.

16.5 Build Equipment for Overcoming Game Obstacles

Here are the contents for a typical ascension kit:

- A good artifact weapon. Get this through offering.
- Very good AC. By the Castle you'll want at least -10, and by the Planes around -40.
- All the resistances you can obtain, but especially poison and magic.
- Very fast speed. You can only really get this by wearing speed boots.

- A means of water travel. Levitation or water walking is best; an amulet of magical breathing will get you through, but your stuff will get water-damaged unless contained in an oilskin sack or greased other bag. In limited cases, you can make do with using scrolls of earth and wands of cold to make bridges.
- A means of distance attack, for taking out sea monsters and other troublesome guys.
- A wand of digging, for zapping down (">") to escape from monsters.
- A unicorn horn (blessed when you acquire the means).
- A lizard corpse (keep it in your main inventory).
- A bag of holding, blessed when you can swing that, same goes for greased.
- A means of reflection: amulet of that type, silver dragon scales/scale mail or silver shield. This protects your inventory from getting burned/frozen/blasted/disintegrated. This isn't a top-priority thing if you keep destroyable stuff in a bag, but in that case make sure to at least get disintegration-resistance, which only comes from eating a black dragon corpse. (Black dragons are the only monsters that use disintegration rays.)
- A luckstone, preferably blessed.
- A stockpile of holy water, for blessing and uncursing stuff.
- Escape items (scrolls and wands of teleport are among the best).

16.6 Know How to Deal with the Gods

Prayer will get you out of these troubles:

- Being low on HP (less than 5 or 1/7 your max, whichever is greater),
- being weak from hunger (not just hungry),
- turning into stone,
- being sick from food poisoning,
- being strangled by an amulet,
- being stuck in a wall,
- and a few other things.

The chances of good things happening are increased if you're standing on an altar of your alignment. Please don't pray on a differently aligned altar; check alignment by pressing colon (":") while standing on one. After praying, you can't pray for aid again until a certain number of turns, usually up to 300, have passed.

If your alignment score (a hidden variable tracked by the game) is high enough, you might be crowned. If this happens, you immediately get several useful resistances and are granted a powerful artifact weapon, but your prayer timeout also becomes much, much longer. Also, occasionally, your god will tell you about the Castle's drawbridge-opening tune, or just outright tell you what the tune is. And sometimes, your god will just outright grant you a minor intrinsic, such as stealth.

Sometimes in the dungeon you'll find an altar. If it's of your alignment then it's safe to offer dead monsters on it and offer them. (Shift-O.) Gods don't like really weak monsters compared to your level (though most monsters are still good at the time of the game where you encounter most altars) and always fail to appreciate kobolds. Also, don't sacrifice former pets or monsters of your race if you're not chaotic. (Since NetHack elves are always chaotic in alignment, elves are thus pretty much always okay to sacrifice.) If a monster corpse is too old (roughly the same time scale as it's good to eat them), then nothing will happen. Only freshly killed monsters will work as sacrifices.

If you offer a corpse on an altar not of your alignment, then if your alignment score is too low you might get converted to the altar's alignment, an extremely bad thing that usually makes the game unwinnable. Fortunately, it's not hard at all to keep a good alignment score by playing normally. If you aren't converted, then there's a chance of converting the altar; if you succeed you gain luck, and if you fail you lose luck. (There is more on the Luck statistic later.) If you succeed but the altar belonged to a temple with a priest, then the priest will become angry with you, will begin attacking you, and you'll lose any divine protection thus far granted.

If you make a good sacrifice, several things may happen:

- If a prayer timeout is still active, it'll get reduced a bit, providing the message "You have a hopeful feeling." If this eliminates the remainder of the timeout, the message is "You have a feeling of reconciliation."

- If you have no prayer timeout currently, and your luck is lower than maximum (10 points), then you get a message about a four-leaf clover and gain a point of luck.
- Once in a while, instead of a four-leaf clover, you'll get the message "An object appears at your feet!" This is usually an artifact, a powerful and unique weapon. Artifacts are rarely found on the dungeon floor, and can be wished for too, but this is by far the most common means of acquiring them. Some classes have a specific first artifact they receive this way. For valkyries, for example, it's Mjollnir. If you were "restricted" in that weapon, that is unable to gain skill in it, it'll become unrestricted and you'll be able to advance to Basic skill.

16.7 Know What Is Safe to Eat

Mostly, if you use common sense, you'll be okay, but there are some exceptions.

- Don't eat kobolds. They cause sickness.
- Anything acidic (like acid blobs and ochre jellies) will do acid damage if you eat it, and if you're low on HP this will kill you. However, acid corpses never go bad, and eating one cures stoning in a pinch.
- If you're satiated, be very careful what you eat! One of the most ignominious ends in NetHack is choking on your food, which tends to happen to players relatively late on their journey. If you're not satiated when you start eating then there is nothing in NetHack that will kill you from choking, but if you are satiated when you start you're pushing it. Particularly, don't eat dragon corpses unless you're not satiated!
- If something has the power to kill you instantly while alive, then be careful about eating it when it's dead. Be careful around these things: chickatrices, cockatrices, green slimes or Medusa in particular.
- If the corpse has been dead for longer than about 15 turns, don't eat it. It's best not to risk eating a corpse unless it's really freshly killed; food poisoning sets in surprisingly fast, and it's fatal unless you have a means of curing it. (Apply a non-cursed unicorn horn, potion of extra healing, successful prayer.)
- If it was undead when "alive," don't eat it, even if you just re-killed it; the corpse starts out old in this case. Exception: wraiths are okay to eat if freshly killed, and in fact eating them is recommended.
- Don't eat creatures of your race; that counts as cannibalism, your god will be angered, and you'll pick up the intrinsic Aggravate Monster.
- Don't eat pet-type creatures: white cats or dogs, or normal horses. You'll get Aggravate Monster, even if it wasn't already your pet.
- Don't eat or offer a creature that used to be your pet. It's a relatively new feature, but the game will punish you for it.
- Don't eat lizard corpses! It's not that they're bad, far from it. They're too good to waste on a quick meal. They never go bad, and if you start turning to stone from a cockatrice's hissing ("You slow down" and "Your limbs stiffen" are the signs) quickly take a bite of one to halt the process and save your life. By the way, only the monster called "lizard" has this effect; other monsters that happen to be lizards, like newts and geckos, don't have the same property.

16.8 Learn about Elbereth

One of the weirdest tricks in NetHack involves engraving the word "Elbereth" on the floor. Once done, if you stand on that square 90% of monsters won't attack you! Generally speaking, only humans, elves, minotaurs, angels and blinded monsters (oddly, not naturally-sightless sightless monsters) will attack someone standing on an Elbereth. Creatures that will "respect" it include all demons and demon lords, and nearly every other dangerous monster. Elbereth protects you against melee attacks only, and pets and peaceful monsters don't respect it.

The tradeoff is that, if you write it in the dust with your fingers, the word will degrade rapidly. If even one letter is changed, the whole thing will cease working, and often it'll have degraded by the time you finish the original writing! Writing with certain wands will do the job quickly, or an athame, or a magic marker (although that may be considered a waste of resources). You can also engrave slowly with a weapon, although doing so will rapidly dull the weapon into near uselessness, or you can use a hard gem. Note that you're a sitting duck when slow-engraving; strangely, the game won't prompt you to stop engraving if you're attacked while writing.

Elbereth is useful in a pinch, but isn't necessary for survival. I win the game fairly often and don't use it. If you don't have the means or desire to write Elbereth for protection, standing on the same space as a scroll of scare monster has the same effect.

(*December 2015*: Some minor facts of Elbereth have changed in the recently released NetHack 3.6. It now does not work in Gehennom or the endgame!)

16.9 Use Some Identification Tricks

The cheapest scroll in shops is identify. If you have unknown scrolls and find a general store or bookstore, find out what their prices are (drop in the shop). If it's less than 30 to sell or 50 to buy it's probably Identify, and if it's not then it's probably light, a harmless scroll to read. It is best not to trial ID scrolls after Identify is known.

To get a good clue as to what a wand does, engrave on the ground with your fingers (what you engrave doesn't matter), then try to add onto it with the wand. The message you get depends on the type of wand. Three wands give the same message, that the engraving disappears. Several wands do nothing special, but that mostly happens with the less useful wands and those that are out of charges. The only real drawback to this method is that it uses a single charge from the wand and, if it's a wand of create monster, it might give you some monsters to fight.

If you have an extra ring of an unknown type, a similar trick can be done by dropping one of them down a sink. In that event, all rings have a unique message, and a couple of them even give the ring back. You can sometimes get a lost ring back by kicking it, but that means you won't get a random ring instead, and can attract dangerous monsters for early in the game.

Enemies use many kinds of items, and if you see them do it you'll often get a good hint as to what the item does. They drink and throw certain potions, read scrolls, zap wands and wear certain types of armor. They will also wear one type of amulet. Notably, however, they never wear rings.

16.10 Make the Most of Your Pets

To get more pets easily, throw food at cats and dogs. Tripe rations always work for this. Horses can be tamed by throwing vegetable food at them. Even ordinary food rations work for this, although they won't eat them unless they're very hungry and it doesn't always work. Sometimes it'll make the creature in question peaceful instead.

Pets will not step on cursed items without a special message, unless there's a food item they're interested in on the same square. Opposing monsters will never attack pets in melee unless the pet attacks them first, and pets refuse to attack anything more than a level higher than it or extremely dangerous to attack (like cockatrices). Pets won't attack you unless they're blind, confused, stunned or extremely hungry or you're wearing a ring of conflict.

Every time a pet kills a monster, it gains a maximum hit point, and when it gains eight points it also gains a hit die, up to a maximum. Dogs, cats and horses are special, however, in that they can promote through three stages as they grow. A horse at maximum level is just barely capable of taking out a shopkeeper. Even so, these basic pet-types are typically only useful up to a certain point in the game.

16.11 Know How to Deal with Shops

Don't try to steal in plain sight of the shopkeeper; they are formidable opponents unless you're already strong enough that you'll probably not have much need for the stuff in the shop, they call in the Keystone Kops who can be difficult to deal with at low level, and money is worthless except for paying shopkeepers and priests anyway. In the early levels you can steal from shops safely by letting your pet do the lifting for you; stuff your pet carries out of the shop is free to take. The space right inside the shop's door counts as outside the shop for this. Don't attack a shopkeeper or zap wands at him, don't teleport while carrying stuff, don't dig holes in a shop's walls of floor, don't kick his closed door down (even if it says "Closed for inventory"), and don't attack him directly.

16.12 Be Aware of Special Areas

The **Gnomish Mines** are the first branch you'll encounter, a second set of downstairs between levels 2 and 4. They have lots of gnomes and dwarves to fight. Gnomes are pretty much fodder, but dwarves sometimes wear good equipment. Dwarven mithril is good armor for this stage in the game. Halfway down the mines is Mine Town, referred to by some as the shopping mall. It's got many shops, including a guaranteed lighting shop run by a beloved figure, and also a guaranteed temple with a priest. Use the altar to ID curses, pay the priest for protection (see below) and check the shops for good items. Notably, both the tool shop and lighting shop may carry magic lamps, possibly the easiest source of a wish in the game. Make sure a magic lamp is blessed before rubbing it (Alt-r/#rub)!

Sokoban is found a little deeper than the Mines. It's entered through a second upstairs found on a level, and all its levels start out pre-mapped. Sokoban is a series of boulder-pushing puzzles, along the line of the Sokoban puzzle game. The game's movement rules are subtly different here: you cannot move diagonally through corners or between boulders. Doing anything that would break the rules of the puzzle of the same name causes you to incur a luck penalty while here, which could be a very bad thing if it goes negative (prayer never works when you have negative luck). To proceed, you must fill in all the pits blocking the way onward with boulders. Because of the puzzle aspects and luck penalties, many players choose to ignore Sokoban, but a lot of food, rings and wands tend to be generated there, and players who make it to the end can claim either a shield of reflection or a bag of holding.

The **Oracle** level is in the main dungeon. It's mostly ordinary, except for the Oracle herself, who can be questioned for game hints. There are also several fountains and statues here. If you're a wizard, you can often find spellbooks by casting force bolt on the statues.

The **Quest**, also known as the "Home" dungeon, is a branch accessed by entering a magic portal. The portal counts as a trap, so you won't find it at first until you happen upon its square. Until the quest is completed, you'll be given a reminder message each time you enter the level. Every character class has a different quest, some harder than others. (Monks have a particularly difficult quest.) The first level of the quest always has a staircase down that can't be used until the quest leader, a particular friendly monster on the level, gives you permission (chat with him to speak). To get permission, you must be level 14 and of your original alignment. Take heed! If you permanently change your alignment (by offering at a cross-aligned altar if you haven't been playing your alignment well, or by offering a unicorn of your alignment on an altar of a different alignment), you will be permanently barred from accessing the quest! Since the Bell of Opening must be obtained from the quest and it's needed to win, this means the game cannot be completed.

Fort Ludios is a little-seen one-level branch that is sometimes, but not always, found from a magic portal in a vault in the middle of the main dungeon. Vaults are hard enough to find, and to reliably find the fort you'll probably need to find several of them. It's a pretty difficult level, with a huge number of soldiers, a number of dragons and King Croesus in the middle of a castle. There is a huge amount of equipment to be found here, and lots of gold and gems besides. Ludios is not present in every game.

The **Medusa** level is fairly deep in the main dungeon. The two main obstacles here are a vast lake between you and the stairs down, and Medusa herself standing on the stairs. Make sure to be blinded when facing Medusa; seeing her alive is an instadeath. If you have a means of reflection then she'll probably turn to stone from seeing her own image. Sometimes there is a statue named Perseus on or near the stairs; if smashed to bits with force bolt or a pick-axe, there is sometimes a bag of holding and/or a shield of reflection inside it. (These should be checked for curses.) After Medusa's level, some of the dungeon levels will be mazes. If you get to Medusa without a way past the lake, you can dig down (">") with a pick-axe or wand of digging to fall past it and move on. Remember, however, you'll still have to cross the lake coming back, and Medusa will be right by the upstairs when you climb them, so remember to blindfold yourself before climbing the stairs on your way back up!

Not much further down than Medusa is the **Castle**. The drawbridge can be shattered with force bolt (bridge the moat with a boulder or wand of ice, or cross the water by other means), opened with a wand of opening or a spell of Knock, or if you have a musical instrument you can play it to open the drawbridge by playing "Mastermind," using the noises received as clues for the notes you need to enter. Be careful, however; if you get in by opening the drawbridge, and you're standing on the two spaces in front of it, you'll be crushed by the falling bridge! Even once open, you can be killed if someone shoots a wand of striking and shatters the bridge while you're standing on it. Inside the drawbridge is a lot of tough monsters, and the moat contains a number of deadly eels, which can instantly drown you if they swing themselves around you. In one of the corners of the Castle is the game's sole guaranteed wand of wishing. Good things to wish for: 2

blessed scrolls of charging (for recharging the wand once when it's out of charges), blessed +2 gray dragon scale mail (if without magic resistance), blessed +2 silver dragon scale mail (if already in possession of magic resistance), blessed +2 speed boots (only permanent source of "very fast" speed), spellbook of finger of death (if experienced in attack spells) and blessed magic marker (for making useful scrolls out of blank paper). There are lots of other good things to wish for; Google up a full spoiler for full details. There is a series of pit traps at the back of the Castle. These are the only way down to the next level.

The **Valley of Death** is the first level of Gehennom; prayer doesn't work here. There are lots of undead monsters and treasure chests. There is a temple to Moloch near the end; although Moloch is the evil god of the game, you can still get protection from paying the priest here. The staircase down is hidden behind secret doors near the end; search for them.

Gehennom, also known as "those stupid mazes," is really annoying to get through. I suggest magic mapping as many levels of Gehennom as you can; it'll come in handy later.

Several demon lords have lairs in Gehennom: **Asmodeus**, **Baalzebub**, **Juiblex** and **Orcus**. Azzy and Bubs sometimes ask for a bribe if you're carrying money in your main inventory; they'll vanish without harming you if you pay them enough. Juiblex can make you deathly sick if it engulfs you, but you can escape being engulfed with a wand of digging and can then cure yourself with a potion of extra or full healing, a spell of cure sickness or applying an uncursed, but preferably blessed unicorn horn (though that has a chance of failing to work each attempt). Orcus has a wand of death, although he'll probably use up all its charges in dealing with you. For more tactics in dealing with them, check the section on monsters.

Vlad's Tower is entered through a second upstairs in a Gehennom level. The tower is three very small levels with lots of traps and locked doors. A number of useful items are guaranteed to appear here, among a few other highly dangerous cursed items. Look for levitation boots and an amulet of life saving. At the top of the tower is Vlad the Impaler himself, who is possibly the easiest-to-kill "boss" monster in the game. He holds the second of the essential items, the Candelabrum of Invocation. Note that Vlad's Tower is not technically part of Gehennom; it is safe to pray here.

There is a series of three levels in Gehennom with a huge, blocked-off rectangular section in the middle of them. This is the **Wizard's Tower**. There is no way in from these levels, however. To enter, you'll have to continue to explore down, where you'll find **Fakewiz** levels and the **Wizard's Portal** level, which all contain a small moat surrounding a few walled-off spaces. Cross the water and dig through the wall. One of these levels will have a portal there to the bottom of the Wizard's Tower. At the top of the tower is the Wizard of Yendor himself, who carries the Book of the Dead. Once awake, the Wizard will harass you periodically until the end of the game. Even if you kill him, he'll just keep coming back. Also sometimes he'll call in a bunch of dangerous monsters to surround you, and sometimes he'll curse an item you're holding; he can do these things even if he doesn't actually show up on the level! He stops appearing once you reach the Astral Plane. (Twice now, I've been able to get the Wizard out of his room on the top level and teleport to attack me by playing a drum of earthquake while outside the tower on that level. I forget if he carries his Book with him in this event, though.)

Once you have the Bell of Opening, the Candelabrum of Invocation and the Book of the Dead, proceed to the **vibrating square** level, the bottom-most level of Gehennom. You'll also need seven uncursed or better candles; the lighting store in Mine Town is guaranteed to carry at least that many. One of the spots of floor on this level, which is impossible to determine until you step on it, gives the message "You feel a strange vibration under your feet." Once you find it, stand there then apply the candles to attach them to the Candelabrum. Then: ring the Bell, light the Candelabrum, and read the Book. The result is very cool and produces a staircase down.

Below that is **Moloch's Sanctum**, which contains more monsters than you've seen up to that point and a walled-off room containing Moloch's high priest, who carries the Amulet of Yendor. To get in, you'll need to get by a bunch a fire traps and find the secret door to the room; a wand of secret door detection is called for here. The high priest is a tough opponent, and while you're in the temple, Moloch will cast lightning bolts at you.

Once you get the Amulet of Yendor, the nature of the game changes. Now you have to carry it back up and out of the dungeon. You'll be completely unable to (on purpose) level teleport, normal teleport often fails, going upstairs in Gehennom has an annoying chance of teleporting you away or even back down into lower levels, and spellcasting requires many more power points than before. If you can get to level 1 with the Amulet and climb the stairs, you'll get to enter the endgame. If you make it there, good luck! We're rooting for you.

16.13 Other Things

Turn autopickup OFF if it's on. Most players eventually find it more trouble than it's worth. To pick things up without it, press the comma key while standing on the object you want.

If you don't know what bags of holding are, then don't put wands that might be cancellation or bags that might be holding or tricks into other bags. Bags of holding explode when these items are put into them! All good NetHack players fall afoul of this the hard way at some point in their careers and are a lot more careful about it afterwards.

Don't pick up a gray stone on a whim. If it's a lodestone you'll get weighed down and put in considerable danger even if it's uncursed, because they can curse themselves, and cursed lodestones cannot be dropped. To check, try kicking one ("k" when playing with numpad on, control-d if it's off) into an adjacent square; if it goes "thud" and doesn't move it's a lodestone. (This doesn't apply if you have very high strength or are wearing kicking boots.) The dangers in picking up a lodestone are great enough to try, if a gray stone is generated in a corner, to try digging around it to give it room to move when kicked. It's safest to not pick up gray stones unless you're reasonably sure it's a luckstone. If you do pick one up, prayer can uncurse it so you can drop it.

A quick way to determine which items are cursed or blessed is to drop them onto an altar. This works even if the altar is not of your alignment.

One of the weird little facts of NetHack is that, after buying from shops, money is next to useless except as a minor score bonus. The best thing to do with money is to give it to priests: if you give a priest (using Alt-C/#chat) your experience level times 400 in gold, you'll gain points of intrinsic protection. It doesn't have to be a priest of your alignment. Since this protection cannot be lost by taking off your armor, and "stacks" with the protection offered by armor, it's an extremely useful attribute to have. Once protected, however, be careful not to do things that anger the gods or you'll lose it. Things that will cause loss of protection: killing an aligned priest, wearing a helm of opposite alignment, praying too often or while in Gehennom, and praying at an altar not of your alignment.

Magic lamps never run out of fuel. That's a good way to identify such a lamp, but since it's the only never-expiring light source in the game, players who are already prepared for the ascension run sometimes keep one on-hand for light. Don't try to fill a magic lamp with oil, by the way; that will convert the lamp into an ordinary oil lamp.

Your character has an invisible "Luck" attribute. It goes up when you offer corpses on like-aligned altars ("You see a four-leaf clover at your feet."), when you convert altars to your alignment, when you throw good gems at unicorns and in a few other cases. It goes down when you fail to convert an altar, when you cheat at Sokoban, sometimes when you anger the gods and in a few other circumstances. Luck "times out" over hundreds of turns, slowly returning to its base value, usually zero. Carrying a luckstone prevents this from happening, which can be either good or bad. A cursed luckstone only prevents bad luck from timing out, and a blessed one prevents good luck from timing out. Luck affects many things, but in particular: it helps chances to hit, and it makes good effects from fountains, sinks and thrones more likely. Bad luck is very bad: if you have luck less than zero, prayer never works, and even wishes might fail.

Get poison and magic resistance as soon as you can. It's possible to win without them, but it's very unlikely and depends, to large extent, on luck.

Get the other resistances soon: sleep, fire, shock, cold, disintegration. They can all be gained by eating the right monsters.

Don't let yourself get surrounded if you can help it. If you see a group of hostile monsters, try to maneuver into a corridor so you can fight one at a time. Swarming monsters, such as hill orcs, killer bees (if you have poison resistance) and rothes, are much less dangerous when faced this way.

Beware soldier ants at low level! Again, they are the deadliest monster in NetHack. Wild big cats are tough opponents, too. Beware of leocrottas as well, and also mumaks, both "q" monsters that can tear you up unexpectedly.

Use weapons you can see yourself using in the long term, so you can build weapon skill in them. You don't have to use #enhance to win the game, but it can help. Not all classes can become proficient in all weapons. If you're a spellcasting class, focus on building your spell skills. If your god gives you an artifact or spell of a type you're not able to build skill in, they also grant you the ability to advance to Basic skill with a little practice; sometimes this is a more valuable gift than the object.

Knowing the bad types of items can be of great help in identifying the others. The bad scrolls are amnesia, punishment, fire, destroy armor, create monster and most cursed scrolls. The bad potions are sickness, blindness, hallucination, confusion, paralysis, acid and most cursed potions. Blessed potions of invisibility grant permanent invisibility, which can make it difficult to patronize shops. Many wands are as dangerous as they are useful. The bad amulets are strangulation (which is extremely bad) and restful sleep. The bad rings are polymorph, hunger, conflict, teleportation, levitation and increase rings with minuses. Some of these rings are sometimes cursed, but many of them are potentially useful too. Additionally, the ring of adornment is of only slight value.

Besides just exploration and survival, the next-most-important thing you can do proactively to improve your chances of survival is to make a holy water engine. You can dip items, even whole stacks of items, into a potion of holy water (which is merely blessed water) in order to uncurse cursed items and bless uncursed things. Most items are much more useful when blessed than uncursed or cursed, so a good supply of holy water can greatly aid you in your quest for the Amulet of Yendor. To do this:

- Step 1: Take all the useless potions you've found and turn them into water. You can do this in a number of ways: dip them twice into fountains (only once you've gotten reasonably powerful, as it's dangerous), drop all your other stuff and walk into pools of water until they dilute, or wear water-walking boots then stand over a pool and dip. If you have a wand of cancellation, most potions can be cancelled to water by zapping them on the ground, and some unhealthy potions can be turned to water by dipping a unicorn horn into them.
- Step 2: Find a self-aligned altar. That is to say, one whose alignment matches your own. If you find one that's not of your alignment and there's no attendant priest, you should try to convert it by offering dead monsters at it (Alt-O or #offer). Once it's your alignment, drop as much water on it as you can then pray to make them all into holy water.
- Step 3: Once you have one potion of holy water it's much easier to make more. Make more potions of water by any of the methods in step 1, identify their curse status if not already known so they'll all stack together, then dip the whole stack into your remaining holy water at once; the whole stack will become holy water itself.

Identify is one of the most useful scrolls. Once you learn it, try not to read them unless they're blessed, since they have a much greater chance of identifying everything you're carrying that way. Because of the chance of identifying everything, try to be holding as many unknown items as you can in main inventory before reading. Identifying a whole inventory of unknown things is one of the best things that can happen in NetHack.

Zap yourself with a wand of speed monster to gain permanent speed. Zap your pets with it to make them permanently fast. Drink a blessed potion of see invisible to gain that property intrinsically. Drinking a blessed potion of invisibility and zapping a wand of make invisible both have permanent effects, which is mostly good but could pose problems in getting into shops. Wear a mummy wrapping to temporarily make yourself visible again.

Lawful characters of level 5 or better who can advance in long sword can fairly easily get Excalibur, one of the best artifacts in the game, by dipping long swords into fountains. The chance is one in six times per dip.

In enhancing your weapons and armor, extremely useful are the scrolls of enchant weapon and enchant armor, each of which permanently increases the "plus" of an item. Blessed scrolls increase plus by one to three points, depending on how high its plus was already. Enchant weapon always affects your primary wielded weapon; enchant armor picks a random worn armor type to work upon, so if you want a specific piece enchanted, take all the rest off before reading. When a weapon or elven mithril armor reaches +5, or any other armor reaches +3, you may enchant it just one more time safely. If these items are higher than the listed plus, enchanting them carries a very high risk of destroying the item.

Some scrolls have different effects when read while you're confused. Some of these effects are very helpful and unavailable in other ways. Scrolls of enchant weapon and enchant armor will fire/rustproof instead of enchant, and scrolls of teleportation will cause you to level teleport. While scrolls may work, after a fashion, while you're confused, spells cast from memory do not. Neither spells nor scrolls will work when you're stunned.

17

Spoiled for Options

June 2007 One of the happiest things that can happen to a player in NetHack is being granted a wish. Wishes are one of those things that distinguish roguelike games like NetHack and ADOM from the vast category of lesser RPGs. Imagine if a Final Fantasy VI player were able to wish for the most powerful weapons in the game from relatively early on? That these two games now only allow this, but are not irretrievably broken because of it, speaks volumes about the care that was taken in putting their supposedly chaotic designs together.

In ADOM the player can only wish for non-artifact objects, but in NetHack, a wish can give the player nearly anything, including artifacts and even one quest artifact per game. The only object types that can't be wished for in NetHack are your role's own quest artifact, and the four objects required to win, one of which being the Amulet of Yendor itself. But obtaining a wish is not easy, and knowing what to wish for is not obvious.

The ways you can get a wish in NetHack involve fountains or thrones (both very unlikely and highly dangerous to low-level characters), magic lamps (quite uncommon, and it requires special equipment to maximize the chance of a wish), smoky potions (same as lamps but much rarer) and wands of wishing (the least common item in the game). All these methods are rare, unintuitive and/or dangerous enough to a new player that many people go for months without realizing that such things as wishes are even in the game.

But eventually a player drinking from random fountains, generally an unwise move, lucks out and summons a water demon, who is grateful for release and grants him a wish. What to wish for?

17.1 A Question with No Right Answer? Well Actually . . .

A new player has never had a wish before. He may be able to piece together for himself that he is supposed to ask for, that is, type in the name of, an object. Most early NetHack players, again, have probably not seen even half the ordinary stuff that can be generated in a game, even less often identified that stuff, and has probably not ever seen a single artifact. It is a case where the player does not even know what is in the game, so he won't know what he can ask for.

As he puts more time into the game he'll find more items, so that eventually he might acquire some objective understanding of how they help his game. Among the most useful items are speed boots, but compared to Stormbringer or an amulet of life saving their effect isn't very flashy. He may even figure out for himself that he can wish for items with a specified enchantment, erosion-resistance, or blessed/cursed status, all at once. Of course, the only opportunity he could have to find out that works is at a wish prompt, and even with obsessive play it can be days or even weeks between those for a typical low-level NetHack player.

Now, let me skip ahead to the end of this train of discovery, and note that the destination is a spoiler, so try to skip past the rest of this paragraph if you care about such things. The best item to wish for, for 90% of NetHack characters, is blessed +2 gray dragon scale mail.

This one item, obtained and worn, will suddenly make most characters about three times more survivable.

It will give him a negative armor class all by itself (dragon scale mail is the best type of armor) so monsters hit less often and do less damage when they do.

It's extremely light so it won't weigh him down like plate mail.

It's not made of metal so it won't inhibit spellcasting.

It doesn't burn, corrode or rust.

It even confers magic resistance, immediately ending the game-ruining effects of level-teleport and polymorph traps, nullifying the effects of wands of striking, magic missile and death, and making the player immune to the worst monster spells: destroy armor and touch of death.

Dragon scale mail is never found randomly in the dungeon, but must be made from dragon scales of the right color (infrequently dropped by the eponymous monster) and then a scroll of enchant armor must be spent to make it, so the chances are slim that a character will find one eventually anyway. And yet, this item is not even an artifact. Dragon scale mail is so useful that all NetHack characters not specifically looking for an extra challenge win the game with it on their backs; even for those 10% of characters for whom gray dragon scale mail is not the best choice it is only because they already have or can infallibly obtain another source of magic resistance. For them, silver dragon scale mail is recommended.

(Spoiler end.)

17.2 "So It's Great, but I'm Still Not Sold . . ."

A character who obtains this thing is suddenly in a position to make excellent progress in the game. The Gnomish Mines change from being a ravening slayer of innocent players to almost a playground. It stops short of being a guarantee of survival (especially if the player doesn't have poison resistance), but it has a profound effect. Finding out about dragon scale mail is as major a step towards becoming a NetHack expert as discovering what's safe to eat, figuring out when to use the #pray command, learning about sacrificing at altars, piecing together how to make and use holy water, and noting how to pay for intrinsic protection. All of these things make a NetHack character that much more likely to live through a general crisis, but none of these things is too terribly obvious to someone making his first trip into the Dungeons of Doom. It is possible to win without knowing any of this, but realistically, that's territory for experts, not the average 'hacker.

This brings us around to the point, which has to do with the relationship between roguelike games and spoilers. There are many players of more mass-market computer games who would never think of tackling a new adventure from the likes of Blizzard, Square/Enix, Nintendo or Rockstar without a strategy guide at the ready. Many experienced players, like myself for instance, scoff at this. We know that computer games are now many times easier than they were in the old days, and we defeated enough in that dusty era to easily give us the confidence we need to power through nearly anything those companies put out.

But with roguelike games . . . with these . . .

17.3 The Guiltless Confession

It is not so much that I am "admitting" to having read practically every spoiler about the game of NetHack ever written. It's that the purpose of spoilers for these games seems to be something different, not just in scale but in nature, than what it is for other games. One cannot really "admit" anything, because winning the game all but implies being spoiled. While people do win at NetHack without being spoiled (they didn't write themselves, anyway) it is surpassingly rare.

Yet the game is chaotic enough that knowing all there is to know about it does not mean automatic survival. In fact, just having the information means nothing unless you have digested it, sorted it out in your head and turned it into a plan of attack. Reading the spoilers for such games doesn't ruin them; it is the barrier of entry to success.

Now some people complain, with some justice it cannot be denied, about this state of affairs, and it has led to the creation and development of an entire class of roguelikes that prides itself on not requiring a master's degree in the game in order to win. But it is worth examining how this situation came about, and how it is that, to a great degree, the situation is fundamentally unavoidable.

17.4 "My Valkyrie Puts All Her Skill Points into 'Google Lore'!"

The first roguelike game was, of course, Rogue, which was a much harder game than any modern example of the breed while having not nearly as much to learn as any of them. A rogue can be killed through pure bad luck. Even an expert player will die many times before he wins. There is a balance in a game between the share of the difficulty that comes from lack of knowledge and that which comes from the game environment. Rogue's balance is tilted far over in favor of environment.

For this kind of game, the chances of winning can be measured as a very low percentage of games, but knowing certain facts about the monsters, the dungeon or how the items work could raise that by a couple of percentage points each. In the early history of Rogue, the game was played mostly in university computer rooms, whether the received wisdom of the game was passed orally, then through the use of text files like the Rogue's Vade-Mecum: https://web.archive.org/web/20170115060237/http://userpages.monmouth.com/~colonel/rvm.html.

NetHack's evolution has filled the game with progressively more ways to ease its difficulty curve, so that the balance is far on the side of knowledge. For a well-informed player the game is much easier, and there is a well-known set of hint files relating to the game dating back to version 3.0, called the WCST Spoilers, widely read at the time. The game is famous for "being fair," that is, providing ways out of almost all situations. This implies that it is the player's fault if he dies, but there is a downside; if there is a way out of every situation, then a perfectly knowledgeable player will be able to survive any situation. But the important thing to understand about this is that there is no middle ground; if the game is going to remain a challenge (and the game's score-based premise means it must be), and not an action game, then a balance must be found between the two poles: pure chaos with no guarantees of survival, or complete survivability to a sufficiently determined, that is to say spoiled, player.

This means that people who expect to be able to win if they play well will come to see reading the spoilers as necessary to play. Spoilers are not required to win at NetHack, but the trail goes on for years without them. You can discover that dragon scale mail exists, that gray dragon scale mail provides magic resistance, that magic resistance is an essential attribute to have, and then piece together that a first wish should be spent on it over time, slowly, over the course of dozens of individual incidents spread across many hundreds of games, eventually forging the essential fact in your head through research independent of the efforts of others. Or, you can spend ten minutes reading a spoiler for it on the NetHack Wiki.

What's it going to be?

By the way, just so it's available to you should you wish to see it, for a long time the major resource for NetHack on the World Wide Web was Boudewijn Waijers' homepage for the game, since long vanished. You can see it, as it was near the end of its life, here: https://web.archive.org/web/20000817004013/www.win.tue.nl/games/roguelike/nethack/.

He had links to a lot of other now-forgotten roguelike games as well: https://web.archive.org/web/20001119161100/www.win.tue.nl/games/roguelike/roguelike.html.

The WCST Spoilers, for NetHack 3.0, still make for interesting, if now inaccurate, reading. A copy of them can be found here: http://protovision.textfiles.com/games/spoil700.nh.

18

Hack Hacks

November 2006 /dev/null's annual NetHack tournament is, as I type this, winding its way towards concluding another successful year. While there have not been a good many surprises this time out (Christian "marvin" Bressler has already won Best of 13 again), there has been a fairly substantial surprise in the game itself.

One of the things that NetHack makes possible, and /dev/null takes advantage of in their contests, is for game administrators to provide customized games for their players. The level description files that NetHack uses to generate levels are separate from the game executable, and can be compiled separately from the main game without even invalidating old saves. The source code itself is also open, freely available on nethack.org, which over the years has made possible NetHack's handful of variants, including SLASH'EM. One might think that a game in which all its secrets are laid bare in the source code would provide no surprises for a player, and it is true that the source itself is the primary NetHack spoiler, but since the source is not always easy to read, and much of the game is randomly generated anyway, this doesn't tend to ruin the game. (In fact, if anything, only spoiled players ever seem to win at NetHack . . .)

So what /dev/null has done is implement a "challenge," a patch to the game that is added each year to the source of their version of the game to mix the game up for long-time players. (There is an option to play without it as well.) This was begun last year, with an appropriately far-reaching mood set by asking players to go over to popular webgame Kingdom of Loathing, which includes a special theme area as an homage to NetHack, and complete a quest there. This year's challenge is entirely in-game, adding new monsters and items and a special procedure to be undergone concerning them.

NetHack patches are fairly numerous in general. Angband, NetHack's primary competitor for the position of most popular roguelike, is also open source but its patchableness, combined with the relatively easy-to-understand code, has steered starry-eyed modders more towards the creation of new variants than just adding stuff to the core game. NetHack, on the other hand, has a notoriously twisty codebase with all kinds of gotchas waiting to pounce upon an untutored programmer, making the creation of full-fledged variants quite difficult for players without an encyclopedic knowledge of both the source and the C programming language, and its play has more unique character than Angband's anyway, so most patch authors content themselves with adding a minor feature or two.

Many of these patches can be obtained from the NetHack Patch Database, a website that catalogues and makes these source patches available for download. Compiling them into the game can be an adventure to itself, especially with some patches that have not been updated since older versions, but for those stout of heart enough to see them through their compilation are rewarded with some fairly radical changes to the play.

Note: when applying patches to NetHack, it's important to note what version of the source code the patches are made for. The current version of the game when most of this was written was 3.4.3. The current version as of publication is 3.6.6. There are plenty of newer patches to find on the NetHack Patch Database, located at bilious.alt.org. Some of these patches have been incorporated in more recent variants for NetHack.

Among the more promising patches out there for NetHack 3.4.3, were:

18.1 Color Alchemy

https://bilious.alt.org/?59
Port to 3.6.1: https://bilious.alt.org/?498

A relatively recent addition to NetHack's formidable feature set is alchemy, which is implemented in the game by dipping one potion into another. It used to be that the result from such a combination was completely random, with a good chance of an explosion. More recently, a system has been implemented by which particular kinds of potions mixed into others would tend to make the same result. For example, mixing potions of healing and gain energy together yields extra healing.

The details of NetHack's alchemy system, as many other aspects of the game, can be learned at the NetHack Wiki, but that doesn't concern us at the moment. Color Alchemy discards that system entirely and replaces it with quite a nifty little idea: that mixing potions should produce results depending on the colors of the input potions more than their types.

Under the Color Alchemy patch, if you mix a potion of a red hue with a yellow one, the result will be orange. To elaborate: if you mix a potion type whose description is a red color with a potion type whose description is yellow, you will get out of it a potion whose description is orange.

This is a fairly ingenious change to the game. Under the old system, once you know what certain potions are, you can fairly consistently create certain other potions, but those mixtures do not change between games, and some of these potions, such as full healing and gain level, are highly desired. Since potion descriptions are randomized at the start of the game, playing with the Color Alchemy patch means entirely different combinations on every play. One game may have highly useful potion mixture combinations; another may have all valuable types combine to make crappy ones. It is possible for extremely useful mixtures to result from this, like two common potions mixing to produce gain level, but in the end the results balance out, since it would be fairly unlikely to happen, the player will have to have learned what the potions are to get real use out of this which implies the player has survived the early game, and in the long run level gain creates problems as it solves others, so it is a fairly well-thought-out change to the game.

Further, there is something intrinsically NetHackish about using a logical aspect of potion descriptions as the basis for mixing them. In a game where players can rustproof armor by reading a scroll of enchant armor while confused, color-based potion mixing fits right in. Because of this, this patch is considered by some to have a good chance of being incorporated into the next version of the game . . . but the ways of the DevTeam are mysterious, and one can never speak for sure as to what they plan to do with the game in the next version.

18.2 Enhanced Artifacts

https://bilious.alt.org/?208

For all its wonders, there are also a fair number of head-scratching things about NetHack. One of the most scalp-tingling of these is the game's collection of practically useless artifacts.

A NetHack artifact, to explain once more, is a unique, named object that carries special properties above the typical example of its class. Most of them are weapons, and some are quite nice to have in your hands. Many games have been won by players wielding the likes of Grayswandir or Excalibur. However, there are at least as many "useless" artifacts in the game, which few knowledgeable players would bother carrying around. Most of these are in a category termed the "Banes," a number of artifact weapons that grant attack bonuses against one class of monster and nothing else. Against monsters that are not dragons, Dragonbane is no different from an ordinary longsword. For a weapon of such superlative quality that only one of it exists in the world, this is something of a letdown.

Even this would not be so bad if the actual bonus was something so tremendous that it could, say, slay monsters of its class with a single blow, but this is not the case. One might think that a weapon whose specialty was the destruction of a particular species would at least be so powerful against it that it would be the obvious choice in such an encounter, but even against dragons, Dragonbane is nothing to write home about.

Neither is Trollsbane all that useful against trolls, nor Werebane against lycanthropes, nor Ogresmasher against ogres. Bane longsword weapons, in particular, are outclassed against any foe by the headliners in that weapon category: Frost Brand, Excalibur and Fire Brand. Even Vorpal Blade, which has a 5% chance of beheading foes but otherwise has a pitiful bonus, is better than Dragonbane. Further, most Banes can be made obsolete by a single blessed scroll of genocide, which may be rare but are far from unique.

What the Enhanced Artifacts patch does is take some of the less useful of these weapons and add extra powers to them. This usually takes the form of extra damage (especially in the case of Vorpal Blade and the Tsurugi of Muramasa), but the Bane weapons in particular have been focused on, granting them a substantial boost in to-hit and damage against their enemy races and giving them powers in addition to their normal weaponly function. Trollsbane grants regeneration and prevents trolls from coming back from the dead (again and again, dammit), while Dragonbane grants reflection, eliminating all threat from dragon breath and wand attacks at once.

The essence of game design is to provide the player interesting decisions to make, but a decision in which there are choices that are obviously good or bad is not a real decision. No player who knows what he is doing will choose Trollsbane over Frost Brand. Ultimately, what the Enhanced Artifacts patch really does is remove a little of the surety behind that decision, and that makes for a stronger game.

18.3 Biodiversity

https://bilious.alt.org/?91

NetHack is a game known for the size of its bestiary. It contains hundreds of vicious foes, most of them with far more, um, personality than that of a garden-variety RPG. NetHack has monsters that quickly kill those unwise in dealing with them (giant eels), monsters that drain experience levels (vampires), monsters that cause amnesia (mind flayers), monsters whose corpses can be used as weapons themselves (cockatrices), monsters who can provide special armor (dragons), monsters who steal money (leprechauns) and items (nymphs) and even monsters who, properly approached, can help the player (succubi/incubi and nurses), and that's just scratching the surface.

But the thing about variety is, it never seems like there is quite enough of it. Even with all its wonders, there eventually comes a time in most players' hacking careers that the basic catalog of monsters begins to seem kind of boring. This is one of the primary reasons people play SLASH'EM, the NetHack variant most likely to cause insanity: while NetHack merely appears to go overboard in every respect, SLASH'EM truly does so.

But there is perhaps a middle ground between "considerably" and "absurdly" loaded with monsters, and that ground may well be occupied by the Biodiversity patch, which adds a number of new foes to the game, including one that fixes shoes, one that disintegrates objects with a touch and even one that changes mazes. In a game that contains Keystone Kops (and used to have the Three Stooges) this may not seem like a big deal, but at least most of the added foes fall into the "monster has special unique powers" category, instead of the "monster has hit dice, three attacks and fire resistance" one, like, say, every monster in Angband.

18.4 Grudge

https://bilious.alt.org/?62

One of the older modifications for version 3.4.3 of the game is the Grudge Patch, which takes one of NetHack's central features, the core concept behind pets and rings of conflict, the idea that monsters can sometimes hit other monsters instead of the player, and runs with it. Simply, Grudge gives certain monsters a greater priority in their lives than killing that particular @-symbol who happens to be traipsing through the maze at that moment. All you people who sat and thought unkind things about a game in which elves happily attack the player alongside orcs, your nerdly objection has been heard!

18.5 Pet Ranged Attack

https://bilious.alt.org/?92

The thing that most people know about NetHack, if they know anything about it at all, is that players begin with a pet, a little dog or a kitten (or sometimes, in recent versions, a pony). This pet will often not last long in the dungeon, but that's okay as a canny player can acquire a new one and can in fact build an army of loyal lackeys to tackle the dungeon for him.

A pet is a monster that fights for, rather than against, the player. But there are more differences than that. Pets can steal from shops, provide hints as to what is safe to eat and help identify cursed objects. Pets can also grow hungry over time, which untamed monsters do not, and the player is punished, sometimes harshly, for not treating his minions with the proper respect.

Many NetHack patches, as we have seen, get their inspiration from fixing some of what are perceived as the more lacking aspects of the game. One can't help but think each of them occurred because the patch author once had a game in which he was bitten by the lack of the expected behavior. The oversight the Pet Ranged Attack patch corrects is the fact that, when a monster becomes tamed by the player, it seems to suddenly forget how to fire missile weapons, use its breath weapons or cast magic. The great majority of NetHack's non-human monsters can be tamed, but this situational memory condition makes some of the most powerful of the lot, liches and dragons in particular, tragically ineffectual once they start working for the player.

When playing a game with the Pet Ranged Attack patch applied, pets will attempt to use distance attacks, including beam-attacks like rays and breath, against the player's foes. They will even make an effort not to harm the player with these blasts. However, since ray attacks may carom off walls and sometimes take random bounces, one should keep in mind that having a pet black dragon while not having a reflective shield, amulet or suit of armor is a recipe for disaster.

18.6 New Bigrooms, New Castles, New Medusa Lairs, New Sokoban Levels

Bigrooms occur on a certain range of levels, relatively early in the dungeon, and are, as the name implies, made of one gigantic room without things like sight barriers or corridors to impede the monsters from merrily sidling up next to you and whacking you to the extent of their joyous monster heart's desire. NetHack Bigrooms are implemented as semi-hardcoded levels with predefined layouts and some randomized aspects, such as monster types and stair locations. When one appears (only in a small percentage of games), it is chosen from one of a number of pre-made layouts, but they are all generally wide-open and easy to get surrounded in.

The Castle appears fairly deep underground and marks the transition between the Dungeons of Doom and Gehennom, the two major halves of the game. Like Bigrooms, it is semi-hard-coded, although there is only one main Castle layout in basic NetHack. It always contains a drawbridge, pits leading to the next level instead of stairs and a certain very powerful aid to the player's quest. It also has many particularly tough monsters, and it serves as the last major trial before the player can seriously undertake the search for the Amulet of Yendor.

The Medusa level is a few floors up from the Castle, and since it is mostly flooded the player usually needs a means of crossing water to proceed. There are two potential layouts to the Medusa level, but both of them have the gal herself standing on the downstairs, and special measures must be taken to prevent turning into a statue at the mere sight of her.

Sokoban is a dungeon branch relatively early in the game, accessed from a second set of upstairs found shortly after the Oracle level. Unlike most branches it leads up, not down, and always contains four levels. Sokoban levels are a bit less random than most and contain a pre-written arrangement of boulders and pits. The level also has special rules patterned after its namesake game, which prevent boulders from being pushed diagonally, or getting past a pit unless it has been filled. Sokoban's layouts, consisting as they are of traditional box-pushing puzzles, are all pre-written, and each floor, of ascending difficulty, is chosen from one of two alternatives when it is first entered.

As for the patches themselves? They simply increase the number of possible layouts for these levels. The Sokoban patch is interesting since it adds 19 more possible puzzles to the 8 included in the game. The Castle patch adds variety to a level that formerly had fairly little, since in vanilla NetHack there is only one Castle layout.

18.7 Heck^2

https://bilious.alt.org/?26

Excluding branches, there are three major sections of NetHack's dungeon. The one most players are familiar with is the Dungeons of Doom, which goes from the surface down to the Castle. Above the upstairs are the

Planes, which make up the endgame and can only be accessed once the player has the Amulet of Yendor. After the Dungeons and before the Planes is Gehennom, which goes from the Valley of the Dead down to the bottom-most level, where the Amulet is kept.

The Dungeons of Doom are composed of rooms and connecting passages drawn between them. Gehennom, in contrast, is made up of a good number of mazes, with the occasional special level thrown in.

These mazes comprise what many consider to be the most boring portion of the game. A player who has reached them has probably cleared the Castle so he is not likely to be overwhelmed by monsters at this point, and the demons that infest Gehennom, while strong, are not much stronger than some of the monsters the player has likely already faced, like xorns and liches. Notably, most of the demon lords and princes in Gehennom are relative pushovers for an even slightly prepared player. There is still the Wizard of Yendor to contend with, but it's some time before he shows up.

Meanwhile, as I said, most of these levels are mazes, and it usually takes much longer to explore a maze than a complex of rooms, while being less interesting to explore. There are no special rooms in the mazes, nor any altars, fountains or sinks. The stairs down might be two spaces away from the entrance, or they might be clear on the other side of the level. Along the way there is the usual mix of increasingly pathetic monsters to slay, which becomes more and more just a formality as the player continues into the depths.

I explained that it is possible to teleport down many levels at once if the player is suitably prepared, yet the player cannot really skip the mazes: once the Amulet is obtained the player must escape with it, and player-initiated level teleport does not work while it is carried. It must be brought, from the lowest level, all the way back up to the top of the dungeon on foot, with the occasional random teleport down a few floors just to be frustrating, so a smart player has planned for this by mapping out all the levels ahead of time. This makes the formerly useless scrolls of magic mapping nearly essential on the way back out of the dungeon. It also makes for a fairly tedious experience, as all those mazes do not have much variety to recommend them.

A number of patches have been created to address this perceived failing of the game. SLASH'EM handles it by cutting out the mazes almost entirely, increasing the size of the main dungeon and making Gehennom more of a collection of special levels than a huge maze. It also gives all the unique demons their own special level, including rarely seen special guest star Demogorgon, the deadliest monster in the game. The Lethe patch makes Gehennom more perilous by introducing rivers of amnesia-inducing water, as well as throwing in more special levels, many of them populated with a selection of Lovecraftian monsters.

Heck^2's solution to the problem is not to make Gehennom shorter, but to make it more interesting by throwing more special levels in to the mix. It comprises 42 special levels that can replace a substantial portion of Gehennom's random mazes. Some of the random possibilities include special levels for the guest demons, but there are plenty of other interesting possibilities, such as one containing a small coven of amnesia-causing mind flayers, and a maze made up of NetHack's least-known terrain type, iron bars, which can be seen through but not passed.

While NetHack is open source, its official maintainers are not promiscuous about the contributions they accept. For all out patch inclusiveness there is SLASH'EM, a game that contains automatic weapons (as in, machine guns), lightsabers, doppelgangers and vampires as a player races, special character abilities (some of which, it must be said, are incredibly geeky, like the Monk's Final Fantasy VI-inspired direction inputs to execute special moves), a load of new character classes and a couple additional legs to the main quest, among other additions. While it is at times disappointing that the DevTeam seems to have become fairly conservative, not to mention slow, concerning the things they add to the game, for players who wish more there is always SLASH'EM. And for those who would like to retain at least a few of their sanity points, there is the world of user-made patches.

19

A Quick Look at the NetHack Sources

December 2007 There are the roguelike games that have closed source code, which for the longest time included Rogue, and still includes ADOM and just about every commercial game out there. And then there are the roguelikes that are open source.

And of them all, there is one game that is particularly identified with open source. Of course, it's NetHack, which was effectively open long before it became fashionable. The game is old enough that its license, the "NetHack Public License," takes GNU Bison's as its model, not the GPL. In point of fact, Eric S. Raymond himself has contributed documentation to the game, and he mentioned it in his famous essay The Cathedral and the Bazaar. It and the other open source roguelikes (Angband and Dungeon Crawl among them) offer the best hope that open source game development can work.

Development is one thing. Design is something else entirely. The model of many random people contributing patches often turns into a classic case of too many cooks. It takes a strong vision to avoid the game turning into an unplayable muddle, because it's so easy to wreck it by adding misfeatures. Computer games not only require strong software design but something else besides, and roguelikes rely on ideas that most other games abandoned long ago, that some surprising people will swear have no place in gaming. David Sirlin, who possesses an excellent understanding of fighting game mechanics, made a series of blanket statements about game saving, using Dead Rising as his example, that would absolutely destroy roguelikes if applied to them. For some reason few commercial developers outside of Japan seem to get how roguelikes are supposed to work; even Blizzard's popular quasi-roguelike Diablo games didn't add permadeath until the second game, and went out of their way to say it was intended for "hardcore" players. Anyway, they succeeded largely for reasons unrelated to being like rogue (6).

Because of the special vision required to avoid ruining 'em, roguelike projects tend to languish without a strong person, or group in agreement, maintaining them. For NetHack, we have the mighty DevTeam, who are just about as mysterious a group as is possible in legal open source software development. What they'll add to the next version is known to few outside their group, or even what its release date is. At the moment it's been longer since a new version of NetHack than any previous release of the game, but we still know they're working, and we know a new version will come . . . some day. Of course it's still open source, and that means anyone can make their own version of NetHack. The DevTeam is even known to sometimes add a selection of outside patches in the official game. But neither do they add tremendous numbers of outside ideas, and what they do add at times seems odd to us mortals.

But yes, the source is still open, so anyone can make their own version of the game with just a computer, a compiler, the code and a whole lot of cursing. Unlike Angband's source, which prior maintainer Ben Harrison cleaned up and made so inviting for people to mod the game that there may be more players of variants than of Angband, NetHack's source looks exactly like you'd expect something with "hack" in the name to be.

19.1 GCC Hits! Your Brain Is Eaten!*

Trying to modify the NetHack source code with only basic programming knowledge is a good way to get frustrated. Changing NetHack is definitely not a task for the faint-hearted . . . or for the C-ignorant, for that matter. It is not recommended that one try to learn C by hacking away at the NetHack sources, due to its many weirdnesses. Some of its code is automatically generated by an included utility called makedefs, and changes made in the wrong place (like trying to add monsters in pm.h instead of monst.c) could cause unexpected problems, or at best be destroyed by the act of compilation. Macros are used in many places. Even C experts may be confused by the identifiers sprinkled around, things like STATIC_DCL and STATIC_OVL. These are dusty vestiges of the 286 days, when the game had to work under real-mode DOS. They had cooked up this impressive overlay scheme to allow everything to work, swapping code in off disk when needed, but while no one has successfully made real-mode NetHack since 3.3.0, the artifacts of the system are still sprinkled around the source code.

First off, to compile NetHack for your system, you'll need a supported compiler. This is actually one of the less troublesome aspects of building the game, for NetHack's source is promiscuous to say the least. NetHack is mostly a straight, pre-ANSI C program, with none of that C++ stuff mixed in. It gets some help from make, which gets a fair workout, and yacc/bison and lex/flex for building levels. On Microsoft platforms, there's support for multiple versions of Microsoft's Virtual C tools (including the free 2005 Express version combined with Microsoft's Platform SDK, which I've personally used to build the game), Borland C++ and GCC (using either cygwin, mingw or DJGPP for protected-mode DOS, still one of the most playable versions of the game). Mac OS/X and Classic are supported, as are many different Unixes, some rather elderly. In addition, the game has official support in the tree for BeOS, Windows CE, OS/2, Amiga and Atari ST. (And of course porting the game to other systems, like the Nintendo DS, is a standard hack for hobbyists.)

Instructions for building the game are straightforward but lengthy, with the docs beginning in README in the source directory followed by system- and compiler-specific instructions in each platform's Install. file. Further help on this step can be found on the NetHack Wiki. In a last-ditch situation, the DevTeam is known to sometimes reply to questions concerning compilation trouble, and if a problem seems intractable

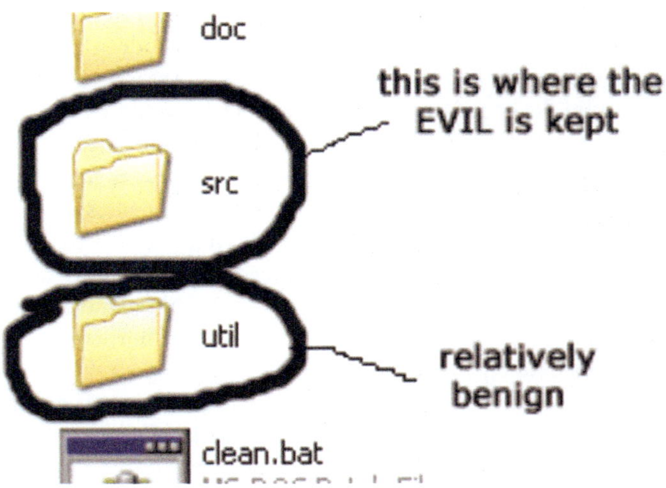

Figure 19.1

Author's notes on a couple of NetHack source directories

* These notes apply to NetHack 3.4.3. The current version is 3.6.6.

it may be worth shooting them an email. (I won't repeat their address here to try to save them from a bit of extra spam, but there's a contact form on their site that's not too hard to find.)

19.2 "NetHack Contains Everything Including the Kitchen Sink," Eh? Not Anymore, *Fool*!

Once the game is compiled, though, then what? The DevTeam provides official binaries for many target systems, so there's not usually a reason to build from scratch unless one is going to modify the source in some way. And there are several different levels of involvement that one can take with this.

The simplest level, which doesn't take much skill with C to mess with, is to add or remove certain well-compartmentalized features from the game. Config.h in include/ is the place to do this, which is where different graphic styles are added to the game as well as wizard mode, a notable debugging aid that can also be used to cheat. Most of the interesting features come in that file's Section 4, suitably named "THE FUN STUFF!!!"

When the DevTeam adds major features to the game, there's often a period when the code is put in conditionally, so players able to compile the game can remove them because they don't like them, or they need to make the game smaller. After a while, as these features become increasingly identified with NetHack, the conditionals are usually removed from the code. But some features take up residence here permanently. Usually these are the crazier features: kitchen sinks, the Rogue level, Keystone Kops, seduction by succubi and incubi, and Discworld-inspired Tourist players can all be neatly excised by commenting out a single line.

In practice this is done but rarely, because the weirdness has become identified with NetHack's style (people who are attracted to NetHack are often so because of the clever jokes, and are loathe to see them go), and because a number of nice sub-features are tied in with these. Commenting out #define TOURIST also removes Touristy items like credit cards, expensive cameras and shirts. Elbereth, a popular feature that some (okay, I) think make the game too easy, can also be compiled out from config.h, but this also removes crowning, a cool game event that happens to players who achieve high standing with their god.

19.3 At Last We Can Add Godzilla as a Monster

Many people who change the game don't want to add huge new features, but just want to customize some of the monsters and items, or add to the dungeon. This is not so easy, but it could be much worse. The Beginners Guide to the NetHack Sources is the bible for making these kinds of modifications, and for detailed instructions one should check there first. Although it was last modified in 1995 most of its information is still good, especially concerning the overall structure of the source, and most of the information in the rest of this chapter ultimately comes from there.

Making a new monster involves editing the file monst.c, and with a bit of intuition it's not hard to add a new entry there, if one doesn't care about it having any abilities not shared by other monsters. Other than that the process is largely automated, for NetHack determines stuff like monster difficulty, experience awards and generation odds automatically. Adding new levels is trickier, but there is support in the game for changing levels without changing the binary. NetHack gets its information on the dungeon and its levels from data files, not the game binary itself, so it's theoretically possible to change the dungeon on a pre-compiled version of the game.

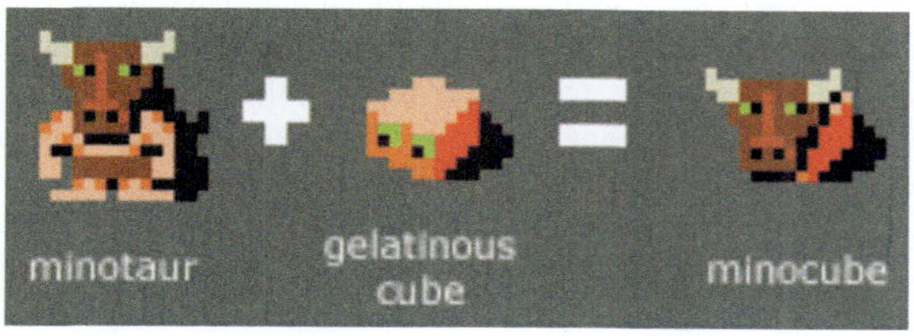

Figure 19.2

A suggested addition to NetHack's bestiary

It's possible, but that doesn't mean that anyone does it in practice. The dungeon and level files usually get made as part of make install, and there are some hard-coded references to various levels in the source, so making any really interesting changes usually means recompiling the game. Changing the level definition files is a notoriously finicky process, prone to break if language terms are specified out of order, or with the wrong spacing character. (Tabs are not the same thing as spaces!)

A few other things can be added relatively easily. Adding a new item isn't so hard, although it'll have only basic object behavior until code is added to cover the neat stuff it should do. Still, that can get you further than you might think. Basic equipment stats like damage, AC and weight can be manipulated just by changing the appropriate numbers, and some things are automatically applied by the code, like silver damage to demons and lycanthropes if the object's material is set to SILVER.

One thing that's easy to overlook is the special characteristics for different item classes. All rings produce special messages when dropped down sinks, and many wands produce distinctive messages when the player engraves on the floor with one. Often potions mix with others when dipped or have special effects on items, and scrolls and spellbooks should have code added to handle when magic markers are used to write them. This is all in addition to the code needed to make the object perform its function, and don't forget that potions, wands and tools have different effects if cursed or blessed, and scrolls have additional effects when read while confused.

New room types are a mixed bag. It's easy to take the code for a monster lair room type in mkroom.c, like the leprechaun hall, copy it, modify it to make a new type of lair, then adjust the room generation probability elsewhere in the source file to make it show up. But this will only produce lair-type rooms. The most interesting NetHack rooms are the ones with special rules, shops and temples, and those are very difficult to write. NetHack shops and shopkeepers do things the hard way because it makes theft into a puzzle to be overcome, and are designed with care. Duplicating that is a task even experienced hack-hackers balk at.

19.4 That's How . . . But Why?

The best advice I can offer towards learning how to get around the code, besides playing the game a lot to know how things operate, and using a code cross-referencing tool like doxygen, is to think hard about using the source code itself as a guide for how to do things. Many things you might want to add to the game are already there, under a different context. I had an idea a week ago about adjusting a unicorn horn's cursed/blessed status one level down when successfully applied for healing, in order to prevent a single horn from making a player practically immune to negative status effects. I happened to remember that scrolls of scare monster, when picked up, lower in blessing status in exactly the same way. A search for SCARE_MONSTER turned up hits in five files, one of them named pickup.c. The addition ended up being only slightly more involved than a copy-and-paste job. When trying to find code to adapt, it's useful to search for the code's name for the item (like "SCARE_MONSTER"), or for a message printed by the game when using it.

19.5 Knowing What Not to Change

The greatest danger, when it comes to modifying the source . . . well, the greatest danger is making the game buggier. But assuming it all works, then the greatest danger is messing up the game's design while doing so. NetHack's various game systems interact with each other in unexpected ways, and one must have encyclopedic knowledge of nearly the whole game to avoid unforeseen balance effects. Some people wonder why drinking a potion doesn't leave an empty bottle that could be later filled with water. The only real answer is because it would make the game too easy: water is one of the most useful potions available to a player who knows how to use it. It doesn't make sense, but it's pretty much mandated by the play.

Maybe there's a way to make empty potion bottles work in the context of the game. It's not impossible. But it's the kind of thing that, if there was an easy way to do it, the DevTeam probably would have implemented it years ago. Most of the weird things about NetHack are like that. Perhaps that budding patch author may have the solution to the problem. It's just likely that he doesn't.

20

Balancing a Game That Looks Balanceless

September 2007 NetHack (and Hack) keeps coming up again and again here because, after the original, it is the most Rogue-like of them all. Rogue is a game with profound design: changing even the tiniest bit affects everything else.

Of all the roguelikes, the Hack games are those which most recognize that Rogue is an interesting game for reasons other than its turn-based tactical combat. Many of these games pay lip service to some of Rogue's more profound features, especially item identification, without really embracing them. In Angband, attempting to ID some things by experimentation is a really bad idea, because of the existence of items that can instantly kill a player who uses them, and anyway players can usually find all the identify scrolls they need through the town shops. Dungeon Crawl's maintainers admit that it downplays its item identification game. And all of these roguelikes weight item generation by level, which upsets the identification game by making it even more unlikely that very useful items will appear early on.

NetHack's deeper features tend to be extensions and elaborations of Rogue's: its identification game, its objects with heavily programmed functions and the secret uses of many items. And these are the things that roguelike fans who don't like NetHack disapprove of. I maintain this is because they've been trained to enjoy "mainstream" gaming first, which tends to be devoid of real strategy, values providing the player with an "experience" more than being a game that can be lost, and are forgiving to the point where he can't really ever die: he can always return to a previous save, after all. The absence of those things allows precisely the aspects of Rogue that make it worth playing at all.

My own thinking regarding NetHack's design has undergone some adjustment over time. Most people who become fans of the game upon first exposure like it for being Rogue Deluxe. After further play, they notice that although there are many more secret features in the game, after learning them all they make the game easier than the original. Some of them appear unbalancing at first, but actually they seem to be rather deviously balanced. After many games, it sometimes turns out that they may not be balanced as well as it seemed at first, and some of it actually overturns some of Rogue's elegance out of the exuberance of adding new stuff.

Yet that exuberance is an important part of NetHack. It is filled with interesting things, and as any worthwhile game designer will tell you, it is profoundly difficult to put something really interesting into a game. There are not actually that many things that can be put into games, and the artificial strictures placed upon them by "modern" game design, like returning to old saves, overbearing balance, hard-coded levels and even the tutorial aspect of the early sections, serve to restrict the designer's imagination even more. NetHack's DevTeam seems to be saying through NetHack that it's more important to add new cool stuff than to make sure it's properly balanced, and provided that it really is cool, I tend to agree with them.

But this is not to say that balance isn't important, nor that the DevTeam isn't concerned with it. What they're really about, in my opinion of course, is adding cool new features yet making sure they "fit" with the rest of the game. Sometimes they get it right immediately, sometimes it takes them some time to figure out the problem and fix it, and sometimes the problem survives. Sometimes it survives long enough that it becomes part of the game, and the thought of removing it becomes unthinkable. Sometimes it even turns out that the misfeature isn't so bad after all, or later features remedy its balance issues, but also sometimes they aren't so fortunate.

Here is a short list of some of the more immediately evident of these features and their current status.

(*January 2016*: Some of these exploits that existed at the time of this writing have been fixed in NetHack 3.6.6.)

Problems that have been fixed:

20.1 Wishing for Wishes

Wishing items used to allow the player to wish for objects that could then be used to get wishes. In the case of wands of wishing (which used to be fairly common in hell), the net gain in wishes would be positive.

This was fixed long ago, although it can be noted that drinking smoky potions, no matter what they might be, may very rarely summon a djinn who could offer a wish. There is no restriction of the wishing of smoky potions, although the wish chance is slim enough that it's hardly an exploit.

20.2 Nurse Dancing

Players wearing no clothes and wielding no weapons get healed, not harmed, from the attacks of nurses. If the player's fully healed, then a few of these hits will raise his maximum hit points.

This is a prime example of a feature that other games would either never have included, or if they did would remove rather than work through balancing it into the game. In NetHack, taking off all your clothes can open you up to quick death from suddenly appearing monsters, especially liches, but there are other checks as well. There's a limit to how HP can be raised this way, and when a nurse heals there's a chance it'll vanish from the game, not just teleport as with nymphs, leprechauns, etc.

20.3 Polypiling

Zapping a wand of polymorph can turn a monster into another kind of monster, but if the invisible ray travels over items it'll turn them into other, random items of the same type, i.e., weapons become other weapons,

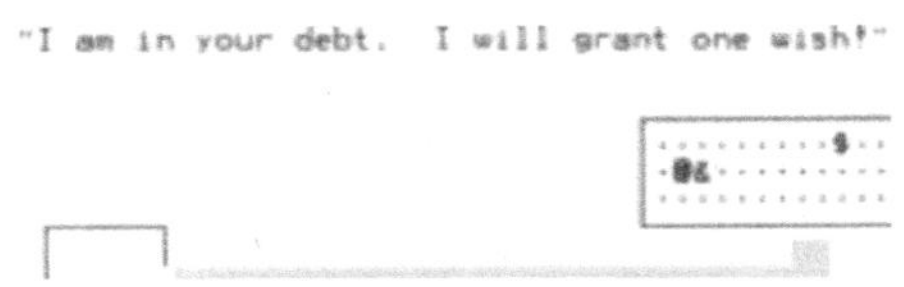

Figure 20.1

Encountering a friendly djinni

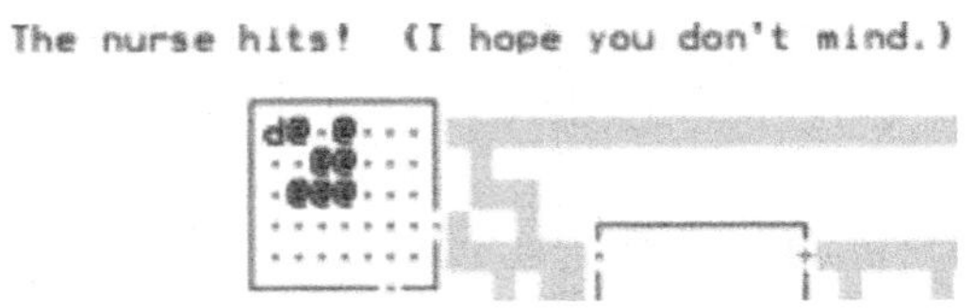

Figure 20.2

An encounter with a medical professional

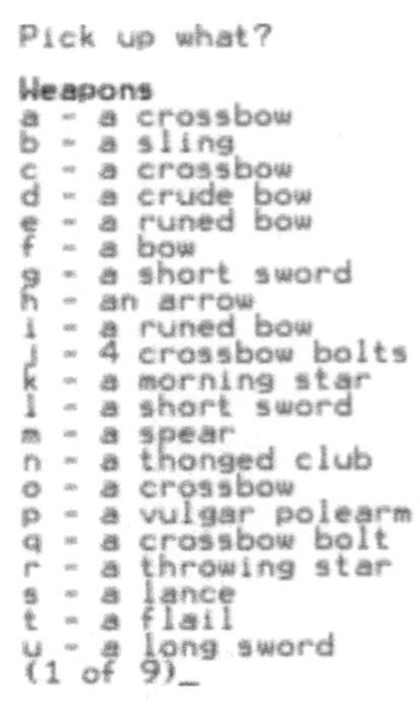

Figure 20.3

A result of a polymorph zap

armor becomes other armor, gauntlets other gauntlets, rings other rings, potions other potions and so on. Equipment keeps its enchantment, wands retain prior number of charges and so on.

The major incentive to explore dungeon levels, as opposed to just heading for the stairs, is to find new random treasure, but if you can get that with a quick zap from a wand? And if it'll affect all items over five spaces, even if there's hundreds on that spot? This got fixed by causing large stacks of polymorphed items to "merge" into smaller piles when changed, discarding large amounts of stuff, and the creation of golems, which are sometimes strong opponents and who also take some of the objects out of the pile.

20.4 Succubus Dancing

Succubi and Incubi are a particular type of demon that can be . . . "consorted with" . . . to make special things happen. With high stats and luck, the chances of the things being good ones can be very high, even guaranteed, and one of those things is gaining an experience level.

The balancing from this is two-fold: the direct method and the indirect. As for direct, such an encounter leaves the player mostly unclothed, and like with nurses, the monster always ends up with "a headache" afterwards, unwilling to do it again for a random number of turns, and after a while getting a severe headache that disables its benefit-generating ability with permanence. To get benefits consistently from a foocubus also requires the player have high scores in Intelligence and Charisma, the two most difficult stats to raise (they don't change through exercise), and the benefit granted is chosen from a list out of which level gain is only one element.

The indirect balance is much more profound, and is actually a balance against all the instant level gains the game offers. In many other games arbitrary sources of level gain are obviously a balance flaw, but NetHack's monster generation system means it's not as bad as it might be. The traditional way to select random monsters is to pick from a list that's hard-coded for each level. NetHack does it by selecting monsters, from a big list of all those that can appear in the current dungeon branch, by taking the average of the player's level and the dungeon level, and trying to generate monsters of around that difficulty. This means that gaining levels itself will increase the difficulty of monsters generated, by about half the rate the player advances.

20.5 Current Problems

20.5.1 Pudding Farming

When monsters greater than a certain difficulty are killed, in addition to sometimes leaving a corpse and always dropping what they were carrying, sometimes they'll additionally leave behind a random item. This may not make sense, but it does fulfill a game role, since monster possessions are not very random but vary according to the monster type. For example, soldiers get military equipment, and elves and dwarves sometimes get cloaks, mithril and appropriate weapons. The random item drop thing provides extra loot incentive for killing strong monsters even if they don't ordinarily get treasure.

One of the monsters that can drop random stuff is the black pudding. Every time a black pudding dies, it can drop treasure. But whenever a pudding is struck by a weapon that does more than one hit point of damage, it may divide into two puddings. Each of these monsters now has a chance of dropping random loot, and they may also further divide themselves. Split puddings end up with half the hit points of the original, but they can heal back up to maximum.

Some players have pushed this into an epic exploit. By engraving a certain word on the ground, one that causes monsters to avoid spots on the floor, around their location except for one space, then purposely filling

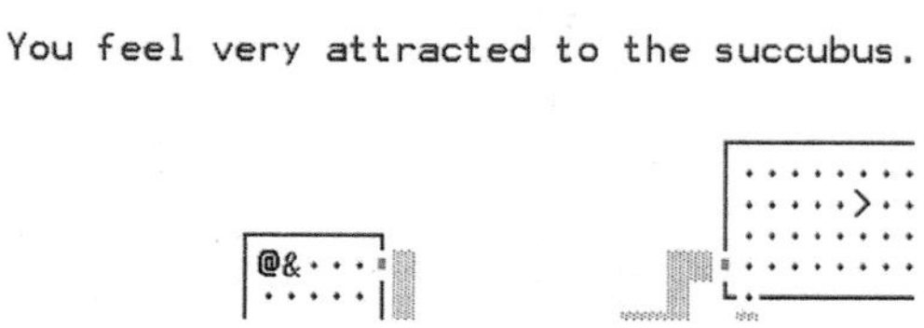

Figure 20.4

What is there to do for fun in a dungeon?

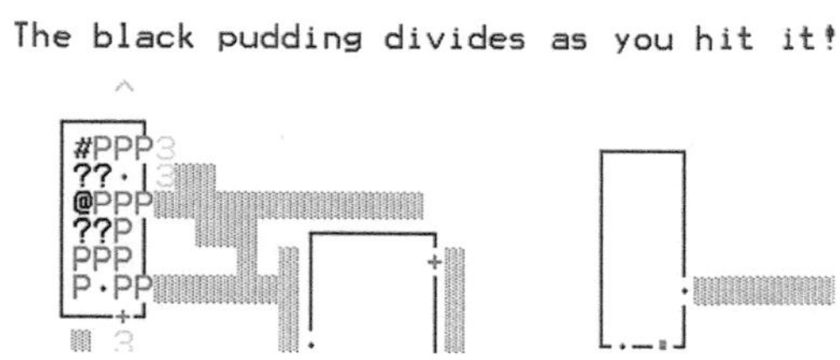

Figure 20.5

Dividing black puddings

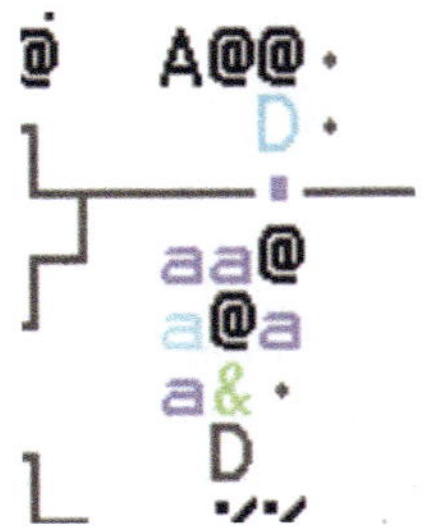

Figure 20.6

An example of a bad idea, if you ask me

the level with puddings through division, they set up what is known as a pudding farm. They endlessly kill puddings, leaving behind vast quantities of loot over time. The chance of getting something from a kill isn't large, and the chance of getting something really good like a wand of wishing is extremely small, but after killing tens of thousands, or more, puddings, the small chances add up.

The only checks on this tactic in the game are the usual ones against sitting in one place doing very little, mostly hunger (pudding corpses, while acidic, are edible), and the tremendous ennui that results from playing the game this way. Players strong enough to divide puddings this much and survive are probably strong enough to win the game already, or could become so with little trouble, but some kinds of conducts become much easier through farming. And by producing huge amounts of loot, gaining high scores becomes much simpler, increasing NetHack's already-great score inflation.

20.5.2 Pestilence Farming

I've mentioned this before (in Giant Eel Stories), but as an advanced case of farming, which has taken scores up to over 2 billion, it's interesting.

Using a somewhat similar setup as with puddings, players can repeatedly kill Pestilence, one of the three Riders at the end of the game, for large score awards. By restricting how other monsters can approach the player, and when playing a telnet game (such as through alt.org), the process can then be automated through a macro, attaining absurdly high scores.

21

SLASH'EM: NetHack Intensified

March 2008

> Commercial games cheat for you and against the monsters: The unarmed orc falls to the ground, dying. "Whirling Blades of Doom . . . backpack," he gasps. "Barbecue sauce . . . left pocket."
>
> NetHack plays fair between you and the monsters: The orc wins the race to the Whirling Blades of Doom. He seizes it, grins, and whirls it at you. You fall to the ground, dying. Your last sight is of the orc reaching for his left pocket.
>
> Slash'em cheats against you and for the monsters: Staggering and more than half dead, you advance to the slain monster. If you can use the Whirling Blades of Doom against the rest of the pack, you just might live through this.
>
> There is no weapon at the corpse. The Whirling Blades of Doom are an intrinsic attack, not a separate weapon. The next platypus in line opens its bill. This one is a fire breather. Thoroughly barbecued, you fall to the ground, dying. When you hit the ground, something breaks in your left pocket.
>
> **—Rob Ellwood**
> *writing sarcastically in rec.games.roguelike.nethack*

21.1 Beyond the Kitchen Sink

Some people consider NetHack to be the game with the "most." The most monsters, the most items, the most places, the most interesting things, the most everything. These people are wrong. They are wrong because there exists SLASH'EM, a NetHack variant that contains everything NetHack does, and then some.

SLASH'EM (capitalized because it's an acronym, standing for "Super Lotso Added Stuff Hack—Extended Magic") is a variant of NetHack that adds in hundreds of things more. It is a super variant, with bits culled from many other versions: NetHack—, NetHack+, SLASH, the Wizard Patch, Lethe and Heck are big influences, but it also has its own unique bits in the stew.

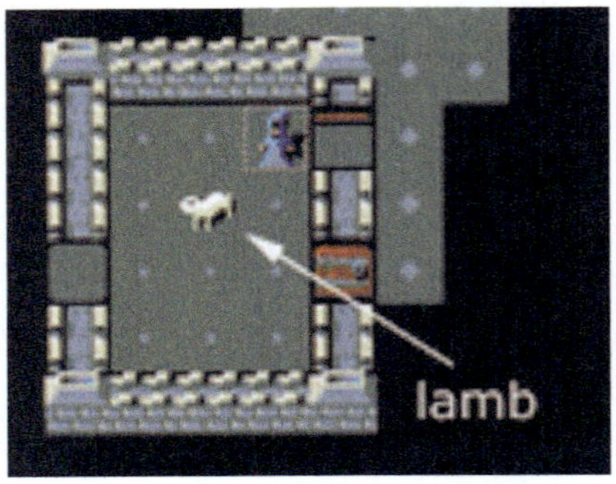

Figure 21.1

Someone thought it was worth it to add sheep to the dungeon

It's interesting to consider the differences between the base game and this one. As we have seen, NetHack's DevTeam used to have a more inclusive development philosophy, but around NetHack 3.1 that stopped, and all the versions since have been much more conservative. But SLASH'EM never stopped adding stuff. In addition to being up-to-date with the features in the most recent vanilla, it has five additional character classes, five new races (hobbits, drow, lycanthropes, vampires and doppelgangers), new abilities called "techniques" for many classes and races, a ton of new weapons including many new artifacts, new magic items in most categories, and a great many new monsters. NetHack's reorganization in 3.1 added dungeon branches to the game, but other than the addition of Sokoban some time ago (itself an import from SLASH'EM) it has steadfastly refused to further expand the dungeon. Meanwhile SLASH'EM has lots of branches, many of them optional.

It may be that there are good reasons the DevTeam reined back their impulse in adding things to NetHack. Or it may not. SLASH'EM has everything NetHack does and much, much, much much more. But it hasn't had the balance work put into it NetHack has. Tougher monsters appear sooner, there are lots more of them, and they have all kinds of nasty new things they can do to the player. Some standard NetHack tricks, like shopkeeper theft, are harder to perform. (Shopkeepers are much tougher opponents, too.) If, in adding a new feature, the developers had a choice between easier and harder, in SLASH'EM it will usually be harder.

21.2 The Dungeon Is Beta Software, Features May Be More Awesome Than Your Universe Will Allow

An imperfect, but useful, way to think about it is being the "unstable" code branch of NetHack, both in design and tendency to crash. There's lots of new features, but much less of a guarantee that the game is fair in any way, or that it won't bomb when you look at it funny. But the NetHack DevTeam has been known to get ideas, and even code, from the game for inclusion in the original. Maybe the greatest example of this is NetHack's most unique role, the Monk, who suffers substantial penalties to wearing armor, wielding weapons, and eating meat. Yet SLASH'EM Monks are still fairly different from NetHack ones.

So what's different? This is far from an exhaustive list, for SLASH'EM has been quite promiscuous in adding ideas from user-made patches, but some highlights include:

Most monster classes have new members. Some of the more interesting ones are:

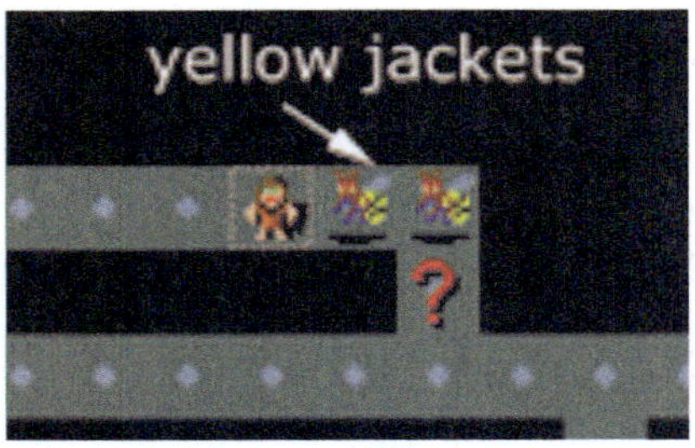

Figure 21.2

Yellow jackets

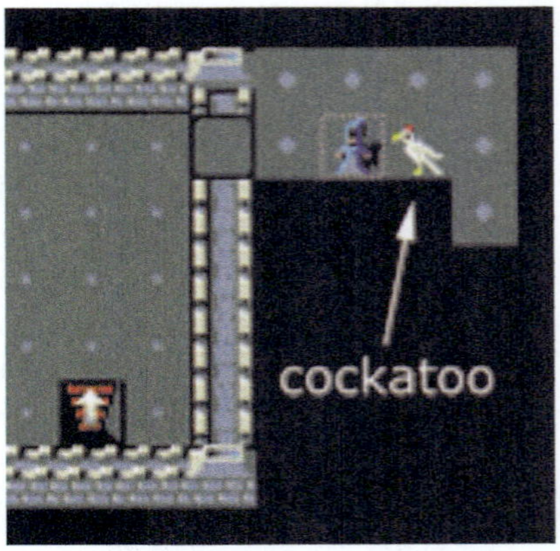

Figure 21.3

Cockatoo

- Gypsies (their term, not mine), which may offer the player draws from a Deck of Many Things as from Dungeons & Dragons.
- Various Lovecraft monsters, like Father Dagon, Mother Hydra and deep ones. Also their invented-for-SLASH'EM cousins, deeper ones and deepest ones.
- Lots of animals, including chickens, cows and sheep. Some of them are more dangerous than experience with their real-life counterparts might lead you to believe. The first screenshot game I started ended due to an irate cockatoo.
- A larger assortment of werebeasts. Since lycanthropes are a new race, and lycanthropy is an acquirable condition, this can also affect the player.
- Some humanoid species have royalty which can appear on special levels. Among them are Kroo the Kobold King, Grund the Orc King, Ruggo the Gnome King, and Aphrodite, boss of the nymphs, who can't be happy about her royal neighbors.
- Some other creatures have new unique versions: Pegasus the winged horse, the spiders Girtab and Shelob, and . . . Jumbo the Elephant?
- Australian monsters! Echidnas, koala, wombats, Tasmanian devils, wallabies, kangaroos, "wallaroos" and platypuses (no, the intro quote wasn't joking about that).
- There are no new mimics, but there are new mimic-like monsters like killer coins (a Wizardry reference), killer food and tripe rations, and a particular favorite of mine, the "bad egg."
- A few other D&D monsters have made their appearance, including a Beholder (undoubtedly irate for being commented out in NetHack for so long) and long-time D&D favorite Vecna the Lich.
- Of course, each new role has its own quest dungeon and unique leader and nemesis.

21.3 More?

There are also a large number of new weapons, including multiple lightsaber types. An entire new category of weapons is modern firearms, which are more powerful than arrows but with much rarer ammunition. They are not generated laying around the dungeon floor, but soldier monsters sometimes get them on creation, making them a much deadlier class of opponent.

The main quest has an additional step besides collecting the three unique items to get to the Amulet. Now the player must also get two out of three aligned keys, which reside on special branches off the main dungeon. Of course, they are guarded by unique monsters.

Most major variants of NetHack these days take it upon themselves to address what is seen as the biggest flaw of the game, how the second half of the game, Gehennom, has become increasingly irrelevant (for its supposed hellishness, few characters die there), boring (maze after maze with no special features) and annoying (that damn mysterious force on the return trip). SLASH'EM is no different, and it has a much shorter Gehennom. To compensate, the main dungeon is much longer, and Gehennom is now composed almost entirely of special levels. Each of the named demon lords has his own now, including everyone's favorite, Demogorgon.

Also along the lines of fixing perceived flaws, unicorn horns in SLASH'EM have different trouble-fixing odds than NetHack. In the original, the factor in telling what a unihorn will do when applied is its curse/uncurse/bless status. At its best, it can fix a wide range of status ailments, and also make many dangerous potions harmless, while also helping to identify them. And it doesn't degrade with use. And it's a moderately decent weapon in a pinch. To increase its curative properties in SLASH'EM, on the other hand, it must be enchanted as a weapon, which is a harder thing to do than just blessing it.

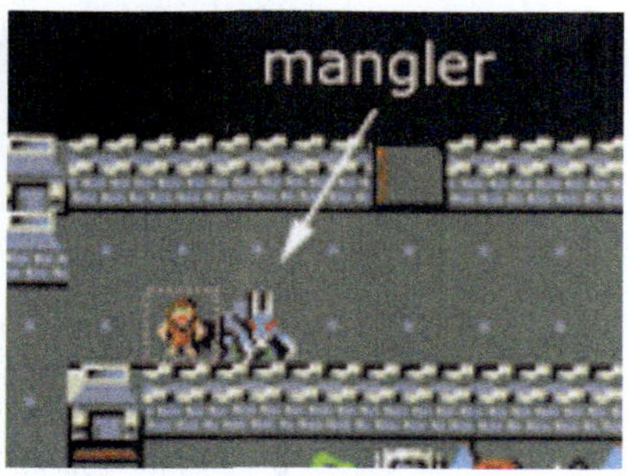

Figure 21.4

A "mangler," whatever that is

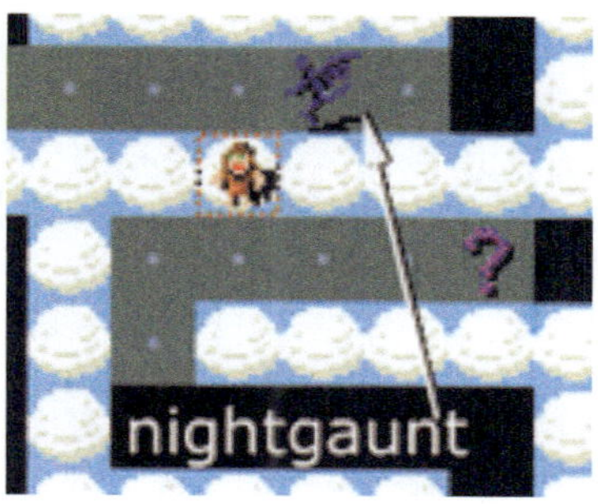

Figure 21.5

Nightgaunt

One of the places SLASH'EM got many of its ideas from is an old variant created by Stephen White, called NetHack+. One of the biggest things in that game was that it allowed shopkeepers to provide services for the player in exchange for some money. This was very good in that it made money a big part of the game again (it's been devalued ever since it lost its central place in game scoring), and it gave shopkeepers more personality. This was very bad because, to prevent higher-level players from just taking advantage of all the services offered then slaughtering the shopkeep to get his gold back, shopkeepers had to be made much stronger, which in turn made it much more dangerous to steal from shops.

21.4 Even More?

Altar conversion is riskier in SLASH'EM. Other gods are much more likely to get mad at you for converting their altars to your own alignment, sending in tough minion monsters to attack you. Conversely, sometimes sacrificing on a co-aligned altar will result in your own deity sending you some help to follow you around and slay stuff on your behalf.

SLASH'EM has lots of new artifacts, which range from interesting choices drenched in D&D lore, like the Hand and Eye of Vecna, to the Bat From Hell, which is not, let's say, the flying kind of bat. The game is a lot more serious about artifact alignment than NetHack, though, so it might help to consult a list to make sure the weapon will like you before you pick it up.

NetHack's reference list ranges far and wide, but it doesn't get as geeky as you might think. The nerdiest gag I have seen in the main game, by a good margin, is a Ranma 1/2 reference on one of the T-shirts. On average, SLASH'EM's references tend to be one Nerd Tier above NetHack's: there is an artifact spoon called a Houchou which instantly kills any one monster it's thrown at*, Undead Slayers sometimes start out with a whip**, and Monks have an ability which causes them to do special moves if the right arrow-key sequence is input.***

NetHack creates bones levels (saved dungeon levels from when players die) less often at later levels. SLASH'EM reverses this tendency, creating them more often the deeper the player gets. The result is that deaths later in the game are more likely to have their stuff preserved for a future player, but the monsters that did the killing are also more likely to hang around.

In addition to new shop types like pet shops, shop prices have been remixed a bit, requiring price IDers to learn anew what everything is. The most useful items, like magic lamps and artifacts, tend to have much higher prices than before.

21.5 Dear God, Still More?

Later on there is a special level, the Black Market, that is one of SLASH'EM's more interesting opportunities. Originally from NetHack+, most of the level is filled with a single gigantic general store. The way shops are

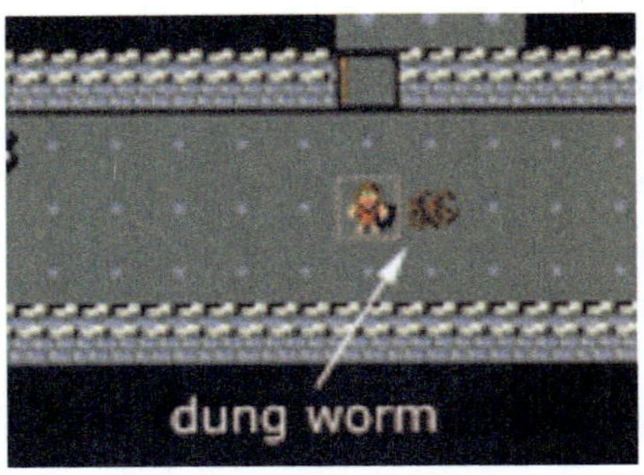

Figure 21.6

Dung worm

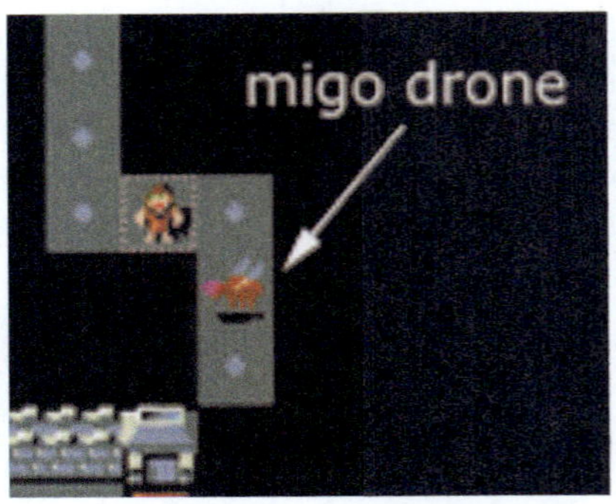

Figure 21.7

Migo drone (from H.P. Lovecraft)

* Final Fantasy IV.
** Castlevania.
*** Fighting games, and also, perhaps, Final Fantasy VI.

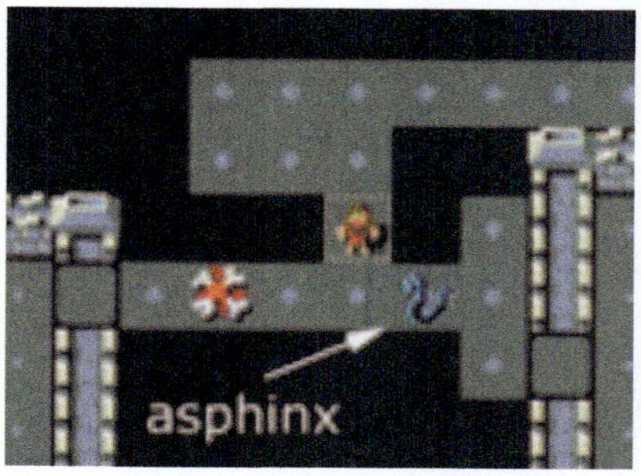

Figure 21.8

Asphinx

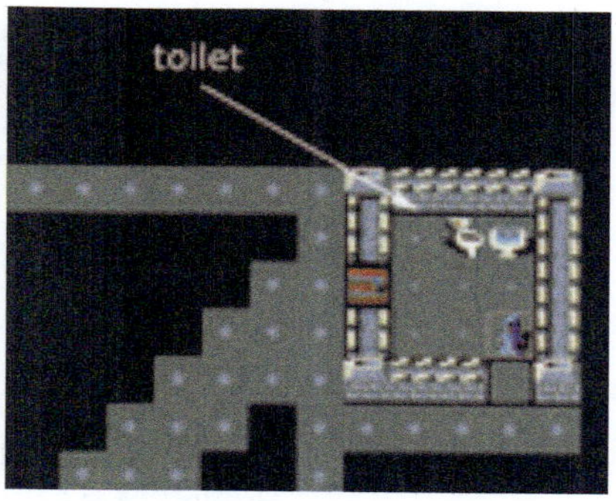

Figure 21.9

A random dungeon commode

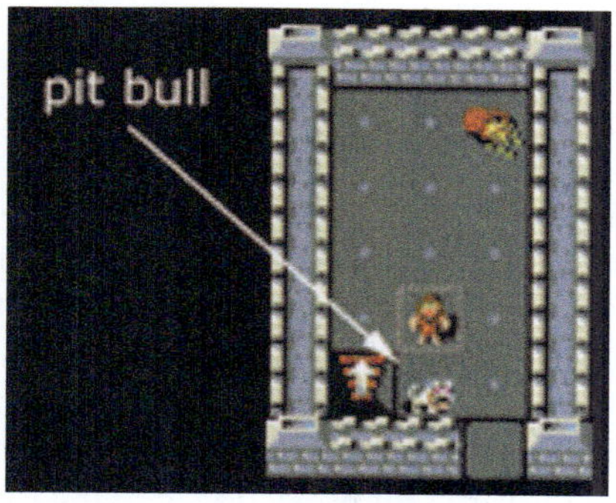

Figure 21.10

Pit bull

generated is, the larger they are, the more varied their contents are likely to be. However, this one is unique among them all: prices are 25 to 50 times greater there, it has special defenses against theft, polymorphed players are not allowed inside, it's on a special branch so one cannot just dig his way out, and the proprietor (One-Eyed Sam) has much greater resources for messing up thieves, including a weapon that has an instadeath effect and a cancellation effect. The result: the shop is large enough that useful things are bound to appear there, prices are high enough that players won't be able to walk out with more than an item or two, and theft is much more difficult to get away with than usual. Fortunately, the level doesn't appear until quite deep.

In NetHack, if the player polymorphs (that is, changes form), the effect eventually will expire and return him to normal, but for monsters and items it is permanent. In SLASH'EM, all polymorph is temporary unless special measures are taken to make it permanent. This means you can't change a pet into something powerful and expect the benefit to stick, even though the usual polymorph risks like death from system shock or polymorphing into something suicidal are still present.

A big, yet often overlooked, feature added to the game is "techniques," which are special command options only certain roles or races can use. This greatly helps define the roles, although some of the techniques are a bit questionable as far as the role's milieu is concerned.

And at last, in addition to doors, fountains, sinks, thrones, altars and graves, SLASH'EM adds toilets. The uses for such a thing I leave to you to discover. As you might guess, they can be helpful in cases of sickness, or of overeating, or for interacting with a particular deity-figure.

21.6 But Why?

What is all this good for, other than blowing the minds of folk who think NetHack is too complex? As mentioned before, a major incentive for variant authors is to fix things in a game they find lacking. With NetHack, the things most often fixed are a loss of difficulty in the late game, ennui once all the monsters and items are fully known, and Gehennom. This may make SLASH'EM's development strategy more evident: it is a game made specifically for NetHack experts.

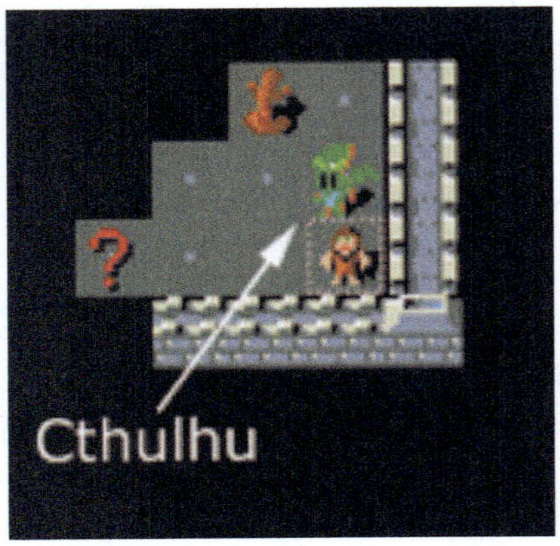

Figure 21.11

Cthulhu

This may be why it's so much harder than NetHack. One cannot get as far here with a lucky start, like a pet polymorphed into a dragon, getting a lucky shopkeeper kill or even an early wish. This evens out the game's balance, but also "fixes" one of those things people like about roguelikes: how a game plays can have a different feel depending on what they find on early levels. There are more different kinds of dangers to prepare for in SLASH'EM, so NetHack's big panaceas, like unicorn horns, prayer and magic resistance, each cover a smaller proportion of them. Level drain, in particular, goes from being trivially defeatable with an elven cloak to requiring special measures for protection, making vampires a serious opponent again.

The tremendous difficulty makes it difficult for me to recommend the game to anyone but die-hard 'hackers. If you're already not thrilled about playing a game as difficult and complex as NetHack, then SLASH'EM may cause an allergic reaction. It is definitely a game with a certain userbase in mind . . . but for that userbase, it can be a lot of fun to play around with . . . at least until the NetHack DevTeam releases its next major version.

(*January 2020*: If SLASH'EM seems overloaded, then you should look at even-more-overloaded variants SLASH'EM Extended and SLASHTHEM. Search for the Variants page at the NetHack Wiki for more information.)

21.7 Source

https://groups.google.com/forum/#!msg/rec.games.roguelike.nethack/v-m55ENZx_0/GpGiOch4wZMJ

22

Ten Years of the dev/null NetHack Tournament, Part 1

October 2008 The most impressive thing about devnull's NetHack tournament is its longevity. This is the tenth consecutive year it's been run. It's old enough that it's spanned multiple NetHack versions. It's been said that it could be the oldest-running computer gaming tournament in existence. It's a difficult claim to prove, but it may well be true.

Despite the great obstacles to making roguelikes work as multiplayer games they have long had a substantial online presence, and a big part of this is the relative ease in setting up terminal-based, ASCII games for playing over the internet via telnet, SSH or some other form of remote console.

Originally intended for local networks, when the internet hit it big suddenly games that were originally shared between a group of students could be enjoyed from the other side of the planet. In the case of NetHack, despite the availability of graphics when played locally, a good case could be made that online play, such as through alt.org, is the best way to play.

It gets you other people's bones files (remnant levels of past, lost games), a community score list (now so bloated that the lowest entry on the top 2000 list is an ascension with over 4 million points), ghost names taken from prior players, real-time game spectating, game recording through TTYRECs and even the sending of messages to players during the game by retrofitting NetHack's mail daemon monsters.

What is probably the best-known public NetHack server isn't even up year-round. The yearly NetHack tournament hosted by dev/null/network only runs during the month of November, usually making the front page over at Slashdot shortly before it lands. (Slashdot stories: 2006, 2005, 2004, 2003, 2001) While light on features compared to alt.org's (mostly) perpetual setup, their tournament is interesting for many other reasons.

Despite NetHack's great suitability for online play, there are some difficulties with running an actual tournament. Probably the biggest is that, in the years since the release of version 3.4.3, NetHack has been extensively analyzed and spoiled, even wikified, and its source code has been made searchable on the web more than once.

Anyone willing to put the energy into it can build an extensive bulwark of knowledge against the game, and a player who has acquired it can play amazingly well. New players are lucky to get to level 7, but people who have really studied the game win all the time. A few players, given enough time and effort, seem able to win on demand.

Three games over on alt.org have earned exactly the maximum possible score in the signed 32-bit integer variable the game uses to record it, over 2.7 billion points, and one of those wasn't even a winner. If more than one player is capable of reaching MAXINT-1 points then, it's sad to say, score is probably no longer the best measure of playing ability.

devnull's award setup takes this into account by measuring some accomplishments other than score. To this end, there's roughly four levels of trophies, with some aimed at nearly every type of person who plays NetHack.

22.1 Things Most People Can Win

The lowest tier simply measures progress towards winning a game. There's an array of several Stars, from plastic to dilithium (the most valuable gemstone in NetHack), that are awarded for making game progress. Each player earns one of these, corresponding to his best progress into the game.

A Plastic Star, for instance, is earned for completing the Sokoban levels. A bit further up the scale is the Iron Star, for beating the Quest dungeon. The Copper Star is awarded for entering Gehennom. The most notable stars are Silver (getting the Amulet of Yendor), Gold (reaching the Elemental Planes), Platinum (reaching the Astral Plane), and Dilithium (ascending).

Notably, one of the stars is earned from reaching the bottom level of the Gnomish Mines, which, with persistence and luck, most players can probably accomplish. Because of this, a good majority of players can win something. (Note that by winning "something," I mean a small gif suitable for linking to a website. I do not think there are physical trophies involved this year.)

Another category that tends to be wide open is the challenges. One of the most distinctive things about the devnull tournament is that it's not played, strictly speaking, with vanilla NetHack. Every year since 2003 2005 the maintainers have written and added a new patch to the game that implements a substantial new feature. The feature is never revealed ahead of time; the player must discover it during the game.

It always revolves around something that a player must accomplish. These "challenges" are sometimes surprising in their wide-ranging scope: the very first one required that players go to popular web game Kingdom of Loathing and complete a quest in a NetHack-inspired parody dungeon! Other challenges haven't required going to another site, but have some fairly heavy Zork references and a Pac-Man maze. (*January 2016*: While most current dev/null optional quests remain in the game from year to year, the KoL quest has been removed due to changes at that site.)

NetHack adepts may shake their heads in dismay at that news, so they'll be relieved to hear that devnull's challenges are optional. The first time the player does something that in any way affects a challenge he's told and asked if he wants to participate, although the nature of the challenge itself isn't otherwise revealed. If he chooses then, he can completely disable challenges and play what amounts to (barring bugs) standard NetHack 3.4.3.

Most of the really good players know that to do well at NetHack requires knowing as much about the game as they can and so pre-disable them in their tournament config file. But to players who don't care so much about winning one of the big trophies, the challenges can be a fun diversion, allowing them to liven up a game of which they thought they had known everything.

Note, especially, that each year all the challenges from previous years remain in the game, in addition to the new challenge. All of the challenges get their own trophy awarded to players who complete it. This year, as revealed by the trophy description page, nine trophies center on the new challenge!

22.2 Things Experienced 'Hackers Can Win

The next tier of awards is for those players to whom ascensions are expected and foregone conclusions, and counts what a variety of ascensions they have during the tournament month. A player ascending a character of each gender (that is, any male character and any female character) has "shot the Birdie."

Ascending a character of each gender and alignment (lawful, neutral and chaotic) in any combination, requiring a minimum of three victories, is "throwing the Double Top." Add in all the races (human, elf, dwarf, gnome and orc, so five wins minimum) to "do the Hat Trick." "Hitting the Grand Slam" is to also ascend every role of the game's 13, which by implication means also winning 13 games during the one-month contest period. Last year, three players accomplished this.

Finally, "going the Full Monty" is doing all this, plus keeping all of the game's conducts in at least one won game. They don't have to all be done in a single game, but a few of the conducts, like Foodless, Weaponless, and Pacifist, are still quite challenging all by themselves. All of these awards can also be earned "With Bells On," which in the jargon of the tournament means meeting their requirements in consecutive games.

So, to win the Full Monty With Bells On is to win 13 games in a row, one of every role, and getting in the Foodless, Atheist and Pacifist conducts along the way. Last year someone won this for the first time in the tournament's history. Predictably, it was won by marvin, maintainer of the Atari ST port of NetHack, scourge of alt.org's scoreboard and probably the best overall 'hacker in the world.

22.3 Things Really Good Players Can Win

Another set of awards goes to the player who earns the highest score with each character role. Score, as mentioned, is no longer the best measure of playing skill, but the game still tracks it, and it does serve an important historic value. It's interesting to note those cases where a score listed as winning a role trophy also appears winning another trophy; in this manner, one can discover that the player who won Most Conducts did it while playing a Monk.

The top trophies are the mutually exclusive (except for ties) ones that record the best games, according to various measurements, played during the contest period. The best scoring game played during the month is recorded here.

In 2007 that top score was 134,520,114 points, obtained in a game played by user nopsled. This was also that Monk game that won Best Conduct, with ten of the game's 12 earned. (I've been unable to find conclusive details of the conducts he kept, but it was probably all of them except Pacifist and Foodless. The reason playing a Monk is significant is that they actually get bonuses for fighting unarmed, so the conduct for never hitting with a wielded weapon is relatively easy to keep.)

22.4 Things the Very Best Can Win

Another top-tier trophy notes the lowest scored ascension, which in 2007 went to theta's game of 25,360 points. Earning an extremely high NetHack score is mostly a matter of patience, but earning an extremely low score for a winning game is a tremendous challenge.

The player gets one point for each experience point earned through combat (no free experience grants are counted), and that score is doubled upon victory, so to do this one must nearly play as a Pacifist anyway. The first ascension trophy goes to the player to get the first victory during the contest period, usually on the first day.

The fastest ascensions in game time (turns elapsed) and real time (only actual playing time counted) are now tracked by separate trophies. In 2007 the fastest game in real time was aardvark's credibility-defying four-and-a-half-hour game, and its fastest counted in turns was r.g.r.n regular rast's playthrough of 10,067 turns, which is even more eye-popping to someone who knows what a player must go through to win.

Getting to the penultimate level of the dungeon rapidly is not hard at all for a player with just the right equipment (controlled levelport has been a trademark NetHack trick since ancient times), but getting that one last floor down requires getting three specific items that usually require a lot of fighting to earn. But the worst bit is that the player cannot purposely levelport while wearing the Amulet of Yendor, so he must walk all the way back up, while getting sent back levels randomly, purely through the malevolent whim of the game.

22.5 Things marvin Can Win

Of the four remaining exclusive trophies, two of them, Most Ascensions and Best of 13, are nearly always won by marvin. Best of 13 is the number of won games out of 13 consecutive ones. Hitting a Grand Slam With Bells On would also earn one a perfect score in this, but I don't know what happens if two players qualify.

22.6 Things You Won't Want to Win

Another trophy notes the "death by trickery" that the game reports when, due to a bug in the game's code, it wrongly counts a game as having been tampered with.

If NetHack thinks it detects tampering with the game files it'll end the game, reporting "A trickery" on the scoreboard. Since the tournament version patches the game software, it is always possible that this will occur (as it did a number of times last year). In that event this trophy is offered as a consolation prize.

The last trophy is a real favorite, awarded to the player who encountered the most unique causes of death during the contest period. In 2007 the trophy for Most Unique Deaths was won by theta who, with 141 different types, had 72% of all the possible demises.

This is pretty impressive in itself; much is made by all the ways a NetHack game can end, but the tournament's maintenance software lumps most monster-caused deaths into a small number of root causes, so one can't just get killed by every monster there is to shoot up his total. Many causes are rather obscure.

Everything that clips even a single hit point is potentially a source of mortality, and NetHack has so many sources of piddling low damage that the great majority of those death types, in practice, only occur to players who are shooting for them. And many death types, like being petrified by Medusa or dying to a demon lord, basically require giving up a game so advanced that winning would be a foregone conclusion to many players.

If this sounds like fun, new players can sign up once the tournament begins each November 1 on the registration page. You can also help the tournament out by purchasing merchandise at the swag page, which has new stuff as well as a few items left over from the very first tournament. Go have a look, and bask in that warm glow of awesome that only a printed adaption of a green-screen terminal display can provide.

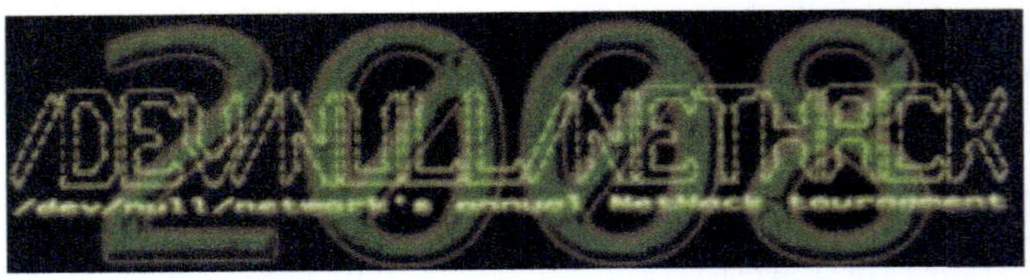

Figure 22.1

23

Ten Years of the dev/null NetHack Tournament, Part 2

November 2008 November 1 marks the beginning of the tenth-annual devnull NetHack tournament. A couple of days ago we provided an overview and took a look at the trophy structure. I asked a few questions of the co-creator and primary maintainer of the tournament. Here are his answers. Thanks to brothers Robin and Mark Bandy for taking time away from the tournament preparations to give us the story!

John Harris: Tell us a bit about yourself.

Robin Bandy: My name is Robin Bandy, I'm 37 years old and married; my wife has played NetHack, but is not exactly excited about how much of my time the Tournament takes each year though she's been extremely patient about it. I grew up on a ranch in southwest Colorado, but I've lived in the hills in east Oakland, California, since '97.

Though my college degrees are in anthropology and history, I've been a professional geek since '94 and have been freelance since '97; most of my work these days is as a consultant running the server farm that runs 1up.com, gamevideos.com and mycheats.com for Ziff Davis Media.

My other main interest after my wife and my geekery is making hard apple cider (and a variety of other fruit wines as well as a small amount of beer); we're fortunate to live in a part of Oakland that was an orchard 100 years ago, so most of our neighborhood has semi-wild apple trees which are great for ciders. Cider bottling time is usually about halfway through the Tournament, which tends to liven things up a bit. ;-)

JH: His brother, who runs another tournament server and has been involved with the running since the beginning, adds:

Mark Bandy: My name is Matt Bandy. I am Robin's older brother. I have a PhD in Anthropology from UC Berkeley and am an archaeologist who works in Peru, Bolivia, and the United States. I live in Boulder, Colorado. I had the idea for the tournament many years ago and co-wrote the code (with Robin) for the first few years. Robin since has taken over the maintenance and development of the tournament and it really is his baby and it has been for at least five years now.

JH: How did the tournament get started?

RB: That was actually my brother Matt's idea; as I remember it, it was basically a case of him saying "Hey, you know what would be fun to do?" and it just kinda snowballing from there.

He and I co-wrote the first version of the control server, and he wrote most of the original game server kit on his own; we still use most of his game server code, but we lost the original control server several years ago when that server lost its primary and backup disks in the same night so I had to re-write all of it from scratch. He runs a game server each year now, but with two kids that's about all he has the time to contribute.

JH: When did the tournament first become really popular? Was it around the time Slashdot first linked to it?

RB: The first time Slashdot posted a front-page link (in 2001) almost doubled the number of players, it's true, but the biggest year was actually the year after that. We don't have anything except the scoreboard files from the years before 2002, but I think we had ~400 competitors in 2000 and 800 in 2001; in 2002 we had 1071 players and haven't had a year that big since.

The time we consider the Tournament to have really become a staple in the NetHack community was with the release of 3.4.3 when the release notes file opened with the sentence "Now that the November tournament period is over, it is time for the NetHack DevTeam to make NetHack 3.4.3 available."; according to VersionTracker that was on 2004-01-08.

This year, actually, we're hoping to be the largest; I'm even trying to write a press release. ;-)

JH: How well does the distributed game hosting software work? Were there any interesting technical challenges in getting the servers up and synced?

RB: It actually does a pretty good job, though the rsync commands could stand a bit of debugging; the cron jobs throw errors when the source directories are empty for example.

The niftiest thing in it, in my opinion, was the way Matt set it up to work via ssh remote command execution so that the one control server can execute scripts on the game servers to get information from them; combined with a clever bit of Perl that lets us use flavor-specific Perl libraries for various commands means that the same script can be called on the various game servers and work the same way even though they're running many flavors of Unix.

I've gone on to use that style of remote command many times since; it's a staple for the entire admin structure on the servers that I built and run for 1up.com, for example.

JH: The trophy system came about as a fairer way to judge playing skill than the old score-based system, which is vulnerable to certain score-optimal playing styles that aren't generally considered normal play. Would you like to discuss the thinking behind the current trophy setup?

RB: The grand prize trophy is basically a stunt (a streak of 13 winning games covering all races, roles, alignments and genders), and now that more players almost managed it in 2007 we are considering how to replace it with an even more outrageous stunt; that's the kind of thing that should be there at the top.

The major trophies, other than First Ascension, are all intended to recognize different play styles that have developed in the community over the years; the Recognition trophies are also aimed at that, but we extended them down to include folks who (like myself) cannot reliably ascend.

OK, another one of them is also not really based on a play style but rather on an aspect of the game: it kills a lot of characters, so the Most Unique Deaths trophy came in as a joke originally; now, though, it has actually developed into a play style that (as you mention below) abandons the concept of "winning" completely.

The minor trophies continue to reflect NetHack's score, since it would be inappropriate to just ignore it. Many folks have made very good cases that it doesn't really reflect the degrees of skill between the top players, though, which is why we brought in the major/minor distinction in the first place.

The Clan trophy is a bit of a joke, as the whole clan system is (Hi EIT!). It would be a lot more meaningful except for the fact that RGRN overshadows everyone else by such a huge margin. This is definitely an area that could use some serious re-imagining.

JH: One of the most interesting trophies, although one that a player has to almost abandon going for wins to shoot for, is Most Unique Deaths. For 2007's Most Deaths trophy, player theta achieved 74% of all the deaths categorized in the game, for a little more (according to my math) than 80 death types. Another neat trophy is the "Death by Trickery" consolation prize. Are there any other clever new trophy types (or any new trophies at all) coming this year?

RB: I really like the Most Unique Deaths trophy, and I really enjoy watching it when it gets competitive; some of the deaths that have been posted can only be achieved by getting a game up to the point where it could be ascended and then doing something stupid like eating the corpse of Famine.

Trickery is actually the game's internal name for what happens to you when something goes wrong with the game files that makes the game give up completely; this is usually caused by an admin screwing something up, so we adopted it as the apology for when something we do kills off a character.

We do have one more major trophy in mind and I've actually done the artwork for its icon, though it won't premier this year; it will be named something prosaic like "Most Extinctions," but I think of the icon image as being "ASCII Chief" since it's based on the iconic helmet from Halo.*

JH: For several years now marvin, a.k.a. Christian Bressler, has won the grand prize, Best of 13. Last year sawtooth game him a bit of a run for his money, tying for most ascensions overall at 14. Now that multiple players are getting to the point where they are competitive for the grand prize, is it possible that you'll have to come up with some other way of measuring playing skill?

RB: Yep; we're really pleased to see more players rising up to those levels. The closest anyone but marvin has gotten to the Best of 13 is sawtooth's 11 from two years ago, so there's probably some life in that stunt yet.

We don't have any ideas in mind for what would replace it, but we've gotten several suggestions. If (or when) we do bring in a new grand prize we'll keep the Best of 13 active, probably by downgrading it to being a major trophy.

JH: Would you mind telling us a bit (officially) about the Challenge system and player reactions to past challenges? How do players "opt out" of a challenge? Are there any difficulties with the challenge patches accidentally changing the logic of the vanilla game, even if the player opts out? Would you like to drop any hints about this year's challenge?

RB: The Challenge trophies I added in 2005 when I had to write a new control server from scratch; they (like the Recognition trophies) were intended to open the scoreboard up to some new folks who (like myself) wouldn't be able to compete at the levels the old scoreboard required. By adding this additional dimension to the Tournament, and by making it one that the serious ascenders would probably avoid, it gives a lot more people a chance to get onto the scoreboard and a lot of new ways to play.

This year's Challenge really expands on that, to the point that it has its own separate scoreboard in addition to the list of players who've completed it that past Challenges have had.

They were also intended to be a bit of an apology to the players, since the old system was wiped out about a month before the Tournament was due to start and I wasn't at all certain that I'd be able to get the new system built up enough to start on time.

Some players have been upset that this changes the Tournament from being a vanilla NetHack build, but from the beginning we've made them optional and I've gotten a lot better about actually limiting their impact to players who accept them; I think I tracked down the last bug in the Grue code this summer that was exposing it to non-Challenged players.

The Grue and PacMan Challenges have been the most complicated, since they both involved creating new levels and changing how light/dark worked for the Grues and overriding the vision system completely for the PacMan level. In both cases many characters (some of whom weren't on the Challenge) died in the first few days from bugs in my Challenge code and players have been rightly annoyed about that.

The basic idea of each Challenge is a narrative, hung onto a single feature of NetHack, which will be unavailable until the player completes the Challenge; last year's PacMan Challenge is a good example: when a player tries to eat a fruit, they'll be offered a Challenge (with nothing to say what it is; the Challenge must be entered into blindly) and the choice of accepting the Challenge, declining it or ignoring it for the rest of the Tournament.

Players who ignore it will not be offered it again in that year, players who decline it will not be offered it again in that game, players who accept it are given a little story about "the necromancers Blinky, Pinky, Inky and Clyde (the four greatest villains of their age)" since I'm very fond of stupid jokes and I also like to make sure there are enough clues around for players to figure out what the Challenge is going to be.

Once the player has accepted, they will be prevented from eating any fruit in the Game until they either complete the Challenge (by playing a NetHack-ified PacMan game) or log onto the web site to block it from there.

Hints? OK, two words: "Bizarro Orgasmatron" . . . ;-)

* This will probably be a trophy for the most complete "extinctionist" game. NetHack keeps a count of the number of monsters of each species that are generated, and when the count hits 120 most of them will no longer be randomly generated except in special circumstances. Extinctionist players seek to do this to all monster types that respect extinction, which tends to make for very long games.

JH: Any plans to expand the tournament to cover notable variants, like SLASH'EM, SporkHack or NetHack Brass? How about other popular roguelike games like Angband or Crawl?

RB: I would definitely be up for that, but I'd really need to do it by working with someone from each game's community who could be responsible for that game's presence; in addition to having to patch NetHack to get it to log the data we need for the trophies, I really think an important part of the Tournament's acceptance has been that we try to build it in NetHack's style as well as we can and I don't really have the experience with any of the other major roguelikes to do that for them.

JH: How about leaving a devnull NetHack server up year 'round?

RB: It's said on the web site for many years that we would do that, and we really should either do it or delete that line. ;-)

At this point, though, I'm leaning towards not. Unless NAO is short on capacity, they do an excellent job of providing a public playground and I really can't take the time to either adapt our system to running a regular server or learning how their system works.

If they do need additional capacity, or if they disappear for some reason and no one else can step in, we would certainly dedicate at least one server to being a full-time NetHack service but as long as we're not needed for that we'll keep our resources focused on the Tournament.

I am, however, working on another roguelike project that will involve providing a server; I mentioned on rec.games.roguelike.development a few weeks ago that after 10 years of running this Tournament I've finally decided to try my hand at developing a new roguelike on my own and (though that won't be a /dev/null project) I will definitely have a public server up for it.

JH: Would you want to say something more to our audience?

RB: It's not a game unless you can lose; in a great game, losing can be at least as much fun as winning. In my opinion that's the core of what the roguelike games contribute, and it's a lesson that could have made a lot of the mediocre games out there genuinely great.

SECTION IV
Dungeon Crawl

24

Before Learning to Walk, One Must First Crawl

March 2007 A note . . . .

I figured what I should do before writing an article on Dungeon Crawl was sit down and give it a good shot at playing it. It has a tremendous reputation for difficulty, though, so my hopes were not high. So I was as surprised as anyone then, after what I estimate are 30 or so games, that I managed to get to the very deepest level of the game, level 5 of the Realm of Zot.

I started out, as in most of my games of Dungeon Crawl, as a Hill Dwarf Fighter. I had heard that the more "dedicated" characters in Dungeon Crawl, the ones who are capable of doing one thing but doing it very well, are easier to play than jack-of-all-trades like Humans (no racial bonuses) and Wanderers (the "General Studies" class of the game). Since Hill Dwarves are very good fighters, with excellent Strength, but they don't have annoying drawbacks like Trolls' increased hunger, and Fighters are traditionally straight-forward, whack 'em from up close types who can take a few hits before dying, I fixated upon that combination. It seems like a good match, and this time it took me up to the very threshold of winning.

What follow are my observations on getting so far in a game after so little time. This is a very long installment, even compared to the usual, and I apologize for that. I have tried to distill most of what I've learned in playing this game. Some of this was gleaned from spoilers, and some is just hard-won discovery. Use, or ignore, it as you wish.

24.1 Shrek Ain't Too Happy to See Me

All Crawl characters, even the strong, straight-forward ones, have points early in their lives where they have to play carefully to survive. Early exploring is dangerous in Crawl, even more so than ADOM, because the game likes to throw in the occasional tough newbie-killer. Fortunately, fighting the likes of soldier ants and mumaks in NetHack left me well-prepared for this kind of thing.

Of all the newbie-killers, ogres are the worst; they can appear on level 4 or maybe even earlier and will kill weak characters without ceremony. Ogres are an interesting monster because, besides their high HP and abnormally huge attack strength, they are otherwise completely average. They can wear no armor, their weapon does lots of damage but is almost never branded (that is, carry a special ability). Most importantly, they have no distance attacks and are of only normal speed.

Thus the best tactic to use against ogres is to use the loop technique, to trade blows with the ogre until he is capable of killing you with one more hit, then run away around a loop until hit points have regenerated enough to continue the fight. The problem with this tactic is that it is vulnerable to interference from other monsters. It relies on being able to infallibly move away from the ogre, so a monster that wanders up from the other direction can force the player to kill it, or move around it, instead of escape from the ogre.

(*Note*: after writing this, I heard some readers remark that they didn't find ogres to be too difficult. It did seem that most of them were experienced Crawl players, though.)

But there are other techniques that can be applied to ultra-strong opponents, and some of them take advantage of those intruders. If a rat is between you and an ogre, it is best to let the rat live, since his attacks will barely dent your armor, and if you escape up the stairs, the rat will follow but the ogre will be stuck on the prior level. These kinds of tactics aid the player in other roguelikes, but Dungeon Crawl makes them essential for survival.

24.2 More Early Bullies of the Dungeon

Snakes (not small snakes, but plain snakes) are another problem, since they're probably faster than you at the start so you can't effectively use the loop trick, and they can poison you before you get resistance. The poison will wear off after a short while, but if you get to low hit points before it does it may be worth it to drink unknown potions hoping for healing (which restore pitifully few hit points but always cure poison, sickness and other conditions like that). If you don't know what healing is yet, it is the most common potion early in the dungeon, so try drinking first the potion type you have the most of.

A bit deeper you'll encounter orc priests (run until you're out of sight to lure 'em close then kill from adjacent), centaurs (similar, but you can use other monsters to block their shots) and invisible stalkers, which move like bats but you can't see them, and they do a lot of damage. Stalkers generally require that you run to the nearest corridor then shoot down it. They don't have a lot of HP, but they are hard to hit unless you can narrow down their location.

The last kind of troublesome early monster is jellies, which are usually a bit slower than you, but other than that can be very dangerous monsters. When you attack them, or they attack you, they can corrode weapons and armor, permanently reducing its plus, unless you're wearing a means of protection or the item in question is an artifact. Worse, they feed on items laying on the ground, and if they happen upon such things they not only destroy them but often spawn more jellies in the process! Their slowness makes the loop tactic very effective against them, over time, but be sure to pick a loop that has no litter on the floor or you'll soon be facing a corridor full of capital Js. Because of their corrosion attribute, often darts are the best way to handle them for non-magic users: run along the loop until they're a space away, then chuck one back with the "f" key. It'll take a long time but eventually, if you've picked up enough darts, you'll destroy the obnoxious little sandwich spread. Alternatively, you can use a wand charge or two.

Once in a while you'll happen upon one of Crawl's unique monsters, who are usually @s with a name. Most of them are not a big threat, but watch out for Sigmund early in the game, for he's a spellcaster who merits using centaur strategy to get out of the range of his deadly magic darts. Also beware of "player ghosts," who have the relative name and power of a prior character who died in the game. They are usually very strong but can often be taken out the same way as ogres.

24.3 Roadmap to Monsterland

Crawl's dungeon has changed a bit since this overview was made, ten years ago.

The Hive and the Hall of Blades have been removed. Lair branches have been shortened.

New are the Depths, the Shoals and the Spider's Nest, and more random extra areas.

The Dungeon itself is now 15 levels, with the Depths and the portal to Zot at the end.

Crawl's dungeon structure is special, even among roguelikes, because it's non-demanding nature. See, Angband and Rogue have only a single dungeon branch, NetHack has multiple branches but requires players venture into many of them (especially the Quest and Vlad's Tower) to obtain the items needed to reach the Amulet, and ADOM has a very complex quest that forces players to wander through many different dungeons. Crawl, on the other hand, has lots of branches but leaves it up to the player which he explores.

The entry to the Realm of Zot, the last area of the game, is blocked unless players can find three "runes," found at the end of certain branches. It doesn't matter which runes, of around 15 to be collected, that he

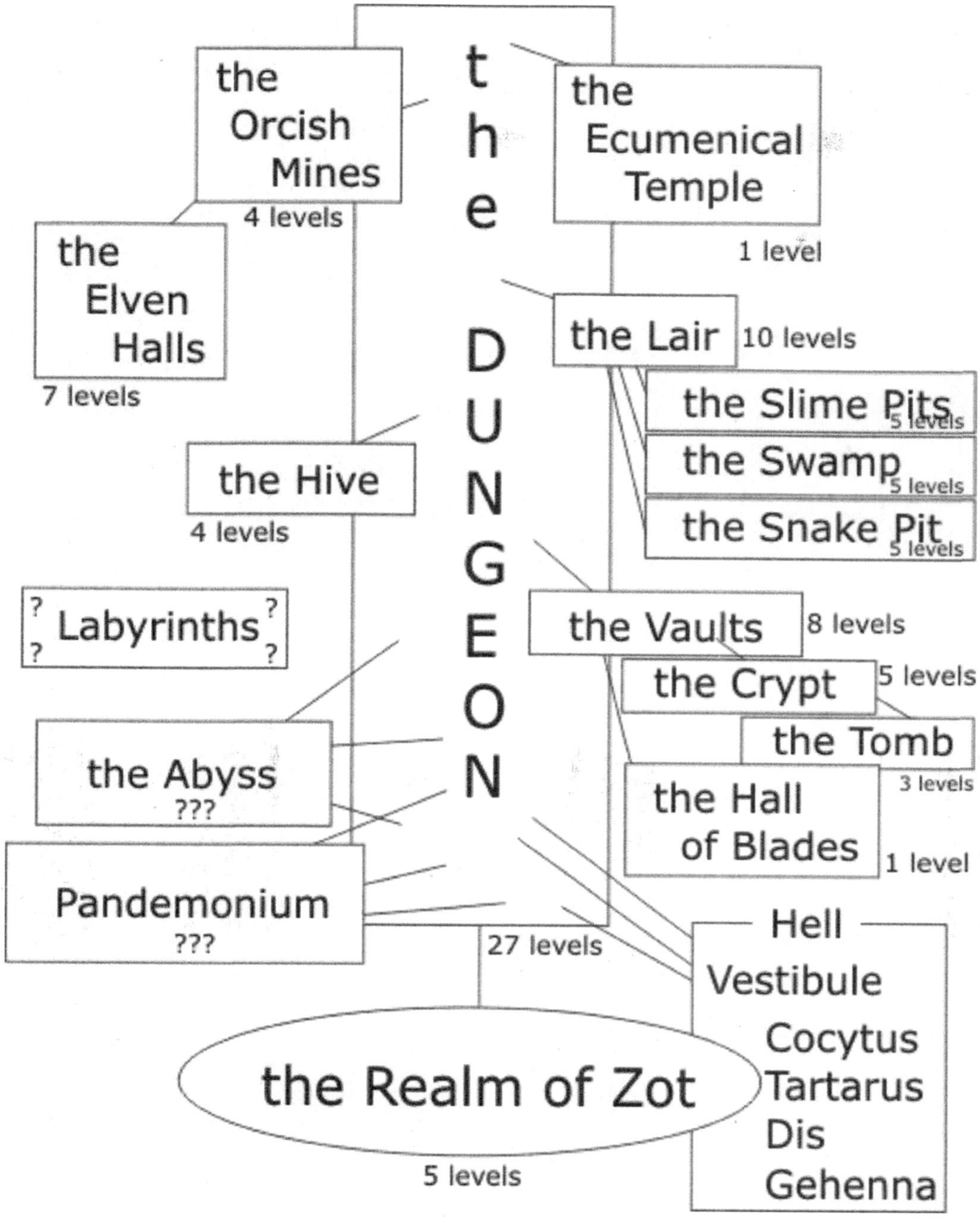

Figure 24.1

An overview map to Crawl's dungeons, circa 2008 or so. Nowadays there may be some small differences. A more accurate overview is on the Crawl Wiki, at http://crawl.chaosforge.org/Dungeon_branches.

finds, but he needs at least three. Each branch poses a different kind of challenge, and different characters, even sometimes those of the same race and class, will find an easier time in some places than others.

One quirk of Crawl's dungeons is that they're often not simply connected: each level usually has multiple up- and downstairs, each leading to a different staircase on the next level. Sometimes you'll even go down some stairs to find out the area you find doesn't itself have a staircase down! If you get stuck like this, sometimes you can search the walls to find a secret door (again, the "s" key searches the eight spaces around you for traps and doors), but usually the best thing to do is go back up the stairs and find another way down. Later on, you can use a means of teleport or digging to get out of those situations. Note that rock staircases,

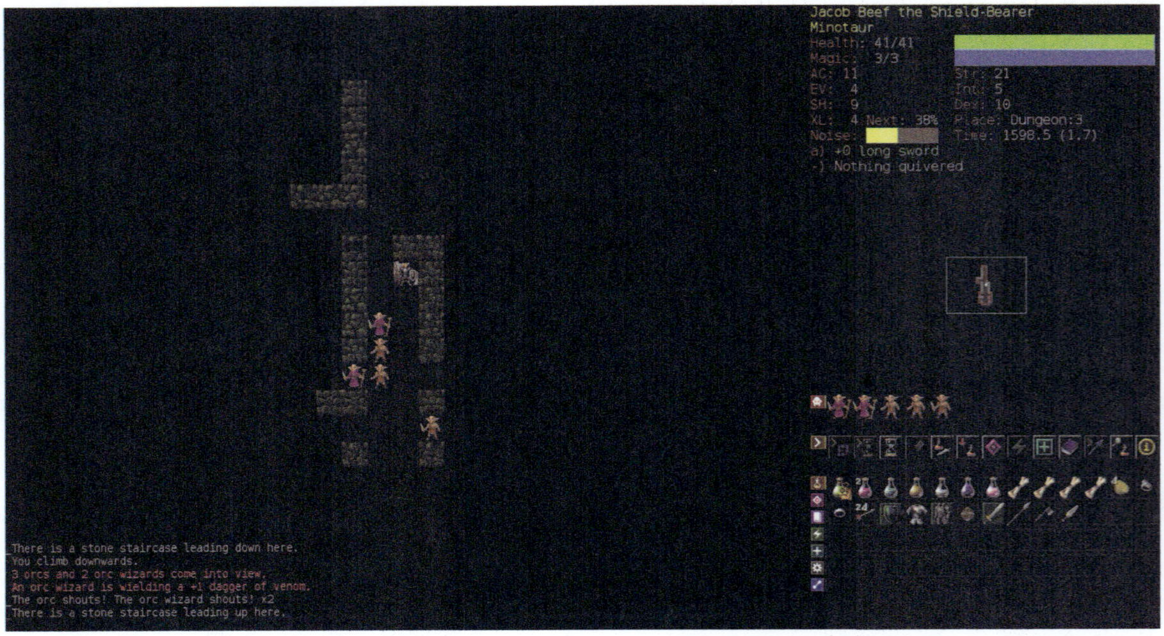

Figure 24.2

Orc trouble

which you find from time to time, are special; they take you to a random stair on the next level, so going down one then up will effectively take you to a different place.

24.4 Tips for Identification, Conservation, Mastication and Eradication

Crawl's items are randomly scrambled, like Rogue's and NetHack's, but unlike those games they are generally not too dangerous to discover by testing them out. The worst potions you can find are generally mutation (which can be good or bad), poison or strong poison (cure that with a healing potion), or degeneration (which can drain stats; cure it with potions of restore ability, which are not rare). The worst scroll is usually immolation, but it can be used by the canny to attack monsters if you don't care about losing some hit points. Armor in Crawl is identified simply by putting on, although that exposes you to curses. Basic weapon brands (things like poisoned weapons, draining weapon, etc.) types are revealed by wielding it, but the weapon's pluses require using it for a while to figure them out. Many players hoard lots of armor and weapons, along with scrolls of remove curse, so that they can wear- and wield-ID them all at once.

Crawl takes after Rogue in its food system, which functions as a kind of timer. Bread rations and meat rations are the best common food, and generally you'll find enough, as well as other miscellaneous food, to survive in the early dungeon. This food never spoils, but just chowing down on those can be a bad idea; this kind of good food is typically only generated upon first entering a dungeon level, so if you do a lot of backtracking through levels you might find yourself going hungry. Plus, some of the later dungeon branches have little or no food in them. (More recent versions have introduced both characters who are less tied to the food clock and other ways to keep the player propelled.)

The solution is to dissect the corpses of monsters you kill (press Shift-D while standing over one), then eat the resulting chunks, which provide not a lot of nutrition but the idea isn't to live off of them but to have them keep you going, so you can conserve the good food for emergencies or late in the game. Some food is poisonous, and some can even mutate you, plus sometimes it'll just randomly make you sick (use healing potions, again, to cure that), but unlike NetHack and ADOM, no monster corpse will provide you with special permanent abilities just from eating them. Most races won't eat raw chunks, however, unless they're already hungry unless they're wearing an amulet of the gourmand. And never eat food if it's started to spoil. And one more "and": you can't dissect corpses without a bladed weapon handy, although the game will ask you if you want to switch if you have one available. If you can make it to the Hive you can scavenge a large supply of food that doesn't spoil, enough to easily last the rest of the game.

24.5 Seventh Floor: Housewares, Home Appliances, Customer Service, and Geryon, Gatekeeper of Hell

Sometimes you'll find a yellow staircase. Standing on one will tell you that it leads to a special dungeon branch, and which it goes to. Eventually you'll have to go into some of them to get runes, but it's usually a good idea to look up what they are in a spoiler list to get a sense of whether your character can survive there. (More recent versions of Crawl have changed the dungeon a bit since this was written.) Summarized, they are:

Ecumenical Temple: There are no monsters generated here, but there are lots of altars, one devoted to each of Crawl's gods. By using the "p" key to pray on one, you can convert to the religion of that god. Each god has certain things he expects of worshipers, and special abilities he provides to faithful followers. Like the dungeon branches, and again, against the popular perception that Crawl doesn't require spoilers to play, the only real way to make a good decision as to which, if any, to follow is to read a spoiler page. My suggestion is to go with Okawaru at first, since he's fairly easy-going. He only really hates it when friendly monsters die, and it's easy to please him by simply praying while killing monsters, and also dissecting them while praying. Eventually he bestows the power to haste one's self, which can come in handy both in combat and escape.

Orcish Mines: Lots of orcs, who are relatively weak, but it is easy to get surrounded by them; there are priests and wizards scattered through them who can attack from a distance; and the level structure makes it difficult to force enemies through bottlenecks in the layout, which help the player by forcing opponents to attack him one at a time. The mines do not contain a rune.

In my game, I found Orcish splint mail of magic resistance there, which became my main armor for the game. It is often better to find artifact armor and use that, because it cannot be damaged by monsters, but it also can't be enchanted beyond its starting pluses. They also can have special powers that are difficult to acquire otherwise, especially in the case of randarts, randomly determined artifacts that are different every game. It is possible to get many necessary resistances taken care of at once with a single randart, if the player is lucky enough to find one, but because there are few equipment guarantees in Crawl it is possible to be undone by a failure to find a good one.

In my game the ultimate cause of death was from fire shots from a pair of Orbs of Fire in a wide-open area, with me only having one level of fire resistance. If I had worn two sources at once their shots would

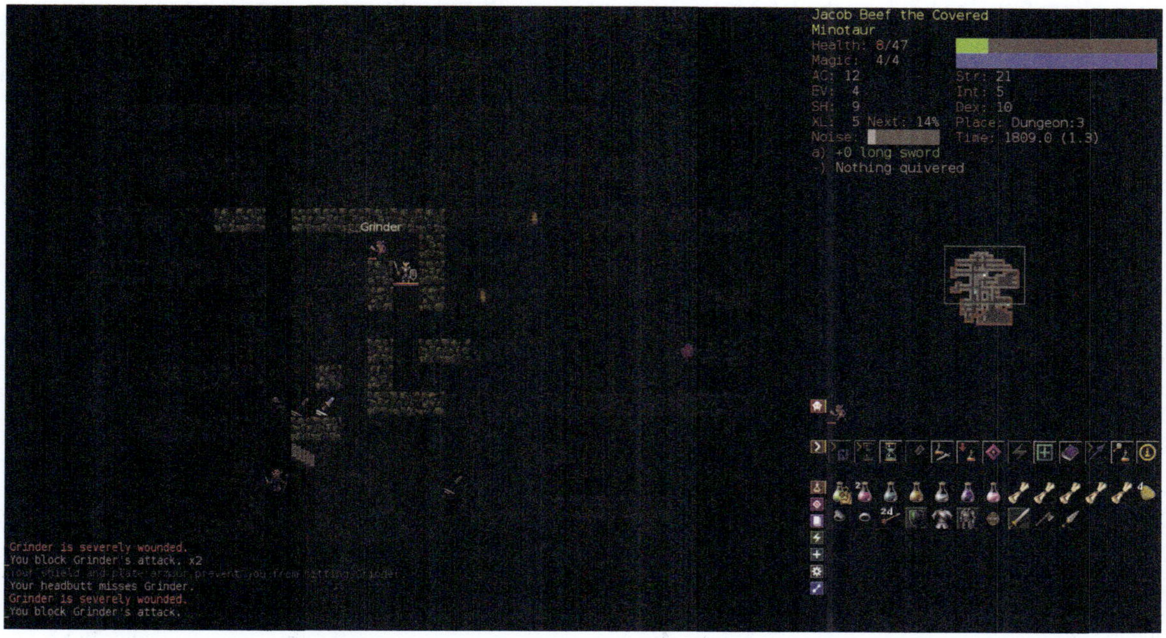

Figure 24.3

A special named monster

have been much more survivable, and with three they would have been barely a threat at all. But one only has so many equipment slots, and so much that can be carried at once, so one usually has to make hard choices about whether to have one kind of resistance or another at a given moment, or use other equipment like rings of slaying instead. But a single lucky artifact can take the place of several pieces of armor or jewelry, if it is generated and the player manages to have it identified so he'll know it has special powers.

Elven Halls: Lots of magic users here. Players must have one or more sources of magic resistance to have any chance here, but there are many demon summoners on the lowest level, and demons can be strong melee opponents. There is lots of equipment on the lowest level, but no rune.

Magic users in Crawl can be tricky opponents because of the power of magic in that game. The direst spell around (well, debatably) is one that banishes the player to the Abyss, a horrible place filled with demons and difficult to escape from. Fortunately, that didn't happen to me in the Elven Halls, although it did later on . . . .

Lair: This is perhaps the easiest dungeon branch of the game, for almost all the monsters here are ordinary animal-types. Near the bottom strong foes like death yaks may be found, but there are no magic users. The Lair has no rune of its own, but it has three branches itself, two of them having guaranteed runes and the other having a great chance of one. Best of all however, the Lair is a great place to gain experience without much risk.

Snake Pit: I got my first rune here. Its primary foes are nagas, which have strong poison attacks, but having just a single level of poison resistance was enough to combat that. Guarding the rune is a small army of nagas, some of them spellcasters, but there is a one-space-width corridor leading from it. A character standing at one end of that can shoot wands of fire, cold or lightning down it to take care of many nagas queued up along it in relative comfort.

Swamp: I got my second rune from here. It's a series of wide-open levels with lots of water. Falling into deep water can be very dangerous so it is bad to get confused here, and the Swamp Drakes that infest the area have a confusion gas breath attack. Shallow water, while not instantly fatal, slows the player down and makes it difficult to fight back. Poison resistance is also important to have here due to the Swamp Dragons that live in the Swamp's deeper levels. The hydras that live here should be defeated, by the way, with a blunt weapon like a mace, instead of a bladed one like a sword. Just trust me on this.

Slime Pits: The last branch off from the Lair, and where I eventually got my third rune. It is a very dangerous area for unprepared players. While I took care of the Snake Pit and the Swamp at around level 13–14, I was level 22 when I finally worked up the courage to tackle the Slime Pits. (For comparison's sake, the highest experience level the player can reach is 27.) Equipment damage is frequent unless the player has items to guard against that. I did, yet I still ended up with a couple of pluses taken off my armor while there.

The most annoying thing about getting runes here is that they are random, not guaranteed, and if they are present they are inside one of four chambers on the deepest level that have undiggable walls, and can only be entered by teleportation. I found not a single source of teleport control through the whole game, and I eventually had to get the rune by wearing a ring of teleport and evoking it many times, until I finally managed to get into a rune-bearing chamber.

Hive: Another place it is unwise to enter without poison resistance, but once the player has it and is strong enough to take care of multiple bees at once, this is an easy place. There is lots of food here, in the form of honeycombs and royal jellies, so players who can clear this place out and manage their food consumption carefully will be able to worry a lot less about starvation. Unfortunately, there is no rune here.

Vaults: The first truly challenging area, there's always a rune here, but it's in the extremely dangerous last floor, which I was scared to visit. Dungeon levels here are strange: each floor is a wide-open plain with lots of rectangular rooms around it, some of them with doors leading inside and some without. Those doors are essential fixtures, since they are the only bottlenecks to be found there. Combat is often against several foes at once because of that.

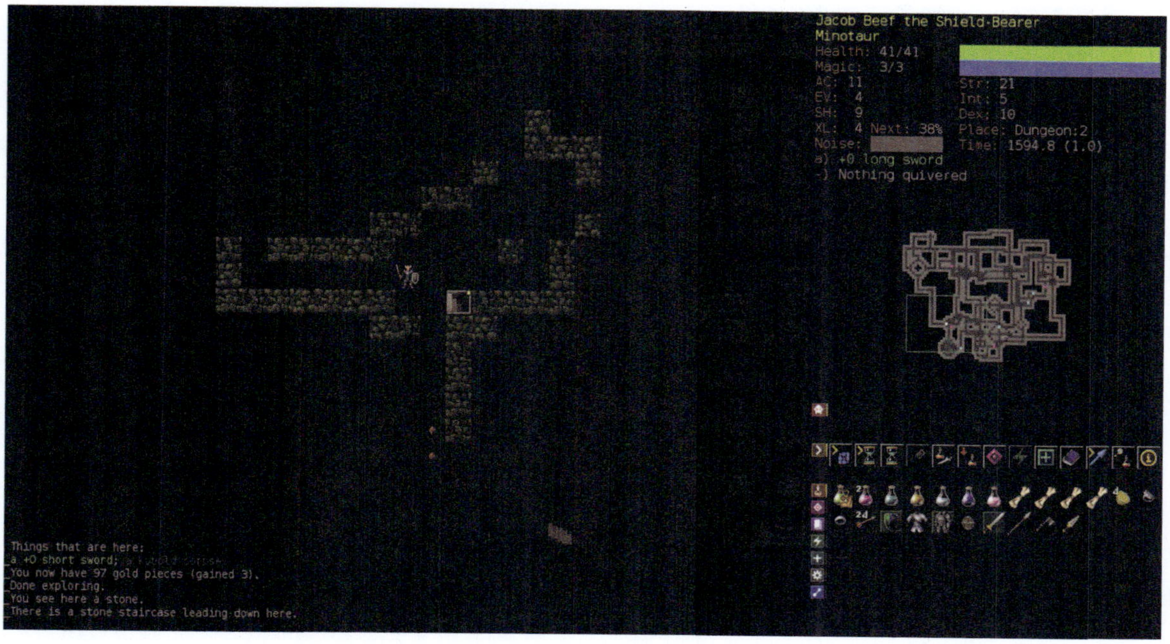

Figure 24.4

Just another day in the dungeon

Crypt: Found branching off the Vaults, there is no rune here, but I was strong enough by then that I wasn't in much danger, either. Undead are very common here, including the feared skeletal warriors, but they weren't much of a problem for me by that time.

Tomb: A very interesting place branching off from the Crypt. The primary monster here is mummies, which have a very special attribute: if you kill one, they bestow a curse upon you. The curses range from just having stuff cursed (easy to counter with a scroll of remove curse) to rotting for a short while (which removes maximum hit points!) to being sent to the Abyss. The only way to safely handle mummies is to summon or charm other monsters so they take care of them for you, but as a very unmagical dwarf who relied on wands for that kind of thing, this was not easy for me. I left the Tomb after only a few hundred turns, and didn't return.

Hall of Blades: A one-level branch from the Vaults, here the only monsters are possessed weapons. Once a weapon is "killed" it falls to the ground and can be used, but while it is "alive" the player will have to face all the effects the weapon possesses. I was banished to the Abyss twice here, once by a morningstar of distortion, and again, once I got back and killed it, by wielding that same weapon. After that, I dropped it in the Abyss and didn't look back.

Abyss: And what of the Abyss itself? It is effectively its own dungeon branch, but always random. If you leave and return it'll be different, and it doesn't "map out" as you explore it either. The level even wraps around, making it difficult to come up with a good exploration strategy. Attempting to teleport here will just send you to a new area of the Abyss. There is always an exit portal in it somewhere, but meanwhile every kind of demon is trying to kill you, and many of them have strange abilities like intelligence draining and summoning in still more demons. While there are lots of random walls around to hide behind, it's also easy to get caught in a dead end. It is possible for even low-level characters to get sent there on rare occasions, who die quickly unless they do lots of running, and use teleport scrolls to get out of tight spots. Rarely, runes are found in the Abyss, but going there on purpose to look for them is often unwise.

Hell: Hell has five sections, four of which are available by killing Geryon in its entry level and blowing his horn. Each of the other areas has a rune to be found, but a few close calls deeper in convinced me to go look in the Slime Pits for the last one I needed. Mostly, this place is a whole bunch of demons supplying a whole lot of hurt, but at least it's not "instanced" like the Abyss is. One rune is in each of its four branches.

- Pandemonium: The third and last of the "underworlds" in Dungeon Crawl, it's like the Abyss in that it's random, tough and hard to escape from (even harder in fact, since most Pandemonium areas only have portals to other areas), and like Hell in that it's mappable. Or at least, so I read. I didn't go there in this game, and I suspect that was a good choice on my part. Several runes can be found randomly here.
- Realm of Zot: The other branches are, to a degree, optional, but once enough runes are found all players must come here, which is a series of five tough, random areas. My game ended here, on the fifth and last level, just one screen away from the Orb of Zot, goal of the game. I kind of expected it might.

But I know why I died, and next time there, I won't. That's what playing roguelikes is about.

25

Crawl: Skills and Advancement

January 2010 This is the beginning of a sequence of chapters on the popular roguelike game Dungeon Crawl. We've covered it once before, but considering the game's importance and continued development we have not discussed it nearly as much as it deserves. Hopefully this and the next few chapters will go some way towards remedying this tragic situation!

Of the five major roguelikes (Rogue, NetHack, Angband, ADOM and Dungeon Crawl), Crawl is both the most recent addition to the list and the one undergoing, by far, the most intensive development. A favorite of the Goons over at Something Awful, it possesses a very strong design which is difficult to exploit, and provides tradeoffs and drawbacks for most important actions. In this it sticks closely to Rogue, and other than the original Hack it is probably the popular roguelike that best recognizes its forefather's great strengths.

Chapters 24–29 are written based on the as-of-this-writing most current stable version of Dungeon Crawl Stone Soup, 0.5.2. (As of publication of this volume, the most recent version is 0.24.0.) Information on the current version of the game can be found at the Dungeon Crawl Wiki.

25.1 Crawl's Experience System

To begin our discussion, I must first describe Dungeon Crawl's unique experience system. (*January 2016*: Crawl's experience has changed a bit since this, to eliminate the need for "victory dancing.")

Characters in Crawl advance in two important ways. The first way is the usual one featured in most role-playing games, through the gaining of experience points towards raising character level from defeating monsters. Crawl is more conservative in its advancement rules than some other RPGs; unlike Moria and Angband or later editions of D&D, monsters do not grant less experience when they are outclassed by the player. The reduced benefit of defeating weak monsters comes entirely through the greatly increasing experience needed to gain higher levels.

But while "character level" in Crawl has certain visible benefits (HP and MP go up, stat increases may occur, and more spells may be learned), a character tends to gain more profound advantages from increasing skill levels.

Characters have a number of skills, which can be examined in-game by pressing the "m" key. These can be divided into fighting skills (which include general Fighting, all the weapon skills and some additional abilities like Dodge and Throwing), utility skills (Traps & Doors being the most universal, but also the

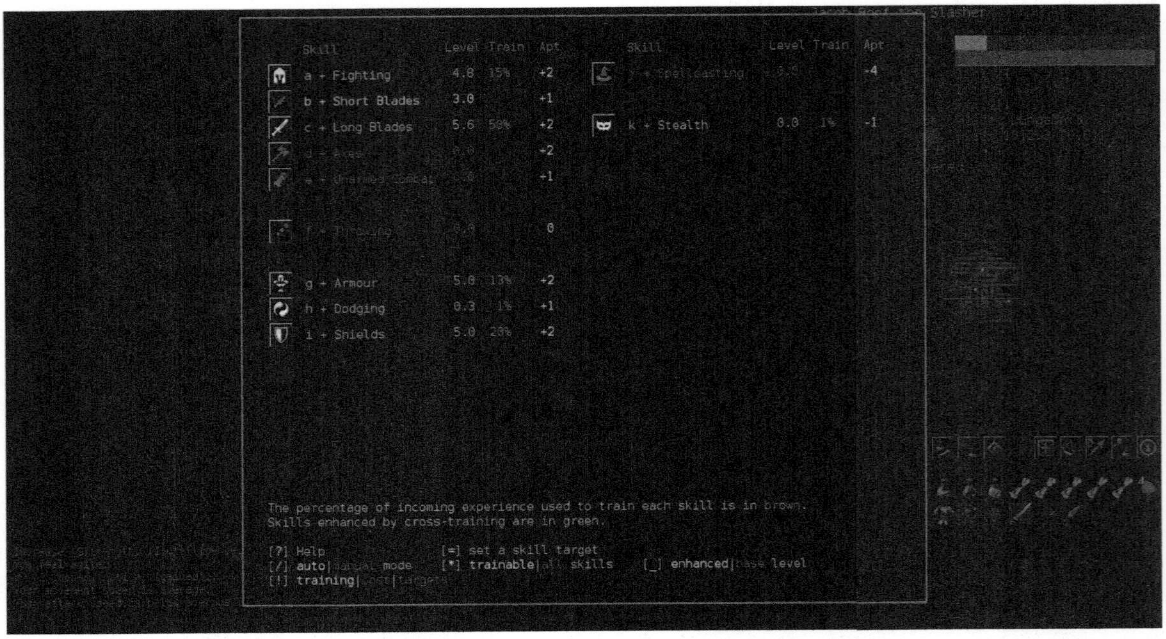

Figure 25.1

The skill screen

specialized magic-using abilities Invocations and Evocations) and magic skills (one per school of magic, and general spellcasting). These skills are what govern most of a character's action success rates and power.

When the player earns experience in Crawl, both the overall experience total goes up and an extra total called the experience pool. Points live in the pool until they get assigned to one of the skills through practice. Pretty much any action the player can perform that has a chance of failure belongs to one of the skill categories, and practicing that action provides a chance that some of those skill points will be moved to that skill. Higher skill levels require vastly more points than lower levels, just as with character level, but will also increase the number of points that are diverted to that skill with a single practice.

The most interesting thing about Crawl's skill system is how it deftly avoids the many problems of a skill-based development system.

- There is no feeling a character doesn't improve over time;
- nor that skills are watered-down to prevent one from being unbalanced compared to the others;
- nor that one is overpowered;
- nor that characters are generic, infinitely malleable bags of properties interchangeable with each other;
- nor that a character quickly maxes out and becomes unable to advance;
- nor that rapid, early advancement in one area makes improving in others impossible or nearly so; and
- nor that a character can easily advance in all areas and become a super character without proper effort and playing skill.

Crawl's system avoids all these problems, or tries to anyway. It is probably the best skill system yet seen in any roguelike; it could make a claim at being one of the best in any CRPG. Aimless practicing only improves skills so long as the player has successes, measured in monster kills, to power them, and also requires an opportunity to train them. The skills are broad enough that no experience diversions feel wasted, but sufficiently narrow that characters don't become, functionally, generalists. If a character has low aptitude in a skill it costs more points to train, a significant but far from insurmountable amount. And most skill practice events require some opportunity, meaning even if the player has pool points to spare, there may not be the opportunity around that the player wants to spend them on.

Oh by the way, the maximum experience level, skill level and (until recently) dungeon level of Dungeon Crawl all are 27. Don't ask why; it's kind of the magic number of Dungeon Crawl.

25.2 Race, Class, Stats and Deity: The Four Facts of Crawl Existence

A starting Dungeon Crawl character is, generally speaking, a combination of race, class, statistics and god.

Races are a bundle of skill aptitudes, some starting equipment, skills and stats, and sometimes a few special rules. Aptitudes determine how difficult it is to train a specific skill. Special rules are sometimes profound changes to the basic gameplay of Crawl, like an inability to use most armor or a rapid metabolism. A hill orc character, of whatever class, will have certain abilities that a deep dwarf of the same class is not capable of and vice-versa. Many of the game's races have special abilities like this. Some of these differences may overcome with the right mutations, but that process is random and dangerous.

A Crawl character's class provides a further development of items and skills, sometimes with a couple of extra perks. Class plays a much greater role in starting skill allotment (but not aptitude) than role, but both factor into it. The following fact is so important to understanding Crawl's class system that it gets a paragraph to itself, and in boldface too, just to impress its importance:

Class provides no benefits to a character beyond startup; once the game begins, everything a character becomes follows from his actions and his race.

Just because you're a "Conjurer" does not mean you have to cast even a single spell. You could pick up a knife and start training combat skills, and win the game with them, and the game will not make it any harder for a character to do this other than the difficulty he will have starting out with no skill in that area, and whatever stat deficiencies he might have, which are due more to race than class. Likewise, a character beginning as a "Fighter" can pick up the basics of spellcasting from reading random scrolls, then find a starter's spellbook in the dungeon and begin using magic, provided he is willing to go with light armor and has a good-enough Intelligence stat. It would not be an easy road, but it is possible.

Those stats are also quite important. Dungeon Crawl has only three: Strength, Dexterity and Intelligence. Their improvement is mostly tied to experience level. At periodic levels one randomly chosen stat (which is picked depends on character race) is increased by a point.

Additionally, every three levels the game asks the player for a statistic to improve. Strength influences combat damage and skill using some weapons. Dexterity plays a role in combat hit chances, attack evasion and skill using the rest of the weapons. Intelligence is needed to memorize spells and to cast them more successfully once memorized.

That leaves deity worshiped. Most, but not all, Crawl characters begin the game without a religion and can choose to remain unaligned in that way. (Characters of the demigod race, in exchange for markedly higher stats and stat growth, are forbidden from joining a religion.) In a special dungeon branch called the

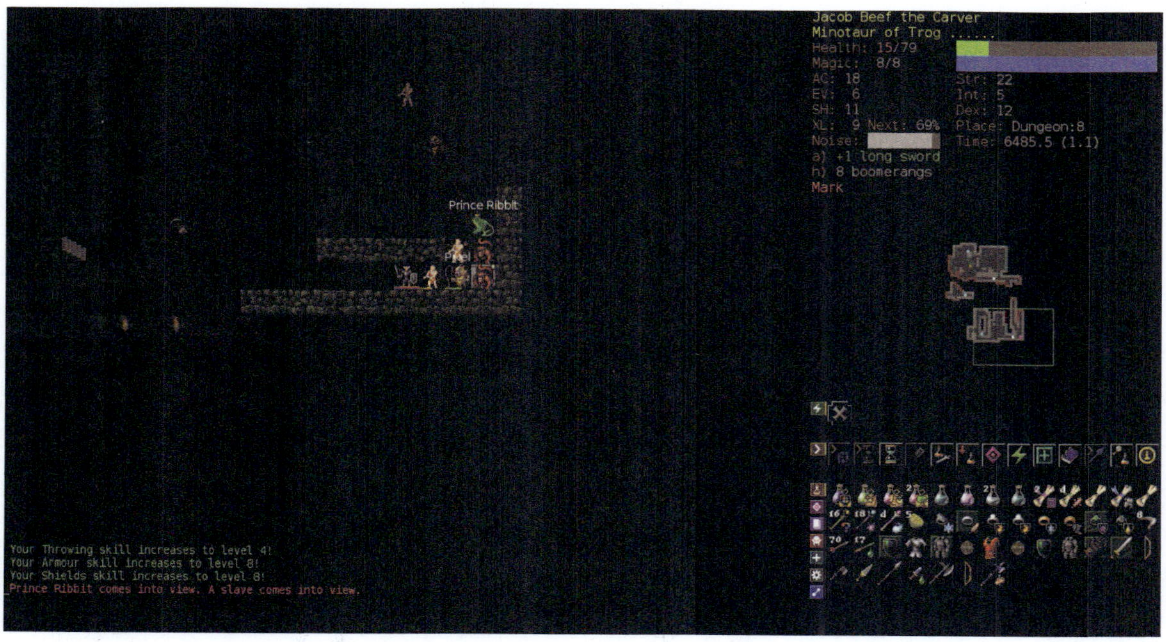

Figure 25.2

Beware the might of the fearsome Prince Ribbit!

Ecumenical Temple some way down, a character can pick out one of 12 gods to worship, each providing special gameplay advantages in exchange for following its dictates. Once a religion is joined, the player can leave at any time by using the Renounce Religion ability, but depending on how much time the player has spent in that religion and which god (if any) he changes to, doing this will incur the wrath of his former deity.

All of these aspects combine to provide a very deep set of gameplay possibilities for each combination of race and class.

25.3 How Crawl Steers Characters along Their Path

A fact that is not obvious to the Dungeon Crawl newbie is that all of the character races and classes have the same skills. When you check your skills at the start of the game with the "m" key, you will only see a few options available. Despite this, all skills are possessed by the player character. The skills not displayed are just considered to be at "level zero," and progress towards advancement in them is still tracked, just not displayed. These skills are also called untrained. Whenever the player does something that involves an untrained skill, a couple of points will be diverted to it. Since one of the functions of having levels in a skill is an increase in the number of pool points that can be diverted to it in from a single practice, even with a full experience pool it may still be awhile before the skill advances as points get diverted to the player's higher-level abilities. (A foresighted player can help prevent this by disabling skills from the "m" screen, which doesn't actually turn them off; it just makes the game much less likely to assign pool experience to them.)

So every character class can learn every skill, and no class uses special rules to provide its gameplay features. How, then, does Crawl avoid the problem of classes being too similar to each other, such as with most of NetHack's classes?

Starting out is difficult without a "gimmick," a system by which a character can prosper in the early going.

A character with no skill in anything would be quite hard to play. The numbers are stacked against such a character; starting stats and skills tend to be just enough that most players will need to rely on class-specific abilities to get a leg-up on the monsters. These skills make possible the character's engine, the system by which he kills monsters and earns experience within acceptable levels of risk. Having an engine is not strictly necessary, and for some race/class combinations is as simple as walking up to monsters and hitting them with stuff, but without one the player will have to resort to making use of random items and extreme tactics more often, strategies that bring with them necessary dangers.

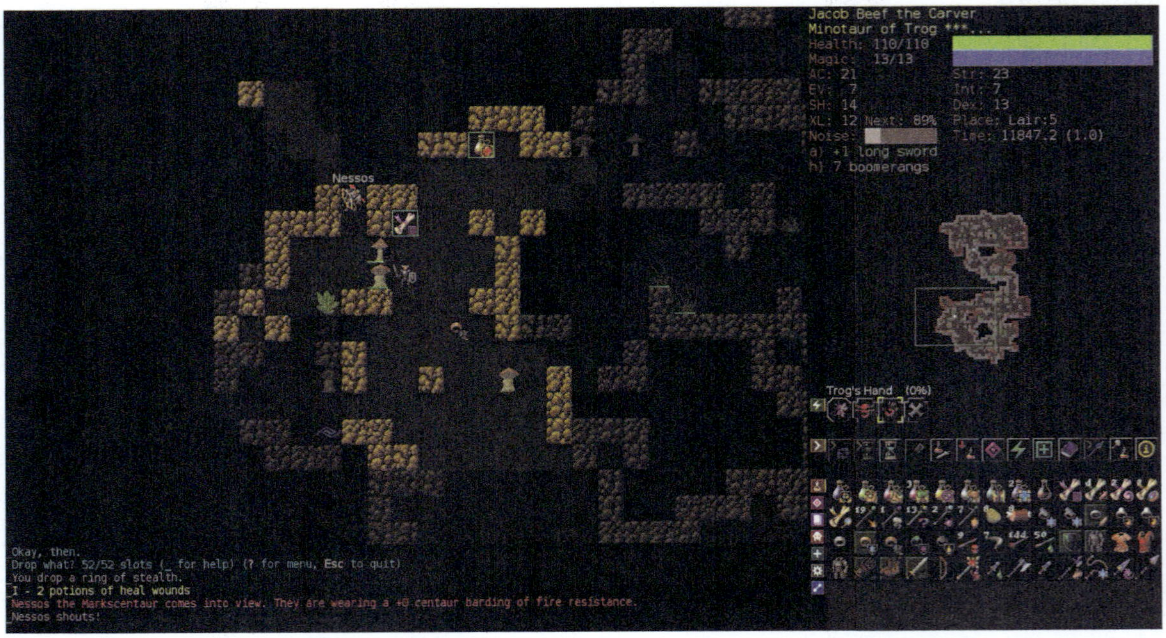

Figure 25.3

Oh, what fresh hell is this?

The hit-them-with-stuff gimmick is more conventionally termed melee specialty. Spellcasters that start out with conjurations can also survive in a straight-forward kind of way. But then there are centaurs, which are very fast and great with missile weapons, but must eat more often than most other races, and so must keep on the move more. And then there's Spriggans, who are extremely weak physically but naturally stealthy, and so they can make a good living off of stabbing sleeping monsters before they wake up. A Spriggan Enchanter (about which more will be said before long) gets a spell that can often put a single monster to sleep long enough to get in a single, almost certain-to-hit, ultra-high-damage critical strike that can wipe out even some very strong monsters instantly.

Many of the races are built off of these kinds of tradeoffs. The more extreme the tradeoff, the more the player will have to deviate from basic walk-up-and-smack-em play to survive and prosper. This can change the game a lot for some classes, restricting some basic abilities and/or making interesting new ones available. In a way, Crawl is actually a variety of different roguelike games that happen to take place in the same dungeon; the path for success for a High Elf Wizard is very different than that for a Minotaur Berserker, but they are both quite alien compared to a Vampire Anything.

Beyond race, it must be remembered that Crawl's classes are, for the most part (but see the next paragraph), identical after the game begins. Chances for advancement are the same for a human Fighter, Wizard, Assassin, Transmuter or Wanderer. What matters is how they make use of the skills they begin with, and how well they can diversify away from it, which usually relies on item generation.

What do I mean by "for the most part?" Some classes start out with a god that other classes cannot pick up until they find an altar, usually in the Ecumenical Temple found between dungeon levels 4 and 7. This is a fairly major advantage for those classes, but it mostly just gives them a good start. Additionally, elemental magic skills, including any levels possessed at the beginning of the game, make other elemental skills harder to learn. These differences may delay character advancement in some skills, but the player can always overcome them with more practice . . . provided he lives that long.

None of this would matter for much if Crawl were not a hard game. The game is very finely balanced, with the knife's edge very close to the limits of most characters' abilities at the start of play. Further, the player does not have the luxury to do much grinding for skills due to the food system which, while not as hard as Rogue's, does limit the amount of food that can be reliably found in a game. It is useful to think of character advancement in terms of experience gained vs. food consumed, with more efficient improvement techniques providing for a potentially more-powerful character later on.

If food were not a resource of hard scarcity, then the player could use the monster generation of early levels as a way to gain experience points, and those points could then be put into skills through practice a lot more easily. So it could be said that Crawl's food system drives its design. Even the small number of Crawl races that do not need to eat have some mechanism that forces the player to search for resources. The need to find more treasure is what makes the opportunities for experience and skill gain meaningful.

26

Crawl: Skill Overview

February 2010 (*January 2020*: Dungeon Crawl development at the time was moving quickly, and it continues to evolve today. The following should still be generally accurate, but some of the specifics may have moved out from under it.)

Crawl's character development system is designed so that, if you don't want to bother with planning your guy's growth, you don't technically have to. Other than being asked to pick a stat to increase every three levels, all advancement is done passively. Since character growth happens using a practicing system, and many times you must take advantage of character strengths to survive and prosper, playing this way will result in a strong focus on those initial strengths, which suits some characters more than others. Strong melee characters can do very well with this, given careful play. Spellcasters, on the other hand, require a bit more care to survive, since an ogre-type monster will sometimes get into melee range without your being able to do anything about it. And even melee guys would do well to diversify their weapon skills a little, in case a powerful artifact of a different weapon type shows up or an interesting spellbook is found.

Increasing skills you don't know requires free pool experience (which, as we discussed last time, comes from beating monsters) and an opportunity to practice. Many of those practice opportunities, especially for melee skills, come from fighting monsters, so we should be grateful that there is an ample supply throughout the dungeon. Increasing Traps & Doors happens on its own, but is greatly accelerated by trying to disarm traps (press Ctrl plus the direction of an adjacent trap to try to disarm). Dodge goes up generally whenever you're attacked in light armor, and Stealth goes up randomly just from moving around in light armor. Shields and Armor skills go up similarly, when wearing the appropriate equipment.

Spellcasting is a bit special. Most of the time you do not need an appropriate circumstance to practice a spell, even if it ordinarily requires a special situation such as a skeleton or a handful of arrows. You won't get much game use out of the spell in those cases, but it still counts for practicing the skill. Even unsuccessful spellcasting attempts practice magic skills, but those can cause miscast effects, which can be extraordinarily dangerous in Crawl's system. Every class of spells has its own assortment of miscast effects, ranked from slight to perilous. The worse ones tend not to happen unless you cast spells well outside your ability. This may come as a shock to players coming from NetHack, where some of the most powerful spells like Identify and Magic Mapping can be made useful even if you have only slight skill just by trying again and again until successful. In NetHack, the penalty for spell failure is wasting a turn and some magic points; in Crawl, depending on the spell, it can include high damage or Abyss banishment, among other harsh punishments.

It really sucks to die due to damage from miscasting a desperation spell, so it is best to stick with spells you know you can cast well in dangerous situations. Casting high-level spells you have no skill in should be avoided unless you have some other factor balancing it out.

26.1 Overall Skills: Fighting and Spellcasting

These two skills are special in that they are overskills, which add small bonuses to multiple other abilities. They tend to train more slowly than the subskills, and their effects are more subtle, but their bonuses extend to every skill they cover. This way, if a player becomes skilled in Conjurations, along the way his Spellcasting skill will improve. If he then tries to learn Enchantments, he'll have a slightly easier time of it than if he started from minimum Spellcasting. One level of that skill is roughly equal to a quarter-level of skill in each individual magic school.

These skills are also special in that, no matter which of Crawl's many classes you choose, your major abilities will likely fall under at least one of them. It can be useful for characters who do not seek to gain major ability in both areas to gain at least a little anyway.

Characters with Fighting skill begin gaining extra hit points at character level 5, with the amount proportional to the amount of skill. If you are already character level 5 then you gain hit points immediately every time Fighting goes up! (There is no advantage based on when you gain Fighting skill; the hit point bonus is applied, effectively, retroactively. Notably, NetHack's Constitution score, which applies bonus hit points in a similar manner, does not do this. This is the source of a subtle, long-standing exploit for that game.)

Characters with Spellcasting may also receive magic point bonuses according to their level in that, although characters can also gain maximum magic points by instead having skill in Invocations. (Why the weasel word "may?" Magic points are actually determined by a complex system that decreases the likelihood of gaining additional magic points as the total increases, so when you have many MP increasing Spellcasting might not help here.)

Spellcasting is useful for one other thing. Without at least one level of Spellcasting skill, spells cannot be learned or cast at all! As I said last time, all characters have the opportunity to gain Spellcasting skill, but seeing as how the way to gain Spellcasting is to cast spells, how does a character do this without being able to use magic? The key is in reading scrolls; if the player has a zero in Spellcasting skill, then reading scrolls with points in the experience pool advances Spellcasting a bit, and when level 1 is achieved (you "gain Spellcasting skill") the wide world of magical aptitude opens up to you.

Similarly, Fighting skill can be trained up to level 2 by fighting inert opponents like plants and fungi. Since that grants maximum hit point bonuses, it is a good idea even for magic-using classes to do that,

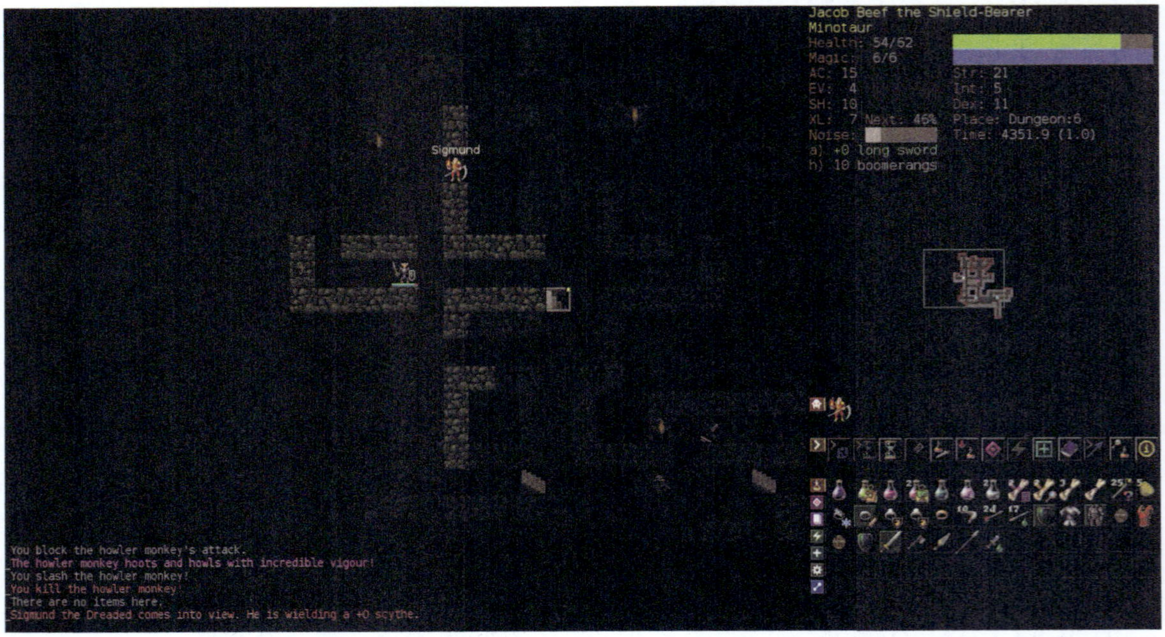

Figure 26.1

although with care Magicians can fairly safely train combat skills against weak monsters like giant newts and goblins.

26.2 Weapon Skills: Short Blades, Long Blades, Axes, Polearms, Maces & Flails, Unarmed Combat

These skills all affect their individual weapons' usefulness, so their worth is tied to the worth of their respective weapons. In brief:

Short Blades: Relatively low-damage weapons, but the best at Stabbing which makes them the best weapons by far for certain classes. Contains the dagger, which is a special case in the Stabbing rules. This skill "cross-trains" with Long Blades, meaning learning one makes it much easier to learn the other to the same level.

Short blades are weak as weapons go, but one area in which they excel is stabbing (see the next synopsis). Additionally, they all provide large to-hit bonuses.

Crawl generates some guaranteed knives in the first few levels of the dungeon, plus daggers are favorite weapons of kobolds, which the early game is loaded with, so there is usually no difficulty in finding a short blade to train with. Some weapons one might consider to be in the long blades category, such as sabers, in fact count as short. To discover which category a weapon belongs to in-game, go to inventory and enter the item's letter. (This can be used to describe any object you can carry, and is excellent for figuring out how to use a mysterious object.)

Some sort of bladed weapon is useful for nearly all characters as a means of chopping up corpses for snacks, among other uses. That use probably does not depend on skills, but if the character can use it in combat anyway it means one less thing to carry around.

Long Blades: Crosstrains with Short Blades. Starting weapon skills are assigned based on the weapons a character begins with, and so only Paladins begin the game with Long Blades skill. Interestingly, long blades are better than most other weapons at stabbing, but Paladins, as worshippers of The Shining One, are forbidden from doing that. Because it cross-trains with Short Blades, the best way for stabbing characters is probably to raise that skill first. Long bladed-weapons tend to do more damage, obviously, than short-bladed ones, but short-bladed weapons are better at stabbing.

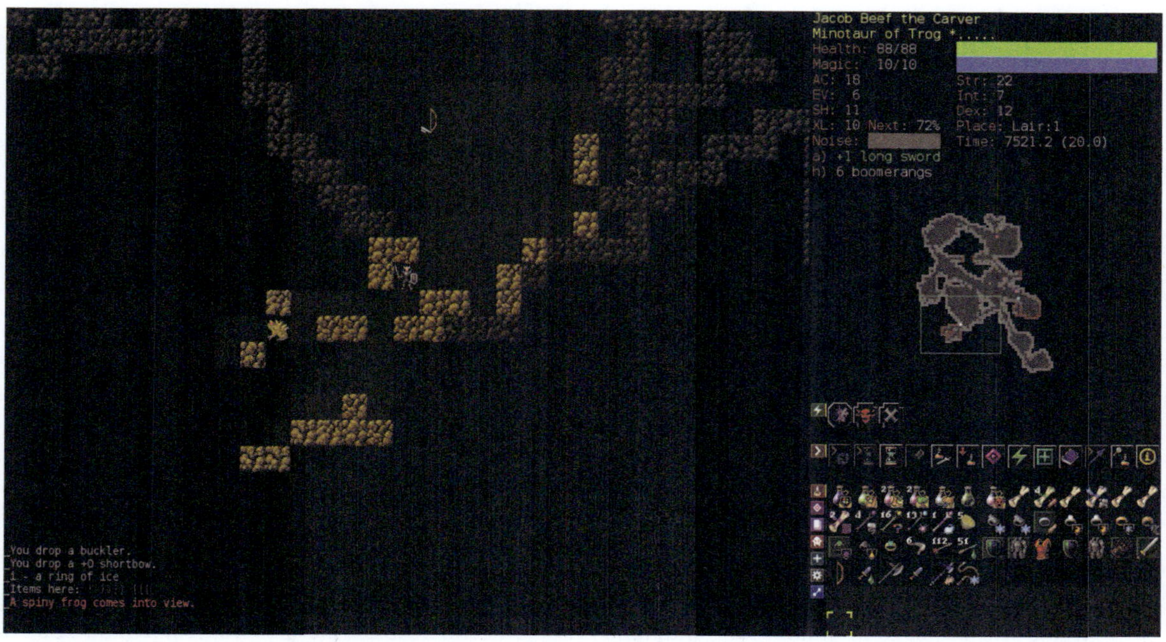

Figure 26.2

Traditionally, in D&D, longswords are the "default" weapon, the most likely one to start with and the most likely to be found enchanted in the world. In NetHack, particularly, many of the best artifacts are longswords. Crawl has a good distribution of fixed artifacts among its weapon classes, but Long Blades ties Maces & Flails for the most fixedart-filled category. (Most artifacts are randarts, which have different properties every game.)

Of particular note, both short- and long-bladed weapons are bad to use against Hydras, which become stronger as their heads are cut off and new ones grow in their place.

Long blades are quite difficult to find in the first levels of the dungeon. Most players find their first off of an orc, such as an orcish falchion.

Axes: Axes are one of the most powerful weapon categories that can be reliably found in the dungeon early on, and are a great weapon choice for the burlier races. The orcs frequently found in the early dungeon often carry them, along with short blades, maces and polearms.

Maces & Flails: This wide-ranging skill covers maces, clubs, flails, whips, hammers and morning stars. The earliest ultra-powerful weapon usually found in the dungeon are the giant clubs and maces usually carried by ogres, but like all the powerful weapons, they are slow and heavy, and using them causes large to-hit penalties. Note that Crawl does not support the traditional D&D prohibition on priests against cutting weapons, so there is no particular reason for them to wield maces if they don't begin with skill in them.

Polearms: Also a surprisingly inclusive weapon category. In addition to the sticks-with-knives-tied-to sorts of weapons it includes spears and scythes too. Sigmund, a deadly unique opponent frequently encountered in the early game, comes with a scythe, but to get it first you have to kill him. Many players try to put this off for when they're a couple of levels up on him.

Two special weapon brands, dragon-slaying and reaching, can only be generated on polearms. The former is limited in application, especially in the early game, but reaching allows you to strike one space away by using the "v" key with it wielded. This feature can be utilized by monsters too, especially by gnolls, who are prone to suddenly having this weapon when you're trying to cast spells on them.

Staves: The least inclusive of all the melee weapons, this category only includes quarterstaves and the exotic and rare lajatangs. The random staves found in the dungeon, as of version 0.5.2, are useful for their magical properties, not too useful in combat. Although there are some special battle applications (some inflict special damage types depending on effect), they cannot carry the enchantments that make other weapons so useful later in the game. Word is that the current development version of Dungeon Crawl Stone Soup, called "trunk" in the developers' parlance, promotes magic staves to full weaponhood.

Unarmed Combat: Okay, so it's not a weapons skill, but it fills the same kind of hole in the skill system. This is best trained if your character has, or is likely to receive, some kind of special attack mutation, like horns on your head or claws on your hands, so you're doing more than just punching damage. It also trains if you're wielding no weapons when fighting in melee. Notably, Unarmed Combat skill allows you sometimes to get in free hits in battle, such as punches with your off-hand and headbutts, even if you're using a weapon, so many melee characters could stand to get a little training in it.

26.3 Missile Skills: Bows, Crossbows, Slings, Darts and Throwing

The choice of missile weapon matters a little more than melee weapon due to some requiring spending a turn to switch to in order to make use of them and availability of both weapon and ammo.

Bows: This skill covers use of both normal bows and longbows. It requires a turn to equip the bow, so it can be a good idea to make the bow your exploration weapon, and switch to melee if the situation demands it. Arrows are very common, on the ground and in the inventory of centaurs. Centaurs always carry bows, too. In 0.5.2 missile weapon ammo can carry a brand. Bows can have a brand too. Either case will impart a magic property to a shot, but will always destroy the ammo in the process. (Exception: if the arrow is flaming and the bow is freezing, or vice versa, the shots will be normal!)

Crossbows: Faster to fire than bows, and hand crossbows can be fired one-handed. (Important note: it looks like hand crossbows will be removed in 0.6.0.) It is much harder to find crossbows and ammo than bows. Sometimes the player will have to wait until the Elven Halls, a dangerous mid-game dungeon, before he can start building his crossbow skills. A useful trick for conserving ammo is to wield a stack of bolts and reading a scroll of enchant weapon; ammo that carries a plus is much less likely to be destroyed by firing than unenchanted.

Slings: These are midway between the power of bows and the ease-of-use of darts. Slings can be used on both sling bullets (which may carry a brand) and stones (which do not). Although it may seem counter-intuitive, the Throwing skill is neither checked nor trained by using slings. The two skills do cross-train, however. Stones are an important missile weapon in the early game for being the best way for a non-magic character to kill jellies, since they do not consume rocks.

Darts: Using darts as a weapon practices both the Darts weapon skill and the Throwing skill. Darts are convenient due to their being able to be thrown without wielding anything ahead of time; they can be tossed directly out of the quiver. Darts are also governed by the Throwing skill. The word from the Crawl DevTeam is that 0.6.0 will remove the Darts skill in favor of using Throwing entirely. (*April 2020*: They did.)

Throwing: In addition to Darts, this skill governs everything else that is thrown, including stones that are not launched from a sling. Although this is technically an overskill like Fighting and Spellcasting, it is very limited in application and doesn't carry extra benefits as do those other skills.

26.4 Miscellaneous Skills: Stabbing, Stealth, Dodge, Armor, Shields, Traps & Doors, Invocations and Evocations

Stabbing: An extremely useful skill for certain character classes, stabbing is Crawl's term for what other games call a backstab, a highly damaging attack made against a compromised foe. Whenever you make a melee attack against a monster with (in the tiles version of the game) either an exclamation point or a question-mark in the monster's tile, there is a chance relative to the level of the Stabbing skill that the character will carry out a stab. The damage done depends on the level of Stabbing, the level of the weapon skill corresponding to the wielded weapon, the kind of weapon, and how incapacitated the opponent was, with the best cases being stabbing with a dagger and a sleeping monster. (*April 2020*: Stabbing was removed from the game in version 13. In more recent versions, your chance to deliver a stab is determined by your skill in the weapon and your Stealth skill.)

A character with full-level Stabbing skill, stabbing with a dagger, and attacking a sleeping monster, does over 12 times his usual damage. He is also practically guaranteed to hit. Even at relatively low levels of Stabbing

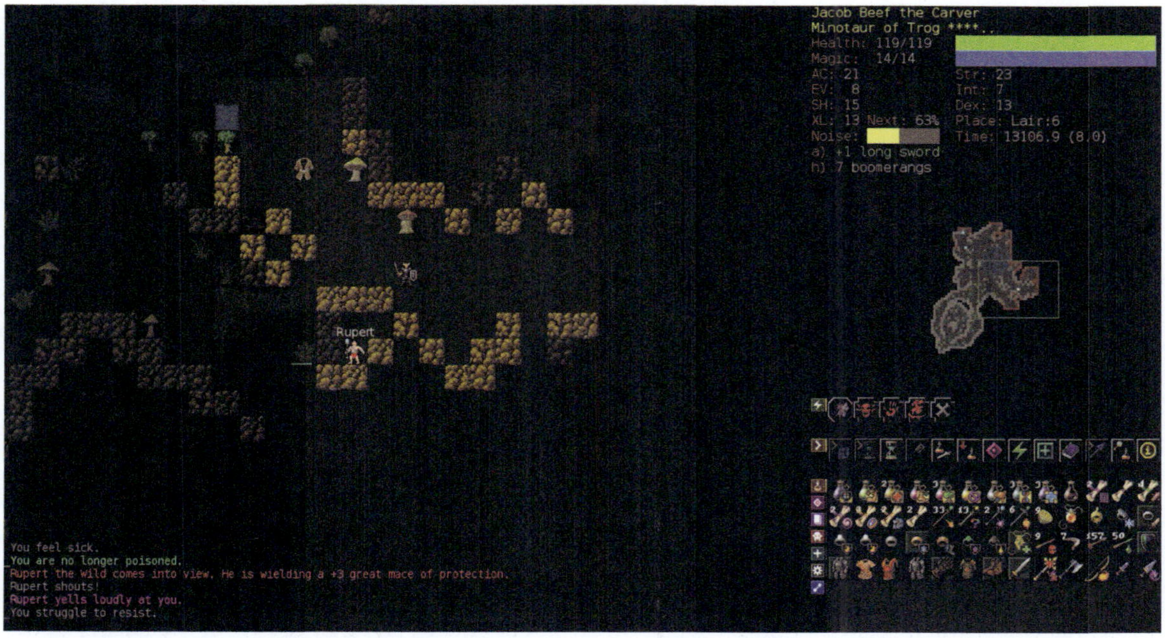

Figure 26.3

the damage bonus is high enough that monsters much stronger, in other ways, than the character can be dispatched in one strike if only they be put to sleep. I recommend the experience of taking out an eight-headed hydra with one hit at low level to everyone. Of course many higher-level opponents tend to resist such sleep effects, or are cold-resistant (sleeping spells in Crawl are cold-based), but considerable damage bonuses can still be achieved against monsters who are merely confused.

Stealth: A passive skill that determines how likely a monster is to notice you approach. Every race has a stealth modifier that Stealth skill is multiplied by to produce a character's base stealth score, to which various other bonuses and penalties are added. Notably, being burdened by carrying too heavy a load or confused greatly increase the chances of being noticed. Armor adds in a substantial penalty to stealth relative to its weight. Stealth bonuses can be provided by items, artifacts, silence and invisibility.

Stealth is most useful partnered with the Stabbing skill. A very stealthy character like a Spriggan often ends up as a natural assassin regardless of what class he began with. Stealth is trained randomly just while moving around while not wearing "heavy" armor, which makes it, for better or worse, very easy to train. For more on this, see the next skill.

The wiki downplays the worth of Stealth, saying that it's practically useless for non-assassins, but it can be of value in escaping from powerful monsters that have not yet noticed you, or getting in an extra missile attack before the foe closes in for melee.

Dodging: Training this skill decreases the chances enemies have to strike your character. Its effectiveness is lessened if your character is wearing heavy armor with low Armour skill. Even with good Armour skill, it is not trained while wearing heavy armor unless the player has enough Armour skill, but if the player's character isn't wearing any it gets practiced frequently whenever an enemy makes an attack against him.

The usefulness of Dodging goes up relative to the player's Dexterity, up to a point which is determined partially by the size of the character. A side effect of this is that, even with high Dexterity, only Spriggan-size characters (the smallest player race) don't receive any benefit from Dodging until they get their second level in it.

Every practice event that occurs in Crawl takes points from the experience pool, and thus makes other practice events that much harder to devote points to. And high skills cause practice events to devote many, many more points to them, exacerbating this situation. Thus it is that, without some planning, high scores in Dodging and Stealth can absorb many skill points the player might prefer go into other areas, especially for spellcasters, who will want to avoid heavy armor, and Spriggans, who can't wear most of it. Some players "turn off" training in Dodging and Stealth early on, from the "m" screen. This doesn't actually deactivate skills; it just makes them much less likely to train. In fact, this can be a useful strategy for many kinds of characters in the early game where every skill point counts.

Armour: If you're wearing heavy armor then Dodging and Stealth do not train; what does instead is Armour skill, which lessens the negative effects of wearing such armor. It can also provide added protection from armor as the player learns to wear it better. For technical reasons, this is potentially very useful for Orcs worshipping the orcish god Beogh.

Heavy armor can produce substantial combat penalties (not to mention those for spellcasting), so melee characters will benefit greatly from training the Armour skill.

Shields: In many ways, as Armour skill is for heavy armor, Shields skill is for shields. A high skill means the negative effects of bearing a shield (hit less often, reduced attack speed, spell fail chance) are reduced and the positive effects (blocking of enemy attacks) are increased. Shields in Crawl are useful even if they provide no visible Armour Class benefit, but they also make it more difficult to hit in battle or cast spells.

Traps & Doors

(*Note*: remember when I said that these chapters are a bit out of date, and that Crawl has seen heavy development, and even redesign, since they were written? More recent versions of Crawl have entirely done away with this skill! I leave this section in for historical interest.)

Relative to other games, Crawl has remarkably lethal traps. The only roguelike with traps more deadly is ADOM, whose door-mounted stone block traps have squished many early characters. But Crawl provides a defense against these traps in the form of the Traps & Doors skill.

The effects of this skill are: it increases the chances of finding a trap by searching; it increases the chances of finding the trap passively, just from passing time near it; it appears to increase the distance from which hidden traps can be spotted; it decreases the damage done by the trap if it hits; it decreases the chance of being struck by it when it goes off; and as a bonus it even helps find secret doors, both passively and from searching or resting. (An interesting feature of Crawl is that, although both search and rest keys are supported by the game, they actually do the same thing. Resting a few turns automatically searches nearby spaces in the bargain!)

It isn't very far into the game where traps start doing substantial damage, so all characters should increase their Traps & Doors skill when they can. The skill is practiced sometimes when a trap is set off or spotted randomly, but the best way to train it is to attempt to disarm traps, by holding the Ctrl key down and attempting to move onto it. (This is also the fight-without-moving command, by the way.) Failing to disarm a trap often results in taking damage from it, so it is best to do this with traps on the earlier levels, since they do much less damage. It certainly is worth making a trip back up the dungeon in order to practice with less risk. Some kinds of traps, notably alarm traps and any magical types, cannot be disarmed.

An interesting thing about this skill is that while, like all skills, it takes a bit of doing to get it to first level, once you get it to maybe level 5 it sort of takes over for itself, and becomes almost a self-training skill. The reason is that automatically finding a trap from a distance is itself a practice event for the Traps & Doors skill, so the better you are at it, the better you tend to get. If this process steals away too much pool experience, you might end up having to turn it off to slow its advancement.

Deep in the dungeon the player will start to encounter Zot traps, which are one of the most diabolical hazards in Crawl, capable of doing a wide range of terrible things to the player's character including banishment to the Abyss. Having a good Traps & Doors skill is one of the few good ways of avoiding these.

Finally, one of the more wonderful things about Crawl is the occasional goodies found in secret vaults. These can be found even on some higher levels, hidden by secret doors. It can sometimes be worthwhile to return to earlier levels once you get Traps & Doors up to a respectable rank and seeing what previously unseen passages call out to you.

Invocations: Many gods, once you gain enough favor, or piety, with them, will grant you special abilities that you can use. The use of these abilities trains the Invocations skill.

The use of many invocations also carries costs, in the form of food, magic points or piety, making them more or less useful for training. The Invocations skill applies to all gods, so theoretically you could train the skill under a god with a cheap power, then switch over to the god with the expensive power to use it more effectively, but most gods will punish those who convert away from their religions very harshly.

Overall Invocations is one of the less generally useful skills in the game (it is completely useless for atheists and Demigods), but it does have an extra benefit; characters with low or zero Spellcasting skill can train this skill to receive extra maximum magic points.

Evocations: Crawl even has a skill for the use of magic items; this is it. The higher Evocations skill rises the more useful useable magic items will be. Most items that use the v or V command to activate train Evocations (but not weapons of reaching). For most characters the most useful function of Evocations is the use of wands, which become more useful generally as Evocations skill rises. Rods, which are like wands but more easily rechargeable, can make this skill quite useful, as well as provide greater opportunity to train it. Rods are rare generally, though.

Artificers in particular, which have magic item use as their focus and begin with wands or a rod, tend to get more lot of use out of this, as do Deep Dwarves who can recharge wands as a special ability.

One particular use of this skill is in drawing from decks of cards. The cards are not changed by Evocations skill, but the ones drawn can become more powerful (which can be good or bad) as skill increases.

26.5 Primary Magic Skills: Conjurations, Summonings, Enchantments, Translocation, Transmutation, Divination, Necromancy, Poison Magic

(Enchantments and Divination have been removed from the game. Enchantments was divided between Charms [which help you] and Hexes [which harm others].)

The individual magic skills affect memorization chances, casting chances and spell power for the spells covered by their corresponding school.

Conjurations: The most direct of magic skills, all the Conjurations spells in Crawl have to do with creating effects out of nothing. It includes direct damage spells of both its school alone (like the common Magic Dart spell) and spells that are mixed with elemental schools (like the awesome Lehudib's Crystal Spear). Spells of mixed schools average the levels of those skills when checks are made.

Conjurers is a class that focuses in Conjurations spells, but Wizards, who are typically generalists, usually end up relying on them as well.

Summonings; These spells call creatures (of many different types) to aid the caster. Or at least that is the intent; not all of these spells guarantee that the called being(s) will be friendly. Higher levels in Summonings increases the odds of the summoned creature, for those spells, of being favorably inclined towards you. The lowest-leveled Summoning spells are Summon Small Animals, a.k.a. "Summon Spammals," and Summon Butterflies, both useful even late at the game as ways to put things between you and slavering horrible monsters.

Enchantments: Enchantment spells are more subtle than Conjurations but still powerful if used correctly. Spells that confuse or put to sleep are excellent early in the game, especially to stabbing characters. Confused monsters cannot cast spells, smite you or fire missiles. One of the most powerful early spells in the game is Mephitic Cloud, which is Conjurations/Poison/Enchantments.

Later on Enchantments becomes less useful as many of its status effects get resisted by high hit die monsters. There are even some monsters that are entirely immune to Enchantment. Back on the plus side, Selective Amnesia, one of the most useful spells in the game, is an Enchantment spell that allows you to forget other spells, freeing up those spell levels for other magic. The only other ways to forget spells are a Sif Muna ability that costs piety and certain miscast effects, which have the added drawback of not letting you choose the spell forgotten. There is also Invisibility and Haste, spells that are so powerful that they cause "magic contamination" if used too frequently.

One of the most useful Enchantment spells is Enslavement, which makes a monster (if it doesn't resist) temporarily into an ally. To digress for a moment to compare Crawl to another game . . . one of NetHack's little strangenesses is that its "pets" are never struck by enemies as a direct attack, they only hit as a counter-attack after a pet hits them first. Crawl's pets/summons/allies/slaves are full-fledged monsters that must be targeted by enemies, so just having a friend fighting with you makes you marginally safer as some enemy attacks will be spent attacking the pet. This seems to me to be a much more realistic way to handle allies.

Translocation: This spell school is about moving things around, either you, monsters or items. A low-level spell of the school is Apportation, which moves an item in sight to your space. At higher levels you can blink or teleport, or control teleports, or banish monsters to the Abyss (although you might find them there when you go there yourself).

Most of the magic schools have low-level spells that help the player in little ways that can be used to gain basic skill in that school. Translocation has Portal Projectile, which can be used, according to the game, to teleport launched projectiles directly to their targets. The result, functionally, is a to-hit bonus. Enchantments also provides such a spell in the form of Corona.

Transmutation: This is the magic school of turning-things-into-other-things. Before you get NetHack-inspired visions of limitless resources, polymorphing objects is not possible in this game. You can polymorph monsters, but player polymorph is limited to a few special forms and a handful of special cases. Many of the Transmutation spells involve morphing into those forms, which each provides for various benefits (and often some drawbacks). Other useful Transmutation spells are Dig, Passwall, Disintegrate and Shatter, which can be very useful in getting around Crawl's complex multi-level dungeon.

One of the Transmutation spells is Alter Self, which inflicts upon the player a number of random mutations. Crawl divides mutations into "good" ones and "bad" ones, and Alter Self (and most sources) picks randomly from the lists. Curing mutations, for most characters, is harder than gaining them; the most common sources of mutation removal are potions of cure mutation, which are fairly rare. (The message they give is "This potion has a clean taste.")

Many of these magic skills have a character class that specializes in them (that is to say, begins with several levels in it). An early-game engine that works for Transmuters is using the spell Fulsome Distillation to extract harmful potions from corpses then Evaporation to use those potions against monsters.

Divination: Roguelikes are almost unique among CRPGs these days for providing spells whose sole purpose is to provide information, and Divination is the spell school in which Crawl's information magic lives. The star of the Divination school is Identify; Crawl's system of randarts means there is rarely a lack of magical things to query even late in the game. Also spells include Magic Mapping and an assortment of detection magic. Other than those things, Divinations seems to be the magic school with the fewest spells.

Necromancy: The magic of dead in Crawl is, in gameplay terms, a kind of hodge-podge of spells with effects like those in other schools. There are direct damage spells like in Conjurations, enslaving spells like Enchantments, and monster zombie-raising spells are a bit like Summoning.

One unusual specialty for Necromancy in Crawl is healing. Interestingly, Necromancy is the only spell school in Crawl with healing magic, and instead of just increasing your health it always has some strange mechanism behind it, such as increasing regeneration, stealing hit points from monsters or sacrificing maximum hit points. This makes healing items (potions of healing, potions of heal wounds, wand of healing) and gods very valuable in Crawl.

Poison Magic: Similar to the elemental magic schools, Poison Magic involves a particular theme of effect. Also like the fire and ice spells of those schools, it is a lot less useful generally against monsters resistant to it. Unlike fire and ice resistance, poison resistance is all-or-nothing; there are no multiple levels in it. I do not know if Poison Magic counts as an elemental skill for purposes of learning (see next entry for more information).

26.6 Elemental Magic Skills: Fire Magic, Ice Magic, Air Magic, Earth Magic

Elemental magic skills are an exception to the rule that knowledge in one skill doesn't hinder knowledge in another. All elemental magic skills other than the one the player has the highest level in are harder to learn, and the one opposed to that skill is even harder to learn. Fire opposes ice, and air opposes earth.

Fire Magic: This is generally the elemental magic school for attack magic. Utility spells include Conjure Flame (which blocks off a space to some enemy movement for a while; it tends to be fairly weak), Ignite Poison (useful both to damage monsters you've poisoned and as a painful way to cure it in yourself), Dragon Form (grarr) and Evaporation (a very interesting spell where you throw a bad potion and it explodes in a cloud of vapor; quite useful combined with Fulsome Distillation).

Ice Magic: Contains the oddly named spells Ensorcelled Hibernation and Metabolic Englaciation, which you might as well think of as Sleep and Mass Sleep. Sleep spells are super powerful in Crawl because the game uses coup-de-grace rules, in conjunction with Stabbing skill, against helpless opponents, for huge damage bonuses. This allows for a potent engine for Enchanters. Note, dear players, that if monster slept with one of these spells wakes up, a further casting won't work on them for around 20–30 turns. Ice Magic has fewer attack spells than Fire Magic, but it's still no slouch.

Air Magic: This is the elemental school that contains Lightning spells, which are powerful and with less common resistances than fire or ice magic. On the defensive side, one of the most dangerous monsters in the Realm of Zot is lightning golems, against which the Air Magic spell Insulation is very useful. Airstrike is one of the few magic attacks in Crawl that use "smite targeting," meaning the attack strikes from above without having to pass through intervening creatures, which is highly useful for taking out summoners. Air Magicians also get the Silence spell, also of tremendous aid against spellcasters. This school, with Poison and Conjuration schools, combine to provide the potent early-game confuser Mephitic Cloud.

Earth Magic: Unique among the elemental attack spells, there is no special resistance against Earth attacks. They tend to be like physical strikes. Possibly the most useful spell in the game, Lehudib's Crystal Spear, is of this school. Utility spells are more frequent in this school than others, with Dig, Magic Mapping, Passwall, Shatter and Statue Form, among others, to choose from.

27

Crawl: Interesting Class and Race Pairs

February 2010 One special feature of the game is that nearly every one of the game's many races can also play all of the classes in the game, and vice versa, and do so in a reasonably consistent way that exposes interesting gameplay options. Unlike other games, Dungeon Crawl has found a way to keep classes differentiated, requiring different play styles, even into the late game, without actually preventing classes from doing anything. It is possible for a fighter type to learn magic and vice versa, but is it wise to put in the effort in doing this? Sometimes yes, and sometimes no.

Here we have a look at some of the many interesting combinations of race and role in Crawl, and their available paths (or lack thereof) to success. The specific combinations looked at are: Spriggan Enchanter, Deep Dwarf Paladin, Hill Orc Priest, Human Wanderer and Minotaur Chaos Knight of Xom.

27.1 Some Words about Engines and Recommended Classes

At the race and class selection screen, you may notice that some of the entries are displayed in light gray and some in dark gray. This is an indication of the Crawl Stone Soup developers' confidence on the survivability of these play options. Depending on which race you pick the names of different classes will be darkened; if you pick class first, then the names of different races will be darkened. Regardless of which race you select, Thief and Wanderer are always dark. Even though they're "grayed out," you can still pick any combination of the two; the only actual limits are those where picking a certain class implies following a god that is forbidden to that race. Those classes that are not grayed out are often those that have a good engine available.

What is an engine? It is one term for the mechanism a character uses to survive the dungeon. In most roguelikes this is a matter of walking up and hitting things, with occasional recourse to magic. In Crawl, the greater dangerousness of the dungeon makes this a bad idea for many characters. An engine is a gimmick, a special trick, a clever way around it that you end up relying upon. For example, Wizards beginning with the flame or frost spellbooks soon gain access to the spell Mephitic Cloud, which is applicable to many early-game situations and confuses many types of monsters. (*Note*: its availability and effect has changed in more recent versions, but describing how it used to work is still useful to explain.) It can be used to easily neutralize enemy spellcasters and hordes, sometimes even causing them to kill themselves accidentally. Confused monsters take more damage in melee, due to the stabbing rules. And if a monster is still too tough to beat, you can choose to just run away. An early game wizard's attack spells aren't that great, but Mephitic Cloud can keep them going to the point where they can be relied upon, and even some ways after that.

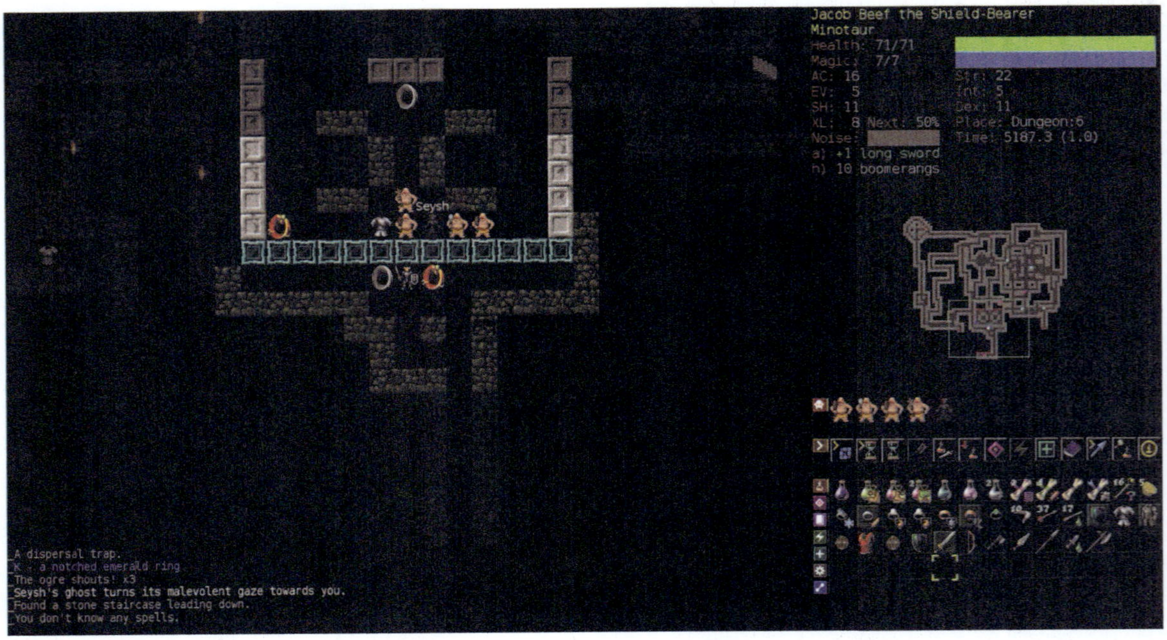

Figure 27.1

A ghost, a dangerous opponent in Dungeon Crawl

Mephitic Cloud is useful enough that it seems game breaking, and in a lesser game it might actually be. But all of the engines (that I know of at least; Crawl characters have many options available) have limits to their usefulness. Mephitic Cloud doesn't work against monsters that resist poison, or those that can't be confused. If you try to win the game with just Mephitic Cloud, you'll eventually reach a point where the engine stalls. At that point, you'll have to either improvise with whatever other resources you've found or die. Canny players will have used some of the experience income from those easy kills to have given their characters more options to use, but this, too, can be dangerous. A character with level 3 in everything is at a disadvantage compared to one who is level 10 in a couple of skills. Being able to intelligently determine which skills to focus on and which to ignore or turn off, this is the beginning of Dungeon Crawl wisdom.

Here are a few interesting race/class combinations. Due to the way Crawl's characters are diversified, some of these tricks apply to other classes of the same race, or other races of the same class. I leave most of those examples for you to find.

27.2 Spriggan Enchanter

"Sweet li'l wee faerie lethal assassin deadly death"

Spriggans are one of the more unusual races in Crawl, possessing a combination of very good and very bad attributes that would break the game if they weren't balanced against each other. In total I'd say they are balanced a little on the easier side, but they must still be played carefully enough that they require a little more skill than a novice is likely to have.

Spriggans are little fairy-like beings. They are unable to fly but are still very very fast characters. They are already so fast that some sources of hasting don't work on them! Unlike centaurs, another race that gets its advantage from speed but pays for it with a greatly increased hunger rate, Spriggans actually have the lowest basic hunger rate in the game. The trade-off comes from what they can eat. They begin with three levels of the "herbivore" mutation, meaning, they cannot eat meat at all.

There are several kinds of food that can be found in the dungeon. Usually the best type of food is meat rations, but Spriggans cannot even try to eat them, nor sausages or beef jerky. They also cannot eat "chunks," the bite-size fragments left over from butchering corpses. Chunks are emergency rations for most characters, an important fallback food in the event the level generator is stingy with the meal service. Even if the generator makes what would normally be sufficient food, Spriggans are still out of luck if it turns out to be meat. Once in a while this produces a game where no suitable food can be found for five or six whole levels. Spriggans' super-low metabolism means they might go up to three levels without having to eat, they always begin with a potion of porridge that provides lots of nutrition, and they get extra nutrition out of those food sources they can eat. Despite these things, it can still be a harrowing early game until that first bread ration turns up.

This isn't even the worst thing about them. They are also completely unable to use most armor! Their bodies are just too dang small to wear armor other than robes (or, strangely, troll leather or dragon armor), and neither can they wear boots, gloves or hats heavier than a cap. This dooms them to having an extremely low AC for most of the game. Low AC means having to play a lot more carefully than otherwise. Some work-arounds are dragon armor (which hinders spellcasting), transformations and the right kinds of mutations.

Furthermore, Spriggans get fewer hit points per level than other classes and can start with the lowest starting strength score in the game. If playing as a magic-using class, it is possible for a Spriggan to begin with a Strength score as low as 2! Dungeon Crawl does not protect players from having stats too low for survival, from whatever cause. If a Spriggan's Strength dips below 1 it dies immediately, even if only from carelessly wearing equipment that provides a minus to Strength. And in many areas they don't even have good magic skills to make up for it; Spriggans are awful at Conjurations, Summonings and Necromancy, the most directly useful types of combat magic, and their elemental magic skills are not that great either.

But as I said before, Spriggans still seem a little on the easy side, at least for the first half of the game, and the reason for that comes down, mostly, to their amazing speed. Faster-than-normal movement speed is an incredible advantage in a roguelike. Most other classes reach a moment of reckoning when they encounter ogres. Spriggans are one of the few classes that can handle them pretty safely, just by keeping their distance, loop dancing and chucking darts behind them along the way. Only a very few monsters can keep up with an unencumbered Spriggan. Being faster than opponents means being able to turn melee range into missile range almost at will, means being able to escape nearly any foe so long as they can get to a staircase in time, means faster exploration, means getting out of enemy sight range and then losing them at an intersection, and means being able to wade lithely through a horde of attackers and getting to a corridor before being surrounded.

Of the magic skills Spriggans are good at, they are amazing. They have extremely good Enchantments, Translocations and Transmutations learn rates, and excellent Divinations as well. In a combat situation, Enchantments is often their greatest ally. It contains the low-level spell Ensorcelled Hibernation, something that other games might call Sleep. This spell puts a chosen monster to sleep so long as it doesn't resist the spell. The way Crawl's sleep rules work, if the monster is asleep a character with even low Stabbing and weapon skill can do huge amounts of damage in one hit. And for some convenient reason, the one melee weapon skill Spriggans are good at, Short Blades, is the one that does the most Stabbing damage. Spriggans

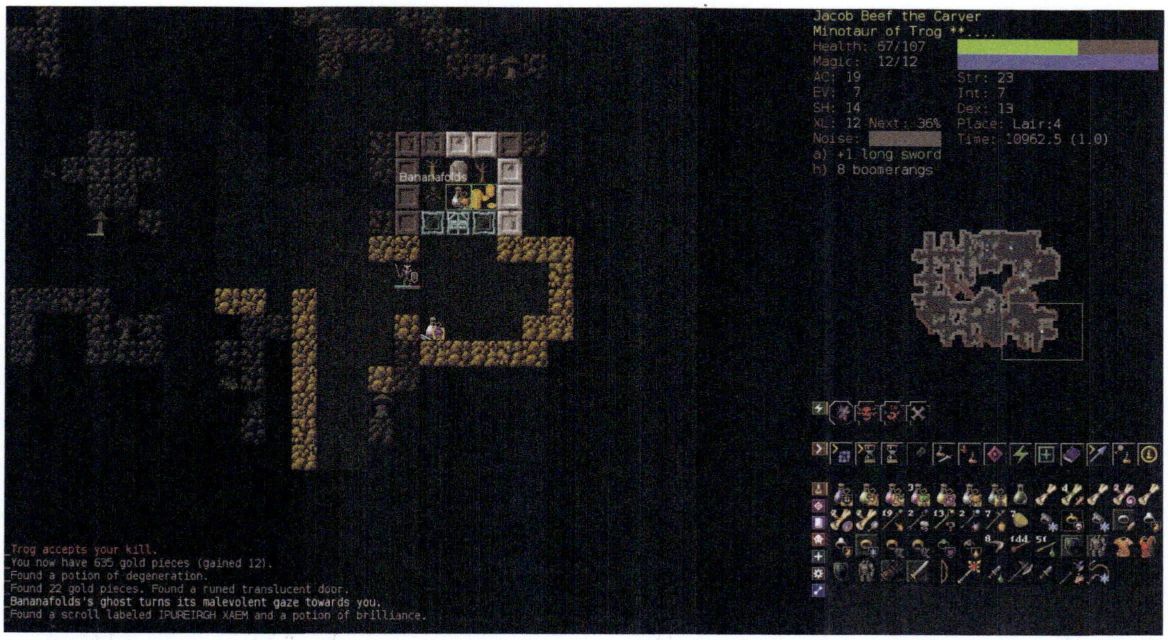

Figure 27.2

Another ghost.

are also naturally stealthy, gain Stealth skill quickly for becoming even more stealthy, can't wear hardly any heavy armor so don't wake monsters up that way, and are super-fast so they can close the gap between the edge of detection range and melee faster than any other race, so they might not even need to put a monster to sleep to stab it to death; they can often do this with monsters who are just taking a nap.

What this means is that Spriggans are what you might call nature's assassins. Even if you don't purposely try gaining Stabbing skill, you'll probably end up getting it accidentally anyway unless you go out of your way to wake monsters up before hitting them. And if you don't start with Stealth, unless you manage to find one of the few Spriggan-wearable types of heavy armor fast, you'll be getting that skill too. And Spriggans may be the only race that can make it pay off.

Whatever class you pick for a Spriggan, you'll want to rely on their missile skills and the magic skills they excel at, so you might as well get a head start in those areas by playing a Hunter or an Enchanter. Enchanter, in particular, is a great choice since your starting spellbook begins with Ensorcelled Hibernation, which makes 95% of monsters you encounter in the early dungeon, the Orcish Mines, the Lair and the Hive a piece of cake. With care and diligent training, you can one-shot hydras this way with minimal danger.

The biggest challenge to playing a Spriggan, besides the food problem, is their fragility. You don't want to get into melee with strong and awake monsters if you can help it. The nature of the game is that sometimes you end up in melee range of a monster without warning, and a small percentage of those occasions you won't be able to back away out of trouble. Slowly improving your Fighting skill and training Short Blades helps out a bit there, but the best solution is probably to teleport or blink. It is good that Spriggans also have an excellent Translocations aptitude.

All character builds have weaknesses, and Spriggan Enchanters have the most trouble with monsters who are even faster than they (there aren't many, but they exist), with cold-resistant monsters who can't be put to sleep with Ensorcelled Hibernation, with monsters that don't sleep to begin with like demons and with those few monsters who are entirely immune to Enchantments. Fortunately, most of these guys appear late enough that you will probably have found alternate means for handling them by that time, such as attack wands, or a hard-built Conjurations skill.

Good gods for Spriggans include Vehumet (who can help make up for their natural lack in Conjurations and Summoning), Sif Muna (who eventually will provide every spell in the game, good for making up for deficiencies) and, perhaps strangely, Nemelex Xobeh the gambler god, since he appreciates sacrifices of items and Spriggans can't use so much stuff they never lack for things to offer.

27.3 Deep Dwarf Paladin

"As unchanging as the mountains, and with the same capacity for healing"

Deep Dwarves are another special race type in Dungeon Crawl. Their gimmick is that, whenever struck for any amount of damage, they "shrug off" a number of points of it. This ability increases as they rise in level, and against basic opponents they frequently take no damage at all. It is much like the D&D attribute called "damage reduction."

The trade off, however, is huge. Deep Dwarves do not regenerate hit points naturally. The passing of time does nothing to lessen their wounds! And equipment, items or spells that work by increasing regeneration don't work either. All of the hit points that Deep Dwarves regain must come from magical or divine healing, and it happens that both are fairly rare in Crawl. The game simply has no analogue for D&D's Cure Wounds series of spells. (It seems the spells may technically be in the game, but their matching book never generates.) Potions of Healing and Heal Wounds are effective and common, but when they are a major source of healing you'll always find yourself wanting more.

A Wand of Healing, which can be zapped at yourself, can be recharged and takes up less weight than an equivalent stack of many potions, is one of the best solutions and Deep Dwarves always begin with one. They also can recharge wands as a special ability, although it costs them a maximum magic point to do it. Crawl's Max MP gaining rules are such that the lower your Max MP, the greater the chance you'll get more on a level increase or other source of gain, so this isn't quite as bad as it seems; the lower score subtly increases the chances of gaining more at higher levels. But it's still pretty harsh, so scrolls of recharging should probably be devoted towards refilling that wand.

Divine sources of healing are another way of getting hit points back. Mahkleb will sometimes heal you a point or two whenever you kill a monster once you get enough piety with him. The Shining One, who you conveniently begin the game with if you choose to play a Paladin, will sometimes heal you for several points of damage when you kill an "evil being." In the early game this includes zombies and imps, but also applies to orc mages and priests. One can also play as a Healer, which begins worshipping Elyvilon, and using the self-heal ability in a pinch. That carries a piety cost however. Classes not starting with a god can pick one up once they reach the Ecumenical Temple.

Even with damage reduction there are still plenty of monsters who can overpower that kind of advantage easily, and you'll probably be cannibalizing your Max MP to recharge your Wand of Healing, so it is probably best to abandon spellcasting and put on the hardest armor you can find. Don't forget, though, increasing Spellcasting skill can also provide you with the occasional extra Max MP, so it can be worth it to wait until you have experience pool to spare before reading identify scrolls.

In the long run, probably the hardest thing about Deep Dwarves is their healing limit. You only have so many potions, recharging scrolls and Max MP for charging that wand. It isn't hard at all to reach a point in the mid game where your character is powerful and ready to kick ass, but is down to 17 hit points with no means for regaining them.

27.4 Hill Orc Priest

"The center of the SWARM"

Hill Orc Priest is one of the most entertaining race/role combinations in Dungeon Crawl. It is nothing to do with the Hill Orc race directly, who are generally unremarkable as far as that goes. It has to do with Beogh, God of the Orcs, who is only available to orcs to worship, and who Hill Orc Priests have the opportunity to start out with. It is certainly an experience.

Consider, for a moment, the plight of the orc. Unloved, unappealing and the go-to-guys for evil wizards looking for muscle to help them take over the world. They do not have the most graceful manners, and they usually either look like pig-men or are green with tusks, depending on which artist is depicting them. That can't help their self-image any.

In the Book of Orc, the holy text of sacred (as far as that goes with an orc god) Beogh, it is told that one day a Chosen One will emerge to lead the Orcs up from their lowly position in the world. Orc priests tend to labor under the impression that they may be that chosen one. As a player race, they have a decent shot at it.

Playing a Hill Orc Priest basically means taking up the sandals of Orc Jesus. Followers of Beogh, fairly early in their career, pick up a very nice little ability. When they catch sight of a particular orc for the first time the game makes a die roll, influenced, I assume, by your piety level. If it's successful, the orc there and then greets you in a friendly manner and joins your team. There is no limit to the number of orcs you can have on your side, all flavors of orc may do this including uniques (the stronger ones may have to get beat down a bit first), and as individual orcs accumulate kills they gain power and can even promote into stronger forms, or gain magic or priest abilities. A friendly Orc Knight that has lasted a few dungeon levels is indeed a great friend, and allied Orc High Priests and Sorcerers, if you are lucky enough to score them, spam-summon friendly demons to aid your cause. While causalities are frequent, as many Crawl players discover early, there are a lot or orcs in the dungeon, so losses are easy to replace. It is that simple, and it is that awesome.

NetHack's pets can be useful to have, but you rarely get the opportunity to have more than two or three at a time due to the difficulty of getting them to the next dungeon level. Dungeon Crawl allows any allies who are visible, can reach your position and are within three spaces of you the chance to come along to the next level. That's up to 48 per trip! You even get an ability later on that lets you summon your henchmen to your side in an instant.

Playing as a Hill Orc Priest feels an awful lot like turning the tables on the dungeon, letting you field your own horde against the monstrous opposition, and does it ever feel good. Using the Ctrl-T command you can order your followers to scavenge the best items they find on the dungeon floor, which is a good way to make use of all those artifacts that tend to get generated that your skills are poorly matched for, or that plate mail +3 of magic resistance you can't make use of because your current plate mail of magic resistance is already +4. A well-equipped swarm of high-level orc knights, priests and sorcerers roaming the dungeon is amazing to behold and recommended to every roguelike player at least once. The funny messages your orcs supply as you traipse throughout the dungeons are icing on the cake. (Those of you who are wary of memes take heed of my warning: these particular orcs are quite loyal. They are known to inform you from time to time how they're never gonna give you up, and that they're never gonna let you down.)

The biggest drawback to leading your horde around is just the unwieldiness of commanding an army. It is very easy to leave orcs behind on a level, even with the Recall Followers ability, and if you accidentally hit one with an attack there is a chance both of him turning hostile and of Beogh giving you a smack for good measure. (Although the game is very good about warning you about that ahead of time.) If you abandon Beogh, your whole army will immediately turn hostile. So don't abandon Beogh, okay?

(*January 2016*: These days, the horde-gathering trick can be done by any hill orc if they manage to convert their religion to Beoghism! DCSS orcs are the first fresh take on orcishness I've seen in a long time. I love those guys.)

27.5 Human Wanderer

"Mr. Average"

Humans, as in many RPGs, are the utterly average race in Dungeon Crawl. All of their aptitudes are straight-average 100 except for Invocations and Evocations at 75 (which require having a god or magic item respectively and so their average is low to represent that outside aid) and Spellcasting at 130 (which is over 100 for everyone except Elves and Spriggans). Higher aptitude values mean the skill is harder for that class to learn.

Humans are the most flexible of all classes and have no explicit disadvantages in play. No class is restricted from them except Priest of Beogh (which, as already mentioned, is unique to Hill Orcs). This is actually a great drawback for human characters, since the game is balanced around the idea that characters will have some above-average ability to help them through the dungeon.

That is bad enough. Add to that the Wanderer character class, which starts the character out with basic equipment and random skills. It is quite possible to start out with a weapon the character has no skill with, and it's very likely that he'll have skill in some school of magic but no skill in Spellcasting, making them very difficult to use useless he's read enough scrolls to get Spellcasting to level 1.

On the race and class selection screen, there are combinations which are recommended, which are displayed in light gray, and combinations which are not recommended, showing up in dark gray. But the game does not actually prevent picking any combination of race and class so long as it isn't logically inconsistent, such as when trying to create a Demigod in a race that begins worshiping a deity.

Very few are forbidden, but lots are considered bad ideas depending on the intersection of race and role. But there are two classes that are considered "challenge classes," which are not recommended for any race. Thief is one of them, since thief skills are under-represented in Crawl and Assassins get most of their advantages and then some. The other, in case you haven't come to suspect it, is Wanderer.

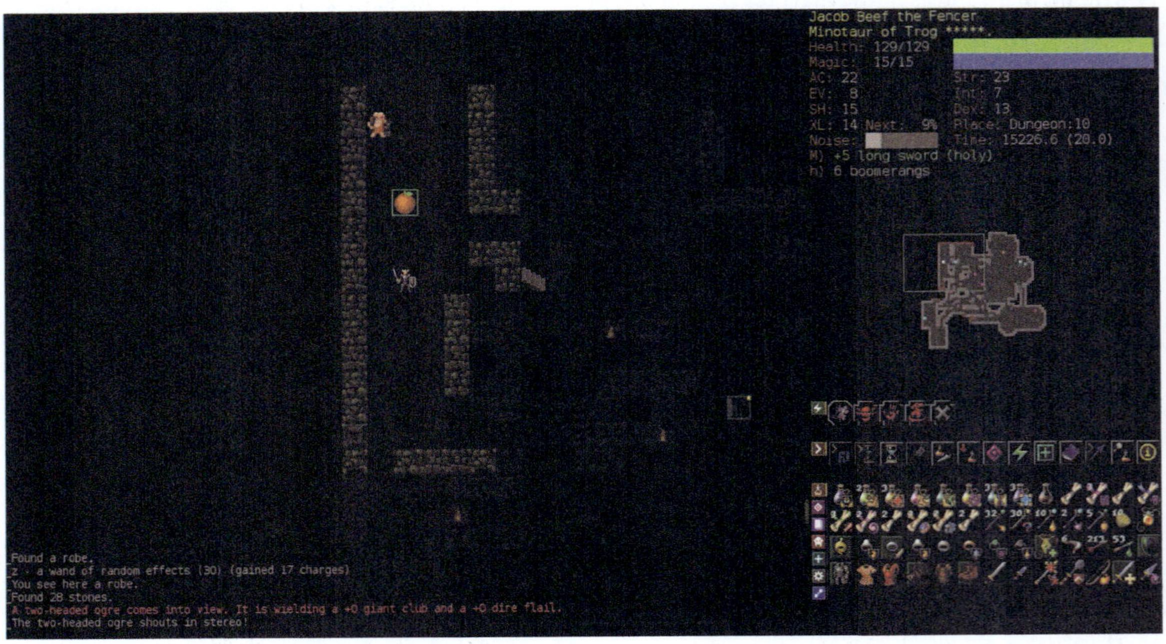

Figure 27.3

It is possible to luck out with a Wanderer. They never start with high skill in anything, but they can more reliably quickly specialize on the first attack-branded weapon they find and have a relatively easy time of the first levels of the dungeon, if they can survive that long.

27.6 Minotaur Chaos Knight of Xom

"Hail Nyarlathotep, the Crawling Chaos!"

So we come to Chaos Knights of Xom, which are almost the mascot of Dungeon Crawl.

Chaos Knight is a class that, like Priest, starts you out already following one of Crawl's deities. The class has a bit of melee emphasis thrown in to help out. When you're following Xom, every little bit counts.

Xom is unlike the other gods in that he doesn't just give you new abilities as you gain piety and follow the god's precepts and generally be a good member of the flock. Xom doesn't actually care what you do, so long as it's entertaining. Entertaining for him, not you.

Every so often, Xom will either do something for you, or do something to you. It could be something good or bad; Xom does have a persistent mood that carries forward through the game, but every time he acts there is a 1-in-5 chance of it getting set to a random value, meaning he can go instantly from absolutely loving you to trying to smash you beneath his shoe, and as quickly back. There is not a lot you can do to affect this, although you can tell generally how he feels by checking the ^ screen; if the message calls you a "plaything" then Xom's next action will probably be bad, if it calls you a "toy" then his next action will probably be good. There is no guarantee in either case.

Some of the good things for your character: being given a (sometimes) good item, the summoning of demon pets, getting granted good mutations, the polymorphing of a nearby monster or having a spell cast on your behalf.

Some of the bad things: being the target of random miscast effects, the summoning of hostile demons, getting inflicted with bad mutations, the polymorphing of a nearby monster or getting sent to the Abyss. Some of these bad things are very bad, although they are balanced (a bit) away towards being overwhelmingly deadly.

One instance in which this system doesn't apply is when Xom is bored, that is, you haven't done anything interesting lately. You get warned when this occurs. While bored Xom only does bad things to you. Just fighting monsters that are reasonably strong compared to you often counts as an interesting thing, but hanging around resting does not.

The key to understanding Xom is in realizing he is not just a system for intensifying Crawl's random number generator. You can use equipment and magic, as well as the better part of valor, to help alleviate the bad things and keep the good items and mutations, so in the long run—provided you can live that long—you should come out ahead. There is a greater variety of bad things he can do to you than good, though, and you should still be prepared to hoof it in a tight spot.

There are some other minor influences on Xom's behavior. He never does something directly lethal to you unless he's bored or he's attacking you for abandoning him. At those times, if an action would do so much damage that it would take you to zero or below hit points, then instead he won't do it. And his chances of doing something good goes up a little when you're in a fight with dangerous monsters, and down slightly if no foes are in sight.

28

Crawl: Travel Functions and Play Aids

March 2010 One thing new players to Crawl may find dismaying is the sheer size of the dungeon. Rogue, NetHack and ADOM have dungeon levels that fit on a single screen, but Crawl's maps are much larger, many more screens in size both vertically and horizontally. They aren't as large as Angband's, but Angband has transient levels anyway; once you leave a level, it is completely forgotten and cannot be returned to, so in a sense they are disposable.

Dungeon Crawl Stone Soup's levels are big enough that they pose challenges of information management for the player. And if a player has a good enough memory to handle them, or a pad and paper for writing things down, that works well, for a while at least. The game did little to help the player to keep track of it all for a while. In fact, the addition of the Travel Patch marks the root of the Crawl code fork that would become Stone Soup. (The Travel Patch and its role in Stone Soup's origins are detailed in a post at crawl.develz.org.) Since its introduction, Crawl has acquired an amazing array of automated play aids, far beyond the call of duty and unique in the roguelike world.

28.1 O: Auto-Explore

Let's start with the first one players tend to discover, auto-explore. When this feature is first discovered it feels almost like cheating. You press a key, not even a shifted one, and the game suddenly begins playing itself....

What happens when you activate auto-explore is: your character takes stock of the portions of the level not yet explored, finds the reachable unseen tile adjacent to its known area that it takes the fewest turns to reach, then pathfinds to it and tries to walk to that spot. Once he sees the target tile, he picks a new spot and tries to get to it. He continues to do this either until something interesting happens (like a possibly useful item is seen, a monster comes into view or a trap is found) or he runs out of new territory he can reach on the current level.

He will refuse to move through traps if he considers there to be any real danger from them and also will not cross dangerous ground or the range of particularly dangerous monsters like Oklob plants or hostile statues. Your smart little guy will automatically pick up useful objects along the way and seems to take their

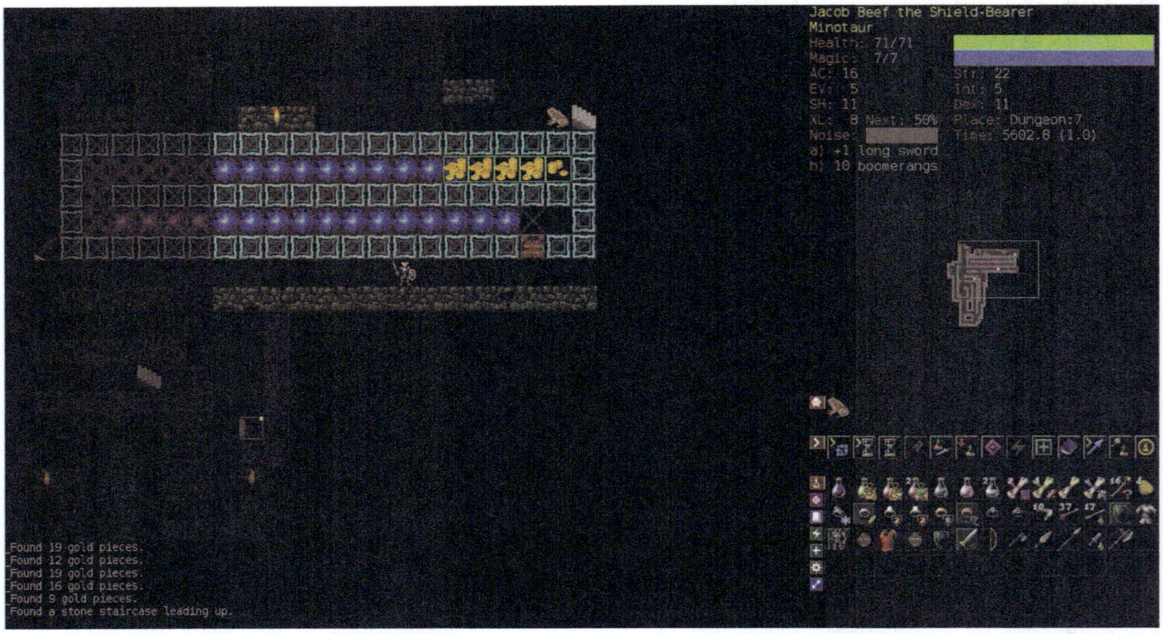

Figure 28.1

A special formation in the early dungeon.

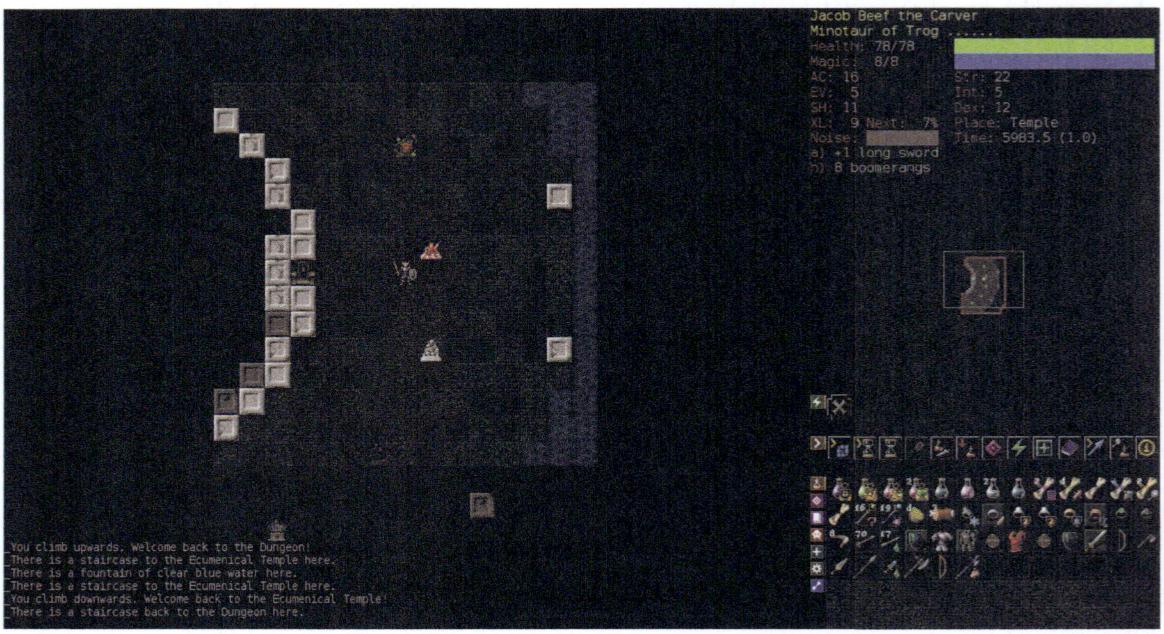

Figure 28.2

An entrance to the Ecumenical Temple

acquisition as a superseding priority. He even ignores items your character cannot use, like equipment a Spriggan cannot wear, eat or gain benefit from. In this respect, a Crawl character often knows how to play the game better than a newbie player.

Moving through Crawl's huge levels takes long enough that hitting a key for every step of the way takes a lot of time, so much that, after you start using auto-explore, it rapidly becomes difficult to see living without it. And it is strange but the nature of the game subtly changes through its use. You no longer have to worry about not spotting a monster and moving too close to it; auto-explore halts the moment so much as a rat

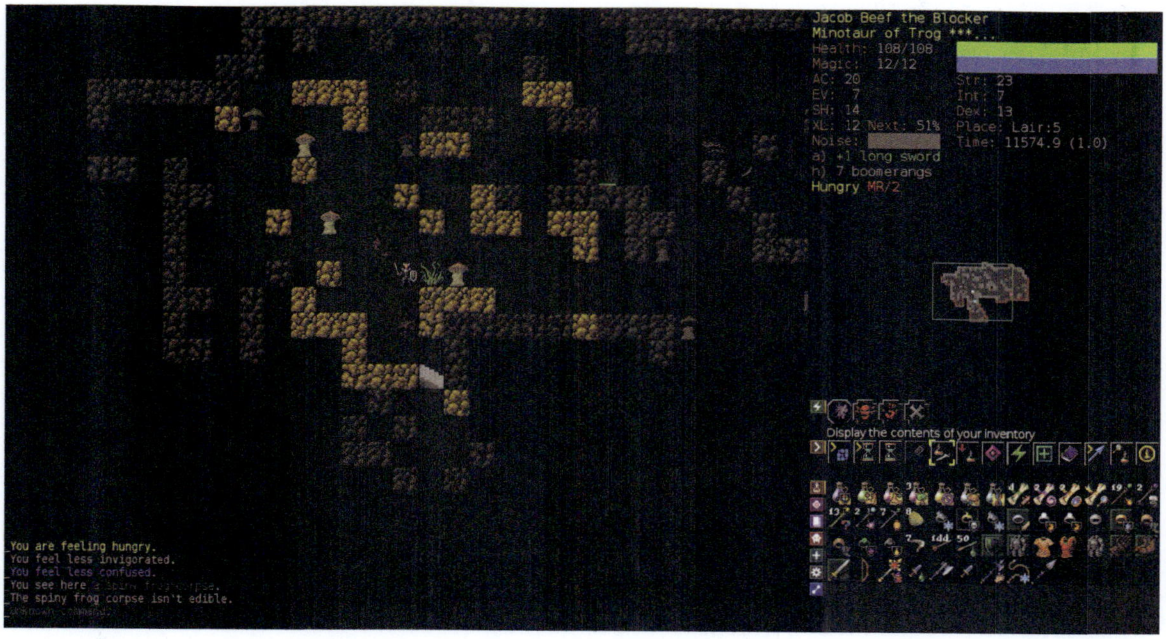

Figure 28.3

Searching for a meal in the Lair

enters sight. Running down long tunnels takes less than a second instead of half a minute. It even enters unseen shops automatically so you can note inventory! It turns the game, almost, into a kind of specialized random roguelike situation generator. And yet, if you ever need to manually walk through an area, all the old roguelike methods remain available.

28.2 Shift-X and Ctrl-G: Level Search and Autotravel

If you want to get to a location you've already been quickly, try hitting Shift-X. This brings up an interface through which you can cursor to the location you want to go and have the game automatically pathfind to it by pressing Enter. The same rules are in place about stopping for monsters and traps as in autoexplore.

Even better, if you hit > or < repeatedly, the game will cycle through all the down- or upstairs you've seen in the currently accessible region of the level, in order from closest (in turns needed to reach) to furthermost. Hitting the tab key will even cycle through shops the same way! Note: if you try this and for some reason the game doesn't want to jump to particular stairs or shops, it's probably because you've yet to find a way to that spot without leaving the current level.

Remember, Dungeon Crawl's level structure is sometimes complex, and it isn't rare for all three downstairs from a level to each lead to separate sections of the level below, and sometimes this discontinuity holds through multiple levels. If the game won't go to the spot you want, try going back upstairs and finding another way down first.

Here is where it gets freaky. What if you've gotten to the bottom of the Lair and realize you need to jump back to the Hive, found earlier in the game, to replenish your food stores? Crawl's levels being as large and complex as they are, the simple act of moving through all those dungeon levels could be a real chore. Wouldn't it be nice if you could just tell the game, in essence, to go to the Hive, and have it take care of all the moving and route finding for you?

Ctrl-G presents a list of all of the dungeon branches you've found so far in the current game along with a key letter for each. Enter the letter, then the number of the level you want to go to, and the game will start your character on his way without further input from you. It'll even find the fastest way there and will wind through other levels if need be.

Once in a while when you do this, the game will say it doesn't know how to get there. This usually happens when you fall down a shaft from a higher level and the explored zone you're currently in doesn't yet intersect with that of the destination. Try exploring a bit more, maybe moving a level closer to your goal manually,

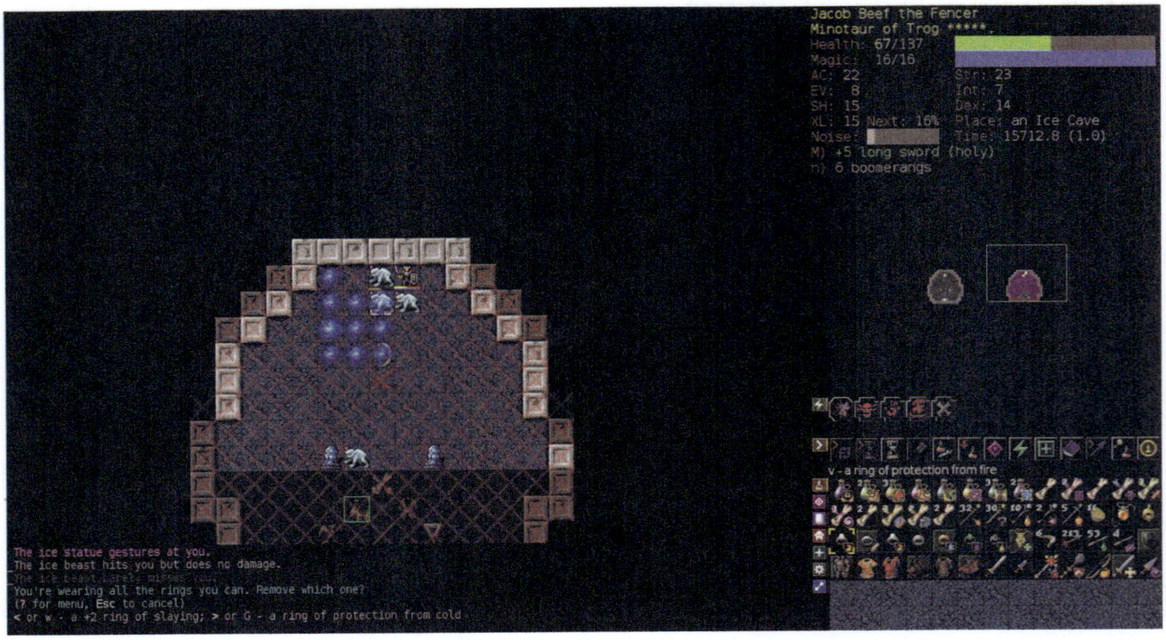

Figure 28.4

Ctrl-G: Level Autotravel.

then trying it again. If you just want to remember where a branch or shop is without traveling there, try Ctrl-O to bring up a helpful dungeon overview.

When a new feature is added to a game and, suddenly, you wonder how you ever did without it? That's a good sign that there was something wrong to begin with that you hadn't recognized. DCSS's travel options are unequaled among almost any game in terms of ease of use. They direct the player away from relatively uninteresting movement chores and focus attention on the items and monsters that make the game fun. It could be argued that some verisimilitude is lost in using them, turning the game into more of a situation generator than an integrated dungeon exploration game, but Crawl is so expansive that it arguably was a bit overdone in that regard.

28.3 Ctrl-F: Stash Management

In NetHack, did you ever find an item you really wanted but didn't want to risk going into Burdened or Stressed, so you left it there to find a good stash location for your less essential loot, but then discovered you'd forgotten where the item you wanted to pick up was?

Crawl has a solution to this kind of problem, and to my knowledge it is the only game that offers nearly so complete an item management system. The game remembers the name and location of every item you see throughout the entire game and allows you to do a text search through them. It will provide you with a list of all the items with names containing the words you specify, and you can pick from any of the hits to begin moving there. You can search for traps, shops and shop contents this way too. With some compilations you can even use regular expressions in your search! Not only is this useful for recalling the location of that object you saw several levels back, but it can even sometimes find objects your character saw but you overlooked.

You can also set a waypoint in the dungeon with Ctrl-W then specifying a number, then travel there by hitting Ctrl-G then that number, great for getting to that stash back in Lair:1 by the most expeditious means possible.

28.4 Other Player Helps

In addition to the question-mark help screens that all sane roguelikes provide, there are several other ways Crawl subtly helps the player to learn how to play. It contains a surprisingly helpful tutorial, for instance, not a mean feat in a game as randomly generated as Dungeon Crawl Stone Soup.

New players may wonder why different items and messages are printed in different colors. Items that are known to be bad to use (in their primary use, if they have more than one) are colored red, and useless items (like stuff you can't equip or that won't provide useable benefits) are dark gray. Artifacts show up in a brilliant white, whether identified or not; this is actually the easiest way to tell if an item is really special, since sometimes the attached adjective on an artifact is similar to one of Crawl's more-ordinary enchanted or ego adjectives. Messages, too, are color-coded by default, depending on the danger or benefit provided, or depending on their source.

29

Crawl: Dungeon Sprint

October 2010 You start up a game of Dungeon Crawl without thinking about it too clearly. You pick name, race and class. Afterward you're asked a question about which "map" you want to play. What does it mean by that? Who cares, let's just get started. You pick the first and begin in a room with one door out, to the right. You go through.

It's Ijyb with a wand of negative energy?! He zaps you and you DIE? What?!

You start a new game, with all the same options. Weirdly, you start in the same room, and through the door is Ijyb again. This doesn't seem very random. . . . You manage to kill Ijyb (he doesn't seem to have the wand this time), and you get a whole experience level for killing him. But in the next room is an ogre. Smack! You die again.

A few games later you get through Ijyb and, somehow, the ogre as well. At experience level 4 after killing two monsters you feel pretty smug, so naturally Sigmund himself waits beyond the next door.

What probably happened was that you accidentally started your game in a special mode included as part of the newest version. Welcome to Dungeon Sprint, Dungeon Crawl's rather more intense variant, now included as part of the 0.7 release.

Dungeon Sprint is an entire game of Dungeon Crawl condensed into a single level. The level is mostly set; randomness comes into it only slightly, putting the focus on set situations above throwing together random challenges. The game doesn't pull punches in difficulty, but you gain 27 times more experience than normal! Countering this, the monsters are very strong relative to your level. The game constantly provides monsters at the upper-end of your ability to defeat.

This makes for a much sharper experience. You either lose or win big, constantly, time after time. Actually I wouldn't doubt it if you graphed character deaths relative to degree of game completion, if the game weren't actually that much harder than standard Dungeon Crawl. You die a lot more often from having your face spiked to the dungeon floor by enemy weapons, but in standard Crawl you die a good portion of the time through plain bad luck. The more times the dice are rolled the more chance they have to come up snake eyes. Reducing the length of the game actually works in the player's favor, which balances out the tougher opponents.

29.1 On Choices: Map, Race and Role

Dungeon Sprint is played on custom maps supplied with the game. The current distribution comes with two choices. Most of my Sprint experience comes from playing the map "Red Sonja," which starts out with the Ijyb/ogre/Sigmund combination described in the opening. The game starts you out with potions of speed and berserk rage and a scroll of blinking, but there are few other guaranteed items. One of the toughest monsters in the early game is Sonja herself, a unique kobold who's fast, can blink, usually wields a sword of distortion and is armed with curare needles. Even one of these things could prove deadly; all of them at once makes for an obstacle that must be treated seriously every game. Useful tactics I've found are ducking behind walls to force her to approach without getting curare'd to death, and using the guaranteed potions of healing and speed you start with to nullify poisoning if it does happen. Spellcasters could use Confuse and Mephitic Cloud to cause Sonja to stop shooting from a distance, or summoning to put obstructing bodies to fight and shoot through between you and her. Closing to fight with her hand-to-hand is hazardous; she can blink away and resume firing easily, and if a needle hits you get strong-poisoned and slowed, meaning you'll probably get hit again several times before you can close again.

One thing that Dungeon Sprint's ramped-up challenge does do is increase, even more, the importance of picking a good character. On Red Sonja, so far I've gotten farthest with my "old standby" character, a Spriggan Enchanter, although I usually have to drink the starting potion of berserk rage to get through Ijyb and the ogre. At level 2 such a character will gain enough spell levels to learn Ensorcelled Hibernation and start with the stabbing of things. But while in normal Crawl this phase of the game can get the player almost through the whole midgame, Sprint's advanced competition make this tactic less reliable. I've managed to get to around experience level 12 this way, but that was with good luck finding things in shops. A major gimmick of the Red Sonja map is that there are many treasure rooms filled with gold and several completely random shops that you mostly rely upon for items. Spellcasting races who don't find a bookshop are recommended to hook up with one of the game's two main spellbook-providing gods, Sif Muna or Vehumut, to gain access to magic outside their starting book.

Another spellcasting race I've had some success with is Deep Elf Wizards, who begin able to memorize Summon Small Animal out of their starting spellbook. That one spell lasts you surprisingly long; it costs only one magic point to cast and it doesn't take much skill with it to call multiple animals per casting. All those little teeth chewing away at once can take down the ogre without much trouble; Sigmund likes to go invisible, but once he's opaque again the Rat Army will prevail. The combination hits its first major challenge when it reaches the jelly, which when wounded likes to eat nearby doors to heal, revealing monsters rather stronger than you're ready for.

One note: be careful about classes whose main abilities come from teleportation. Means of teleportation other than blinking are disabled in Dungeon Sprint.

29.2 Sprint: Dungeon Crawl Intensified

I may actually like Dungeon Sprint a little better than stock Crawl, because you don't end up playing for six hours only to die while trying to get a third Rune. If you're going to die, it's gonna happen fast, and then you can try again. It gets to the good stuff much more rapidly. A more randomized version of Sprint might be quite interesting. The other map included in 0.7, "The Violet Keep of Menkaure," seems to recognize this, but seems rather harder than Red Sonja. Sprint's theme of a game where the player is always pushed to the edge of his ability is harder to balance well with randomly generated opponents.

The stereotype of the normal role-playing game, a long quest that takes the player through a lengthy story and allows him to play a character through many adventures, actually works less well for roguelikes since every minute a game continues effectively increases the stakes a little bit. In this, Dungeon Sprint is one of the most interesting roguelike games I've seen recently. It takes Dungeon Crawl's quick-start philosophy and then removes the somewhat-tedious early-level exploration. It's not a game for beginners but works well for players who are already familiar with much of the game's strategy and lore. I suggest you give it a try; there is a lot to like.

29.3 To Save a Few Dozen Lives: A Guide to the Early Rooms

What follows is strategy discussion of the early stages of the Red Sonja map. If you want to find everything out for yourself, you may want to stop reading now. Dungeon Sprint feels a lot like classic "old school" dungeon crawling, where the surprise is part of the fun, but the dungeon is so hard that you're unlikely to complete it on your first, or even your hundredth, try. You might want to come back to it if you try playing Sprint but get stuck.

This map is of the areas most commonly seen by early characters. The walls are black, the doors are brown, secret doors are purple, yellow represents treasure (usually gold), shops are dark green, and random

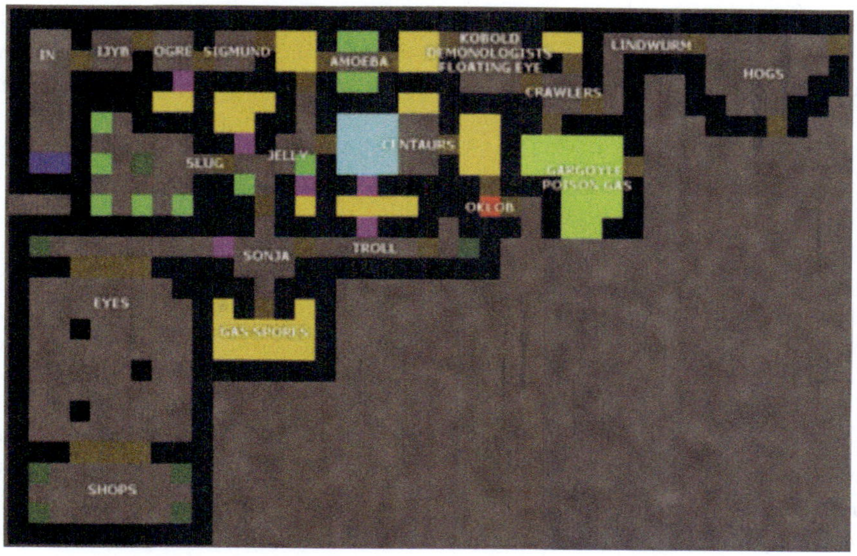

Figure 29.1

Map of early areas of Red Sonja (circa 0.6.0)

altars light green. Don't confuse either of those, however, for the poison gas area, which contains neither. Some other aesthetic colors are used as well.

As alluded to in the introduction, most of the monsters are contained in their own rooms, and your survival desperately depends on your ability to keep them out of your hair before you're ready for them. This puts an emphasis on stealth, another reason stabbing-type characters have a bit of an advantage. Magic users should be careful not to use loud magic; a lightning bolt is a fine attack spell in many cases, but not when it'll pull in centaurs, Sonja and kobold demonologists all at once.

Here is a description of each marked area:

In: The entrance. This room is a good place to exercise your starting 25 experience points and memorize a spell if you can. The dark blue spaces are fountains.

Ijyb: The first monster in the dungeon is a moderate challenge. Melee types can probably take him, but spellcasters might have to use one of their starting potions to kill him. Poison works well against him and the other two starting humanoid opponents.

If you choose Speed you might be able to get through Ijyb, the ogre and Sigmund on one potion if you're lucky, but you'll probably also have to drink a heal wounds potion before it's over. Surer is your potion of bezerk rage, which if drunk while standing by the door to the ogre room can pretty reliably take out both monsters before it wears off; be sure to let it expire and then wait for the slow period to wear off before opening the next door!

Ijyb is often generated with a wand or a potion of his own. Stalker-types who manage to one-shot stab him before he wakes up can take this item for themselves.

Ogre: Many games will end here; this ogre isn't any weaker than the ones who frequently kill unwary characters in standard Crawl, there aren't any pillars to dance around with this one, and you're probably only level 2 to boot. He is well-capable of killing even melee types in a single hit. My suggestion is to drink your potion of berserk rage, and if you're going to do that you might as well have taken Ijyb out with it too. (Sigmund is more dangerous; if he goes invisible you probably won't be able to kill him before the potion wears off.)

Sigmund: The soldier ant of Dungeon Crawl, in the standard game Sigmund is probably the deadliest unique relative to when he appears. By the time you reveal him you're probably at experience level 4. He'll probably turn invisible if he wakes up; if a stalker-type doesn't kill him before then he might have a problem.

A good spell to use on him, if you have it, is Mephitic Cloud, since he can't cast spells if he's confused. Stalker-types often can learn it by now. He can also confuse you, though. A tough opponent, know that once you manage to get past him consistently you're well on your way to becoming an advanced Crawler.

Amoeba: If you're sure of yourself you can try to take this monster out a little earlier than you'd usually and get access to these four random altars.

Unlike the humanoids preceding it, this giant amoeba is immune to poison, so you can't Sting it for damage or Cloud it to confuse. This is a much stronger opponent than Sigmund; fortunately, it's slow and can't open doors. Some character types might be able to stab or slash it to death; if you can't, take advantage of its slow speed by luring it back into the starting room, running by and closing the door behind you. Even if you come back with many more levels it's possible to get killed if you underestimate this dangerous blob of cytoplasm.

Jelly: If you melee this monster you stand a good chance of having your armor and weapon corroded. It's not marked on the map, but there's actually a couple of items in the entrance to this room; if you run from the jelly without picking them up, it will eat them and heal, or even multiply. (It can even do this during a normal move, which seems almost buggy.) This multiplication, however, is one of the few opportunities you'll have to get ahead of the expected experience level. It's not that big a deal in the long run; you're starting to approach the period where experience requirements are great enough you won't be gaining levels as quickly. Note: unlike the amoeba, jellies are not immune to poison. But also unlike the amoeba, jellies are not hindered by closed doors. There are two random altars in this room, and secret doors to some items. The items are usually gold, but sometimes items appear in the bottom room.

After dispatching the jelly, most characters will want to kill the giant slug to the left.

Slug: A giant slug is a slow but very strong opponent. It will be difficult to confuse, but if you retreat and let it chase you you'll have many chances to use magic on it. Strong melee characters might be able to just smack it to death, but don't try this if you don't have lots of hit points and good healing. In emergencies it can be ditched in one of the starting rooms.

In the room beyond the slug are five altars and what is probably the first shop you've seen. Shops provide options and advantages outside of the "usual" game of Dungeon Sprint, and this map provides you with plenty of funds, so you should closely examine the inventory of every shop you find for useful objects.

Sonja: The map's namesake, she's described in the text above. Be very cautious about opening that door! Its proximity to a potentially door-eating jelly is dangerous.

One way to handle her is invisibility then sneaking up and stabbing, but that tends to be highly dependent on race and role. The Repel Missiles spell is valuable if you have it, although it's not infallible. That potion of healing you begin with cures poisoning. The slowness caused by her curare needles can be negated with one of your starting potions of speed. Summoners might be able to spam her to death with summoned animals. She is usually (but not always) generated with a sword of distortion that allows her to blink away. If you kill her, that sword can be a powerful asset, but remember that unwielding distortion weapons can be dangerous. Finally, you should know that there is a slim chance upon her striking you with it that you might get banished to the Abyss. That might actually be helpful since that means random monsters with experience points outside the set amount contained in the level, but it's possible to get overwhelmed with foes while there. If you do get banished, keep moving, keep your eyes open for exit portals, stay away from monsters, and don't let yourself get trapped.

Gas Spores: It's more than possible for an unlucky character to open the door, for one of the two spores on the other side to get the first move, move adjacent to the player, explode immediately for high damage, and in the process set off the other spore which also immediately explodes. I have had a character die from this, no other actions after opening the door. At the very least you should be at full health before swinging it open. On the other side is a fairly large amount of treasure but no other exits, so it can be safely skipped. Keep in mind that, since the previous chapters on Crawl, gas spores have learned a new trick: they now sometimes leave behind ballistomycetes when they detonate. You don't get credit for killing a Gas Spore until you've killed all its ballistomycetes.

Eyes: This room offers little direct danger, but it can potentially make your character unplayable if not treated with respect. The room contains two floating eyes and a few shining eyes. Neither can harm the player directly, but the giant eyeballs can paralyze you for several turns with a glance, which is often fatal if a monster with a physical attack is around. Giant Eyeballs are one of the few monster types that is not shut down from confusion. The shining eyes have a mutation gaze attack. The mutations could be either good or bad, but usually you won't be getting the good ones from their attacks.

Several shining eyes gazing at once can quickly turn your character into a mutant freak, and being frozen in place by giant eyeballs while it happens is even less fun. It's best to lure these babies back into Sonja's room, or farther, and kill them one at a time. Still, some mutation is almost unavoidable unless you manage to one-hit them or have come across a source of mutation-resistance. They can't open doors, so maybe you can trap some in the early rooms. Shining eyes are worth a lot of experience. There is little direct danger here, so if you're stuck you can pretty easily smack your way through here to the room beyond . . .

Shops: Your reward for making it through the eyes is this room with four random shops. There are no other exits, so you can skip the eyes if you need to. Keep in mind, the hall immediately in front of the eye room contains one shop.

Troll: On the other side of Sonja's room is this Troll. There is also treasure in this room (which I neglected to depict). By this point a troll may not be all that difficult of a foe, but it can still pack a wallop. At the end of the hallway is a shop. North is a secret door hiding even more treasure.

Centaurs: At the right-hand side of this room are two centaur warriors, quite dangerous foes. Working in your favor is the fact that this room is naturally hazy, often blocking line-of-sight to you from their deadly arrows. Working against you is the shallow water blocking both entrances to this room; if you just step splash into the puddle you'll wake the archers and then you'll probably have a hard time surviving. Repel Missile spells work fairly well. Better would be a way to levitate over the water so you can stab them (provided you're playing a stabby type). Confusion spells are another useful tactic against missile firers.

Oklob: South of the centaurs' treasure room is a one-space chamber containing an oklob plant, one of the most obnoxious monsters in Crawl. Oklobs take huge amounts of punishment and shoot powerful corroding blasts at you while you're in line-of-sight of them. The textbook way of destroying an oklob is with a disintegration wand, but chances are high you haven't found one by the time you encounter this room. I've yet to look at the passage beyond, even though it's technically possible to get into it without killing the plant by moving diagonally from doorway to doorway.

Kobold Demonologists and Floating Eye: If you keep going beyond the amoeba room you find these tricky opponents. Kobolds of whatever level are not very strong, but their being demon summoners put the odds in their favor. Most tricks like confusion, poisoning, sleeping and the like don't work well against demons and, being summoned creatures, they don't even give you any experience points. If you can kill the kobolds and then run, eventually the demons will expire naturally. Keep that in mind.

The kobolds alone would be bad enough, but there's also a giant eyeball in here. Unlike the one in the eye room, this one accompanies monsters who hit for damage, so this is a dangerous room even for high-level characters. It's your choice which is the greater priority: kill the kobolds before they can summon demons so it doesn't matter if the eye paralyzes you (difficult, as there are two summoners), or kill the eye first so it can't freeze you in place while infernal claws cut you to ribbons.

Crawlers: This room contains four demonic crawlers to harass you even if you somehow wipe out the kobolds without trouble. They are not actually extremely difficult monsters, but their demon nature gives them a lot of resistances. Frequently when you approach this room the door will already be open, for some reason.

Gargoyle + Poison Gas: The gargoyle is actually a *metal* gargoyle. Making it tougher is the poison gas clouds that infest this area. Poison gas can cause confusion, making getting out of the clouds harder than getting in. There are also traps throughout this room.

Lindwurm: A low-level dragon with fire breath. It's a good thing that it seems relatively easy to sneak up on for stealthy characters.
Hogs: After all of the trouble with the other rooms this room is something of a break. This entire room is filled with hogs, which are fairly ordinary animal monsters. They're not weak, but they don't have resistances, and they're still worth good experience.

This is a good room to end with. If you continue on you'll find hydras and fire giants, divas and Pandemonium Lords. There's gold to find, too, and lots of treasure. It's good to use the shops as larders, coming back to them as you get the money for them and cleaning them out of the good stuff. Red Sonja's map packs a lot of Crawl's most interesting special obstacles in close proximity to each other, including multiple types of special gasses, transparent walls and deep water, so stay on your toes.

Section V
ADOM

30

ADOM, NetHack with a Goatee

February 2007 This is a game that does things that sometimes defy belief.

Many people have wondered over the sheer range of possibility here. They see the huge array of random items. They see wishing and item transformation, altars and prayer. They see that players can eat dead monsters and gain (and lose) abilities from their meal. That items can be blessed and cursed, and have different effects depending on that state. The tremendous variety of monsters. That players can take potions of water, make holy water out of them at an altar, then use that to bless other items. They see that the game implements special rules on certain real-world dates, like Friday the 13th.

All of these things, as we've covered before, are true of NetHack. But now, we are not talking about NetHack. We're taking a look at a copy of NetHack that came to our world after falling through a wormhole from a mirror universe. We're looking at ADOM.

That ADOM bears so many features first seen in NetHack indicates pretty strongly that its creator and maintainer, Thomas Biskup, was inspired by that game, and borrowed many of its aspects. And like NetHack, there is far too much to say about the game in one chapter. I shall attempt to give a good initiate's-eye view of the thing. Again, and as usual, I am more concerned with examining the game's play, its innate coolness and its problems than with avoiding spoilers, although, again as with NetHack, most players must be spoiled greatly to have even a slim chance at winning.

(*December 2015*: ADOM has returned to active development lately, so some of this may no longer apply. *January 2020*: It's even on Steam now, with graphics and a new interface!)

30.1 The Guise of the Overworld

Perhaps the first thing that players notice upon beginning a game is that they do not begin in a dungeon level or town, but in a screen-sized overworld map reminiscent of (although less graphical than) those from some of SSI's Gold Box AD&D games. The map is dotted with towns, clearings and dungeons, some challenging to find, and some accessible only by finding routes through some of the dungeons.

Some of the dungeons are relatively small, while others, such as the Caverns of Chaos and the accurately named Infinite Dungeon, are much larger. They usually start easy and get tougher the deeper a player gets, but there are exceptions ready to catch the unwary, as anyone happening upon Darkforge will discover.

One thing that's important to note about this map is that it is not randomly generated, but is always the same. Although the actual dungeon layouts and item identities are mixed up anew for each game, the properties of the dungeons and towns do not change. But this is not necessarily a point against ADOM, for no major roguelike has yet to make random overworld generation work satisfactorily. Some of ADOM's dungeons are uncommonly harsh if entered at the wrong time, so it is possibly a good thing that the player can know which these are with experience.

30.2 Our Very Special Quest Stars

ADOM's quests, as with much of the rest of the game, can be considered either good or bad things. To many they will be both. Roguelikes are usually relatively straight-forward games which, while they may have the occasional detour into a dungeon branch for some necessary object, are still primarily played from the surface down. New players can generally keep hitting the downstairs and be reasonably assured they're going in the right direction.

This contrasts with ADOM's complex itinerary of dungeons, levels and opportunities. Some of them become unavailable after certain game thresholds, or are open only during a small window of the player's adventuring career. If a player doesn't know how to talk to people (Shift-C, for Chat) then some locations, which can only be entered after talking to particular folk, won't even appear on the map. Most roguelikes can be explored, though maybe not survived, easily by new players and, while their chances of success may be minimal at first, at least they can be assured that they aren't missing out on something happening halfway across the world that they aren't even aware of, simply because they hadn't met some invisible appointment. ADOM does not have that assurance.

The game is still winnable, overall, despite this, but there are special opportunities for players who know what's up.

30.3 For the Love of Purple 't'

The quests themselves are pretty cool, and sometimes they contain surprising verisimilitude. Some of the types of challenges a player may engage in are unknown anywhere else in the roguelike genre. To pick one easily observed example, there is an early quest in which the elder of a village asks the player to ease the suffering of the village carpenter, who has gone crazy and run off to the bottom of a nearby dungeon. The wording of the quest is such that the player considers that he is expected to kill the carpenter to accomplish this. However, on level 4 of that dungeon is a healer, who helpfully offers to heal the player should he speak to him.

Early in my own ADOM-playing binge, which took place while the game was still under active, heavy development, on one of the first visits to the dungeon, I got it into my head to try something strange. What would happen if I lured the carpenter, who follows the player through the dungeon and will also chase him up through staircases, to the healer? Would the two fight? I was startled to discover that the healer then healed the carpenter, restoring his sanity and causing him to drop some items! Later versions of the game even made this a prerequisite for learning the Healing skill and Bridge Building skills.

(*December 2015*: When reviewing this piece for publication, the game I was most reminded of with its alternate solutions to confrontation, perhaps oddly, is Undertale. Brogue also lets you get out of most encounters without fighting, or at least the player isn't penalized for avoiding killing monsters, but there is no exclusive benefit to either pacifism or violence.)

The experience of happening, purely by accident, across this interaction played a big role in my early fascination with the game. I suspect the players who come to love ADOM, who discover this kind of thing through spoilers, cunning or accident, feel the same way about it. However, it can also be seen as one more instance where spoilers are practically required to win at the game; the Healing skill, which improves hit point regeneration, greatly helps the player in making headway into the game, yet it is easy to kill the carpenter accidentally or for survival's sake, making it harder to acquire.

But because of this proliferation of quests, there are times when ADOM doesn't feel quite as random as it should be. The items that are found in a play of a roguelike game determine its character. A game of NetHack with, as a lucky friend of mine discovered recently, Mjollnir resting happily at the player's feet on the starting square of the game will feel different from one where artifact weapons are harder to come by, or one with few scrolls of identify, or one with an early ring of slow digestion, or pair of speed boots and so on.

But NetHack also contains a number of hard-coded items and areas, and sometimes that makes the game feel less random than it should. ADOM, unavoidably, has the same problem.

30.4 Why Is the Trollish Warrior Fleeing from That Kitty-Cat?

Another prominent example of an element of ADOM that is difficult to discover without spoilers or being bitten, in this case one that could result in the end of a player's first potentially winning game, concerns cats. There are three monsters in ADOM that are considered to be of this type: wild cats, cave lions and cave tigers. As far as monsters go they are apparently ordinary, just another monster type in a game that also contains dogs, rats, spiders, lizards, bears and greater molochs, but there is a secret peril regarding them.

Late in the game there is a guaranteed monster, the Cat Lord, whose strength is proportional to the number of cats slain by the player during his adventures. There is no known maximum to the strength he can attain through this, and it is possible for him to become a rude surprise indeed. If the player manages to kill no cats on his quest, the Cat Lord will actually be peaceful and give the player a very powerful item for his trouble. But this Cat Lord business is remarked upon hardly anywhere in the game; it's only alluded to in a fairly obscure way, hardly enough warning to prompt a player to avoid killing all of a certain type of monster (which tend to get in the way at the least opportune times) unless, of course, he's already been spoiled.

It is not my job to apologize for roguelikes, but to honestly report on them for good or ill, and in the end all roguelikes, even those supposed friendly towards novices, like Rogue and Crawl, have this problem built into their design. It is just a bigger version of that shock players receive upon first encountering a powerful, previously unknown monster. ("A capital T, huh? How hard could it be?") But the further a player gets through a roguelike, in which the game must be begun anew after each loss, the more it stings. And when that loss comes from a hitherto unknown, seemingly arbitrary cause, it stings hard.

With ADOM, these stings are many. Kill a cat? Bad move. Hit a karmic lizard with a melee weapon? Bad move. Stand on an altar with an intelligent monster nearby? Really bad move. Once again, NetHack also has its fair share of arbitrary peril, as anyone who's smacked a floating eye knows, but at least in that game, for the most part, it is the obviously fantastic beasts and objects that cause the problems.

ADOM reserves a special kind of smackdown for people who kill cats. Because of this, and a great many other idiosyncrasies, it is difficult to recommend the game to roguelike newcomers.

Although really . . . it hardly matters what roguelike game you choose, you're in for some version of this. Even Dungeon Crawl Stone Soup, which takes great pains to avoid being unfair to the player, still teaches through death sometimes. It is a difficult mode of play to avoid for this kind of game, at least while still remaining challenging.

30.5 Damnation by Degrees

Perhaps ADOM's most defining element is corruption, by which is meant a series of mutations that the player's character undergoes during the game according to a timer. There are 19 corruptions in the game, each of which being a different, specific mutation the player undergoes, and they function as both rising difficulty level and an ultimate time limit on the game. If the player lives without winning long enough eventually they'll all happen, in random order. Some of them are helpful, but most are mixed blessings. A couple, Poison Hands and Mana Battery, are obnoxious effects that make it extremely difficult for the player to make use of some of his inventory. (*April 2020*: There are now more possible corruptions in ADOM, and you are not guaranteed to encounter all of them.)

If a player receives all the corruptions, he only has a little while longer to play before he devolves into a puddle of chaos. Like Rogue's food supply, this isn't a hard limit but can be pushed back by using certain items (some are available for completing specific quests) or by wishing for them. There is a quest that will wipe a player's corruption slate clean once. Still, corruption removal is rare enough that none of these means can (typically) be relied upon indefinitely, and there exist traps, items and especially monsters that can corrupt a player early. Players who never get past the midgame may not even know that corruption exists, or that it's time based, because there is a good buffer of radiation that can be absorbed before the first corruption occurs, because many early locations in the game have no "background corruption" that hurries the clock, and because corruption doesn't become a big problem until the 90th day, when the rate doubles. Once the player gets in gear and begins exploring dangerous areas, corruption is unavoidable and must be taken into account in any long-range strategy.

30.6 The Bizarre Cathedral

One thing about ADOM that bears mentioning is the fact that, unlike almost all the other roguelikes currently played today, it is not open source. It is beer-free, not freedom-free. (Dec 2015: These days, the Steam version ordinarily goes for $14.99.) The reasons Thomas Biskup gives for keeping the source to himself, and a handful of people who write ports to other operating systems, varies according to the citation: that he prefers to keep some aspect of mystery in the game; that he'd like for there not to be a plethora of variants such as with Angband (although its variants are common because of the relative ease of modifying that game); that he was scared by some people who angrily demanded, via email, the source; that he someday plans to make a commercial version with graphics; and that it wouldn't be as much fun for him to write it if others were looking over his shoulder.

Whatever the reason—and with it being his program, he doesn't have to give one—it does preserve some aspect of mystery in the game's workings. The route to the "ultra" endings of the game, special extra quests that can be completed for greater glory, took dedicated players on the ADOM Usenet group a long time to determine. To this day, despite the presence of that special brand of obsession only diehard roguelike players can muster, there are still things about the game that are not known. Meanwhile the promiscuously open source NetHack has no mysteries to the sufficiently determined, and there are dozens of die-hard players and modders who can quote the source chapter-and-verse.

But there are also real disadvantages this decision presents to the game's maintenance. Of course there is the quality argument, for there are almost always bugs in a computer program and the more eyes looking the fewer there will be, but it also presents problems for its design.

NetHack's vaunted verisimilitude did not arise fully-formed from one person's brain, or even entirely from within its DevTeam, but from the work of many dozens of developers submitting their modifications. A good proportion of the most-recently added features originally came from popular variants NetHack+ and SLASH'EM, variants which could never have existed if the source were not open. Over time, many of the rough edges of NetHack's design have been worn down by a legion of coders, each fixing what they cared about, and adding stuff as they liked. As noted earlier, there are many patches in existence now that arguably improve the game. NetHack grew up through the accretion of these patches, but ADOM relies entirely upon the skill of one person. At the best, an open source game can seem like the product of a godlike intelligence, greater than any one of its contributors, but ADOM is the product of Thomas Biskup, and whatever brilliances or blindnesses it has are, for better or worse, his.

In the end, the greatest danger is that the game will eventually turn out like the Lost Roguelikes: Advanced Rogue, XRogue, SuperRogue and URogue. NetHack is immortal due to its widely distributed source, while those other games are only recently being recovered. In 20 years NetHack will still survive—whether it's the DevTeam working on it or someone else. One cannot say that so confidently about ADOM.

- ADOM, or Ancient Domains of Mystery
  - Homepage: www.adom.de/
  - Guidebook: www.adomgb.info/
  - Wiki: http://ancardia.wikia.com/

31

Things to Do While Visiting Ancardia

May 2007 NetHack has gotten a lot of talk here, and it remains perhaps the most complex roguelike out there due to its profusion of object interactions, but it is by no means the roguelike with the "most to do." That is, the objective of NetHack, although more complicated than the old days where ultimately all you had to do was just get fire resistance, level teleport down to the Amulet, get it, then climb out, is still relatively straightforward. The game got a lot more complex in version 3.0 and more complex still in 3.1, but in this respect it really hasn't changed too much since Hack.

The roguelike with, by far, the most to do is ADOM (Ancient Domains of Mystery), which is perhaps the example of the genre that takes the most ideas from the world of other RPGs. Nowhere is this made more evident than when examining the game's complex web of quests. NetHack has four (although one is different for each character class). ADOM has dozens.

Here is a very small sampling, chosen for a mix of ease of observation by beginning players and raw cool factor.

31.1 Save a Puppy!

The little girl in Teryino, the first town, asks you to save her dog from a nearby cave. The cave doesn't appear on the map until she asks you. The cave always has a good number of ants in it.

The "cute dog" must be generated (its level reached in the cave) before four game days have passed for it to remain alive, which is a very strict time limit considering that the required overworld travel will necessarily take up some of that time. Because of this, the player has almost no opportunity to advance in level except in transit, making this fairly difficult.

31.2 Make the Plains Safe for Adventurers!

The sheriff, Tywat Pare of Teryino, assigns two peacekeeping missions to the player during the game. Kranach and his band of raiders appear as a random overworld encounter near Teryino until you reach experience level 6, meaning that sometimes the player won't be able to complete this one due to bad luck. Wilderness encounters also get more difficult over time, and wandering the plains uses up a lot of food, so it's not recommended for beginners. The reward is 3,000 gold pieces, which some players will find more interesting than others.

The other involves killing the crime lord Hotzenplotz in the nearby outlaw town Lawenilothehl, a task that's either challenging or simple to a character at about that point in the game, depending on whether he has ray attack spells. As in, if you don't know any, then his bouncers will probably bounce you to death. If you do know one, you can beat him and his cronies without taking a hit. What else can be said, except, "Wizards rock?"

31.3 Kill the Mad Carpenter! (or Cure His Madness)

Later in the game the player must cross a piranha-infested lake. There are only two ways across the water, and one of them involves learning the skill of Bridge Building. This means something must be done about Yriggs, who carries the only source of that skill in the game, the Manual of Bridge Building.

The Yriggs quest (which I also mentioned last time, should this sound familiar) is one of the coolest features of ADOM, and it comes early enough that it can be done first if the player wants. After talking with Rynt in Teryino, the player can go down to the dungeon approximately to the south-east and descend to level 7 to find him. If killed he drops the objects necessary to build bridges, but, usefully, he can also be saved by purposely running away from him, letting him chase you to Jharod the healer on level 4. (Like with many of NetHack's features, there aren't many hints within ADOM that this is possible.) Doing this will satisfy Jharod that you are worthy of learning the extremely valuable Healing skill, increasing your rate of natural hit point restoration.

Like many quests, this is also worth a bit of an Alignment change towards Law, which some players will appreciate, and some find annoying.

31.4 Perform Last Rites for a Dying Sage! (or . . . .)

ADOM contains multiple dungeons. The "main" one, usually not seen until the player already has a few experience levels, is the Caverns of Chaos. And in this dungeon, some way down, is the endangered sage, Khelavaster.

The opponent philosophy of roguelike games is, in essence, "everyone is a monster." Characters considered NPCs in other RPGs get full stats and can usually be attacked and killed, in a roguelike game. Usually they will become angered in the process and made hostile. They are controlled by AI just like the dungeon opposition. Khelavaster is an interesting case, however, because unlike the roguelike tradition, he is part of a scripted encounter.

Khelavaster is generated peaceful on the downstairs of his level, surrounded by chaos servants. In ADOM, there is no way to descend dungeon levels without using stairs, so the player will eventually have to get Khelavaster off them to continue with the game. This is typically not a problem, as talking with him (with the chat command, Shift-C) will cause him to immediately die and leave his stuff to the player.

This is the story. See, Khelavaster is the sage who originally predicted this chaos stuff would plague the game's fantasy world. He went into the Caverns of Chaos to try to do something about it And Was Never Seen Again. While Khelavaster is not actually fighting the chaos servants, he is "in stasis" on his level, about to die. But he is actually immortal until the player talks to him; he always perishes in the conversation, in dramatic fashion.

However . . .

While ADOM's treatment of the encounter may not be roguelike normal, there is a very clever thing the player can do concerning him. It requires finding one of the game's more useful items, an amulet of life saving. As with NetHack's item, if worn by the player or a monster it will save his life one time, remedy the fatal condition, then disintegrate. Also like in NetHack, these are not too common to find. Actually they're pretty rare in ADOM, even more so considering that the game is thought to weight item generation according to dungeon difficulty.

If the player can find an amulet of life saving before talking to Khelavaster, then instead of chatting with him, he can give him the amulet, which logically enough will save his life. This is a fairly nifty trick, right up there with curing Yriggs the Carpenter. It makes the stuff gained from the sage much better (somehow) and late in the game enables the player to attempt an "ultra" ending if he wishes.

The problem is that amulets of life saving are quite rare and usually don't appear until later in the game, while Khelavaster is typically found about one-quarter the way down the Caverns of Chaos, fairly early.

None are guaranteed to be generated, and even if the player searches all the available dungeons before reaching that point frequently he won't find one. They can be wished for, but wishes are not much more common than the amulets are, and there are plenty of other things that the player might want instead. But then, it isn't called an "ultra" ending for nothing. (And there are worse things the player must accomplish in order to achieve that . . .)

31.5 Collect . . . Um . . . Strange Items!

Ah, the si. For a game that has dozens of artifacts, hundreds of monsters, devious quests, secret features and ultra-endings, it's amazing how it's the little things that come to define the game in one's memory.

The si was a relatively early addition to ADOM's equipment list, and despite the fact that it has no "purpose" and doesn't even have much of a logical explanation, it's still there. Probably because were Thomas Biskup to take it out, he'd probably have to fend off a hundred enraged ADOM fans with a stick.

"Si" stands for "strange item," and if you're expecting more of an explanation than that, well, you won't get one, mostly because there isn't one to give.

No one knows what a si looks like. We know the level it's on is filled with a strange smell. We know that the si is a kind of tool. We know it weighs 10 stones. And we know that the si is an artifact, of sorts, despite the fact that the major defining attribute of artifacts, uniqueness, doesn't apply to it.

This is because the si multiplies. So long as one is carried, they will slowly make more of themselves. The means by which this happens is obscure. No message is printed on the screen when it happens. It doesn't seem to happen if it isn't in the player's inventory.

Because they will periodically add an additional 10 stones to your carry weight, careless players will eventually get weighed down by them if they don't notice what's happening and drop some of them. Like other artifacts, it cannot be destroyed except by special means, but it has little other use, except for generic artifact things: they can be sold for cash, they can be sacrificed to make your god happier with you, and should you need something that's generally indestructible, they more than fit the bill.

Ultimately, what the si is is a whimsy. It's not a reference to anything. It's kinda silly and cool, even though it's not an explicit joke. Like naming the fruit in Rogue, it's just a neat thing that got thrown in just because.

It's good enough for me, anyway.

31.6 Source

ADOM Guidebook: www.adomgb.info/. Most recent update, April 1, 2010. Authorship was a joint effort between the members of Usenet group rec.games.roguelike.adom. It has been dedicated to the public domain.

32

Interview: Thomas Biskup on ADOM

July 2018 Although marketing and endless cloning have devalued the meaning of the term "roguelike" in recent years (most of which should be called "roguelites," if even that), there are six games, I say, that should be considered the Major Roguelikes, the canonical ones, those that combine fidelity to the concept with popularity and size of player base: Rogue itself of course, NetHack, Angband, Dungeon Crawl Stone Soup, Brogue and ADOM, a.k.a. "Ancient Domains of Mystery."

Of all of these, only the last two could rightly be considered the work of a single person. And of them all, only ADOM's source code is not available to a curious player. (Rogue was never released as open source, but the common variant Rogue Clone IV was.) Thanks to the 7DRL competition ("7-Day Roguelike"), thousands of people have made toy roguelikes of their own, but to create one on the scale of ADOM, a game arguably as complex as even mighty NetHack itself, is a terrific feat.

Fortunately, ADOM creator Dr. Thomas Biskup is both friendly and willing to talk about the game he has spent so much time and energy on, and he recently spoke with us about both ADOM and its in-development sequel, Ultimate ADOM.

The first part of this interview was done around October 2016. The second half was done in October 2018 and is generally up-to-date. The whole has been trimmed somewhat and edited for publication.

John Harris: So, first question: How did ADOM get started?

Dr. Thomas Biskup: ADOM got started when I, during my days as a student of computer science, decided to learn a new programming language (C specifically). I learn best when I have some kind of project in front of me and at that time I had played games like DND, Rogue, Hack and NetHack (and seen Omega) and loved the genre. I was fascinated by the random generation parts as well as the single player exploration style of these games and felt I needed to understand how they work. So trying to use my growing C skills to that effect seemed natural. But when I started diving into the NetHack sources (which seemed to be the most detailed and thus most interesting candidate) I quickly learned how advanced and complicated those sources were. Which led me to believe that it might be much simpler to write a game of my own. And it definitely seemed to be a lot more fun to figure things out for myself instead of spending many hours understanding the genius of others. So I started writing my own roguelike game, first trying to create a map, then figuring out how to dig tunnels, place the '@' on the screen and get it to move. All in all, things were a lot

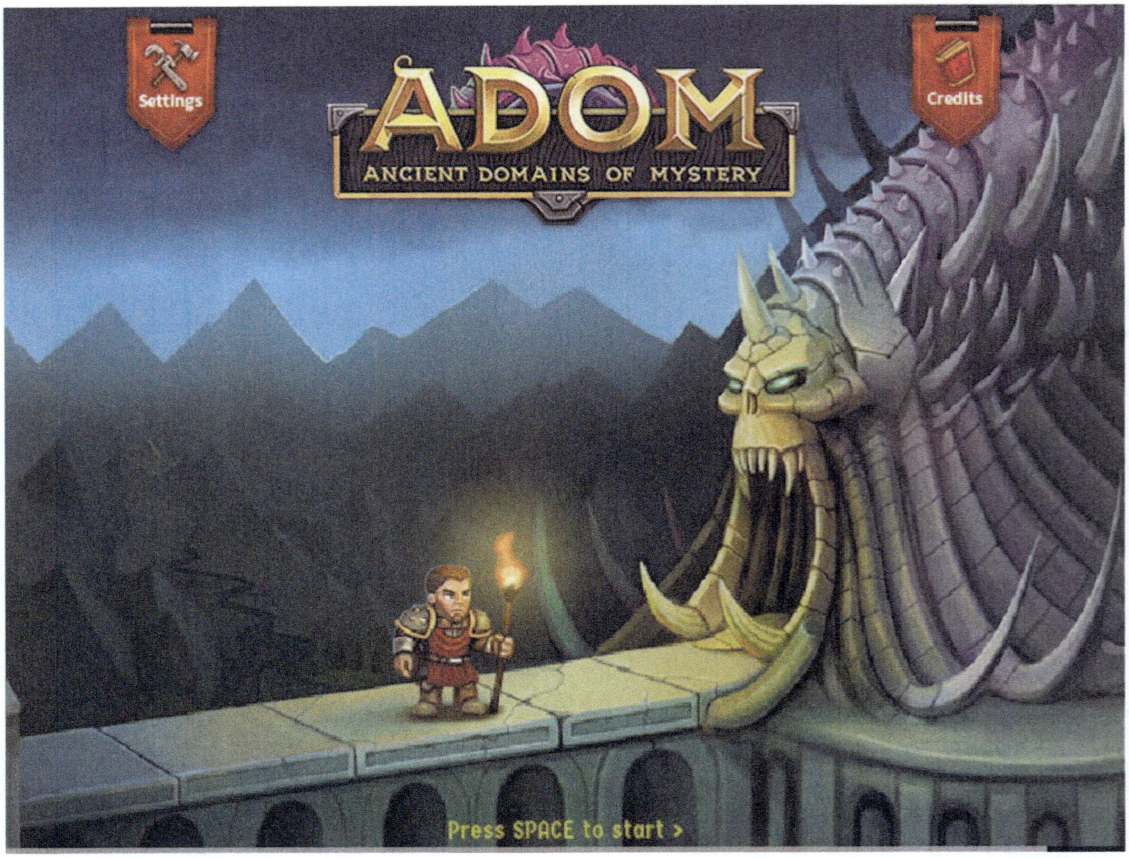

Figure 32.1

New ADOM title screen

more complicated than I had expected, and so about two years passed until, in summer of 1994, I finally had something in my hands that seemed like it could be the base for a working game. And that's the true (source code) roots of ADOM. Things started to progress a lot more quickly once I had figured out the real structure of what I wanted to build and so ADOM began to take form over the next two years that led to initial releases and finally to the well-known and quite widespread game that ADOM is today.

JH: Ah! I've had a look at the NetHack sources myself and can vouch for the complexity, a lot of which comes from its having a lot of people work on it for such a long time, bolting on features here and there. It's surprising that it holds together so well given its development history! I remember reading that NH 3.0 was the occasion of a big code cleanup, and the (then) recently released NH 3.6 was another such cleanup.

That has to be one advantage of working on a project largely by yourself, you don't have to worry so much about breaking something someone else has written, either technically or in design. Actually, that's an assumption on my part. Do you have any help on developing ADOM now, or is it still largely yourself?

TB: Having a project of your own IMHO has several big advantages:

1. Your learning rate is exponentially higher compared to extending stuff other people have created. Because you need to figure out everything on your own.
2. You can more easily (or better: at all) realize your vision of how a game should be and feel. If you build on someone else's work lots of assumptions already will have been built into the game and if you don't like that stuff it's a hell of a lot of work (if at all possible) to get this stuff removed. Especially if you are getting into that project as a newcomer.
3. Forking an existing project probably will make you unhappy as you will have a hard time keeping up with ongoing work in the parallel project, both due to technical reasons

(integrating parallel code changes can be impossible) and for design reasons (e.g. figuring out what all the minute changes all over the code mean and how they affect the vision behind your fork). And you'll always be compared to the original, which can be good and bad, but IMHO in the end distracts from your own design.

Team ADOM nowadays includes myself, as the maintainer and programmer for the core game and content; Jochen Terstiege, as the only other person worldwide with access to the ADOM sources, he's managing the build infrastructure, the Steam deployments, fixing programming bugs and working on the integration of sounds and NotEye and is a column of stability and quality for ADOM; Zeno, who's the genius behind NotEye and thus the reason for ADOM having graphics nowadays; Lucas Dieguez, who's our master composer and responsible for the incredible soundtrack that ADOM has nowadays; and Krzysztof Dycha, who's our head artist and Michelangelo, having single-handedly created each and every image in the graphical version of ADOM, literally the work of years.

So on one hand I'm still working alone on ADOM (e.g. the core game), on the other hand I'm part of the best team ever, as those guys are so immensely creative and resourceful that we keep pushing each other. I love working with each and every one and believe that we have a lot of awesome stuff in store for the future.

Finally, there's our incredibly loyal, and once again growing, community. There are so many people out there that spark new ideas by using our bug/rfe database at www.adom.de/bugs and thus also help in evolving ADOM. The game wouldn't be what it is today without all these awesome people!

JH: When I first played ADOM, I came to it from NetHack, which contains many references to classic Dungeons & Dragons, in its monsters and its story, as well as many literary and pop culture references. When I came to ADOM from there, I was taken aback a bit by how the game struck out

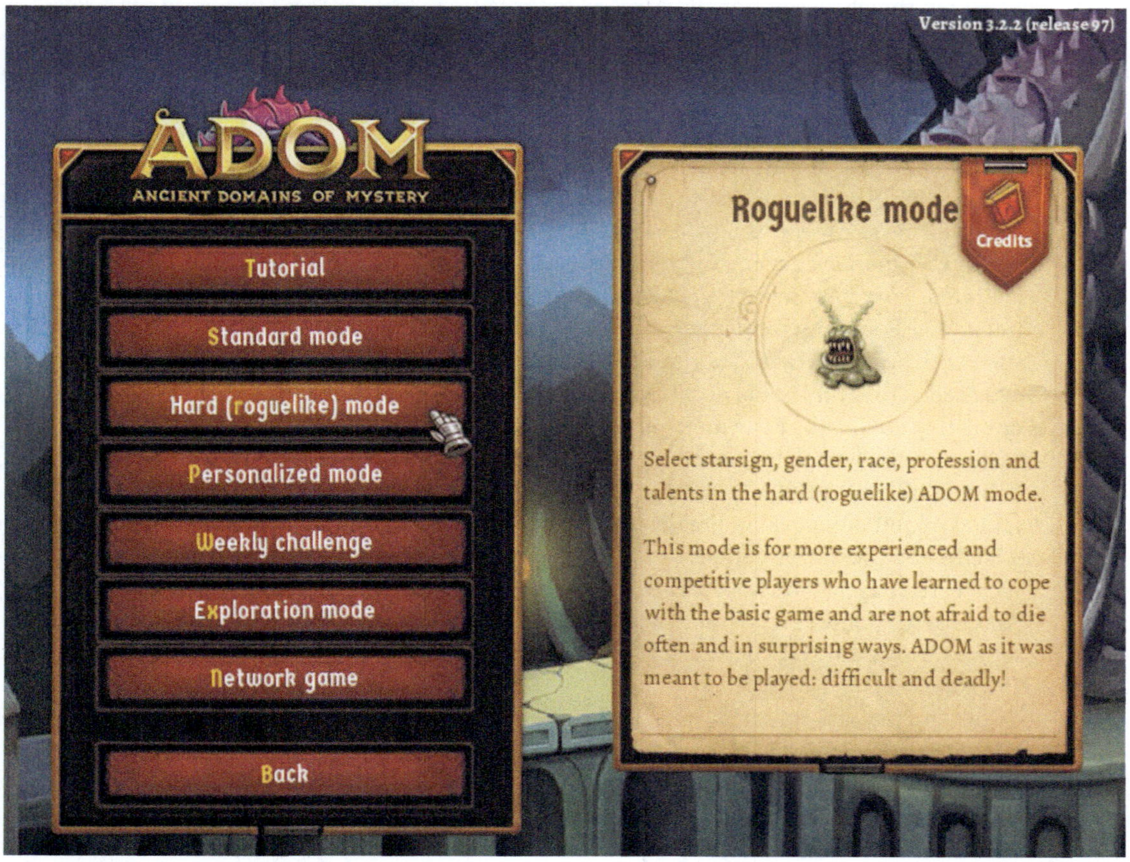

Figure 32.2

ADOM's startup menu

on its own, largely with its own self-contained mythology and setting. Now, I think that setting is one of ADOM's strongest aspects. It seems to me now that part of the game is discovering the unusual, sometimes terrifically unusual, properties of items like the si, or all the herbs, or the many artifacts. Were these created specifically for the game, or do they draw from some other source, either outside or self-created?

TB: I would say that most of the content is "self-created" or "other-created" but inspired by a variety of existing sources. E.g. the general idea for corruption came from the Warhammer Fantasy Role-Playing Game with its notion of Chaos encroaching upon civilization. Andor Drakon as the god of Chaos goes back to an AD&D character of mine (1st/2nd edition), who started as an evil cleric worshiping a minor demon and at some point killed his god and managed to ascend to immortality. Imagine the original Andor Drakon in his immortal form a bit like Sardo Numspa from The Golden Child. The "si" also comes from a very long-running 1st AD&D campaign where a friend of mine and I played two dwarves, Gorko Galgenstrick and Groron Garman. One day my friend suddenly discovered a "si" in his hand-written equipment list and we had no idea how it got there. We made fun of it and months later we suddenly discovered a second "si" on this equipment list. From there the inside joke about a reproducing artifact started which in the end made its way into ADOM.

Many other details, like Aylas scarf, Brannalbins cloak and Rolf, come from characters I or friends played during D&D and AD&D campaigns.

Another huge part of influence have been the comments from the ADOM community over so many years. There are tons of awesome details that have been suggested directly or indirectly by fans of the game. I try to select those things that IMHO match the tune of the game best.

Finally, some parts have been created only for ADOM, especially the whole elemental mythology thing that is still evolving. The outlaw village, Terinyo, the black druid and such elements have been specifically created for ADOM.

So, all in all, it's a big hodge podge of influences. The main criteria for inclusion being that I either am somehow emotionally attached to the various parts or that I just loved the suggestions or ideas of others so much that they needed to become a part of the game.

JH: I like that, it gets in some of the community aspects of open source game creation, while allowing the source to remain closed and thus preserve some mystery for the players.

ADOM development had to pause for a while. Could you tell us why it ceased, when it picked back up, and give us a current status report? It's on Steam now, how is that treating you?

TB: ADOM basically paused from 2001 to 2012. The reason behind it was real life. In 1998 I started working full time as my life as a student came to an end, which already ate up lots of free time, and by 2001 we founded a company, QuinScape. I'm still working their today with my two founding colleagues. We have more than 100 employees these days and are a healthy and experienced IT integrator. Founding a company takes so much energy, more than many people think, that my time with ADOM really deteriorated. Then in 2003/2004 I, for some reason, decided that my ego needed to see if I could do a PhD as a hobby project while building the company. So I started doing that during the early morning and late night hours. Then my then girlfriend and I decided to get married, which happened in 2009. Luckily she blackmailed me to finish my PhD by then.

But I was quite busy, to put it carefully. And I had started programming ADOM II (JADE) in Java as a kind of sequel. So I really just did neither have the time nor the inclination to work on ADOM and the longer you pause the harder it gets to come back. Luckily my very good friend Jochen Terstiege, who's now part of Team ADOM, kept pestering me about doing more with it. And at some point in 2010 he showed me an iPad prototype he had started. (He had access to the sources because he had been doing lots of ports starting with the Amiga port from as early as 1996 or 1997.)

That got me back up somewhat, and I restarted work on JADE after a kind of meditation about my hobbies during a vacation in Thailand in 2010. At that point I had been running four or five blogs, been writing various pen & paper RPGs. (I even got published in Germany with the only true world-wide pulp RPG magazine. I don't mean the RPG genre but the RPG format. Search for "Maddrax" and "Thomas Biskup" and you should be able to find some traces.) But I kept wondering: what am I looking for and in the end I noticed that I was looking for something that I already had found with ADOM: A great community to exchange ideas with and then put them into some kind of game.

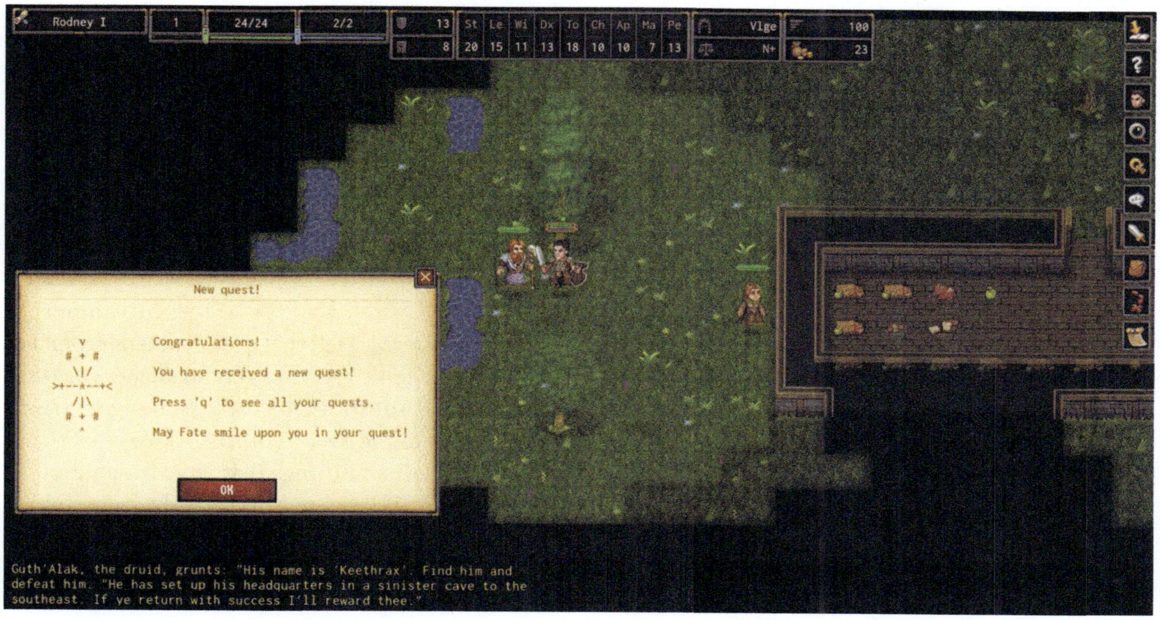

Figure 32.3

ADOM: the first town

So I said, "OK, let's scratch all that stuff and resume work on ADOM." Which led to the release of JADE 0.0.1 on the 2nd of July, 2011, which led to more polite pushing from Jochen, which led to us devising the ADOM crowdfunding campaign which started on the 2nd of July, 2012, and was quite successful giving us about $90,000 to work with. The money led to the formation of Team ADOM and the actual resurrection of ADOM development.

While we still have a couple of rewards to finish from the campaign (it's been a very long run), we are immensely proud on how ADOM has turned out in the past four years, with scores of soundtracks, amazing graphics, a modernized UI (although we can do so much more in that area) and so much new content.

The most recent high point has been the release on Steam in November 2015. This has opened up a new source of revenue, which is important. I yet have to earn a single dollar with ADOM. So far all the money is going into paying the Team members while I continue to work for free.

While initial sales have decreased overall sales still are on a good level that should allow us to continue for years to come. We now are working in the next level. Which means: Finally getting done with the remaining crowdfunding promises and then moving into a bright future for ADOM. We have collected tons of awesome ideas but so far lacked the time to work on them since we mostly are focused on the crowdfunding stuff. It will be a kind of relief to have that done and be able to do create stuff more freely.

Just pick it up on Steam (www.adom.de/steam). It's an awesome, yet difficult, game.

JH: Wait, so you got your PhD? I should be calling you Dr. Biskup then! And it's so great to hear ADOM's back up and running!

If you don't mind, I'd like to move more into game design issues. One of ADOM's most distinctive elements is the corruption clock, which replaces Rogue's food clock as the primary force pushing the player forward. While there are ways to counter it, I think it does a good job of forcing the player onward, especially since a few of the corruptions, such as Mana Battery and Poison Hands, have the potential to make the game much more challenging to play. What inspired the idea?

TB: Yeah, I got a PhD. But only people that annoy me need to call me "Dr. Biskup," so you are safe.

Regarding corruption: I always loved Warhammer Fantasy Role-play, and how the chaos creatures sported various kinds of corruptions. I also loved how the Broo in Runequest were kind of randomly corrupted. And I always loved mutations in Gamma World. I'm a huge Gamma World fan and in ancient times I even ran the official Gamma World mailing list, when mailing lists still were the greatest thing on earth.

All this came together when thinking about corruptions. I always liked the phrase "power corrupts, and absolute power corrupts absolutely." So I thought that it might be kind of cool to have something in the game that can make you more powerful but at the same time can cause all kind of trouble for you. (Don't ask me about my idea for chaos wizards and chaos necromancers as PC classes . . .)

As I also liked the idea of having an ongoing story in ADOM, I felt that the battle against Chaos might be more tangible due to a kind of lingering corruption effect that gets stronger over time. In the beginning it was not imagined to be a replacement/substitute/rival to the hunger system, but rather as something that connected you more closely to the overarching story.

The specific corruptions evolved from a mix of my ideas and things that were brought up by ADOM fans during those early golden days. Mana battery, if I remember correctly, is something that was brought up by one of the community people and I loved it so much that it had to be integrated.

Nowadays I love corruption as a rather unique mechanism to intertwine game design issues (the time clock you mention) and story issues (the world becoming a darker place). For ADOM II and ADOM III, if I ever were to do the latter, corruption would be a lot more prevalent in the overall world. Other beings and monsters also would slowly corrupt and degenerate, the weather would be more noticeably affected (it is affected by corruption in ADOM but probably nobody's noticed), plants should mutate, and I have this vision of the world slowly turning into this purple corruption haze. Tentacles everywhere.

And I would love to add more means where you consciously have to trade power for corruption, such as a means for players to strengthen their spells by absorbing corruption. I love tempting people I guess.

JH: Have you tried D&D 5th edition yet?*

TB: I actually own most of the books but haven't done much with it to be honest. I like what I see but I am a firm believer in simple skill systems and I am kind of angry about them for not even considering to do a simple standard skill system. And I was a little scared away because I thought that the very flat power curve doesn't nicely mirror the hero's journey I personally expect from D&D. There is just too little difference for me in the skill abilities of a 1st level fighter compared to a 20th level fighter.

But I really like how they otherwise smoothed the system. I hate 4th edition with a passion and 3rd just was too complex for my tastes.

JH: Yeah, I hate lots of things about 4th edition. Two members of our group played a great deal of 3rd edition and are, by all accounts, experts at it. That made it very imposing to run. They know all the exploits, and so it was almost impossible for me to challenge them! In 3rd edition, it felt like I was either handing them a few XP, or handing them a ton of XP.

TB: I'm a 1st/2nd edition traditionalist, and actually there is yet another RPG I'm writing on the sidelines that collects all my house rules for my personal "perfect edition of (A)D&D." But who isn't these days?

The exploitation topic also is one of the things I disliked about 3rd edition. It just seemed to allow for far too much min-maxing for my tastes, and tended to lead people to search for optimal builds and stuff. I don't like that. I'm more into storytelling.

I like kind of crunchy systems nonetheless but I'm more into winging stuff when I am the GM. I need a kind of loose system of mid complexity. And complexity-wise, 2nd edition was perfect for me. We heavily used the skill system and were kind of loose with races and classes and that came pretty close to our favored style. Because we had enough crunch for the gaming side but mostly focused on the stories.

* The following questions represent the recent portion of the interview.

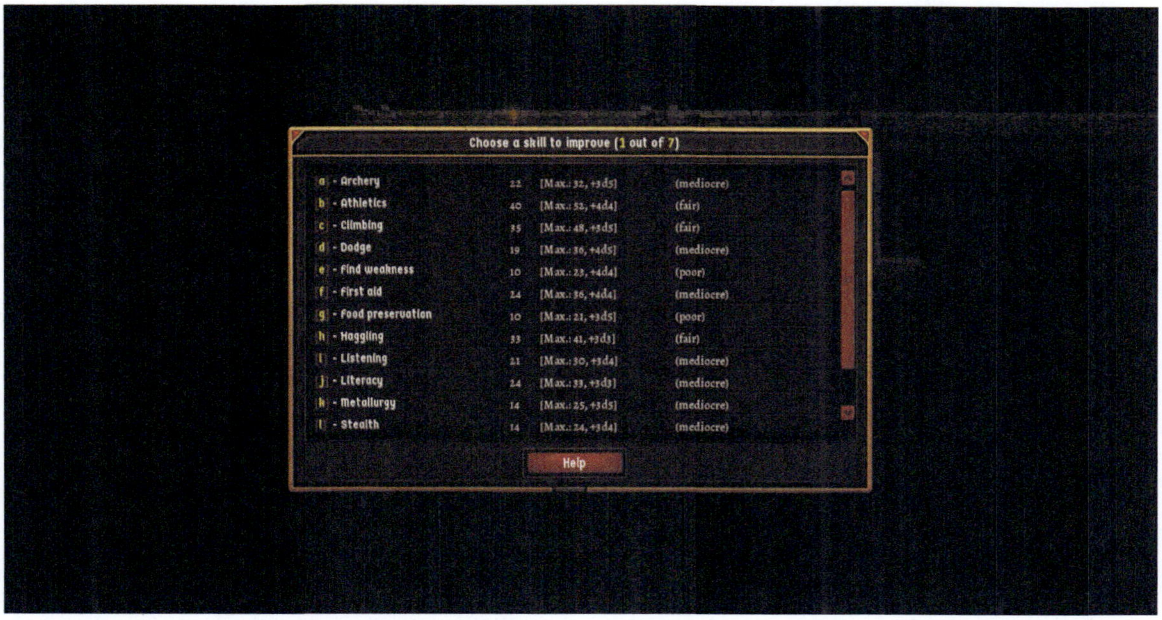

Figure 32.4

ADOM: skill improvement

JH: Yeah. I think there's less min-maxing in 5E, but it's still there. I've been working on a megadungeon to lead them through, it's been lots of fun for everyone.

TB: Mega-dungeons are an awesome topic. I really would love to do one of my own these days but sadly, with our recently born daughter, my already pressed schedule now is even worse.

It's an awesome idea, Castle Greyhawk kind of stuff. Like in the golden days of RPGs. I love that! I was so eager about the first part(s) published by Troll Lord Games, but sadly the trolls were too slow. And Gail Gygax somehow doesn't seem likely to do anything with the inheritance. A true shame.

I was at last year's GEN CON, with all the special sessions on its 50 years. It was a mind-blowing experience meeting all the old legends and hearing them talk about the early days. Amazing days. I loved every minute, and got many nice pictures with them I'm such a fanboy. We actually plan to have some of them writing stories for Ultimate ADOM. I'm kind of excited about that and hope it all works out like we plan.

JH: That must have been awesome. I never get to go to conventions, except for DragonCon, which happens to be relatively close to me.

TB: I have been to two GEN CONs but that's about all I do. We have the Spiel game fair over here in Essen. It's the largest gaming convention in the world for traditional board games. Sadly, RPGs these days are a minor topic there. But I have been to each and every Spiel since 1988. A great tradition I hope to keep up for many years. It's brilliant. And luckily just a 30 minute drive (roughly) from me.

JH: I still can't help but think of ADOM as a new kid on the block, even after all this time, even though Dungeon Crawl Stone Soup and Brogue both came out after it and have been around for years. What do you think about those cocky upstart games? And how about the phenomenon of "rogue-lites," randomly-generated action games inspired by roguelikes?

TB: I personally think the problem with ADOM is that it had this long pause in the middle. That's IMHO why it sometimes feels young and ancient at the same time.

JH: Considering how long NetHack's pauses are, I think you have no need to feel insecure there.

TB: I still remember when Dungeon Crawl took its first steps and Linley started showing the source code. It was a brilliant mess. I was kind of wowed by all the things he did but kind of scared by the way how he coded it. I am highly impressed by what these games achieved and how many innovations they introduced.

Games like Brogue and DCSS are really inspiring to me. They urge me to hopefully push the boundaries even further with Ultimate ADOM. It's great to see such games because IMHO they are very important in keeping the roguelike flame alive. And I love how alive the scene feels. So many people working on innovative games. It's just great how procedural generation, permadeath, randomized game settings and stuff are more and more becoming mainstream.

I also kind of like rogue-lites, although they aren't my personal favorite. But it's interesting to see roguelike principles being applied to other gaming genres. What I hate is the kind of confusion that seems to get created in the wake. Many studios seem to enjoy trying to derive marketing benefits by calling their games roguelike, although they really aren't. That's kind of annoying. But it's a personal pet peeve and probably doesn't matter to the world.

So overall, I'm happy to see so many roguish activities and feel both inspired and challenged by them.

JH: Yeah, it seems like half the games on Steam these days claim to be roguelike.

TB: It's really bad, especially on Steam. But Steam generally is a rotten swamp in many ways, although I'm grateful for the benefits it offers to ADOM! ;-) I'm annoyed about them killing Greenlight, although it was not really brilliant. But it was better than the "give us $100 and publish a game" approach. I wish they'd ask for like "give us $5000 and publish a game" or at least $2000. Something that stops the crap from appearing.

JH: Last year I had a short gig for MobyGames, helping to fill out their database. It involved going through a list of new games on Steam and filling out their information. Some of them were hilariously bad. One was basically a love letter to Donald Trump. A first person shooter where the player was "American President, John Trump," and went and shot up mafia guys. [The game is "The Last Hope: Trump Vs. Mafia."]

TB: Aargh. That sounds truly bad.

JH: Perhaps predictably, it was put out by a Russian publisher.

TB: LOL If it were a Hollywood story everyone would be saying "Nah, unbelievable crap."

JH: Here's another question. One of the things about ADOM is how it takes ideas from NetHack and Angband and extends them. Like NetHack's shops, item systems, complex monsters and clever item uses, and Angband's monster memory and (in the Infinite Dungeon) regenerating levels. I

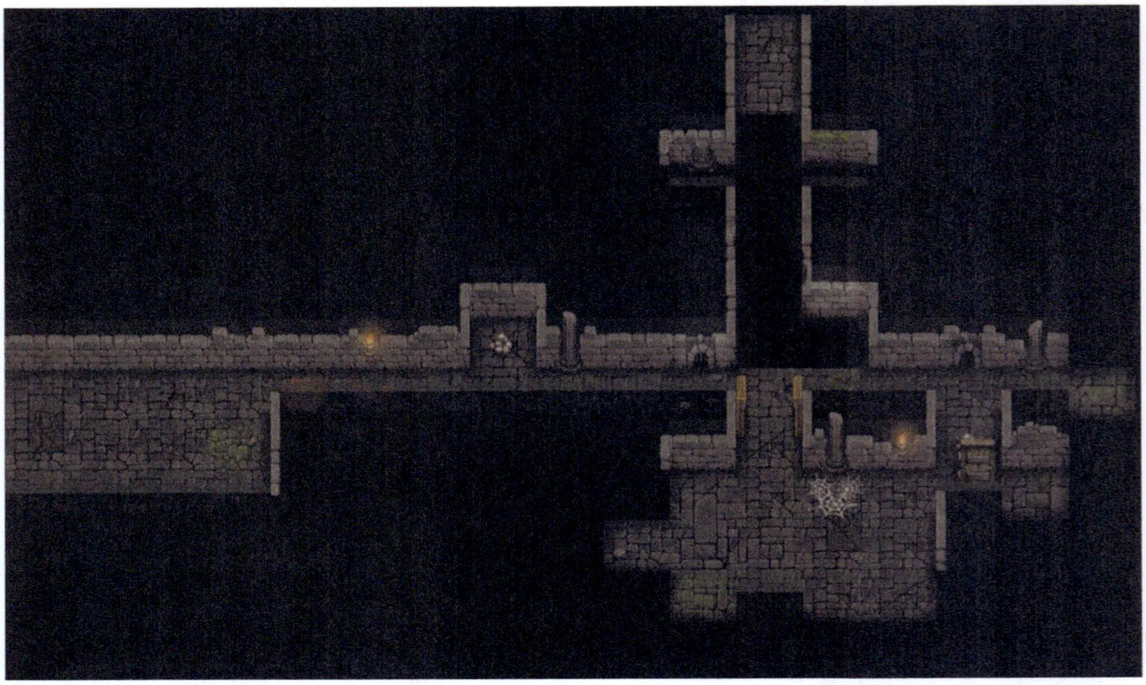

Figure 32.5

ADOM: Dungeon exploration

really like that aspect of it, how it's willing to take those ideas and present its own take on them. I guess it's less of a question and more of a statement, heh. There's more there I'm sure that I've missed.

TB: "Imitation is the sincerest form of flattery." That's a true observation. I basically took the features from other games I loved and kind of tried to impress my own tastes. And in many cases the community also provided awesome variations on ideas that I loved.

Design for me has a lot to do with trying to improve on things that work well. So you'll find a lot of that in ADOM.

JH: Yet there's so many new things. Especially the quest structure. I don't think there's really any other game that uses quests like ADOM does. I think they're so effective. They're what really give the game its form.

TB: The quests again come from my preference for storytelling. I know that many players consider roguelike games more like a tactical challenge or puzzle to solve. For me it always has been about trying to tell an interesting story and enrich it with all the random things to make it endlessly replayable.

JH: Yet it's a form of storytelling that structures the game. In a lot of games, storytelling kind of comes at the expense of gameplay. ADOM is a huge counterexample to that, that you can have pre-defined quests that are enhanced by randomness.

TB: That's also something we hopefully will hugely improve on in Ultimate ADOM. We have plans for very extensive story lines that overlap and touch each other . . . but in different random ways in each game. Including factions with their own goals that will drive the world forward and leave it to the player to decide, when he/she wants to interact with what parts of a huge flowing and ever-changing story line.

JH: My favorite example is trying to save Yriggs.

TB: Why do you like that example so much?

JH: I remember first finding out about it, discovering it in the game myself. I remember trying to get Yrrigs up to the healer, just on a whim, and being surprised that it worked.

What I like about it especially is that its nature is heavily dependent on the randomness of the dungeon. It's a very interesting tactical challenge, it could be very easy or hard depending on how the levels lay out and what monsters get in the way.

TB: I personally feel these days that tiny constant blimps of static storyline in a hugely random world leave for the best emergent experiences. Such experiences get people to talk about their emotions when they played their particular variant of e.g. the Yrrigs quest, and that's just wonderful.

Did you already manage to do the new ice queen quest and solve her secret mystery. You'll love that. It's a kind of mega-Yrrigs story.

JH: I've not gotten to the Ice Queen, I haven't had much chance to dive into post-revival ADOM unfortunately.

TB: Ah, you'd love it. But it's very very high level. And the ramifications of that secret quest actually carry over to Ultimate ADOM.

JH: My guilty secret is, for how much I write about games, I don't get to play them a lot these days.

TB: LOL, it's the same with me and programming games. No time to play them. That's why I am so bad at ADOM.

JH: What other kinds of games have you played, or consider inspiring? CRPGs, like say the D&D Gold Box games? Any Legend of Zelda?

TB: Ah, I'm a fan of some ancient games. Regarding ADOM, the two most influential games probably have been the original Wasteland, for its incredible amount of secret side quests and mysteries, and Bard's Tale III, just for the complexity of the dungeon story. I also love Realms of Impossibility, on the Commodore 64, for the sense of wonder it instilled into me as a child. I loved the very first "Fate" game for the "every action has a consequence" tag line, and that's again something I'm trying to stress to death for Ultimate ADOM.

JH: Ah Bard's Tale. I played almost to the end of BT2, only to get caught up in that annoying last puzzle snare.

TB: I liked Phantasie III on the Amiga for its brutal combat, weird races and again the sense of wonder it instilled in me. I solved all of the first three Bard's Tales spending endless hours on them. BT III was simply brilliant.

JH: I never got the chance to play 3, but I still have my BT2 maps somewhere. I hope they do a good job with the new BT game. By all accounts people like Wasteland 2, so hopes are running high.

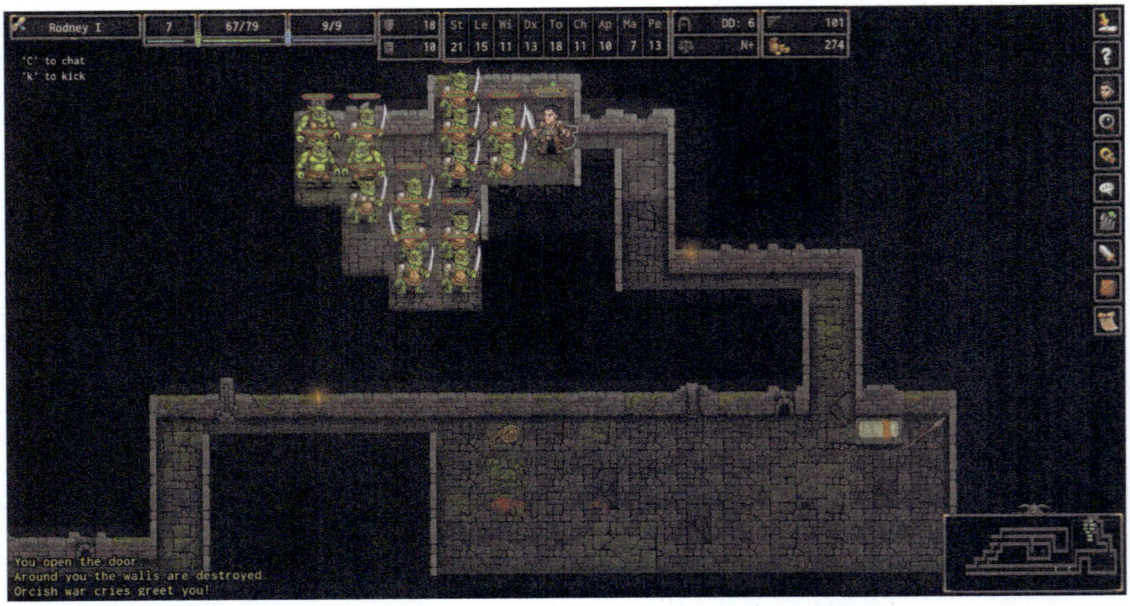

Figure 32.6

ADOM: Orc ambush

TB: Naturally I played some of the Gold Box games. Pool of Radiance was brilliant. And that strange special extra end fight with the Beholder corps finally inspired a super difficult new end quest in recent ADOM releases, that you only can play after actually winning ADOM.

JH: Aaaah interesting! Which means I'll probably never see it.

TB: That new end quest probably will be seen by 0.0001% of all players.

JH: Which means 100 people will probably blog about it Tuesday, and they'll speedrun it at next year's SGDQ.

TB: LOL, yeah. I backed the new BT and am kind of curious if they will manage to be successful. I also backed Wasteland 2 and have the limited edition box standing here on my shelf . . . and sadly so far had no time to even try it.

JH: I wonder what the dungeons will look like. Will it still have Wizardry-style mazes?

TB: I hope they go that way. But I only have seen a few combat scenes. Again, no time to follow on the details.

JH: Let's talk about ADOM's skill system a bit.

TB: Interesting topic, as it will be completely different in Ultimate ADOM. I'm thinking a lot about it these days as soon we are going to add the new skill system to UA.

JH: It's probably my favorite thing about the game, because of its similarity to classic Runequest/Call of Cthulhu percentile skills.

TB: Interesting. I dislike it with a passion these days, although I loved it when I initially implemented it.

JH: That is interesting! How are you dissatisfied with it?

TB: On several levels:

1. I find it too granular these days. It's kind of fiddly and more recent players seem to wonder about all the numbers. As small steps in the skill have barely any noticeable effect it IMHO wastes mind space by appearing more crunchy than it needs to be.
2. These days I dislike that some skills work automatically and others need to be activated manually. It's kind of complex to understand for players.
3. They do not feel very balanced as far as usefulness goes. You have stuff like Bridge Building beside stuff like Alertness or Concentration. It's not necessarily a bad thing but it feels kind of ugly.
4. These days I also feel that games become more interesting if the choices you have to make are kind of painful. In ADOM it's more like "pump points into the skills until they are at 100 but the road to that score doesn't matter too much."

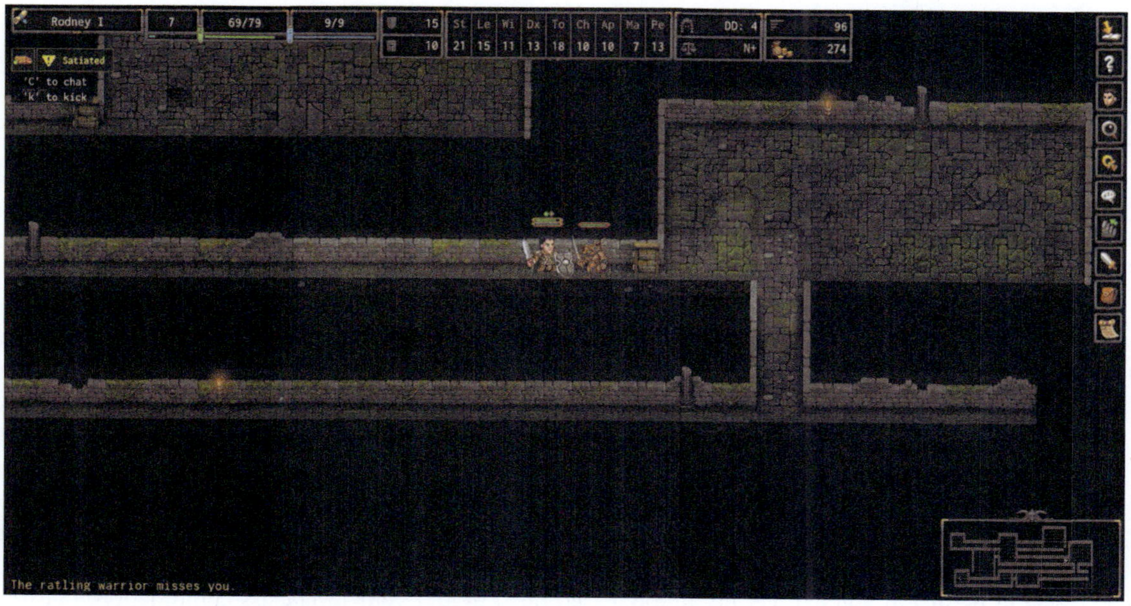

Figure 32.7

ADOM: Fighting a ratling

JH: I can't disagree with any of those things. I think Point 4 is particularly insightful. Games are basically about the choices the player makes, and if the choice is painful it means it's important, and thus of particular interest. It is good design in general to eliminate no-brainer choices.

TB: So for UA I have different plans which currently run along the following lines: Skills probably will have but five or six levels (apprentice, journeyman, expert, master, grand master, legend—something like that). Each and every level will add something very meaningful. E.g. "Observation" at level 1 might yield basic data about monsters and items, at level 2 you might learn about PV/DV/hit-points, at level 3 about power points and spells, etc. It's kind of gamey but has actual meaning. And if every skill is as useful at every level every choice will be painful. To increase the pain you probably will get but 1 or 2 skills per level to increase by one single level. And suddenly you get something that allows for vastly different play and character experiences.

I'm still working on the design details (and the skill list and levels in particular) but the basic design will be the one just described.

JH: I agree about the need to accommodate different play and experiences. Expanding the possibility space of gameplay.

TB: I actually also will be doing some brutal things like removing the need for identifying items. It might be an option for some kind of hardcore mode, though.

JH: That is interesting. It might be a good decision, depending on the rest of the design.

TB: I feel that it doesn't add much to the game for most players these days. It's very hard to identify items, and the presence of cursed items (in their current state) makes it even more dangerous and often ruins fun. So instead of something exciting (myriads of wonderfully alien items), we have a kind of dreary task ahead (what do I do with all that stuff I don't understand). Which is the reason why cursed items in UA also will be very different.

Curses will be much rarer and they will vary. Things like, "can't be unequipped for the next 100 turns," "will cause 4d8 damage if you unequip it," "will confuse you for 2d10 turns when you unequip it," and similar stuff. So, curses that add interesting choices.

JH: Item identification is a weird thing, it can be done well, but the game that did the best, arguably, is still the original Rogue. Because means of identification were fairly rare in Rogue, and so often you had to use unidentified items, and take on the risks of using a bad one. Because you also relied heavily on your items in Rogue. It was that combination, you had to use items, but often didn't know what they were, that gave weight to that game's bad items and identification.

TB: Considering the tons of items in ADOM, I feel that having constant risks while using them bar a large fun part of the game from you. I'd rather add a lot more interesting uses and combinations to the game regarding what you can do with items.

JH: I'm sure you'll find the best solution. You made ADOM, I feel like we can trust you on that.

TB: LOL, thanks. No pressure here.

JH: I had something in my notes about "item power" vs. "level power." Like, I see NetHack as a game mostly about item power. If you have the right stuff you can go pretty far, even at experience level 1. And that game doesn't generally weight item generation by dungeon level, so you can potentially find good stuff (rarely) on level 1.

Whereas I see Angband as being a game about level power, about what your character's experience level is. And ADOM I see as being a synthesis of the approaches.

TB: I see. Personally I believe in striking a better balance. Levels and their effects IMHO should be interesting, otherwise you kind of could get rid of levels and classes and that stuff. But interesting items should be able to change the mixture. Because items are somewhat random and randomness adds to emergent storylines. ("Man, I found that nasty eternium long spear of devastation at level 3 and it allowed me to . . .") So I am a believer in the middle ground here.

JH: It is a good approach, and I like that idea of emergent storylines. The story of your character. The events and adventures that make him memorable, defined by his situations.

TB: It would be nice if you can get far simply based on skill and your level/class combination, but item powers should be able to steer you on new paths and approaches. And sometimes it's just nice to require certain items for certain quests or monsters. And I love how people find new approaches to defeating monsters by using items in interesting ways, such as all that stuff with wands of door creation and limiting movement of certain monsters. I never thought about that when I designed the wand.

JH: What I see as positive about that approach is, most commercial gamedevs would see something they didn't intend as an exploit that has to be stamped out. A lot of Big Designers come to see player ingenuity as something to be fought.

TB: I really take the opposite position, unless something totally unbalances the very basic experience. But it's great to have these incredible innovative solutions to complex problems, and I intend to offer a lot more of that in UA because you will have pretty new innovative new ways of combining things.

JH: I was reading the ADOM Wiki a bit to prepare for this, there's some weird stuff there.

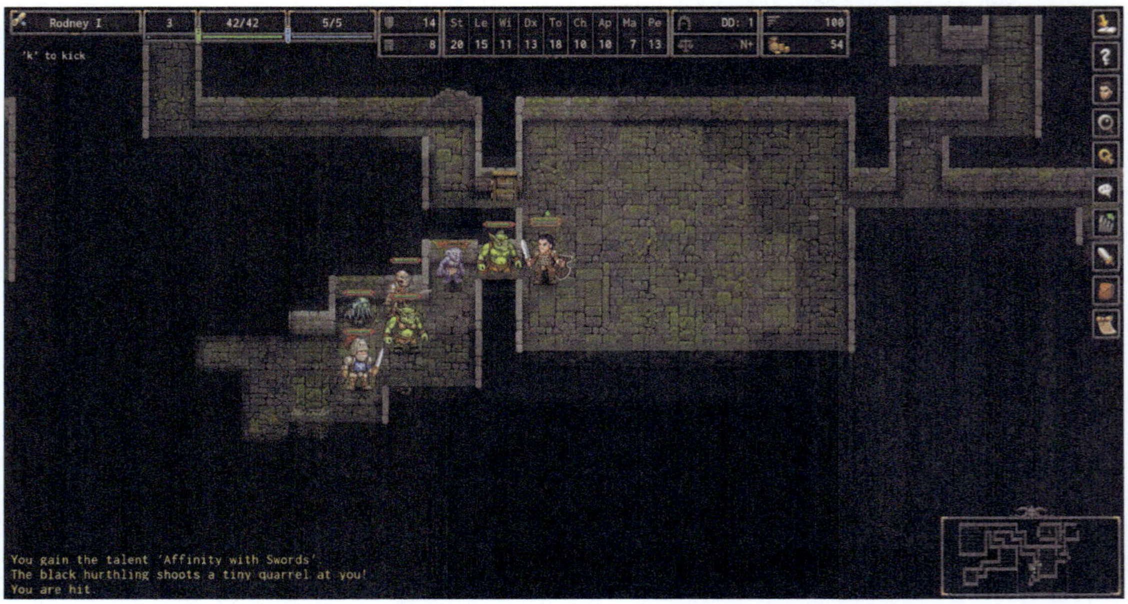

Figure 32.8

ADOM: Group of opponents

TB: So you probably know more about ADOM than me. (Starts digging up the source code . . .)

JH: The wiki mentions code diving to get information, which is cheating. But it also mentions a player called Anilatix who cast the Create Item spell over 150K times. And made a webpage with the results in spreadsheet form! I have the link here. All to try to figure out the item generation algorithm. I'm amused, amazed and kind of frightened of that level of player obsession.

TB: Wow. I didn't know that. LOL, ah, I see. I am humbled by these incredibly persistent people. Reading the binary code probably would have been less painful.

JH: I remember the early days of the Ultimate Ending, when no one knew what it was.

TB: Glory days.

JH: I kind of wonder if a secret like that would be found faster now.

TB: That's why there is the scroll of omnipotence in the game now . . . and nobody so far has managed to read it . . .

JH: I've been watching SGDQ, the speedrun marathon, and some of the things people have discovered in these games kind of make me despair that people will ever be able to hide game secrets in code ever again. Well, the scroll of omnipotence kind of proves it's possible then!

TB: I'm not sure. In the days of yore there were amazing players from Russia that disassembled the binary and were able to point out bugs to me in a precision that I found unbelievable, for someone not having the actual source code. Such skills more and more seem to get lost these days. It's extremely hard I guess. And usually can only succeed if people do not have the right combination of skills. Grond e.g. is an extremely skilled player and he is so fast in figuring out things (and reporting bugs) it's amazing.

JH: That was nice of them. I shudder to think of what their skills would be used for now.

TB: LOL, yeah.

32.1 Acknowledgments

Thanks to Dr. Biskup for spending time to talk with me, and for being patient between the two interview sections. ADOM, one of the greatest roguelikes of all, is available on Steam. Other versions are available from the game's home page, at www.adom.de/.

Section VI
Mystery Dungeon

33

The Delights of Mystery Dungeon: Shiren the Wanderer

March 2008 In recognition of the U.S. release, after more than ten years since its Super Famicom origin, of the DS version Mystery Dungeon: Shiren the Wanderer, we now turn to that game.*

This chapter is focused mostly on new players. If you're an old-hand with the Super Famicom game, following is a list of some of the differences between it and the DS version. Thanks to Teasel from the NeoGAF forums and Gabikun of GameFAQs for some of the items. Further thanks to Lord Gek for pointing me to Gabikun's list.

33.1 Part 1: Why You Should Play This Game

What is it that reviewers have against Mystery Dungeon: Shiren the Wanderer? (*December 2015*: Some of the linked reviews have been taken down and so I removed links, but the quotes remain here as a mark of shame.)

> Everything about this game is excruciatingly painful to anyone who associates the words 'video game' with fun and exciting.
>
> (Britishgaming.co.uk)

I take serious issue with dismissing the game as "painful." Getting killed in ludicrous ways is part of the fun.

> However, due to the turn-based nature of the game, the entire experience feels stop-and-go. Attacking enemies is a quick, no frills affair with only the minimal amount of animations. Granted, this is a port of a Super Nintendo game, but even other SNES RPGs managed to have a little more pizzazz. When we bust out a Lightning Staff or breathe fire thanks to Dragon Herb, we certainly wouldn't mind a smidge more style. We just lit some undead soldier on fire after all, give us something to 'ooh and ah' over!
>
> (IGN DS)

If this guy played an ASCII roguelike it'd probably burn his eyes. And I can't believe he is criticizing a game for being "stop-and-go." I can recognize that he's trying to say something unique, but what does that even mean?

> On the downside, the dungeon generation can be moronic and if Shiren dies, he loses everything—all the items, money, and powers he attained through hours of questing are gone. Games, in general, have gotten easier since this title was originally released on the SNES and this unforgiving style simply won't fly with players raised on newer games.
>
> (GamesRadar)

* Screenshots here are from the Super Famicom fan-translated version, which is easier to get images from.

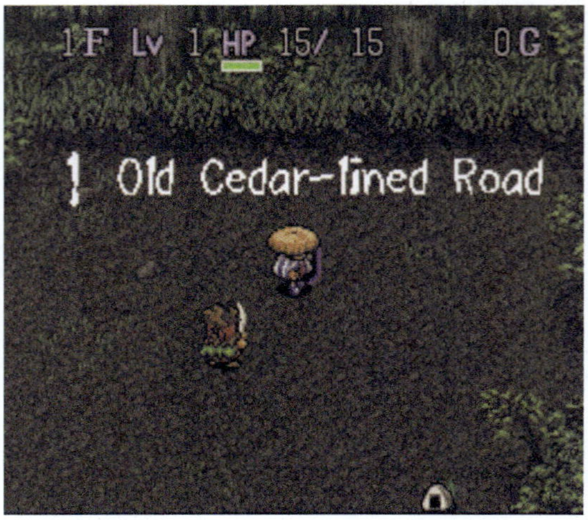

Figure 33.1

Mystery Dungeon: Shiren the Wanderer

Re: moronic, realism is less important than being fun, and the layout of the dungeon levels is less important than what they contain. The fact that games have gotten easier is not seen, universally, as a good thing, even among people who only recently started playing. There must be some reason torture games like I Wanna Be the Guy have gained in popularity, and the main quest of Shiren, while hard, is far from torturous.

> All told, there's not much special to Mystery Dungeon: Shiren the Wanderer. The game is boring in the early going, and then it becomes scary. Who wants to explore so badly that they'll die and go back to zero? This could be yet another example of a product that makes much more sense in the region in which it was initially created. And so, I'd suggest Shiren go back to Japan.
>
> (Geek.com)

The boring early levels are there to fortify the player character for the later levels. Players need to use the treasure found in the first half of the game to survive the second half. This is all by design.

> Imagine if Satan were to create a video game. If he did, he'd probably join forces with ChunSoft to create Mystery Dungeon: Shiren the Wanderer.
>
> [. . .] The game is a roguelike dungeon crawler that spews Japanese gaming out of every orifice imaginable.
>
> (Sega Nerds)

The reviewer misspeaks: roguelikes are really more Cthulhu's bag. "Spewing Japanese gaming" sounds like something I did when I watched a roommate play through Kingdom Hearts. I won't touch upon the "every orifice imaginable" phrasing, except to say that my nightmares feature some pretty funky orifices, and only a few of them show up in Shiren.

With all these reviewers lining up to take shots at the game, you'd almost think it was already out for the Wii . . . .

I can't fault them to some extent, as roguelikes are still kind of obscure. (I hope that my writing will eventually help to alleviate this condition.) But to hear people whose job it is to recommend games for people to play rag on one of my favorites of all time, and I've played a great many, is kind of infuriating. And it looks like I'm not the only one who really likes it, either. So the best thing I can do, as I see it, is present my own view. Here it is.

The first thing you should know about Mystery Dungeon: Shiren the Wanderer, and something that I wish each of the above reviewers had been told before they wrote their pieces, is that it is a game.

That may seem like an obvious statement, but it's not as simple a declaration as it may first appear. While the G in RPG stands for Game, many are not games in the strictest sense: they care more about storytelling than play, and there is no real way to lose. The definition of game has been only recently expanded to cover the kinds of things most CRPGs are. Some still hold that opinion even now. The kinds of persons who turn their nose up at RPGs are probably influenced by those old definitions.

In a Final Fantasy or a Dragon Quest, if your party is wiped out it is not a real failure, for you can always return to your last save. So long as the player doesn't do something grossly stupid, like selling all

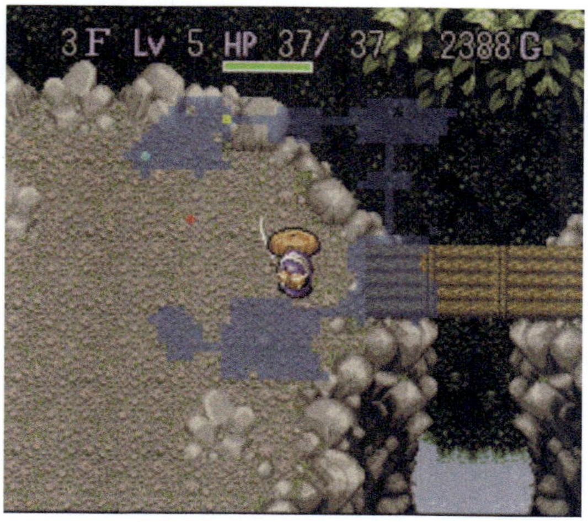

Figure 33.2

Mystery Dungeon: Shiren the Wanderer

his equipment and wandering the wilds naked, he's not going to fail at the quest. Meanwhile, Shiren the Wanderer is a game in a more fundamental sense, the sense that you can actually lose at it, and probably will many times before you earn your first win. While it is not real time, it is still much like a classic arcade game, where games nearly always end by losing. As Dwarf Fortress reminds us, losing can be fun.

But it is still a role-playing game. It and other roguelikes arguably have better claim to that title than other CRPGs. There are games that got inspiration from the earliest incarnations of Dungeons & Dragons, but even now roguelike games, with their "no do-overs" policy, their dependence on player preparation, strategy and volition, and their opportunities for creative play more profound than just hitting the X button repeatedly, feel more like a pen-and-paper RPG session than many Western RPGs, and nearly all other Japanese ones.

The word volition up there isn't used casually, and it gets to the core of what makes roguelikes and traditional CRPGs, which both spring from the same ideas and ancestor games, so different from each other. In traditional games, the player is told, pretty much, exactly what to do and where to go. There may be some subquests, but the focus is on the main story, and there's not a lot the player can do to affect the route he will have to take. Roguelikes require that the player, instead, perceive what his needs are himself, take advantage of the opportunities that present themselves and make his own way through the dungeon. You cannot play a roguelike passively, letting a story wash over you. You must drive yourself forward and accomplish the game.

Of all roguelike RPGs, Mystery Dungeon: Shiren the Wanderer may be the best first-time introduction that has yet been created. It is challenging, but not overwhelmingly so once you learn the rules and how to escape from trouble. While new players still tend to die a lot, they can still make some progress in each game that makes later attempts easier. The artwork, animation and writing are entertaining enough that players can have fun even if they die. The controls are much simpler than the every-key-does-something norm of the genre. And, there are few "instadeaths" compared to a game like NetHack.

Mystery Dungeon: Shiren the Wanderer is a DS game, but it is based on a Super Famicom game released over ten years ago that was never released outside of Japan. The dungeons are random, but there is logic to what happens in them. This logic means it is a game in which amazing things can happen: a monster that attacks the player with an explosion might accidentally kill another monster, thus gaining a level, and becoming a far deadlier monster in the process.

Back in 1996, a guy named Alan Kwan wrote up a couple of stories about the game, based on his own playing, and posted them to Usenet. These stories are how I first learned about the game, and they are still excellent introductions. If you really want to know what playing it feels like I cannot recommend them more highly. I have saved copies that you can read here:

Story 1: Dark Owls, Super Tanks and Menbells: https://sites.google.com/view/extendedplay/replay-ficsfc-furai-no-shiren-replay-fiction-1-long

Story 2: Theft, Master Chickens, and Staves of Misfortune: https://sites.google.com/view/extendedplay/ficsfc-furai-no-shiren-replay-fiction-2

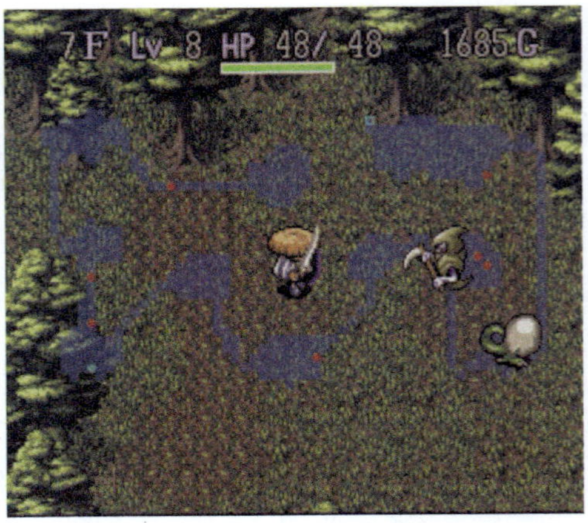

Figure 33.3

Mystery Dungeon: Shiren the Wanderer: Forest scene

Some things Shiren the Wanderer is not:

- It is not impossible. People do win this game. You'll win too if you stick with it, at least the main Table Mountain quest, I guarantee it.
- It is not mindless. Far from it, it requires far more strategy than nearly any other non-roguelike RPG.
- It is not badly made. Shiren the Wanderer is really very well-designed. It has the tightest core game system of any top-tier roguelike other than Rogue itself. Nearly every item, even supposedly bad ones, has a purpose. Every monster, even those with tricky attacks and abilities, have strategic ways to make them less dangerous, some even harmless.
- It is not unfair. The great majority of situations have ways out of them. Sometimes, it is true, you may have to make a sacrifice, or the way out is not to have gotten into it to begin with, but there are usually ways to have seen them coming. With good planning and economical use of resources, you can do a lot to ensure you'll have the tools to survive the latter half of the game.
- It is likely not the same as other random dungeon games you may have played. Although most random dungeon games are inspired by roguelikes, many of them neglect important features. Even among roguelikes, Shiren's a bit special. In the taxonomy of the genre, it's closer to being a Hack-like game than a 'Band, but it's really closest to Rogue itself.

33.2 Part 2: For New Players

Some tips for players going through Table Mountain for the first time:

The beginning of roguelike wisdom is in recognizing critical moments. A critical moment is a turn in which, if you don't do something important, you may die before you get your next turn. For example, if you're next to an enemy who has just hit you for 20 damage, and you have less than 20 HP left, that is a critical moment because you may die if it gets another attack. If you swing and try to kill the monster, you might either not do enough to finish it or miss, in which case if he doesn't miss you may take 20 HP of damage. Even if you know you could kill the enemy with one blow nine times out of ten, you should not take that chance unless you can certainly kill it or have no alternative. There are lots of monsters but only one Shiren, so over the course of the adventure luck tends to favor the enemy.

That is a simple example, but there are so many special monster abilities that it can sometimes be difficult to recognize danger. Most critical moments in this game are caused by damage done by monsters. One of the most reliable responses to a critical moment caused by damage is to push a Chiropractic Jar, which fills up your hit points. These jars are common and can be used multiple times each, make healing easy if you have a spare turn, and you can't heal yourself if you're dead. If in doubt, heal.

If you often find yourself running out of food, consider trying these things:

- There is a free Big Riceball available from talking to a guy across the counter in the tavern in Canyon Village. After adventuring some and finishing some subquests, you can eventually get free fill-ups in Mountaintop Town.

- Sometimes completing one of Fay's Puzzles is worth a free riceball.
- There are ways to get a little extra fullness without eating a riceball. Herbs and meat give you 5% and 10% fullness, respectively.
- The longer you wait before eating a Big Riceball, the more use you get out of it. In a sense, every percentage point a source of fullness will take you over maximum is wasted food. It's usually best to wait until you're actually starving before eating it.
- Riceballs are harmed by Rotten Traps unless they're in some container. With a little searching, quite suitable containers are not hard to come across and identify.
- While finding riceballs in the dungeon is random, there are monsters in the game that make food, and monsters are less random than items. Making effective use of them is tricky, but not hard with a little thought.
- There are two guaranteed shops in the game that often have riceballs in them. New to the DS game, you can leave these towns and return to them to regenerate their stock.
- Staying at an inn fills up your hunger meter. If you're approaching a town with an inn in it, you should probably not eat a riceball, but wait until town.
- Don't wander around too much. You get hungry as turns pass, and walking around is how most turns are wasted. Don't take the long way around a dungeon level if you can help it, don't waste too much time healing up, don't run from fights more than you have to, and don't spend a lot of time grinding for levels.
- Some monsters make you hungrier as a special attack. Deal with them quickly to save your stomach.
- Finally, if you're really out of food, you can still make do for a few turns. Running out of fullness doesn't mean you die instantly; you just are unable to heal naturally and lose one HP a turn until you eat. If you have reliable means of healing, you can keep going for a short while. If you're getting near the end but your food stores are depleted, a sprint to the stairs can be effective. I've won a game while in starvation mode.
- If you've got extra stuff, use excess resources first. Dragon Herbs are one of the more useful items, able to destroy most single monsters in one turn, but if you have several of them they should be an early recourse in a tricky situation.

If your inventory is full and you really want to pick up another item, you might have to make a hard decision as to what to take with you and what to leave behind. One option is, instead of just dropping something, think if something you're carrying can be usefully used up first. Of special note is when you're carrying Medicinal Herbs, Restoration Herbs and Chiropractic Jars. Chiropractic Jars are the best healing items in the game: they fill all your hit points instead of 100 at most, and they can each be used multiple times. If you have several Chiropractic Jars you're probably set as far as healing goes. In this case, if you're suffering from full pockets, consider eating the Medicinal Herbs and Restoration Herbs when you're at full hit points. This both frees up inventory space and increases your maximum hit points by a small amount. Of course, if you haven't found any Chiropractic Jars you'll need those herbs for healing.

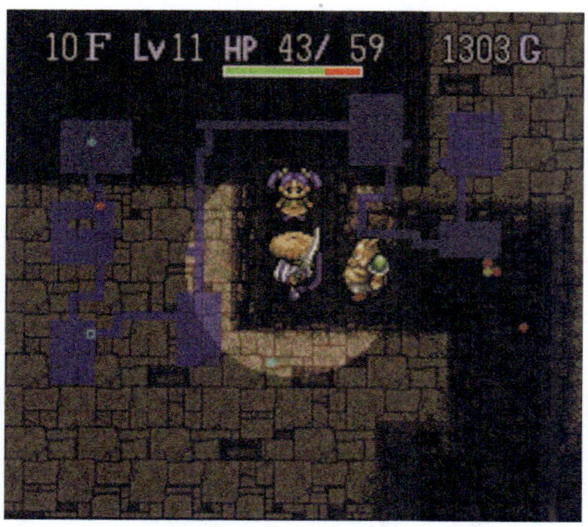

Figure 33.4

Mystery Dungeon: Shiren the Wanderer: Dungeon area

One of the hint-providing characters in the game offers a tip that makes it sound like all shields make you hungrier but the Armor Ward shield makes you more hungry than usual, and Hide Shields make you less. This is not exactly true. Most shields don't affect your hunger rate at all. Only the Armor Ward shield makes you hungrier, and the Hide Shield makes you less hungry than even if you had no shield. Without a shield, you lose 1 fullness point every ten turns, but with a Hide Shield you lose 1 every 20.

The walls in dungeons are interesting because, unlike with water, trees or pits, you cannot cut across their corners by moving diagonally, either to move or attack with a weapon. This means, if you're standing in a doorway, usually only one monster can attack you. But a few monsters have attacks that can hit through corners, particularly any monster with a flame attack. While most swords cannot attack across wall corners, the Razor Wind sword can, as well as arrows, staff blasts and thrown items.

In a tight spot, one-use items should be used before wands. Shiren has very limited inventory space, and a wand is potentially several escapes in one slot while a Dragon Herb is only one. There are plenty of exceptions to this though: Dragon Herbs are the most powerful instant damage item, and some scrolls, such as Blastwave, Confusion and Sleep, can affect a whole room.

Blastwave Scrolls become less useful for clearing our Monster Houses later on. In Table Mountain, even reading two such scrolls will probably not clear a Monster House, although it'll probably make it much easier to kill the monsters in melee. A FAQ for the SNES version on GameFAQs claims that reading a Powerup Scroll before reading a Blastwave increases its power. I have yet to confirm this, however. (It also says that reading multiple Powerup Scrolls have a cumulative effect.)

Keep food in Jars of Holding to protect them from Rotten traps.

Most item-destroying enemies cannot destroy your currently-used equipment.

Curse Girls and family can now curse any item. Non-equipment cursed items cannot be used, but can still be thrown.

Don't keep all your food in one jar, so you don't lose access to all your food because of one inopportune curse.

If you really need the contents of a cursed Jar of Holding, you can get your stuff back by throwing it at a wall. The jar will break and your stuff will be released onto the floor. But if you can wait, it's best to use a Scroll of Blessing so you can keep the jar.

The Fowl family of enemies can electrify items. Charged items cannot be used, dropped or thrown, and vanish once off the floor. It's unknown, currently, if there is a way to rescue a charged item before it evaporates. Fowl-class enemies don't seem to be able to affect jars, but this may be inaccurate.

Rice Changers CAN affect jars. Make an effort to kill them before they get into melee range. If you're trapped, you can protect important items by dropping them, for Rice Changers can only transform stuff you're carrying. (Note, however, that Field Raiders also appear on the Rice Changer floors, and they can turn items on the ground into weeds.)

Here's a table of which monsters can affect which items, based on personal observation. I do not claim that it's perfectly accurate, especially for Fowl, but it seems to hold up for me:

Table 33.1 Item destroyers in Shiren DS

	Effect on items	Equipment?	Jars?
Fowl	Destroy (electrify)	N	N
Rice Changer	Transform into Rice Ball	N	Y
Curse Girl	Curse	Y	Y
Walrus	Steal	N	Y
Slime	Corrode	Y (only in-use)	N

When you hit a normal-speed enemy with a Wand of Sloth, slowing it down, you have one turn before it gets its next move. If you slowed it because it can kill you in one turn and it's adjacent, the best move to make is to step away from it, so it'll use its next move to catch up. Then you can kill it easily using hit-and-run tactics.

The most common wands, in order from most useful to least, are: Bufu, Paralysis, Postpone, Sloth, Doppelganger, Knockback, Lightning, Switching and Steadiness. But each has particular instances where they excel. Doppelganger is the only wand that can potentially save you from a whole Monster House, although at the cost of allowing foes to promote. Lightning is good if you have no arrows. Switching is best

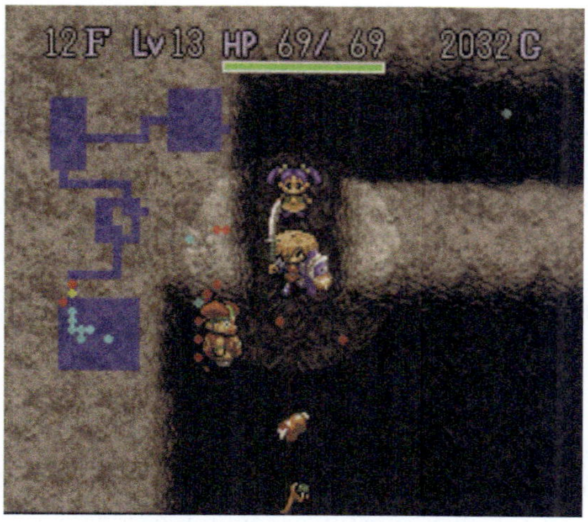

Figure 33.5

Mystery Dungeon: Shiren the Wanderer: A shop

in opportunistic situations, but can sometimes instantly get you from the middle of a Monster House to the door or staircase. Steadiness is hard to identify, but in the Table Mountain adventure it's usually the wand that doesn't cause anything to happen when swung at a monster.

One of the most frustrating situations in the game is being attacked by a wall-pass monster inside a wall. Monsters that can pass through walls are unique in that, while embedded, they can attack without you being able to hit them back. One of the deadliest later monsters, Death Angel, has double-speed, double attacks AND wall-pass! If you're in a corridor and don't have a pickaxe, the only effective way to fight them is to move along the corridor, offering it free attacks, until, in the process of following you, it moves into the passage. Don't skimp on the healing if this happens to you.

Room-affecting scrolls, if not used in a room, work only on the spaces immediately surrounding Shiren. A notable exception to this is the Monster Scroll, which turns a room into a Monster House, complete with loot. If it's read in a corridor, the game will teleport Shiren to a room before it takes effect.

New to the DS version is the ability to go backward through the stairs, to previous levels, up to a point, but items usually aren't generated on the ground on such levels except in shops. But monsters that drop items upon death do still appear and leave loot behind, and if you go back a floor because you fell through a pitfall (which happens on the Table Mountain levels, which go up instead of down), then you WILL find items on that level.

One of the cooler things about the game that people don't suspect at first is that some items have special effects when thrown. Dragon Scrolls, when read, blast in front of Shiren with fire breath, but they also have a similar effect when thrown, and if thrown with a Pitcher's Armband they can affect a whole line of monsters. Bottomless Jars, if thrown and broken, create pitfall traps. Break a Walrus Jar and its walruses become monsters on the current level—useful because they leave behind loot if killed before they steal from the player. If a Monster Jar is pressed, its monsters jump out and surround the player, but if the jar is thrown and broken the monsters will be generated confused. If you really need to kill an enemy from a distance, you can throw spare weapons and shields. Finally, while the game suggests throwing staves if they are out of charges to get one last effect, it is possible, though rare, that a thrown staff will have no effect.

Three floors in the Table Mountain quest, in particular, are unusually dangerous and should be evacuated as soon as possible. Levels 15 and 16, the marsh right before Table Mountain, are the "drain floors." They have several monsters that can lower your strength, corrode equipment, destroy items and drain levels. The experience you could earn from defeating them, and even the loot you could get, is generally not worth the resources lost in exploring them, so my advice is to head through the exit as soon as you find it.

The other super-dangerous floor is 26, the Ravine of Illusions, a somewhat-open level containing Skull Wraiths. Skull Wraiths are the third level of the Skeleton Mage monster and have much more dangerous wand effects. They can paralyze, confuse or put you to sleep; turn you into a monster or even a riceball; temporarily seal your inventory; and drain levels, all from a distance. Just being in line with a Skull Wraith is a critical moment: a single unlucky shot can end your game. If you get paralyzed or slept, they may well get the chance to get several more shots off on you before you get another turn. Skull Wraiths are among the most dangerous monsters in the game and should be neutralized as soon as possible. If you paralyze one, it's recommended that you do NOT wake it up to kill it unless you can finish it immediately.

From 26 on to the end, the game spikes up in difficulty. In addition to Skull Wraiths, dragons appear on these floors. Sprinting to the stairs is often a good idea.

To handle level 30: the boss monster, Tainted Insect, looks imposing and has a bucket full of hit points but can be affected in all the ways the other monsters can be. In practice, the Skull Wraiths on this floor are much more threatening. But when the boss is killed, all the other monsters die as well, and the boss won't appear on later runs through Table Mountain.

33.3 Sources

Britishgaming.co.uk: page, indeed the whole site, is dead. URL was http://www.britishgaming.co.uk/?p=271. They appear to be vanished from the web.

GamesRadar: Review at https://www.gamesradar.com/mystery-dungeon-shiren-the-wanderer-review/. Written by Raymond Padilla.

Geek.com: page is dead, site seems to be down. Article was at: https://www.geek.com/review-mystery-dungeon-shiren-the-wanderer-for-ds/

IGN DS: page is dead. URL was https://www.ign.com/ds/articles/856/856601p1.html The review is still extant however, at: https://www.ign.com/articles/2008/03/04/mystery-dungeon-shiren-the-wanderer-review. Written by Jack DeVries.

Sega Nerds: Page is down. Article is no longer online, it appears. Review was at: http://www.seganerds.com/2008/03/09/review-mystery-dungeon-shiren-the-wanderer/

34

Architecture of the Mystery Dungeon

June 2007 I've mostly been covering the traditional roguelikes of late, which are primarily terminal games with roots back to the very origins of computer gaming, to the neglect of the extensive Japanese console branch of the genre. They've had commercial roguelikes all over the place, thanks mostly to a little company called ChunSoft, known for the "Mysterious Dungeon," a.k.a. Fushigi no Dungeon, games.

The first game was a licensed game based off of one of the player characters in Dragon Quest IV, and since then it has crossed over with the Final Fantasy, Tower of Druaga and even Pokémon franchises, as well as a "default" character, Shiren the Wanderer, whose games are usually the best of the series.

As ChunSoft has found inspiration from the roguelikes, so have other Japanese publishers found inspiration from ChunSoft, and so the Mysterious Dungeon games have quite a lot of imitators. Off the top of my head, there's Azure Dreams, Climax Landers (Time Stalkers in the U.S.) and the Ancient Cave segments of later Estopolis/Lufia games. Lufia: The Legend Returns for the GBC makes that the entire game.

Sega made a rather uninspired roguelike in the form of Fatal Labyrinth for the Genesis. The recent Izuna: Legend of the Unemployed Ninja is a fairly close example of the type, and the popular homebrew WonderSwan game Dicing Knight has some roguelike aspects as well. Even Parasite Eve has an optional random section in the form of the Chrysler Building.

34.1 Mysterious Lineage

The chain of inspiration here is important. From playing them, it seems unlikely that the makers of most of those other games have ever heard of NetHack or Angband. Their source of inspiration is clearly the Mysterious Dungeon games. Take note, class, for this is how a subgenre gets its start. Their designers invariably mistake the idiosyncrasies in Mysterious Dungeon as essential design aspects, and not knowing about those features it leaves out, an entire field of games has sprung up without wishing, bones, player ghosts, vaults, resistance building or any of the other clever little features the maintainers (or players, in the case of open source games) of traditional roguelikes cooked up from scratch. Not knowing their importance, they usually care little about identifying items, dungeon room shops, traps or equipment advancement. Some of them don't even feature grid-based tactical movement.

This isn't to say that none of these games are good, but the best ones continue to be those by ChunSoft, whose designers display in their work a great fondness for Rogue and NetHack. And ChunSoft is not

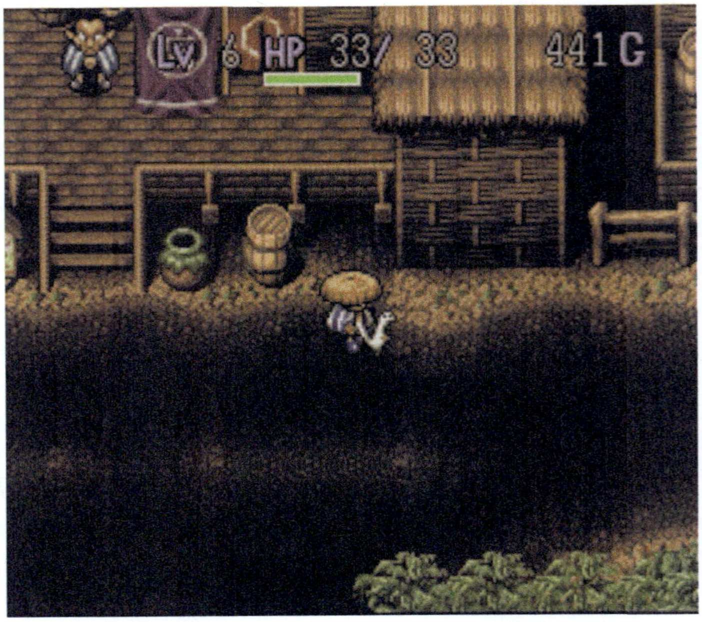

Figure 34.1
Mystery Dungeon: Shiren the Wanderer A town

merely acting as a plagiarist; there are some genuinely novel ideas to be found there, additions that the traditional roguelike developers would do well to take notice of, which I'll get around to mentioning . . . later.

Before covering Shiren, it would be helpful to cover the play metaphor of the games, which originated with the original Torneko no Daibouken, and is so copied by all the other games of this subgenre that its presence is the surest indicator that we're talking about a Japanese roguelike.

What do I mean by a play metaphor? It's something so deeply ingrained in computer gaming that few players spare it a thought. It's in the association of the player's identity, in the depicted game-world, with that of a protagonist character. It's in the translation from the abstract events taking place on-screen to a pretend reality constructed in the player's head. And it's in the nebulous "space between the games," the idea that it is okay for games to feature continuity across play sessions, and to play around with the separation between the real world and the virtual one.

The process of setting up the game world is substantially different for roguelikes, of all types, from other games that can just load environments off disk, that even the initial play requires some setup. A freshly installed copy of NetHack is different from one that's had a few games played; the played install will probably have some bones laying around, and its score list will have a few entries. It may be easier to be the first to play an installation of Dungeon Crawl than the tenth, as there won't be any troublesome player ghosts to be encountered.

But traditional roguelikes use these features as curiosities. Japanese roguelikes greatly expand their role, using this idea to construct a meta-game that wraps around the dungeon exploration mode.

34.2 The Afterlife Looks Familiar

When a player begins a game of the original Mysterious Dungeon game, Torneko no Daibouken (Americanized as "Taloon's Great Adventure"), he is not thrown into the first level of a sprawling dungeon. Nor does he appear in a "town" dungeon level with shops and low-level opponents, or an overworld populated with random encounters and dungeons. His character begins in a field, talking with his wife and son about his dreams of opening a shop.

Soon after, he meets with the king and is told of the Mystery Dungeon, which contains lots of stuff to sell. But the dungeon is a dangerous place, so first the king asks Torneko to retrieve an item from a trial dungeon as a test.

In he goes . . .

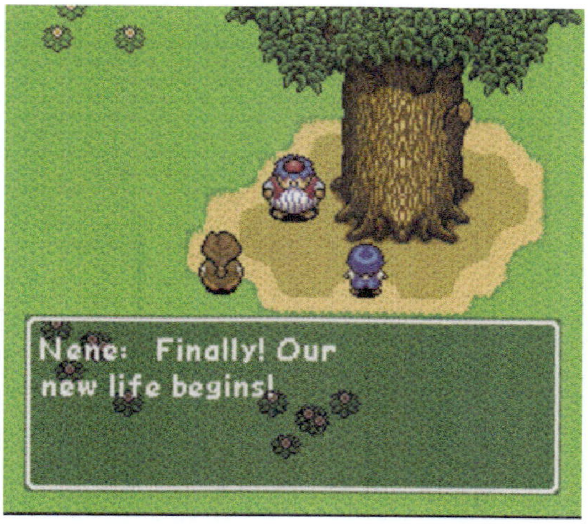

Figure 34.2

Torneko no Daibouken: Opening

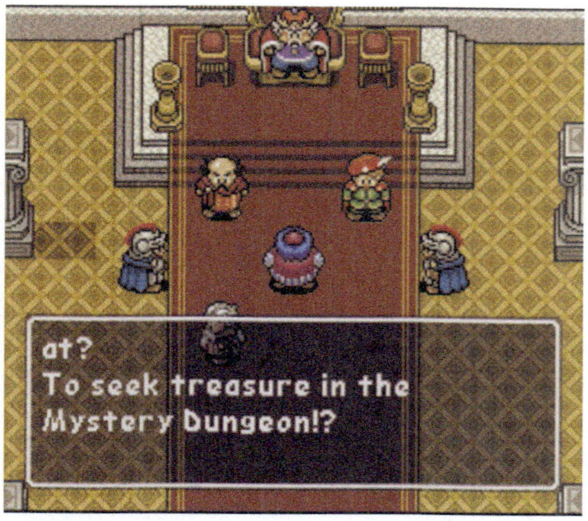

Figure 34.3

Torneko no Daibouken: Audience with the king

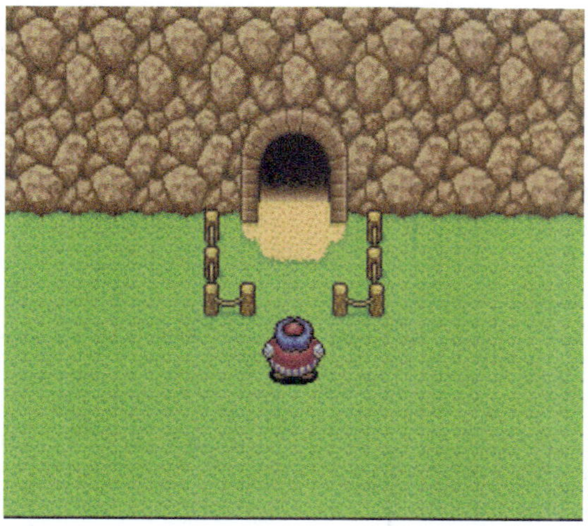

Figure 34.4

Torneko no Daibouken: Into the dungeon

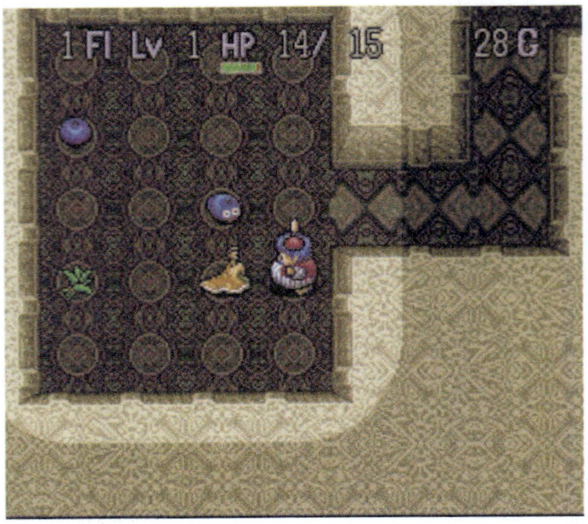

Figure 34.5

Torneko no Daibouken: Monsters!

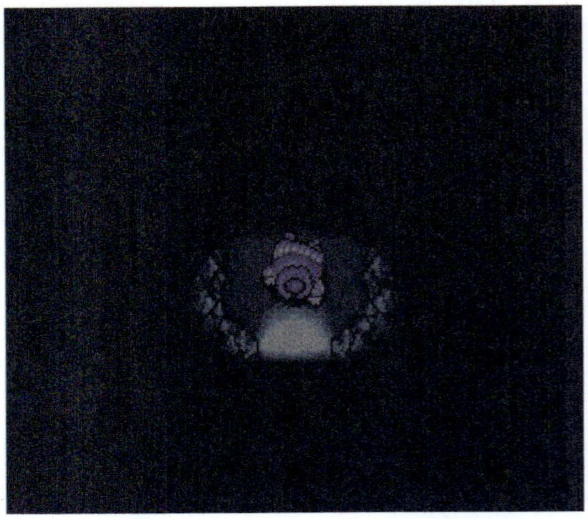

Figure 34.6

Torneko no Daibouken: Oops

He's in a random level. Ah, there are some monsters! He's going to try fighting them . . .

Oh, he got killed. So it goes.

But what is this? I thought he was dead! Are those guys throwing out his decaying corpse as part of some monstrous Keep Our Lair Beautiful program?

No, he's back at the king again. Does the game not have permadeath? How can it be called a roguelike without that?

It's because there's really two games here. There is an outer game that plays like Dragon Quest, what with the narrative and the talking and the storing and the buying, and an inner game that plays like Rogue. Not coincidentally, Torneko no Daibouken is set in the Dragon Quest IV world. The player character never dies in the outer game; in fact, there are no dangers there. It is no accident that it takes place in towns and castles; the player is just as safe from monster attacks there as he is in Generic Fantasytown. From there the player enters the dungeon, in some games just by leaving town, some by finding an entrance somewhere, and the inner, or real, game begins.

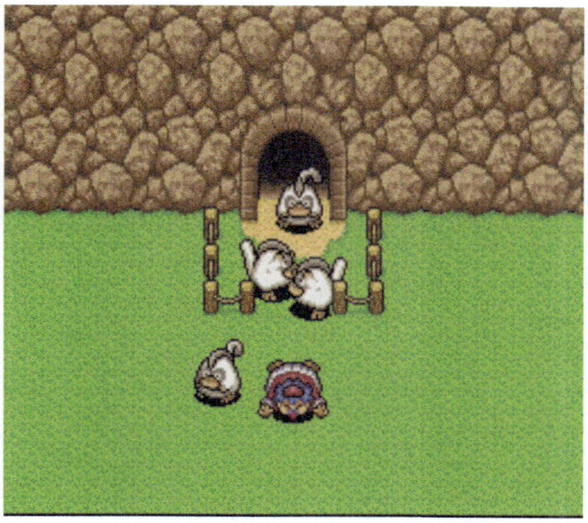

Figure 34.7

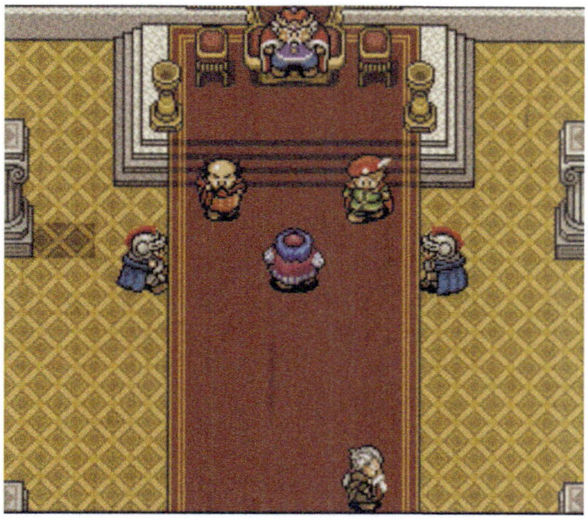

Figure 34.8

Torneko no Daibouken: Back at the king

34.3 Level 3 Town, with Population 750 and 40 Hit Points

The distinction isn't just for show. When our player finishes the trial dungeon, he'll find himself in a typical RPG town. The town gets larger as the player saves up money found in the dungeon. Eventually new resources open up to him as he goes which make the dungeon exploration game easier.

Here, town serves as a shell by which the player gains access to the real game. The town's services function similarly to NetHack's bones and Crawl's player ghosts: they are actually an outside-the-game influence. Later Japanese Roguelikes greatly expand on this idea. Shiren has warehouses for item storage, blacksmiths for improving equipment, special quests to complete to gain access to new items and helpers, and eventually bonus dungeons with special rules.

None of these features are necessary to win the game, but they make it a bit easier. A popular sub-subgenre of the Japanese Roguelikes, including games like Azure Dreams and Pokémon Rescue Team, mix the roguelike aspects with a dinobuddy monster-raising simulation. Azure Dreams resets the player's level to 1 every trip into the tower, but the player's monsters retain their level and grow ever stronger. These monsters are kept in a stable between trips to the dungeon, which allows the player to keep track of them. In these kinds of games, the outer game's amenities are not optional, and their maintenance grows to rival the roguelike play in importance. Whether this improves the outer game is a question I will not answer, but I think it is obvious that these aspects cannot help but dilute the inner game, where the focus should lie.

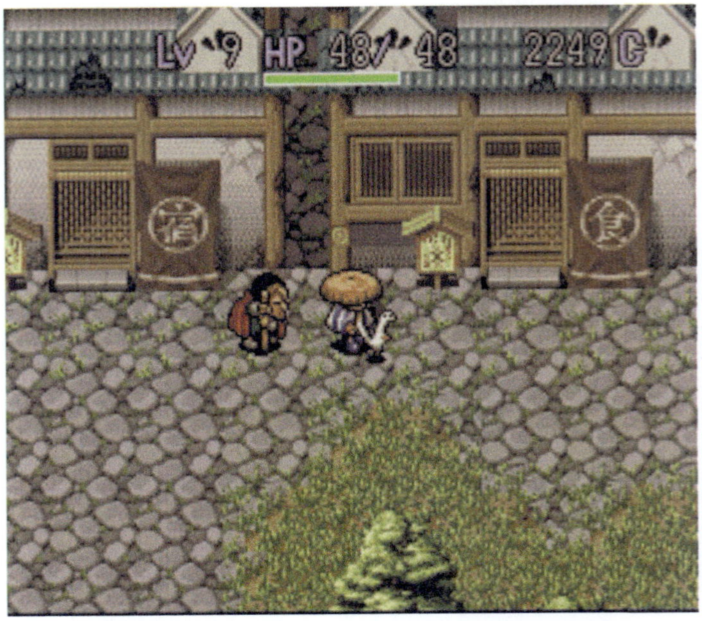

Figure 34.9

Shiren the Wanderer: Another town

The dual advancement tracks of the Japanese roguelikes, that of the inner game (player experience and equipment) and the outer game (town growth, quest status, saved equipment, monster pets, what have you), give them a different dynamic than traditional roguelikes. In Rogue, every character starts off from square one. In the Mysterious Dungeon games, the dungeon effectively becomes easier after a while.

35

Fei's Problems

August 2007 Let's have a quick look at one of the more interesting parts of Shiren the Wanderer, the series of puzzle dungeons called Fei's Problems. In the starting town there is a building that contains a shopkeeper-looking guy called Fei, who's constructed a series of 50 non-random single dungeon levels he wants you to attempt.

Most of these dungeons are arranged so that there's only one way out of the situation presented. Some of them rely on obscure aspects of the game rules. Because of this, they serve as an excellent step-by-step tutorial for learning how to play the game. Only one can be tried on each "life," but they yield helpful items, occasionally very nice ones. Later on they get quite diabolical. For example, there's one that relies on the fact that, if you're standing on money without having picked it up, it can be thrown at monsters for high damage!

But as far as deviousness goes the last problem tops it easily . . .

In addition to Fei's Problems, there are three "bonus dungeons" in the game, each with subtly different item generation qualities and monsters. The first starts the player out with a Bufoo's Cleaver weapon, which often turns killed monsters into meat, but contains less normal equipment than usual. Monster meat is a fairly powerful item, which lets you either turn yourself into a monster, or turn other monsters into its type. Facing a Sky Dragon? Just chuck the meat of a Mamul (an extremely weak monster) at it.

The second bonus dungeon gives the player a Trapper Bracer, which makes him immune to traps but causes monsters to be affected by them.

The last bonus dungeon becomes available after the main quest has been defeated and all 50 of Fei's Problems have been completed. Then, if you go speak with Fei, he'll revealed that his digging has uncovered an unusually large and difficult dungeon. It's a 99-level random dungeon with every monster and item in the game showing up. It also scrambles scroll and herb identities, which in the other dungeons are always known. In short, it's just the challenge that roguelike experts relish. It's Fei's Final Problem!

I've completed this dungeon. While it can be difficult to get started, it's not quite as difficult as escaping with Rogue's Amulet of Yendor. This is because of an interesting little trick that seems to be intentional.

There's an item in the game that raises the player's maximum hit points by 5. There is a kind of item in the final dungeon, the Angel Seed, that raises the player's experience level by 5. There are items that increase stomach capacity and that let pots contain more items or "Backs," and there's even one, the Synthesis Pot, that lets you take base weapons and shields and combine other like-type items with it, adding together not only their pluses but their special qualities.

Another item in the dungeon is called the Duplication Pot. When an item is put inside, it creates an identical duplicate, which also appears in the pot. When the pot is thrown and broken, thus, the player gets twice what he put in. Imagine how useful it is to do this with an Angel Seed! Duplication Pots are rare, of course, so this can't typically be used more than once. Unless . . .

There's also an item in this dungeon, the Withdraw Scroll, that lets the player, once, remove the stuff from a pot without breaking it. Use it on the Duplication Pot and you can use it again, making more copies of whatever you want. Of course, Withdraw Scrolls are also rare.

But just imagine if the player had a Duplication Pot and two Withdraw Scrolls. Then, he took one of those Withdraw Scrolls and put it into the Duplication Pot. If he read the remaining scroll, he could get out of the pot two Withdraw Scrolls. He's gotten the stuff out of the pot without breaking it, and he hasn't lost any items. He could do this again and again and lose nothing except the turns necessarily to perform this little ritual.

This would be just a curiosity if the pot was only big enough to hold the Withdraw Scrolls, but it's usually bigger than that. If expanded with other scrolls, the pot can be made big enough to contain up to ten objects. In addition to duplicating Withdraw Scrolls, up to four other items can be duplicated each time.

Do you see where this is going? The player can duplicate Angel Seeds and, in just a few turns, reach maximum level (70). He can duplicate Life Herbs and reach maximum hit points (250). He can duplicate Expansion Herbs and get to maximum satiation (200%). And best (or worst, depending on your point of view), he can take a +1 weapon and a third Withdraw Scroll, then duplicate them to make two +1 weapons, then use a Synthesis Pot to combine them into a +2 weapon while using the extra Withdraw Scroll to get it out. Repeat over and over to get to +4, then +8, then +16 . . .

The maximum plus a weapon or shield can have is +99, which in D&D is power possessed not even by the gods, but because item special functions can also be added in, the numeric limit doesn't have to be the end. A +99 shield is extremely strong, but how about a rustproof +99 shield which makes half of enemy attacks miss and also defends against item theft, stat draining and dragon fire?

But here's the thing about the Final Problem. By the time the player reaches around dungeon floor 70, the only monsters appearing are the strongest in the game. These floors are infested with the top-level dragon monsters, which in any other context would be over-powered. The easiest dragons can breathe fire on the player if he's in a straight line with them. The middle dragons can breathe fire if the player's anywhere in the room. The highest-level dragons can flame the player anywhere on the floor, regardless of sight, walls or even knowledge! They breathe, wherever they are, and Shiren is hurt. They breathe, each of them, for there can be several on the level, around one turn in five. Even with the Dragon Shield's fire resistance ability folded in that's enough damage per hit that 250 HP can be depleted in a few attacks. But on the other hand, the player can also duplicate healing herbs, undoing that damage in a couple of turns, and they don't breathe fire every turn.

This is what the end of Shiren becomes. It is powergaming taken to its ultimate extreme, ruthless exploitation of the system because without it, the player is toast. It is interesting once, but honestly? Once a good

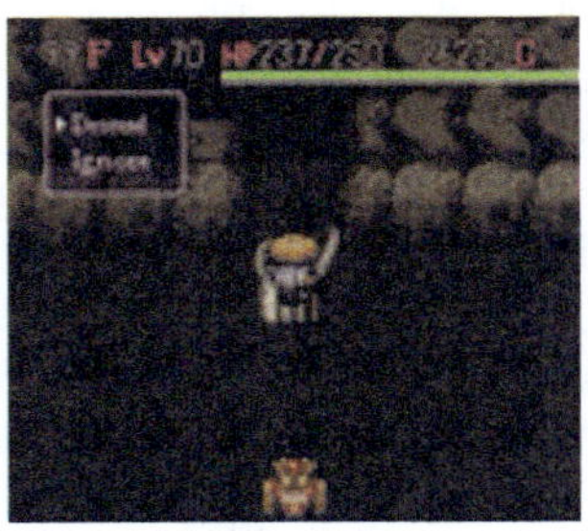

Figure 35.1

Shiren the Wanderer: The end of the dungeon!

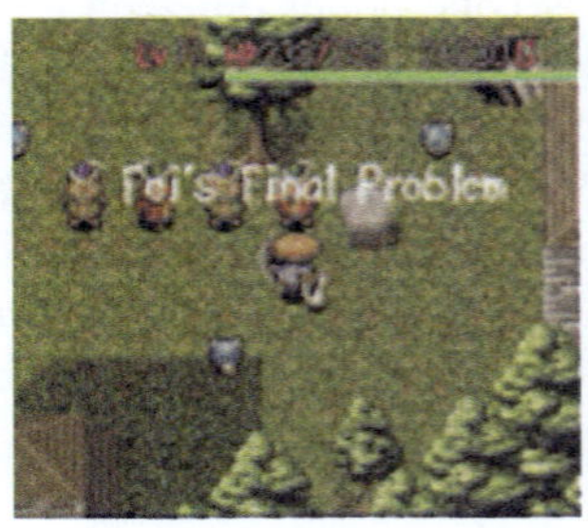

Figure 35.2

Shiren the Wanderer: Some strange place

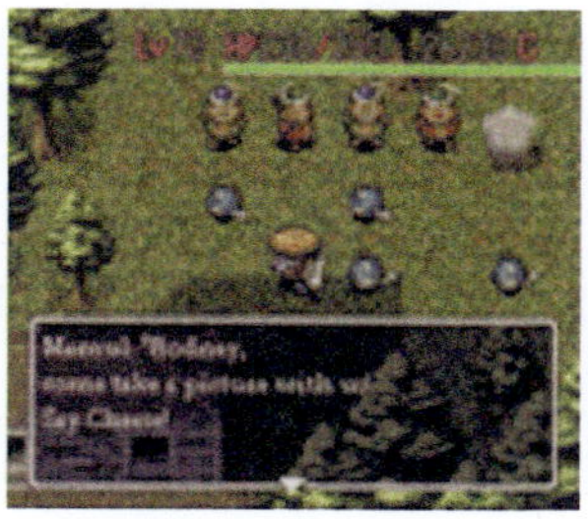

Figure 35.3

Shiren the Wanderer: Sightseeing at the end of the world

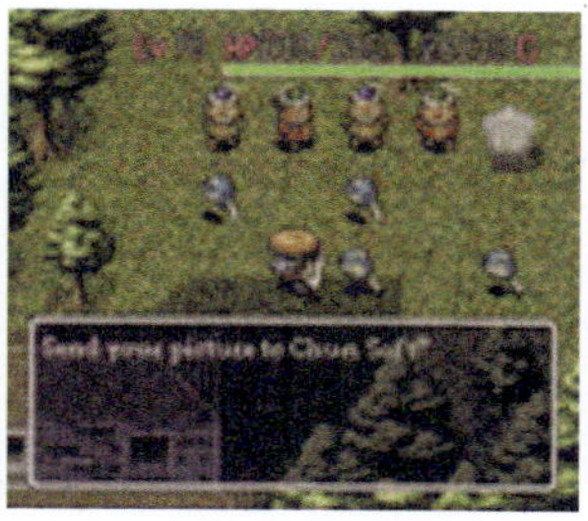

Figure 35.4

Shiren the Wanderer: Please don't send this picture to Chun Soft

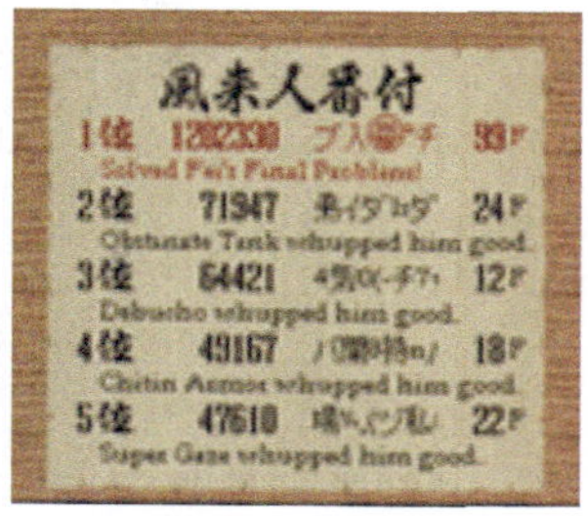

Figure 35.5

Shiren the Wanderer: The End

duplication engine is going scarcity is destroyed, it's like dungeon exploration after the Singularity, and the game becomes much less interesting, even with all the items unidentified at first. It's probably intentional by the designers (it is "Fei's Final Problem" after all, implying they expect the player to use a trick to succeed), but it's just a trick.

Visual record of the end of Fei's Final Problem (complete with glitchy text, presumably resulting from the translation patch authors not having tested this part of the game):

36

Taloon's Mystery Dungeon, in Great Detail

July 2007 Figure 36.1: Here is Taloon, our hero, making his way through the first level of the Mystery Dungeon. His objective is the Happiness Box around level 27. Let's follow him along for a while, shall we?

First off, take notice of the blue silhouette overlaid on the screen. This is the automap. It can be turned on and off from the menus.

Since only a very small portion of the dungeon will fit on one screen, this provides an alternative to being able to see the whole layout in Rogue. Monsters that are in Taloon's range of sight, even if they don't appear on the main screen, show up as red dots. Items are blue dots, and the stairs to the next level appear as a tiny blue box.

Next, see the light-colored circle around our hero? That is the range of his vision. As you can see, walls and corridors are visible beyond that range, but monsters are only visible if they're within that circle. Here Taloon is in a dark corridor and you can only see a single space around, but in a room the circle expands to the edges of its walls.

At the top of the screen is the status line. "1 Fl" is the dungeon level he's on, "Lv 1" is his experience level, then there's his hit points displayed both as a number and a life bar, and finally the gold he's carrying. In this game, as in Rogue, money is just a score. Nothing can be purchased with it.

There's some other status info as well, including "Belly," which is how full Taloon's stomach is, and "Strength," which is actually physical strength. Those show up on another status window that appears when Taloon stands still, or when the player opens up the action menu. We'll see those soon enough.

Figure 36.2: Here you can see a room. A slime, eternal mascot of the Dragon Quest games, is over to the left. Notice how you can also see it on the map as a red dot?

Figure 36.3: Killing it was enough to get Taloon to level 2. His maximum hit points went up to 22. Like in other roguelikes, and like D&D, the number of maximum hit points gained is random. He got 7 this time, which isn't bad.

Figure 36.4: Here's what he's carrying. There can be up to two pages of stuff. The Big Bread is starting rations, enough to fill his stomach to capacity once. The Identify scroll and Bronze Shield +2 were found lying around. Equipping the shield was a risk, since it could have had a minus instead of a plus, and be cursed. I could have read the scroll to find out if was cursed before wearing it, but that would have used up the scroll. Generally, it is better to use Identify scrolls on magic items than equipment unless the player has a surplus of them. And among items, it's usually better to identify rings first, followed by wands. So far, herbs (the game's

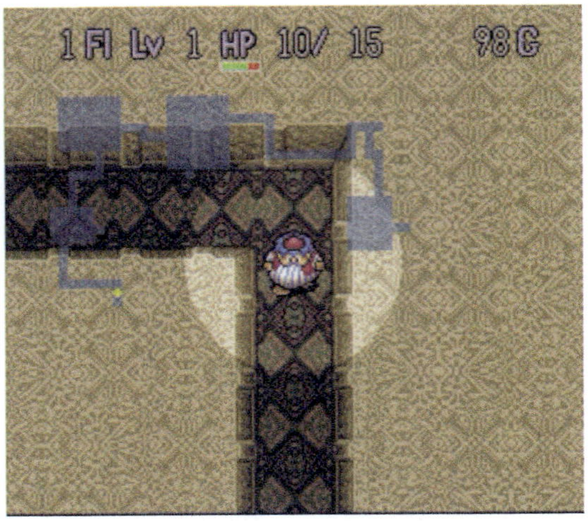

Figure 36.1

Torneko no Daibouken: Level 1

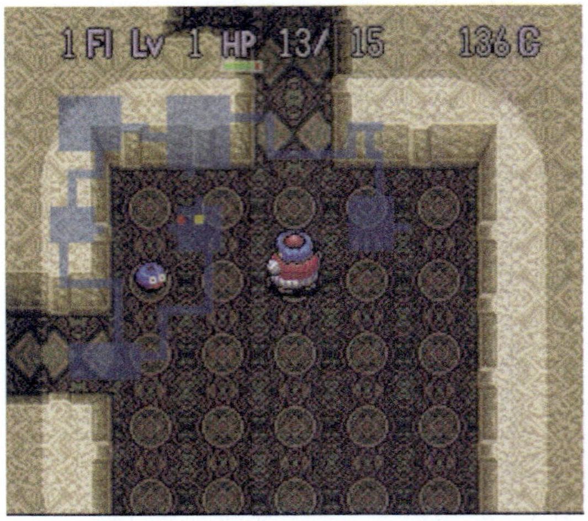

Figure 36.2

Torneko no Daibouken: Room on Level 1

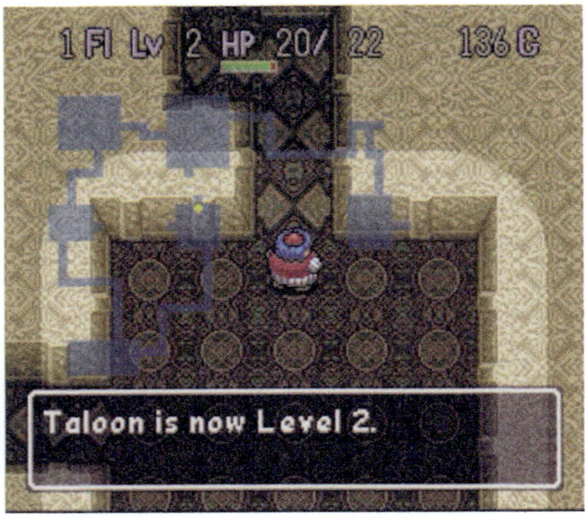

Figure 36.3

Torneko no Daibouken: Experience level 2

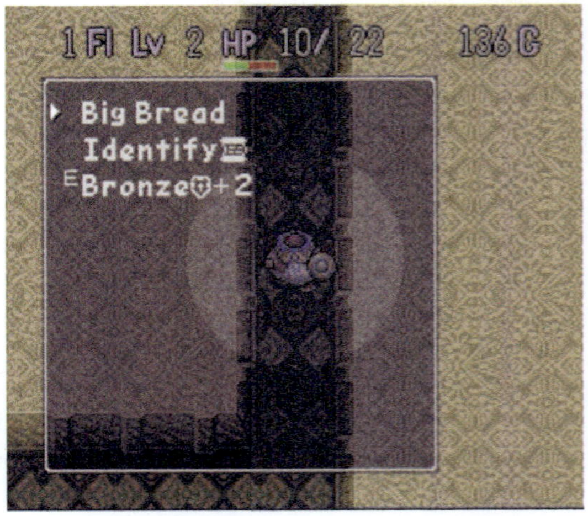

Figure 36.4

Torneko no Daibouken: Early inventory

analogue for potions) and scrolls are not randomly scrambled in the game. Once the player escapes with the Happiness Box, further forays into the dungeon will have more items scrambled.

Figure 36.5: This is actually from a different game, since I died soon after that last pic. Notice that Taloon's maximum hit points are different. Here, we're on dungeon level 2. Entering a new level is always a bit of a risk because there could be a difficult monster right by the stairs, so it's usually good to be free of any easily solvable conditions before going down. Notice also that Taloon is carrying a sword here. He found a Gold Sword +1 on level 1. While it isn't a terribly good weapon, it is worth some extra score if brought back to the surface, and it is rustproof.

Figure 36.6: By later on the same level, I've found these things. Having a shield and sword at this point is pretty nice. Unlike Rogue, Taloon begins the game with no equipment. Until he finds something on the floor, he must rely on his fists for weapons, and his comical pinstriped shirt for protection.

The other stuff he's carrying is mostly useful. The best is the Bang scroll, which does moderate damage to all enemies in the room. If it's used in a corridor, it'll only harm enemies in the eight spaces around him. The Muddle herb is better thrown than consumed; that way, it'll confuse the enemy instead of Taloon. (Confusion here, as in other roguelikes, translates to moving randomly most of the time and not being able to control what you attack.) The Eyedrop herb cures bad eyesight, but that's a fairly rare condition. Finally,

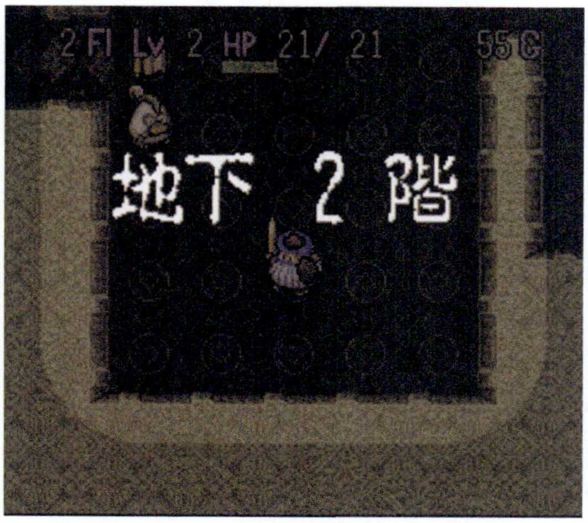

Figure 36.5

Torneko no Daibouken: Level 2

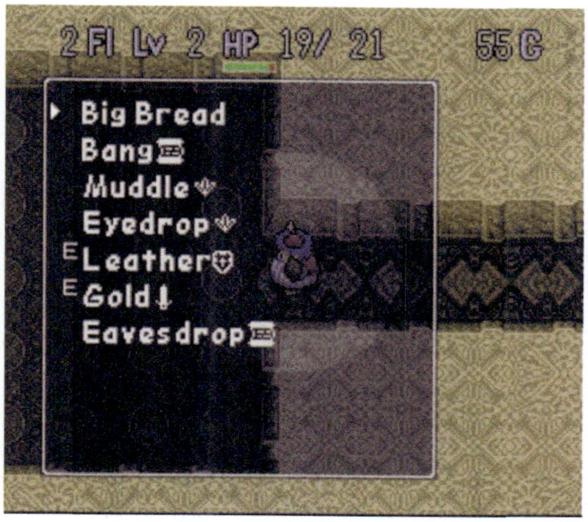

Figure 36.6

Torneko no Daibouken: Got some stuff

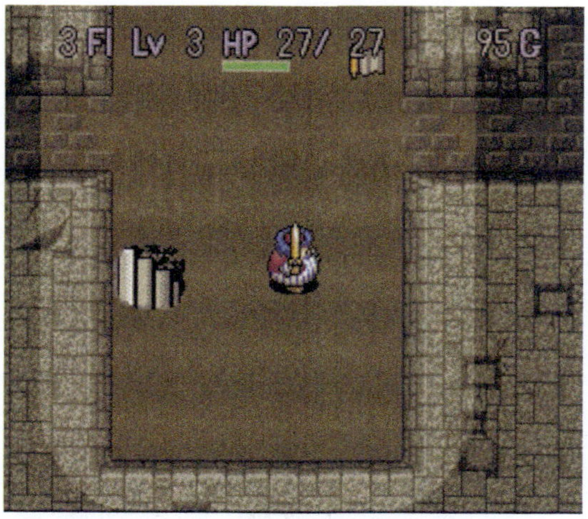

Figure 36.7

Torneko no Daibouken: Level 3

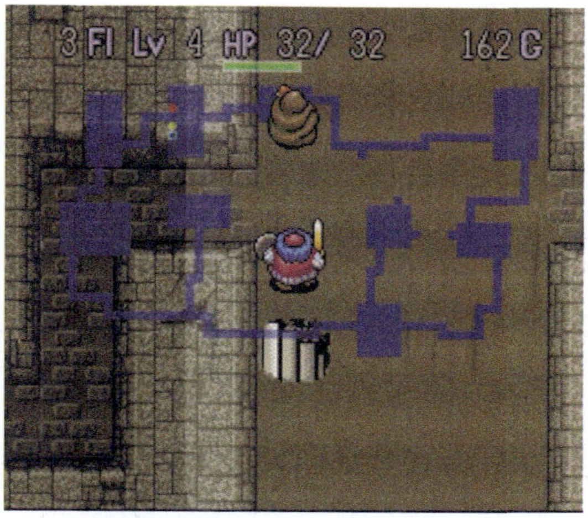

Figure 36.8

Torneko no Daibouken: Magician

the Eavesdrop scroll shows the locations of all monsters on the automap until the player leaves the level. It doesn't reveal which monsters they are; the player will have to figure that out for himself, or go to them and see.

Figure 36.7: A bit later still. Now I'm on level 3, and luckily the stairs to 4 are in the same room.

Here is the dilemma. I could dive, going to the next level right away. I'd save lots of food this way, and have no risk of dying here, but I'd miss out on the treasure and experience. Some of the treasure on this floor could be food.

Each roguelike has a different level of food rarity. The Mysterious Dungeon games tend to lean towards Rogue's "hard" scarcity, meaning, it's important to conserve food because the only reliable way to get more is to explore more rooms. The player must explore to find more food, but he'll be doing some exploration regardless. Does one dive when he can, or go out of his way to check every room? What I do is explore complete levels unless approaching starvation, in which case I dive. If you are carrying a goal item like the Happiness Box, all normal food consumption stops!

Figure 36.8: I've gotten to experience level 4 by now, and I encounter my first Magician.

Magicians are a troublesome enemy in this game. If they're in melee range, they could either attack for a bit of damage, but not really much, or they could put Taloon to sleep. That would be very bad.

If Taloon is put to sleep he'll be stuck until he wakes up naturally. Most of the time, the Magician will have killed him by then. Magicians are like the Ice Monsters, or Floating Eyes, of this game: they seem harmless at first, but they can prove fatal.

On the other hand, Magicians are the first type of monster in the game that could drop random items when killed, and are worth 12 experience points each. They're often generated asleep and compared to other monsters are fairly difficult to wake up. If you can kill one from a distance they are worth it in the early game, but it is a very bad idea to fight one in melee, even if you're of a high level.

Figure 36.9: On level 5 I finally eat that bread I've been saving. Big Bread completely fills Taloon's stomach, so there is an advantage to waiting as long as possible before eating it. However, if the player waits until he's starving (losing hit points each turn from lack of food) he might end up encountering a monster that must be taken care of on a turn he'd like to eat. It's best to put off eating when you can but not to the point where it could become an eat-or-fight situation.

Figure 36.10: Later on the level I find a Magician and a Drakee, and I tackle the Magician by blinding it, with a thrown Blinding herb. For the monsters, being blind is about the same as being confused. There's still a chance the Magician could attack me each turn instead of one of the seven other spaces around him, and if he did that he could choose to cast sleep instead of hit, but the odds are against it. I'm not too concerned about the Drakee because they are like Rogue's bats: they often move randomly instead of chasing the player, and they're pretty weak anyway.

Figures 36.11 and 36.12: Oops! I decided to take care of the Drakee first, and in the process of moving stumbled on a gas trap! If I hadn't blinded the Magician I'd be in trouble here. Fortunately, the chances that he could find me before I woke up were slim.

Unfortunately, soon after that I died to a Mummy whose strength I woefully underestimated. Moving on to the next game . . .

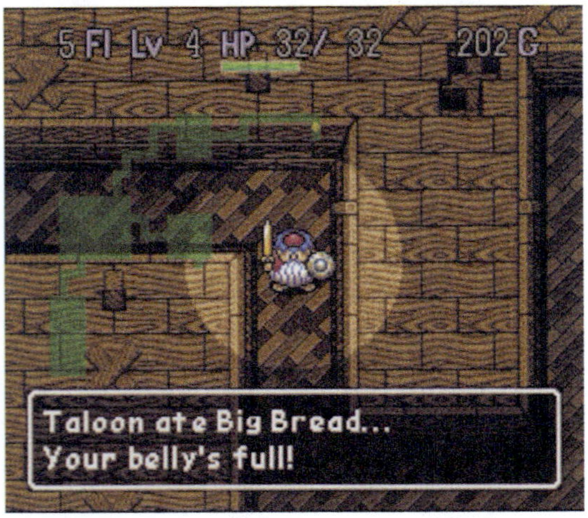

Figure 36.9

Torneko no Daibouken: Eating food

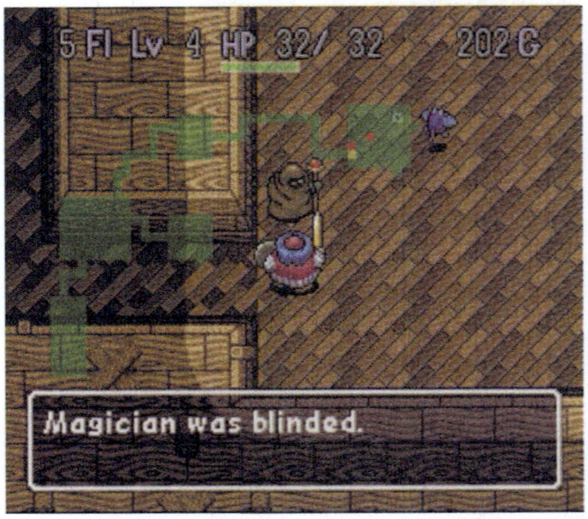

Figure 36.10

Torneko no Daibouken: Blinding an enemy

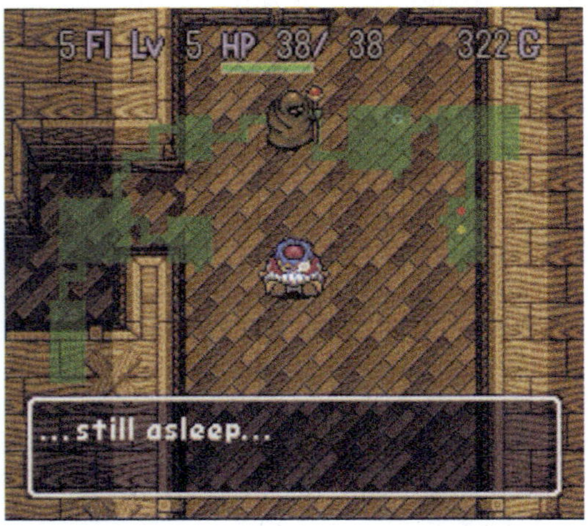

Figure 36.11

Torneko no Daibouken: Gas trap

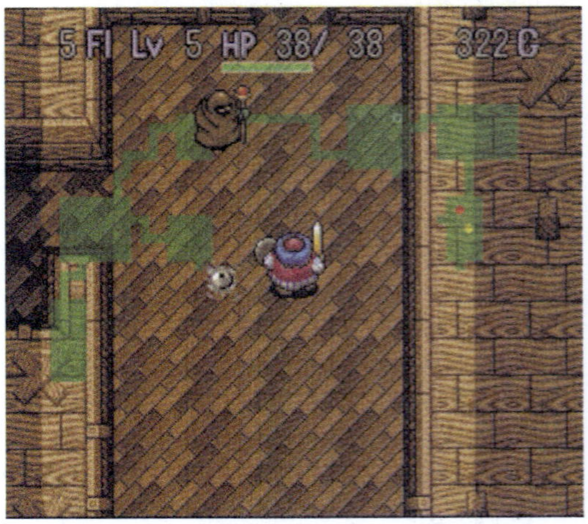

Figure 36.12

Torneko no Daibouken: Woken up

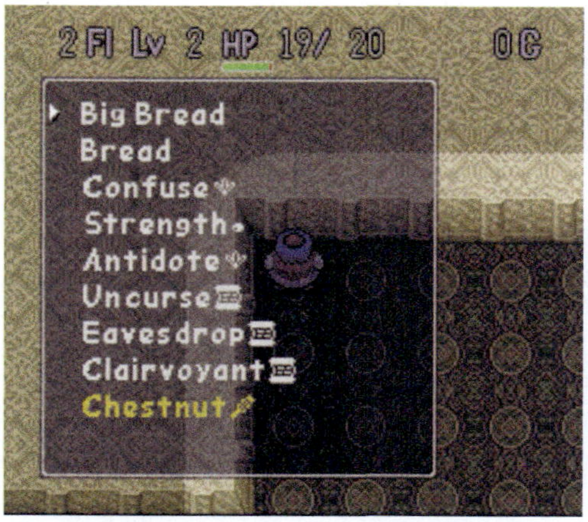

Figure 36.13

Torneko no Daibouken: Lots of stuff on Level 2

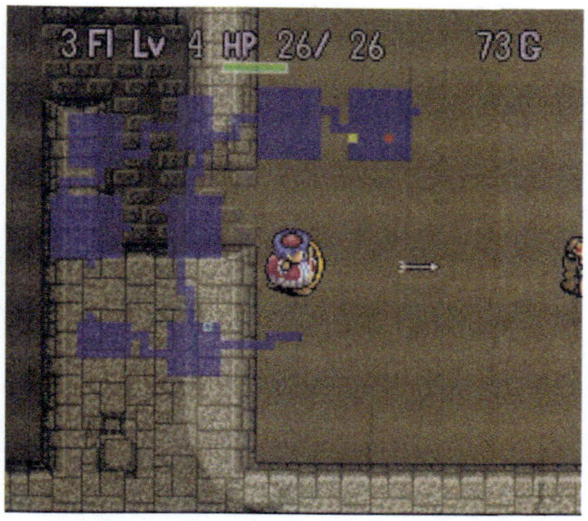

Figure 36.14

Torneko no Daibouken: Firing an arrow

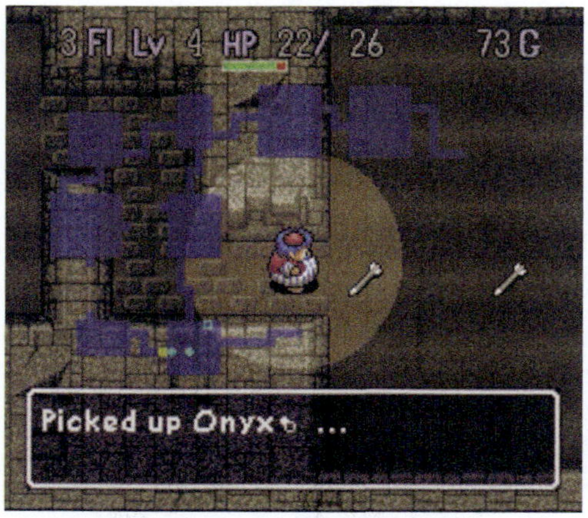

Figure 36.15

Torneko no Daibouken: A ring!

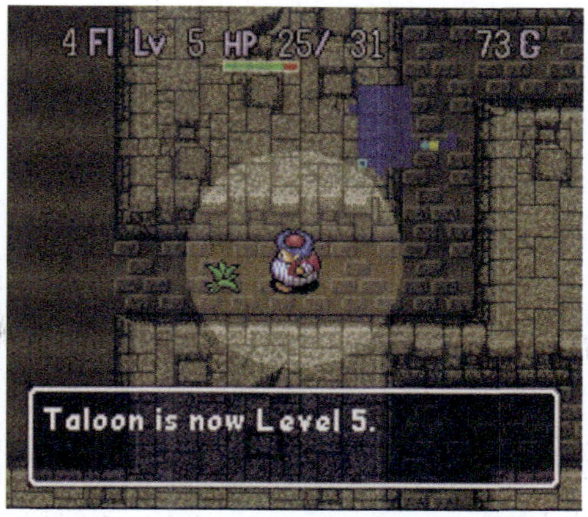

Figure 36.16

Torneko no Daibouken: Experience level 5

Figure 36.13: Another good haul for level 2. Of special interest is the Chestnut staff, which is unidentified; the Clairvoyant scroll, which shows item locations on the level; the Antidote herb, which restores lost strength back up to maximum; and the Strength seed, which increases strength by one point.

Strength seeds and Antidote herbs are analogous to potions of gain strength and restore strength in Rogue. It is best to eat a Strength seed when the player is at maximum strength, because then it'll also raise the player's max strength by 1. Then, if a later monster strikes and drains strength, the next Antidote will restore to the new maximum. But sometimes Antidotes aren't easy to find, and if the player's strength gets really low, he might have to consume Strength seeds just to remain viable.

Also in the inventory here is some normal Bread. Although the message reported upon eating it is that it fills Taloon's belly, in fact, it only fills it by 50% of capacity.

Here's a question: which is better to eat first, Big Bread or normal Bread? The answer is normal Bread, because the player's inventory capacity in this game is limited. The types of bread fill Taloon's stomach by different amounts, but they both take up the same amount of inventory space. Thus, it is best to use up the least valuable item first. That'll free up a spot for other treasure sooner, while keeping the extra 50% of food for later.

Figure 36.14: This, if you can arrange it, is the best way to handle Magicians: kill them with arrows. (You don't need to find a bow. Apparently, Taloon carries one at all times.) You can either select them and choose Fire, or you can equip the arrows and fire them off with the L button. The latter is recommended in cases where no enemies are around, but if near an awake foe and with no arrows equipped, it's better to Fire them, as equipping an object uses a turn.

Figure 36.15: Ah, the Magician dropped an Onyx ring! Things are looking up. It's best to identify these babies before putting them on.

Figure 36.16: Level 5, not bad at all.

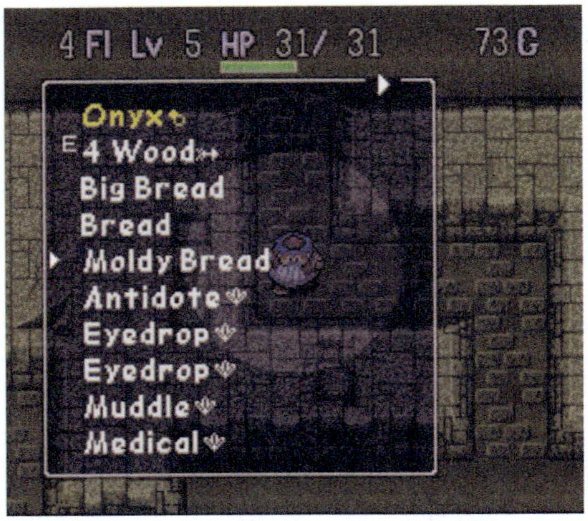

Figure 36.17

Torneko no Daibouken: Food choices

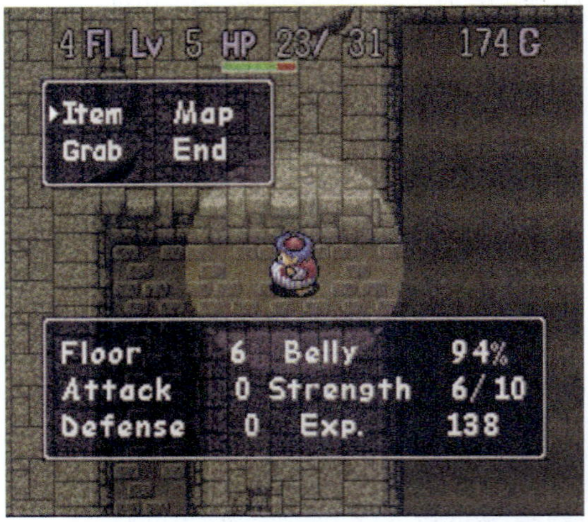

Figure 36.18

Torneko no Daibouken: Stats window

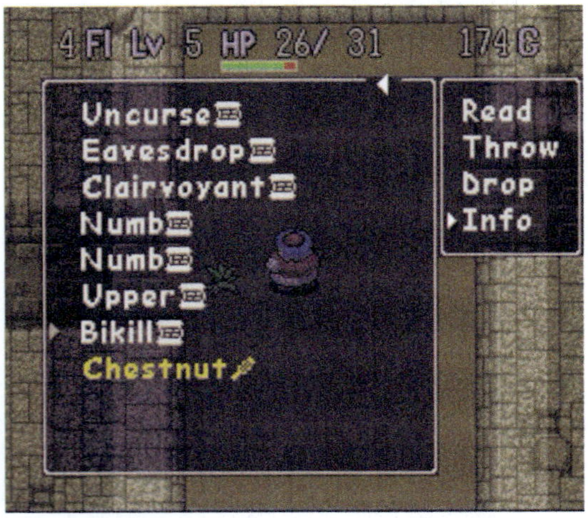

Figure 36.19

Torneko no Daibouken: Bikill Scroll

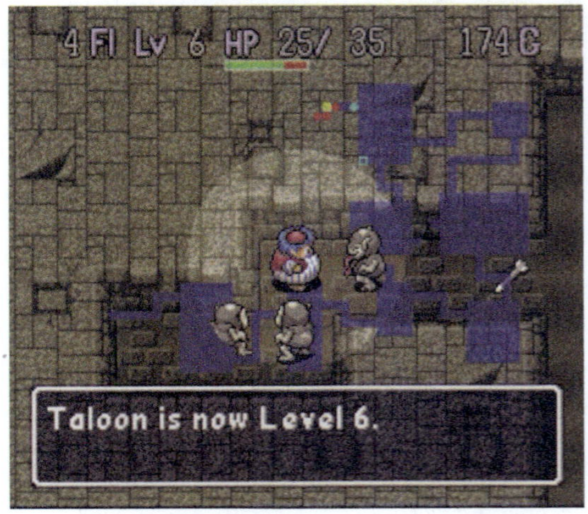

Figure 36.20

Torneko no Daibouken: Surrounded!

Figure 36.17: Notice that Taloon is carrying Big Bread, normal Bread and Moldy Bread. He's also carrying an Antidote.

Eating Moldy Bread fills up the stomach all the way but does a little damage and drains a point of strength in the process. One can undo the drain with an Antidote, but Mushroom enemies might drain it again. Eating an Antidote cures all strength loss, so the player is usually better off using it as late as possible.

Figure 36.18: Except in the case where he's already low on strength. If Taloon is already going to use the Antidote, he might as well wait until he's starving, then eat the Moldy Bread and taking the strength drain. Then he can eat the Antidote and undo both the original loss and the point from the mold.

Figure 36.19: A Bikill Scroll increases the strength of the player's weapon by one plus. It also uncurses it in the process. Unfortunately, in this game I've yet to find a weapon!

Figure 36.20: Taloon may have reached level 6, but take a look around him . . . Yikes! How did this happen?

The monsters here are Liclicks. When one takes damage, there's a chance that it could split, resulting in a second monster with as many hit points as the original had. Further, the new monster is also capable of dividing! I got careless and hit one a few times, and I was soon mobbed.

But with a little thought, I was able to salvage the situation. You see, monsters cannot attack diagonally in corridors like this. I can't attack diagonally here either, but that's okay. The idea is to reduce the number of monsters pounding away at those goofy pinstripes at once.

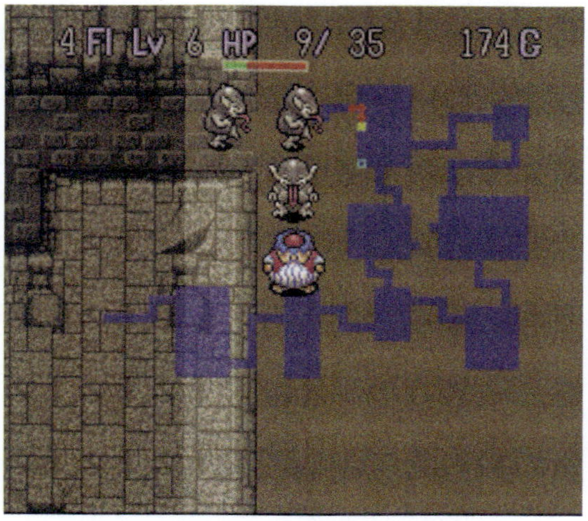

Figure 36.21

Torneko no Daibouken: Running for my life

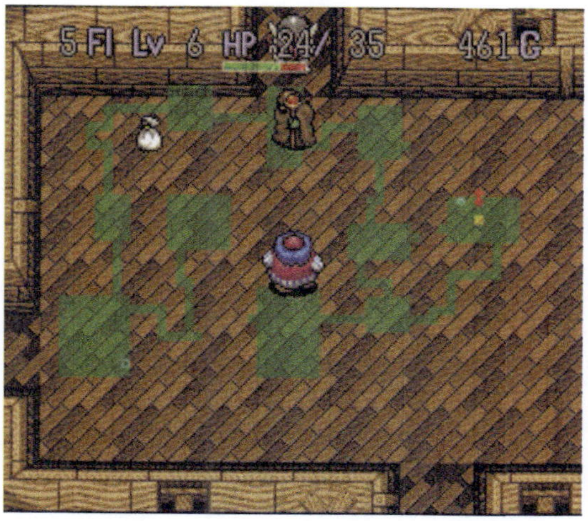

Figure 36.22

Torneko no Daibouken: Level 5

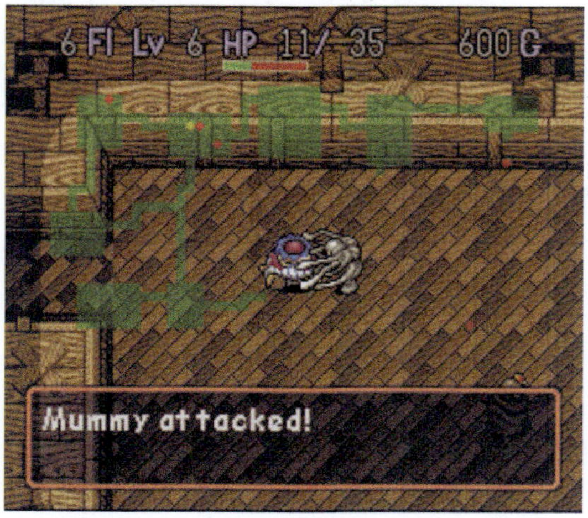

Figure 36.23

Torneko no Daibouken: Another Mummy

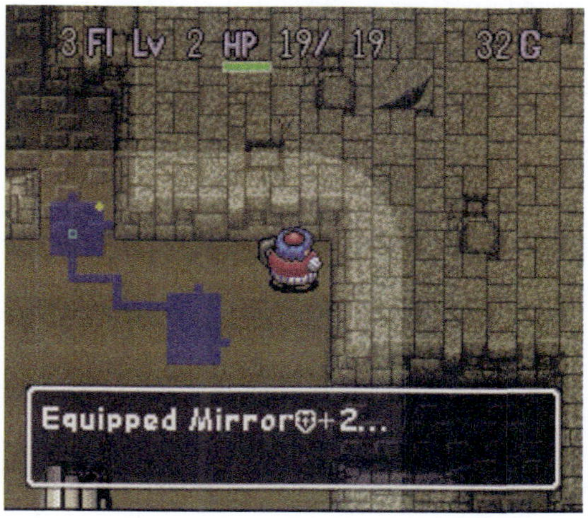

Figure 36.24

Torneko no Daibouken: Mirror Shield +2!

Also, notice how the Liclick south of Talon isn't facing him? That's because I had thrown a Confuse herb at him. Not only are there only two monsters that can hurt me, but that one can only attack one turn in eight. And Liclicks can only multiply if there are empty spaces nearby into which to divide. In a corridor, those fill up quickly.

Figure 36.21: Even so, discretion is the better part of valor. Especially when they got me down to 9 hit points so quickly. Time for the next level I think . . .

Figure 36.22: Sometimes it's best to let sleeping monsters lie. There are two reasons not to disturb this Magician. First, he's a Magician, and we already know to be careful with them. Second, he's taking his nap in front of the room's entrance, blocking that Liclick! This is a case where the small chance of treasure in that last room up there is probably not worth the danger of waking up the Magician and having to deal with *two* dangerous opponents.

Figure 36.23: Alas, shortly after that I stumbled upon a gas trap, and that allowed another Mummy to end that trip in to the Mystery Dungeon. I never even got to find out what that Onyx ring was. Ah, but the next game . . . the next game went very well indeed.

Figure 36.24: For starters, I found a Mirror shield on level 2. They're rustproof and quite strong, and this one turned out to be +2.

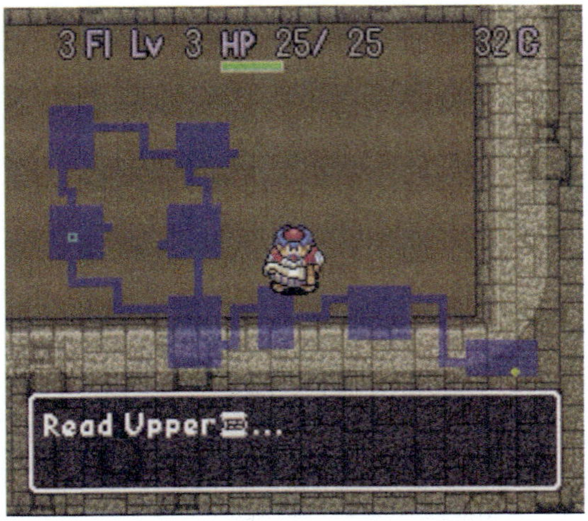

Figure 36.25

Torneko no Daibouken: Upper scroll

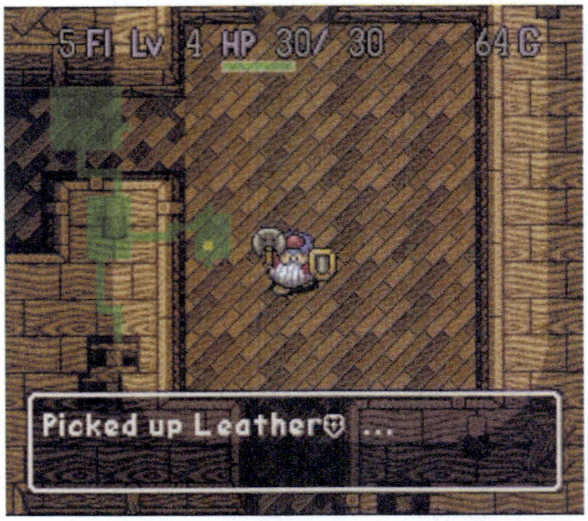

Figure 36.26

Torneko no Daibouken: Leather Shield

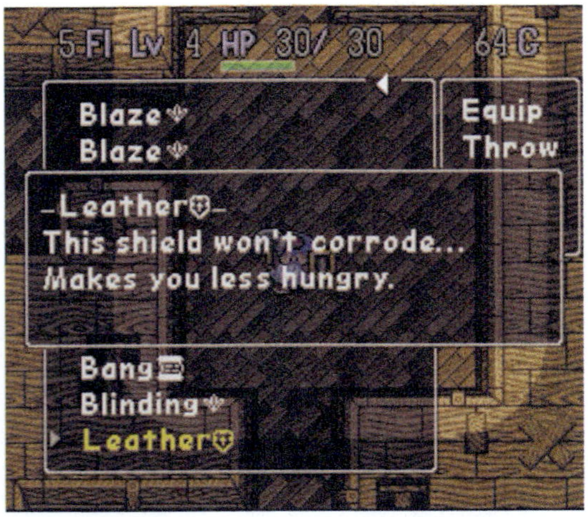

Figure 36.27

Torneko no Daibouken: Leather Shield description

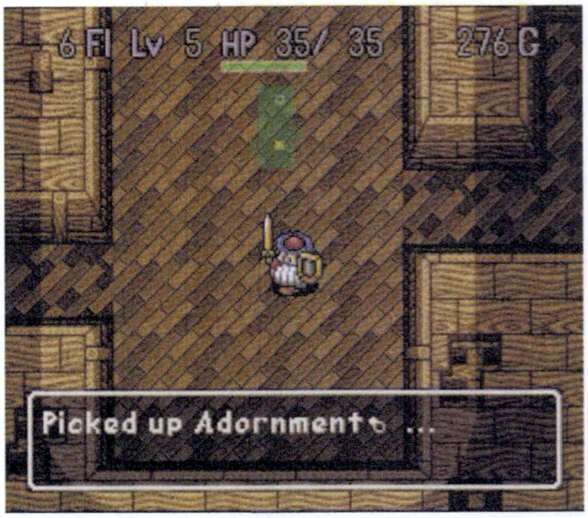

Figure 36.28

Torneko no Daibouken: Ring of Adornment

Figure 36.25: And using an Upper scroll got it to +3!

Figures 36.26 and 36.27: A short while later I found a Leather shield. They're weaker than Mirror Shields, but they're also rustproof. They can be quite useful because one quirk of the Mysterious Dungeon games is that, for some reason unknown to me, as long as you have a Leather shield equipped, your food consumption is lowered. Very interesting.

Figures 36.28 and 36.29: This game I had very bad luck with rings. I found three, and they were all Rings of Adornment, which in roguelike-ese means "worthless."

Figure 36.30: On level 7 I start meeting Derangers. They get that name because the first Dragon Warrior game they appeared in, they had a confusion spell that could cause your party members to attack each other, so the English localization team gave these lumpy wizards that name. But it's misleading here; the special power Derangers have in this game is to teleport you randomly. (Still, one might think it makes more sense than calling them Quantum Mechanics.)

But still, things are going pretty well, and it looks like I'll be able to win bef—

Figure 36.31: Sweet merciful heavens, a monster lair!

Take a look at that room on the map. Look at all of those red dots! This doesn't look good.

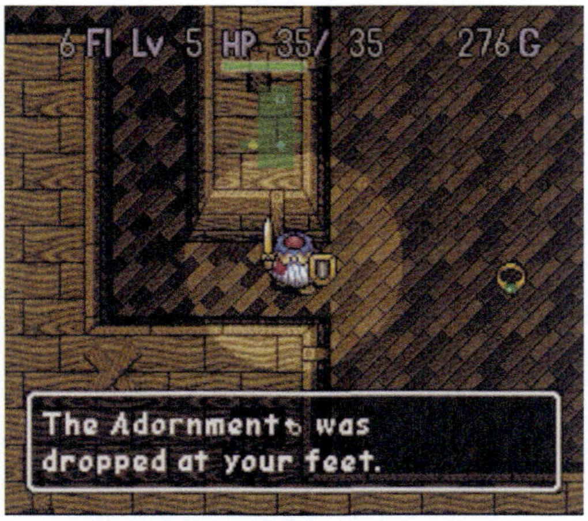

Figure 36.29

Torneko no Daibouken: Not a great find

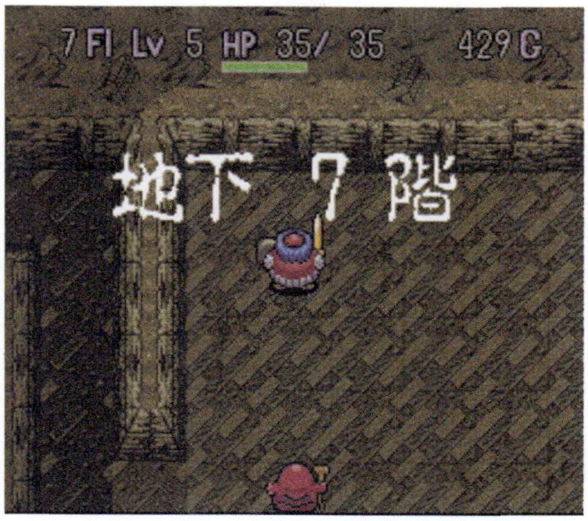

Figure 36.30

Torneko no Daibouken: Level 7

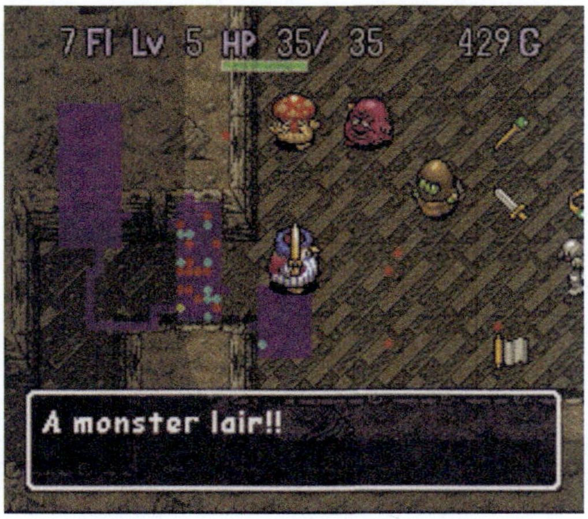

Figure 36.31

Torneko no Daibouken: Monster lair!

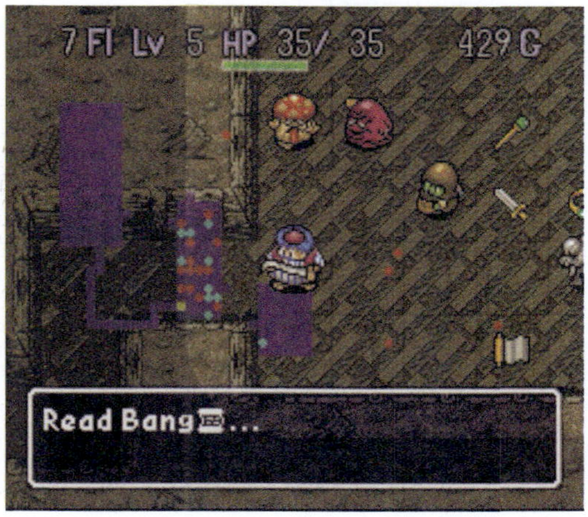

Figure 36.32

Torneko no Daibouken: Bang Scroll

There's also plenty of treasure in monster lairs (they're this game's version of Rogue's zoos), but surviving the opposition to use them is not a trivial problem.

Times like this, the best thing to do is STOP AND THINK. There is a very good reason roguelikes are not real-time games.

Let's look at the monsters. Hm, there's a Mummy among them, on the far right edge of the screen. With my Mirror Shield +3 they're a lot less dangerous than the last two games, but he's not the only monster to worry about. There's an archer in there too, and a Mushroom, and several monsters off-screen. Haven't found any solutions yet . . . .

Well, none of the monsters are adjacent yet. Maybe there's something in inventory that'll help out . . .

Figure 36.32: Ah! I have two Bang scrolls! Oh boy, this is going to be awesome . . .

Figures 36.33, 36.34, 36.35: Remember, Bang scrolls damage all monsters in the room. It's not huge damage, but at this level it's significant. It's like they were made to take care of mid-level lairs like this one. I've clipped about 20 pages of damage messages here.

Figure 36.36: After reading both scrolls, it's just me and the loot. Woo-hoo!

Notice what I was able to do because I didn't panic? (Well, not panicked much, I've been killed many times by zoos and lairs before.) Standard procedure in lair situations is to retreat into the hallway and take

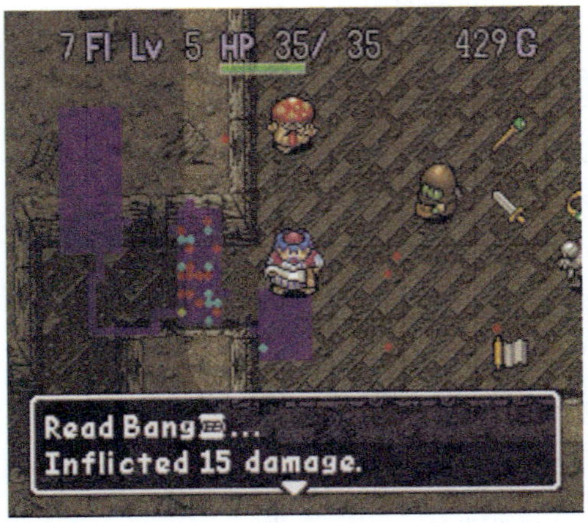

Figure 36.33

Torneko no Daibouken: Doing damage

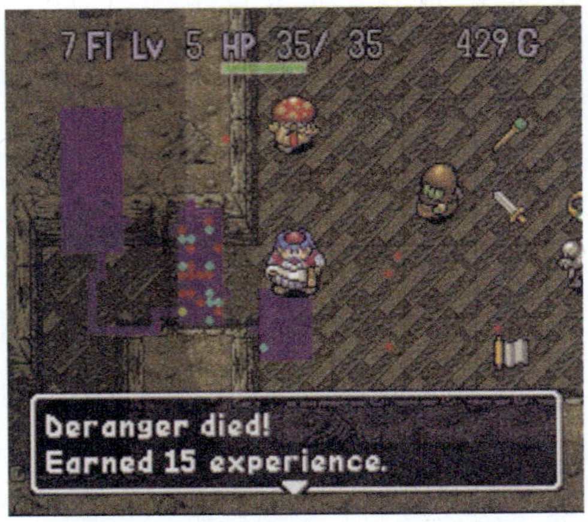

Figure 36.34

Torneko no Daibouken: Earning experience

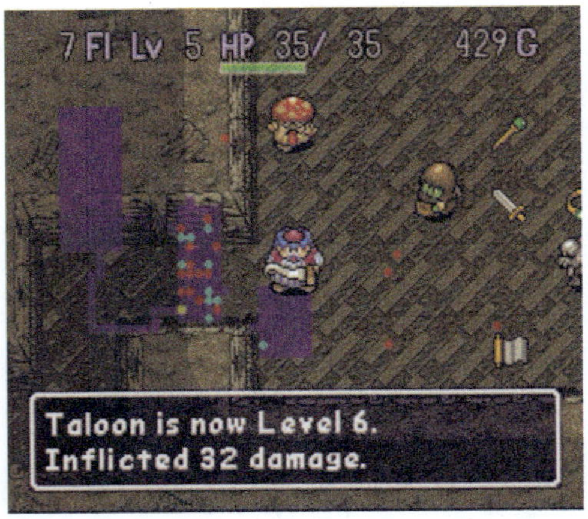

Figure 36.35

Torneko no Daibouken: Experience level 6

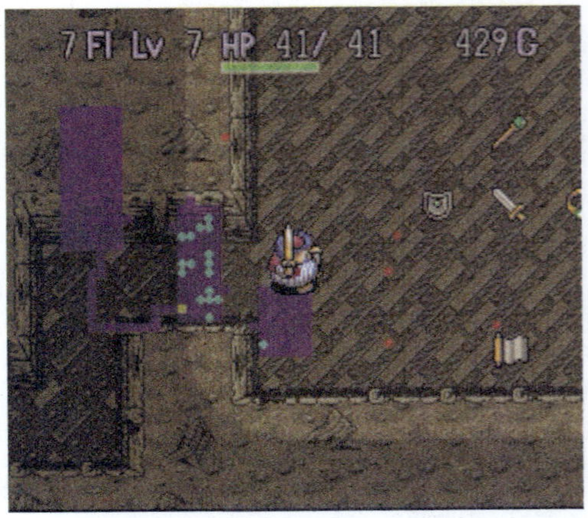

Figure 36.36

Torneko no Daibouken: Loot!

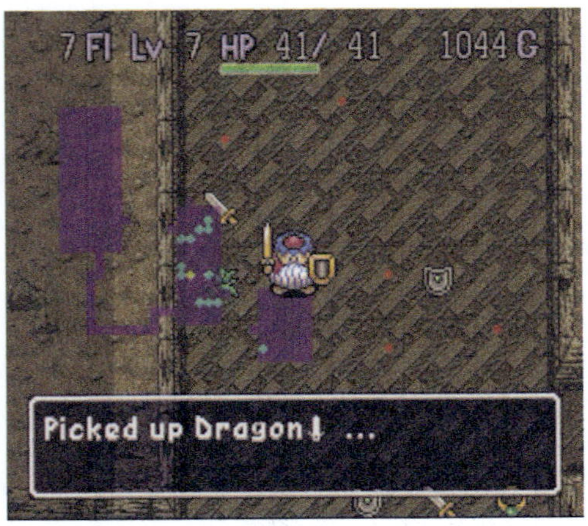

Figure 36.37

Torneko no Daibouken: Dragon Sword

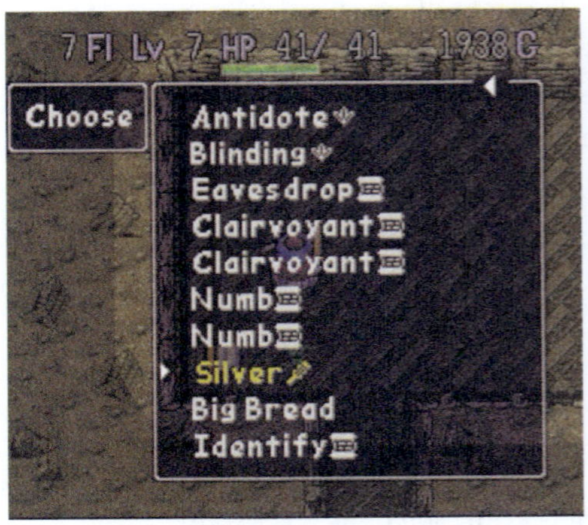

Figure 36.38

Torneko no Daibouken: Inventory

the monsters on one at a time, but then the Bang scrolls would have been far less effective, and they probably would have worn me down.

Figure 36.37: Ah, a Dragon Sword! The hardest monsters in the game are green dragons, and Dragon Swords do extra damage against them. I've had lots of good luck so far. I hope it holds.

Figure 36.38: An unknown wand and an Identify scroll. Let's have a look.

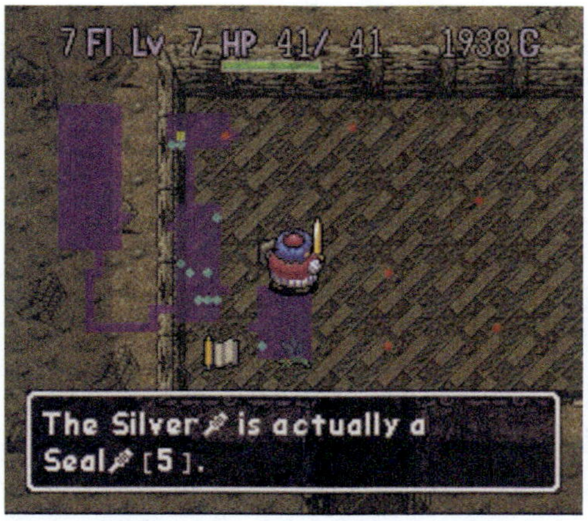

Figure 36.39

Torneko no Daibouken: Found a Seal Wand

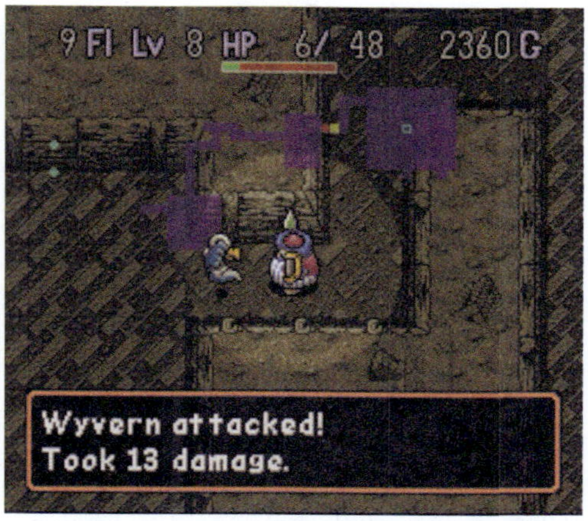

Figure 36.40

Torneko no Daibouken: Desperate times

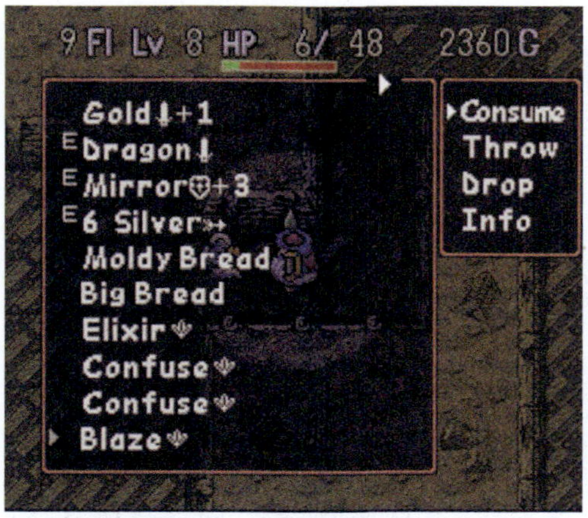

Figure 36.41

Torneko no Daibouken: Desperation action

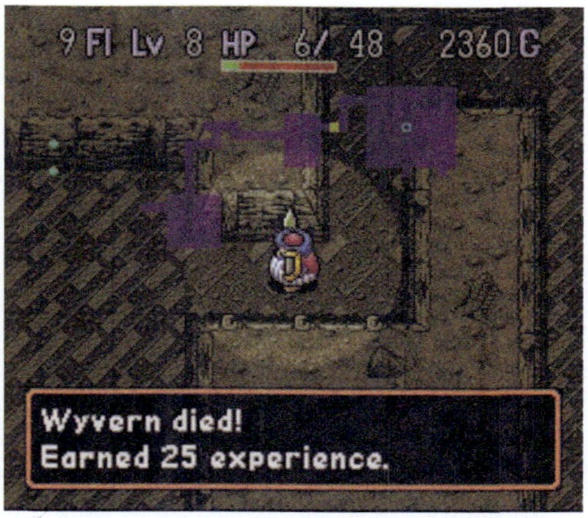

Figure 36.42

Torneko no Daibouken: Reward for victory

Figure 36.39: A Seal Wand. This disables the special ability of any monster you wave it at. Magicians lose their sleep spell, thieves can't steal or teleport, and dragons can't breathe fire. Very useful when used at the right moment.

Figure 36.40: Here, we see the importance of keeping "escapes," ways out of arbitrary danger. Taking on this Wyvern in hand-to-hand has proven to be a bad idea, and with only 6 hit points left I probably won't survive another round if I just stand here. Let's have a look at my stuff.

Figure 36.41: A Blaze herb will do nicely.

Figure 36.42: Blaze herbs do tremendous damage! Almost every enemy in the game will die to one, but they only work at melee range, if you're facing your opponent, and they only affect one monster. Thus, they are best saved for emergency use.

Figure 36.43: On level 10 I found the safe that is the subgoal for the dungeon. If you die when carrying a safe, instead of losing half your gold you get to keep all of it. Gold taken out of the dungeon improves the state of the town (the "outer game"), so it helps to build up its amenities faster.

Figure 36.44: This enemy is called a Lethal Armor. It's hard not to get spooked by that name. But I'm doing pretty well, and I've got enough general escapes handy, so I'm going to take a risk and use-test a wand.

Figure 36.45: The wand made the Lethal Armor not attack me next turn, but face a random direction. Ah, a wand that causes confusion, those are called "Chaos wands," aren't they?

Figures 36.46 and 36.47: We should make a note of that. Using the "Name" command, we can label all items of a specific type with a reminder of its use.

Figure 36.48: That Mirror Shield I've been building up pays off. Horks (similar to rust monsters/aquators in Rogue) do no hit point damage but lower the enchantment on your shield by one point . . . if it's not immune. Other shields can be protected by reading a Plating scroll.

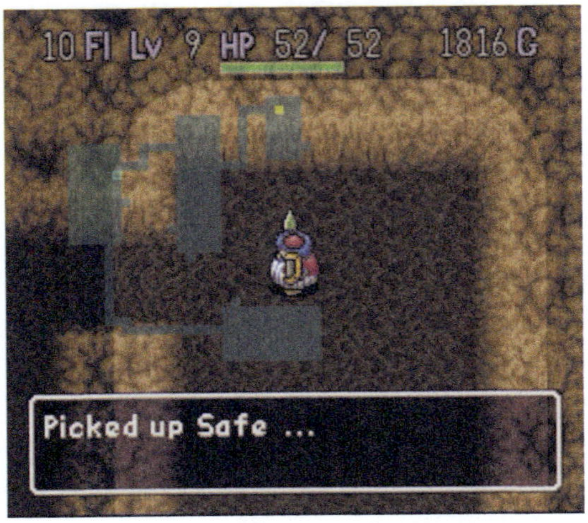

Figure 36.43

Torneko no Daibouken: A Safe

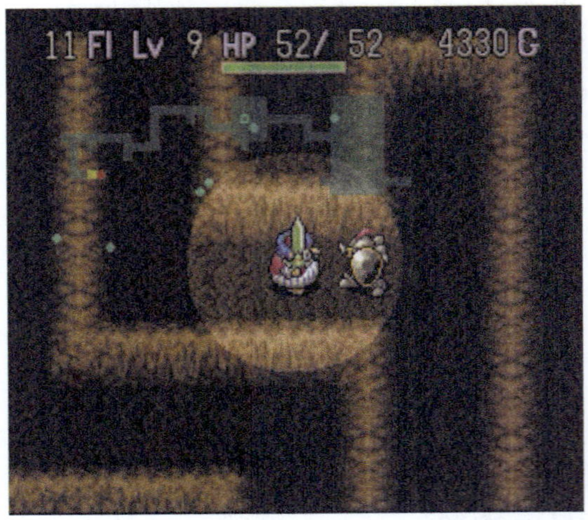

Figure 36.44

Torneko no Daibouken: Lethal Armor

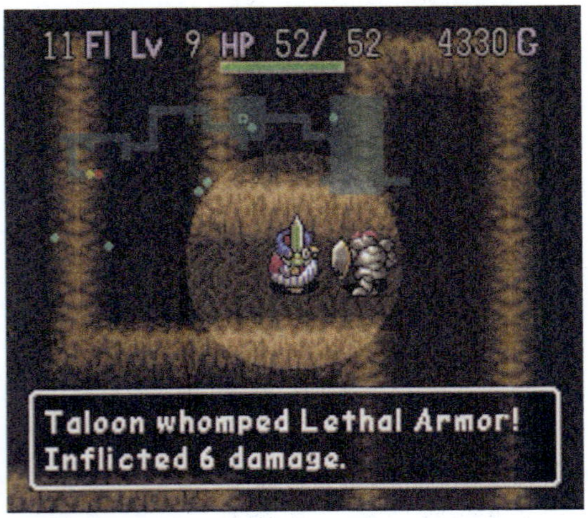

Figure 36.45

Torneko no Daibouken: Identification by use

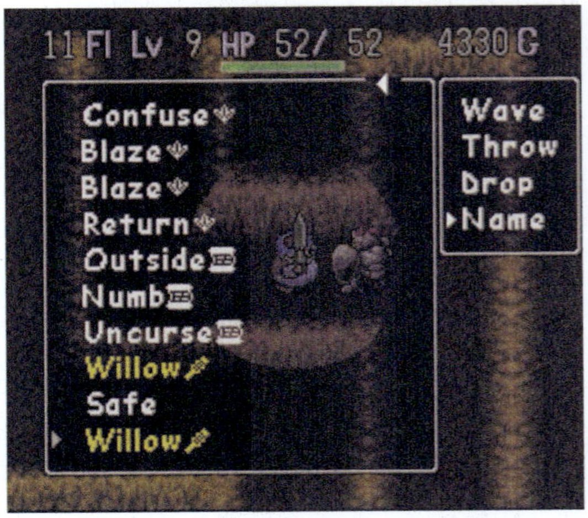

Figure 36.46

Torneko no Daibouken: Naming the item

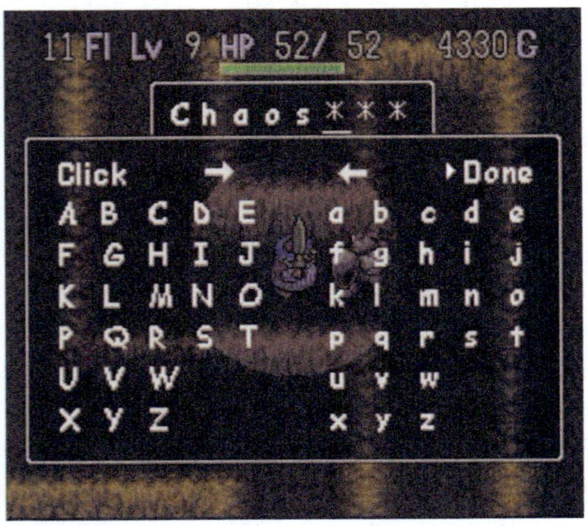

Figure 36.47

Torneko no Daibouken: "C-H-A-O-S"

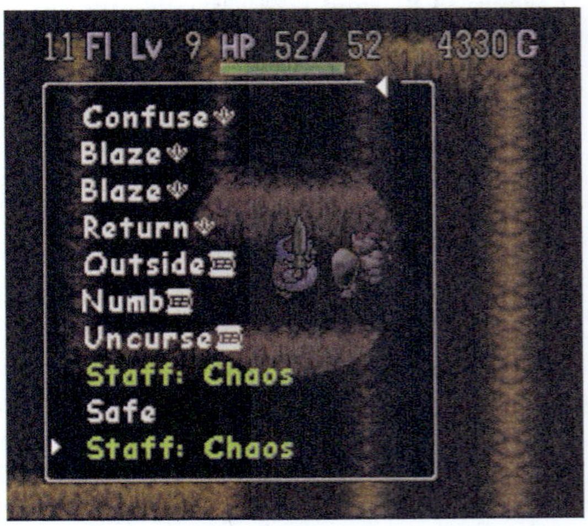

Figure 36.48

Torneko no Daibouken: Named items appear in green

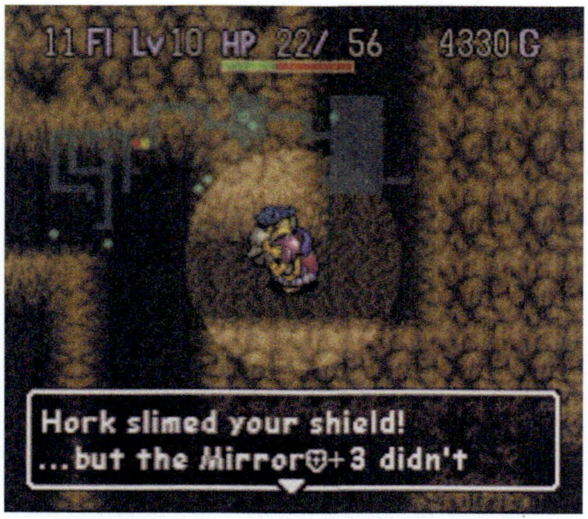

Figure 36.49

Torneko no Daibouken: My shield is protected

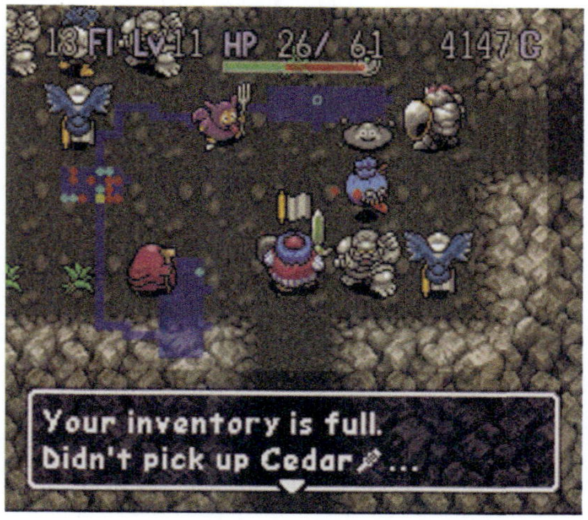

Figure 36.50

Torneko no Daibouken: Another monster lair!

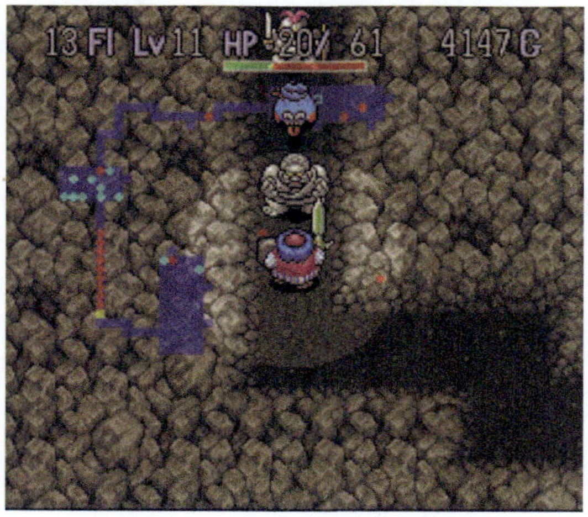

Figure 36.51

Torneko no Daibouken: Lining them up

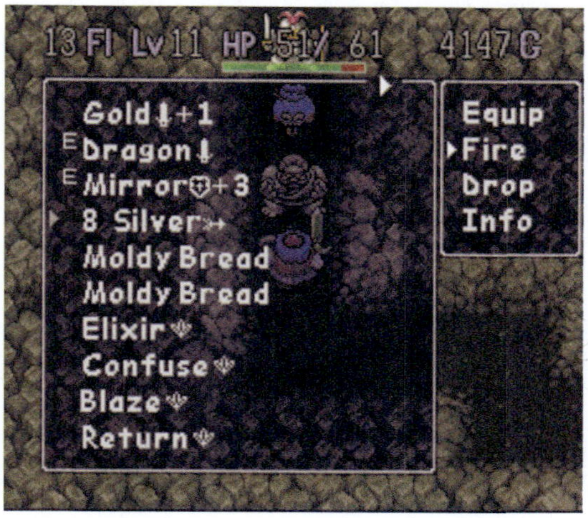

Figure 36.52

Torneko no Daibouken: Silver arrows

Figure 36.49: Oh no, another monster lair! The quality of monster in this one is much greater than the last. Wyverns are still giving me trouble, and there are also Stone Hulks in here. There's even a Metal Babble in the lot. This is a serious test.

Figure 36.50: But I have a plan. Take a look at the map in the figure and notice how the monsters are arranged in the picture. I ran back into the long hallway I had emerged from, and all the monsters followed me in.

Figure 36.51: After consuming an Elixir herb to get my health back up, I notice that I have a supply of Silver arrows! They aren't equipped, but as stated before, I can save a turn in an emergency by firing them from their item menu.

Silver arrows are unique in that they don't stop with the first monster hit. They continue in a line, damaging all monsters in their path. They even go through walls!

This means that, if a Silver arrow misses, it can't be retrieved and reused, since they always sail out and leave the map. But clearing monster lairs is no time to skimp on the resources. Fire away!

Figure 36.52: It worked! There's so much loot in here that I have to make some hard choices about what I can take out of this place. Still, that's the kind of decision I like to make!

Figures 36.53 and 36.54: Argh . . . this lair also has a good number of traps in it. Mine traps remove half your hit points and destroy any adjacent items!

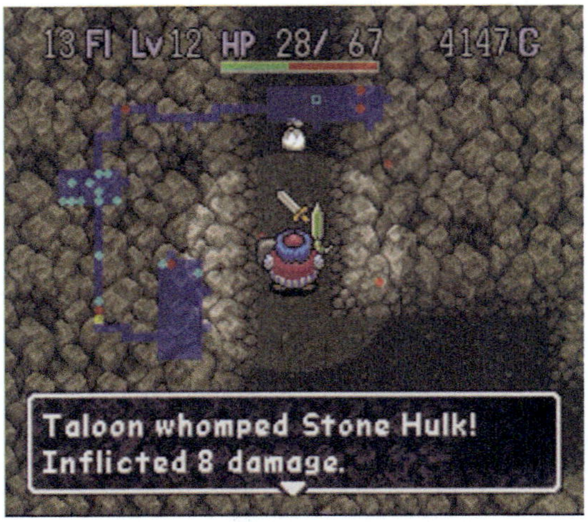

Figure 36.53

Torneko no Daibouken: Massive damage

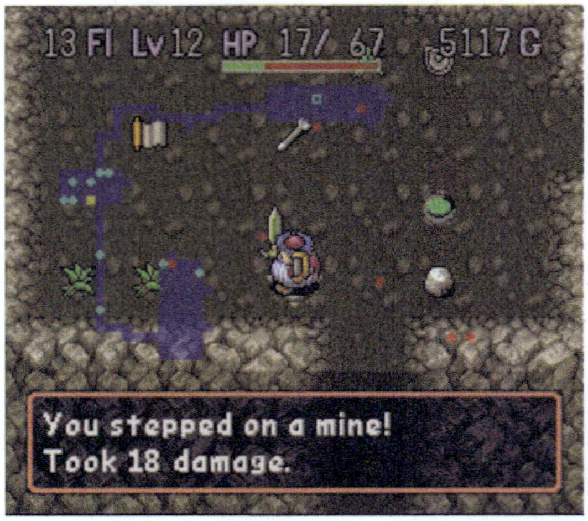

Figure 36.54

Torneko no Daibouken: Still not safe though

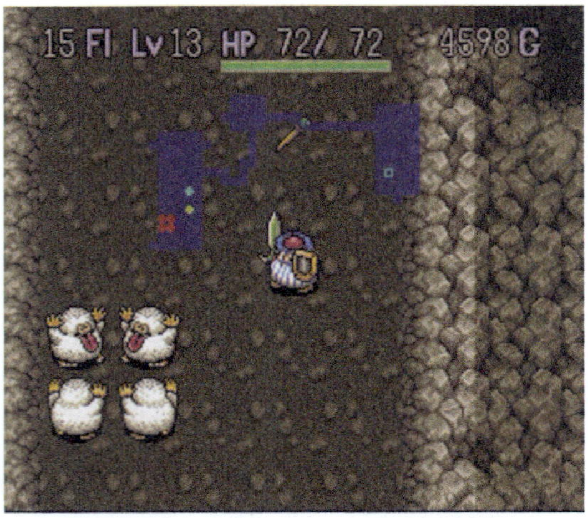

Figure 36.55

Torneko no Daibouken: Ice sloths

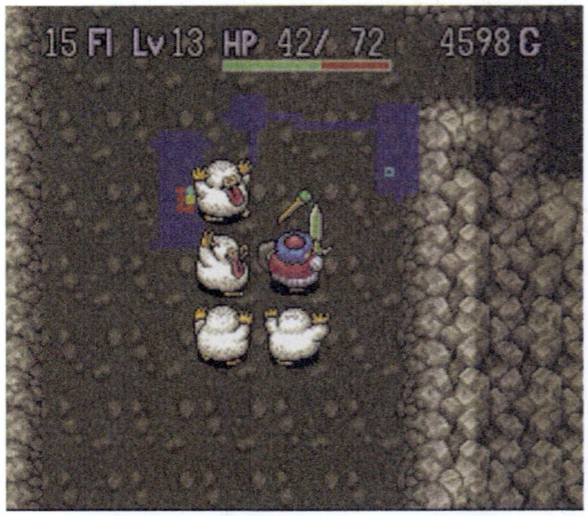

Figure 36.56

Torneko no Daibouken: Surrounded again

Figure 36.55: Monster lairs are good places to check for traps. In these games, the way to do this is to swing your weapon into a space where a trap might be. Note that items cannot be on the same space as a trap, so as long as I only step on spaces that held loot, I'll be okay.

Figure 36.56: A new enemy type, Ice Sloths. Hm, I don't remember how to handle these. They're asleep at least. I've got a lot of resources at hand, though, let's see if I can kill them.

This is bad . . . they all woke up at once, and despite being sloths they're actually double-speed! I probably won't be able to make it back to the corridor at this rate. This is no time to skimp on the resources, let's get out of here!

Figure 36.57: Ah, an Outside scroll. That should do the trick. Here goes . . .

Figure 36.58:. . . whua?

Figure 36.59: WHAT?! I escaped the dungeon?!

Figure 36.60: WHAT THE HELL?

Figure 36.61: Ah, I remember now. I know what happened.

There exist, in the game, two items with confusing names. There is the Outside Scroll, which I used and which teleported me out of the dungeon, and the Return Herb, which teleports me elsewhere on the current level. Notice the names! Both are legacies, like the lumpy wizards being called Derangers, of the American names of the localization of the spells in the Dragon Quest/Warrior video games that Taloon comes from.

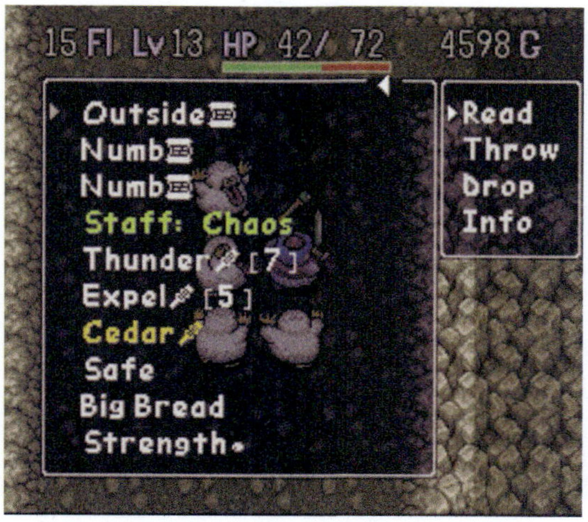

Figure 36.57

Torneko no Daibouken: Outside scroll

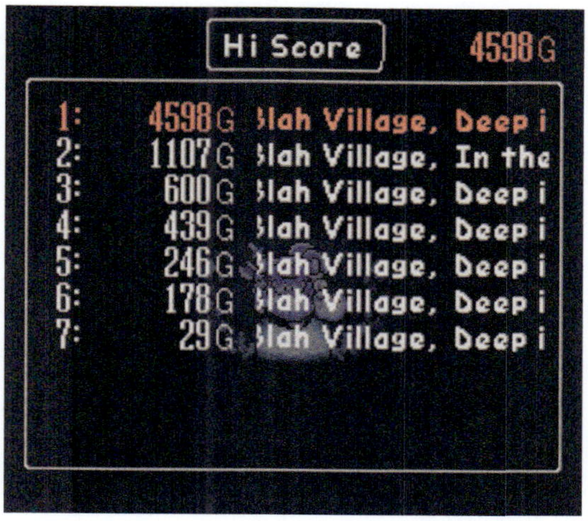

Figure 36.58

Torneko no Daibouken: Scoreboard 1

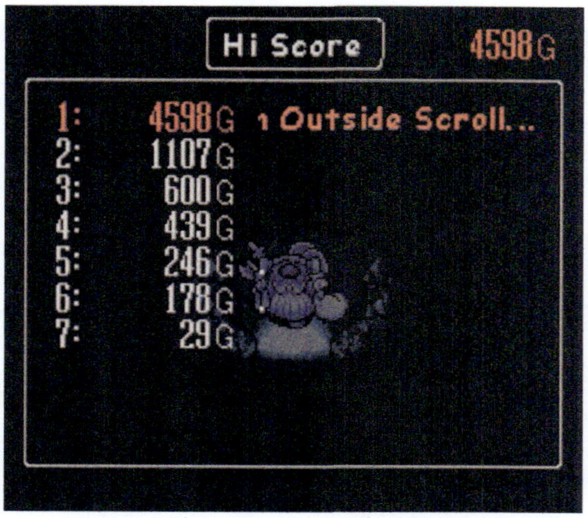

Figure 36.59

Torneko no Daibouken: Scoreboard 2

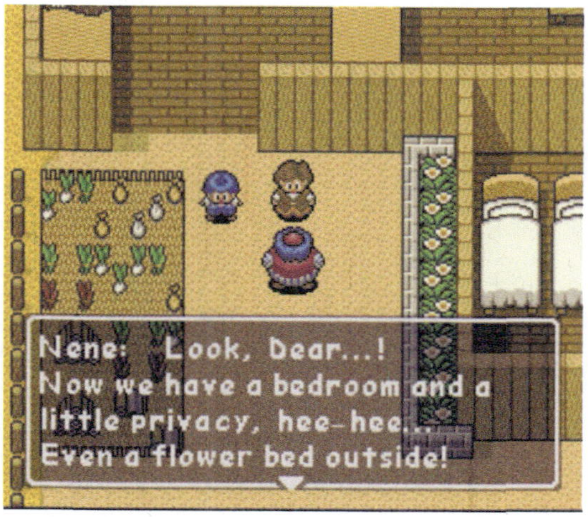

Figure 36.60

Torneko no Daibouken: Back home

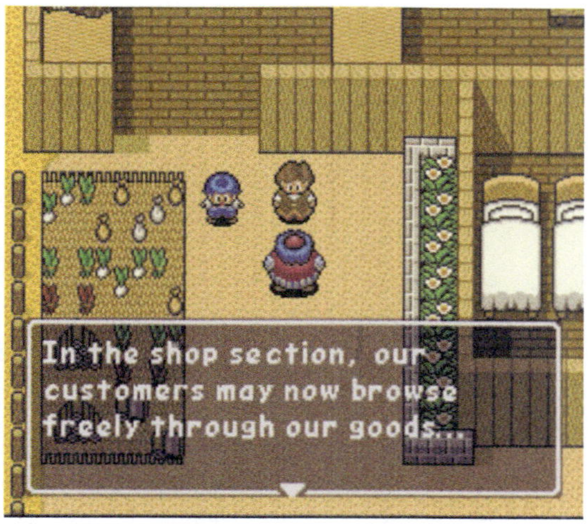

Figure 36.61

Torneko no Daibouken: Thanks for the info, dear

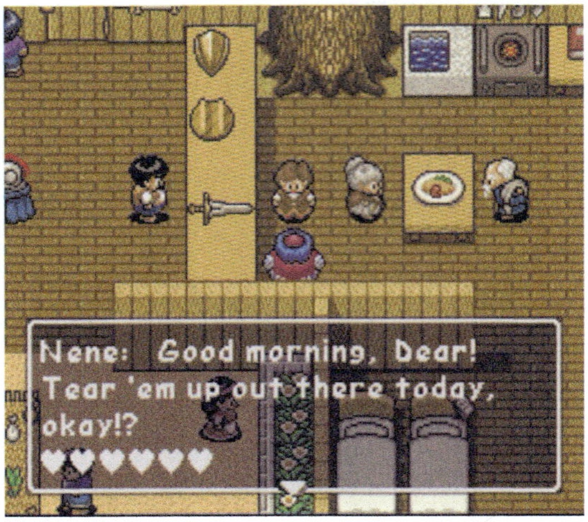

Figure 36.62

Torneko no Daibouken: The wife is happy, at least

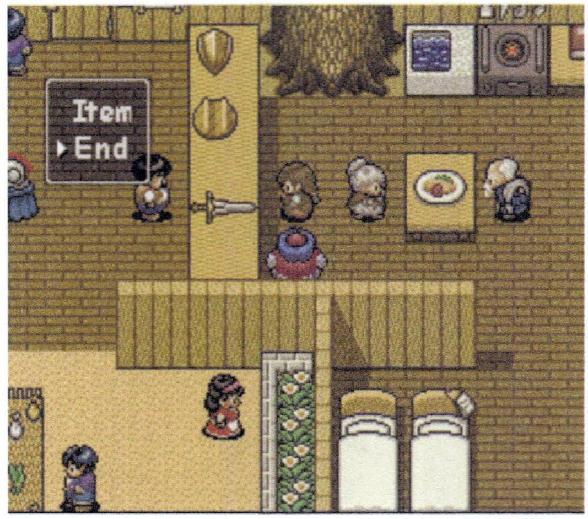

Figure 36.63

Torneko no Daibouken: Farewell

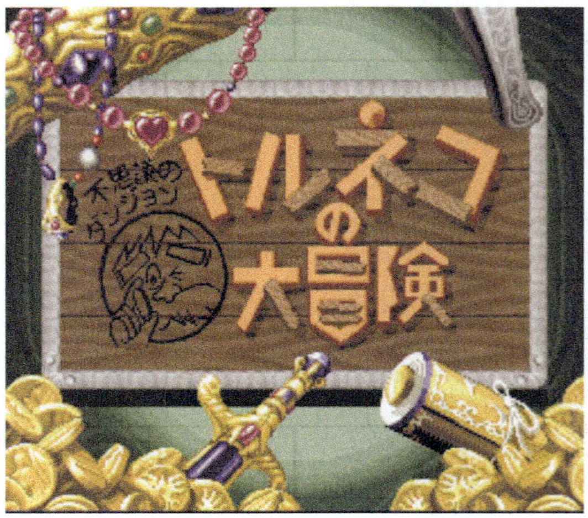

Figure 36.64

Torneko no Daibouken: Title screen

The fan translator used the same names in his romhack even though they are less suitable here. I assumed that the Return herb was the exit item (as in "return to the surface") and that Outside scrolls would teleport (as in "outside the room"). Alas, I was mistaken.

Ah well, I didn't really want to spoil the ending for all you folks anyway.

Figure 36.62: Yeah honey, go to hell.

36.1 Acknowledgments

Thanks to Anna Anthropy for the reminder that the translation I played was made by Magic Destiny, with an unofficial release made by necrosaro. Here's the romhacking.net entry on the translation (https://www.romhacking.net/translations/480/).

37

A Journey to Table Mountain, Part 1

July 2007 So, you've probably just read my description of scenes from the Super Famicom Torneko Mysterious Dungeon. The screenshots came from multiple games, but I think they illustrated what the game is like nicely. This time we're going to do the same thing with the Super Famicom Shiren the Wanderer game, the second Mysterious Dungeon game, and still possibly the high point of that series. But this isn't a pieced-together narrative from multiple games. Everything you are about to see happened in one game, and a long one at that. Think of it as being like Let's Play, but with more death!

As an experiment I started a new file and started playing from scratch to see how far I could get. I didn't have the benefit of upgraded towns, or the "helpers" you can eventually earn through playing many times. I didn't have the benefit of "Staves of Bufoo," an extremely useful item that not only immediately kills foes you swing it at but turns them into meat you can eat and gain special powers from. And most importantly, I didn't have the use of the equipment from a cleared game; when you win, you get to keep the things you won with for later games, making the next play much easier if you choose to use them.

For this game, I started over from turn one. I nipped by the cafe in the starting town to pick up my free Big Rice Ball, then went and did the first Fei's Problem (more on those in a later) and got a very useful Todo Shield +2. Then I started the real game.

For the record, this isn't the first time I've tried doing something like this. Over a decade ago, playing around with the computer game NetHack, I decided to make a website devoted to the game that, using screenshots (laboriously acquired using the Alt-Print Screen keys and Microsoft Paint) and Microsoft Publisher (for compositing the images together), would be kind of a visual journey through the Dungeons of Doom.

The result was, I won. It was my first victory at NetHack, too.

While I didn't win this game of Shiren the Wanderer, I did get quite far. The very act of recording one's progress through a game is apt to make one a much more careful player, and thus enable better play than usual.

Anyway, on to the game . . .

Note: I use a fan-made English translation of the Super Famicom game. Since this was written, Sega and ChunSoft released a DS port with an official English translation. The quality of the translation there is better, but unfortunately the game was subtly redesigned and, although it has more "content," in the form of bonus dungeons, it is also less thrilling to play. Still, it is not a bad game at all, and well worth tracking down.

37.1 Overview

Torneko/Taloon is not actually very hard, the deaths I had last time notwithstanding. But Shiren now, it can be quite a challenge.

It's also a much more interesting game. While both games take inspiration, of course, from Rogue, Shiren also steals a few features from NetHack. It has got sealed rooms like NetHack's vaults, it's got in-dungeon shops that work a lot like NetHack's (down to calling guards after you if you're caught stealing), it's got an analogue for NetHack's pets in the form of the helper characters you can acquire, and it has Scrolls of Genocide. It even has Blank Scrolls that you can write (and Genocide is an excellent choice in writing one).

In general, good items are better in Shiren than Torneko/Taloon, and there are a lot more of them, but the monsters and traps are likewise much more challenging and numerous. Shiren also has special levels, like occasional big rooms and set challenges, and other similarities. It is also the first Mysterious Dungeon game to have a boss, the beginning of the series' slide into the increasing RPG normality that dilutes later installments of the series, although this one at least can be taken care of instantly by a suitably ingenious player.

Figure 37.1: Here we are at level 1. Like in Torneko, you don't begin with anything you didn't obtain in the starter town. Until you complete the main quest, you can get one free Big Rice Ball by talking to the chef in the tavern, and one free miscellaneous object by completing one of Fei's Problems. This time, the item turned out to be a Todo Shield +2, pretty good as far as defense goes, and provides perfect defense against thieves. This is one of the better objects in the game, and getting this is just about the only advantage to starting with an empty file, for it seems that the first Fei's Problem always gives this as the prize.

Figure 37.2: The game looks very similar to Torneko on the face of it. There's the same overlay map, the same colored dots and the same status bar at the top of the screen. The only major difference on the face of it is the graphics. Shiren contains outdoor levels that are sometimes strikingly beautiful. At the very least they mix up the levels a lot more than Torneko's rectangular rooms.

Figure 37.3: I found a Katana! Not a bad weapon, although there certainly are better. Unfortunately, the best weapons are named ambiguously to English speakers. In classic roguelikes you can assume that a "two-handed sword" is going to be a very strong weapon, but here you have to guess at how strong a Dotanuki is supposed to be.

Figure 37.4: An Identify Scroll, eh? Well I found a bracer some time back (this game's version of rings), let's see what it is . . .

Figures 37.5 and 37.6: Oh my.

I wrote once about Pokémon Mystery Dungeon (a distant descendant of this game), and I believe I noted it contained an item that told you the location of all monsters and items on the current level, all the time, and that it was absurdly useful. Well, it is, and it's almost as useful in Shiren the Wanderer, enough that by finding one this early, my chances of winning have gone up considerably.

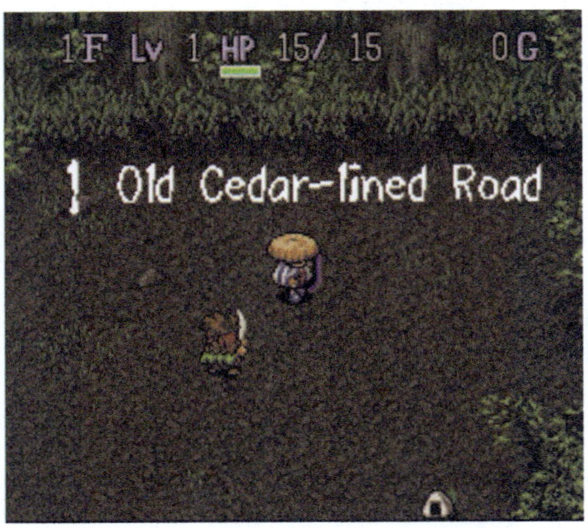

Figure 37.1

Shiren the Wanderer: Level 1

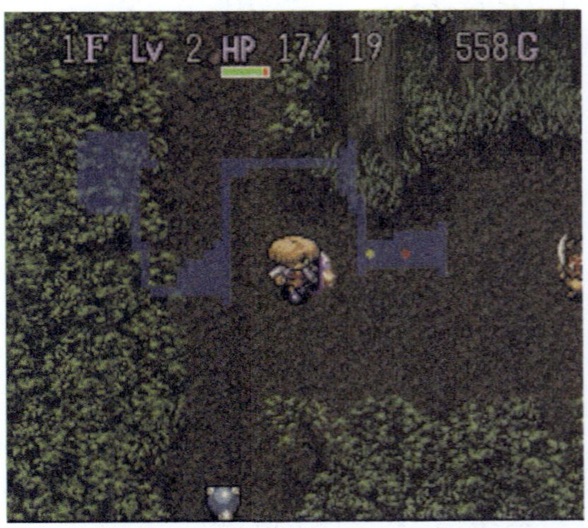

Figure 37.2

Shiren the Wanderer: Looking for the exit

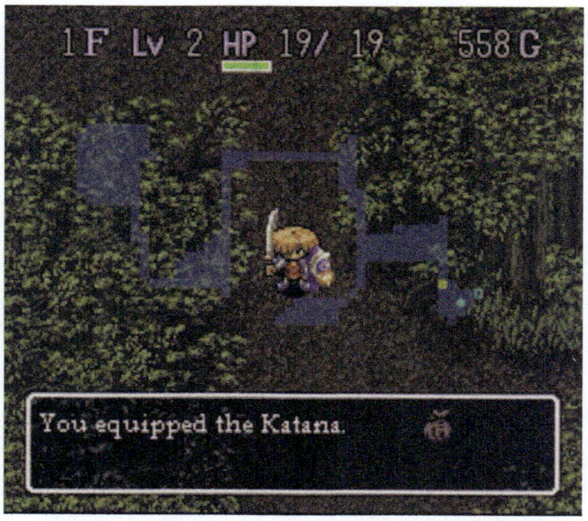

Figure 37.3

Shiren the Wanderer: Found a Katana

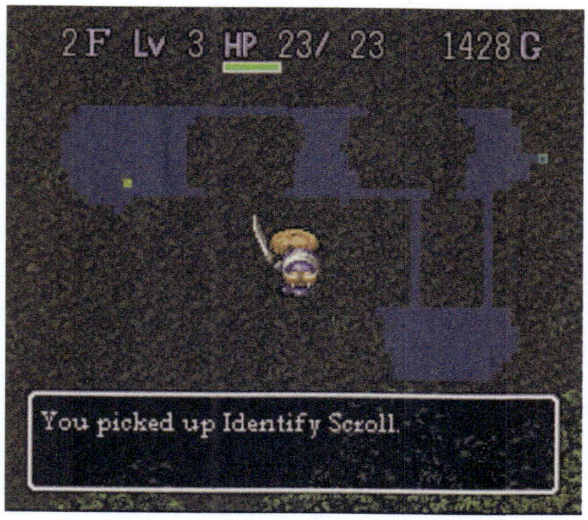

Figure 37.4

Shiren the Wanderer: Identify Scroll

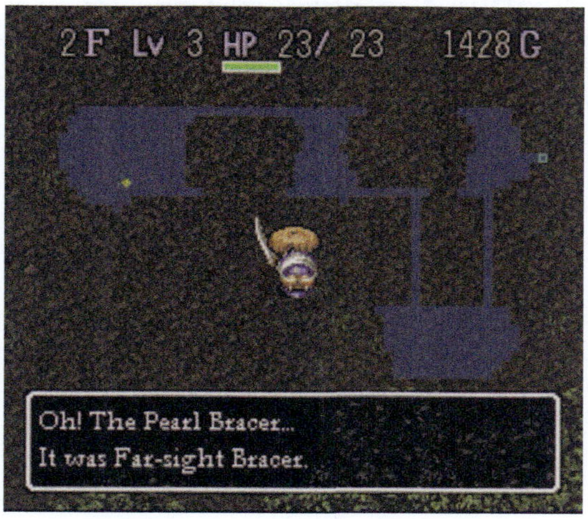

Figure 37.5

Shiren the Wanderer: A far-sight Bracer (Armband in the DS version)

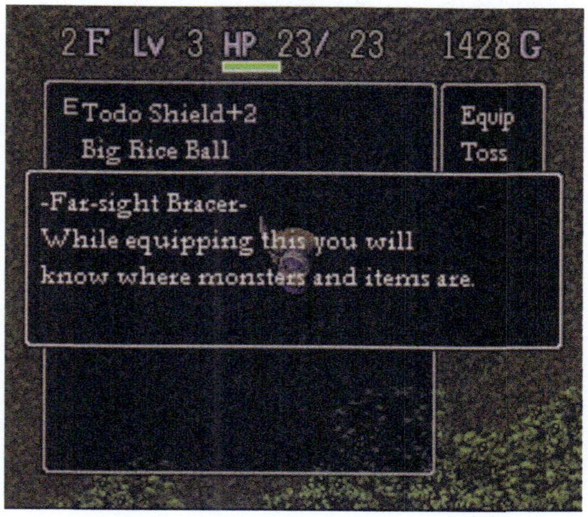

Figure 37.6

Shiren the Wanderer: Far-sight description

In Rogue, this ability is only available as an instant effect or as a short-term ability. NetHack characters can only get a limited version of this unless they are blind or are wearing an amulet of ESP. So by including a ring-type item that provides this ability permanently, this is one way that Shiren is easier than those games.

Why is this ability so useful? You'll find out next time, but for now note that this is why the map in all the screenshots to come have all the item and monster locations marked. Because I am *not* taking that thing off.

Figure 37.7: Gamara is watching to see what happens. In both Torneko and Shiren, this is what the game says when a thief monster fails its steal check. And because I'm wearing a Todo Shield, they will always say this.

It is generally the case in roguelikes that thief monsters leave good loot, and Shiren is not an exception. The trade-off is that Todo Shields are relatively weak in terms of defense, but the +2 enchantment of mine makes up even for this.

Figure 37.8: Life Herbs, when eaten, increase your maximum HP by 5.

Roguelikes that trace their lineage through Hack generally retain the special ability of the healing potions in Rogue. If you drink one when you are at full hit points, you gain *maximum* HP. Shiren does this too, but it also contains an item that specifically increases maximum hit points.

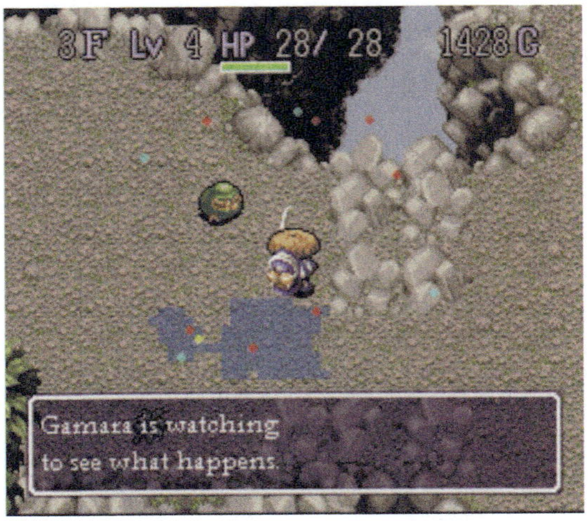

Figure 37.7

Shiren the Wanderer: Gamara

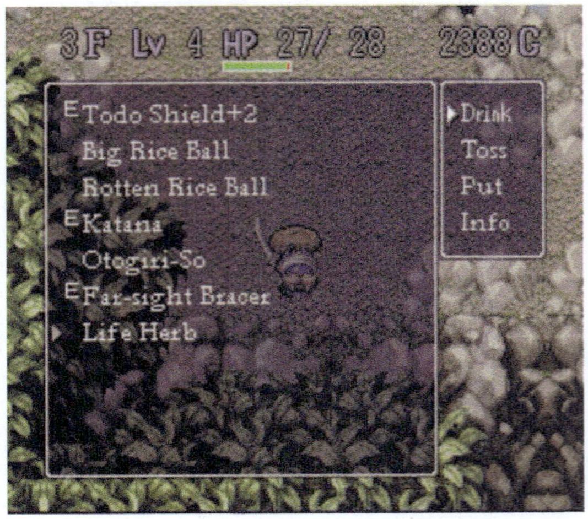

Figure 37.8

Shiren the Wanderer: Life Herb

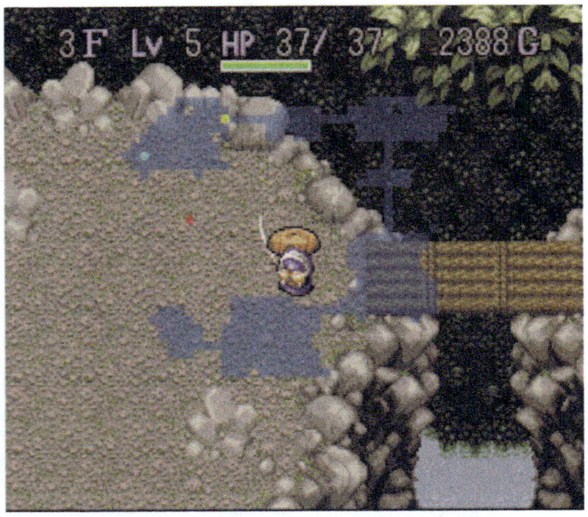

Figure 37.9

Shiren the Wanderer: River crossing

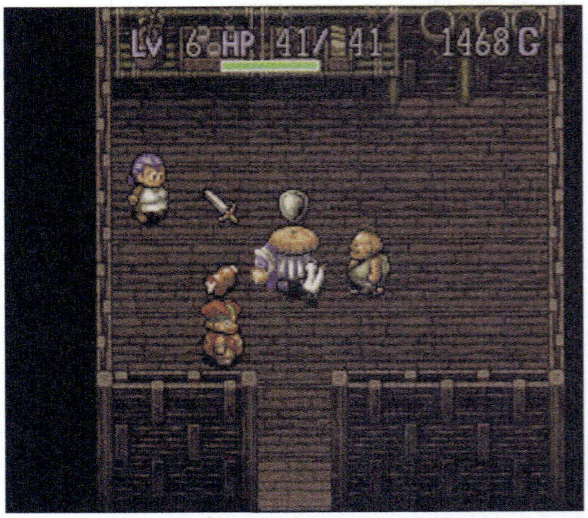

Figure 37.10

Shiren the Wanderer: Town shopping

Note that neither Torneko nor Shiren scramble herb or scroll identifications in the basic game, so finding a Life Scroll is essentially finding five free hit points lying on the dungeon floor. There is no danger from finding a bad item because they're all known at the start. The super dungeon after the main game, Fei's Final Problem, does scramble them. I'll describe that elsewhere . . . .

Figure 37.9: Sorry for the digression, but . . . look at those graphics! Hard to believe this is randomly generated, isn't it? We've come a long way from Torneko's plain stone rectangles! Not that there aren't a lot of those in Shiren the Wanderer as well, but for now let's enjoy the sights while we can.

Figure 37.10: I'm in the second town, located after level 4, and in the guaranteed shop there. Unlike towns in NetHack or ADOM, Shiren's towns are perfectly safe unless the player does something to piss someone off.

Let's take a look at this shop for a second. There's a single door, a shopkeeper standing by it, a bunch of things on the floor. . . . Yep, if this isn't enough to convince you that the Shiren guys played a *lot* of NetHack then you're a lost cause. Only NetHack, and games directly inspired by NetHack, do shops this way.

There are a lot of advantages to doing this. To buy or sell something, one just picks it up or drops it, then talks to the shopkeeper. It makes theft not the business of a die roll but a logic puzzle: how do I get the stuff out the door when the shopkeeper blocks the way when I pick something up, and how do I survive the guards that appear when I make it out?

There are also a couple of other people in this shop. The guy to Shiren's right is one of the helper characters who may join in the journey if their requirements are met. This is my first play on this file and it takes several games to finish his storyline, so he won't be coming along this time. (I don't like him anyway.)

Figure 37.11: Another thing some towns have is a smithy who'll improve your weapon by one plus for a fee.

One possible strategy for building a nice weapon is to play through to the third town, having the weapon improved at the two smithies to be found along the way, then use whatever means can be found to have the weapon sent back to the warehouse in the first town, where the player can pick it up at the start of his next game. He can then take it through again and get it improved two more levels, and repeat.

In practice this is risky however, since there are some tough levels in the early game, and there's always the chance a means of sending the weapon back won't be found in time.

37.1.1 Field Raider

Figure 37.12: It would be wrong to assume Shiren is just a copy of NetHack. There are plenty of cool new things in it to amaze and confound players! Field Raiders are one such thing. A Field Raider, when he's not concentrating on beating you to a pulp, has a second mission in life: to roam the dungeon finding all items and turning them into weeds.

What is a weed good for? Not much! If you eat one it's got pitiful worth as food, and that's it. It's best to not carelessly drop things on levels Field Raiders appear on! As time passes on the level Field Raiders will eventually get to all the treasure, so it's a good idea to loot these levels quickly . . . just one reason that Far-sight Bracer will come in handy.

37.1.2 Kimen-Musha and Ghost Musha

Figure 37.13: Another of the monsters that appears around this part of the game is the samurai-like Kimen-Musha. As far as monsters go they're fairly uninteresting, right up to the moment they're killed, for three turns later they reappear, coming back to life as Ghost Musha, and then the trouble begins.

First, I must explain about one of Shiren the Wanderer's coolest, and deadliest, features. Nearly all the monster types exist, not as individual species, but as ranks in a monster hierarchy. Torneko had monsters that could gain experience levels, but this happened but rarely. In Shiren the Wanderer, a monster that gains a level doesn't become numerically stronger; it promotes into a monster of the next higher rank.

NetHack has something like this; a monster that drinks a potion of gain level can promote to another form (so a hill orc can become an orc captain), but that's relatively uncommon. In Shiren, any time a

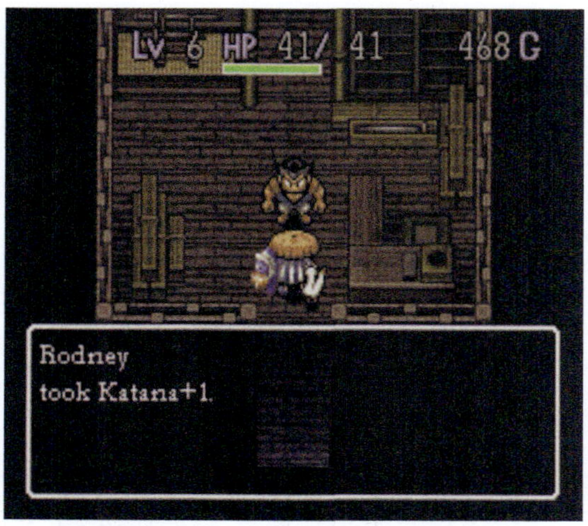

Figure 37.11

Shiren the Wanderer: Blacksmith's shop

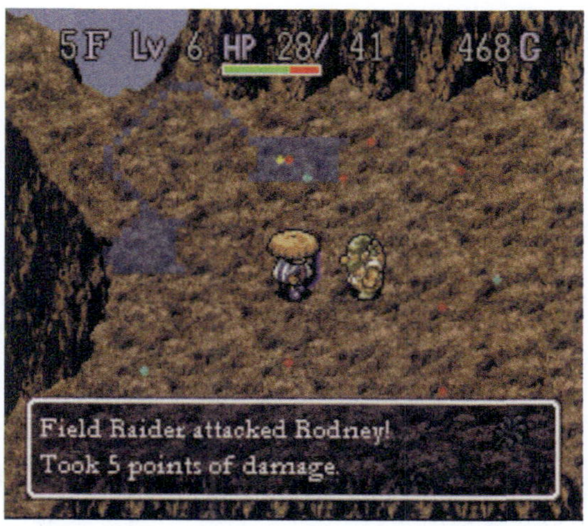

Figure 37.12

Shiren the Wanderer: Field Raider

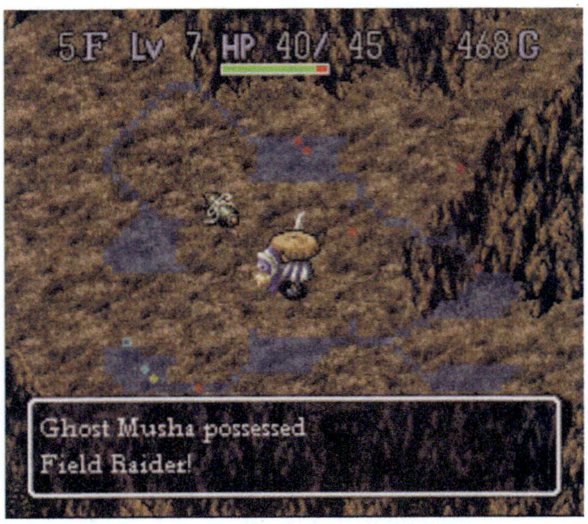

Figure 37.13

Shiren the Wanderer: Ghost Musha (Soldier in DS version)

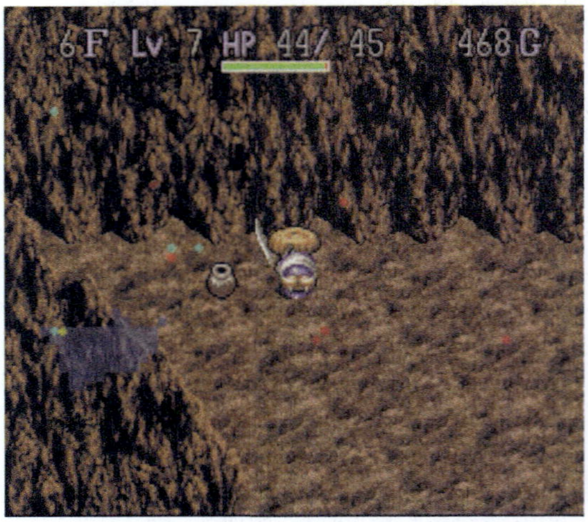

Figure 37.14

Shiren the Wanderer: Random pot

monster kills anything, it promotes. For the most part monsters are trying to kill you, not each other, and when you die it doesn't matter what happens next. But sometimes monsters kill each other by accident, or kill one of your allies, and for most species even one promotion's difference is enough to produce a deadly opponent.

There are other ways for monsters to promote too, and that's where Ghost Musha come in. They don't attack the player, but run and find other monsters. When found, they "possess" it, which in game terms means the monster promotes. The only way to prevent this is to exit the level or kill the ghost first. Ghost Musha only have four hit points, but they constantly try to flee, weapons only hit for one point of damage, and they frequently teleport before they can be killed.

Figure 37.14: It's a pot! Many items in Shiren have analogues from Rogue and NetHack, but pots are the game's great innovation. Nothing like pots exists in anything other than the Mysterious Dungeon games, and other roguelikes could do well to copy them for a change.

Pots are a kind of random container. Like herbs, scrolls and bracers, there are lots of kinds of pots, and each has some effect upon the items put into it. For example, the Strengthening Pot increases the plus of equipment placed inside. But there are also bad pots, such as the Bottomless Pot that destroys items put into it. Like the other kinds of items, the uses of pots can be figured out through deduction or the use of an Identify Scroll.

Most pots store items inside, but don't allow you to remove them easily. To get the contents, Shiren must throw the pot against a wall, causing it to shatter and spill its contents onto the dungeon floor, and all pots have limited uses.

There are also a few special types. Holding Pots have no special effect, but you can put stuff in and take stuff out freely, and so are a way around the 20 space inventory limit. Back Pots don't hold items, but if "pushed," heal the player.

Figure 37.15: The first step towards figuring out a pot's use is to look in. Pots never come with items hidden inside, but some pots say "Back" if you peer into them, which could mean it's a super-nice Back Pot. This one says "Nothing's Inside," so I know it's not that kind.

Figures 37.16, 37.17 and 37.18: Hmm, a Ghost Musha got to another of his Musha friends and promoted it into a Hannya-Musha. Not only are they much more fearsome than Kimen-Musha, but if it gets promoted again it'll make a Shogun, which could easily wipe me out.

Figure 37.19: Fortunately, I have a Dragon Herb, this game's version of Torneko's Blaze Herbs, to take care of it quickly. The defeated opponent is still a Musha, though, so it'll leave another ghost. Time to head for the next level perhaps . . .

Figures 37.20 and 37.21: I found another kind of pot, and looking inside this one shows it to contain Backs. If it's a Back Pot I'm in luck, but if it really is one of those I don't want to waste any of its healings. Let's save it for later.

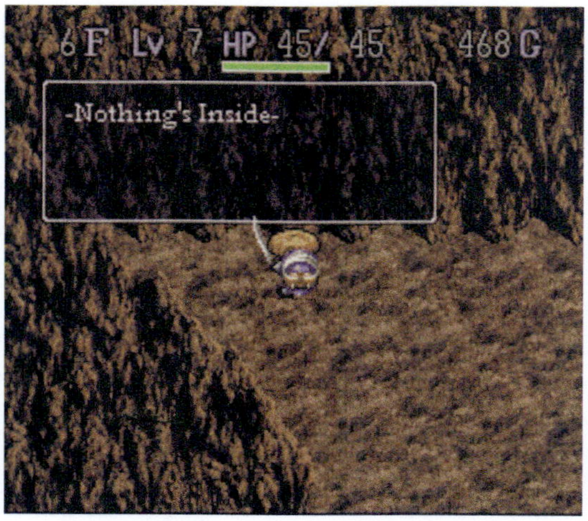

Figure 37.15

Shiren the Wanderer: Empty pot

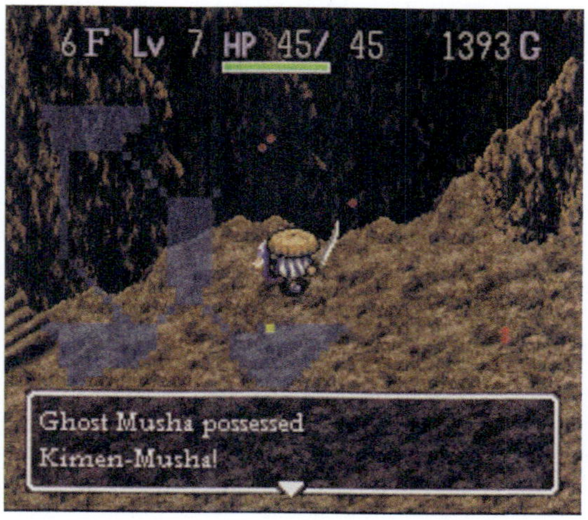

Figure 37.16

Shiren the Wanderer: Monster . . .

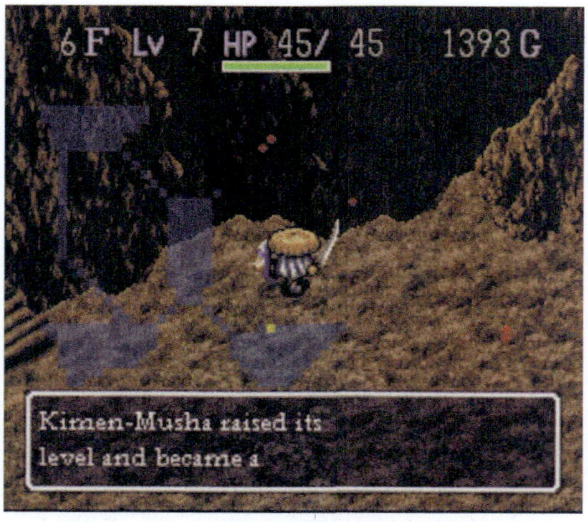

Figure 37.17

Shiren the Wanderer: . . . level . . .

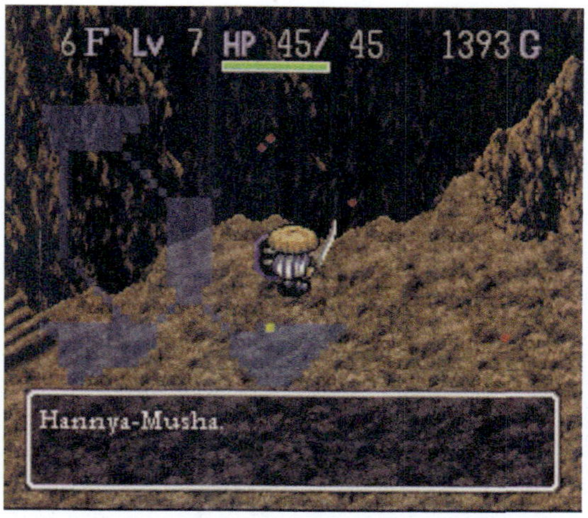

Figure 37.18

Shiren the Wanderer: . . . up!

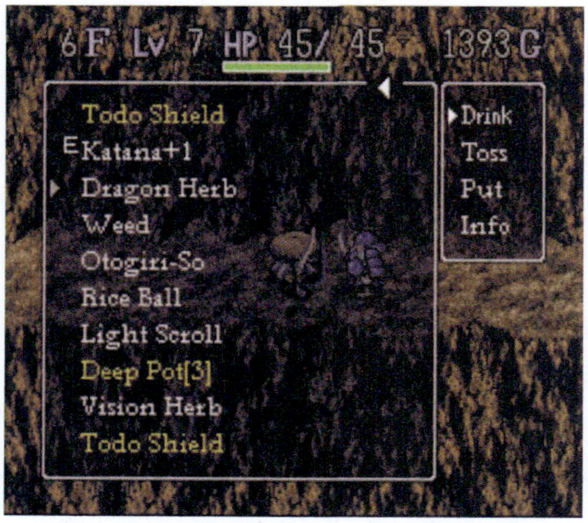

Figure 37.19

Shiren the Wanderer: Dragon Herb

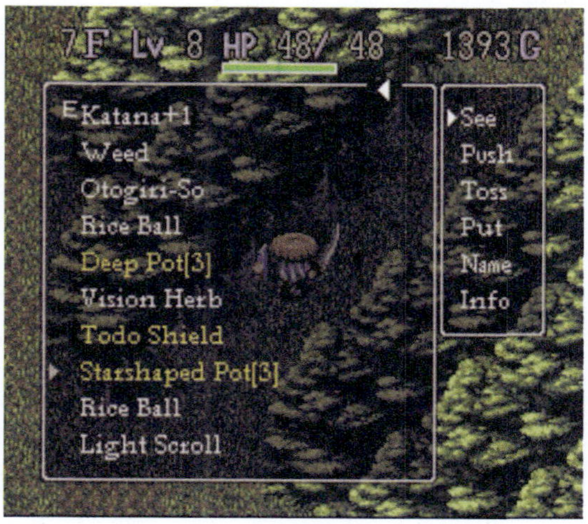

Figure 37.20

Shiren the Wanderer: Starshaped Pot

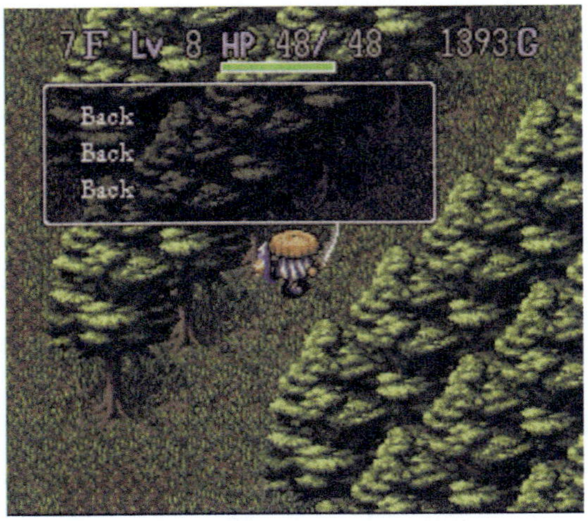

Figure 37.21

Shiren the Wanderer: Back Pot (Chiropractic Pot in DS version)

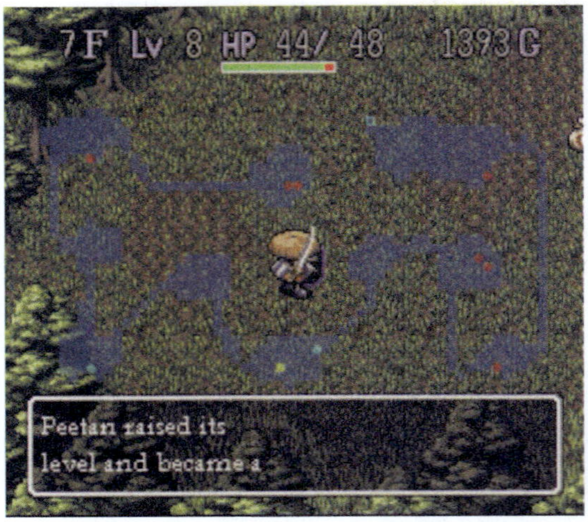

Figure 37.22

Shiren the Wanderer: Peetan promotes

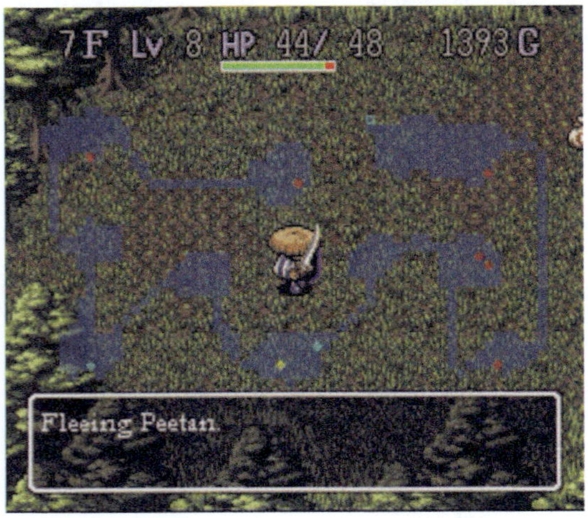

Figure 37.23

Shiren the Wanderer: Fleeing Peetan, somewhere on the level

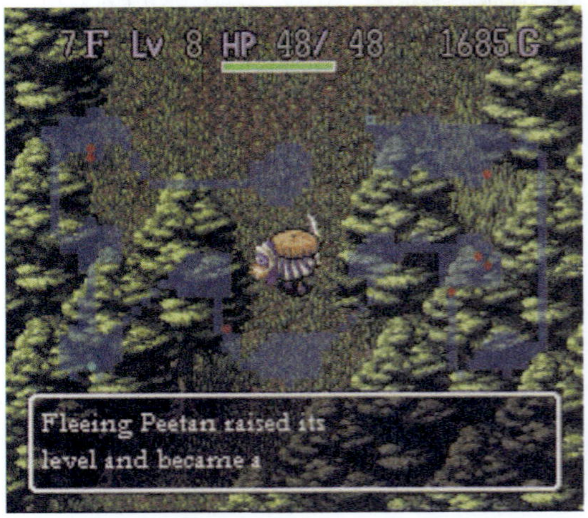

Figure 37.24

Shiren the Wanderer: It promoted again!

37.1.3 Peetan

Figures 37.22 and 23: A Ghost Musha on this level found a Peetan, turning it into a Fleeing Peetan . . .

Figures 37.24 and 25: . . . and then another found it, promoting it into a Flying Peetan. This is actually probably the best monster in the area the ghosts could have possessed. Peetans are pacifistic and never attack the player, choosing instead to run away. They're good at running, for they are double-speed monsters, but if I do manage to slay one they're worth a good number of experience points, and they always leave food behind for me to collect once killed.

37.1.4 Minion of Death

Figure 37.26: That egg-like thing in the screenshot is a Peetan, by the way, but of more interest is the cloaked, scythe-wielding monster in front of it, a Minion of Death.

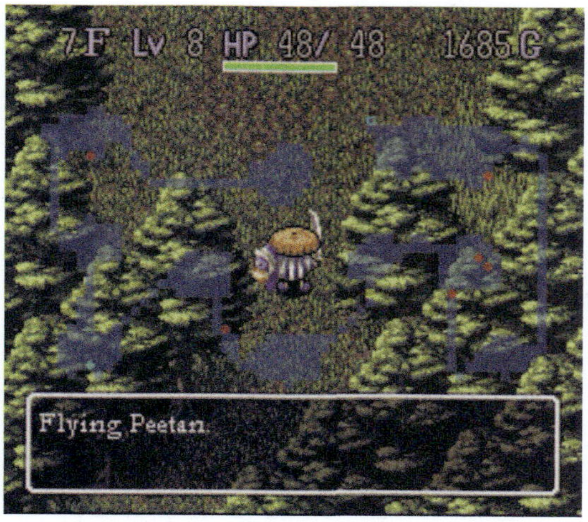

Figure 37.25

Shiren the Wanderer: I'll never catch it now, but at least it's harmless

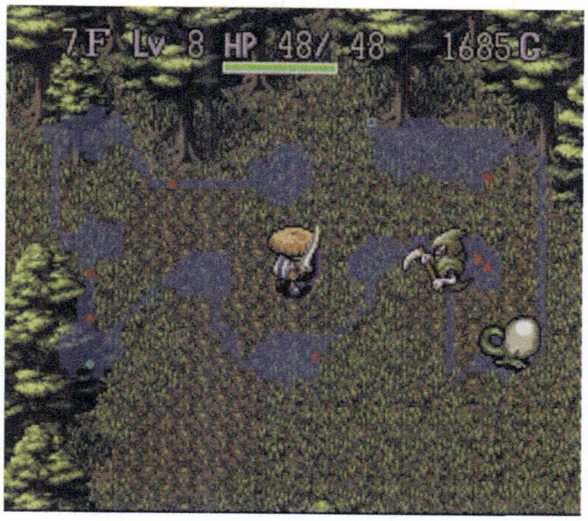

Figure 37.26

Shiren the Wanderer: Minion of Death

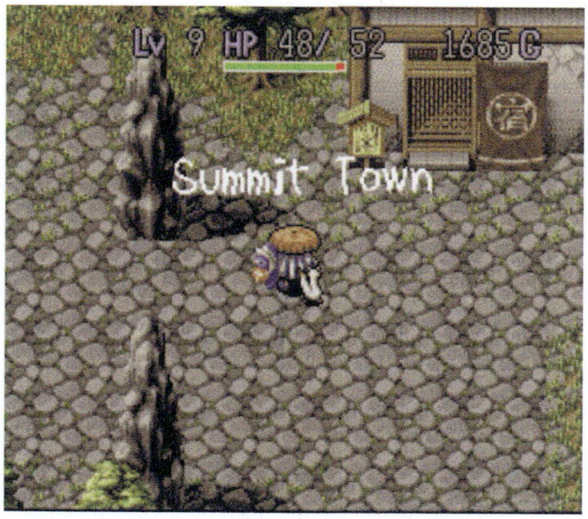

Figure 37.27

Shiren the Wanderer: Summit Town

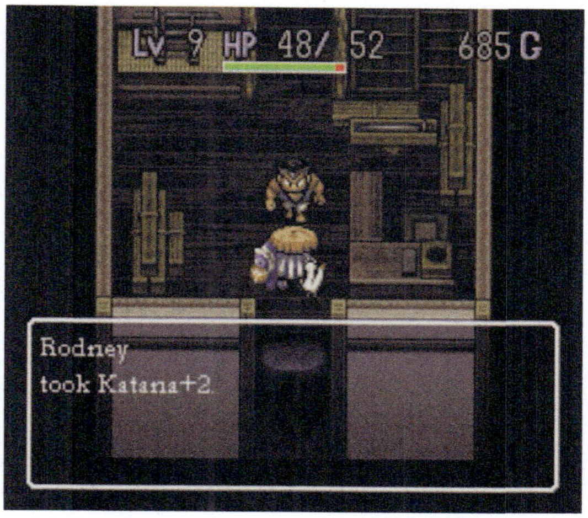

Figure 37.28

Shiren the Wanderer: Another blacksmith

These undead beasties pack a mean punch for this phase of the game, and they move at double-speed. They don't fight at double-speed, which is good, but their high movement rate means I can't just flee from it; it'll use its free move to catch up to me, then strike immediately. Escaping one requires magical means, so it's usually best to kill it if possible. If one gets promoted via Ghost Musha, the resulting monster gets two moves *and* attacks, so I should slay it before that can happen.

Figure 37.27: Summit Town is the third town of the game out of five and is home to the most involved side quests, but we're not here for the tour.

Figure 37.28: Summit Town won't have a shop until one of its side quests has been completed, which won't be for many games, but it does have a smithy.

Figures 37.29 and 30: It also has a warehouse, a place where items left remain between trips. I've got a good amount of junk lying around my pocket, so I might as well drop some of it off to pave the way for later runs. It is the nature of roguelikes that items in abundance one game will be hard to come by the next, so this way I can help to dull the sharp edges of the random number generator.

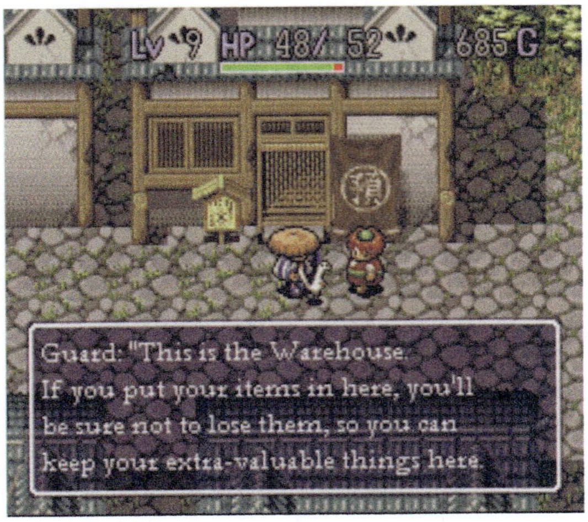

Figure 37.29

Shiren the Wanderer: A warehouse

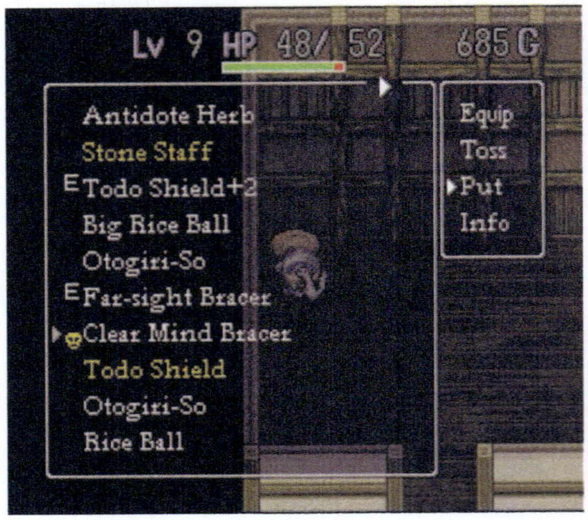

Figure 37.30

Shiren the Wanderer: Dropping things off for later games

38

A Journey to Table Mountain, Part 2

38.1 Skeleton Mage

Figure 38.1: Back in the dungeon, here is one of the more interesting enemies to be found in the game. Skeleton Mages come with a magical ranged attack. The effect is random, usually bad, but one of the possible results speeds the player up for a fair number of turns. It's nothing that can be relied upon, but it is not unknown for a dire situation to suddenly turn survivable because of one of those capricious zaps.

Figure 38.2: Here's one of those side quests I've mentioned. Sometimes a little girl shows up in these levels asking to be taken back to her family. If the player agrees she becomes an ally, which is not all that different from NetHack's pets, a helper who follows you around the monster, absorbing enemy blows. Unlike NetHack's pets, however, this one doesn't attack enemies. She is stronger than she looks, but not really all that survivable. While the monsters frequently won't attack her unless they have to to get to me, if they do attack and

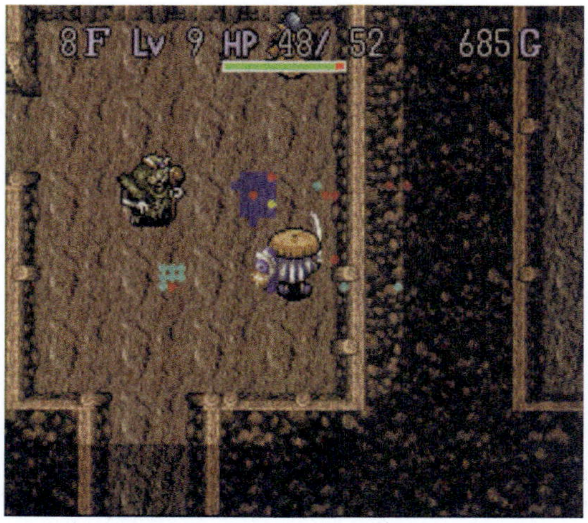

Figure 38.1

Shiren the Wanderer: Level 8

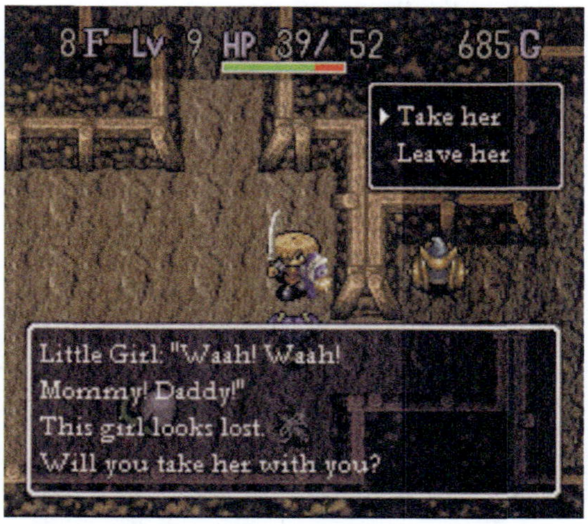

Figure 38.2

Shiren the Wanderer: Lost little girl

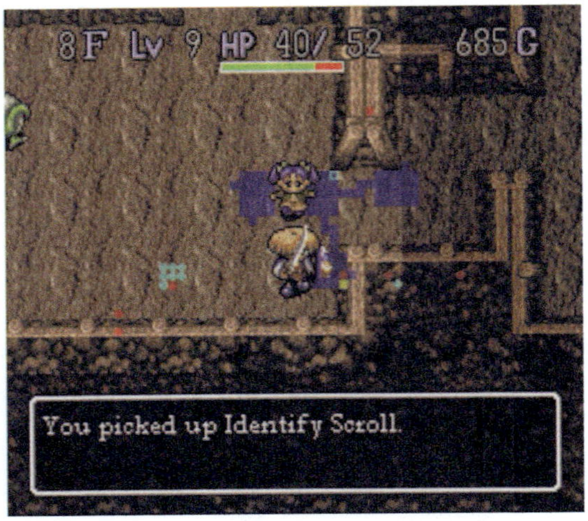

Figure 38.3

Shiren the Wanderer: Another Identify Scroll

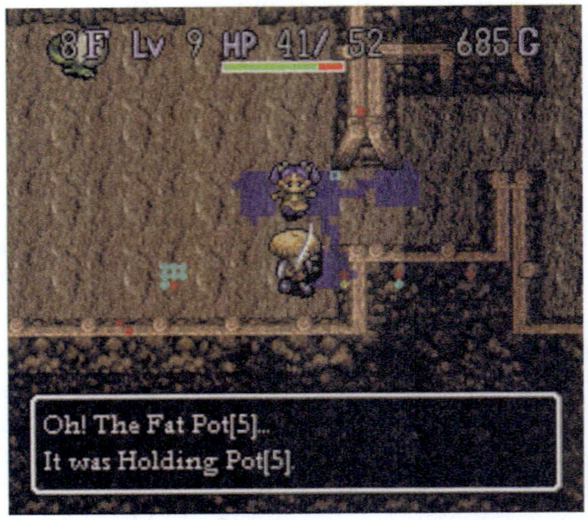

Figure 38.4

Shiren the Wanderer: Holding Pot

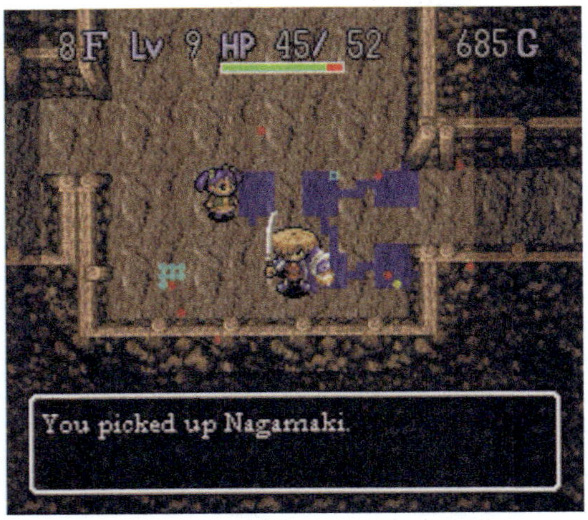

Figure 38.5

Shiren the Wanderer: A Nagamaki

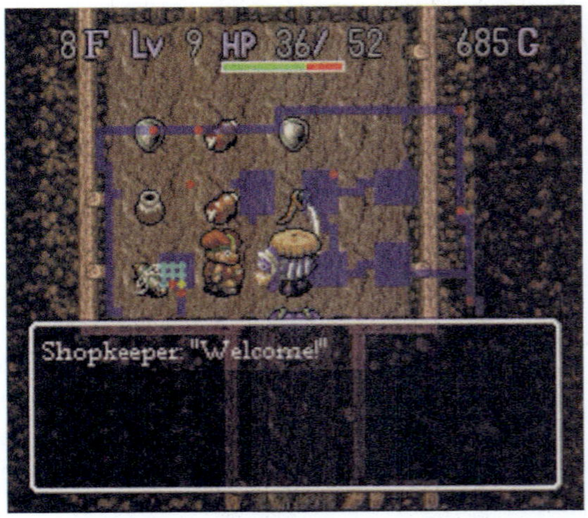

Figure 38.6

Shiren the Wanderer: Level 8 shop

kill her they'll get promoted and probably have me for dessert. But it is nice to have what amounts to a mobile wall following me around.

Figures 38.3 and 38.4: Ah, a Holding Pot! Good thing too, my pockets were getting a bit cramped.

Figure 38.5: A Nagamaki . . . is this better than my +2 Katana? I think I remember that it is, but not tremendously so. I switch to it in a little bit.

Figure 38.6: Why shopkeepers set up in the dungeon I don't know. They must have picked up that strategy from Mr. Asidonhopo's Money-Making Seminar. ("You *will* become rich within 40,000 turns or double your zorkmids back!")

Figure 38.7: Dungeon shops are an important source of items, actually. Rare goods appear in them much more often than in the main dungeon, and sometimes they stock very nice things indeed, like this Battle Counter shield . . .

Figure 38.8: or, they might have mimic-like Ndubas. ("I'm not sure why Mr. Asidonhopo said I needed to have disguised monsters among my inventory, but he's the one with the fortune in gold pieces.")

Figure 38.9: The pot he has in stock also contains "backs!" Don't ask me what a "back" is. To my recollection, there are only two back-containing pots in the game, so one of them must be that potent source of healing, a Back Pot. It isn't very expensive either, so lucky for me!

Figure 38.10: The Heaven Scroll is the game's analogue for Torneko's Bikill Scroll, from the last chapter, and Rogue's scroll of enchant weapon. As in those games, it'll increase the power of my currently equipped weapon. This one will go towards boosting my Nagamaki.

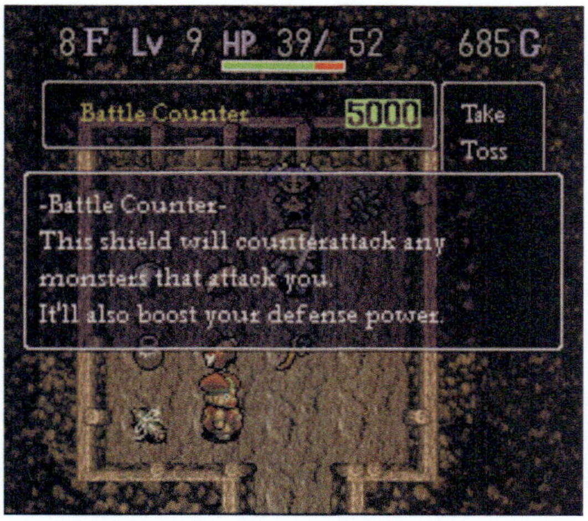

Figure 38.7

Shiren the Wanderer: Battle Counter shield

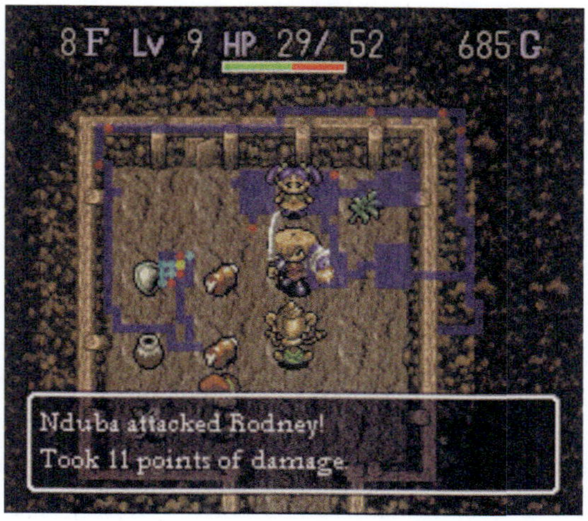

Figure 38.8

Shiren the Wanderer: Nduba

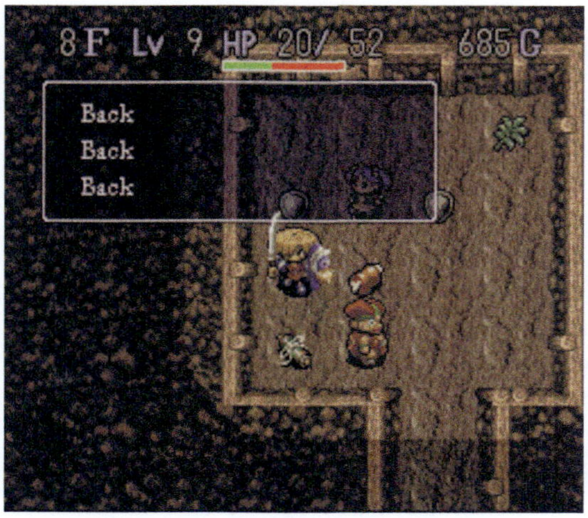

Figure 38.9

Shiren the Wanderer: Another pot with "Backs" in it

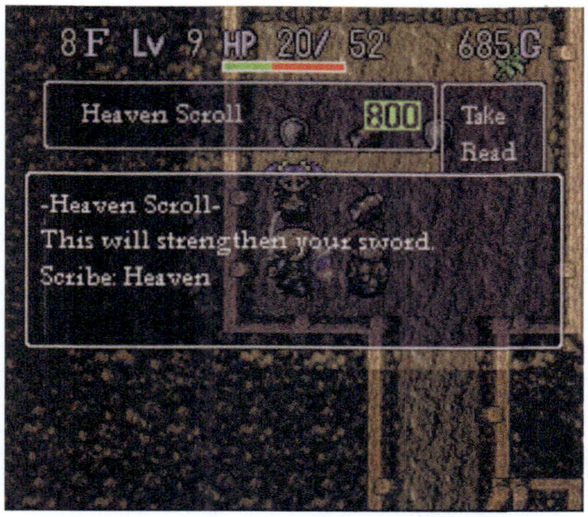

Figure 38.10

Shiren the Wanderer: Heaven Scroll

Figure 38.11: Another Todo Shield. Given the rising crime rate in the dungeon I think the shopkeeper should be wearing this instead of selling it.

Figure 38.12: Yes it's okay, let me pass!

Figure 38.13: A Blank Scroll is one of Shiren the Wanderer's most prized finds. You can make it into almost any other kind of scroll in the game, if you just know its name. In NetHack you need a magic marker to write scrolls; here you just need the paper! Can you guess what this one's going to become?

Figure 38.14: G-E-N-O-C-I-D-E. I knew you could. Actually you can write any eight letters onto the scroll, but only certain combinations will work. They are helpfully listed in the Info text for each scroll. By the way, Anna Anthropy notes that the scribe function was one of the most troublesome things to implement for the patch authors, since it meant they had more work to do than just translate text strings.

(*Note*: the name of the Scroll of Genocide is an unfortunate legacy from the original Rogue, from where it passed to Hack and NetHack, and is preserved in this translation patch for tradition's sake. In the official English Nintendo DS translation of Shiren the Wanderer, it was named Sealing instead.)

Figure 38.15: The "Todo" in the Todo Shield stands for Thieftodo, one of those annoying item stealers I mentioned before. Of course, with that shield they are unable to even touch me, and they become essentially free items if I can catch and kill them.

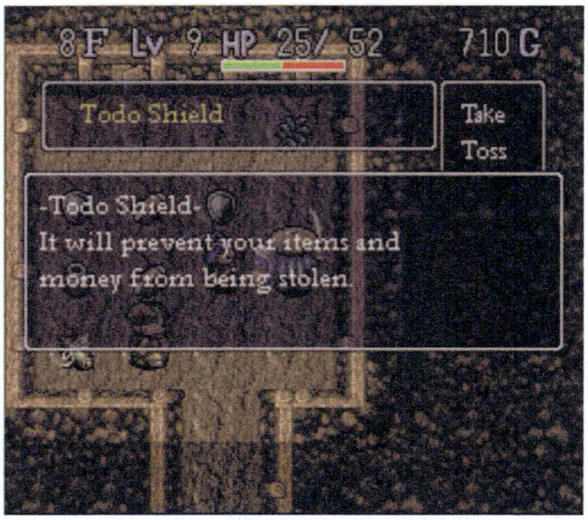

Figure 38.11

Shiren the Wanderer: Todo Shield

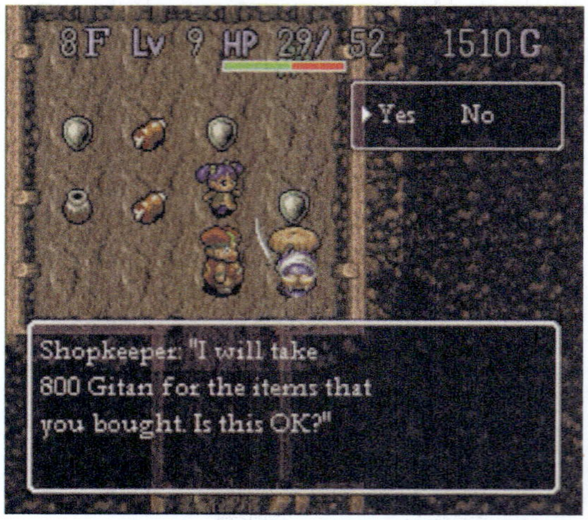

Figure 38.12

Shiren the Wanderer: Paying the bill

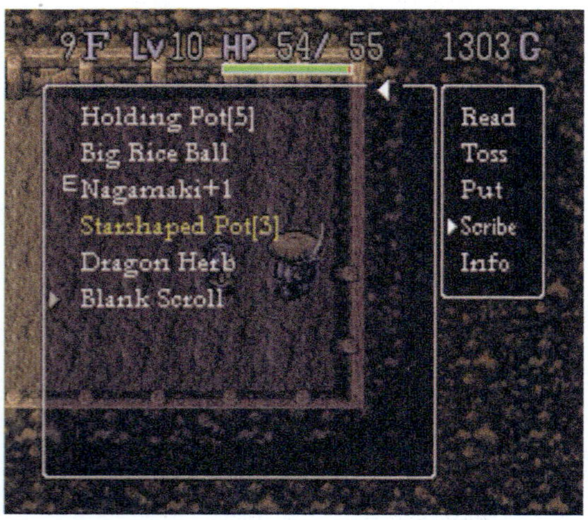

Figure 38.13

Shiren the Wanderer: A Blank Scroll!

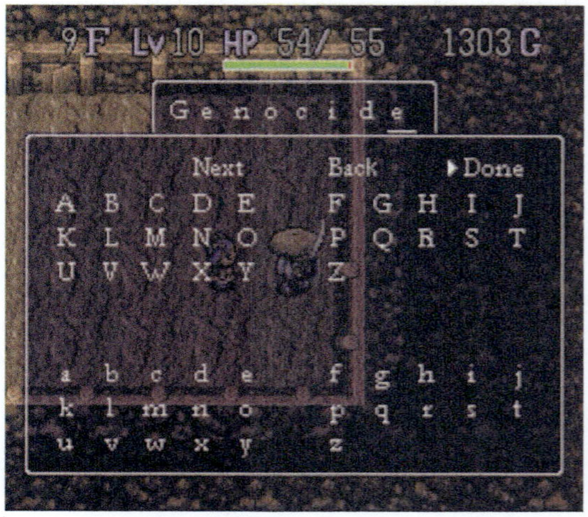

Figure 38.14

Shiren the Wanderer: Writing a Genocide Scroll

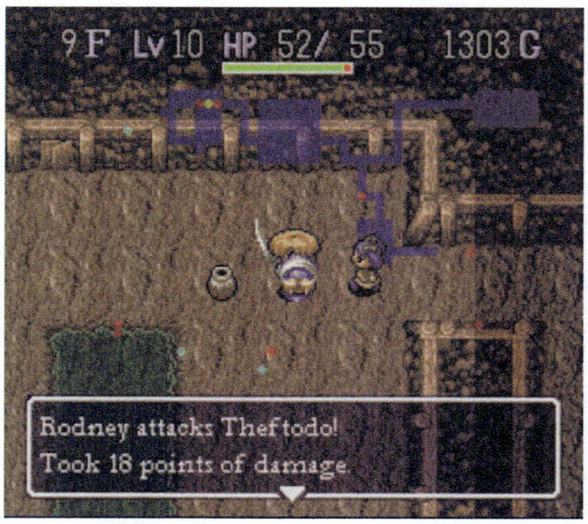

Figure 38.15

Shiren the Wanderer: Thieftodo

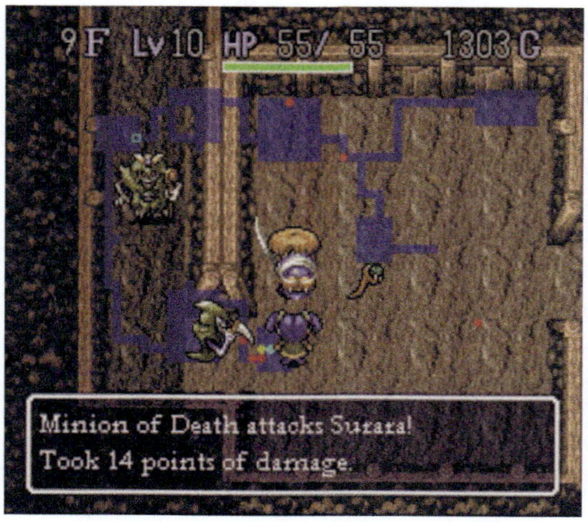

Figure 38.16

Shiren the Wanderer: Minion of Death

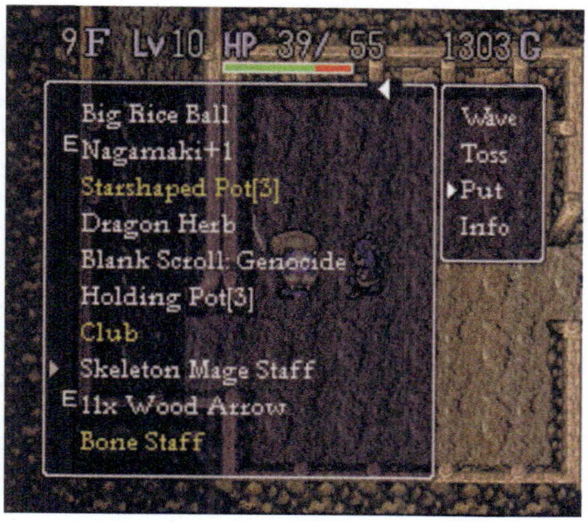

Figure 38.17

Skeleton Mage Staff

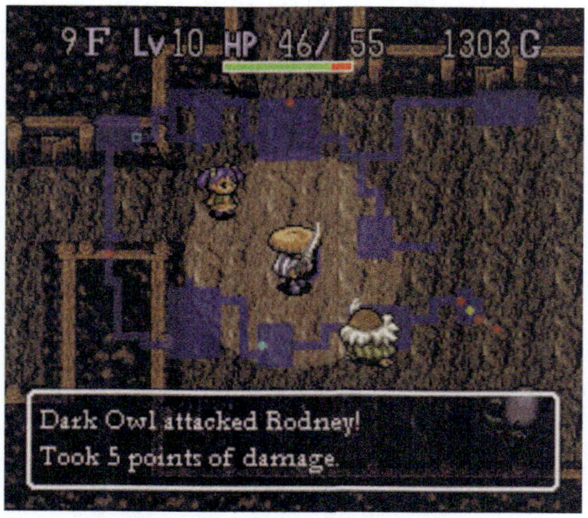

Figure 38.18

Shiren the Wanderer: Dark Owl

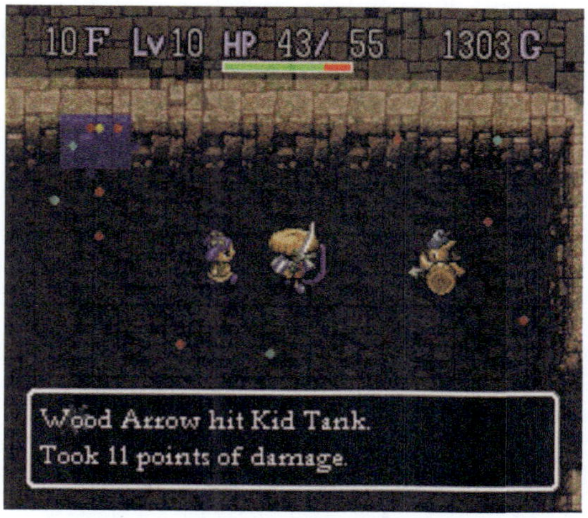

Figure 38.19

Shiren the Wanderer: Kid Tank

Figure 38.16: This was a bit of a worrisome moment, a promoted Minion of Death a single space away could mean a rapid demise, but the girl is stronger than you'd think. She takes that 14 points of damage like a trooper. Remember: a level 1 Shiren only has 15 hit points.

Figure 38.17: Sometimes a defeated Skeleton Mage leaves his staff behind, but they aren't really that useful since the same flaw that sometimes hastes Shiren will sometimes work in favor of your monstrous opponents.

38.2 Dark Owl

Figure 38.18: These are fun opponents. They aren't difficult to kill, but as long as they're alive the room is dark. By the way, notice how I can see that Peetan in the corner, behind the message window? That's because of my Far-sight Bracer. It doesn't just affect the map; it also reveals enemies in dark areas if they're close enough to be on-screen.

38.3 Kid Tank

Figure 38.19: There were a few tough opponents earlier that I neglected to mention. In the big outdoor areas there were the annoying Monster Daikons who sometimes throw herbs that leave the player slowed, and Monster Nigiri Beasts who can turn your possessions into Rice Balls (that is sometimes an affliction it's good to have). And then there were the Bowyas, archers who can attack from a distance.

Funny thing about Bowyas. When they shoot, they pay no heed to monsters in the line of fire, and so they are by far the monsters most likely to get promoted. Supporting this, the developers gave them far more promotion ranks than any other monster in the game. Most monsters have three forms, but Bowyas have six or seven, each far more deadly than the last. The Kid Tank, pictured here in its natural habitat, is just level 3.

Kid Tanks are double-movement monsters, but they still only get one attack, and they have no special vision ability, so the usual way to handle them is to retreat to a corridor where they can only fire when adjacent to you, so at least they can be hit back.

Promoted Kid Tanks quickly ascend the ladder to godhood. The next rank shoots a cannonball every other turn that inflicts 20 points of splash damage, and the next rank above that can fire every turn. Monsters are not immune to the cannonball explosions, so promotion is rapid at that point unless measures are taken. The highest rank, Obstinate Tank, is among the deadliest monsters in the whole game, including those that are only generated in the secret super dungeon. But none of these forms is able to see more than one space in darkness, so if you can flee into a corridor escape just may be possible.

38.4 Pumkorepkin

Figure 38.20: Another ghost monster, these guys move randomly sometimes, but that's made up for by their ability to pass through walls. If one is in a wall yet adjacent to you he can attack but you can't hit back!

Figure 38.21 and 22: A Crisis Scroll is like Shiren's version of a Get Out Of Jail Free card. When you read it, you are completely healed and all adjacent monsters are put to sleep. They also fix many status problems

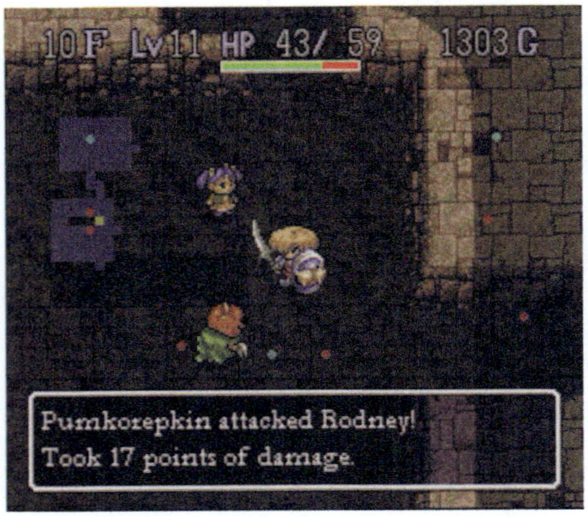

Figure 38.20

Shiren the Wanderer: Pumkorepkin

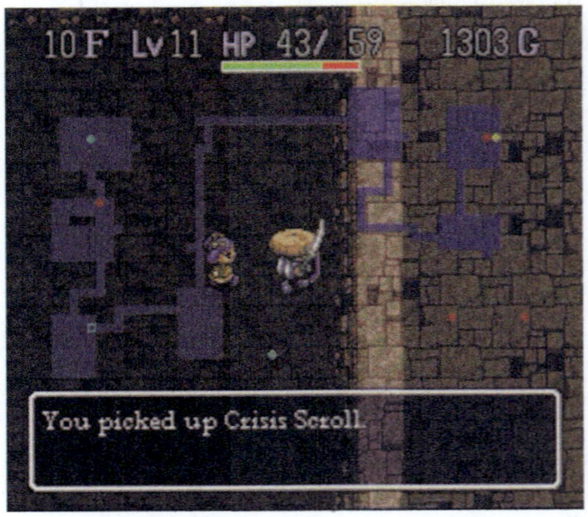

Figure 38.21

Shiren the Wanderer: Crisis Scroll

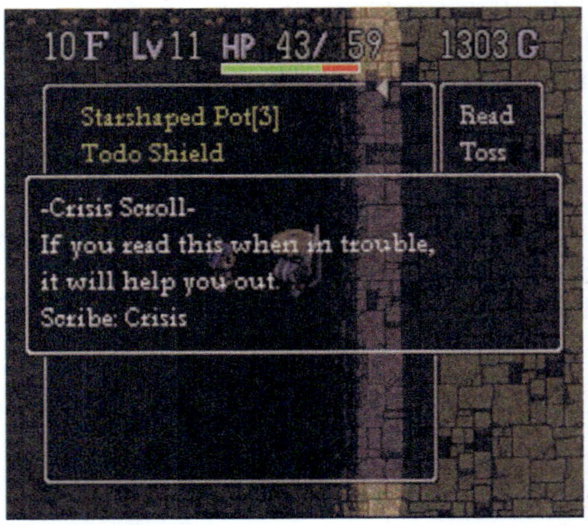

Figure 38.22

Shiren the Wanderer: Crisis Scroll Description

in the process! They are the closest thing in the game to NetHack's universal panacea, the amulet of life saving.

38.5 Debuta

Figure 38.23: This charming orc-like monster has only one special quality. He can throw rocks at the player from a distance, even if he's not in a straight line. The rocks don't hurt much, but the range is surprisingly large and they can wear you down if you don't get up to him and ask him to stop with your sword.

Figure 38.24 and 25: Ah, a Bigroom Scroll.

Remember what I said before, that Shiren contains the occasional Big Room level? They're not just random. You can *make* one by reading these items, the result being that all the walls on the level are destroyed. This can be great when cornered, but one should then immediately head for the exit, because with no corridors around to hide in Shiren will get overwhelmed fast.

I hear that, if one is used on a level containing a shop, the result is that the shopkeeper will run to the stairs so he can block them in case you pick up his stuff . . .

38.6 Healer Rabbit

Figure 38.26: Oh, how I hate these bunnies. By themselves they're pretty harmless, but if one finds a strong monster to fixate upon he can make it almost unbeatable, spending his turns on healing him. If one doesn't have a way to kill the rabbit or take out the dangerous monster in one turn it's best to flee.

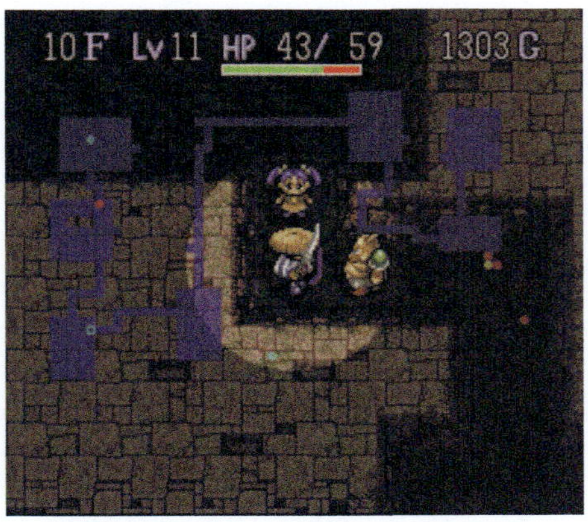

Figure 38.23

Shiren the Wanderer: Debuta

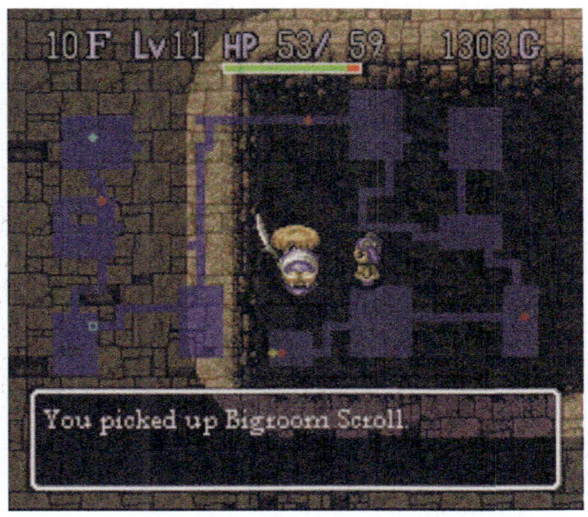

Figure 38.24

Shiren the Wanderer: Bigroom Scroll

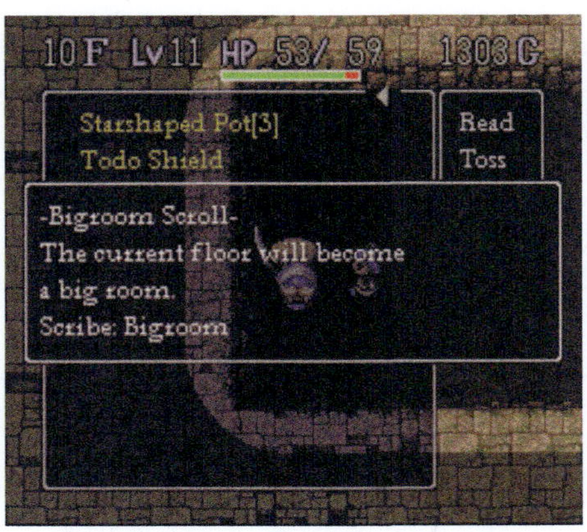

Figure 38.25

Shiren the Wanderer: Bigroom Scroll Description

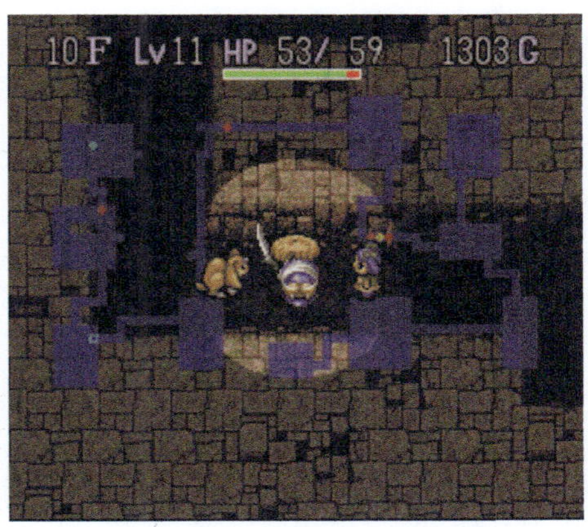

Figure 38.26

Shiren the Wanderer: Healer Rabbit

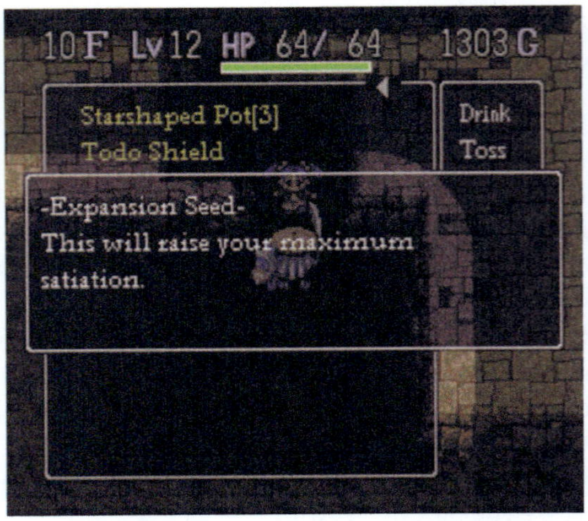

Figure 38.27

Shiren the Wanderer: Expansion Seed

Figure 38.27: Maximum hit points isn't the only malleable statistic in Shiren the Wanderer. Expansion Seeds increase your stomach size by 10%. If you eat a Rice Ball while already full, you'll receive a more modest gullet increase.

That's it for part two. Next time we'll descend deeper and slay gazes, chickens and minotaurs, find out just why that Far-sight Bracer is so useful, and we'll see a sure-fire way to steal from shops. Won't that be fun . . .

39

A Journey to Table Mountain, Part 3

August 2007 Early in part one I had found one of the best objects in the game, a Far-sight Bracer, which reveals the locations of all items and monsters while it is worn. Few roguelikes offer items like this because such knowledge can be extremely useful in those game. Items are the primary reward for exploration in roguelikes, and knowing where they all are also shows the player when no more are to be found. Monsters are the primary source of danger, and knowing their locations lets the player know where to avoid. And both reveal, indirectly, the locations of rooms and corridors. Even NetHack's Amulet of ESP only works over the whole level if the player is blind.

39.1 Flame Priest

Figure 39.1: Many of the monsters later on in Shiren seem quite overpoweringly difficult. Not only do Flame Priests hit hard with a flame attack that the player's shield doesn't help much with, but if a Dragon Herb is used on one it just makes things worse . . .

39.2 Norojo

Figures 39.2 and 39.3: These monsters aren't so bad, but they can curse equipped shields. They don't damage shields, though, only curse them, and it costs them a turn to curse that they could have used to smack the player around. Curses in Shiren follow the Rogue pattern: they only affect equipment, and the only effect is that it makes them impossible to take off, usually, without aid.

So the Norojo isn't a huge threat. But behind it is a Kigni Tribe, and we'll find out more about them in a bit . . .

Figure 39.4: Ah, another shop. They can't get that much business this far into the game, can they?

Figure 39.5: Disposable Shields are interesting items. They have the highest natural defense of any shield in the game, but every time one takes a hit it loses a point of protection strength.

There is a trick regarding these shields and monster meat items, which transform the player into the form of a monster when eaten in a manner similar (again!) to a NetHack feature, player polymorph. While transformed, the player's equipment still affects his stats, but the degrading quality of Disposable Shields doesn't function. The player gets all that protection without loss.

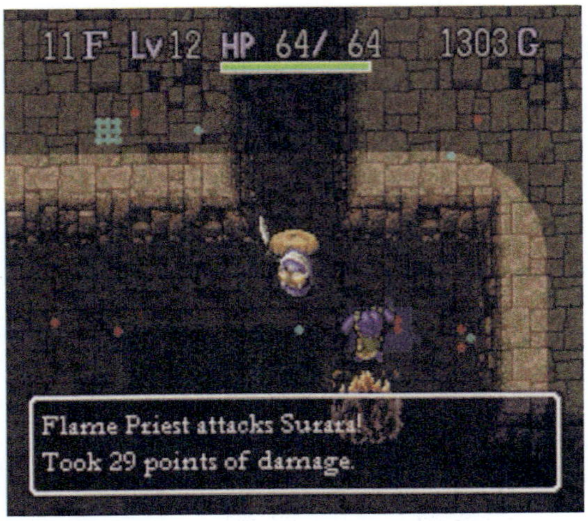

Figure 39.1

Shiren the Wanderer: Flame Priest

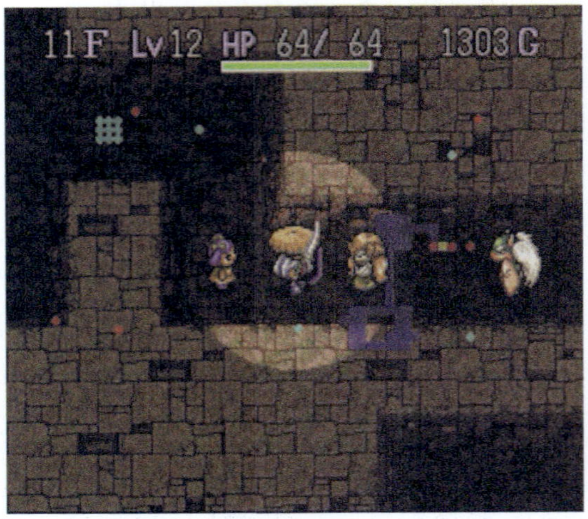

Figure 39.2

Shiren the Wanderer: Norojo (Curse Sister)

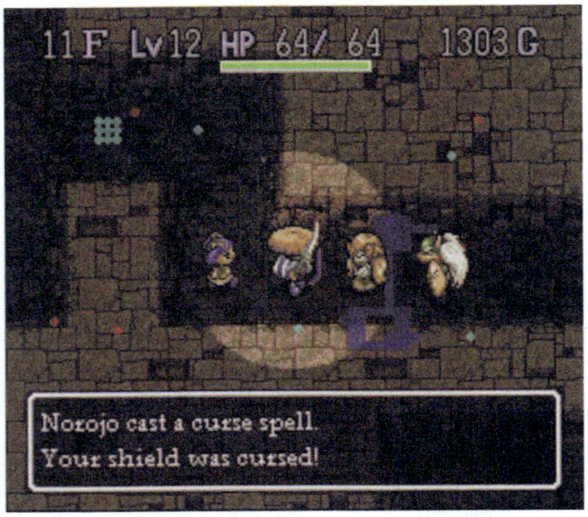

Figure 39.3

Shiren the Wanderer: Getting cursed

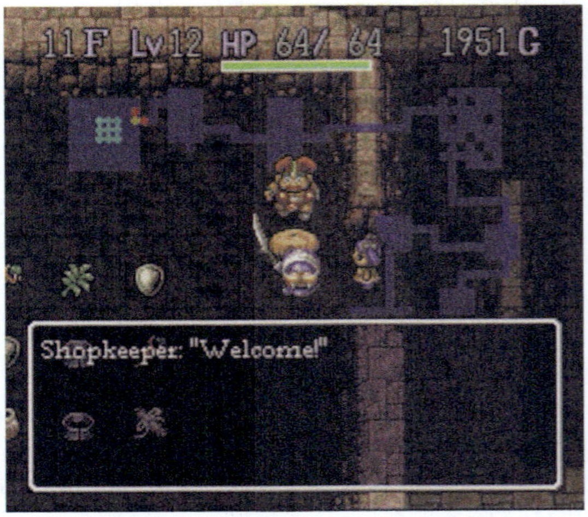

Figure 39.4

Shiren the Wanderer: Level 11 shop

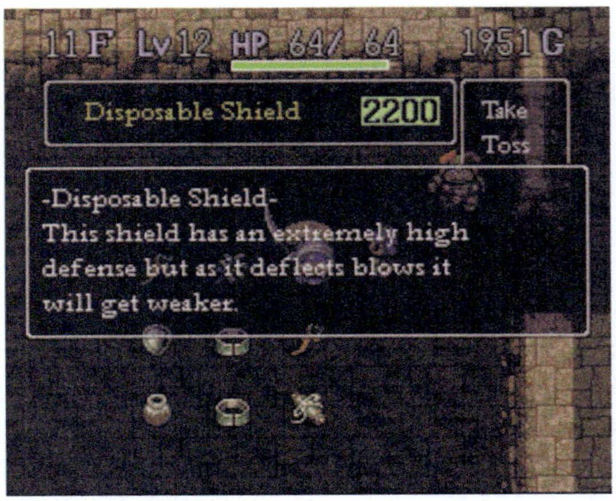

Figure 39.5

Shiren the Wanderer: Disposable Shield

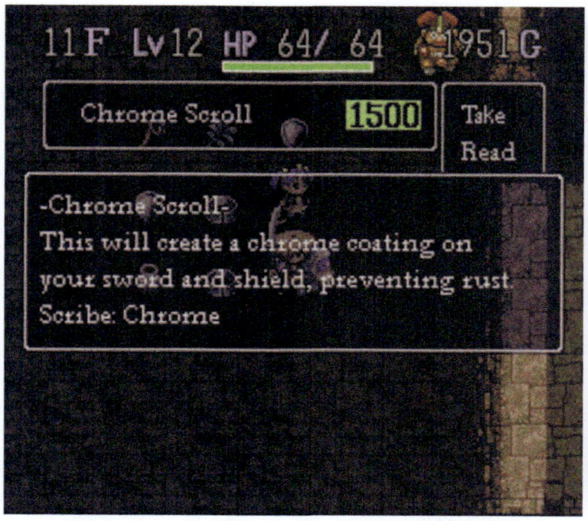

Figure 39.6

Shiren the Wanderer: Chrome Scroll

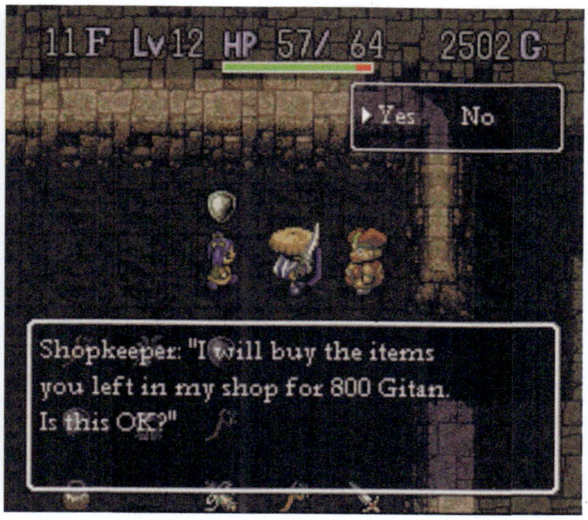

Figure 39.7

Shiren the Wanderer: Pawning stuff

The trick is a little over-powered since polymorph doesn't actually make the player stronger or weaker in Shiren, it just makes it harder to use items and maybe gives him a special ability or two. I don't use it in this game, however, because the only sure way to acquire monster meat is to use a Staff of Bufoo, and they don't appear naturally in the dungeon until a certain subquest has been completed.

Figure 39.6: Chrome Scrolls protect the player's current equipment from damage from monsters or traps. There really couldn't have been a better time for me to find one of these, as the drain floors are coming soon . . . .

Figure 39.7: Shiren doesn't just take good ideas from NetHack; it takes a couple of (in my opinion, of course) bad ones too.

One of the more unbalancing advanced tricks in NetHack is price ID. It's based on the fact that shopkeepers in NetHack know what all the items are even if the player doesn't, and price them accordingly. A player who knows the going rates for stuff can greatly narrow down the possibilities by simply dropping things in a store and seeing how much he's offered. Rogue-type roguelikes depend on hiding item identities to make things more challenging, and a lot of the balance is geared towards test-identifying, but experienced players tend not to test-ID so much in NetHack anymore because there are so many other ways to identify things.

Note, however, that NetHack does, in more recent versions, attempt to make this less useful. There's some variability depending on player Charisma (one of the very few things that stat affects), which must be accounted for. Item prices are arranged in tiers, with a variety of objects of each type having the same price, which helps to keep some info hidden. More deviously, a few items are randomly determined to be more expensive than others, and the price differential has been chosen to put items into the next pricing tier, so once in a while an object will get placed outside its normal price zone. Yet, because there are only a small number of bad items in each tier, a lot of the risk of price-IDing goes away once one of those objects is known. The strange thing about all this is that gold in NetHack is nearly worthless these days beyond the early game, except as a source of protection. If they had completely randomized prices the result would probably be less unbalancing than leaving price ID in the game.

Shiren's system uses some of NetHack's price tier idea (you don't see it in these screenshots, but during this game I found two different bracers that cost 10,000), but not taken far enough to foil a determined player.

Figures 39.8 and 39.9: Here's a little roguelike secret. In most games, items that enchant, vorpalize, protect or otherwise improve equipment almost always remove curses in the process.

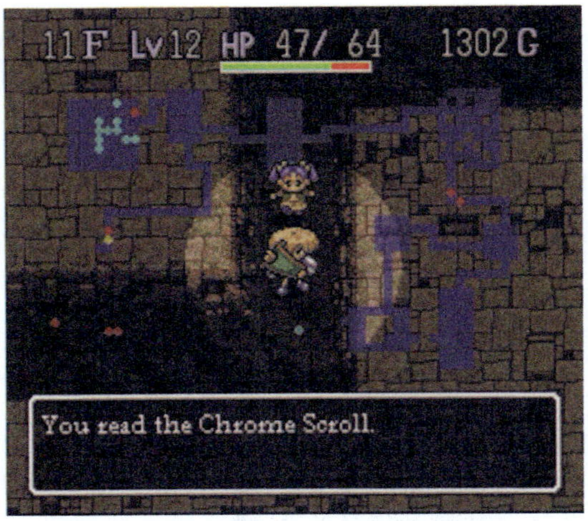

Figure 39.8

Shiren the Wanderer: Reading a Chrome Scroll

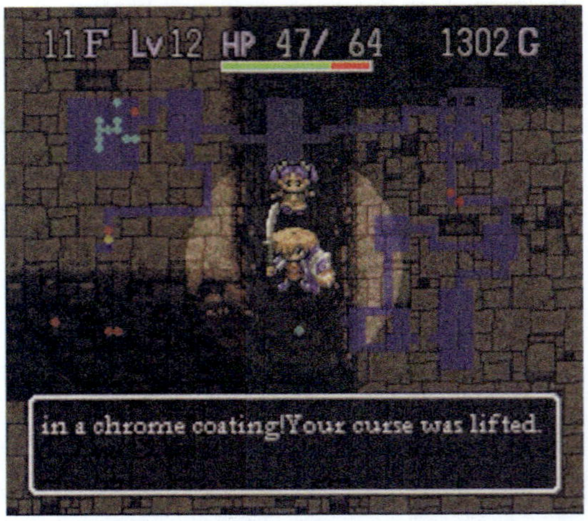

Figure 39.9

Shiren the Wanderer: Item protection with curse lifting thrown in

39.3 Kigni Tribe

Figures 39.10 and 39.11: This is a fairly interesting monster. In ability they're completely ordinary, except for their willingness to purposely slaughter other nearby monsters to improve their own strength!

There are actually several levels of Kigni Tribe, all of which share the same name and appear similar to each other, so it's not always easy to know just how powerful one of these monsters is when encountered.

Figure 39.12: Once in a while there are levels where lots of things happen. The random number generator had a lot in store for me here on level 12 . . .

Figure 39.13: It was here that I managed to identify my back-filled pot, and found it was a Todo Pot. That's still not too bad, as these items allow the player to steal easily from shops, as we'll see later.

Far more ominously, in this screenshot, take a close look at the dungeon map. Do you see that roughly box-like region with lots of red and blue dots?

Yep, it's a lair, or as it's called here, a "Monster House." In Torneko they were troublesome, but Shiren has far trickier monsters than that game, and also far more powerful treasure to find. Monster Houses can even contain "out of depth" monsters, stronger than usual for that floor. They should never be taken lightly.

If I hadn't been wearing a Far-sight Bracer, I probably would have stumbled upon it by accident.

Figure 39.14: Next on the list of things scavenged from NetHack: a digging item, the pickaxe.

There are other roguelikes with digging too, but Shiren also contains vaults, rooms disconnected from the normal level structure, to find by digging. How does one find these rooms without digging every square? Oh, if only I had some item equipped that revealed the location of everything on the level . . .

Figure 39.15: Yet another another shop again.

Figures 39.16 and 39.17: Another pot with backs inside. Since we know what the Todo Pot is now, this one's probably the healing type I talked about last time, good.

Figure 39.18: Okay, here's how to steal with a Todo Pot. Move the store's inventory around so that the stuff you want to steal is directly in front of the door. Then stand outside in the doorway and "push" the pot. A Thieftodo monster will pop out and run forward in a straight line, grab the first item it finds, then return it to the pot and vanish. The item ends up in the pot in place of the "back," and the shopkeeper doesn't notice the object's missing!

Some items are so expensive that, in a normal game, this is the only reasonable way to get them from a shop.

Figure 39.19: Remember, with most pots, you must throw it against a wall and break it to get its contents.

Figures 39.20 and 39.21: The Swap Staff trades your position with the monster hit. This may seem like a minor thing, but it actually can have surprising applications. We'll get to those in a bit.

Figures 39.22 and 39.23: Related to the Swap Staff is the Blowback Staff, which pushes a monster backwards until it hits something. It inflicts very minor damage in the process, but again, pushing has interesting uses.

Figure 39.24: So then, what did I do with that Monster House?

Why, I left it the hell alone! Sometimes it's best not to take chances. Tackling Monster Houses is something best done when you've got a good stock of nifty magical aids at the ready to deal with them for you or help you escape if things start to get pear-shaped. Without some of those, it's often best to leave them alone if at all possible.

Figures 39.25 and 39.26: These levels are where Old Man Tanks start appearing naturally.

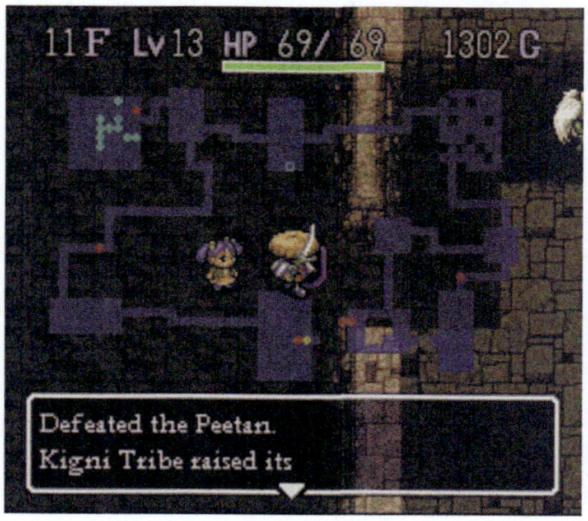

Figure 39.10

Shiren the Wanderer: Kingi Tribe

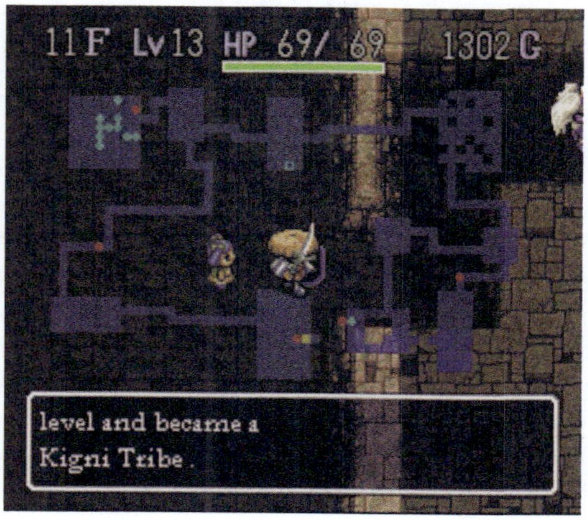

Figure 39.11

Shiren the Wanderer: Kingi promotion

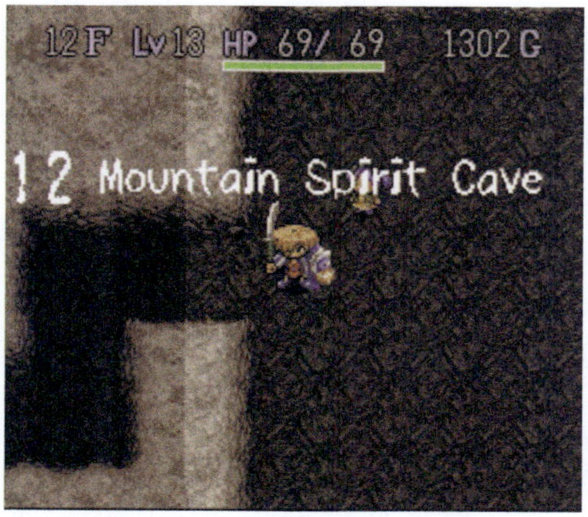

Figure 39.12

Shiren the Wanderer: Level 12

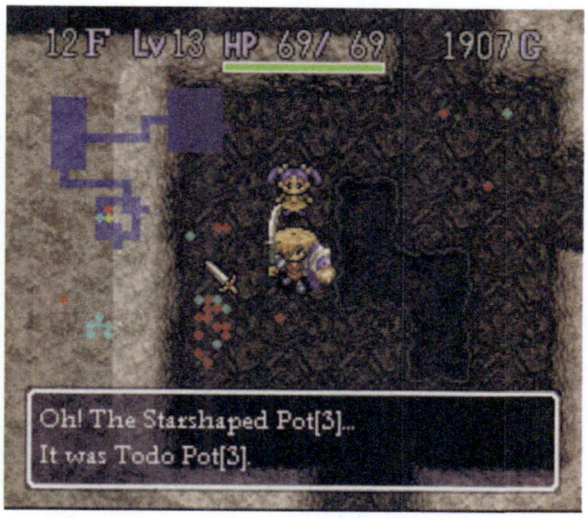

Figure 39.13

Shiren the Wanderer: Todo Pot

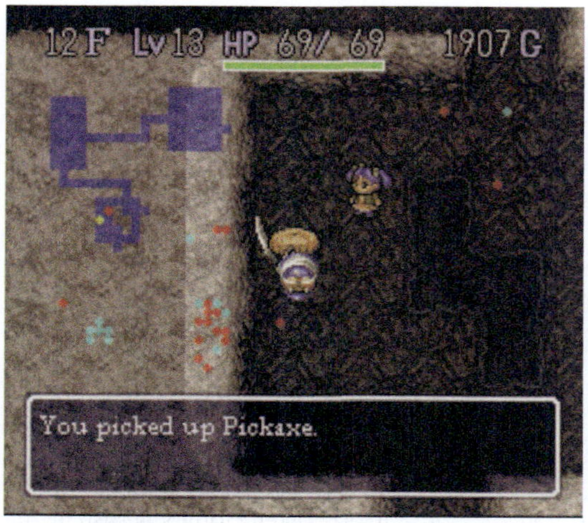

Figure 39.14

Shiren the Wanderer: Pickaxe

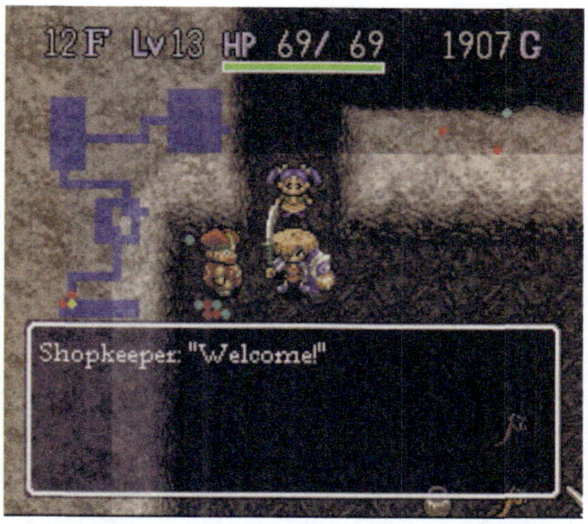

Figure 39.15

Shiren the Wanderer: Level 12 shop

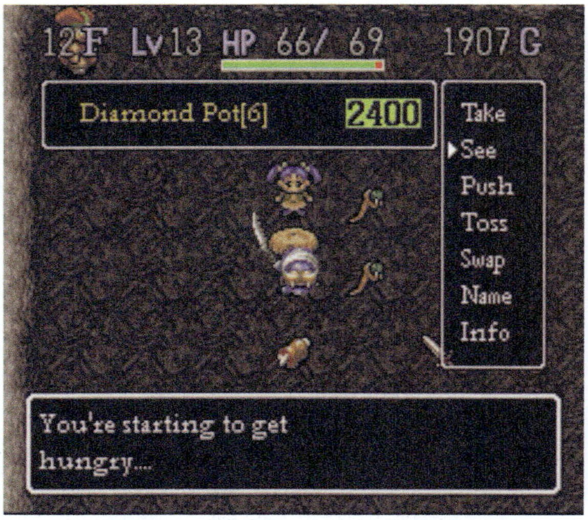

Figure 39.16

Shiren the Wanderer: Pot deduction

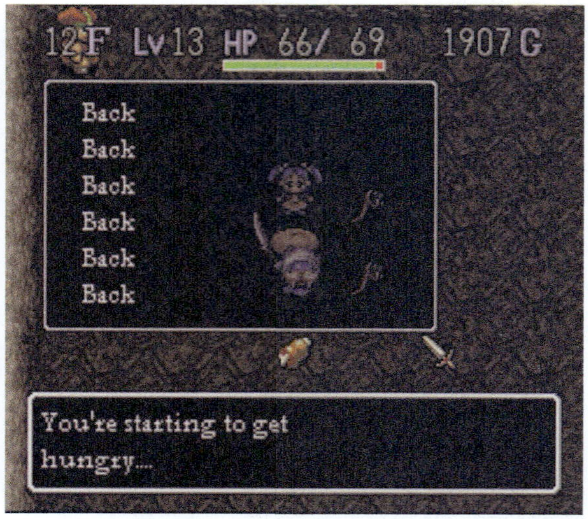

Figure 39.17

Shiren the Wanderer: Back Pot

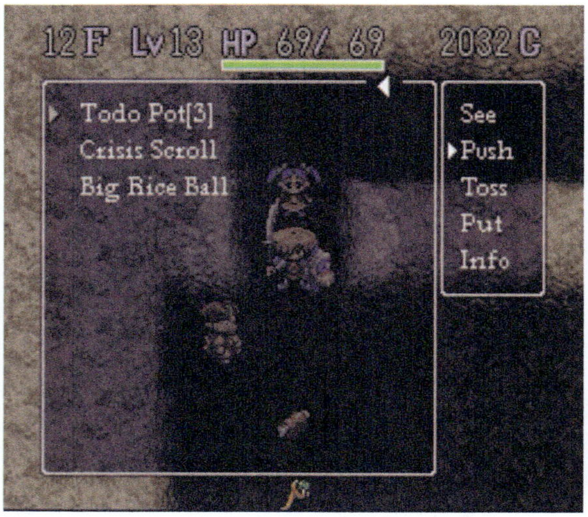

Figure 39.18

Shiren the Wanderer: Theft with a Todo Pot

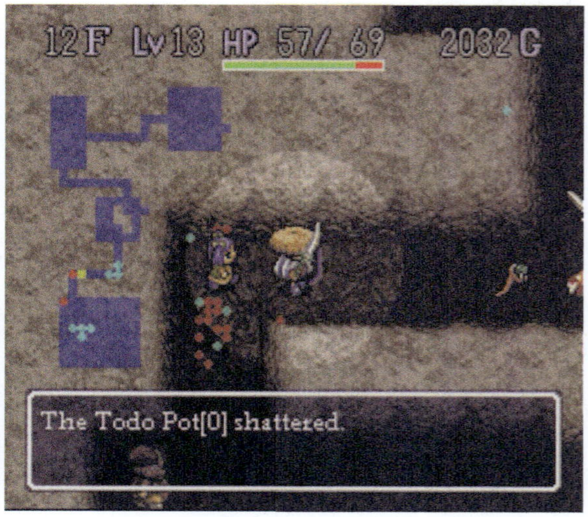

Figure 39.19

Shiren the Wanderer: Getting stuff out of a pot

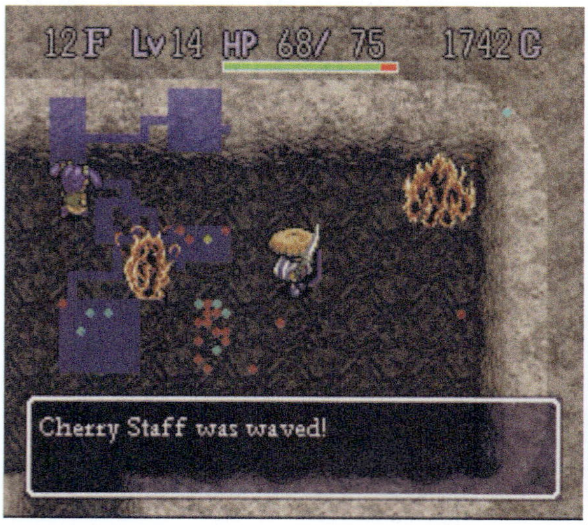

Figure 39.20

Shiren the Wanderer: Staff item deduction

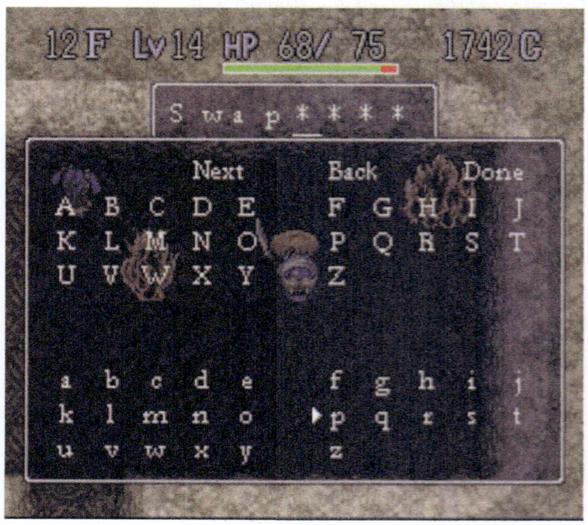

Figure 39.21

Shiren the Wanderer: Naming a Swap Staff

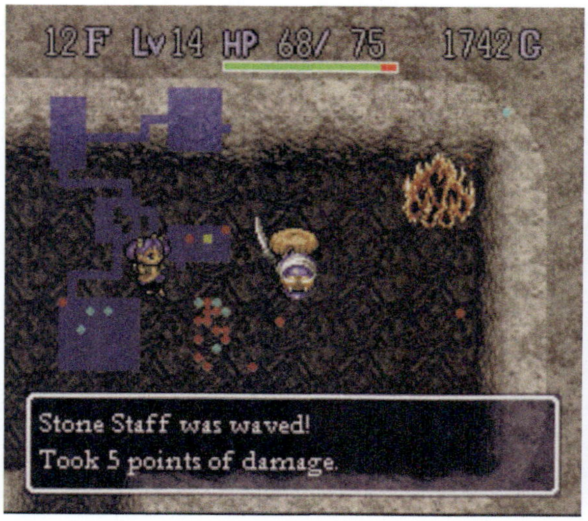

Figure 39.22

Shiren the Wanderer: More item deduction

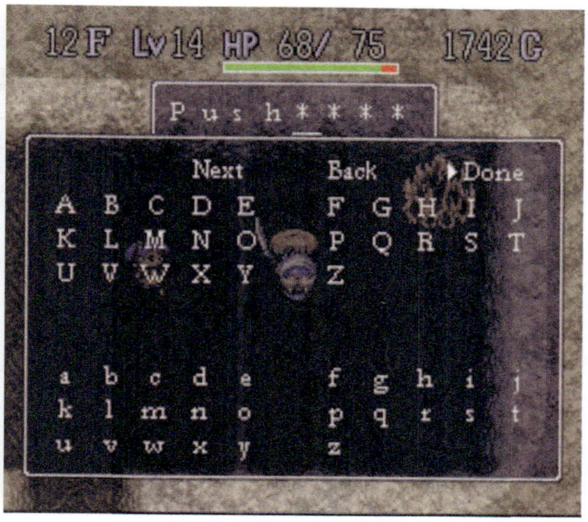

Figure 39.23

Shiren the Wanderer: Push Staff (Blowback in the DS version)

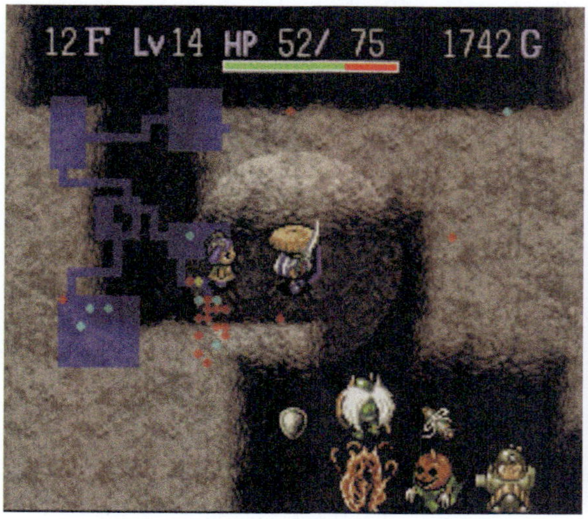

Figure 39.24

Shiren the Wanderer: NOT entering the Monster House

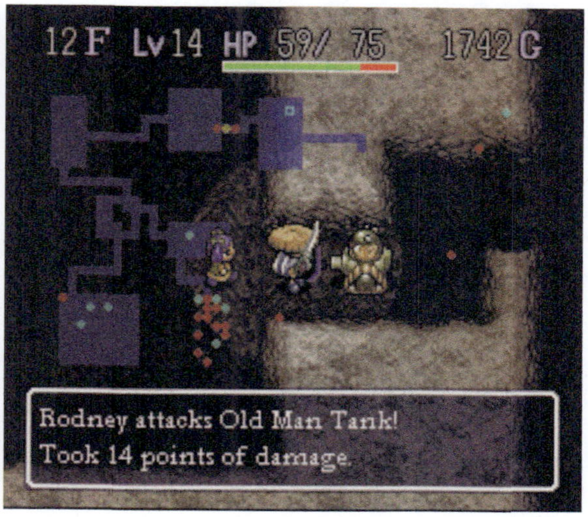

Figure 39.25

Shiren the Wanderer: Old Man Tank!

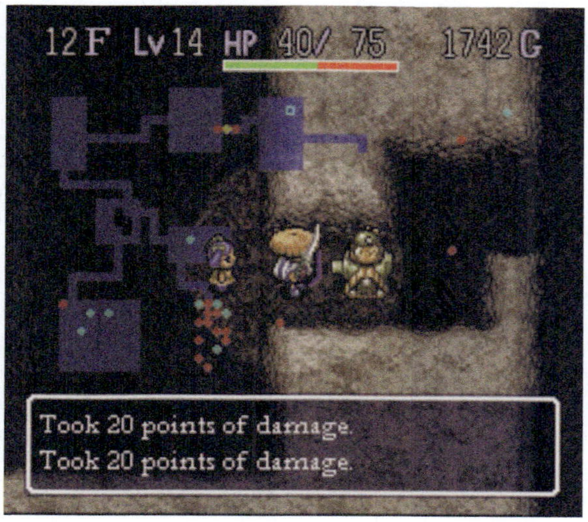

Figure 39.26

Shiren the Wanderer: Bad news!

39.4 Soldier Ant

Figure 39.27: Shiren also contains a type of monster that's a natural digger, able to do it as a monsterly power. Soldier Ants in NetHack are extremely menacing monsters relative to the level they appear at, but in Shiren, while not harmless, they aren't too difficult either. They mostly ignore the player in fact, concentrating on digging new corridors in a partly random fashion.

Figures 39.28 and 39.29: Monsters you hit with a Paindividing Staff (here still described with its unidentified, randomized description of Paulownia) take whatever damage they inflict on you. That'll prove to be quite useful soon.

Figure 39.30: I've not shown you guys too many traps so far, but these levels are the ones where they get to be a problem. Mine traps take off half your remaining hit points. There's another kind that takes off all but one hit point! Both also destroy adjacent items on the ground. Mines hardly ever kill the player but can make him easy pickings for the monsters.

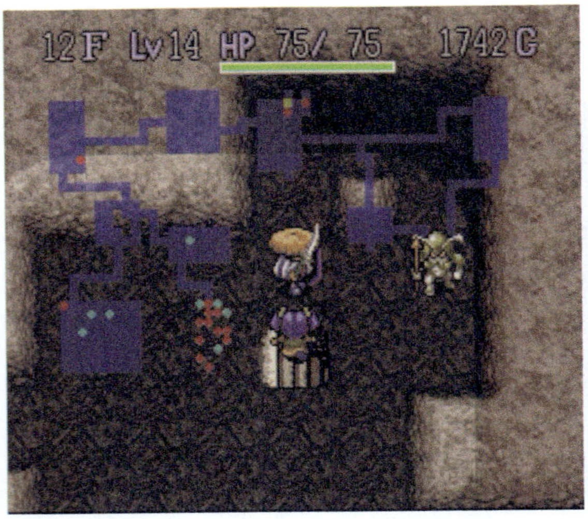

Figure 39.27

Shiren the Wanderer: Soldier Ant

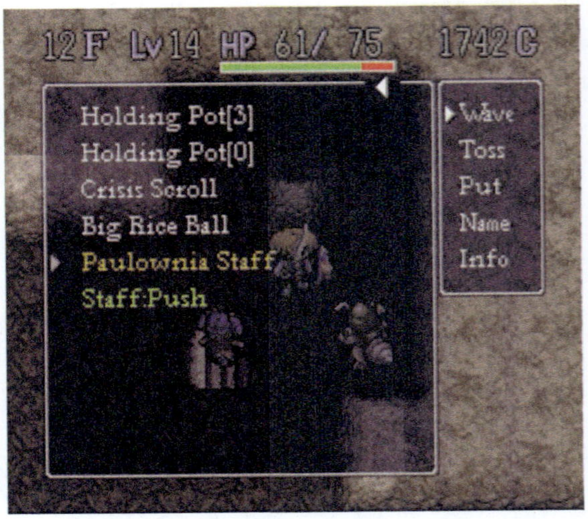

Figure 39.28

Shiren the Wanderer: More item testing

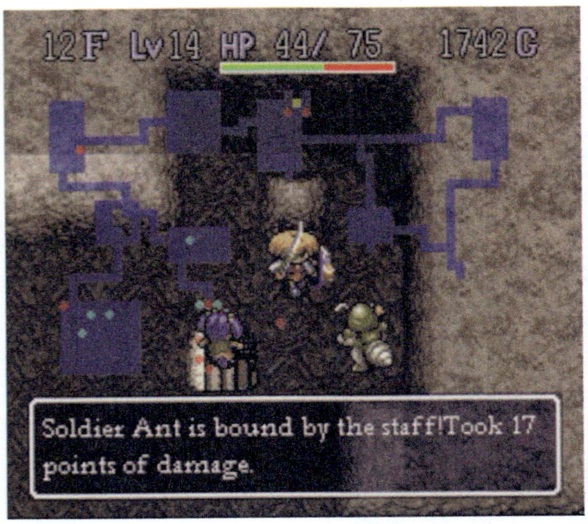

Figure 39.29

Shiren the Wanderer: Paindividing Staff

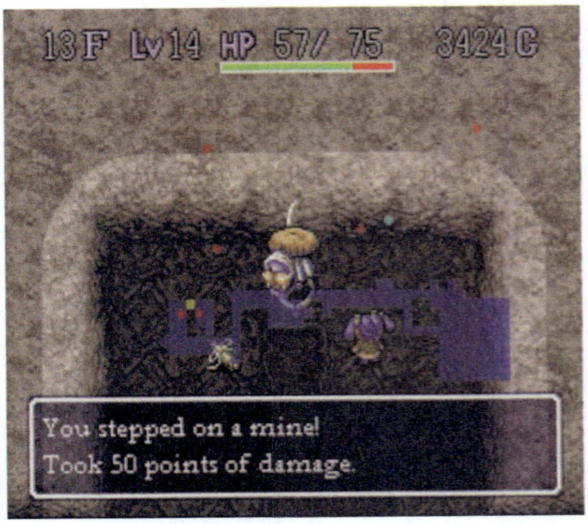

Figure 39.30

Shiren the Wanderer: Landmines I a dungeon?

Figures 39.31 and 32: These traps are harmless in themselves but pepper the whole rest of the level with random traps! Some of those traps, themselves, can be trap-making traps, so stepping with caution is a must.

Figure 39.33: It was here that the little girl who was following me around finally got whacked, promoting an Old Man Tank into a Stubborn Tank. Stubborn is the next-to-last tank level, just below Obstinate Tank. Attempting to close and kill one of these in melee is suicide, so the best thing to do is run. In that, the Far-sight Bracer once again proves its worth.

Figure 39.34: Tanks only shoot at Shiren if he's visible to them. If it finds Shiren, and it's in direct line with him, it'll be nearly instant death. But with the Far-sight Bracer, I can see what its red dot is doing and not take the passages that lead to it.

Figure 39.35: It also helps in getting him off my trail, but I'll explain more about that later, when I get to the Minotaur levels . . .

Figure 39.36: Escaped to the next level. Whew!

Figures 39.37 and 38: But Old Tanks still appear, and are a great danger. Their shots even ignore armor! In these levels, it's never a good idea to go around with less than 20 hit points because of them.

Figure 39.39: Another shopkeeper, on the 14th floor. This can't be a good location for him. Rent down here must be incredibly low.

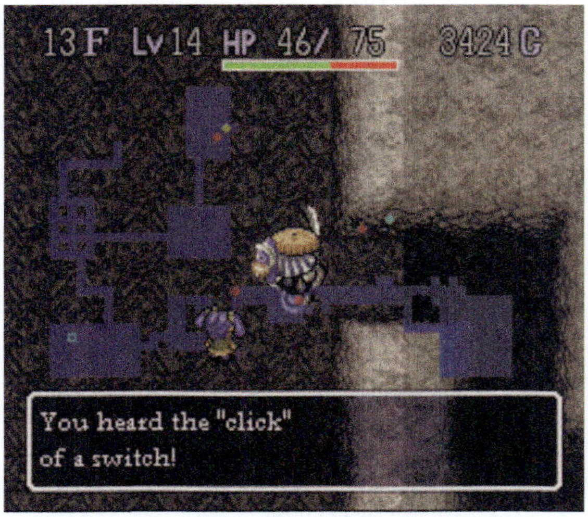

Figure 39.31

Shiren the Wanderer: Trap-making trap

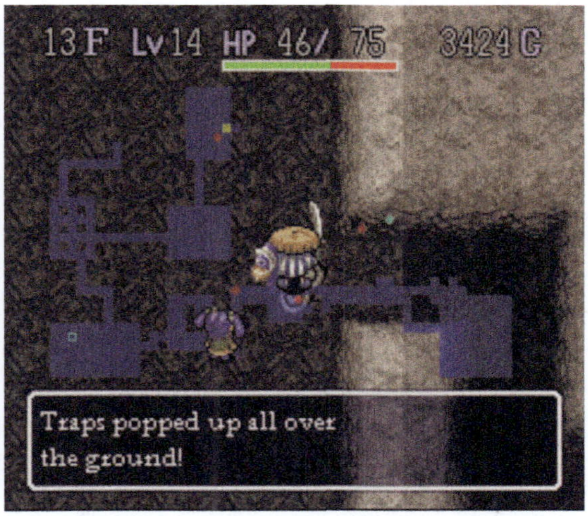

Figure 39.32

Shiren the Wanderer: Trap making trap effect

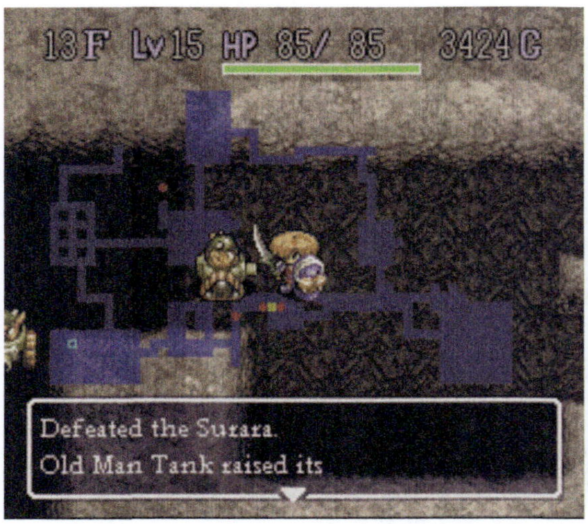

Figure 39.33

Shiren the Wanderer: Tank promotion, oh no!

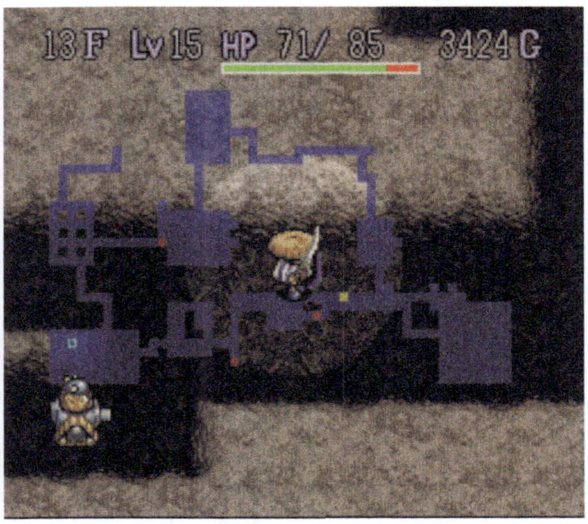

Figure 39.34

Shiren the Wanderer: Escaping the tank

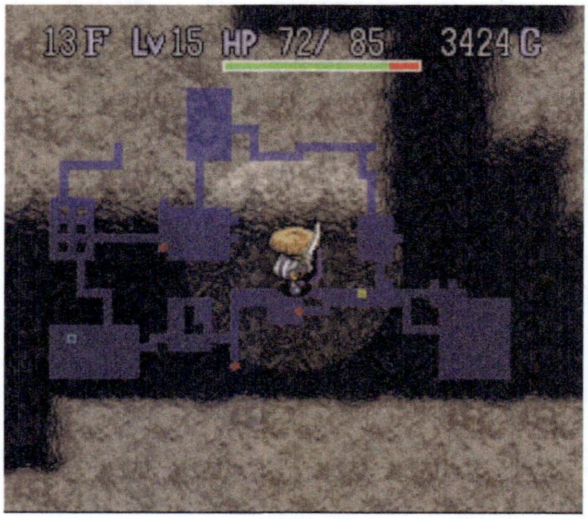

Figure 39.35

Shiren the Wanderer: Nerve-wracking adventure

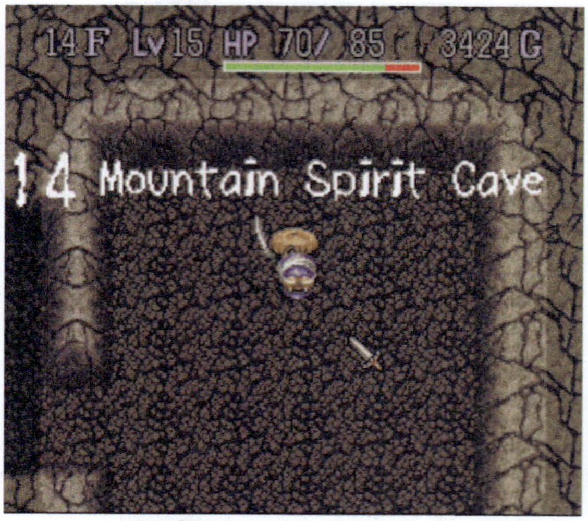

Figure 39.36

Shiren the Wanderer: Made it!

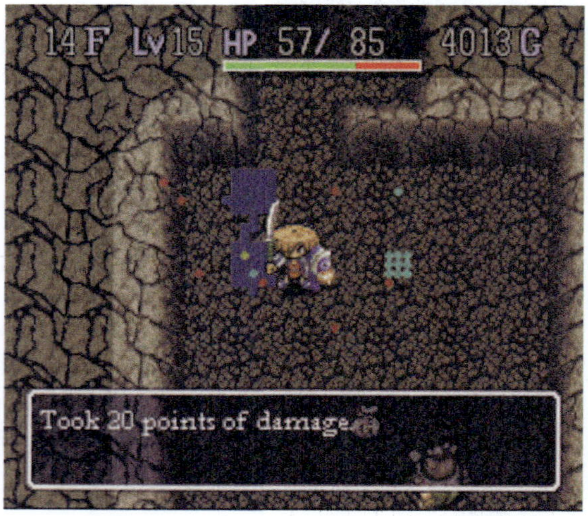

Figure 39.37

Shiren the Wanderer: Level 15

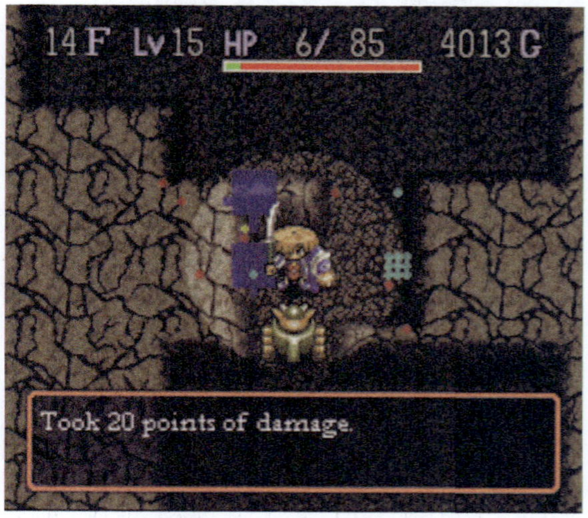

Figure 39.38

Shiren the Wanderer: More tank trouble

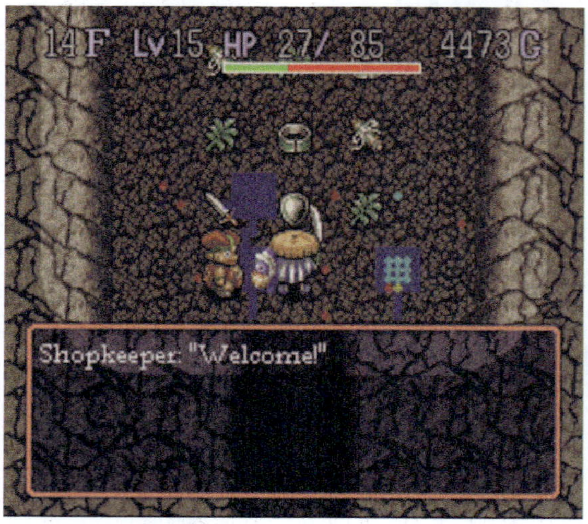

Figure 39.39

Shiren the Wanderer: Level 15 shop

40

A Journey to Table Mountain, Part 4

Figure 40.1: Reflex Shields are okay in defense, but they have a special ability: monsters who try to hit you in melee have a much greater chance of missing than usual.

The thing about the special abilities of weapons and armor is that, while there are a good number of these abilities, they're generally mutually exclusive. I can wear a Reflex Shield, with its increased chance of monster's wiffing, or I can wear a Dragon Shield for protection from dragon breath, or I can wear a Todo Shield to guard my stuff from thieves.

There is a subquest, however, that adds Synthesis Pots to the game. With one of those, the special functions of equipment items can be merged, to produce a super-item. In conjunction with the smithies and warehouses, this could potentially produce very powerful items that bestow huge bonuses to the player. When the player gets to the super dungeon in fact, he basically must do this to have a chance of surviving, and take advantage of many other tricks too.

Figure 40.2: The Dotanuki in this room is a very good weapon. Actually, I probably should have bought this one, but then I wasn't sure if my Nagamaki was better. (I discovered later that it wasn't.)

Figure 40.3: Invincible Herbs are awesome items that make the player completely impervious to damage for ten moves. Nice things to have when facing, say, the final boss.

Figure 40.4: Slumber Scrolls put all monsters in the room to sleep . . . but what its description doesn't reveal is that they wake up after a few turns, and they'll be double-speed. This fact plays a substantial role in my character's downfall.

Figure 40.5: A naturally occurring Genocide Scroll. But it costs 50,000! Maybe I should have saved a use of that Todo Pot for later?

Figure 40.6: Pit traps send the player to another level. Stop and think for a moment. Unlike Torneko (or indeed most roguelikes), Shiren's dungeon doesn't just, in concept, go down towards the center of the earth. The mines go down, but Table Mountain, the final section, goes up. Pit traps take you either to the next level or back a level, depending on which way the dungeon progresses.

Figure 40.7: Crooked Boulder Valley, the next-to-the-last town. There's not much interesting to see unless I manage to get Surara, the little girl from earlier, here safely, which makes a warehouse available.

Figure 40.8: Onward . . . the next two levels of the game are special, in that they contain lots of draining monsters. There are foes that can weaken strength and shields, and even drain levels here. They're generally not worth the experience for killing them or the loot to be found on these levels, so the faster the stairs are located the better.

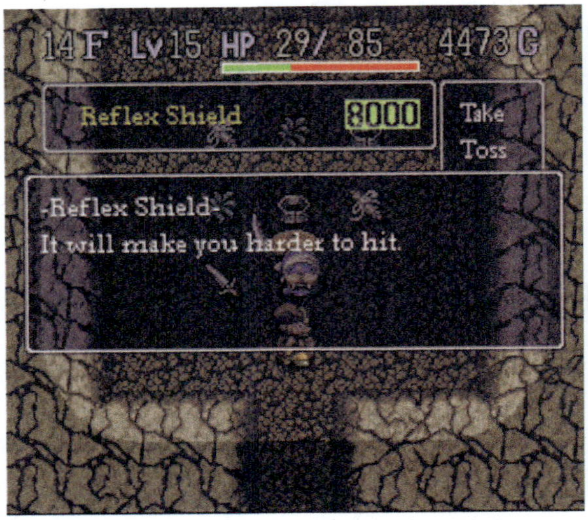

Figure 40.1

Shiren the Wanderer: Reflex Shield

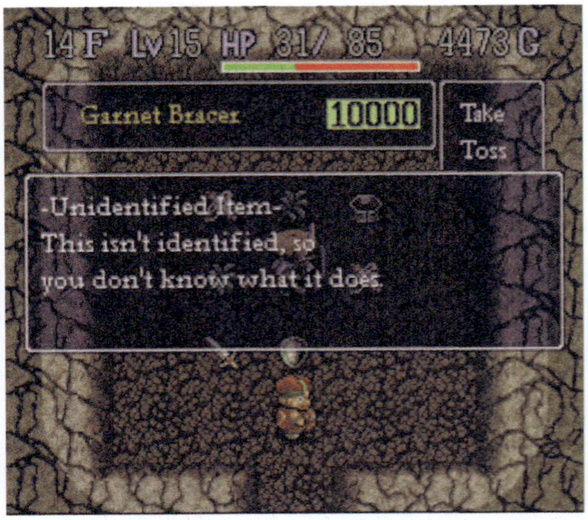

Figure 40.2

Shiren the Wanderer: Garnet Bracelet

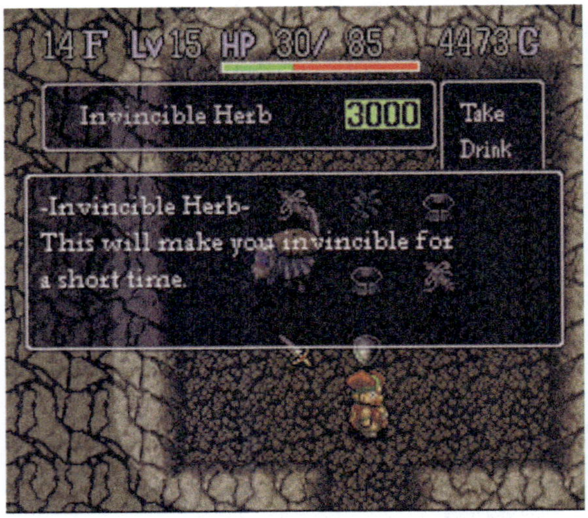

Figure 40.3

Shiren the Wanderer: Invincible Herb

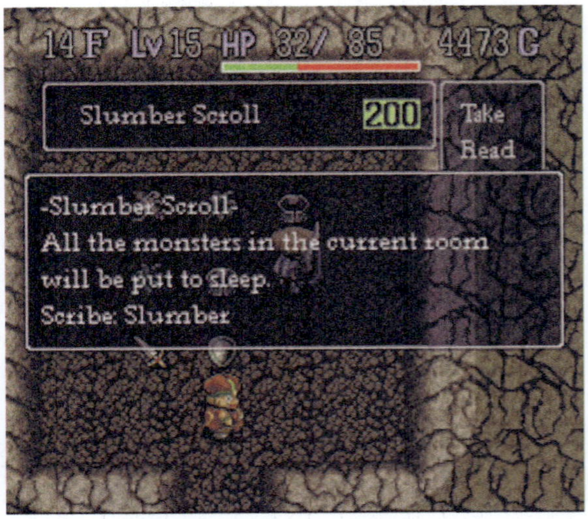

Figure 40.4

Shiren the Wanderer: Slumber Scroll

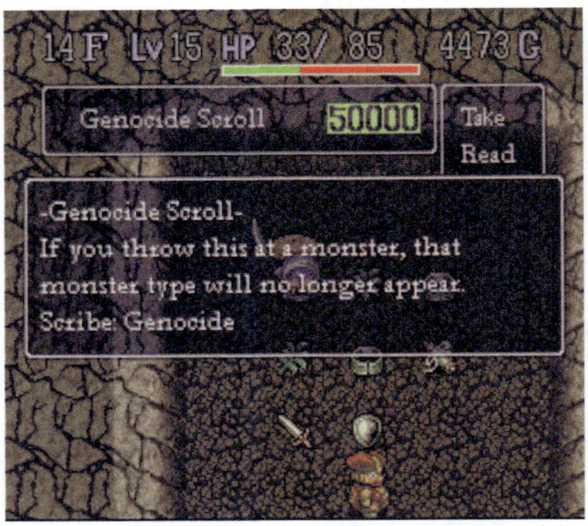

Figure 40.5

Shiren the Wanderer: Genocide Scroll

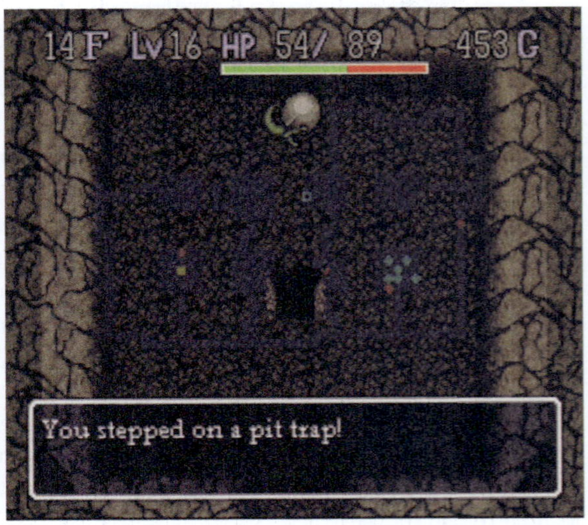

Figure 40.6

Shiren the Wanderer: Pit Trap

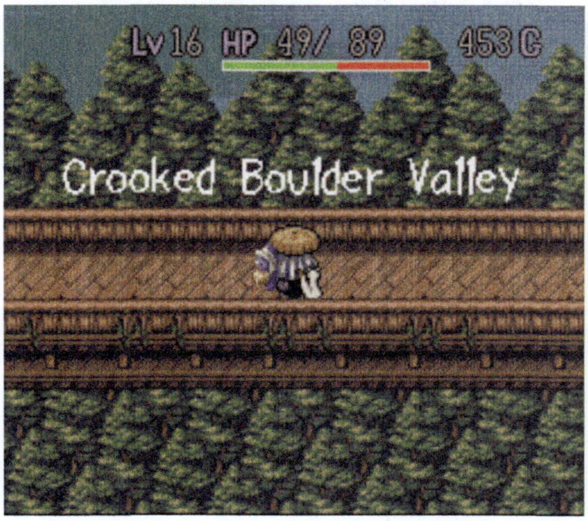

Figure 40.7

Shiren the Wanderer: Crooked Boulder Valley

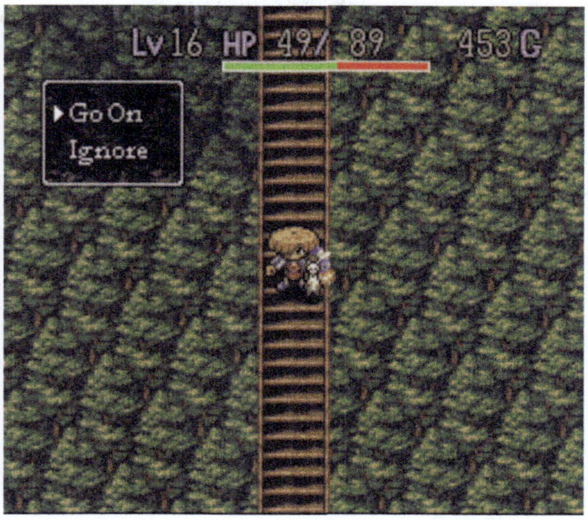

Figure 40.8

Shiren the Wanderer: Into the breach

40.1 Gyazar

Figure 40.9: They also contain Gyazars, who are kind of the opposite idea of the Minion of Death foes from back in the forest. They're single-speed move, but they get two attacks! Even a single hit from them isn't to be sneezed at.

Figures 40.10 and 40.11: That's why that Back Pot I found is so useful. Eating an Otorogi-so fills up your hit points one time, but a Back Pot fills you up once for each "back" inside it, plus cures strength loss and status ailments.

Figures 40.12 and 40.13: Even a Back Pot isn't too useful if you get caught in a cycle of having to spend all your moves healing. In Shiren, all moves take the same amount of time, whether it's fighting, moving, reading a scroll, using an herb or pushing a pot. Two hits from a Gyazar is usually enough to put you into the danger zone, but if you spend the next turn healing instead of running he'll get in another two hits!

Figure 40.14: Buy-time Staves are interesting items. Swing one at a monster and it'll be teleported onto the exit space and paralyzed. It'll block escape unless some creature is already there, so you'll probably have to fight it eventually, and it'll wake up the moment it takes damage. However, if multiple monsters are hit with this staff on a single floor, they'll appear in a cluster around the exit. Since each one only wakes up when struck, often only the first monster hit with the staff must be fought! The lesson here, if you've got more than one charge on the staff, is to try to use it on a weak monster first.

Figure 40.15: This ominous cave is the entrance to Table Mountain. It's the last leg of Shiren's journey! There's still one more town between here and the end, although I don't reach it in this game.

Figure 40.16: And right off the bat it's bad, bad news. Have a look, a Minotaur AND, visible behind the level name, a Master Chicken, both extremely strong opponents.

Figure 40.17: Strong enough that measures need to be taken. It is situations like this for which successful players build up a stock of *escapes*, items good for getting out of trouble. In this case, using that Invincible Herb would allow me to not only survive, but safely kill these guys for lots of experience points.

Figure 40.18: Zero points of damage are the best points of damage.

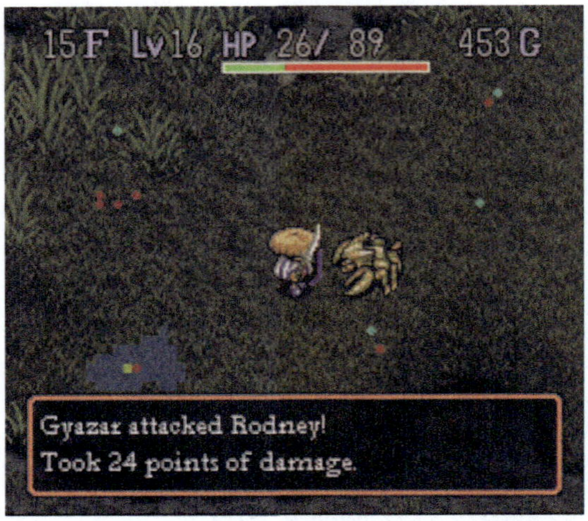

Figure 40.9

Shiren the Wanderer: Gyazar

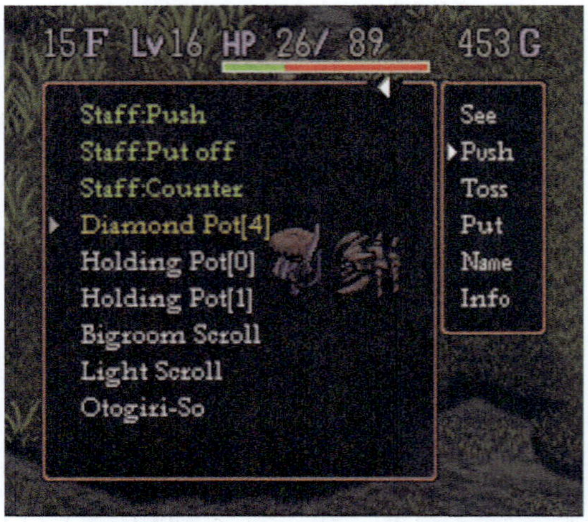

Figure 40.10

Shiren the Wanderer: Testing the back-containing pot

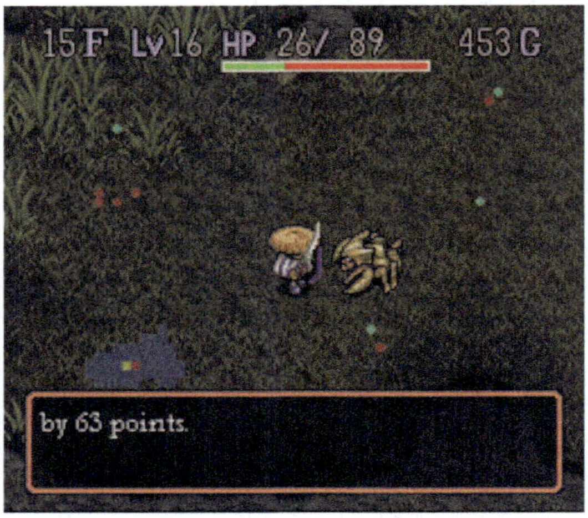

Figure 40.11

Shiren the Wanderer: I'm healed!

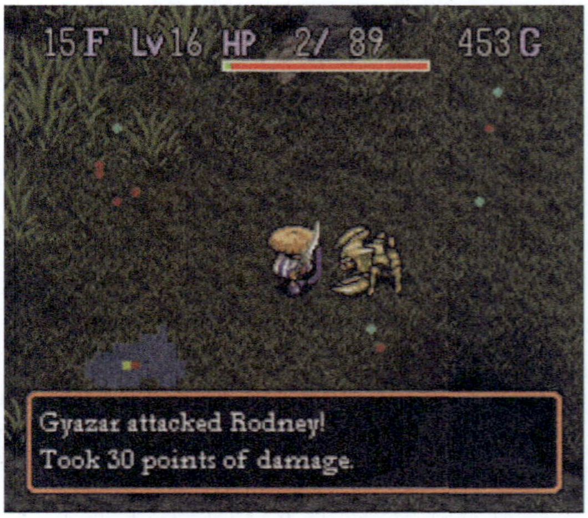

Figure 40.12

Shiren the Wanderer: That hurts!

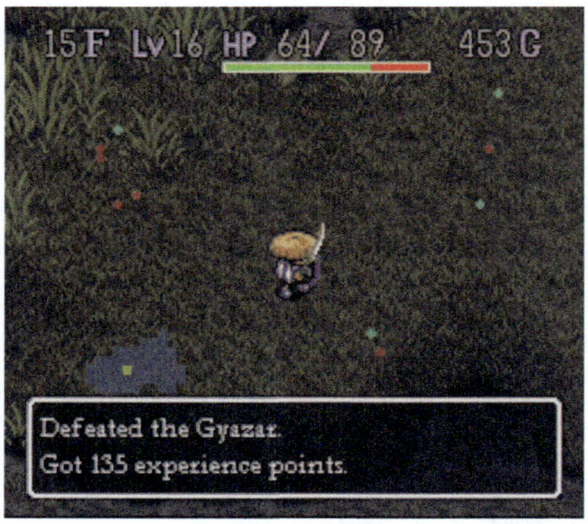

Figure 40.13

Shiren the Wanderer: But it's worth a lot of experience!

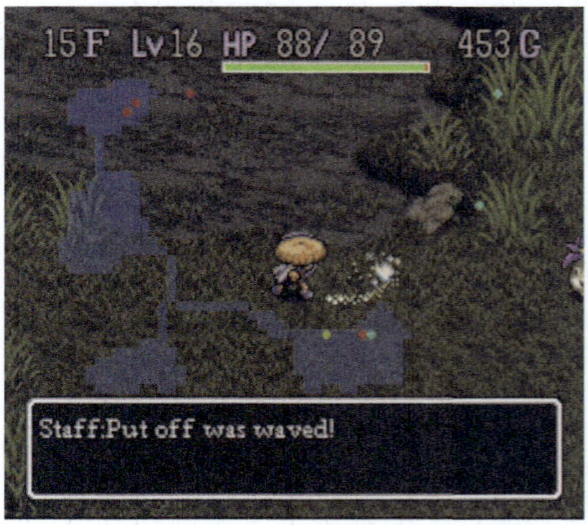

Figure 40.14

Shiren the Wanderer: Buy-Time Staff (The name here is the one I gave to it.)

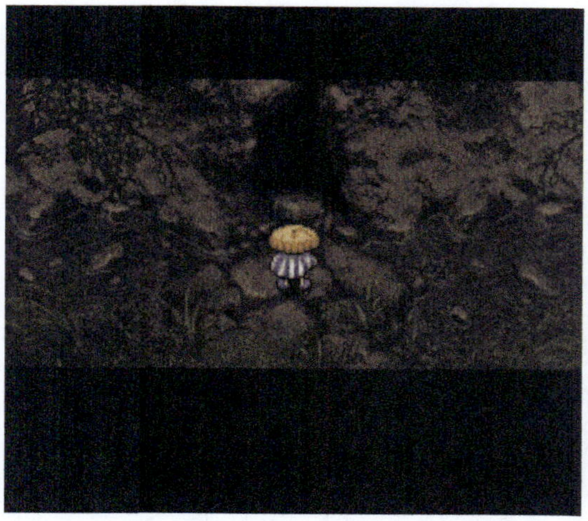

Figure 40.15

Shiren the Wanderer: Table Mountain!

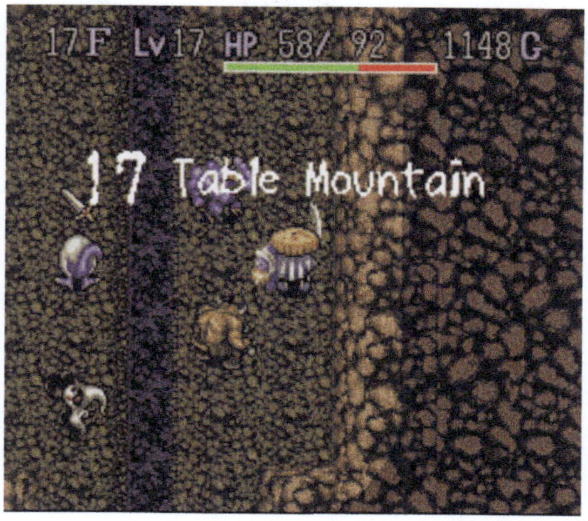

Figure 40.16

Shiren the Wanderer: Level 17

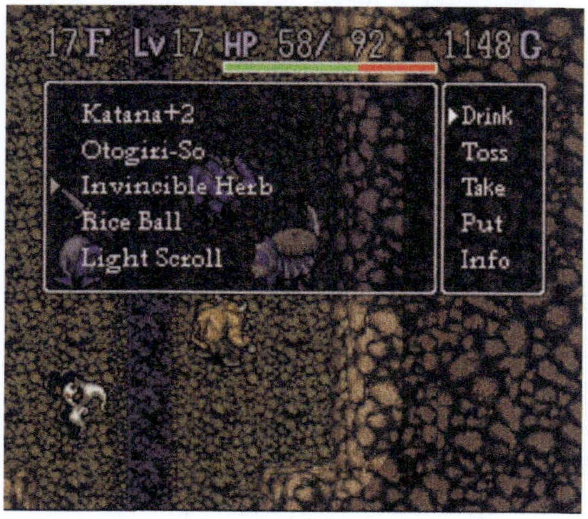

Figure 40.17

Shiren the Wanderer: Consuming the Invincible Herb

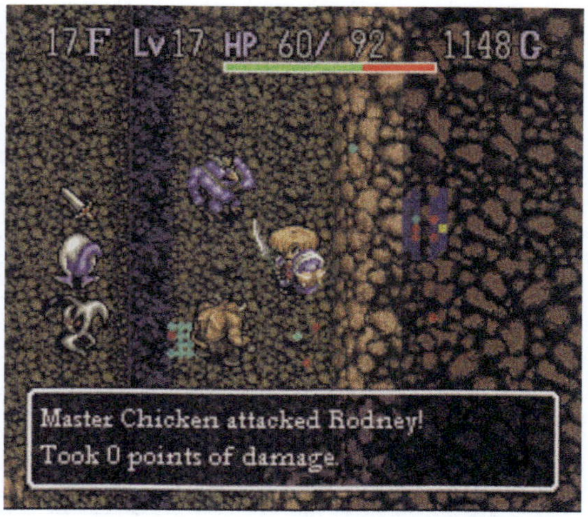

Figure 40.18

Shiren the Wanderer: Complete protection

40.2 Master Chicken

Figure 40.19: Master Chickens, if killed in combat, are worth 400 experience points, which is a lot for this stage of the game. They're strong fighters, though, and it's rare that Shiren actually kills one before it pulls off its special trick. Instead, when one gets to low hit points, it demotes into a plain old Chicken. Chickens don't fight back but flee at double-speed, and even if cornered and killed are only worth half the experience. In the DS version, they're worth almost no experience!

40.3 Minotaur

Figures 40.20 and 40.21: Master Chickens are one of the two toughest opponents in this area. Minotaurs are the other. They're really strong fighters on their own, but randomly (far too frequently) they'll get in a critical hit, which does lots more damage!

Around here we find another great use for Far-sight Bracers. Once you start to get to levels where most any monster, handled improperly, can kill you, avoiding danger becomes very important.

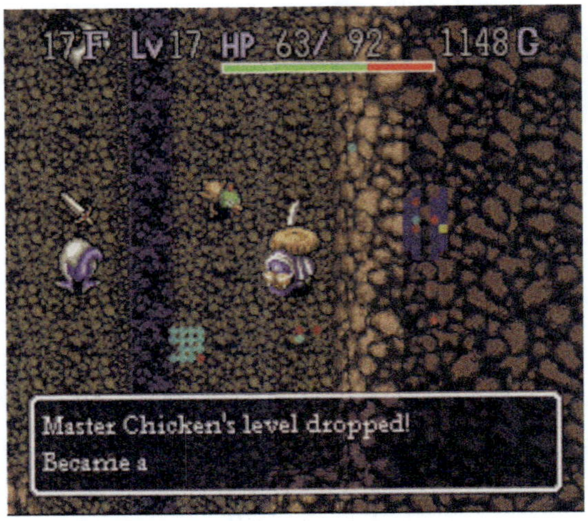

Figure 40.19

Shiren the Wanderer: (Regular) Chicken

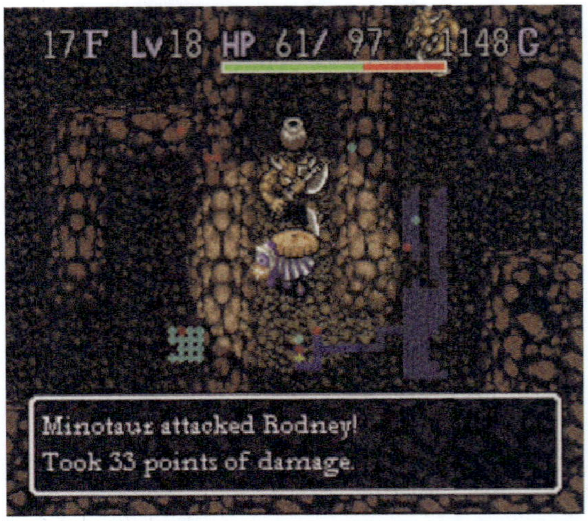

Figure 40.20

Shiren the Wanderer: Minotaur

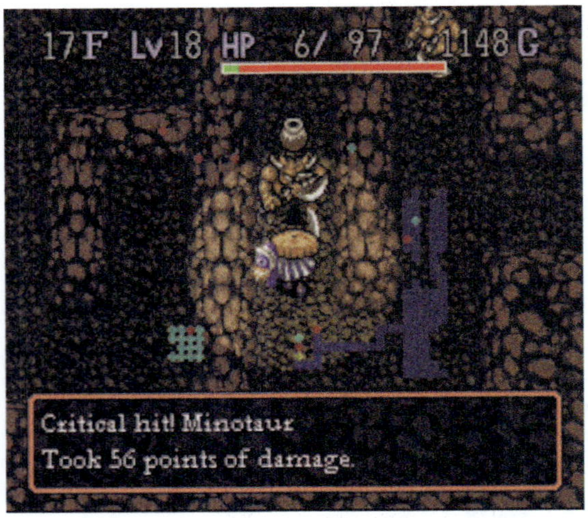

Figure 40.21

Shiren the Wanderer: Critical hit!

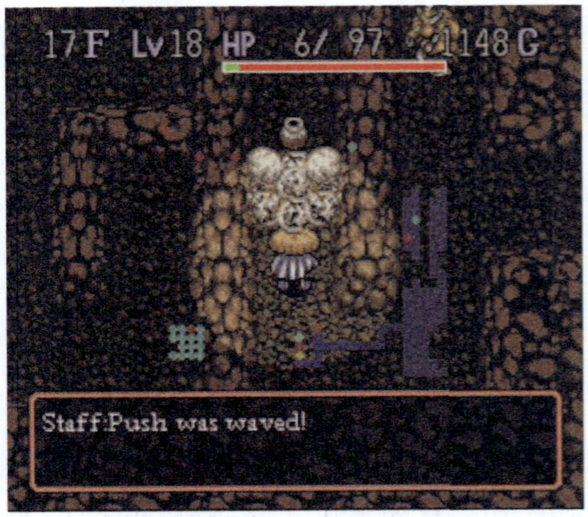

Figure 40.22

Shiren the Wanderer: Push Staff

Many of these monsters can be defeated, with difficulty, one-on-one, but are overpowering in groups, or if the player isn't completely healed at the start. Since the player heals over time, a Far-sight Bracer can help Shiren stay clear of monsters until he's ready to fight.

Figure 40.22: Push Staves also help somewhat. The monsters in Shiren don't have any special ability to see over what the player normally has. It may seem like this is a minor thing, but it's a useful fact to know when being chased.

In a corridor, both Shiren and monsters ordinarily can see only the spaces directly adjacent. If a monster is in space right beside Shiren (or the characters in Rogue or NetHack for that matter) and can move as fast as him, then he'll always be able to close the gap, and running won't be very helpful. If the player can get a space away, however, and run into a corridor, then the monster won't be able to see the player!

Yet . . . how useful is this really? Roguelike monsters are often smart opponents, even way back in Rogue. If a monster loses sight of the player in a corridor he still remembers the direction it saw the player leave, and since it knows the player probably couldn't have gone elsewhere will continue running down the corridor, following its twists, until it finds the player or a branch in the path.

Once the monster finds a branch however, it can't be so sure of where the player has gone. Which path did they take? All it can do is guess. In this way, monsters who are following the player from more than one

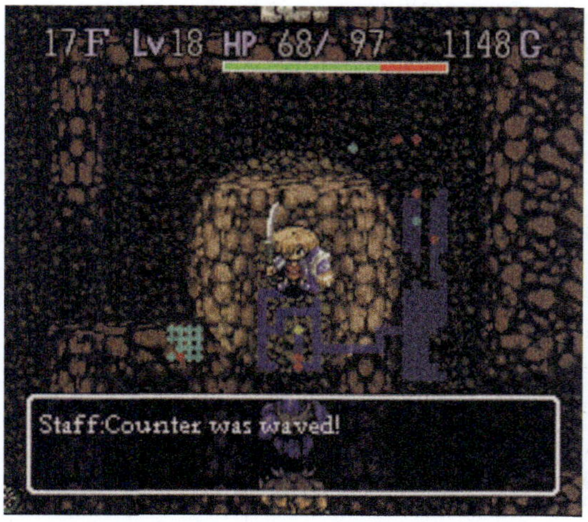

Figure 40.23

Shiren the Wanderer: Paindividing Staff

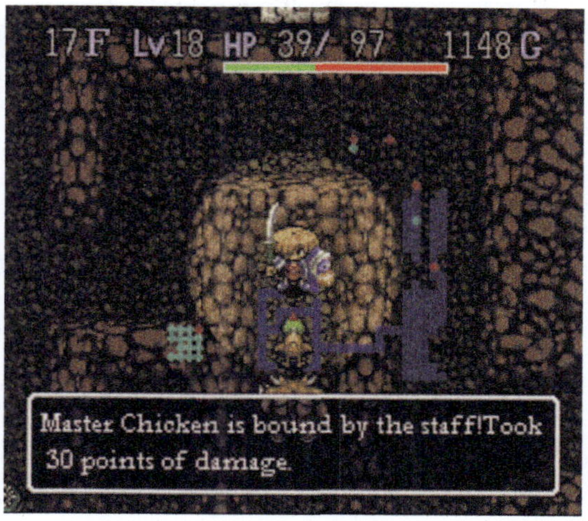

Figure 40.24

Shiren the Wanderer: Turning the tables

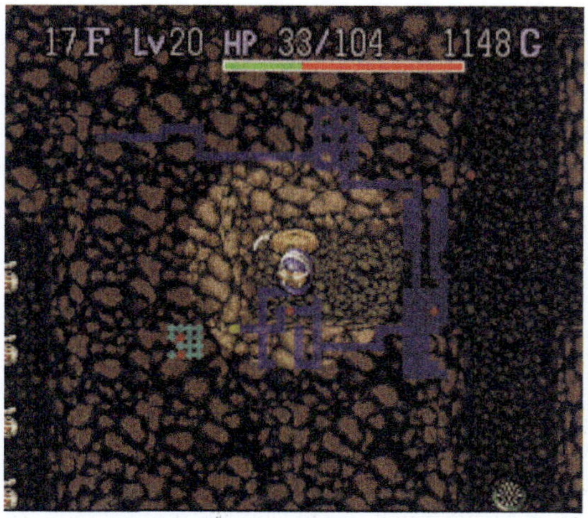

Figure 40.25

Shiren the Wanderer: Digging through the wall

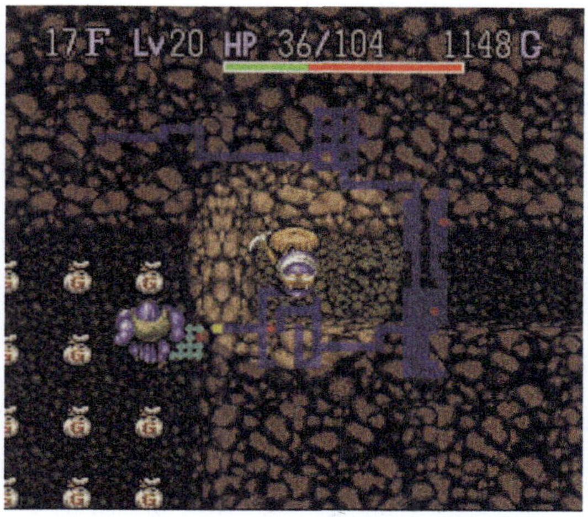

Figure 40.26

Shiren the Wanderer: A secret room

space away can be eluded. But the player's sight is also limited, so Shiren can't be sure the monster has taken the wrong road without going back, and if the monster picked the right road that'll put the player right back into danger again.

But with other means of determining monster position, such as a Far-sight Bracer, that uncertainty is gone! The player can see which way the monster went, and if he went down the player's corridor, he can continue running, maybe to another branch, continuing to flee until the monster has gone the wrong way.

I explain all this because, as we've seen, Minotaurs are serious opponents. A lucky hit by one of them can take off 60 hit points. It's hard to see in my screenshots, but I did a lot of that kind of monster evasion in this portion of the game. That's why a Push Staff is useful; it can knock a monster back down a hallway and make it easier to escape by going through a fork. If this strategy seems like rather a lot of trouble to go through . . . well, it is a little tricky. But it is an example of how roguelike environment simulation allows the player to apply deep strategy to playing the game.

Figures 40.23 and 24: Paindividing staves are very nice to have in this area. A monster might be able to attack your weak point for massive damage, but at least this way it'll end up taking that damage as well, and while many of these beasties may be able to dish out, they aren't very good at taking it.

Figures 40.25, 40.26 and 40.27: Vaults are a NetHack feature that arguably is much more useful in Shiren, which has scarce money, ultra-expensive items and even more dangerous shopkeepers, than NetHack, where players usually find far more money than they'll ever need.

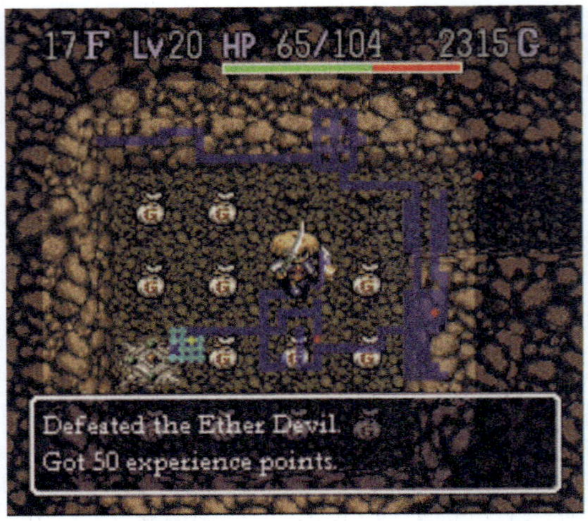

Figure 40.27

Shiren the Wanderer: Lots of money!

Both games contain provisions to allow players to escape from them if they get sent there accidentally. In NetHack, eventually a vault guard will come in and, in exchange for all the money the player is carrying, will lead him back to the main level through a spontaneously appearing, and disappearing, passage, a highly programmatic solution that seems very NetHackish. Meanwhile Shiren just puts a teleporter in each vault to allow a stuck player to escape.

(Note, I don't compare these vaults to the Angband, Crawl or ADOM features here, because those are substantially different, and really more interesting, things in those games.)

40.4 Norojo's Big Sister

Figure 40.28: Just a somewhat stronger Norojo, but these curse weapons too.

Figures 40.29, 40.30, 40.31 and 40.32: These screenshots illustrate identification by use, in this case figuring out a Slanted Pot. A Drain Buster is an okay item, but I'm already past the worst stat draining floors and my weapon is proving capable enough to get me through. I don't have much use for yet another weapon, so it's a perfect candidate for test-IDing by throwing it into a pot.

And it turned out to be a good choice! Notice in the second screenshot the item's name is yellow, but in the third it's white? That's because, while it may look the same otherwise, the item is now identified. It's an ID Pot, which identifies anything put into it! Very nice find, this is.

Figure 40.33: Decoy Staves are a bit of a mixed blessing. Zap one at a monster and it turns into another Shiren, one that, for some reason, the monsters are far more willing to beat up than the player's Shiren. The monster so zapped is even confused as a bonus! But remember what happens when a monster defeats another monster? That's right, promotion time. Because of this the best use of a Decoy Staff is either to confuse a single monster, or to distract other foes while you run for the exit.

Figure 40.34: Aaaa, I went down the stairs and arrived in a Monster House!

This is where my game ended, but it could be useful to illustrate just what I did and why it didn't work, and what I could have done to have survived. First, notice that the stairs are just two spaces away from me, I can get there with two moves, and from diligently leveling from killing ultra-tough monsters I have 120 hit points.

Figures 40.35 and 40.36: I could have just run for the stairs, and with some clever actions I might have made it, but I was cocky. Not so cocky that I wasn't going to use an item to try to clear this room though . . .

Figure 40.37: I read a Slumber Scroll. I remembered that they'd put all the monsters to sleep, but I forgot that the effect was temporary, and that they'd be double-speed when they woke up.

Figures 40.38 and 40.39: I could have run for the stairs at almost any time. Even so, I got to kill a few monsters before they woke up, like this Super Gaze and Flame Priest 2.

Figure 40.40: It was while I was fighting a second Flame Priest that they revived.

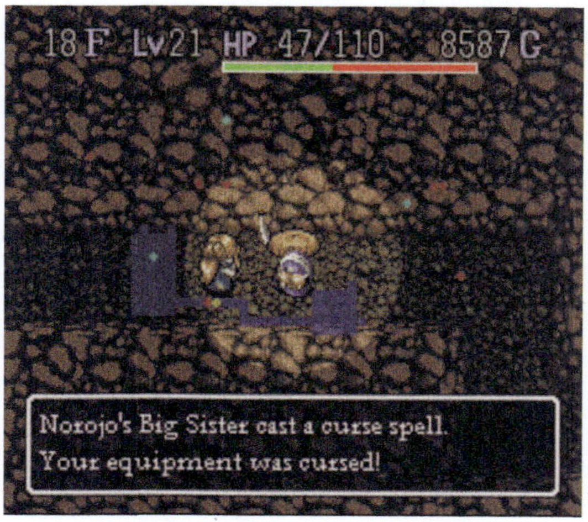

Figure 40.28

Shiren the Wanderer: Norojo's Big Sister

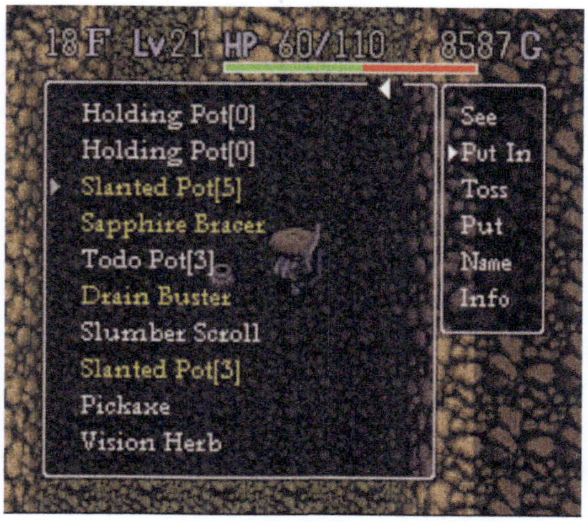

Figure 40.29

Shiren the Wanderer: What could this Slanted Pot be?

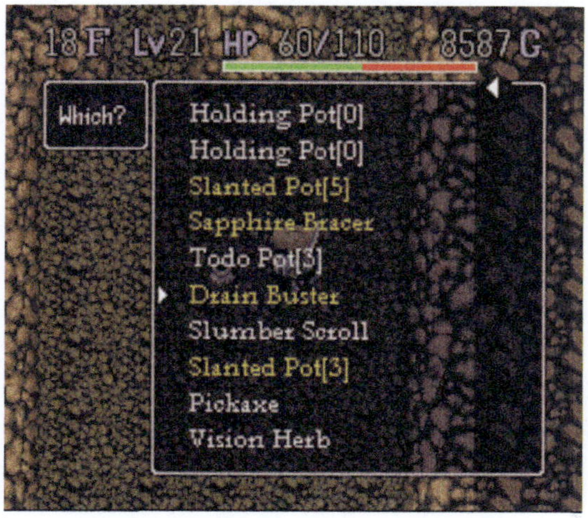

Figure 40.30

Let's put this unidentified (yellow) Drain Buster into it

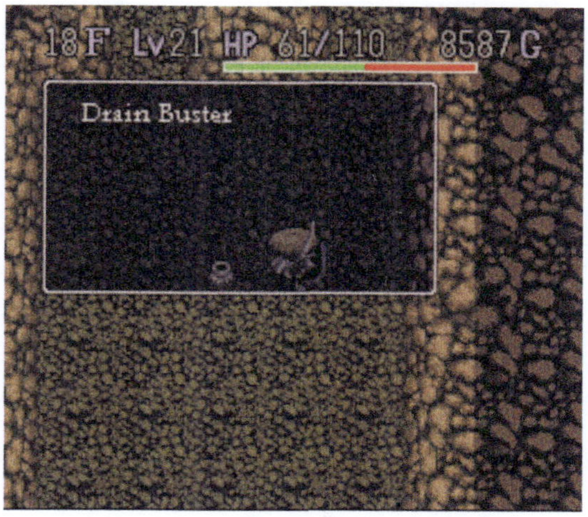

Figure 40.31

Shiren the Wanderer: It turned white (identified)!

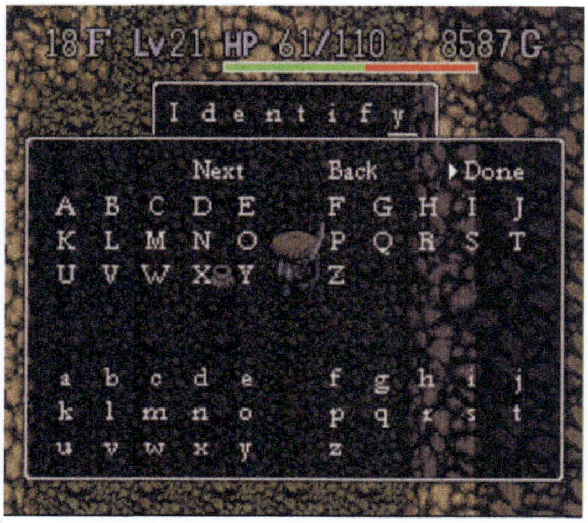

Figure 40.32

Shiren the Wanderer: It must be an Identify Pot!

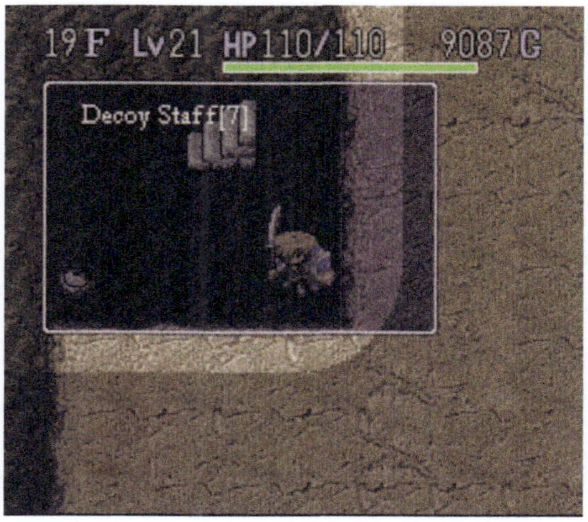

Figure 40.33

Shiren the Wanderer: Decoy Staff

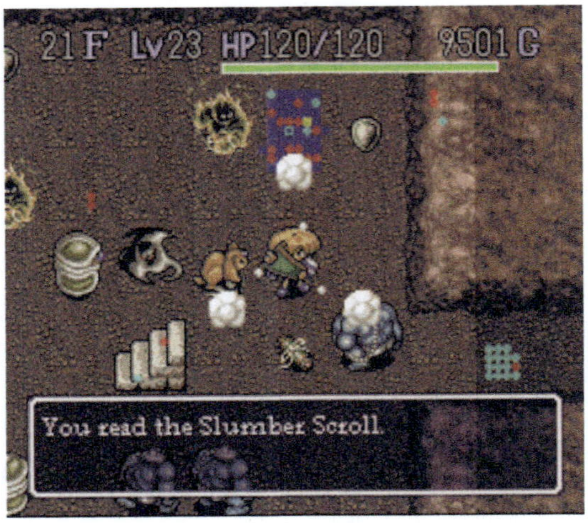

Figure 40.34

Shiren the Wanderer: Monster House!

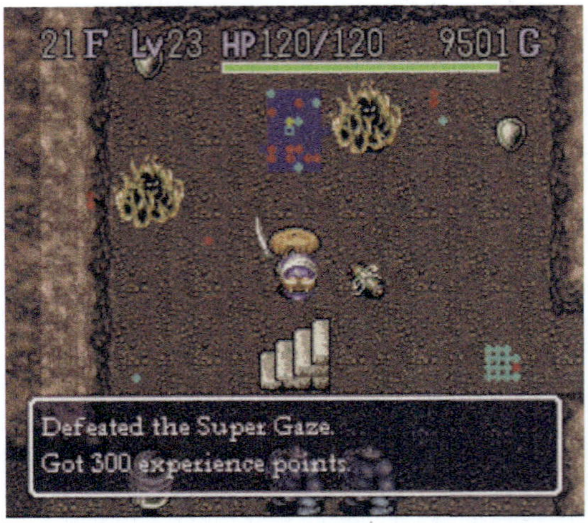

Figure 40.35

Shiren the Wanderer: Trying to clear it out

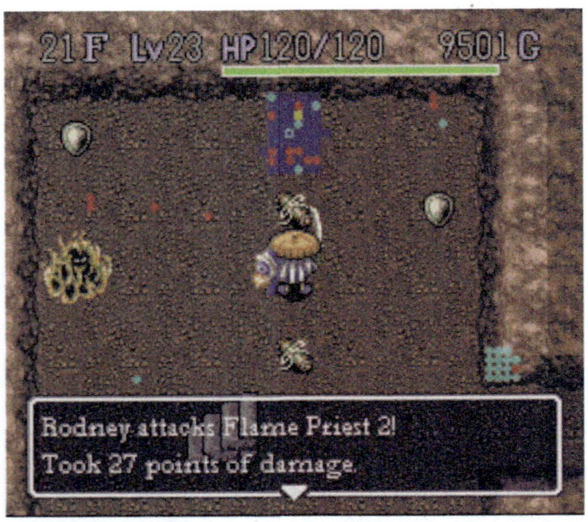

Figure 40.36

Shiren the Wanderer: Flame Priest 2

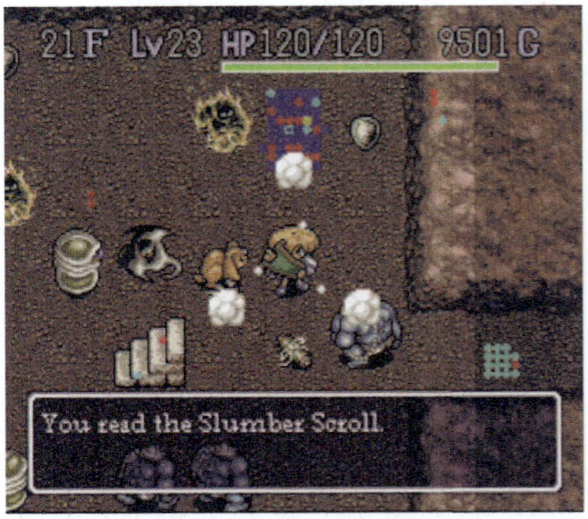

Figure 40.37

Shiren the Wanderer: Slumber Scroll

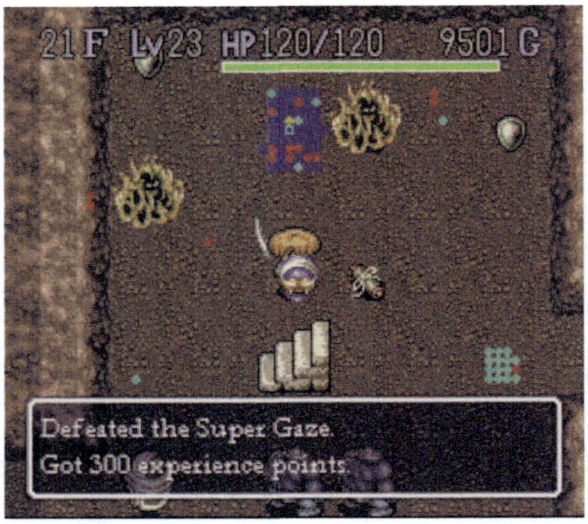

Figure 40.38

Shiren the Wanderer: I should be running away

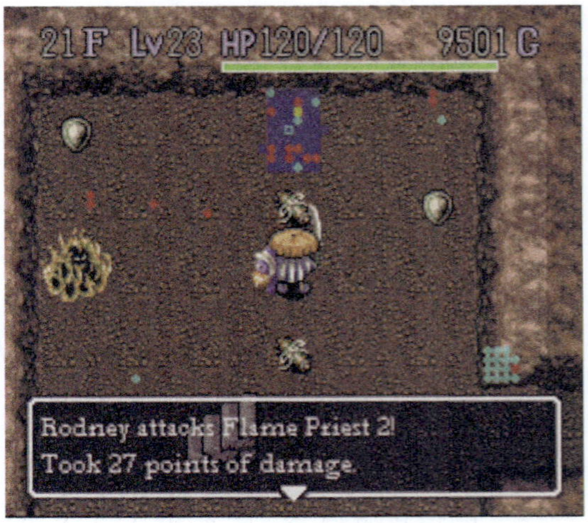

Figure 40.39

Shiren the Wanderer: Bad moves, Shiren

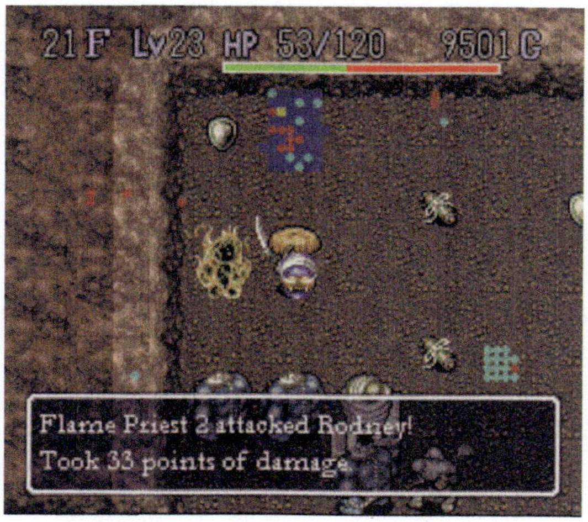

Figure 40.40

Shiren the Wanderer: What are you doing get out of there

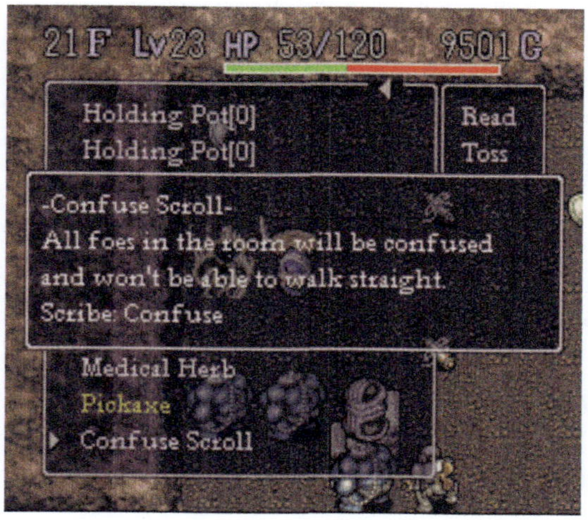

Figure 40.41

Shiren the Wanderer: I've made some bad decisions, but maybe this Confuse Scroll will save me

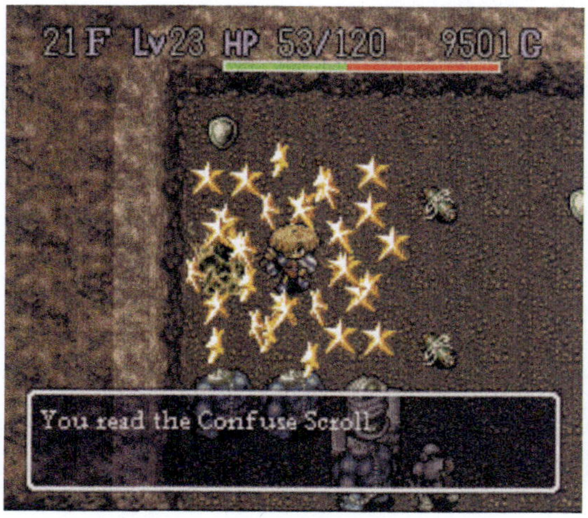

Figure 40.42

Shiren the Wanderer: My god, it's full of stars

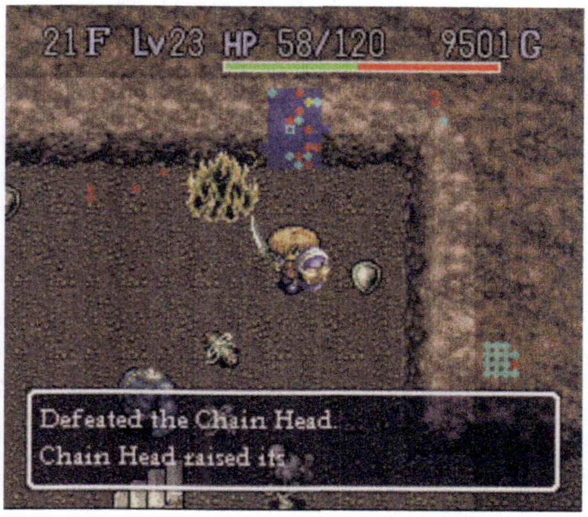

Figure 40.43

Shiren the Wanderer: Chain Head

Figures 40.41 and 40.42: I had a Confuse Scroll in my inventory, though. Now, if I had remembered the drawback of the Slumber Scroll I definitely would have used this first, and saved the Slumber Scroll for an escape. Confuse Scrolls are nice in that each adjacent monster gets a hit in only on one turn in eight, but in a room full of monsters, the chances that one of them will get lucky once in a while is still rather high.

Figures 40.43 and 40.44: And even worse! Confused monsters are as likely to attack other monsters as the player. More likely here, in fact, because there are so many more of them. A Chain Head, already a burly foe, got promoted into a Giga-Head, best described as death in roughly humanoid form. Basically, every turn next to it is a one-eighth chance the game ends there, and I don't like trusting that kind of thing to luck.

Figures 40.45 and 40.46: Time to pull out the big gun, that (insensitively named) Genocide Scroll I scribed. I was trying to save it for the big boss at the end of the dungeon, who for all his hit points and raw terror and taking up four dungeon spaces at once can be dispatched forever with a single thrown Genocide Scroll. But if I never get to him I can't use it, so away it goes.

In NetHack, a Scroll of (ugh) Genocide wipes out one species of monster from the game. In Shiren, only one family can be genocided at a time, so if I found another scroll and used it, the Chain Head family would be back, but the monsters on the level back when I first used it would still be dead.

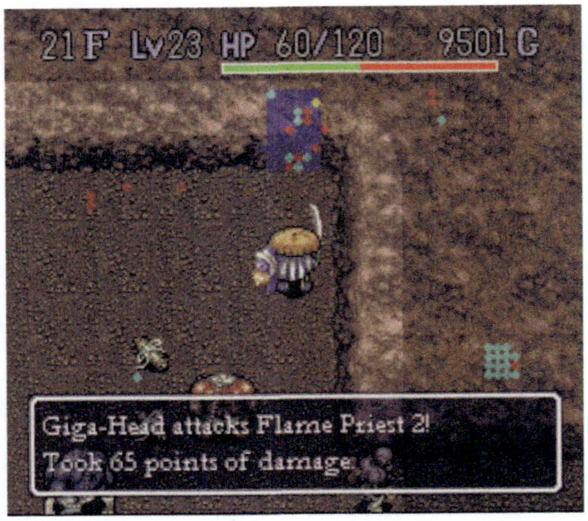

Figure 40.44

Shiren the Wanderer: Giga-Head!

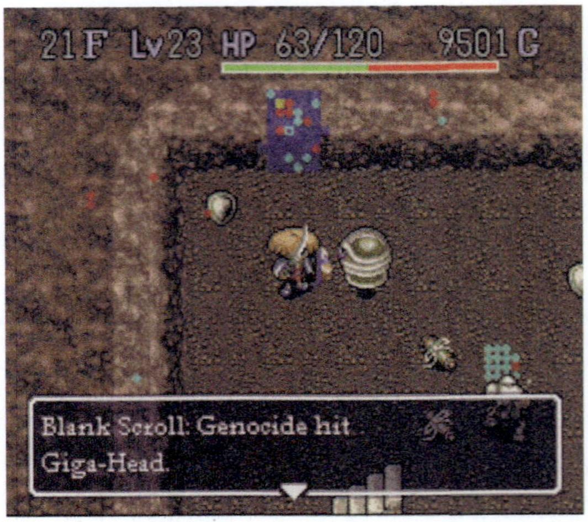

Figure 40.45

Shiren the Wanderer: Using a Genocide Scroll

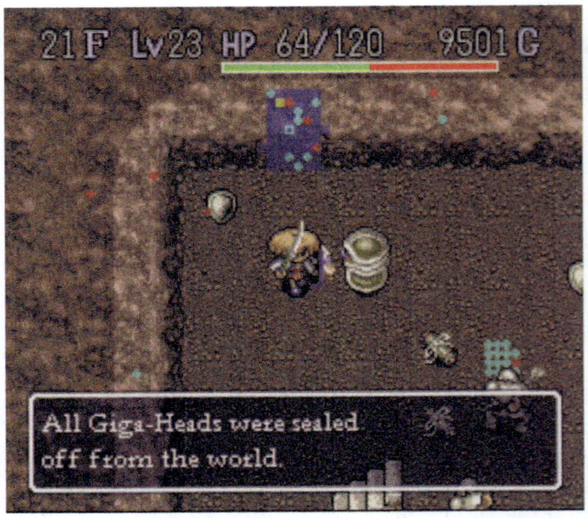

Figure 40.46

Shiren the Wanderer: Pretty drastic!

40.5 Karakuroid

Figure 40.47: These monsters set traps as they go, but they can also hit fairly hard. One of these was the one that got in the last swing.

Figure 40.48: Got on the score list, though . . . .

Figure 40.49: Third place, in fact. It was my best non-winning game in the end.

Figures 40.50 and 40.51: That's it. Notice the first save file, by the way. It's got the bird icon signifying a victory over Table Mountain, but it's also got a Mamul icon meaning a win in Fei's Final Problem. I talked about that back in Chapter 35.

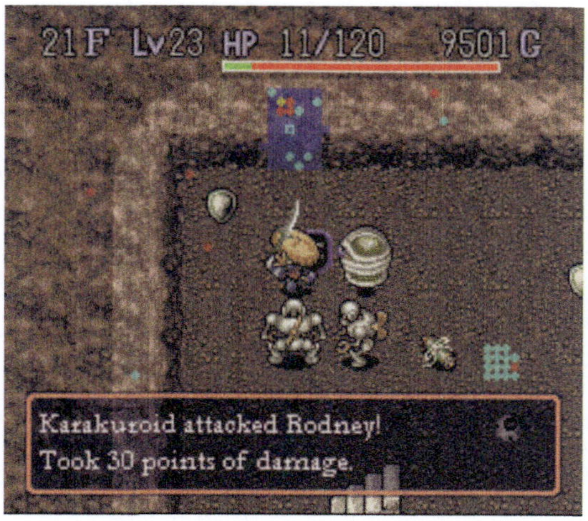

Figure 40.47

Shiren the Wanderer: Karakuroid

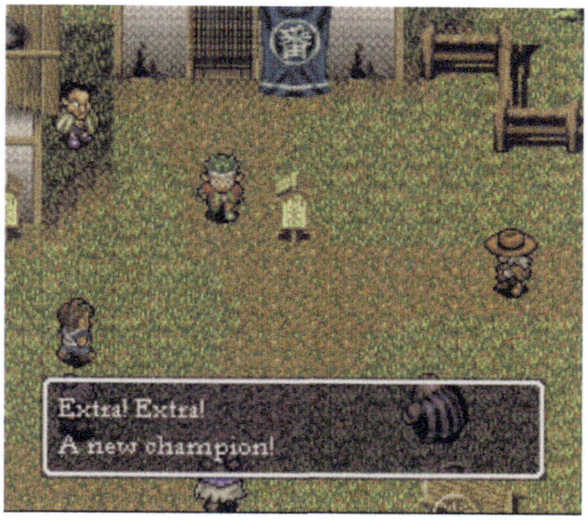

Figure 40.48

Shiren the Wanderer: Extra! Extra!

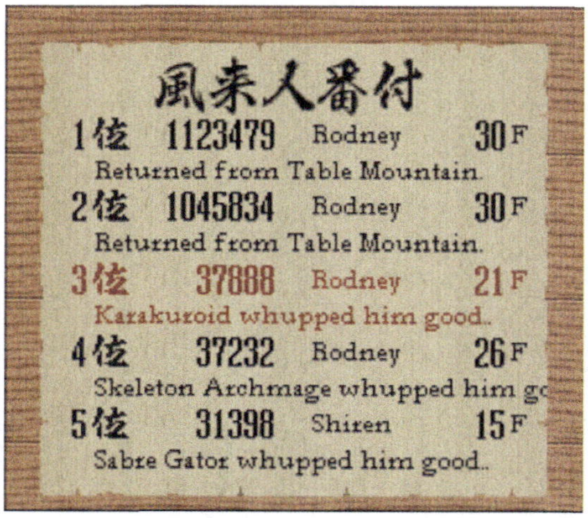

Figure 40.49

Shiren the Wanderer: The scoreboard

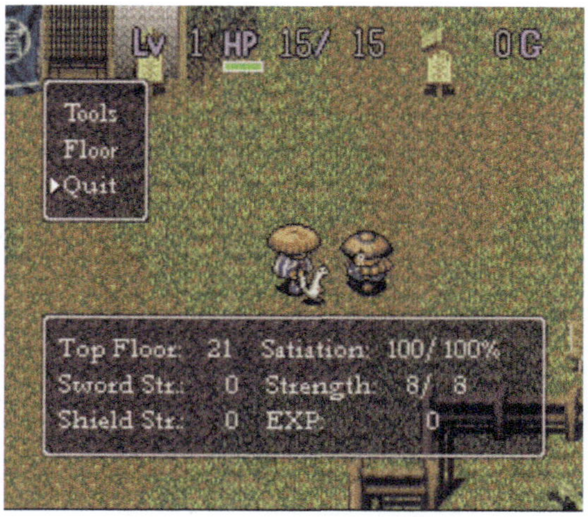

Figure 40.50

Shiren the Wanderer: Back in the first town

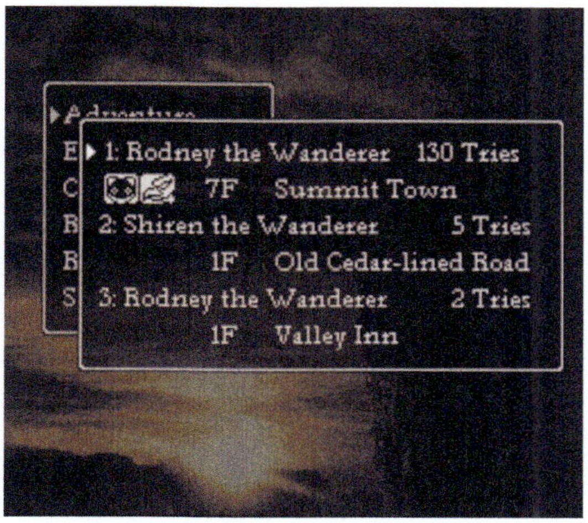

Figure 40.51

Section VII
Various Roguelikes

41

Angband: At Last!

January 2008 I've put this one off for a long time because of the sheer bulk of the game, and the time it takes to get good at a game as large as Angband. NetHack is pretty involved too, of course, but at least I have the advantage of having played it for many years. Still, something has to be said.

Unlike many of the other games we've discussed, especially NetHack, Angband is a moving target. The active development it undergoes really is active, and various things about the game may change in the future.

While it's possible that everything I've said about NetHack will be invalidated by some upcoming brilliant release by the DevTeam, few seriously believe it will happen. (In fact, I would be one of the most anxious to have my notes invalidated.) Thus it is that, everything I say here should be considered provisional, although I will attempt to stick with the more permanent facts about the game.

(*January 2020*: NetHack development has sped up considerably since I wrote that!)

41.1 The Journey of a Hundred Levels

The object of Angband is, starting from a town level on the surface, to descend into a gigantic dungeon, find Morgoth on the 100th floor and kill him. That's right: 100 floors! Or 5000 feet as the game puts it, for each floor is 50 feet deeper than the last.

The dungeon actually goes deeper than that, and the player can continue to explore for higher scores, but level 100 is hard enough for most. Killing Morgoth earns the player the attribute "*Winner*" even if he later perishes. NetHack's dungeon at most contains about 80–85 levels, and they're all solidly limited at being one ASCII screen in size, while Angband's scroll around all over the place. A NetHack game may take days, Angband, weeks.

On the one hand, Angband is a more random game than NetHack. The latter game has slowly been progressing towards giving the player more guaranteed rewards to balance out the random number generator (RNG). Angband takes the opposite tack, providing very little that's certain in every game. Most of what is reliable comes from the shops in town, which provide renewable quantities of some important items like scrolls of identify. This, and its many well-differentiated character classes, mean that Angband is far less likely to come down to a static game later on than NetHack, where most classes play similarly after the halfway-point.

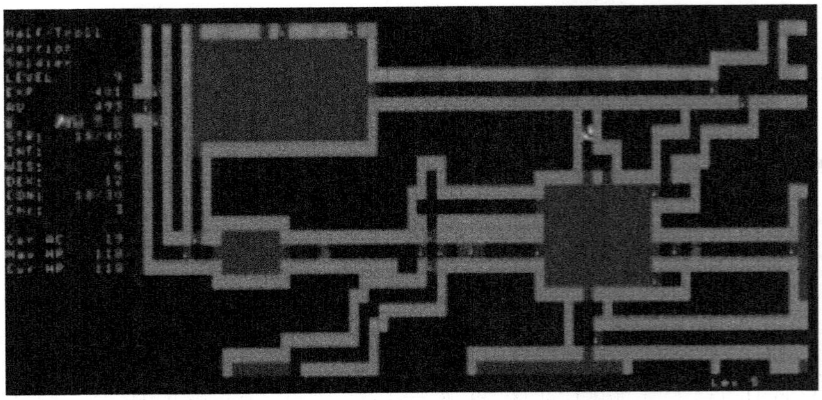

Figure 41.1
Angband

On the other hand, Angband lacks NetHack's complicated, 1st edition D&D-inspired system of object uses and mixtures. An Angband item is generally more straightforwardly useful, or useless, on its face. While items must still be identified, the steady supply of identify scrolls in town, and other sources of this service, makes this more a formality in Angband. Use-identifying in Angband is a sucker's game, and later on it can even be instantly fatal. Use-testing isn't the best way to play NetHack either, mind you.

The source of these differences is probably the game's different lineages. All roguelike games owe their inspiration to Rogue, of course, but after that there evolved two different major philosophies of play, represented by the Hack branch and the Moria branch. (There were a few others yet that didn't thrive as well, like the Larn branch, and the various SRogues and UltraRogues.)

Hack stuck pretty closely to the Rogue basis, and took its greatest inspiration from the clever little bits, like standing on scrolls of scare monster and gaining max hit points from drinking healing potions while at top health. Moria, on the other hand, focused more on tactics and the turn-based, step-by-step movement and fighting. Hack had a couple of competing versions that were merged and became NetHack. Moria became UMoria, and ultimately Angband.

41.2 Because a Game Called "Valinor" Would Be Boring

But what's this? "Moria?" As in, the Mines of Moria? Yes, one of the series' enduring trademarks is the huge number of Tolkien items and monsters that have been playfully thrown in with other D&D and invented creatures. "Angband" itself is the name of one of Morgoth's fortresses in the early days of Middle-Earth. Nearly every weapon Tolkien wrote about, and a good many he didn't and were assumed by the creators, are in Angband somewhere as an artifact. If they're not actually in a book you'd be forgiven for not realizing it, for they were given suitable Tolkien language names just like the others. The One Ring itself can be generated and used by the player, although it's the rarest item in the game, not completely positive in effect, and permanently cursed.

It's important, by the way, for all you Tolkienophiles to not look for rhyme nor reason in the included artifacts or monsters. The developers just threw 'em in to increase play variety, but many are far from contemporary in the books. Much inspiration was found from the Silmarillion, and please forgive me for not cracking that book open again to find the details. While the main guys of The Lord of the Rings have been avoided (except for Smeagol, aka Gollum), one can find such notable bit characters as Farmer Maggot, Bullroarer the Hobbit, orcs Shagrat and Gorbag, and even the trolls from The Hobbit. The major uniques of the game, Sauron and Morgoth, are found on levels 99 and 100 of the dungeon respectively, and their deaths in the pits of Angband won't be found in any work written by John Ronald Reuel.

But what if you don't like the idea of playing the Generic Tolkien Roguelike? It's no matter. Perhaps Angband's most astounding attribute is that, after former maintainer Ben Harrison got done with it, it was perhaps the roguelike with the cleanest codebase of all. While not technically Free Software because a few bits of it were written by folks who have yet been found to obtain their permission to license the lot under a compatible license, the code is effectively open source and has been used as the starting point of literally

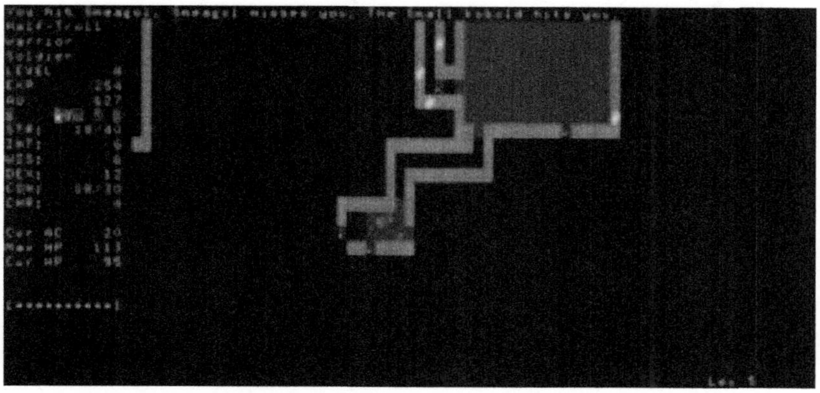

Figure 41.2

Angband

dozens of variants. Many major fantasy book series have served as the basis of an Angband variant at some point, the most notable ones being Amber and Pern. Most of them retain Angband's cheerful chucking together of monsters and artifacts, sometimes retaining a portion (or all) of Tolkien's for good measure. There's even another major Tolkien Angband variant, ToME (Tales of Middle Earth), which includes aspects from other major 'Bands and has a more complex world structure than Angband's 100-level downward dungeon.

(*January 2016*: Current-day ToME is a much different game . . .)

41.3 Ancient Foes Compared: Angband vs. NetHack

One thing that Angband unquestionably does better than NetHack is preserve its sense of danger. Even expert players can never take the game for granted. It is possible for a perfectly outfitted player to die to an unfortunate arrangement of monsters, even with pretty good play. A character missing an important resistance can find himself dead within a turn. There are monsters in the game that do so much damage with a single unresisted breath that they can empty a max-level player's hit points in a single attack.

I said unresisted. In NetHack, gaining some resistance will make the player nearly immune to that type of attack. A player with sleep resistance will never have to worry about being put to sleep, and if he gained it from eating a sleep-resistant monster (the most common source) he'll have that attribute for the rest of the game. The same goes for poison, fire, cold and electricity. A successful player will normally acquire all of these, and they're all binary, either 100% effective or not at all. A poison-resistant player will never again be affected by poison! Gaining poison resistance is actually an important game milestone, because it eliminates a common source of instadeath.

While resistances are just as important in Angband, the game implements them by way of a tiered system. For one thing, "resistance" is different from "immunity," which is more similar to NetHack's resistances but (only comes from certain artifacts?) is fairly hard to get. Angband has no way of gaining intrinsic abilities; all the resistances the player can get are through items or spells. A lot of its artifacts grant them, but there are so many possible artifacts, and no generation guarantees along the way, that the player must generally make do with what he finds and use caution to make up for the rest.

And there are a lot of resistances to acquire! Angband characters begin by aiming for the basics of fire, ice, lightning, acid and poison. Eventually they'll want to gain resistance to confusion, blindness, paralysis, fear, disenchantment, life draining, light, dark, sound, shards, chaos, nether and nexus. (What is nexus supposed to mean? It's the awful power of shuffling player attribute scores around.) In addition to equipment-granted sources, there are also potions that provide resistances for a short time. The permanent sources don't "stack" with each other, but the resistance from a temporary source and a permanent source does. Just one of them cuts elemental damage to a third, but two lowers that to just one-ninth. So, wearing two items that provide fire resistance doesn't provide any more protection than one, but wearing one then drinking a potion of resist fire will greatly decrease damage taken from flame while it lasts.

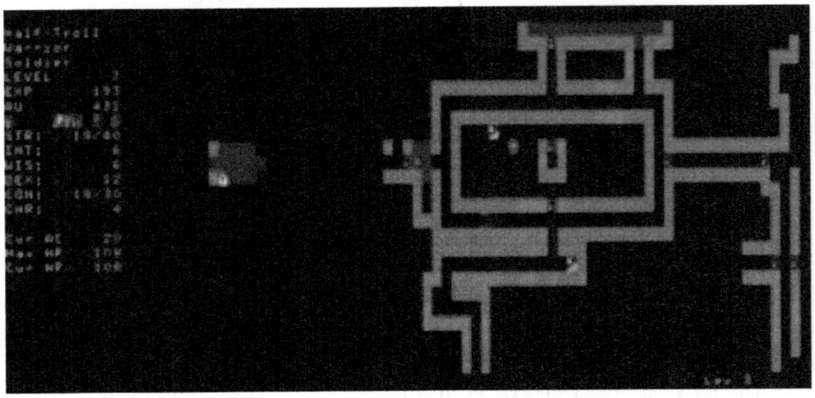

Figure 41.3

Angband

Because of the immense danger of taking unresisted breath damage from the wrong monster, gaining resistances is an important goal in Angband play. NetHack's like this too, but there are more common sources, fewer to gain, and because eating monsters can provide permanent intrinsics the player doesn't need to use up equipment slots to keep them. But this also means that, once acquired, a NetHack intrinsic resistance figures very little into later game strategy. Meanwhile, decisions concerning which ego items or artifacts to keep and which to dump lend depth to Angband's higher-level play.

41.4 "You Enter a Maze of Down Staircases . . ."

Resistances help defend against sudden death, so it's essential to obtain them before encountering a monster which could cause that death. This is where knowing how the dungeon changes in character as the player delves deeper becomes important. Angband monsters and items are generated by dungeon level, so a player who knows the levels that Great Wyrms appear on can be prepared for their ultra-damaging attacks. Angband levels are discarded when the player leaves them and regenerated when returned to, with new monsters and treasure. Because of this, the player can explore the same levels as many times as he likes to find needed stuff. This eliminates the drive to explore ever downward to collect more stuff, but items are also generated by depth, so to find better types of stuff he'll eventually have to go deeper anyway.

The generation algorithm carries some other implications. There is a set of levels, around the 30s in the dungeon, that are colloquially referred to as "stat gain depth." These levels are the ones on which permanent attribute potions are most often produced. Many players stick around here until their stats are boosted as high as they'll go, because the stats will be helpful later in the game and there's no real penalty for doing so.

Because of things like this, while there is generally less for an Angband player to learn to survive than a NetHack player, it's not a great deal less. NetHack is about as difficult as Rogue if the player knows nothing about the dungeon, but once he learns all the many gotchas, commands and hidden uses for stuff it's much easier. The essential knowledge for successful Angband players is more things like generation probabilities, the abilities of monsters and the advantages offered by X weapon or Y artifact. A perfectly knowledgeable player must still be careful, more careful than the equivalent NetHack player in fact. NetHack makes players remember facts; with Angband, what's learned is more like strategic knowledge.

Another basic play difference is that NetHack's play is more purposeful than Angband's. NetHack games in which the player just clears out levels and descends levels at his own pace are nearly always losses. A NetHack player must know what things he needs and how to get them, a process that, unlike Angband, is never as simple as searching shops and/or re-exploring levels at the best depth. Building a supply of holy water is a NetHack tactic that winning players learn is of vital importance. It requires finding an altar, sacrificing at it if it's not of the player's alignment, keeping in good stead with one's deity, obtaining potions of water (most often by diluting or cancelling other potions, itself a process with its own nuances) and finally prayer. The player must judge when he's running low and then take a break from exploration to initiate the process of making more himself.

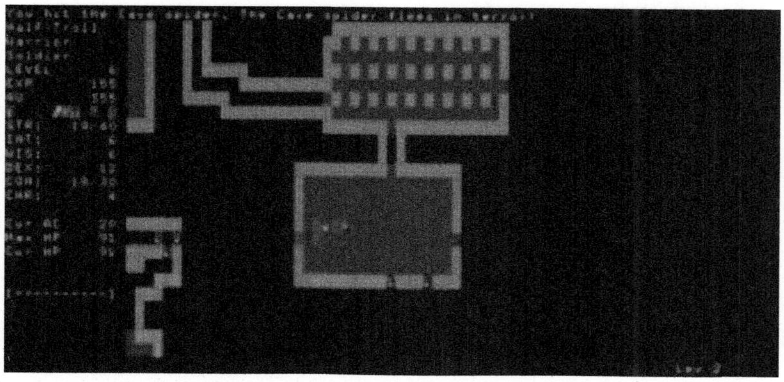

Figure 41.4

Angband

It's nearly a side quest all in itself, and lots of other stuff in NetHack is also like this: gaining protection, making proper use of magic lamps, building AC, using enchantment scrolls without destroying items, gaining artifacts through sacrifice, making dragon scale mail, using wishes. To do these things a NetHack player must be more obsessive than an Angband player, sometimes tripping back through many levels to get to a stash or altar. Ang-players may regenerate levels many times to get stuff they want, but that's a more open-ended activity, and its regenerating levels mean that it still involves dungeon exploration.

41.5 The Game with the Vaunted Vaults

This introduction wouldn't be complete without mentioning Angband's infamous vaults, perhaps the greatest risk/reward activity in any roguelike. First off, there exist in Angband things called pits. A pit is a middle-sized room with a lot of a theme monster, maybe easy ones, maybe tough. The contained monsters range from jellies to undead to dragons. They might have okay treasure.

Then there are lesser vaults, which are larger, contain a variety of monster and come in many designs. The monsters and loot in a lesser vault are "out of depth," that is, it's generated as if the level were a bit lower in the dungeon, so it's a good way to get a leg-up on the difficulty curve. But since the player is probably not ready for the monsters inside, stumbling on a vault is a bit of a heart-stopping moment, like wandering into a zoo in Rogue (and not like finding a throne room in NetHack). But if he can survive or otherwise remove the monsters there's good treasure to be found there, including artifacts.

Finally, there are the greater vaults, which are always generated away from the main complex of rooms. Not only must the player dig to them, but they're surrounded by undiggable walls, and the player will have to excavate around to find the way in. And once he finds entrance, he'll face a truly awe-inspiring challenge: a large number of greatly out-of-depth monsters, with treasure to match. It isn't uncommon to find multiple unique monsters, named opponents with powers greatly above the average foe. Likewise, multiple artifacts are a frequent feature of these direst of rooms.

Now, Angband games can be of two types, determined by the player upon starting, those with "preserve mode" on or off. The difference is what happens to artifacts, those supremely powerful unique items, if one is on a level when it is exited. Remember, Angband levels are discarded once left, the layout and contents determined anew when the player returns. If there was an artifact on that level, then what should happen to it? Sometimes the player will have not discovered it, or maybe he wisely decided not to challenge a vault.

When preserve mode is on for that game, then artifacts on discarded levels are returned to the generation mix. It's really unlikely, but it's possible that the artifact could be found again later on. If preserve mode is off, then the artifact is lost forever! If it was a particularly good artifact then that can be a grievous blow to a promising game, and if the player fails to pick up many artifacts then it's possible to reach a point, in a very long game, when there just aren't many left to generate. This provides a tremendous urging of a player who has a greater vault generated on a level to make a run at it, or else not even know which artifacts were just removed from the game.

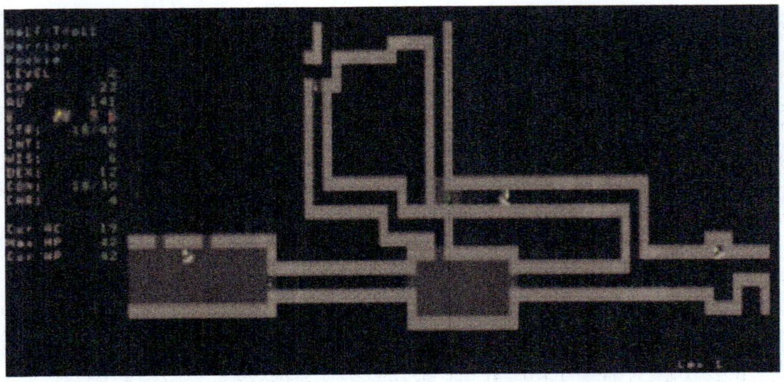

Figure 41.5

Angband

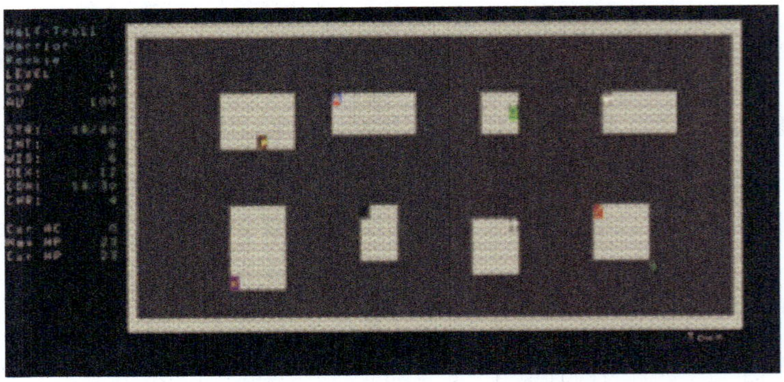

Figure 41.6

Angband (Town level)

To make up for this, the player receives a "feeling" upon entering a level, a brief message letting him know, in vague terms, the general quality of the stuff there. If preserve mode is on these feelings reveal little information; Calris (a much-loved artifact) could be on the level, and the player would have to explore it all to find out. If preserve mode is off, the level feeling will imply something very nice is on the floor, but the player must find it before he leaves the level or it is lost forever.

There, that should serve as a suitable introduction to Angband. We've now covered all five of the major roguelikes! Honestly, this one's not my favorite of the lot (it's all a bit too grindy for my tastes, like most MMORPGs), but Angband is perhaps the purest representation of roguelike tactics in any game. Later on we'll have a look at some of its variants, many of them rich games in their own right.

41.6 Source

The Angband Newbie Guide: www.thangorodrim.net/TANG/index.html

42

Cause for Incursion

January 2009 This game has been requested in comments several times now. While not one of the better-known in its genre, the freeware roguelike Incursion seems to have a fairly rabid community, and examination shows it to have some rather addictive play, a good attention to detail and one of the most "realistic" dungeons yet seen in the genre.

(*January 2016*: This game is still being developed and had an update August of 2015! It's been six years since this was written, so once again, this information may be out of date. I encourage you to download it and check for yourself!)

(*January 2020*: The energy of development has passed, and the game now appears to be unmaintained. Its website is down. It looks like it can still be obtained, for now, from a bitbucket repository: https://bitbucket.org/rmtew/incursion-roguelike/. Get it while it still exists, it's cool!)

To clarify something I see as important . . . I refer to the game here as "Incursion," because it seems to me to be the best thing to call it. It is projected, however, that this game is actually a prototype for an even-more-ambitious roguelike, which will be called "Incursion: Return of the Forsaken." (*January 2020*: Sadly, this never materialized.)

For starters, Incursion is the only roguelike of which I'm aware that follows D&D 3rd Edition rules. Well, technically that's "Open Gaming License" rules, the format by which Wizards of the Coast, custodians of the D&D brand, made them available for others to build their own products off of.

Of course, most roguelike games have always been based off of Dungeons & Dragons, though usually a much simpler, older version and not "officially." 3rd edition D&D does have its interesting aspects that lend interest to such a game, and there is nothing in the 3rd edition rules that prevents it from being used in an old-school, roguelike dungeon-crawling context.

The basic premise itself is fairly ordinary, go-to-this-level and defeat-this-monster. The fun comes from the journey. The random dungeon is perhaps the most complex yet seen in a roguelike; nearly every room is special in some way, and the game even prints descriptions the first time a type is encountered.

There are non-rectangular rooms, caverns, partitioned rooms, complexes of rooms, summoning rooms, polytheistic temples, flooded rooms, frozen-over rooms and lots of other types too. Roguelike dungeons tend to be interesting mostly for the shapes of the terrain they produce more than the actual places; the plethora of special types is a great innovation and does a lot to flesh out the game's sense of place.

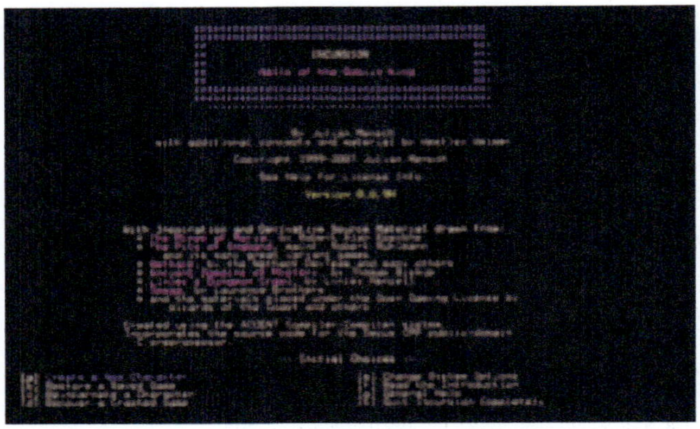

Figure 42.1

Incursion: Title screen

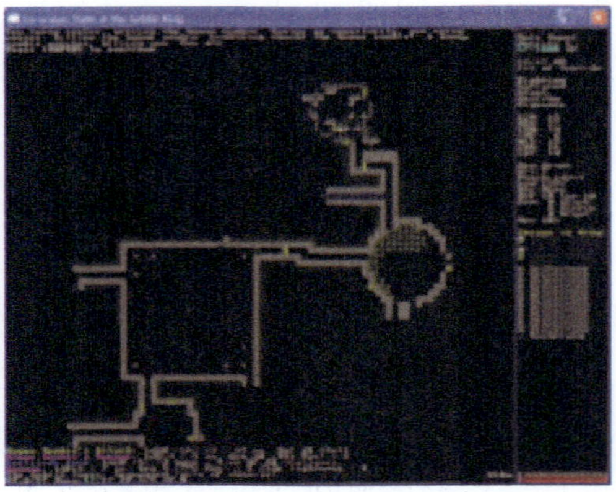

Figure 42.2

Incursion

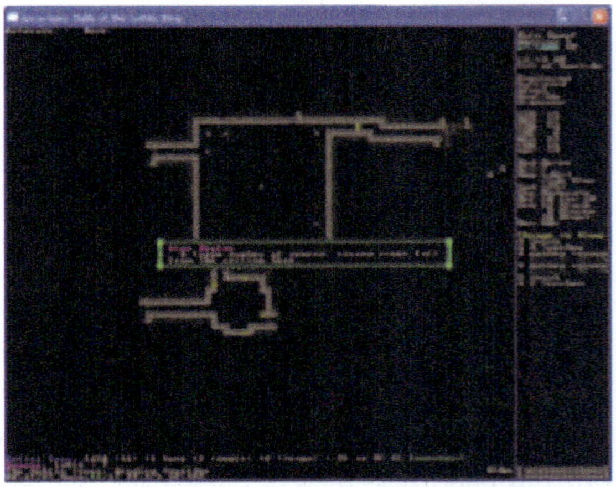

Figure 42.3

Incursion

Another thing about it is that Incursion's dungeon, unlike the dungeon in every other roguelike I'm aware of, is spatially-consistent in its levels. If you go downstairs, travel 30 spaces north-east to an upstairs, then climb them, you'll be back on the previous level 30 spaces north-east of the original downstairs. This may seem like a minor thing, but it's almost unheard-of in this field, and can be surprisingly difficult to implement when dungeon levels are generated on demand instead of all at once.

(Think about this: what would happen if the player found a way to explore the levels out of order, and after going down from 1 to 3 then returning to 2, two sets of stairs needed to be generated on the same space?) Chasms, too, may extend through multiple levels, so falling into a crevasse on level 3 could send the player deeper than level 4, in a realistic way.

42.1 Inexpensive Timeshares Now Available in the Caves of Carnage

The game uses a unique, for roguelikes at least, expedition paradigm for trips into the caves. Lots of roguelikes treat the entering of the dungeon as something that must be done only once for a character. Hack, NetHack and Crawl all call the adventure completely over when the player goes upstairs from level 1. (Players who escape with one of NetHack's "plastic imitations of the Amulet of Yendor" rue this feature.)

Original D&D, the version of that game that roguelikes take the most after, allowed for trips to town to rest up and restock provisions. The three games listed are all designed around not allowing for such trips, which is further proof that roguelikes are not necessarily mere D&D recreations.

But the other major roguelikes that do allow leaving the dungeon without ceasing play (Angband, town level; ADOM, overworld) do it by effectively making those areas also part of its "dungeon." They're not safe havens at all. ADOM's overworld in particular is often more dangerous than the early dungeon levels. In Incursion, the player can leave the dungeon and rest up in town, tackling the caverns afresh after a stay in the inn. This gives low-level players the ability to use the stairs up from level 1 as a base of operations, an interesting dynamic for one of these games.

42.2 Missing Fingers Surprisingly Reluctant to Grow Back

The regaining of hit points is handled differently from roguelike norm as well. Healing in roguelikes has always been kind of iffy, from a realism standpoint, a way to keep up the pace of the game. Even Conan couldn't go from almost dead to unhurt in the space of what amounts to a couple of hours, but most roguelike players do it regularly. But then, the only major game that doesn't, ADOM, goes maybe too far in the other direction.

Incursion's hit system takes after traditional D&D, and it works fairly well. No hit points are regained just from passing turns, but the player can regain them all by using a rest command ("z"). Resting restores all the player's hits and magic. It is balanced by it using a lot of food (about half of a full stomach) and because resting in the dungeon provides a chance to get attacked by wandering monsters, giving them free hits at the player at his most vulnerable.

The ability to leave the dungeon to rest, and the presence of safe zones further down, pulls the balance back into a reasonable zone. This means that food limits provide more of a barrier to resting than turn count. Resting in the Inn does cost food; they provide room but not board, it seems.

42.3 Not Exactly a DM's Guide Put through a Compiler . . . .

While the game covers the spirit, and often the letter, of D&D 3rd Edition rules fairly well, it knows when it's best to depart from them. The need to identify stuff, dating to D&D's earliest days, is close but not quite the system used in Rogue. In this, Incursion follows D&D in item generation probabilities but Rogue in its general magic stuff, which is to say that magic items are related according to their descriptions. (Stock D&D purposely includes bad items that exactly resemble good items.) I haven't noticed any particularly bad items in my playing, but there do seem to be a good variety of things.

Another place where the game leans away from 3rd Edition is in eschewing Vancian magic, the memorize-cast-forget cycle spellcasters in D&D have long used. This isn't meant to imply that this couldn't

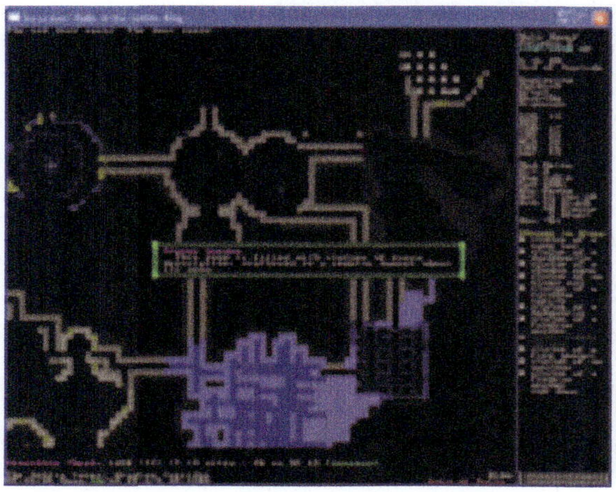

Figure 42.4

Incursion

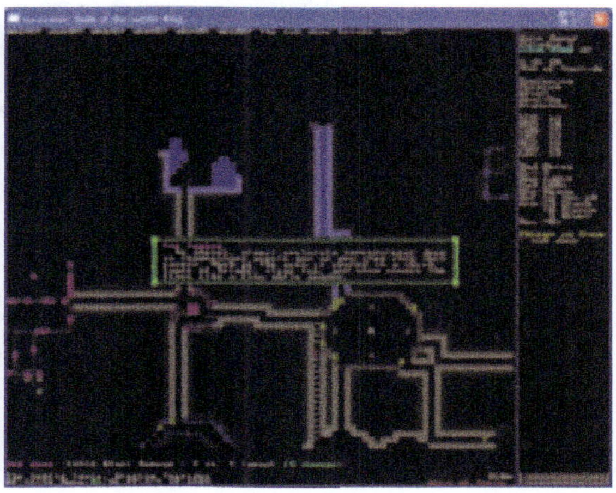

Figure 42.5

Incursion

work in a roguelike game, at least if that game had spells that mirrored their use in the fantasy novels they were inspired by (Jack Vance's Dying Earth), but it might require more of a rethinking of roguelike concepts than one might expect. (More on this matter is left, for interested readers, for the end of this piece.)

Treasure finds tend to follow the traditional D&D model. In roguelikes, items are something that randomly appears on the floor. Incursion has some of those, but most good treasure seems to be found in chests, in the possession of monsters (who know how to use them), or, later, in vaults.

The result is that the player must typically defeat a monster to gain loot instead of just happen upon it, a change that could be called slightly more realistic, if traipsing your enchanted elf around throwing fireballs at cave pelicans isn't realistic enough for you. (Yes, cave pelicans, their feathers black as night, their floppy bills filled and dripping with the blood of the innocent.)

42.4 15 Minutes to Roll Up, 5 Minute Life Expectancy

One of the biggest . . . well, let's not call it faults, but annoyances, is how excruciatingly long character creation can be. This is the place where adherence to 3rd edition D&D harms Incursion the most; while characters are lots faster to roll up than 2nd edition AD&D, maybe even 1st edition, the options do take many minutes simply to sift through, while Rogue, NetHack and Crawl characters are running seconds after they are invoked.

It should be said, however, that Incursion offers a way around this start-up time, by offering the chance to start over from scratch with the last character generated. (This could be abused mind; a player beginning with unusually good character stats could potentially keep them forever with this system.)

The game includes an autoroller that attempts to find good stats for your character, but stats are determined after race and class, and the autoroller appears not to take either into account when rolling. This sometimes results, for instance, in choosing to play a mage but then having to go with a score of 15 for Intelligence.

Neither is character creation easy to abort at this point. The game's solution is to offer the opportunity to switch to a point-buying system, which can be found annoying for its own reasons. These problems are far from a deal-breaker with Incursion, but they are a little head-scratching.

Another bizarre aspect of character generation in this game: it doesn't allow the player to decide on his name. I don't consider this to be a great drawback (I'd probably just name him "Rodney" again), but some people might be taken aback by this. Anyway, it's another strange decision. Of course, many computer RPGs don't allow players to name their characters at all, but among roguelikes, which are among the most simulationist of all fantasy games, it's highly unusual.

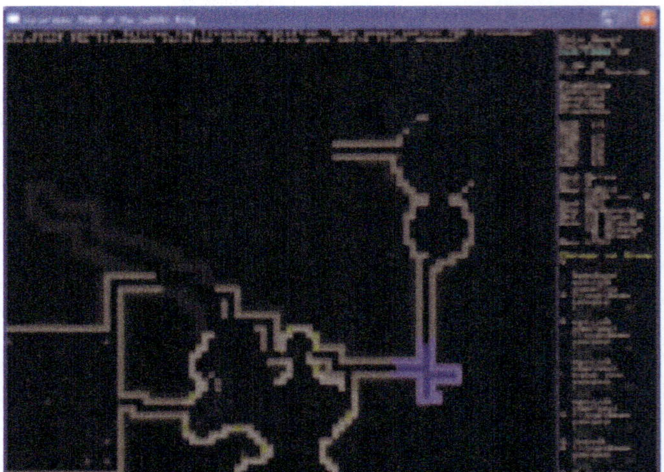

Figure 42.6

Incursion

42.5 "The Key Does Not Fit That Horse!"

One of the most frustrating things about it is that the interface has been changed just enough from roguelike standards to bring the learning curve back to old-hand roguelikers. It may first seem a positive thing that the game doesn't rely on a bunch of Shifted, Ctrl-ed, even Alt-ed key combinations to access commands, but the solution arrived upon takes a bit of getting used to.

The worst example I encountered: the "m" command to cast magic makes it easy for a Paladin to find the "Mount" spell to begin riding, but dismounting requires first pressing the "y" key, then finding which one of the 63 options provided will do the trick. Some other class abilities are hidden under another menu brought up by the "u" key. Some commands, such as buying things in a shop, are harder to abort than they should be. (The standard is to always allow Esc to return from a menu selection at any time.) And the equipment and container management functions take more than a little getting used to.

As the game stands, there are still a good number of unimplemented abilities that are present in the game but don't actually do anything. The game does mention some of these in the ability descriptions when characters are created, but they aren't marked as useless on the selection screen itself, and it's disheartening to see some wonderful power listed only to be told, effectively, "never mind" when it's highlighted.

42.6 "Congratulations, Mortal! You Have Won thBRRGG^^&#-General Protection Fault at $0CFF3E"

The worst thing though is that the game still has lots of bugs.

Unfortunately, Incursion's development pace has slowed considerably. The game autosaves often but the save code itself is a bit buggy, and an autosave crash killed my first decent game. The game does keep a backup of the previous save, thankfully.

The game's balance could also use a little work. As an example, here's how that first decent game ended. The furthest I've ever gotten is a dwarf paladin who got to experience level 3. He was bopping along okay when he encounters a hostile human priest. After smacking him about a bit, he began to flee. Okay by me, I smack him again and am told, in purple letters, "You feel guilty!"

Evidently this is a result of either being a paladin or lawful good alignment, but the guy had already summoned a water elemental so it seemed a good idea to take care of him now. (Previously, I had spared monsters when asked "Attack fleeing opponent?" with the result that, the next trip into the dungeon, they once again tried to take a piece out of me. A lizardman chieftain went through this cycle four times by the time I offed him before he began to flee.)

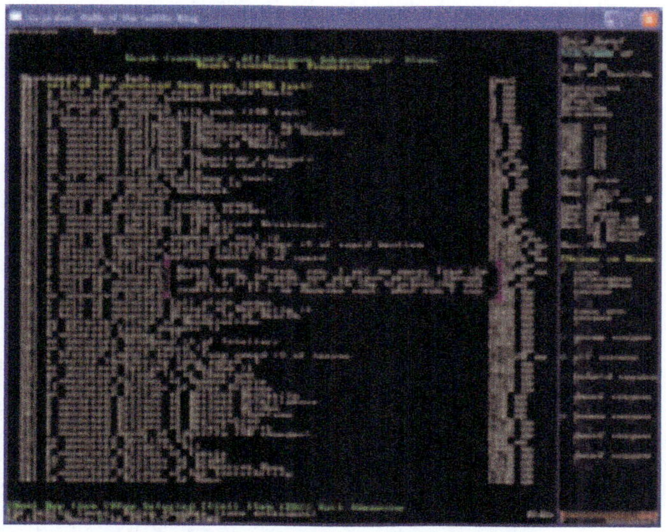

Figure 42.7

Incursion

In any case, the attack doesn't kill the human priest, but something weird happened in the fight that I missed in the flurry of messages. (Incursion does love to throw messages at the player.) As a result, several turns afterwards, my used items started disintegrating, with no explanation as to why. Ring of Good Fortune +2? Poof. Eventually my weapon crumbled as well, and Incursion has a horrible mis-feature that, if you aren't wielding a weapon, you will be told every turn, in a red-bordered box that must be dismissed, "You are empty-handed!" Over and over again, until you wield something.

I switched to my backup weapon . . . and it disintegrated a few turns after. Nothing left to wield, I was faced with a long trek through the caverns looking for something to hold in my hand in order to stop the box from appearing, which would probably itself disintegrate a few turns afterwards. I quit the game soon after.

As roguelike games get more ambitious, they get longer. As they get longer, the sense of loss when the player dies increases. As that happens, the player gets more likely to quit forever out of frustration. Designers, seeing this, make the game easier, which removes the challenge, the whole reason for playing a roguelike game in the first place.

To Incursion's credit, it seems to recognize this. While its premise as a D&D 3rd Edition roguelike imposes an unavoidable complexity to startup time, the ability to use "reincarnated" characters cuts down on this drastically. The dungeon is unusually atmospheric for a roguelike, and the array of treasure and opponents seems to be above average. While there are problems to be found, some serious, we have every reason to think they will eventually be fixed. Incursion, and its expanded sequel should that ever see our hard drives, are unquestionably games to keep an eye on.

The game has a wiki here: http://incursion.wikidot.com/. (This still works!)

On the wiki is an HTML version of the game's manual. On there is a section of tips for players of other roguelikes, which may offer some useful tips to readers.

Additionally, the FAQ page on the Wiki makes for interesting reading. For example: apparently, many of the skills the player can learn have special applications. The Climb skill, it turns out, can be used to scale crevasses, and cross lakes and lava by crawling along ceilings!

42.7 Supplemental: What Is Vancian Magic, and How Does It Apply to Dungeons & Dragons and/or Roguelikes?

Gary Gygax was widely read in the literature of fantasy, especially pulp fantasy such as H. P. Lovecraft and Robert E. Howard, and Dungeons & Dragons drew from an astonishing array of sources. Lots of people have remarked that the games borrowed heavily from Tolkien, but it should be noted that most of those borrowings were superficial. The game borrows some items and races, the Ranger class is pretty much a direct carry-over, and there are a few other things.

But the mood of the game is antithetical both to Tolkien's world and worldview. Dungeons & Dragons characters (and roguelike characters too), in their original form, are all adventuring rogues. The thief class wasn't introduced until the first supplement of the original books, probably because it hadn't occurred to Gygax and Arneson to codify that role into a character class. Why? Because all characters were thieves! They're venturing into dark tombs in order to take treasure away from those who currently own it. What else could they be?

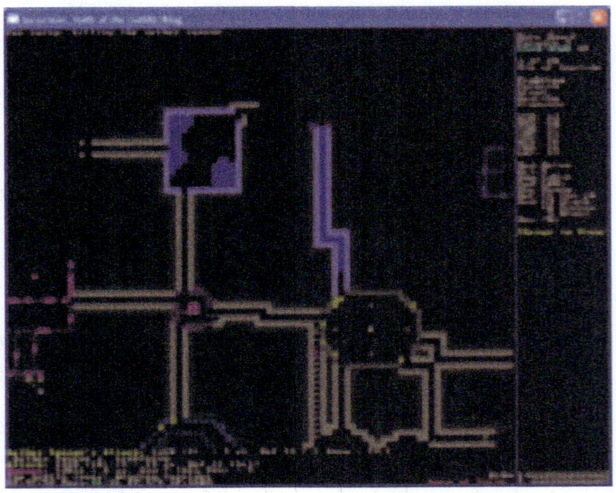

Figure 42.8

Incursion

Another strange thing about the old days of D&D is the way that wizards used their magic. Few wizards in fantasy literature are able to call upon their powers without limit. Even Gandalf became fatigued if he sent out too many fireballs.

The simplest way to simulate a limited resource is to assign a number to it, one that goes down when expended, and is refilled when refreshed. Hit points are the most obvious example of this, an abstraction of damage that makes little realistic sense, but has become so pervasive that few people question it. (Aside: popular fantasy game Dwarf Fortress does question it, and its developer Tarn Adams has some quite pointed things to say on the subject.)

Most RPGs, roguelikes included, also use a straight number to simulate access to reserves of magic power, presenting them as either "MP" or "PP." But this is innovation; Dungeons & Dragons did not use such a concept. Instead, it took the opportunity to add in yet another flavorful borrowing from fantasy literature, a magic system inspired by Jack Vance's Dying Earth books, and thus most-often called Vancian Magic.

It is a decision that has caused many gamers who have not read those books to scratch their heads; it seems like such a complicated way to do things. What a player would most like to do is allow his wizard to draw upon a fireball spell whenever he wants, to the limit of his store of power.

Instead, what he must do is decide, at the beginning of each day, what spells he wants to carry around with him and memorize those. He can memorize multiple copies of a spell, but if he hasn't memorized it, even if he has the spell written down in his personal spellbook, he can't make use of it. And when a spell is cast, that copy vanishes from memory.

The result is if a player gets poisoned but the mage hasn't memorized Slow Poison, then it's as if the spell was never known in the first place. A D&D party may end up encountering all manner of strange things in a dungeon. A wizard must be able to anticipate what kinds of dangers he will encounter that day if he's to make a good choice on which spells to take with him, and sometimes he just won't have the right thing handy.

The spell Feather Fall is great if the player falls into a deep pit, but who, waking up in the morning, says to himself, "I think I'll plummet into a hole today. Better take that one along!" It doesn't help that low-level characters have a pitifully small number of spells to choose from; unless he receives a bonus from somewhere, a first-level magic user can only remember one spell at a time! Bonus spells, thus, are highly sought-after by players of novice wizards.

Compounding this is the fact that, by a good margin, wizards are physically the weakest characters in D&D. The least likely to have good constitution scores, the most restricted in armor and the least proficient in weapons. The most hit points a wizard can start with, assuming no Con bonus, is 4. They'll have just one 25% of the time. Magic is their trick, the whole reason to play a wizard. So to be useful in combat, that most common activity of adventuring parties, a first-level wizard can't take any of those utility spells that only might come in handy; it'll probably be good ol' Magic Missile, once again.

Lots of players, over the years, have wondered what kind of bizarre design point Gygax was trying to make with this. Mages do become the most powerful characters in D&D at high levels, but at low levels keeping them alive was extremely difficult, although keep in mind, no character had a great chance of survival

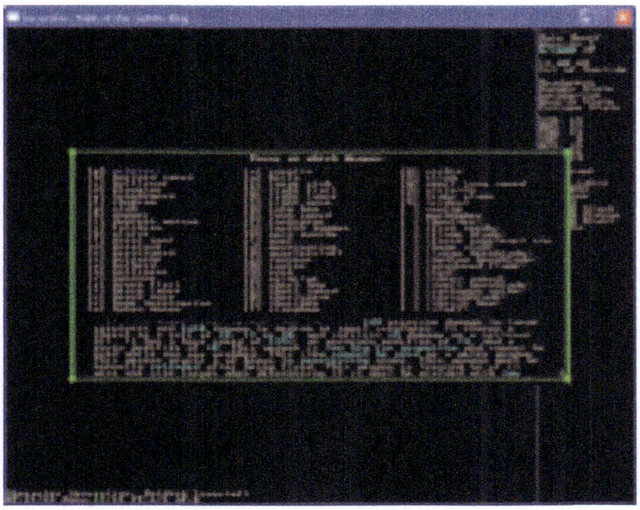

Figure 42.9

Incursion

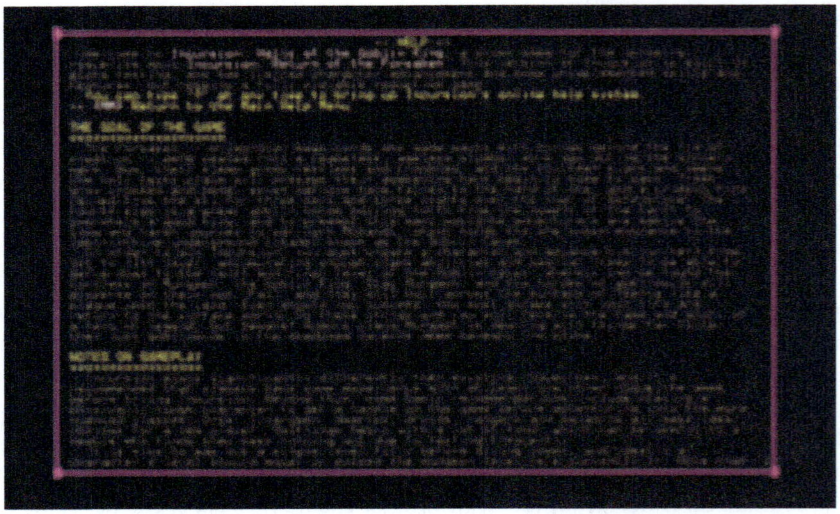

Figure 42.10

Incursion

in the early days. There was a strong sense that a powerful wizard was the reward for a player that had "paid his dues," surviving with such a weakling for so long.

The answer snaps into focus, however, once one reads *The Dying Earth*. Gygax must have been entranced by this vision of magic. But Vance's magicians are anything but weaklings: they are potent individuals, some with formidable physical skills. Your choice of class in D&D, unless you multiclassed which carried its own drawbacks and didn't exist until AD&D 1st edition, precludes having many hit points or the use of protective equipment. Vance's creations would not be so restricted.

In the original D&D books, the only real restriction on wizards in combat is having to go without armor. They receive the same hit points as the other classes (d6) and are capable in wielding weapons just like any other character, and all weapons do d6 damage anyway. Even if they were restricted in choice of arms they'd be just as effective in straight battle as a Fighting Man. Only the lack of armor restricts them from participating directly in fights, and in D&D armor reduces the chance of being hit, not the damage done, so most characters will probably die from damage unless they take great pains to avoid it anyway.

So what does this have to do with roguelikes? They present a generalized dungeon, randomly created. A roguelike adventurer has little chance to determine the nature of the areas he'll enter in a day, and just as little control.

A Vancian magic-user would be forced to make do only with general-purpose spells. (If the game is larger than a single dungeon, maybe with branches or an overworld, then this is less onerous.) Also, a physically fragile character (such as most roguelike wizards are) will have to make up for his weakness with combat magic to have a hope of surviving; as noted above, if the character can do things other than just magic then this is much less of a problem.

But in the case of a hypothetical, default roguelike, as monsters get stronger, wizard combat ability wouldn't keep pace, so combat magic would be the overridingly most-memorized spell. Most other magic would simply lie unused.

For these reasons, it's probably for the best that Incursion goes with a point system rather than Vancian magic. But it's difficult to read through *The Dying Earth* and not feel, like Gygax must have, that this is a system that would be marvelous to play in a game. If it's to be a roguelike game, however, then great care must be taken as to its implications.

I am indebted to Jeff's Gameblog for his remarks on D&D's Vancian magic system, and for cluing me in to the *Dying Earth* books. His site is here: http://jrients.blogspot.com/.

43

Brogue and the Abandoning of Experience Points

January 2016 (*January 2020*: On Windows at the moment, Brogue appears to have some graphics bugs. I suggest executing the game with the command line `brogue--size 8`, or maybe even 7, depending on the size of your display. While running, the plus [+] and minus [–] keys increase and decrease the font size, and correspondingly the window size, and key F12 switches the game in and out of full screen mode. The game is well worth the effort to figure out how to run it well.)

For a long while I had taken to identifying the major roguelikes as Rogue, NetHack, Angband, ADOM and Crawl.

I think adding a game to a list like this isn't a simple matter of picking what's popular, but that the game should emblemize roguelikes in some way. So, while Spelunky gets down the essence of roguelike play very well, it's not a canonical roguelike, if such a term makes sense, because it is an action-platformer. There is also a benefit to keeping all such games either freeware or open source, although this isn't really necessary.

Anyway, Brogue is a game I add to the list. As major roguelikes go, in fact, it is probably the most like the original game. This is not just in terms of gameplay; in some ways the game styles itself as being like Rogue. You're again going after that all-purpose McGuffin, the Amulet of Yendor, and it's again kept down on the 26th level of the Dungeons of Doom.

Brogue parts company with Rogue in a lot of interesting ways, though. One of the biggest is that it doesn't seek as much to be a D&D simulation like Rogue did in its original incarnation. It doesn't abandon the tropes of Generic Fantasyland entirely, which helps players to intuitively understand relative monster strengths and special abilities, and also to generally perceive item functions from their names, which is always a good thing, and a general problem with randarts in other games.

More recent versions of Brogue have diverged from Dungeons & Dragons further, in a daring and interesting way. Brogue has removed experience points and levels from the game.

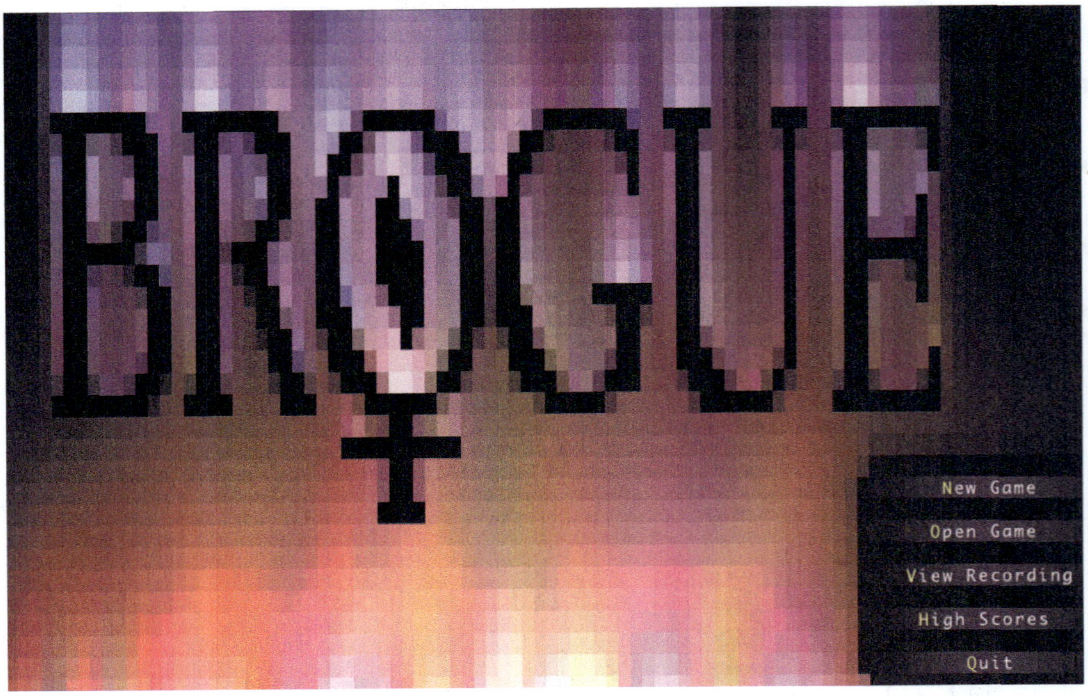

Figure 43.1

Brouge

43.1 Brogue Has Removed Experience Levels from the Game?!

Yes, that's what I said, there's no need to repeat it.

It is a huge change, and I can seriously respect it. The other changes it makes to the play are profound, and probably greater than I can exhaustively cover in one essay. We'll try to go over the general implications.

The biggest thing is it removes one of the powergaming routes of roguelike play, the strategy of defeating hugely powerful monsters early in order to gain large experience awards. Play of this sort is a huge part of the charm of the Mystery Dungeon games, and also of the quasi-roguelike Desktop Dungeons, so it's safe to say that it's not a good decision for every game.

Just because there's not experience doesn't mean there's no character growth. What Brogue has done is take an aspect of character development that's generally gone hand-in-hand with experience growth, that of obtaining and improving equipment and improving one's character through item use, and made it the primary method of growth. In short, your character's equipment matters for even more in Brogue than other games, and the growth of your character's abilities is directly tied to what you've found, and thus how well you've explored each floor.

Three of Brogue's items (used correctly) have important long-term effects on the player's state, and effectively replace player experience growth. The scroll of enchantment has long been one of Brogue's signature items, replacing the scrolls of enchant armor and weapon found in Rogue and other games with a more generalized version that also affects wands, staves, charms and rings. Potions of life replace potions of healing, refilling the player's hit points entirely and also increasing his maximum by about one or two levels' worth. Potions of strength return from Rogue in their normal form, permanently increasing the player's Strength by one point, but increasing the role of Strength in the game by requiring it in order to be able to use weapons and armor effectively, and removing the aspect that causes players to effectively waste the potion if they've been poisoned.

All three of these items, and food besides, are part of an item generation rubberbanding system that seeks to ensure that the player has enough opportunity for advancement to be ready for deeper levels and harder enemies by the time they show up. This, it needs to be said, damages realism. Of course it was always unrealistic that you'd find, say, food in dungeons, or that monsters could survive on their own so separated from non-adventurer sources of food. Does supposing the existence of an unseen hand that supports the player by ensuring that he periodically can find necessary items go beyond that? Anyway, it should be said

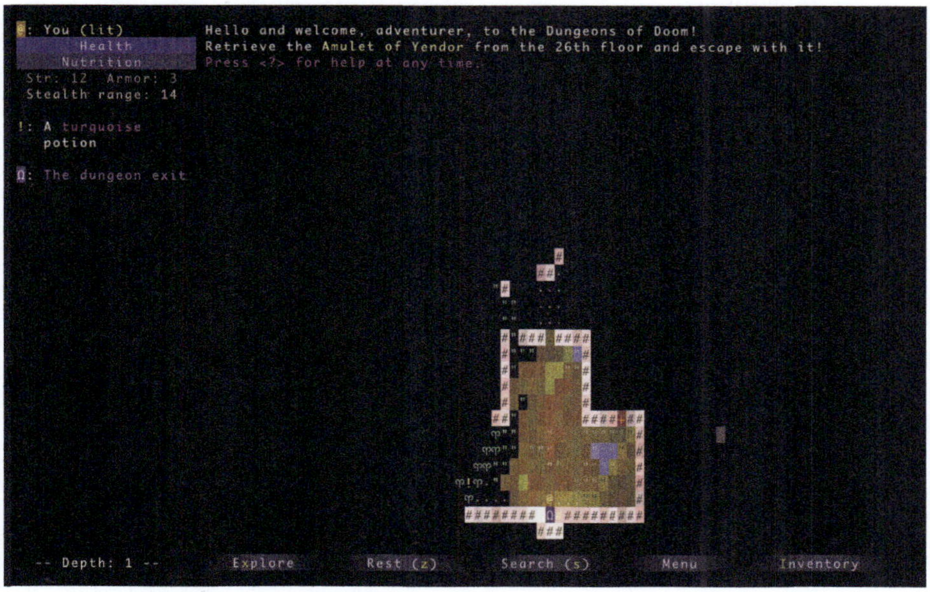

Figure 43.2

Brouge

that this affects only generation; nothing says the player will find the items once generated, although, which sometimes Brogue can hide items pretty well, determined players can still usually loot a level effectively enough to find what they need.

One thing that's interesting to consider is that, in its way, this kind of advancement brings Brogue closer to adventure gaming. One way to look at The Legend of Zelda's system of Heart Containers and found equipment is as a real-time, non-randomized version of this.

Because the direct need to kill enemies to improve player statistics has been removed, adventurers need not engage in wanton slaughter earlier to make it through later levels. Now, most of the monsters are still trying to kill the player, and a monster killed ceases to be a threat in the future, and if not killed those monsters will continue to wander the level, in greater numbers as wandering monster generation kicks in, so in terms of strategy it's still best to slay monsters, when safely possible. But for short-term exploration a player can rely on stealth, especially when magically augmented, both as a means of combat avoidance and to critically hit sleeping and unaware monsters.

One reason that this decision works for Brogue is its huge depth of interrelated game systems that gives players other ways to effectively attack than melee or missile combat. In addition to the roguelike usuals like items and monsters, Brogue supports a complete system of growing plants, liquid depths and multiple types of gas effects. A room covered in grass-like fungus can be set afire to burn monsters carelessly standing around, as can rooms naturally filled with flammable gas. A couple of monsters in the Bloat class seem designed around the idea of this kind of exploitation.

Additionally, lighting, or its lack, is an important part of the game, affecting how easily monsters can spot the player. And player allies in Brogue are relatively common, and feel more like full-fledged helper characters than NetHack's pets (who lose some of their most interesting monster abilities when tamed). Players usually find a number of staves and charms that, when improved with scrolls of Enchantment, can be melded into a successful game strategy.

43.2 Variety and Continuity of Play State

What Brogue's item advancement contributes to is an essential aspect of roguelike gaming, something I call variety of play state. Differences between the resources and abilities available to the player, and between which monsters he's fighting, their positions in the terrain, and any other relevant environmental features around, the variability of these things all provide variety of play state. While the rules to the game remain the same each time, the situation, the scenario changes. Variety of play state increases replayability, but it also customizes your game, makes your experience different from that of other players.

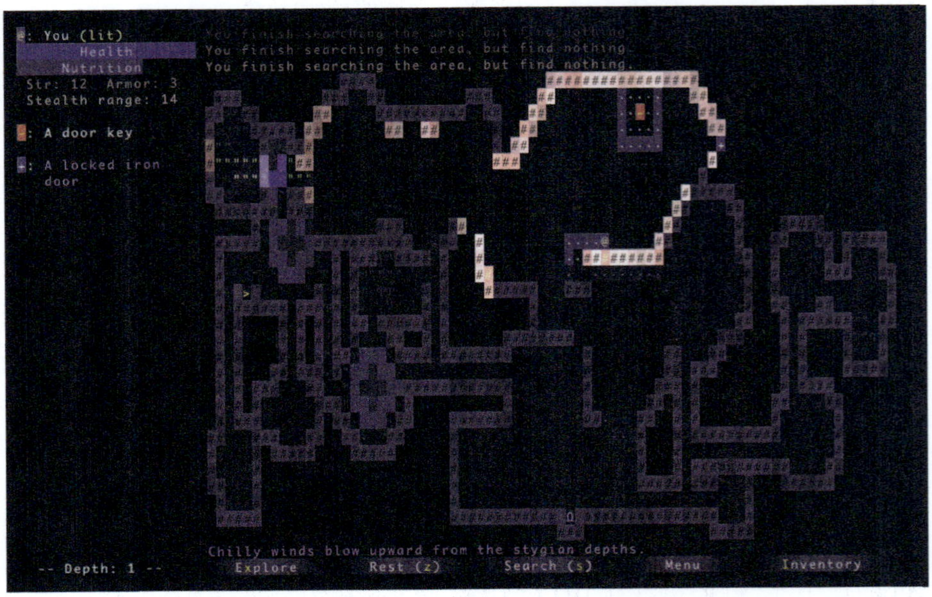

Figure 43.3

Brogue

The player's ability to adjust that scenario, through his actions, to gain advantage going forward into the game, that's something I call continuity of play state. The player's actions affect the scenario, and the scenario affects the player's actions, in an iterative cycle. The combination of the two influencing each other is what turns a game from a static set of challenges into a narrative that the player can relate to, personifying his character's adventures as something that is his, instead of something outside his or herself, created by a level designer.

When you play a puzzle game, those tend to be isolated series of disconnected scenarios. They're generally made to ensure they are solvable, but they must also be made to minimize chaos, differences in possible state going in and during. Narrative is all about changes and variety of state, so puzzle, and their variants adventure games, have to supply a pre-written narrative to give context to their puzzles. At their best, roguelike games turn up the chaos, but to a limited degree. The interplay between player volition and randomized situations is what makes them playable, is what makes them magical.

The more possible ways there are for either or both of the world generation and the player's actions to vary the game state, then potentially the more replayable it is. You can tackle a situation, say, through melee combat, or allies, or staves, or stealth, or taking advantage of the environment, but you can't do all of these things each game.

43.3 "I Am Better Than You, I Have a Higher Score!"

The problem with most games' use of experience points is that they make the player better. In a shallow Dragonball-Z power level kind of way, one character or monster is objectively better than another. This is an assumption, a foundational idea even, that goes back to the origins of role-playing games. Dungeons & Dragons rates everyone, people, monsters, even gods, according to a number of basic statistics, originally compared to player level, and then universalized into an attribute called hit dice, which is kind of a more profound version of level. Even if a monster has no other indication of its power, it still has hit dice lying behind it all, which is basically how the monster designer scales the monster's power relative to character levels.

The real world doesn't work like that. It doesn't make sense to say X person "is greater than" Y person. All comparisons between people are according to some subjective standard that says as much about the measurement, and often the measurer, as it does about the ones measured. The act of combat between two people genuinely trying everything in their power to overcome the other is an inherently chaotic thing, and far more random than most RPGs would imply, where in some games even as much as a couple of levels

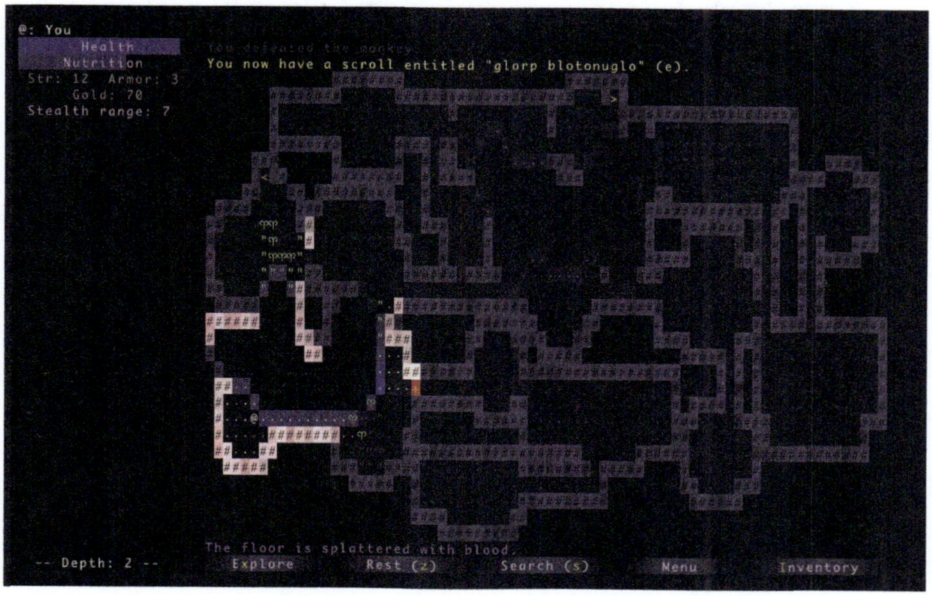

Figure 43.4

Brogue

of difference can be enough for one combatant to easily outclass the other. In reality, people don't improve generally so much as become more specialized.

When a game pegs character power on level, it's generally making a statement that the player's character (as opposed to the player himself—the distinction is important here) is improving relative to the monsters. Historically this improvement takes several forms:

- Higher maximum hit points—the player is further away from dying, directly.
- The player has a greater chance to hit in combat—he has higher chance to inflict damage on a foe he's attacking.
- Improved saving throws—special abilities foes have are less likely to affect the player.
- Greater magic potential—if it's a magic using character, he'll have more power to draw from, and more spells through which to use that power.
- Better abilities—similarly, other abilities the player may have, which vary by class, may also improve.

There are other advantages too. This "more levels = better than" assumption runs deep in D&D. There's a reason a hero (as per the game Chainmail and the potion of heroism) is defined as a character who's reached level 4, and a super-hero is one at level 7.

The problem with this, especially regarding roguelikes, is that at a given level, one character of a given class looks a lot like another. In D&D there are other things going on to distinguish characters, but these things tend not to be as important to roguelike characters, who are in a game type that generally demands quick play and thus don't have much practical means to make them varied from each other. So, many roguelike characters, as they advance in power, end up looking similar to each other, with only their equipment and statistics to distinguish them. In a number of games, you need to have certain abilities, resistances or statistics by certain points or risk death from specific sources. NetHack and Angband both fall prey to this, NetHack with its famous "ascension kits" and Angband with its list of attributes you need by certain depths.

Many of these advantages end up coming from player experience level, which ends up being an automatic bundle of advantages you get just for playing. A character with high level has good hit points and higher to-hit and better saving throws and better skills, etc. Everything in this bundle of advantages could be broken apart and made a different way a character can exist, a different interesting situation for the player to consider.

Brogue basically breaks levels down into a certain number of objects you are guaranteed to find in the dungeon, provided you search long enough. Potions of life increase maximum hit points, potions of

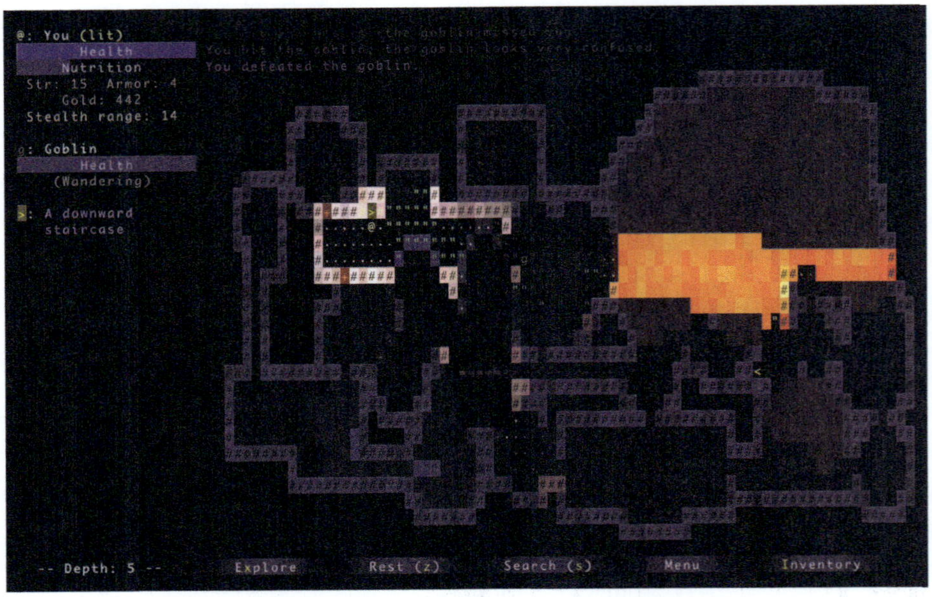

Figure 43.5

Brogue

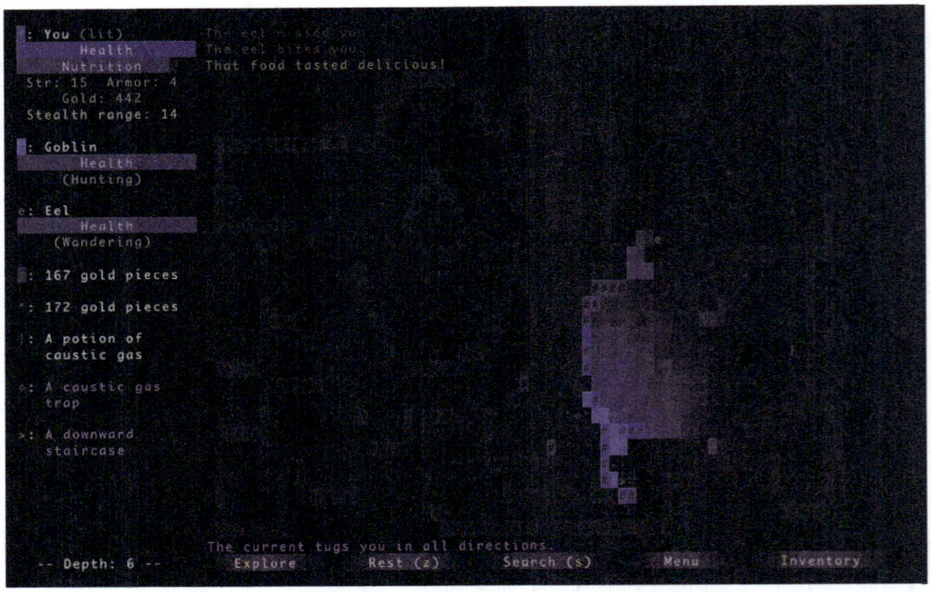

Figure 43.6

Brogue

strength increase damage and make it easier to use weapons, and scrolls of enchantment take the place of both skills and magic improvement.

A disadvantage, in design terms, of guaranteeing the items is similar to those games where players automatically advance in level, regardless of their actions, just to give the player a sense of character advancement, or their kin, games where monsters are generated or adjusted in ability to match the player's experience level. Since all the power you can find in Brogue is lying there, waiting to be found, in the dungeon, the PC's (that is to say, Player Character's) improvement is capped, relative to his location, in a real sense. It's basically another version of programmed advancement, with no way to escape the treadmill. It's still tied to skill somewhat in that the player still has to find and use the items to get the advantage from them, but most people find the great majority of items in each level as it is.

One other problem with tying advancement entirely to carefully doled-out items is the absence of that phenomenon of level boosting a character, discovering ways to defeat monsters of much higher level and getting rewarded for doing so, although really that's more of a thing in the Mystery Dungeon games than others. In those games, it is effectively a self-balancing aspect, if the player is unlucky and ends up facing tough opponents early, if he is willing to devote the resources to overcoming them as opposed to just surviving, he'll be rewarded with greater experience gain. By abandoning experience, Brogue has also abandoned this aspect of game continuity, where the player's past history affects (numerically) later performance.

But then, all game designs come with tradeoffs and roads-not-taken. Whether Brogue is better or worse for the amazing direction it's gone, it is different, and exciting for it. Give it a try, and see if you agree!

43.4 More Reading

Brogue home page, with downloads: https://sites.google.com/site/broguegame/

How Brogue generates levels: www.rockpapershotgun.com/2015/07/28/how-do-roguelikes-generate-levels/

Brogue subreddit (official): www.reddit.com/r/brogueforum/

44 HyperRogue

January 2016 One of the most interesting roguelikes to come around lately, a game that is obviously close to the lineage (down to having "Rogue" in the title) and yet brings new clever and amazing ideas to the table, is a little thing called HyperRogue. You can download some versions of it for free from creator Zeno Rogue's itch.io site, or you can download the newest version for just $3. It's also available on Steam, and for Android on the Google Play store, either free or paid.

44.1 Lessons in Non-Euclidean Travel

At first it seems like a fairly simple game, and at the beginning it kind of is, but the difficulty ramps up wonderfully smoothly. The most immediately interesting thing about HyperRogue is that your guy, lost in a weirdly geometric world surrounded by spaces and thick, clumpy, apparently irregular walls, has only one hit point: if you take even a single hit from any source, you immediately lose. Fortunately, most enemies are likewise restricted, so the result to the gameplay is that you have to get the first hit on any enemy or you immediately lose the game. If you manage to strike first, although you use up your turn doing it, you'll always kill the foe; there is no miss chance in combat. There are exceptions to this rule (some very interesting!), but those are the basics.

One consequence of this is that Zeno Rogue has moved the strategy window (see Chapter 64, Interface Aids and the Strategy Window) up a little, and the game won't even allow you to make moves that result in immediate death. Effectively it works like "check" does in chess. The game will simply ignore moves that would be fatal on the next turn, explaining its refusal with a warning message. To drag out another previous coinage, it guards against immediate critical moments. It doesn't prevent you from making moves that might result in certain death more than one turn in the future. You still have to be on the lookout for those, although they are rarer.

The one hit point limitation forces you to adopt some interesting tactics to survive. If you are hemmed in by walls and have an adjacent enemy, the only move you can make is to attack it. In the same situation, if the enemy is one space away the only thing you can do is pass a turn and let it approach you. For the most part your opponents only act to approach and attack you, which helps the player to anticipate trouble spots and plan ahead to escape them. There is no experience system in HyperRogue, so for the most part you're better off avoiding enemies if you can, although sometimes it's good to turn around and confront a horde of pursuers in a controlled fashion rather than let them corner you in a dead-end.

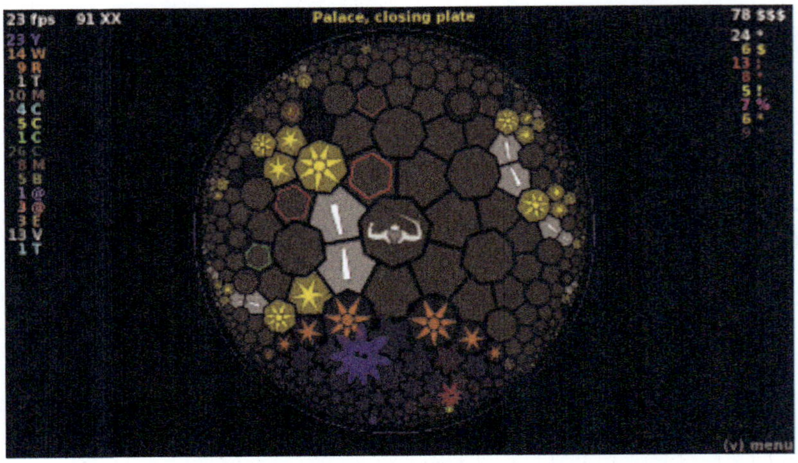

Figure 44.1

HyperRogue (in one of its weirder locations).

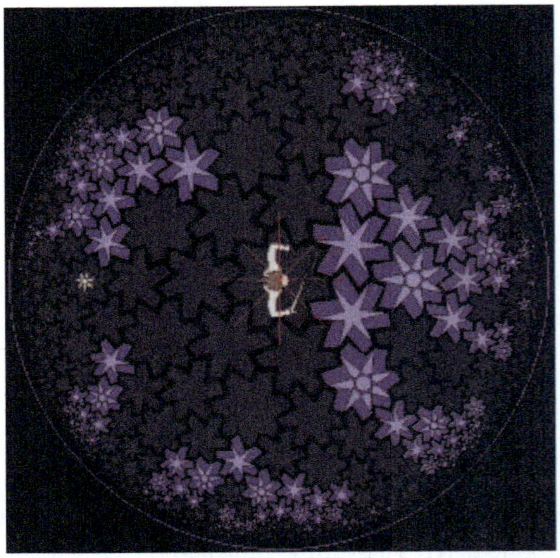

Figure 44.2

Ice Caves

If two enemies are adjacent to you, you cannot attack either of them because his friend would attack and kill you. In that case you must flee, and if you have nowhere to flee to the game ends immediately, and suddenly. Your rogue has effectively been checkmated, and the game doesn't even let you make a move in that case. So the basis of combat strategy is to get enemies to line up so you only face one at a time. Even if you are facing 20 enemies in a row, so long as you kill each one as it approaches you, you'll survive. But if even one additional enemy comes in and doesn't queue up with the others you'll have to flee, and if an enemy approaches from behind, so there's an enemy in both directions and you can't escape both in on turn, then it's all over. Most dangerous is when enemies approach from the same distance in opposite directions; you're better off approaching one of them at an angle before they get too close.

(The one hit point model of roguelike design was described in greater detail, making these points and more, in an excellent presentation given at IRDC 2012 by prolific roguelike designer Darren Grey. Search for it on YouTube.)

Most enemies behave this way. Some are slower than others, but they usually have some visual indication that they're about to move. A few enemies cannot be killed immediately through melee, but your attacks stun them, and often after a certain number of stuns it'll be finished off for good. Other enemies are completely invulnerable unless defeated through special means.

44.2 Your Passport Is Printed on a Mobius Strip

At the start of each of the game's "lands," which are sort of like NetHack's dungeon branches, enemies are very low in number. So when you enter a new zone, you probably won't have to worry much and can easily take out the single foe that harasses you occasionally. Throughout each land you'll randomly find treasures. Treasures don't give you abilities themselves, but each land has a different type. Nearly all the treasures in all the lands are worth just one point towards your score (the game scores very low), but collecting treasure opens up the way to more advanced areas. At the start there are only a few lands you can visit, but once you get a total of 30 points a new set of lands becomes available to find in addition to the ones you started in. At 60 and 90 yet more lands open up. There are over 30 lands in all, but some of the last ones have special requirements for entry, like having killed a minimum number of foes.

The thing about collecting treasures is that collecting them is what increases the enemy encounter rate. Every treasure you get in a land increases the frequency with which monsters are generated, but only in that land.

For the minimum to enter Hell, where the primary objective the Orb of Yendor is kept (there's that name again), you have to have gotten ten treasures from each of nine lands. It doesn't matter which lands, so the easiest way to go about it is to get ten treasures from the easier regions, then vamoose, exploring wildly until you find a Great Wall that signals a border into a different zone. Of course, collecting more treasures than that helps your score.

Each land has its own kind of orbs that give you special temporary powers if collected. If you get all the way up to 25 treasures you can unlock those orbs to appear in some other lands too, which can help you out in tight spots later . . . but by the time you get to 25 points from a single land, you'll be harassed by foes frequently. It's the age-old decision, you can play more daringly now to make the later game easier, or you can get by with the bare minimum and take your chances in the end-game. Neither decision is necessarily better than the other.

44.3 There Are No Snake Enemies on the Hyperbolic Plane*

The one hit point system is interesting, but there's another, even cooler, aspect about HyperRogue. It doesn't take place in a "Cartesian" space, but on a kind of geometric construct called a hyperbolic plane. Like Jeff Lait's amazing, brain-bending 7DRL game Jacob's Matrix, HyperRogue takes place in a "non-Euclidean" space, which has strange properties. For one thing, "parallel lines," which on an ordinary plane stay the same distance from each other forever regardless of how far you go, actually diverge in HyperRogue. Take for example those "Great Walls" between lands that you see frequently in special zones like the Crossroads, like here:

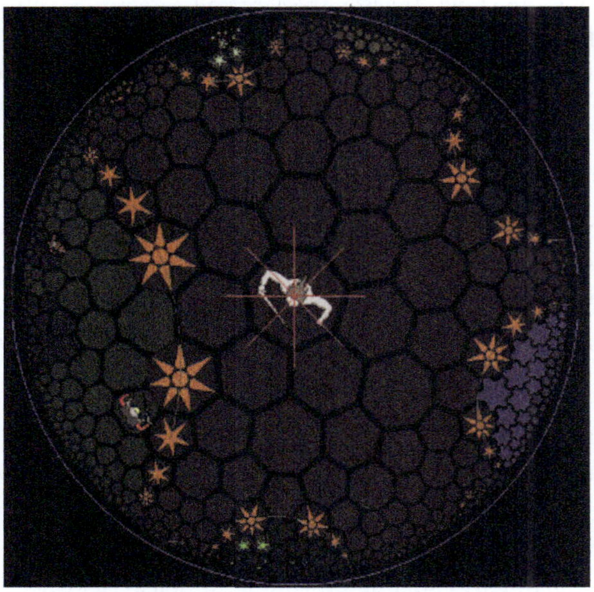

Figure 44.3

One version of the Crossroads

* A correction, sent in by Zeno himself: one region does, in fact, have rock snakes.

The red spaces in the above screenshot are the Crossroads land, which connects many other lands. The orange star spaces are pieces of the Great Walls, and the colored regions they border are the other lands. The weird thing is, although they look curved, all the Great Walls are straight lines in the game's topology, a fact that gets more obvious the closer you get to crossing over into a new land. Although they're not parallel, they never intersect with the other walls, but actually diverge from them as they go on instead of eventually crossing at some point.

It's a strange place, and a little confusing. You can't see it in these images, but as you move through adjoining spaces the world in the direction you're traveling sort of broadens, appearing to distort around you, and the area behind you sort of shrinks. The effect is most visible near the horizon. The bizarre topography of the hyperbolic plane makes it very difficult to return to places you've already explored and have passed out of sight unless you closely retrace your steps. Try watching some landmark while walking around in a circle; you'll find that your view rotates as you turn. You tend to keep missing places to try to go back to unless they're still in vision range. Fortunately, there's an infinite number of lands and of all things in those lands, or else you might end up searching a long time to get back to an essential place you had once been.

Other consequences of the hyperbolic plane are that circles are much larger than you might expect. There are other interesting shapes, and consequences of those shapes, too. Zeno Rogue posted on his site an excellent light math description of some of the shapes that can be encountered, written by Fulgur14, many of which serve as the basis of terrain generation in the advanced lands.

44.4 To Show Your Vacation Slides You'll Have to Use a Poincaré Projector

The soul of HyperRogue is the many varied and intriguing lands there are to find and explore. Each land has its own kind of treasure to collect and tracks your best score even for that area.

Here is a selection of the earlier lands and their rules, to give you a taste for what's to come. If you're ever confused as to what rules are in effect in a given region, you can get reminded in-game by pressing V (to go to the menu), then O (to go to the world overview screen), then clicking on one of the region names on the left side of the screen.

Icy Land: This is always your starting area. Nearby walls will melt away from your body heat if you stand close to them for too long. The Bonfires you find here can be activated, which will both melt close walls and attract some of your enemies.

Crossroads: There are three different versions of this land, which can be distinguished from each other by the ground color. Most areas are bordered by one of the three types of Crossroads. As I said before, the walls here separating other areas from you are actually straight lines: they just appear curved due to hyperbolic geometry.

Jungle: This place is full of vines that grow and grow out from a central point. The center of each plant is cyan; the vines growing out from it are green. Each vine surrounding a plant takes turns growing, each one space at a time, clockwise around the plant. A vine turns yellow the turn before it moves, and is dangerous when it does so. However, you can prune a vine back by attacking it. If you manage to hack your way to and destroy the center, all its vines die at once and you get a ruby as a reward.

Land of Eternal Motion: You can't rest! Every turn must move to another spot, and every space you move from falls away into the void. All your enemies here do the same thing. Since enemies cannot follow directly behind you, they must adopt a parallel course to follow, and as we learned earlier parallel lines diverge on a hyperbolic plane, so it's relatively easy to leave pursuers in the dust here. The only problem is that new chasers will get generated over the horizon in front of you, so you're constantly having to steer away from them too.

Living Cave: The walls in this area grow and shrink according to cellular automation rules. Collectible treasures push close-by walls back until picked up, and the corpses of killed Rock Troll enemies in this zone will tend to draw nearby walls in to "bury" it within their surface. If you get entombed in rock you automatically lose!

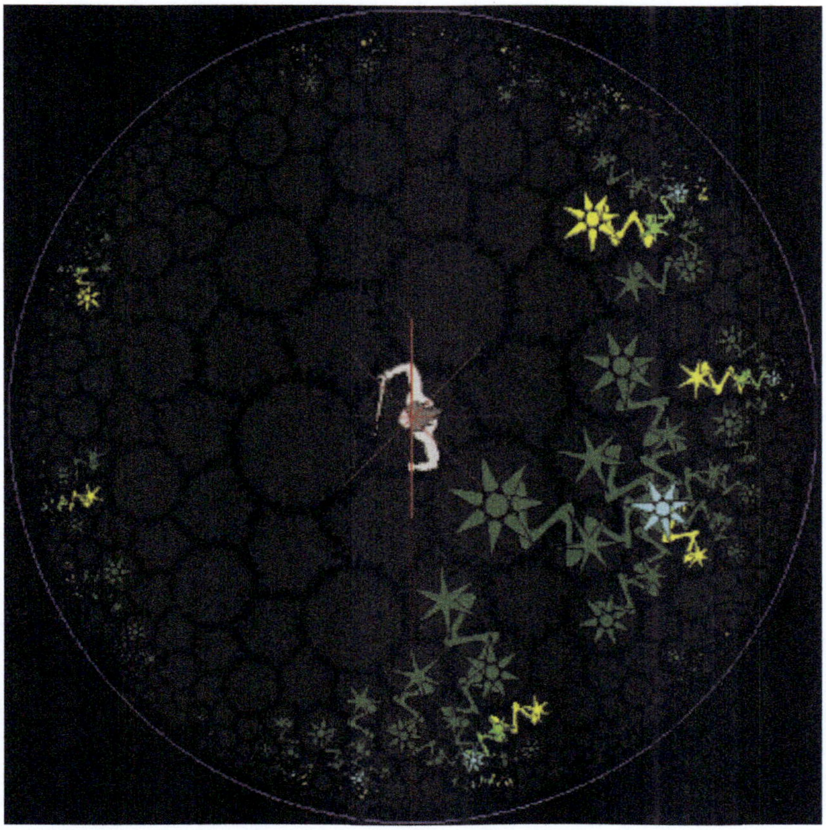

Figure 44.4

Jungle

Minefield: Not all the areas you explore rely on special properties of hyperbolic planes. This entertaining zone is full of invisible mines you must avoid, natch, by playing minesweeper. The number of mines on adjacent spaces is clued by messages and colored dots: blue dots are adjacent to one mine, green dots to two, and red to three. Ground enemies lured in from other lands can set mines off too, but that can be a bad thing: exploded mines erupt in spaces of permanent fire, and if you get surrounded by impassable walls you immediately lose. Because the spaces you pass through are marked as you travel, it's easier to retrace your steps in this land than most others. The enemies here, "bomberirds," are rare, but create new mines when killed!

Mirror Land: There are lots of mirrors here, which double as the treasures you collect. If you break one by running into it, allies that move relative to your movements appear around you, and help you fight approaching attackers. Your helpers tend to be fragile, but are of so much help that this seems to be one of the easier lands.

Alchemist's Lab: All the ground is either red or blue. If you're on blue ground, you can only move to another blue ground spot, and vice versa. Colored slime enemies appear, moving on and matching one of the colors. When a slime is killed, it makes a big splat that overwrites the other color around it, including the spot you're standing on.

Desert: Here are sandworms that slowly (every other turn) grow bigger over time and can only be killed by trapping their head so they can't grow further.

Zebra: The terrain in this whimsical area looks very much like a zebra's stripes. You can step on the light stripes okay, but the black stripes will crumble beneath your feet like in the Land of Eternal Motion.

Ivory Tower: This clever area has "gravity." When you enter, the camera rotates to pick the direction of the Great Wall you entered from as "down." The way the game's description describes it,

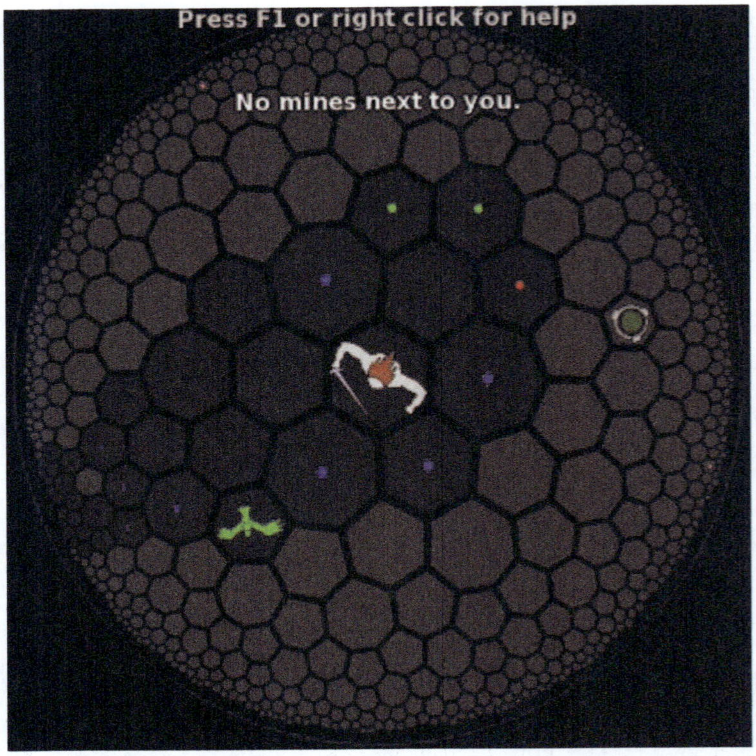

Figure 44.5

Minefield

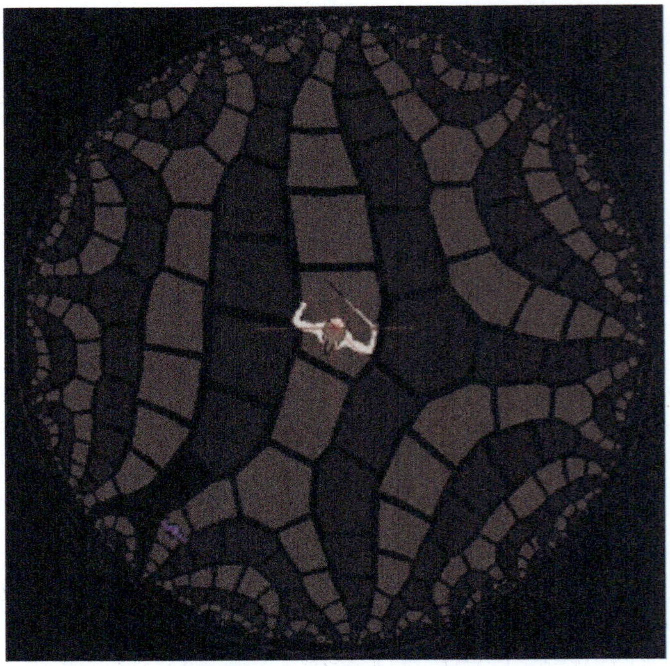

Figure 44.6

Zebra

there are "stable" and "unstable" spaces. Stable spaces have walls beneath them, or are "platform" spaces. You can go any adjacent space from a stable space, but unstable spaces you can only leave by going in a "down" direction, unless it's to a stable space. Depending on how you move, gravity can change direction. Moving up from stable into unstable spaces feels kind of like "jumping," like in a platformer, and going from unstable to stable spaces above you is like grabbing hold of a ledge. Because your movements are unusually limited here, be careful around enemy gargoyles. It's easy to get caught in inescapable situations.

44.5 Further Reading

HyperRogue's website (https://roguetemple.com/z/hyper/). Also from that site, the game's FAQ and a light math description of some of the shapes that can be encountered. Creator Zeno Rogue has a blog and a list of other projects and is on Twitter.

(*January 2020*: In the four years since this chapter was written, HyperRogue has grown significantly and now contains many new lands and other features besides. Check it out!)

45

Super-Rogue, Banished to the Deeper Dungeons

June 2008 Rogue was certainly not the first CRPG. Wizardry: Proving Grounds of the Mad Overlord probably made it out months ahead. Before then, there were interesting, relatively unknown Dungeons & Dragons-inspired games for the PLATO computer network, which might get looked at themselves here, eventually. But Rogue's take on the basic concept adapted some aspects of Dungeons & Dragons that usually got ignored by the others. As D&D evolved, in fact, that game itself abandoned the very ideals that Rogue took to heart: discovery, player improvisation and the amassing of tremendous piles of loot.

Rogue was not a niche game at this time. It was one of the most played games in campus timeshare computer labs, a genuine phenomenon among its audience. Rogue keeps a score list because it was designed to be played in this kind of environment, with lots of people shooting for a spot on the board; later roguelikes lost that sense of competition and community, but kept the score lists anyway. These days, unless the game is played on a public internet server like alt.org, roguelike score lists tend to fill up with the same player. Back in Rogue's heyday, however, competition for the top spots could be fierce.

Soon after Rogue's original release, a number of similar games began to make the rounds of these computer labs. They were the original roguelikes, games that took inspiration from Rogue itself more than even Dungeons & Dragons. Some of these games incorporated Rogue's name in its own: XRogue, Ultra Rogue, Advanced Rogue and Super-Rogue.

45.1 History of the Early Games

This was still a couple of years before the first modern roguelikes appeared on the scene. The first of those was Moria, a game that takes the same format as Rogue but has a more varied design. (*Note*: Moria actually seems like it was created contemporary with the early roguelikes, but didn't get released outside its home school for a while.) Hack and Larn, with their own changes to Rogue's core play, came years afterward. We call the newer games roguelikes, but the early games really put emphasis into that word.

That is, they tended to be very difficult, with monsters that got stronger faster than the player could improve. They had a limited number of character classes, if any at all. They had relatively simple

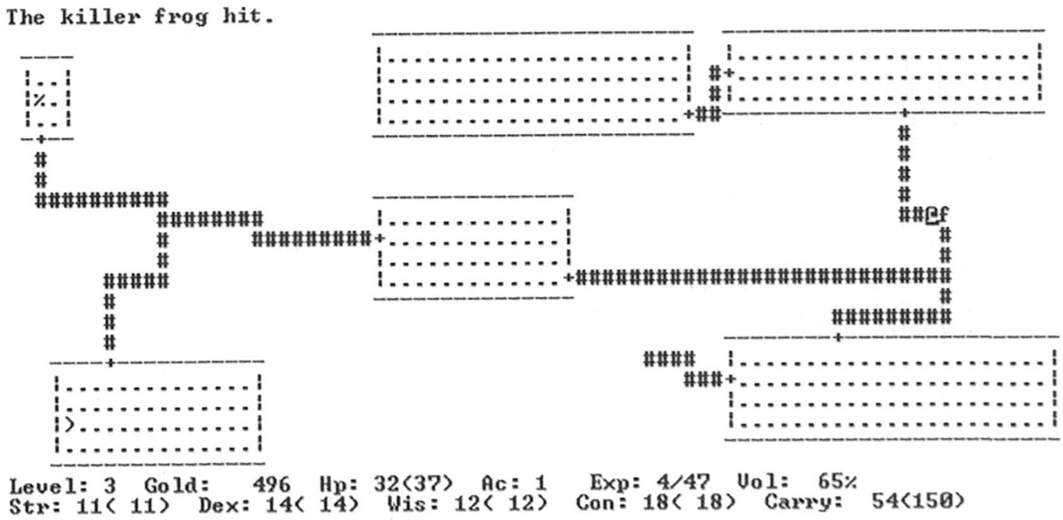

Figure 45.1

Super-Rogue

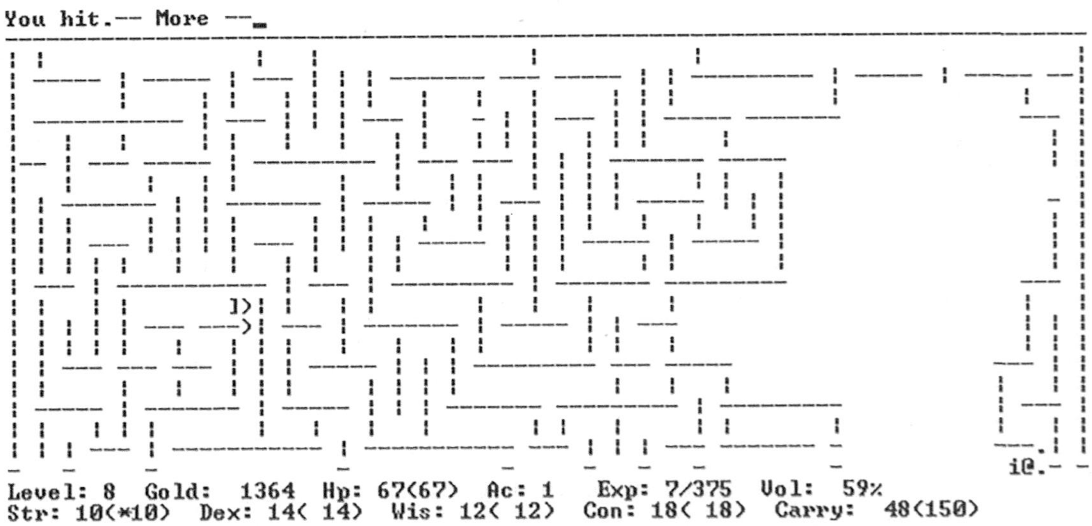

Figure 45.2

Super-Rogue

dungeons, often plundering Rogue's three-by-three grid generation algorithm. They were generally one-way trips through the dungeon until the player found a goal item. They had dungeons of practically infinite length, with the choice of winning or going on for higher scores figuring prominently at Amulet-depth.

And they used an item identification system identical to Rogue's, where scrolls of identify were in short supply and most items had to be discovered through trial and error. They most often used Rogue's basic items, with some extras thrown in. The new monsters and items were really what made the game; they were Rogue-with-extra-toppings.

These games are sometimes called the lost roguelikes, and the reasons for that are sad ones. This was back in the day before there was such a thing as an open source movement. Computer programmers had already begun to look at their source code with a proprietary eye. Rogue's own developers, after some public releases (a version of Rogue is still included with some distributions of bsdgames), began guarding against further source exposures, and in fact even produced commercial versions of the game for play on home computer systems; these are the Epyx Rogue releases. What is probably a pirated version of one of these (although it identifies itself as "Public Domain") is what is now known as "PC Rogue," which these days may be the most played (and hardest) version of the game.

45.2 How Games Become Lost

It's important here to note that Rogue may exist in a playable form now only because of those bsdgames releases and commercial games. The early roguelikes were lost because they had closed source and never got a release for home computer systems. Since they were developed solely for play on then-current, now-ancient, flavors of Unix, they could really be played only by folk who owned that increasingly esoteric flavor of hardware. Even if the source were available, it turns out they were often coded carelessly, relying on bizarre programming tricks like raw memory dumps for save functionality, making it difficult to run it on anything but the system it was made for.

As the years rolled by, it became harder and harder to get together the combination of hardware needed to play them. And if you could get the hardware, you were probably going to use it for some serious purpose, removed from the influence of playful college students.

So for a long time these games were simply forgotten. The middle-era games Moria, Larn and Hack arose, each either with public sources or with versions for systems with more longevity. The later-era roguelikes Angband and NetHack sprung from those. Then the internet reared up, surprising the hell out of everyone, and roguelike games began to find audiences of players who were long done with college, or had never attended. This is where ADOM and Dungeon Crawl enter the picture. All this while, the lost roguelikes receded further back in memory, remembered by few, mentioned but rarely.

For a while there, if one searched for "rogue" on the internet, after throwing out the X-Men links, and after reading through Boudewijn Waijers' excellent roguelike homepages (for a time the only real source of information on these games on the web), one would find a few tantalizing glimpses of the lost games, usually in the form of hint guides or FAQs socked away in the dustiest corners of FTP servers, still informing a vanished audience of enthusiasts about the best ways to conquer the lost dungeons. For a while it looked as if this sad affair would continue forever. Until . . .

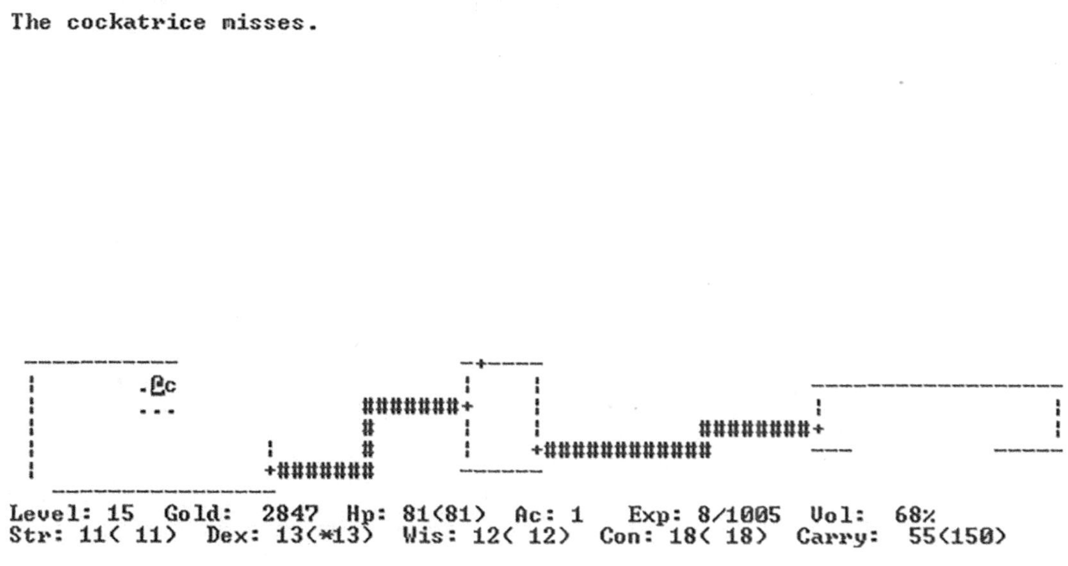

Figure 45.3

Super-Rogue

45.3 Please Contribute Today to the Save the Umber Hulk Foundation

The Roguelike Restoration Project remembers these old games and has for a couple of years now attempted to revive them. For all the reasons given above, this quest they have assumed is extremely difficult. Yet they have done, for the most part, an excellent job in hunting down the sources for these games, cleaning them up, and returning them and compiled binaries available to the gaming world. One of the games they've restored is Super-Rogue, a revision of the original game that, at first, doesn't seem to change the original that much at all.

Super-Rogue has the same one-way-dive, then-return quest format that Rogue has. Like Rogue, it uses nine-sector dungeons that aren't terribly challenging to explore. And the monsters get steadily more deadly as the player gets deeper, forcing him to turn to the wide array of random magic items he finds to survive.

In many ways, Super-Rogue is easier than the original game. Its food system is a lot more lenient. Characters get hungry in proportion to the weight of the stuff they're carrying compared to maximum capacity, and as a result, it's easy to build a big food surplus in the early levels when there's not that much stuff to carry. The least useful items to carry extras of, as in most roguelikes, are weapons and armor, which are also the heaviest things. Players will usually hit maximum pack volume before the weight limit, which is also worth a nice cumulative nutrition bonus.

Just before writing this column, I had finished a game of Super-Rogue that got to level 34. When I died, I had nearly a dozen food rations in inventory, and I had gotten up to 17 at one point. Even though I wore rings, which consume extra food, through most of the game, the only time I was in serious danger of starving was when I zapped a staff that turned out to be "of food absorption."

Rogue may have its roots solidly in Dungeons & Dragons, but it notably only took one statistic from that game, Strength. Super-Rogue also brings in Dexterity, Wisdom and Constitution, which each seem to function in the traditional, if obscure, ways. The monsters have been adjusted to account for this; many more foes have stat draining attacks than before. Rogue, in fact, only had giant ants (or rattlesnakes depending on the version), poison potions and poison dart traps to drain Strength, but it seems like half the monsters in Super-Rogue can inflict stat damage. The potion of restore strength from Rogue makes its return as a magic item. Although its name is unchanged, it also seems to restore the other stats. And finally, although it takes a great while to do it, it seems that stats regenerate naturally over time.

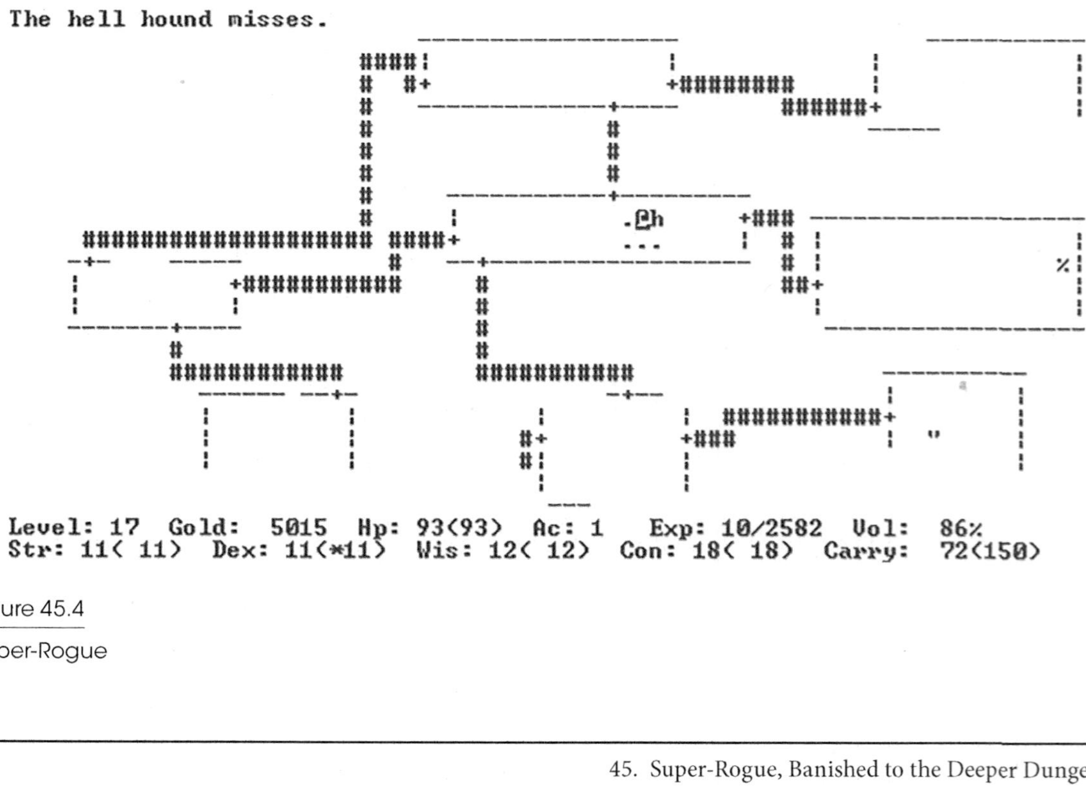

Figure 45.4

Super-Rogue

45.4 The Vrock's in the Details

But mostly this is Rogue with a longer dungeon (the Amulet was on level 26 in Rogue), and with new monsters and items. Some highlights:

It is the word that makes all NetHack players cringe in fear. I fought exactly one cockatrice during the long game. Whether they have an instant-stone attack as in Hack, or are just another monster, I was unable to determine, thank god.

Other monsters don't have some abilities one might presume given the game's origins in D&D. Xorns cannot travel through walls, and vampires don't seem to drain anything. Vampires, however, are instantly killed by lit spaces, which they won't enter willingly. This makes wands and scrolls of light extremely helpful deep in the dungeon. You even get experience for vampires that die because of light, whether they're visible to you or not.

The first difficult enemy in the dungeon is the imp, who can sometimes slow the player temporarily on a successful hit.

Wands of curing heal you, and also cure bad conditions. They are almost essential equipment when Umber Hulks start showing up with their dreaded confusion gaze.

Rings of speed carry a plus, and that plus is the number of extra turns you get per round. Were this unchecked, it would certainly make it among the most powerful items in any roguelike. However, they increase hunger a bit, and after many turns their pluses drain down to zero. If a +0 ring of speed is put on (not if it drains down to +0 from use), it seems that it becomes cursed.

One type of scroll teleports the player back to level 1 of the dungeon; this seems like a good thing. Another scroll "banishes you to the deeper regions," which sent me down to level 15 when the deepest I had seen was 7. I died soon after. The moral: scrolls can be a lot more treacherous here than in Rogue.

Rings of illumination permanently light up rooms as you enter them. A lot of the terror of the later levels of Rogue came from not being able to see more than one space in any direction. This makes the game seem a lot fairer, all by itself. (And yes, vampires hate this item.)

Finally, if you should decide to play this game (I do recommend it), here are a few other things that might help:

The Z command initiates a general, omni-directional zap of a wand. To direct it in a specific direction, use the P key. I also feel I should warn you that, unlike some other games they've ported, the Roguelike Restoration Project's edition of this game does not support keypad controls. You're stuck with the vi arrangement (hjkl & yubn) for this one.

You begin the game with a random weapon and armor here. My level 34 run got so far, in part, because I began it with +2 plate mail. Nothing quite like starting out with the game's best armor!

Some later levels take the form of full-screen mazes. Expert 'hackers might quake at the mention of this, as it is widely regarded that NetHack's play gets annoying in the second half of the dungeon, where most levels are mazes, but they only show up once in a while in Super-Rogue.

An attraction new to the dungeon, and largely ignored by later roguelikes, is the magic pools that occasionally crop up, about one per eight-or-so dungeon levels. Items can be dipped into them with Shift-D, which seems to increase the pluses on weapons. A given pool can only be dipped into once.

This may be the first roguelike game in which monsters actually may decide to run away if wounded in battle. Unlike in some games, here this is actually an effective tactic for them, and they usually resume the attack only if cornered or after they've had time to heal.

There is now the occasional shop in the dungeon, represented by a caret. While it may seem at first like a prototype of NetHack's shops (it's a room with stuff on the floor), there seems to be no way to steal. You aren't told what items are before buying them, but upon purchase they are fully identified. Shops only remain open long enough to make a few purchases, and upon leaving the level is regenerated.

Healing potions grant extra maximum HP as in Rogue, but you don't have to have maximum HP to take advantage of them. They are awarded whenever the potions are drunk.

Sometimes multiple items, especially potions, are found in one "bundle," another presaging of a later feature.

As in Hack and some other modern roguelikes, player possessions are identified at the end of the game.

Finally . . . this is probably a bug, although it might be one in the RRP's implementation of the game more than the original. The player gets a healing turn every time any key is pressed. Even illegal keys that don't allow the monsters to get a turn. This means, by pressing some unused key over and over, players can get all

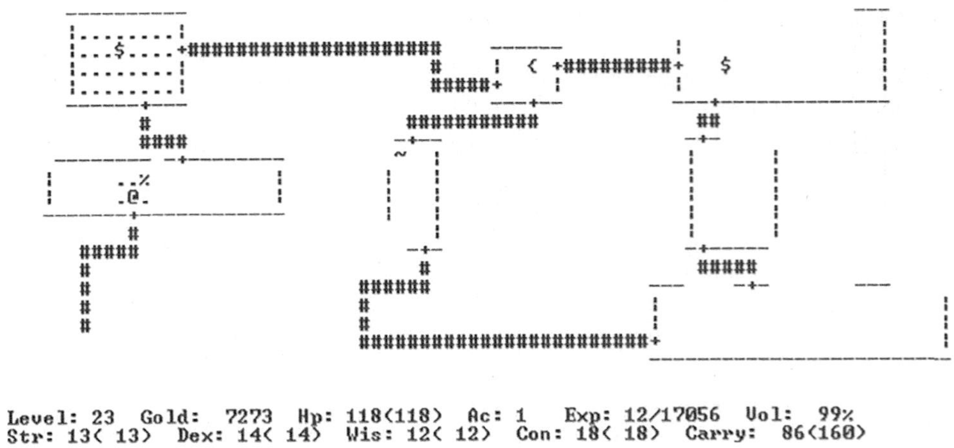

Figure 45.5

Super-Rogue

their hit points back without danger. I did not take advantage of this in my 34-level game; if I had, I suspect I could have won without trouble.

45.5 Playing Super-Rogue Today

As of January 2020, Super-Rogue 9.0 is difficult to obtain. You might be able to get source and a working version at coredumpcentral: https://coredumpcentral.org/roguelikes.html.

As you can probably tell from the screenshots, this is a seriously old-style roguelike. It's all ASCII, it uses no extended characters in its graphics, and it doesn't use color or character attributes. It only supports vi-style keys for movement. Still, from playing it over the past couple of weeks, it seems clear to me that there is more game here than its age might imply. Super-Rogue deserves recognition in the lineage of roguelike gaming. The Roguelike Restoration Project has done us all a great service in making it, and the other lost roguelikes, playable in the 21st century.

Extra fun for those who have read this far: a Usenet post from 1996 in which the creator of Moria talks about writing it and the early history of his game: https://groups.google.com/forum/#!original/rec.games.roguelike.moria/gFiS2tV_-AA/Gp7g-TfuJmUJ.

46

XRogue Has Not Yet Ceased to Be

March 2009 With the aid of the work of the Roguelike Restoration Project, let us return to the early days, when Rogue was the big thing in campus Unix labs and its several imitators became the first roguelike games.

Two games in particular concern us this time. Advanced Rogue was developed from 1984 to 1986 by Michael Morgan and Ken Dalka. It was a considerable expansion of the original game, with different monsters, multiple artifacts, trading posts and other ways to buy things, and a lot of other new features.

It introduced many features that Hack and NetHack would later pick up and run with, such as a three-level curse/bless system, a basic form of shops-as-rooms, charmable enemies and many kinds of enemies. This is also the game that introduced items of "miscellaneous magic," which brought to the game many different things that were explicated in the 1st edition Advanced Dungeons & Dragons DM's guide. Those items include gauntlets, boots, chimes, bracers and other objects, and probably form the inspiration for Hack's many equipment types and tools.

On the item curse/bless thing, also called "beatitude," NetHack and ADOM are best known for it today. NetHack picked it up, so I piece together from the NetHack Wiki page, as late as version 3.0.0. Curses are an important part of the identification game, and all of the major ones use them, but in most games it functions merely as a kind of glue for bad objects. Wearing, wielding or otherwise putting on a cursed item will make it impossible to remove until the curse is lifted, and that's all.

What NetHack, ADOM, Advanced Rogue and XRogue bring to the idea is two things. First, they expand the concept of curses to apply to all kinds of items. Equipment curses work the same way, but cursed one-use items like potions and scrolls perform their functions in a somehow diminished or even negative way. Whatever that way is depends on the thinking and/or sadism of the developer. A cursed potion of healing does a lot of damage in Advanced Rogue, but in NetHack it just heals less.

Second, these games implement blessings, which are functionally the opposite of curses, and cause objects to behave in a more useful, or at least less harmful, manner. A blessed item that comes under a curse will instead become uncursed, or "normal" in Advanced Rogue parlance. For equipment items this doesn't matter much, but blessed one-use items are often much nicer than the normal version, enchanting items for more than one plus, restoring more than one lost attribute point, and so on.

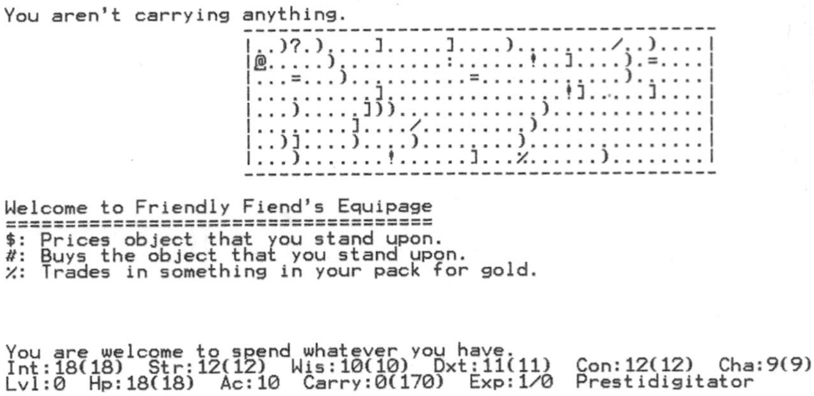

Figure 46.1

XRogue

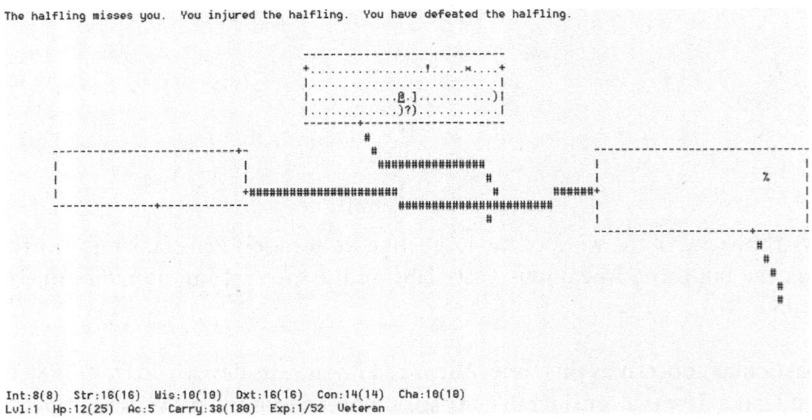

Figure 46.2

XRogue

46.1 People Come in Different Flavors, but Dragons Are Not Picky Eaters

Both games also present a large number of classes for the player to choose from. The selection reads just as if it were directly taken from the AD&D Player's Handbook: Fighter, Ranger, Paladin, Magic-User, Cleric, Thief, Assassin, Druid and Monk.

Five of the nine classes are spellcasters. Clerics and Paladins use "pray" spells (used with the "p" key). Druids and Rangers use "chant" spells ("c," lower-case). Magic-Users and Rangers can "cast" spells ("C," upper-case). Notice that Rangers get access to two of the spell categories; they are the only class able to use more than one variety. Only the magic specialists get the full ability in a class. Spell selection appears to be determined by the combination of experience level and relevant statistic. Magicians, for example, gain extra spells when either their level or intelligence increases. Most classes eventually get 16 different spells, and get them fairly early. The non-specialist spellcasters get them at a slower rate.

It is important for you to know, should you decide to play this game, that even magic-users will do a lot of hand-to-hand fighting. This game doesn't use the traditional concept of what an RPG magic-user is like. You will do far more killing hand-to-hand here than blasting from a distance. In my longest test game I had a magic-user get to dungeon level 31, learning all the spells for that class, and while he did pick up several attack spells they used up so much magic power that they were almost valueless. Most of my magic points went into casting Identify, which as usual is a tremendous advantage in a game like this.

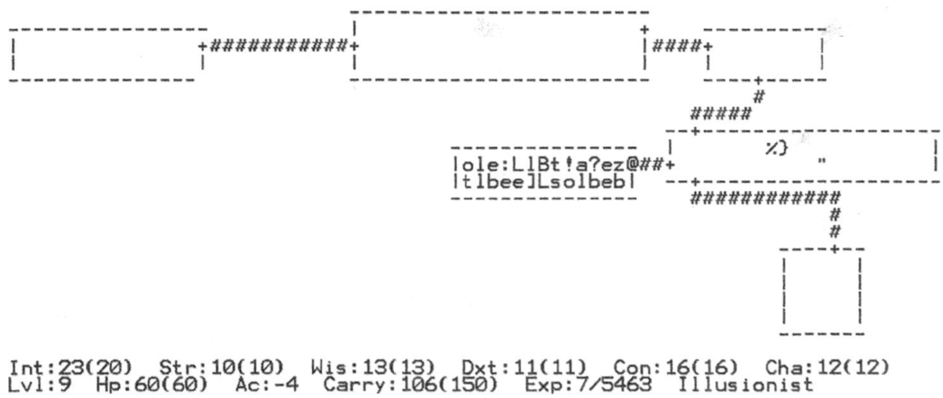

Figure 46.3

XRogue

46.2 The Stuff That Games Are Made Of

To return to the items, there is a surprisingly large number of things to discover, in XRogue in particular. The game doesn't have as many items as Angband or NetHack, but the number is still quite high. One thing about roguelike games that don't bias item generation depending on depth or difficulty is that most things become identified fairly early. This tends to be especially true of NetHack, but in XRogue I was still identifying things through to the last level I was able to reach. The relevant ratio is items possible over items generated during a game. The lower this value, the more likely, and the sooner, the player will be able to identify everything in a single game.

More dungeon levels generally mean more items generated. It's easy to make the dungeon longer in a roguelike since each level is procedurally generated, but there is currently no easy way to procedurally design and implement an item. Each item type must be custom designed and programmed while generating larger dungeon maps is usually pretty simple, so most roguelikes have a much larger amount of dungeon relative to the number of possible items. This is unlike the original Rogue where the ratio was balanced fairly well between the two, and many items didn't normally appear in a single play. XRogue has a lot of repeat items, but it does provide a good supply of possible loot.

Advanced Rogue was one of the earliest roguelikes to support the full range of D&D statistics (even NetHack didn't use Charisma until version 3.0.0), and some of the most useful items in these games are potions of gain ability. Unlike Hack's version of the potion, this item comes in different "flavors," one per statistic, which are revealed for all of them upon identifying one. These potions are fairly common, and drinking one (provided it's not cursed) adds one (for normal) or two (for blessed) points in its chosen attribute score. The thing about this is that while players are forced to begin the game with no stat above 18, in-game stats can get as high as 50, and with rings can go even higher. Some food items also increase stats.

Stats can go down, especially from the attacks of some monsters, but that can be undone with restore ability potions, and the upward pressure from all those stat potions is considerable, greatly increasing a character's power as they consume the potions they find. It's harder to design monsters when player abilities can vary so greatly, so most roguelikes have fairly low limits on maximum stat growth for this reason, but that design strategy itself has a drawback: at the end of many won games most characters look fairly similar to each other, having had long ago boosted all their stats to the maximum allowed. Even though stat-raising potions in XRogue are fairly common, the ceiling is so high that even by the end few players will have reached it. Between the two approaches, I think I actually prefer XRogue's.

Another highly useful item is the scroll of enchantment. Other roguelikes usually separate enchantment scrolls into weapon and armor, but these games combine them into a single item that can be used on many kinds of things. When used on miscellaneous stuff, the scroll most commonly serves to bless the item. Permanent equipment plus-raising is a characteristic of Hack-style roguelikes, and again, most of those games impose strict limits on enchantment levels. Dipping an item into a magic pool may also increase its plus, but this is risky as there's also a chance it'll randomly decide to set the item's pluses to negative levels and curse it! Most pools will enchant items, but the higher the item's plus gets, the more the player stands to lose if the next pool is cursed. XRogue doesn't seem to have an easily obtained limit on pluses, again unlike most other roguelikes. The longer the dungeon gets, the higher stats become unless they're capped, but capping them would make those enchantment sources less valuable to the player.

One thing these two games do that's entirely different from all other roguelikes I've seen is that they allow the player to wear up to eight rings, far more than the two that are standard in most of these games. They appear to increase hunger a little bit each (except for rings of slow digestion), but food is common enough that it doesn't tend to be a problem. The tradeoff is that there are so many useful ring abilities, and potentially great benefits from stacked stat-increasing rings, that the player must choose between the special powers he receives from them. Also, the inventory in Advanced Rogue and XRogue is limited to only 26 items. There are magic items that allow the player to get around this limit for scrolls and potions, but there is no such item for rings, and to be worn anyway they'd have to be in the main inventory. Inventory limits get harsher the more possible items the player can find and have. While 26 items is the same limit as in Rogue, there are many more items in ARogue and XRogue, enough that the player must often think about what to leave behind.

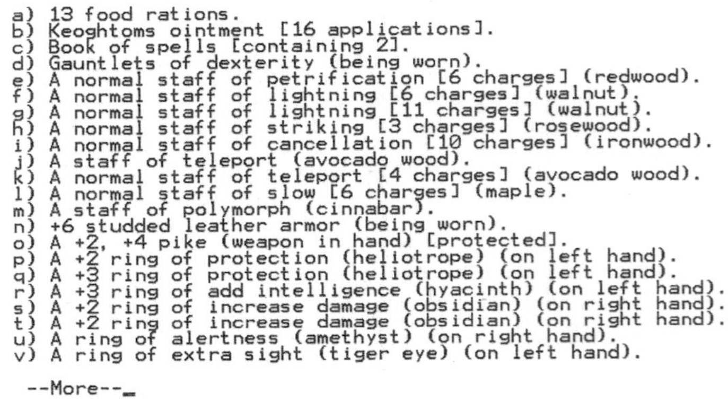

Figure 46.4

XRogue

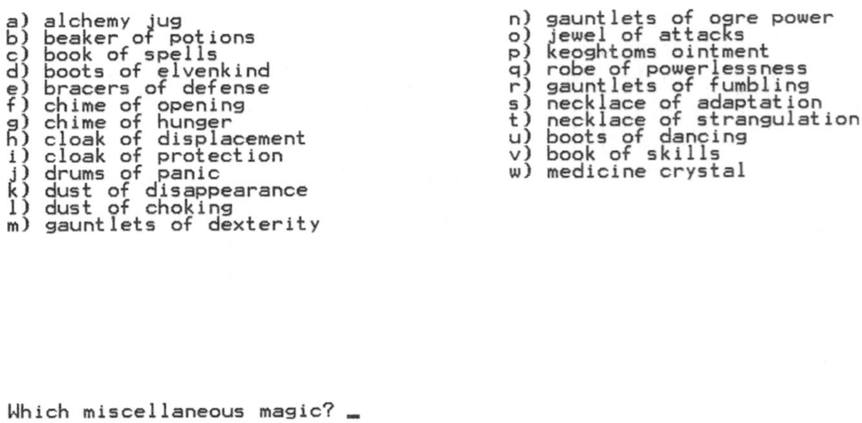

Figure 46.5

XRogue

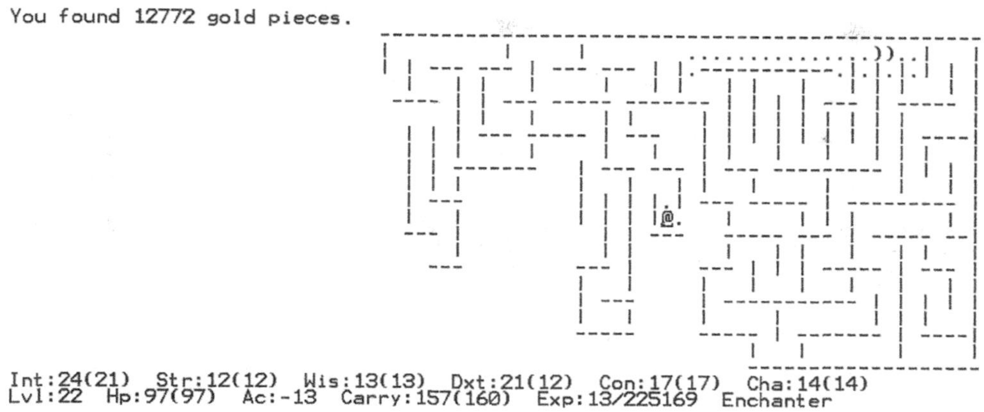

Figure 46.6

XRogue

Another interesting item present in the game is the scroll of charming. Yes, XRogue allows players to have pets and even take them between levels with him if it's in the same room. Yes, this is also a NetHack feature. I don't think pets grow in power naturally as they do in NetHack so they tend not to be useful in the long-term, but they make good cannon fodder. The game doesn't seem to punish you for pet abuse as NetHack does.

There is even an extensive selection of artifacts in the game, which are used for goal items as well as having functions of their own, but I have so far been unable to get deep enough into the game to report on those . . .

46.3 Here Be Dragons . . . and a Selection of Five Other Monsters, Chosen Randomly

The monster selection of XRogue is fairly extensive. Cockatrices are in there, as are Lava Children (special in that weapon hits go through armor; a couple of wands are useful against them, though), several varieties of dragon, and many many many many more. Interestingly for such an early roguelike, enemies can pick up and use some items they find lying around the dungeon floor, another surprisingly NetHackish feature.

Kobolds, a weak enemy among the first seen, can pick up and use any weapon, potentially transforming one into a heavy-hitter. Lamias, found in the middle-to-deep dungeon, can use wands, which is especially dangerous because unlike NetHack, wands don't feel like they've been nerfed here in case of accident or monster use. An "ordinary" attack wand can do significant damage even to a high-level character.

The monster generation routines at work here should be explicated, to bring it into the larger roguelike picture. The primary monster generation algorithm in roguelikes, and the one used here, is the one introduced by Rogue, generation by area. Each level has a selection of monsters that can show up. As the player makes it to deeper levels, some monsters are retired and others introduced.

This gives each level a consistent character that doesn't change even if the layout and precise mix of monsters present does. Some games that do this, like Angband, force the player to rely upon it in order to avoid running into certain highly powerful monsters before he's ready. NetHack, on the other hand, mixes the foes up a bit by partly using the player's experience level to influence generation; even if the player stays indefinitely on a single level, if he gains experience the monsters will still slowly improve.

There are also a couple of special areas the player can accidently end up in, which have a few special monsters of their own. But we'll get to that soon . . .

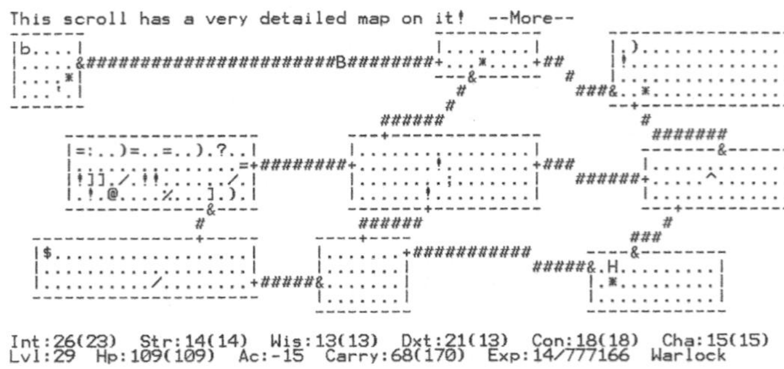

Figure 46.7

46.4 In the Outer Region . . . We Control the Horticulture! We Control the Vertebrates!

The most surprising thing to find in the game is the varied dungeon areas. There are two primary types, each of which tied to a certain type of trap; a later version of this concept features heavily into the later areas of Dungeon Crawl, when the player can get banished to labyrinths, the Abyss or Pandemonium.

The first type of area is quite similar, in fact, to Crawl's labyrinths. It's a single-screen maze with an exit hidden somewhere within. Unlike Super-Rogue these are not in place of a regular dungeon, and unlike Hack and NetHack it's not the entirety of the deeper dungeon, which often becomes tiresome there. They are filled with an abundance of monsters, but also many items, more than on a typical level. There appear to be some monsters that are either more common there, or only appear in mazes; in my long game, I think I only met lava children while in one, a trying predicament since the usual "Hulk smash" enemy handling technique is useless against them.

But yes, we've seen the first kind of special area before. The second type though . . . wow.

Picture this. It's the mid-'80s and you're in a Unix computer lab. You're wandering around an ASCII dungeon, killing monsters, finding loot. It's a cool game, you might think, but all the levels have been pretty much like you've seen in other Rogue variants, the 3x3 grid of rooms and passages. But then you accidentally step on a "wormhole" trap and suddenly you're in a confusing screen filled with non-dungeonish character types. Monsters are everywhere, but there are no items to be found. After a while you might see a message, "The sun goes down," and most of the characters, all those except those right around you, disappear as your range of vision decreases.

Further, and you probably only discover this accidentally, if you walk to and off the edge of the screen, the whole board changes. Walk back on and the board changes back to how it was. The layout of this strange area is persistent! It does reset the monsters in the area, though. Getting out of the zone turns out to be rather difficult, as not many of the screens contain a staircase back into the dungeon!

This unusual zone is called the "outer region," the strange ASCII characters turn out to represent mountains and forests, and it's strange how, even today, happening upon it the first time can be a bit of a shock. It has a day and night cycle, and is persistent within the same game. It originated in Advanced Rogue, but XRogue improved it in a number of ways, such as allowing items to be generated there. (Including food, because it was easy to starve in the original game's outer region.)

Also, while Advanced Rogue's outer region monsters are simply those that were in the dungeon, XRogue's are all prehistoric monsters, including a good number of dinosaurs. In fact, the level of the dinos is adjusted to be similar to that of the dungeon level you left. Facing them can still be a challenge regardless, since the relatively wide-open layout, and good number of summoning monsters among them, make it easy to get swamped by foes. The outer region is not necessarily bad, however, because whatever level the dinosaurs are generated as, they tend to be fairly ordinary monsters. Some of the XRogue dungeon opposition in certain levels can be very trying to deal with; the "jermilane," a tenacious monster with many annoying attacks and some immunity to weapons comes to mind. It's easy to gain a surprising number of experience points during even a few screens of outer region travel.

(By the way, if you would like to explore the outer region yourself, if you take the upstairs on level 1 of the dungeon without your goal artifact, the game will transport you to a level 1 outer region zone. Good luck finding the way back in!)

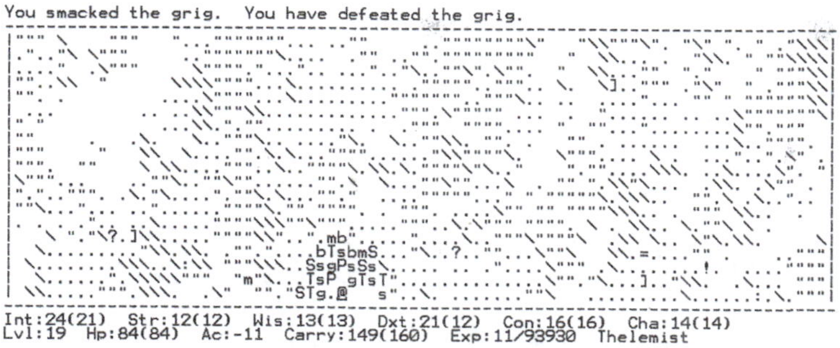

Figure 46.8

Xrogue's outer region

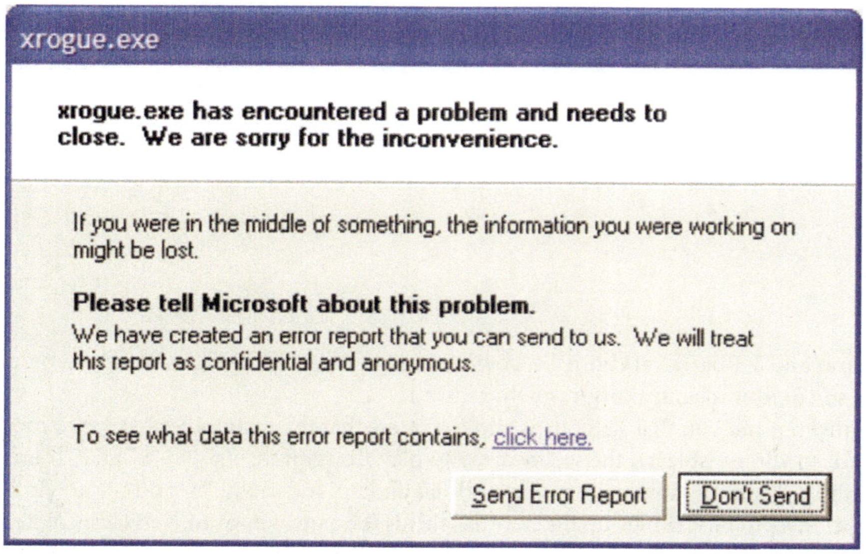

Figure 46.9

The result of some XRogue bug

46.5 You'd Think a Stone Dungeon Would Be Sturdier . . . .

I wish my experience with the game was all this positive, but unfortunately, like Super-Rogue, my best game was ended not by getting attacked by a dangerous monster or stumbling upon a deadly trap, but from the game crashing. I had managed to get through over 30 levels at the time and had identified nearly all the non-artifact objects in the game. Artifacts start showing up around level 40, so I was particularly upset to have my adventure ended in so ignominious a manner. All I can suggest is, if you decide to play XRogue yourself, be sure to save and back up every few levels. Yes, I know you're not supposed to do this, but games aren't supposed to crash either, and yet it obviously happens with this one. My warning is delivered. Of course, you are expected to delete the backup save if you honestly die. Duh.

It is telling, really, how many features Hack and NetHack appear to have lifted from Advanced Rogue. XRogue plays a bit like an alternate universe NetHack, with many similar features but different strategies. It is definitely far less reliant on spoilers to do well, and in overall difficulty is probably on the easier end of the spectrum.

I am sad to say, however, that we will never see another official version of XRogue. Its creator and developer Robert Pietkivitch died in a car crash in 2002, becoming the third roguelike developer, to my knowledge, to have died in the 28 years since Rogue's creation. (The others are Noah Morgan, creator of Larn, and Izchak Miller of the NetHack DevTeam.) It is still possible that the current maintiners of the Roguelike Restoration Project will add in features like numpad support (ARogue already has it).

A

Some Information of Use to New Players of Advanced Rogue and XRogue

Advanced Rogue and XRogue can both be obtained, as of January 2020, from the same place as Super-Rogue, at: https://coredumpcentral.org/roguelikes.html.

First off, I must remind you that XRogue is another game that the maintainer has yet to modify to support the number pad, so you must learn the vi key array to play. To remind: "h," "j," "k" and "l" are left, down, up and right in order. "y" and "u" are diagonals up-and-left and up-and-right. "b" and "n" are down-and-left and down-and-right. Also, to pick things up hit comma (this is the same key as in NetHack). Note that Advanced Rogue is an earlier, simpler game, but it has been modified to allow the keypad for movement; however, if you turn autopickup off, the pick-up key is Shift-P.

In both games, Ctrl-"r" repeats the last message. In XRogue only, Ctrl-"e" reveals your hunger level, and Ctrl-"o" provides a list of active effects both positive and negative. One command weirdness, compared to other roguelikes, is that wearing both armor and rings is done with the Shift-W, Wear command, and Shift-T, "Take Off," removes them. Most roguelikes use other keys, Shift-P and Shift-R, to handle accessories.

You begin the game in a trading post, but empty-handed except for a good quantity of gold. To check how much you are carrying, press Shift-8 (that is, an asterisk). The shopping keys are printed on-screen while you are here. The starting trading post has no limit on the number of things you can buy, but posts you find in the dungeon do. You do not begin with any items, so make sure to pick out some good equipment with your starting funds. (Note that only "fighter-types" can use two-handed swords, so if you're primarily a spellcaster don't bother buying one. I haven't yet tried to see if a mage can wear heavy armor.)

The impulse to start off in a new role-playing game is sometimes to play a fighter, but in fact your first games should probably be as a magic user, which are not actually weak physically so long as you give him average strength in the point-assign character creation. And as long as they start with high intelligence they'll begin with the Identify spell. You should only use spells for identification and curse removal for many levels. Even when you get attack spells, they cost so much that you'll not be able to rely upon them.

Natural healing, in XRogue, is a bit slower than usual in roguelike dungeons until (I believe) your Constitution gets sufficiently high. Experience level also likely plays a role.

An odd thing about both games is that, while Rogue's corridors always meandered at right-angles, here they can have diagonal extents. You must travel diagonally through those corridors, even if it looks like you should be able to walk orthogonally. In mazes, too, corners cannot be cut diagonally around walls, and neither can they be even in the outer region—unless the game determines that two spaces are meant to be diagonally connected, in which case *only* the diagonal move will work. Still, so long as you realize what's happening when your @-sign refuses to take a step, this is only a minor problem most of the time.

In difficulty, the game is a bit easier than Rogue and NetHack in the early going, although death is still common. A lot depends on how quickly you can get your equipment improved. In my level 31 game, monsters almost never hit my magic-user in the later levels, possibly because he was wearing +10 studded leather armor and two rings of protection. I believe I would have had a good shot at winning if the game hadn't been killed by a monster named ntdll.dll.

I don't pretend these lists are exhaustive, but they might help out a bit. These are spoilers, so don't read these if you wish to discover everything for yourself. Really, I discovered all of this from only a couple of games of playing an identify-happy magic user, so it's not like this stuff is a particularly big secret. If you've played some amount of Hack or NetHack, some of these things may seem a bit familiar.

- Scrolls
  - Identify.
  - Cure disease.
  - Hold monster.
  - Remove curse (asks for an item to work on).
  - Monster confusion.
  - Gold detection.
  - Trap finding.
  - Light.
  - Enchantment (works on many kinds of items).
  - Protection. (Shields a given item from damage. However, this will not save an item from a cursed fountain.)
  - Create monster.
  - Runes (fireball goes off when read, damaging reader).
  - Petrification (not tried, too scared).
  - Acquirement. (A predecessor of NetHack's wishes, this allows you to choose from nearly any item in the game!)
  - Aggravate monster.
  - Genocide.
  - Magic mapping.
  - Scare monster. (The secret use of this is the same as Rogue and Hack, but doesn't seem to operate if it's cursed.)
  - Charm monster (picks a nearby monster to operate on).

- Potions
  - Magic detection.
  - Monster detection.
  - Haste self (lasts surprisingly long, but don't drink when already fast though or you pass out).
  - Lightning protection (turns skin blue).
  - Fire resistance.
  - Cold resistance.
  - See invisible.
  - Healing. (Increases max HP when at full health. Note that the game contains no "Extra Healing" or "Full Healing," although a blessed potion is similar.)
  - Flying.
  - Skill (temporary level boost).
  - Phasing (allows walking through walls for a good while).
  - Invisibility. (A drawback is that it makes your character symbol a space. Use the blinking cursor to determine your position.)
  - Poison.

- Raise level.
- Clear thought.
- Restore ability (Unless blessed only restores one point. This is changed from Rogue.)
- Gain ability. (There are six versions, one per stat. Identifying one covers all the others.)

- Wands
  - Cold.
  - Polymorph.
  - Disintegration.
  - Charging.
  - Teleport.
  - Lightning.
  - Cancellation (disables monster special abilities).
  - Fire.
  - Curing (heals the player when zapped).
  - Wonder.
  - Staves (seem to be heavier than wands but otherwise similar).
  - Drain life.
  - Magic missile.
  - Confusion.
  - Petrifaction.
  - Teleport.
  - Striking.
  - Charging.

- Rings
  - Alertness.
  - Add (stat) (carries a plus, there's types for Strength, Dexterity and Intelligence at least, and probably others).
  - Teleportation.
  - Increase damage (carries a plus).
  - Aggravate monster.
  - Extra sight.
  - Heroism.
  - Warmth.
  - Teleport control (also borrowed by Hack).
  - Carrying (halves weight of stuff carried, but provides no help with the 26 letter limitation).
  - Fear.
  - Fire resistance (probably Cold Resistance and Lightning Resistance, too).
  - Slow digestion.
  - Protection (carries a plus).
  - Sustain ability.
  - Illumination.
  - Searching.

- Food

  (*Note:* some food items have special effects upon the player. It seems that these may change from game to game.)

  - Food ration.
  - Slime-mold (can be used to bribe monsters).
  - Soursop.
  - Sweetsop.
  - Peach.

- Banana.
- Strawberry.
- Candleberry.
- Elderberry.
- Caprifig.
- Guanabana.
- Pitanga.

- Miscellaneous Items (Most Used with Ctrl-"u")
  - Keoghtoms ointment (heals some damage and removes some afflictions).
  - Book of Spells. (Storage for scrolls; can hold up to 20 each. Items in storage weigh nothing.)
  - Beaker of Potions (same, but for potions).
  - Alchemy Jug (contains a large quantity of potion liquid, it seems).
  - Gauntlets of Dexterity (sets Dexterity to 21).
  - Gauntlets of Ogre Power (same for Strength).
  - Gauntlets of Fumbling.
  - Jewel of Attacks. (The 1st Edition AD&D Dungeon Master's Guide says it's a bad item that increases the chance of encountering monsters and makes them more tenacious.)
  - Dust of Disappearance.
  - Cloak of Displacement.
  - Book of Skills. (Grants free experience level, but class specific. You should probably beware of using this if your class does not match.)
  - Chime of Hunger.
  - Chime of Opening.
  - Boots of Elvenkind.
  - Necklace of Strangulation. (In both AD&D and NetHack this is a very, very bad item. It's probably about as bad here.)

- A Few Selected Monsters
  - Quartermaster: Non-hostile, tries to sell an item to the player. The only monster that appears throughout all levels of the dungeon.
  - Xvart: Appears in groups, can throw daggers, often drops daggers when killed
  - Fire beetle: Lights rooms while it's in them
  - Troglodyte: Emits a foul odor that can discomfit the player
  - Shrieker: Shrieks when hit. Probably attracts other monsters. AD&D says the shrieking might attract a purple worm, an extremely strong monster.
  - Lemure: Can summon a swarm of bats
  - Grey Ooze: Rusts armor (when it strikes) and weapons (when hit with one)
  - Zoo spore, Gas spore: Explores when hit, doing considerable damage. Note that the explosion does not destroy the spore, and it can explode again if struck once more. These can also harm other nearby monsters, and attacking one from a distance can be an effective way to help clear a room, even if the monsters are tough.
  - Giant ant: Can sting to reduce strength
  - Blink dog: Teleports around the player
  - Violet fungi: Can shriek as a shrieker, and can summon in more violet fungi near to the player
  - Shadow: Can chill with a touch, doing major damage and draining strength; can move through walls; a dangerous opponent
  - Blindheim: Can blind with a gaze; difficult to deal with
  - Cockatrice: Beware
  - Lava Child: Cannot be hit with weapons; also immune to lightning (try cancellation before whacking)
  - Jackalwere: Can cause sleep
  - Basilisk: Can cause paralysis with a gaze (thankfully, appears to be unable to turn the player into stone)
  - Treant: Can summon other treants

- Jacaranda: Can steal gold; can summon Zombies; can cause uncontrollable dancing; can cause blindness; difficult to hit with weapons; a tough customer
- Wererat: Can summon Giant Rats
- Zombie: For some reason, they're often invisible.
- Outer region monsters: Grig, Trilobite, Pterodactyl (flies), Theropod (flies, explodes), Sauropod (can summon grigs), Brontosaurus, Sloth (can summon trilobites), Mastodon

47

Larn, or, I Hocked the Car to Buy a Lance of Death

April 2008 We've covered all of the current big-name roguelikes, at least nominally, at this point, so let's look at one of the older games. Released back around 1986, Larn was one of Hack's chief competitors for the title of successor to Rogue.

Hack was known for killing characters with distressing frequency, and dismaying glee, so Larn was popular for being a much kinder game, although still not a pushover. It was one of the premier roguelikes on the Amiga side of the PC fence.

While it wasn't the first roguelike to use a town level (that was probably Moria), it was the first to give us multiple dungeons in the same game.

47.1 The Taxonomy of Larn

Roguelikes may be categorized into those that take after Hack (like NetHack) and those that take after Moria (like Angband), but Larn borrows from both. Like Moria, it uses menu shops, the character's experience growth is more important than the stuff he's carrying, item generation is weighted by dungeon depth, and there's a surface town that must be returned repeatedly.

But like Hack, levels are persistent, the dungeon itself has a kind of character, there are "features" in the dungeon that can be taken advantage of or cause problems, and there is a strong ethic of powergaming: of trying find ways to use the rules in such a way as to gain an overwhelming advantage.

In other ways Larn takes most after Rogue, and it has several unique ideas all its own. The most Rogueish thing about it, besides its being a roguelike of course, is the game's hard time limit. Rogue starts the player off with a single food ration, and the player must explore fast enough to find more as he descends into the dungeon or he'll starve to death.

This mechanic constantly pushes him downward to find more food, since the only reliable way of generating more is to explore more levels, and prevents him from hanging out on the upper levels, endlessly killing weak monsters to build experience. Larn doesn't have food other than fortune cookies, which aren't of nutritional value but provide hints to the player. It does, however, have a time limit.

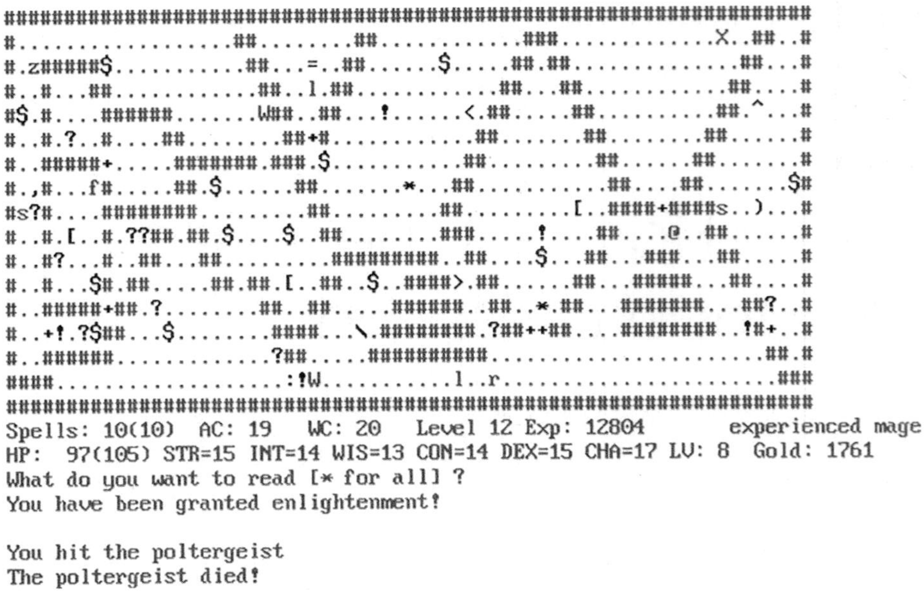

Figure 47.1

Larn

At the start of the game, the player is informed that his character's daughter is ill and will die of "dianthoritis" in 300 "mobuls" of time. It is rumored that somewhere in the dungeon there is a way to cure it, and that is what the player ultimately searches for.

Unlike Rogue, the player may travel freely between dungeon levels and use his time in different ways. In addition to exploring the dungeons, there's a bank in which deposited gold earns interest over time, and there is a university in the town level in which the player can spend mobuls taking courses in fighting, spellcasting or "contemporary dance."

The limit isn't as hard as it might seem, as one type of item that can be found or purchased, scrolls of time warp, has as its sole purpose the setting back of the clock a random number of time units. It's never a huge amount, but usually enough to be useful.

47.2 The Solution to All Your Monster Needs! Easy Installment Plan: One Installment, You Pay Now

To get back to Larn and the concept of powergaming. . . . The tradition of finding ways to game the power curve has its roots in the earliest days of Dungeons & Dragons, and is an essential aspect of most roguelikes. But Larn takes things to an entertaining extreme. One of the places in the town level is the DND Store, which helpfully sells nearly every object in the game, from clubs to scrolls of pulverization.

Unlike most roguelikes, many items can only be found in the store, including the most powerful equipment items. Among these is stainless steel plate armor, not only the best armor but it's completely rustproof. It's expensive, but not tremendously so, and it provides sufficient protection that most weaker monsters won't be able to even scratch the player.

Stainless steel plate armor is quite valuable, but there are still better items for sale. Foremost among them is the lance of death, quite possibly the most formidable weapon ever to be put into a roguelike game. This thing has incredible power, enough that it is bound to cause the player, the first time he gets one, to question the judgment of the game designer in including it. For the lance of death lives up to its name: any monster the lance strikes, from the lowliest kobold to the princes of demons, dies in one hit. All the power of a cockatrice corpse, but none of the risk.

Of course the lance costs a wheelbarrow of gold pieces. But its availability in the game's store, while seeming injudicious at first, turns out to be remarkably ingenious. The existence of the lance works because of Larn's unusual structure. You see, after starting out in town, most players descend into the game's ten-level

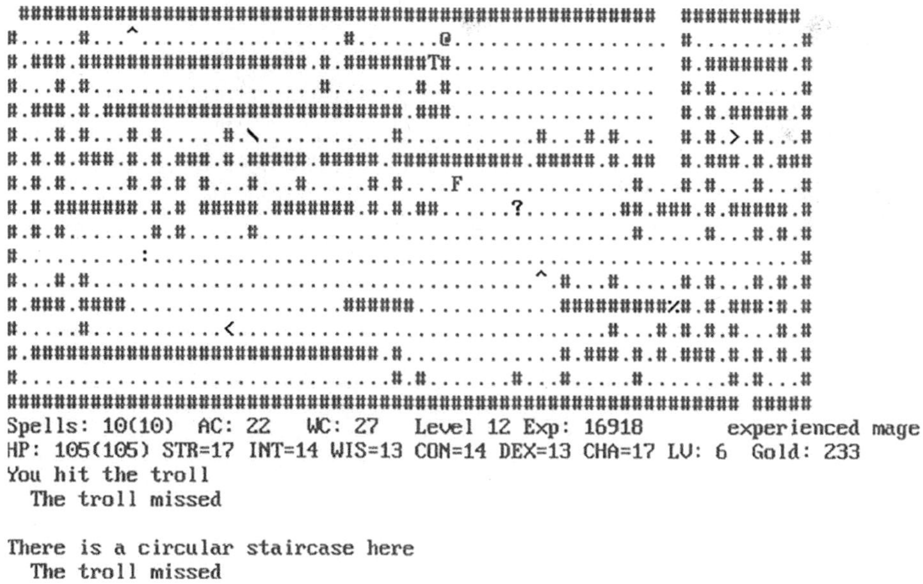

Figure 47.2

Larn

main dungeon to collect the game's big sparkly, the Eye of Larn, building experience and collecting equipment and gold pieces along the way in the traditional D&D manner.

Yet it turns out, the player doesn't want the Eye because of powers it grants, any protection it offers or because the gods will reward the player in exchange for it. He wants it because it can be sold to the bank for over 160,000 gold pieces, and the lance of death costs 165,000! See the connection?

But the Eye is at the bottom of the main dungeon. Why would the player need the lance if he can already defeat the demon guarding it? It's because there's a second dungeon to explore, which contains the magic potion that can save your daughter.

While it only has three levels, it is far more difficult than the main one and is chock full of dragons as well as other high-level opponents. An invisible demon prince stands over the potion you're looking for, which is about the only monster the lance of death doesn't immediately vanquish, just because it's so hard to hit the darn thing.

47.3 Larn Gameplay FAQ

If you should decide to play this game, and I greatly recommend it to first-time roguelike players for its relative lack of keyboard-smashing difficulty, here are answers to a few possible questions:

47.3.1 Where Do I Get It From?

Playing it from Windows is something of a mess, so it's probably better to use a Freenix to play the game. Word is that Larn is available from the NetBSD games collection.

(*January 2016*: The passage of time has not been kind to one's efforts to play Larn. There was a section in the original version of this chapter here on how to obtain a working version, but in the time since then most of the links have died. I must abandon you to your own means to find a working copy of the game. A version is on Steam as XLarn. The homepage to variant ULarn is at www.ularn.org/ An unofficial homepage for original Larn is at https://larn.org/.)

47.3.2 What Are the Basic Keys?

The DOS version has an option to use the numberpad instead of vi keys for movement; activate it by editing the configuration file. Typing a question-mark during the game brings up the help screens, which

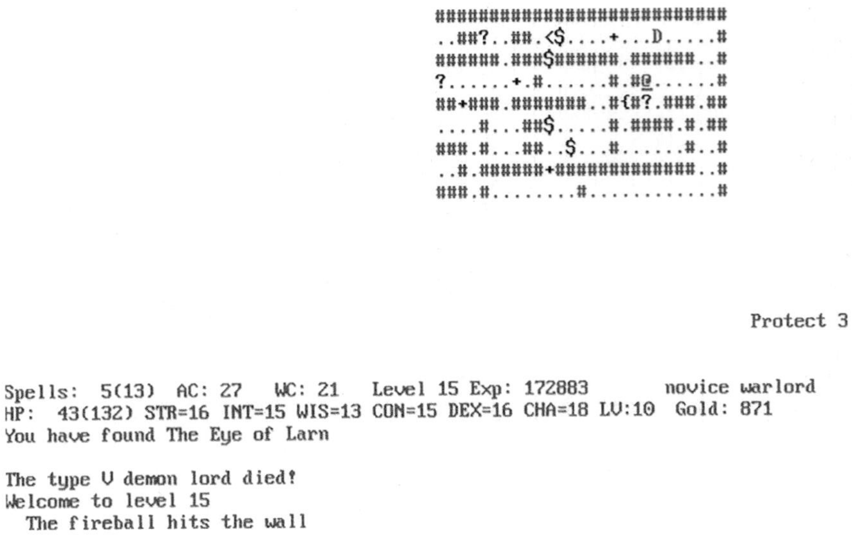

Figure 47.3

Larn

lead off with a list of commands. After that, it's mostly as in Rogue. Here are the basics; refer to help for the others:

Shift-E: Enter a location
Comma: Pick up an object
Period: Wait a turn without doing anything
I: Inventory
D: Drop
Q: Quaff, that is to say, drink
E: Eat
R: Read
W: Wield (a weapon)
Shift-W: Wear (armor or shields)
Shift-T: Take off (armor or shields)
C: Cast a spell
Shift-O: Open a door
Shift-C: Close a door
>: Go downstairs
<: Go upstairs
Shift-S: Save the game (but see below)
Shift-Q: Quit the game

Some of these commands will automatically prompt you if you're standing on the same space as a relevant item if you want to use it.

Note: the only version of Larn I could get to work satisfactorily on Windows XP was a DOS version of Larn 12.4.0. Yet even this version doesn't work perfectly: saved games work, but the game misidentifies them as having been modified and disqualifies them for the scoreboard.

47.3.3 I Started a Game and Now I'm in a Field with a Bunch of Numbers. What Does This Mean?

You're in the town level. The numbers are the locations of the various services available here. They are:

1. The player's home
2. The DND Store

3. The trading post
4. LRS Office (Larn Revenue Service)
5. The bank
6. The college
8. The main dungeon
9. The volcanic shaft

While the town is mostly safe, monsters can be generated here, and the clock does advance while walking around town.

47.3.4 How Do I Enter a Store/the Dungeon/the Bank/Whatever?

Press Shift-E, for 'e'nter. While Larn's keypresses mostly take after Rogue, including using < for upstairs and > for downstairs, Shift-E must be pressed to enter most numbered locations. The exception to this is 9, which must be entered with >, but you probably don't want to go there just yet.

47.3.5 The Messages at the Bottom of the Screen Seem Not to Make Any Sense, Is There Something Wrong With Them?

It's a weirdness of the game. There are five lines at the bottom of the screen reserved for messages to the player, but they don't scroll. Instead, the game reuses the lines over and over, replacing old messages with new ones in a cyclical manner. When the messages reach the bottom, the next one starts at the top again. There is always a blank line after the most recent message. It's not hard to get used to once you know what's happening.

47.3.6 Why Does My Inventory Consist of Five "a Magic Scroll"s and Four "a Magic Potion"s?

Larn uses a typical roguelike ID system, but it's implemented a little differently than in most games. Items' types are distinct from each other before identification, but the player isn't given any way to tell them apart until then. If you have eight magic potions they could all be the same type, or all different types, or a mixture.

If after drinking one it turns out to be healing, looking at your inventory afterward you might find that some of the other potions are now marked as "magic potion of healing." It's the same system as Rogue, but you don't get item descriptions like "bubbly potion" or "scroll labeled THANX MAUD." The upshot is, you don't have the information of how many of each unknown type of potion you have, a minor but important difference.

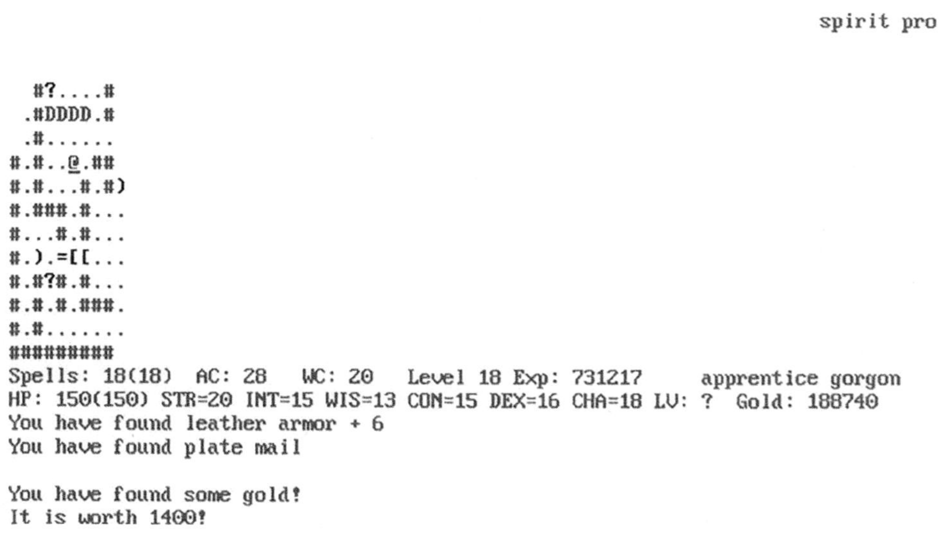

Figure 47.4

Larn

47.3.7 I Went Up/Down a Circular Staircase, but When I Came Out the Other Side I Wasn't at the Stairs from the Previous Level! How Come?

It's weird how many different roguelikes handle staircases in different ways:

- Rogue (and Shiren too for that matter) has only one staircase per level, which goes both up and down, but when you come out the other side you're actually put at a random location on the next level, which could be in the same room as the stairs but probably won't be.
- NetHack and Angband will always put you on a staircase back to the level you came from. NetHack has persistent dungeon levels, and so the staircases lend a kinda-sorta consistency across the levels.
- Larn mixes the two approaches. It has persistent levels, but still puts the player in a random location on the next floor when taking the stairs. Further, each level has separate up- and downstaircases for going to the next floor.

47.3.8 I've Found All These Rings and Things, but I Can't Find Any Way to Put Them on! Help!

This is one of the nicer idiosyncrasies of Larn. You're already wearing them! You get their effects just by carrying them around in your inventory.

This works well because there are no scrambled ring types in Larn, and generally no "bad" equipment items. All rings are known the moment they are found, none of them will mess you up, and you can wear as many as you can find. The tradeoff is that you can only carry so many items at once in Larn, fewer than even Rogue, so the more rings and such you're holding, the less treasure you can bring back on each trip, and thus the more trips necessary, and thus the more mobuls you end up using.

There are some other items in the game with special functions, like belts of striking, and they also work just by carrying them around. Generally, the only items you have to explicitly equip for use are weapons (command w for wield), and armor and shields (both Shift-W for wear).

(Quick trivia: Larn's system of no bad equipment, but unidentified potions and scrolls, is exactly the opposite of the system used in most of Shiren the Wanderer, in which one-shot magic items are known but magic equipment is unknown.)

47.3.9 What Are These Statues, Thrones, Mirrors and Altars Good for?

Various things actually. Gems can be pried off of thrones with a key command (Shift-R) and sat in with (s), and one can (p)ray to donate money at altars. Walking over an altar without giving up a proper donation, in fact, often results in summoning a monster. There are other risks involved with altars I'll leave it to you to discover, as well as with looting thrones. Statues can also provide the player with some material benefits, but utilizing them is not as straight-forward in this case. As for mirrors . . . well, I actually don't know about those. Any ideas?

47.3.10 What Is This Rectangular Region with the Door on One Edge?

That's a room, a small area typically filled with monsters and treasures. Actually there are normal rooms later on in the dungeon, but it's common to find monster lairs even in the early going. You can open a door by pressing Shift-O, which also works on chests. Both doors and chests are often trapped, and some of the traps are quite damaging (near the end level drain traps are common), so care should be taken when opening these.

47.3.11 What Do I Do with the Books and Chests?

You (r)ead them or (O)pen them. Books provide spells, and chests spill forth loot. Both disappear when used, and the effects of both vary in awesomeness according to the dungeon level they were found on. Chests are probably trapped. Both can be sold to the trading post unused for large amounts of gold, also varying according to the level they were found at.

47.3.12 How Do Spells Work?

When you read a book you get a three-letter code for a spell. You should probably write this down, as to cast it you'll have to enter it from the spell prompt (Shift-C). The prompt provides no indication of which letters you've typed by the way, like a password, so be careful in entering it. If you get the letters wrong, or on a random chance, the spell won't work. Most players will need some kind of distance attack spell to succeed (popular example: fireball), and some of the spells available later on in Larn are extremely powerful. The codes don't change from game to game, but they won't work unless you've gotten them from a book during the current game.

Some versions of the game will print a list of currently known spells and codes if you press Shift-D at the spellcasting prompt.

47.3.13 A Scroll of Gem Perfection? What Does That Do?

In increases the value of all gems you're carrying when it's read. This is another of Larn's clever bits: exploring while your inventory is full means you can't pick up the stuff that's lying around, but is good if you find a scroll of gem perfection to make all the jewels you've found much more valuable, or if you find a scroll of identify, which affects your whole inventory in Larn.

47.3.14 I've Been Teleported, but Now the Dungeon Level Is Listed As "?," What Gives?

Pits and teleport traps can send you to different levels of the dungeon. The question-mark represents the uncertainty of your character of which level he might be on. This seems like it's an attempt to replicate that D&D-brand horror from falling down a shaft and not knowing how bad the monsters around you are.

47.3.15 I've Made It to Level 10 of the Dungeon but I'm Being Attacked for Major Damage by Something I Can't See!

That's the demon who guards the Eye of Larn. He's invisible! You should stockpile as much healing as you can for this fight.

47.3.16 If I'm Just Going After It for Money to Buy the Lance of Death, Do I Really Have to Get the Eye of Larn?

Actually, no.

You need the lance of death to survive in the volcano; if you thought single dragons were bad in the main dungeon, wait until you face an entire densely packed floor of them. But it's possible to raise the money in other ways. As detailed at Master Gorgon's wonderful site The Larn Blog, there is a good alternate strategy for raising the cash.

Books and chests from the deep levels, if you can do without their contents, sell for huge sums at the trading post, some of them well over 10,000 gold. Even those from the early dungeon are worth surprising amounts of lucre. And money left in the bank accrues interest over time. It is completely possible to get the

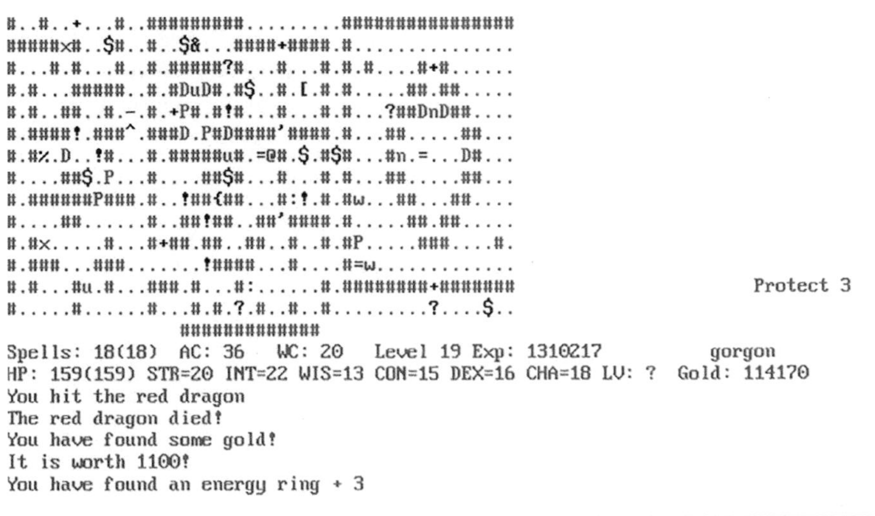

Figure 47.5

Larn

lance by building up funds this way, then jump straight into the volcano. Whether this is wise or not is left for you to decide, but gaining experience is easy with a lance of death.

47.3.17 Any Other Tips?

Some of these things may be seen as spoilers . . .

- There are purposes for many of the things found in the dungeon, but some may require some equipment to make use of.
- Don't step on a Holy Altar, if you can help it, unless you intend on paying some cash as a donation. The gods tend to get irate if their altars are crossed but ignored. Paying enough money can score you a long-lived protection spell.
- Be careful with traps late in the volcano, some pits may be bottomless.
- Potions of healing and fast healing can increase your maximum hit points, as in Rogue, when quaffed while uninjured.
- The game also uses Rogue's stat maximum system, where some monsters can drain stats but they can be instantly restored to maximum status with the right potion, and other potions increase maximums if drunk when that stat is at maximum.
- As is common in roguelikes, the game will let you wield nearly anything in your hands, including items that have little worth in battle. But in Larn, if you read a scroll of enchant weapon when holding such an item, you can increase its plus! In this manner, you can raise the plus on rings and miscellaneous items, and armor too, even though there exist scrolls of enchant armor.
- Get the stainless steel plate armor as soon as you can, as rust monster are common in the middle levels.
- Scrolls of pulverization can destroy a wall, but they can also damage monsters.
- There is a scroll of annihilation in the game that cannot be bought in the DND store.

47.3.18 Hey, I Just Won, but on the Next Game I Didn't Start with Any Equipment, and I Got a Message about Taxes! What the Heck?

Perhaps the most interesting of Larn's features is that, unlike most roguelikes, it has a dynamic difficulty level. There are ten levels of difficulty in the game, and the current game's challenge level is felt in various ways. For example, players at any difficulty greater than 0, the lowest level, don't begin with any equipment, and must make do as they can before they can raise the funds to buy the basic stuff from the store.

The default difficulty of the game starts at 0 on a new installation (or user, on a multiuser machine), but when the player wins, the next game will be one level harder. If you want to explicitly play a given difficulty, you can by invoking the game with the -H command line switch and the digit of the level you want to play, as in, "larn -H9."

In addition, after a player wins the game, the Larn Revenue Service will begin to take notice of him. In subsequent games, the player will be expected to pay a tax relative to the money he had upon winning. On Unix systems, the game will even send local email to the user's account informing him of the gold pieces due . . .

47.4 Acknowledgments

Some gameplay information was taken from The Larn Blog: http://larn-game.blogspot.com/.

48

Hack's Lost Brother

May 2007 The thing about roguelike games is the genre is seriously old. Rogue, a computer game with random dungeons, a full inventory and tremendous strategy, was created in 1980, about the same time as Pac-Man. In those 27 years since Rogue's birth we have seen a good many roguelike computer games, and it is no longer so easy to get to play some of them.

48.1 Genealogy of the Dungeons of Doom

Along those lines, the Roguelike Restoration Project is the incredibly noble effort to take some of these ancient games and make them playable under common operating systems. Among the eight games that can be found there are three versions of Rogue, two of Advanced Rogue and three other games with "rogue" in the title but that take increasing liberties with the play. Like Rogue, all of these are fairly playable today. Unlike Rogue (and like NetHack), they lose some of Rogue's clarity by adding so much to the game. But at least they still exist.

There are some other roguelikes it's getting harder to find nowadays. Moria, Hack, Larn and Omega were the first ones to branch further off from the tree, and there is little, if any, development going on in those branches now. None of these are so easy to find. At least Moria evolved into Angband, while Larn and Omega mostly stagnated. Hack, of course, would become the imposing NetHack, also called Gradewrecker and Thesisbane.

Hack, itself, inspired a few variants back in the day, and one of those is our focus this time: the game HackLite, a little-known variant that is most difficult to play these days because its main version was for Amiga home computers.

Hack was originally the branch-off roguelike to stick closest to Rogue. For example, it and its descendants still call many Rogue monsters by old names. NetHack's latest version contains giant ants, floating eyes, violet fungi, gnomes, invisible stalkers, jackals, kobolds, mimics, purple worms, quasits, rust monsters, umber hulks and xorn, but Rogue's does not, despite all these foes first appearing there. (Trivia moment: rumor has it the monster names and symbols were changed specifically as an attempt to thwart the automatic Rogue player Rog-O-Matic, but we've already covered that little program.)

In between Rogue and NetHack there were a few different Hack versions, games that were only in currency for a moment compared to their descendant's lifespan, but are still referenced fondly by NetHack's history file. Another version of Hack, one that doesn't get a lot of mention anymore because it was not part of NetHack's lineage, is HackLite, of which versions were made for DOS and the Amiga personal computer.

48.2 Meet the Wizard of Yendor's Lost Brother, Neil Yendor

Even while NetHack survived and prospered, HackLite sunk into obscurity, perhaps for two reasons. The first is right in the game's readme: "It is interesting to note that, in the world of Hack descendants, HackLite is the only one I know of that believes a limit on game complexity is a good thing." At a time when players seemed interested in the most detailed game experience possible, the existence of NetHack, which was composed by taking the best ideas from multiple Hack variants, must have seemed awfully compelling. These days there is a thriving side of the roguelike genre composed of games that try to rein in some of the complexity of which they are capable, so it could be said that HackLite was ahead of its time.

The other limitation was a longer-term issue. Hack's source code has long been public, even if not expressly open, back in those heady days when code was considered free by default if available. Thus it was that HackLite forked off of Hack and NetHack's source code right before NetHack switched to the "NetHack Public License," which was based off of the Bison license, and the nature of that beast should become obvious when I tell you it was produced by Richard Stallman. While NetHack ended up with a license that looks more than a little like the GPL, HackLite's source code was never released and remains obscure today. No source means no variants, no user-made patches and no development by anyone other than the author and his agents. Meanwhile NetHack has drawn repeatedly from the work of interested users, fosters a patch-writing culture, and its open nature early on attracted the infamous DevTeam.

There is one advantage to keeping a lid on the source. The workings of HackLite are more mysterious than those of NetHack. While its origin came from the folding together of a version of Hack and NetHack 2.3, the game was changed in other ways than that. No one really remembers all the specifics of the resulting program. When it comes down to it, a lot of the dissatisfaction many have with NetHack comes, not from the fact that it requires spoilers (which it technically does not, all information needed to win is available

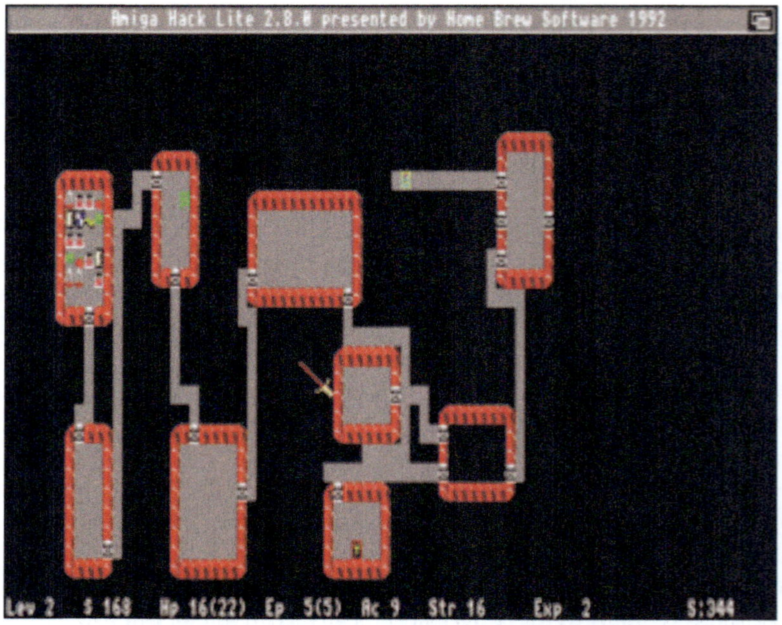

Figure 48.1

Amiga HackLite 2.8.

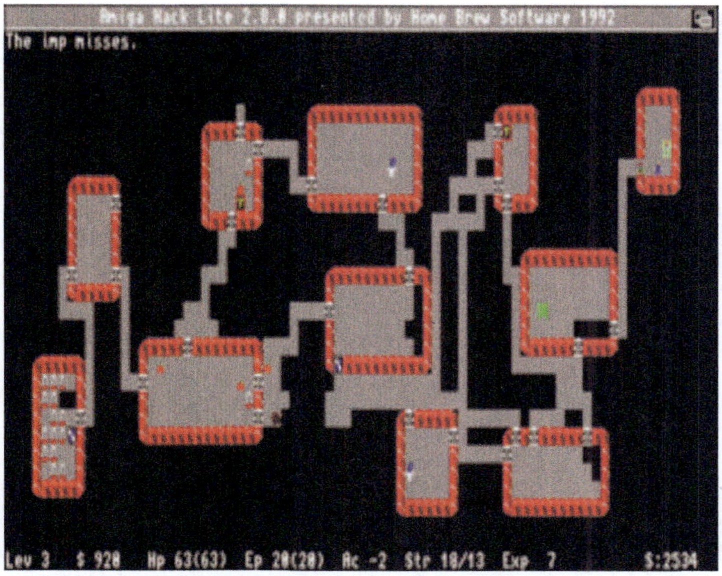

Figure 48.2

HackLite

in-game, although it takes a whole lot of play to see enough of it), but that those spoilers are easy to obtain and exhaustively correct. How did they get that correct? By source diving, of course.

So that leaves us with the mysterious game itself. The opinions here come from playing the Amiga HackLite v2.8.0, scavenged from Fred Fish disk #799.

48.3 "This Corridor Seems Dusty. [More] Perhaps If You Cleaned More Often?"

HackLite is based off of earlier versions of Hack and NetHack 2.3. Importantly, this was before version 3.0, which instituted many changes to the game system (blessed items came around here) and version 3.1, which gave us the modern dungeon layout. This means that the player is in for a game a good deal more like Rogue than he may be expecting.

Importantly, while HackLite has prayer its purpose is obscure. It does not seem to be a general-purpose plea for aid, and it doesn't even work unless the player has taken a certain measure first. Monsters do not seem to be much worse than NetHack's, but neither is food in greater supply, and without prayer for early emergency feedings lots of players run out. Many of my trial games were ended by starvation, it being a far more potent killer than any of the monsters.

HackLite also is missing all player stats other than Strength, level sounds ("You hear someone cursing shoplifters.") and burdening levels (plate mail seems to "weigh" the same as a gemstone). The burden level thing is a much greater change than it may seem at first. One of the more head-scratching things about modern NetHack is the proliferation of weapons and armors that go unused. 3.1 players soon learn to avoid plate mail because of its tremendous weight; only those with high strength can carry both it and basic equipment without becoming burdened. Meanwhile mithril is not hard to find in the Gnomish Mines, while being much lighter, Mid-game characters usually wish up or make dragon scale mail, which has the best armor class, is extremely light, and provides a free resistance to boot. By doing away with burdening, HackLite restores plate mail's usefulness.

But HackLite is more than reduced NetHack; it makes some additions of its own as well. One interesting positive change made to the game, that NetHack itself could gain benefit from, is that items in shops are a lot more similar in price to each other. Scrolls of Identify no longer stick out like a sore thumb as the cheapest thing in bookstore inventories, which may seem like a little thing but actually

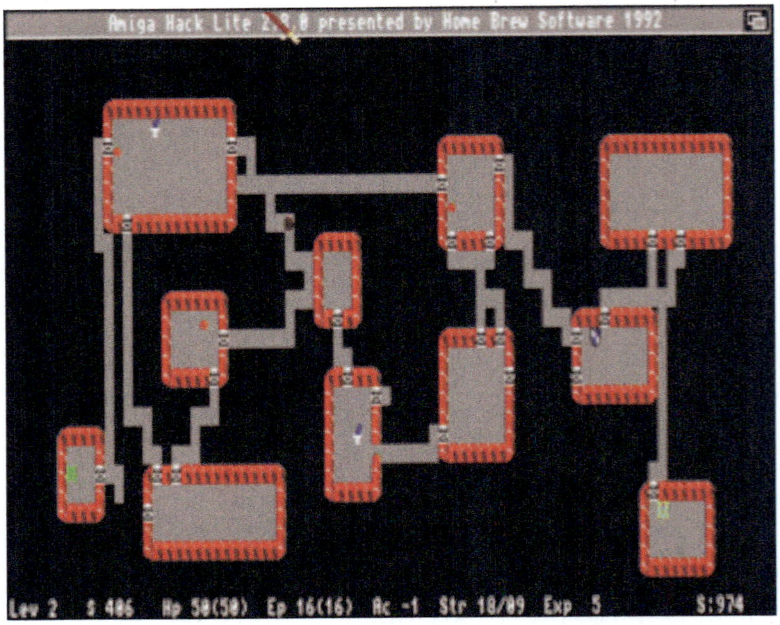

Figure 48.3

HackLite

changes the game quite a lot. Finding that first ID scroll is a milestone in Hack-family games, since the player must happen upon it by chance and test-read to discover its type. This, plus the inclusion of a few additional item types like rings of addiction and wands of futility, can throw players expecting fewer tricks for a loop.

48.4 Plays Great—Less Taxing

So, why is HackLite still entertaining to play? It is simple, the same reasons that games like Dungeon Crawl and DoomRL have become more popular in recent years. It is a roguelike that doesn't require what amounts to a Master's degree in the game to be successful at it. Some tricks will help, and there are secrets, yes, but NetHack has entire game mechanics that are secrets. HackLite, on the other hand, does without many NetHack 3.0 and 3.1 features that are sorely missed (like player attribute scores other than Strength), but it still contains bones, engravings, vaults and the like.

This is a general feeling one gets while playing the game. NetHack has become so balanced (to some, "easy") over time that successful play is most often attained by playing ultra-cautiously, price IDing items when possible, avoiding testing scrolls if it can be helped, using dipping and other means to figure out the bad potion types, being cagey with wand charges to ID them and so on. Many experienced NetHack players manage to avoid trial and error identification nearly all the time. HackLite has fewer of these features, so item information must more often be traded for (by usage, which often wastes resources and inflicts bad effects) instead of obtained for free. This makes it a much more chaotic game than NetHack, even despite its simplified game world.

A note about playing this game:

HackLite actually evolved out of an Amiga port of Hack, which was then converted into a DOS version. The Amiga port is still the nicest way to play, due to its interesting, though idiosyncratic, graphics. If you wish to try the version pictured here, you will either need a stock Amiga, or the UAE emulator and images of the Kickstart and Workbench disks, the rights to which are currently owned by Amiga Forever, who sells copies for about $10 here: www.amigaforever.com/shop/?product=value.

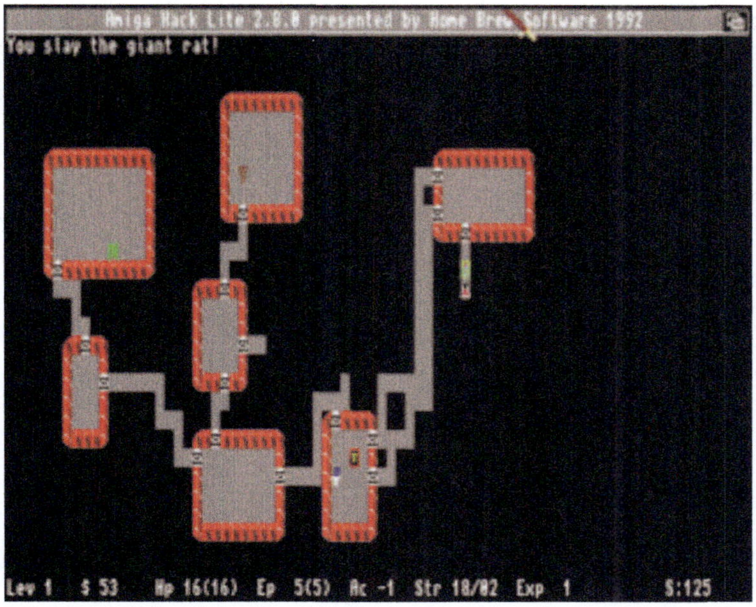

Figure 48.4

HackLite

48.5 Sources

Amiga version: http://ftp.funet.fi/pub/amiga/fish/701-800/ff799/
Dungeondweller's awesome Roguelike archive: http://roguelikedevelopment.org/archive/index.php
HackLite Dos version: http://roguelikedevelopment.org/archive/files/executables/hacklite283.zip
Readme for HackLite—Lost. This may be it: www.pcorner.com/list/GAMES/HACKLITE.ZIP/READ.ME/
The Rogue's Vade-Mecum, defunct, available via Wayback Machine: https://web.archive.org/web/20160115164335/http://userpages.monmouth.com/~colonel/rvm.html

Here are my notes concerning differences noticed between HackLite 2.8.0 (2.8.3 is the most recent version) and the NetHack 3.1–3.4 line.

SPOILERS FOLLOW! Do not continue if you wish to avoid them!

Different:

No dungeon branches.
No pet displacing. (Very annoying, this.)
No exercise.
No stats other than strength.
Shift-X learns spells (not the read command).
Absent commands: no #chat, no #untrap, no #monster.
Shops sell objects for more.
Some messages are different.
"You don't know how to/still can't/will probably never learn to walk through walls."
General items cannot be blessed or cursed. Equipment can be cursed only.
Monster attacks that damage weapons reduce pluses, instead of causing "rusty," "burnt" or "corroded" states.
There are now "preserved" items, probably analogous to NetHack erodeproofing.
Dungeon levels have more rooms.
Some polymorph monster abilities implemented via special extended commands (#? to get list).

Doors cannot be closed; they're always open.

Tins contain food types instead of monster types (salmon makes fingers slippery like french-fried food in modern NetHack). Also, each tin contains random food instead of a predetermined type that could be ID'd.

Dead rats always make you "feel sick."

"Reading this scroll confuses you. You are awarded the Yendor Prize for Poetry!" (Confuses player for a good while).

No level sounds.

No burdening levels: plate mail weighs the same as a gemstone.

Dead zombies are edible?

New items: Ring of Addiction, Wand of Futility.

Fountains can be generated in shops.

Eating rock moles can result in message "You feel tougher!"

Starvation is a much bigger problem.

No partially eaten things.

Similar:

Monster corpses do grant intrinsics.

Eating floating eyes does confer.

Bones levels are in the game.

Overaged corpses can kill players via food poisoning.

Polymorph is in the game.

Potion dipping seems to be in the game, but I don't know its use.

Prayer: #pray. (However, it is not as useful as a generic escape from trouble. Speculation: punishment makes prayer available? When punished and praying, I got "the gods accept your tithe.")

Doors cannot be passed through diagonally.

The engrave trick for identifying wands does work.

Vaults are in the game, as well as the teleport traps that lead into them.

Monsters can use weapons, including thrown weapons.

49

Interview: Keith Burgun on 100 Rogues

August 2009 100 Rogues is a popular commercial roguelike for the iPhone with an abundance of whimsical personality and unique gameplay. In this Q&A, conducted shortly before the game's release in August 2009? I ask the game's lead designer Keith Burgun about the game and its inspirations.

(*January 2016*: I've kept in touch with Keith over the years. His views on game design have changed a bit, but he's still out there and doing interesting things. His most recent designs, both very interesting, are Empire, Auro and the card game Dragon Bridge. Keith Burgun has a website at keithburgun.net, and he's doing the Clockwork Game Design Podcast. Keeping busy!)

JH: First off, tell us about yourself, your company and your team.

KB: I'm Keith Burgun, lead designer at Dinofarm Games. We're a four-man team consisting of myself, Jonathan Bryan (producer, programmer), Blake Reynolds (artist) and Wesley Paugh (programmer). Our publisher, Fusion Reactions, and its office are in Rochester, NY. Blake and I both live in Westchester however, so we end up making many long trips.

JH: Your project is called 100 Rogues. Would you like to tell us generally about the setting of your game?

KB: The setting is a mysterious, scary, yet silly dungeon. The mood or voice of the game can be best explained as "fantasy by guys who don't know fantasy, and who are pretty strange." I get a lot of inspiration from teaching children's art classes—some of the stuff kids come up with is just so outrageous and hilarious, and I would love to see a game with that kind of spirit. So we have a basic fantasy dungeon setting, with your standard fare: skeletons, ghosts, rats and the like.

But we also have a cowboy-ish looking Bandit, a flying baby with bat wings, and quite a few other oddities like that. Also, it's a class-based game, and we've been working hard to make sure that the classes all have not only their own style of play, but also a personality. Not enough personality in games these days, if you ask me.

JH: Teaching kids art classes! That sounds interesting. Did the bucket-head Crusader come from that?

KB: Not directly, but in spirit I think so. The Crusader is very childlike, so having the simple bucket-like shape for his helmet helps to bring that out. There's nothing in this game that has been directly stolen from a child's artwork, however, we did take lots of inspiration, and even a monster, from a strange obscure Famicom game called "100 World's Story." It's not a roguelike, but I highly recommend it!

[JH's note: I have played 100 World's Story, and can vouch for it. It's a Famicom RPG board game, like Sugoro Quest in a way, but with a very different style, simulationist .and competitive.

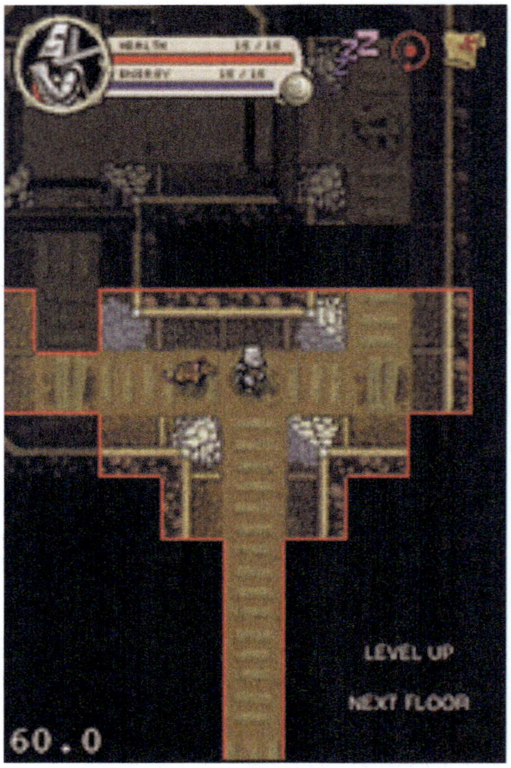

Figure 49.1

100 Rogues

It's very much a multiplayer game, and it's entirely unique. There is an English translation available from Romhacking.net.]

(*June 2020*: The game 100 Rogues, discussed here, despite being named by some their favorite roguelike, is no longer obtainable from the App Store. Because non-jailbroken or developer software cannot be run on iOS devices, and 32-bit software is no longer obtainable from the App Store, the game is simply unplayable now. This is the fate of a lot of older iOS software. An Ouya version vanished when its software store went dark in 2019. There was a Mac version, but it also seems to be gone. 100 Rogues is a great game; that it is no longer possible to play it legally is a shame, and a symptom of the terrible attitude towards software preservation displayed by the tech industry in general, and Apple in particular. It's 2020, and we've been dealing with this for four decades now.)

JH: Personality is something that could be considered to be lacking in roguelikes, which usually go for generic adventurers the player can then overlay his own character impressions upon instead of making him follow a designer's conception. If a roguelike features strongly-defined characters they'd really have to be winners. Obviously you think the ones in 100 Rogues stack up; care to give any specific examples?

KB: Well, it's one thing if you intentionally go for non-characters and allowing the player to imagine his own personality. I would never complain about that. What I don't like is when games do have characters, but they're just forgettable, boring, cliché stereotypes.

Of course, I do think our characters are interesting enough to warrant their existence. Currently, we've got four classes, two of which will be available upon initial release, and the other two will be released in free downloads shortly after. The Human Crusader (male) is a child-like paladin-type with an invincibility complex—in fact, he even is at a tactical advantage when surrounded. The Fairy Wizard (female) is a brooding, angsty fairy who summons perfect beautiful crystals, and then simply bludgeons her foes with them.

Later, we will release the Skellyman Scoundrel (female), who's sort of a thief/rogue type class. As well as being (predictably) very sneaky, she has a taste for poetry and melodrama; she's got one spell where she lifts off her skull and recites a magic poem which causes all sorts of havoc. And finally, the

Dinoman Bruiser (male). He's somewhat similar to a barbarian, although soft spoken and pragmatic, and with an ability called "Ancestral Spirit" which allows him to turn into a Dinosaur for awhile.

Anyway, the personality is something that is difficult to express in mere words. It's something you get from experiencing all of the game's elements—the music, the art, the illustrations—and I hope it gets across to people.

JH: How closely does 100 Rogues hew to the system created by Toy, Wichman and Arnold in Rogue? That is, are there any significant changes to the ruleset in your game?

KB: Well, our goal is to bring a true roguelike into the mainstream. So, I looked at what the core elements of what makes a roguelike, which I see as being turn-based gameplay, randomly generated content, permadeath, to name a few. So our game has all those. Now, there are some other things that generally come along with roguelikes which we are not including in our game.

What has always bothered me is the learning curve—in "Rogue" and in "NetHack," it's not at all obvious for a new player how they interact with objects, or even what objects actually are. I don't think it's good if your player has to learn what the difference between a lowercase and capital B represent on the screen. I am all for representative, simple graphics, but I do think clarity is very important, especially when you're going for a mainstream reception. We also have a very smooth, clear GUI which was designed to be as easy to use as possible. Another similarity we will have with most roguelikes is high levels of un-forgiving difficulty.

JH: Difficulty sounds good. David Ploog of Dungeon Crawl Stone Soup has identified high difficulty as an essential roguelike characteristic. Do you think, however, that this will harm your audience?

KB: I don't think it should harm our audience. Look at Tetris. I've been playing for twenty years, and I still always die at some point before level 10, yet that doesn't make it any less fun. With most video games these days, there's an expectation that the game will hold your hand all the way to the very end. So I think that our game will break that expectation, but people will be happily surprised and reminded of the fact that winning isn't everything in games.

Plus, there will be little victories throughout anyway—celebratory confetti and balloons over the player's corpse when they've died but reached a high score. This way all players will get some positive feedback and learn early on that it's not about beating the game, it's about seeing how well you can do (much like Tetris).

JH: What other games, roguelike or otherwise, would you say have inspired your game?

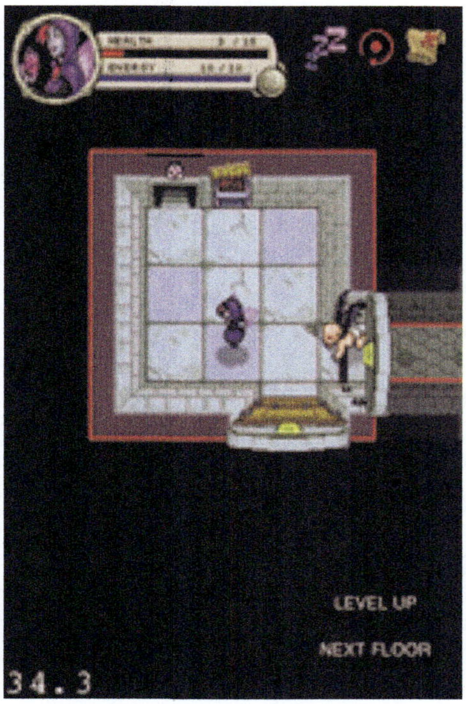

Figure 49.2

100 Rogues

KB: Diablo (especially the alpha version which was turn based), Shiren the Wanderer, Chess, WarCraft III, Team Fortress 2. I've always had a deep love for randomly generated content, as well as turn-based gameplay, which is what led me to discover the Roguelike genre. The first Roguelike I actually played was POWDER, which I still absolutely love, and when we first started making this game our original idea was "hey, let's make a POWDER clone for the iPhone!" It ended up becoming much different.

I put WarCraft III in there because our game is skill based, and I was very inspired by how the heroes in that game really ended up playing and even feeling different because of the skills. Team Fortress 2 because of their system of balanced weaponry—the weapons in their game (and in our game) are all simply tools, each good for a specific job, none being simply *better* than any other. Chess because we want each of our battles to be strategic in a similar way as a game of Chess.

JH: Randomization plays a big role in nearly all roguelikes, lending the genre its characteristic replayability. Does 100 Rogues make any/effective use of randomized elements?

KB: Absolutely. All our maps are entirely randomized, as well as item drops and monsters. The only element we have which is not random are our bosses. We have a few bosses in our game which function similarly to some of the more clever bosses you'd find in a Super Nintendo game that have a set of behavior patterns.

JH: In the old days of computer gaming, social play, even for essentially solo games, was important. Many popular roguelikes were played in campus computer labs and sport high score lists. Does 100 Rogues support score lists?

KB: Yes. We have a set of online scoreboards, as well as a local scoreboard, so that you can dominate your unskilled friends and family, as well as be schooled globally by Koreans. In addition, we also have several tabs, such as "Highest Score," "Highest Score with Crusader," "Highest Score while Inebriated," just to name a few.

JH: I've heard you talk before about how character skills, as opposed to items, are the focus of your game. Would you like to elaborate upon this? Give any examples?

KB: For a long time, I've felt that the items situation in RPGs was a bit out of control and illogical. The main issue that bothers me is the fact that you constantly have to go to the item shop, simply to get all the benefits of your experience levels. So, okay, now I have 10 STR, now I can get the Super Sword, better go do that. Oh now I have 12, now I have go to get the Super Duper Sword. Better go do that. So essentially, games are forcing you to do an action which is simply an extension of your character level.

In other words, there is no strategic reason why you wouldn't buy the Super Duper Sword, it's just, you either do it, or you aren't getting the full benefits of your level. I find this to be unnecessarily burdening the player with a repetitive action. Even if a game doesn't have an item shop, it will work by dungeon level instead of character level. Oh, now I'm at dungeon level 10, now I have a chance to find the Super Duper Sword. Once I find it, what am I going to do with the Super sword? It's garbage.

I hate how in Diablo, most of the items you find are just clutter because of this reason—nothing but something you have to go and sell (once again, a burden on the player). Some may argue It's FUN to sell stuff and to buy the newest available sword, and I agree, it's just that I think actually playing the game is MORE fun.

In addition to this, we're just a few guys on a small budget, so we are limited by the amount of *stuff* we can put into the game. We figure we need to work smarter, not harder. I looked at Chess, and thought to myself, "all they needed to do was change the way things can move and attack, and look how much strategy and depth they created!" So we designed a few character classes which each have their own set of abilities which will not only define how they can attack, heal themselves, and move around, but can be used in concert to create large advantages for the player when used wisely. Simple examples of this would be an area-of-effect skill that fires in a straight line, requiring you to line up as many bad guys as you can, or positioning yourself safely behind a strong summoned creature as you use ranged or magical attacks.

JH: How have you adapted the roguelike control system to the iPhone's touchscreen? Any use for the tilt sensor at all?

KB: It's just as you would expect—click in a direction to move in that direction. Touch a monster to attack it. We developed a radial menu system that appears when you touch your character, allowing you to use their abilities. No use for the tilt sensor at this time.

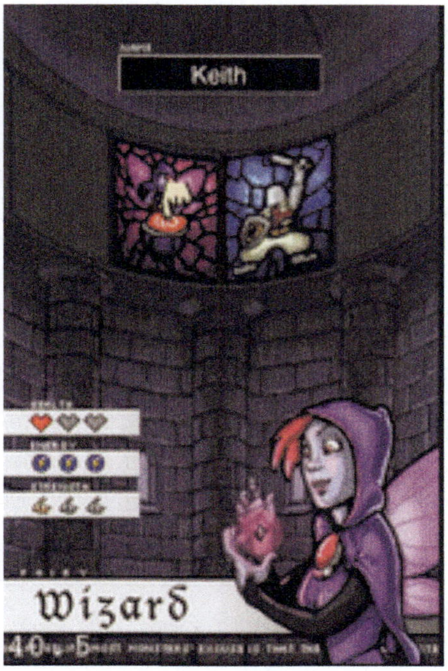

Figure 49.3

100 Rogues

JH: One of the tensions of roguelike design is the difference player knowledge of the game world makes upon the game. NetHack is (in)famous for this, how you have to nearly have an Associate's Degree to play the game well, but all that stuff does lend the game a certain personality, unlike the more-generic, but fairer to unspoiled players, Dungeon Crawl. Where does your game fall between these two?

KB: Right. Well, our game is designed for everyone to be able to play by making how everything works as obvious as possible. Of course, there is still stuff the player just has to learn. For example, it's difficult to imply to the player that a metallic monster is immune to magic, but we figure once you cast a spell on it and it has no effect, you'll get the idea.

We are planning to add a lot of content to the game post-release (something on the order of two to three times what will be there on release), but I am personally against adding anything that requires arbitrary knowledge. I want all of the elements to be there, simple, visible, but add up to something complex. Again, look at Chess. There aren't any secrets about the way units work. It's just that, when you play a lot, the complexities start to naturally occur. That's what we're going for. In terms of personality, I agree that the arbitrary-knowledge-requirements in a game like NetHack do indeed give it personality. Our game has a lot of personality too, it just comes from a different place.

JH: The visual arts are not something that traditionally has had much to do with roguelikes; NetHack's VGA graphics turn out to be a hacked-together version of the graphics from an old home computer version of Rogue. Tell me a bit about the art style of the game, which from the Crusader concept video at least looks fairly charming.

KB: There's a lot that's different about our game, visually. One of the tenets of our art style for 100 Rogues was that, for all the in-game art, every single pixel was placed by an artist. So there's no anti-aliasing, vector art, 3D art, resizing, anything like that. The pixels you see in the end are exactly the pixels the artists put down. That may sound like something insignificant but we believe it makes a difference overall in the end.

Our art director Blake Reynolds was behind the visual look of almost every character in the game, and he and I agree that these days, it's difficult to find a game that isn't typical Japanese anime style, or going for some sort of realism. What we really were going for was a sort of "classic American illustration" look. We're highly inspired by the Walt Disney animation style, especially films like Beauty and the Beast, and so there's definitely an element of that in there. I think when people sit down with this game, they will immediately notice that the game is totally visually unique.

JH: About how long will it take to play through the game?

KB: Most games will not result in completion of the game, as it is very difficult. It's hard to say exactly how long the game will take to beat, but we estimate somewhere around 30–45 minutes.

JH: Are there any cool development or testing stories you'd like to share?

KB: Yeah. This one time, Blake and I were on a trip up to Rochester. It's about a five-hour trip, so we stopped at a rest stop to get some MacDonald's. So I ordered a Cheese Hamburger and some Chicken Nuggets. So I finally get my order, open up the bag, and sure enough there's no food inside, but rather a swirling black Doom vortex. It sucked me and Blake both into the vortex, where we landed in the Dinosaur Days. Just then, we fought a GALACTIC DEMON! Blake rocket jumped up on the palm tree and began kicking coconuts at the creature. "RAGHHH . . . I'M TOO EVIL FOR THIS" said the demon. Then a Dinosaur came! The End.

50

Interview: Josh Ge on Cogmind

November 2018 Cogmind is a unique roguelike game. It is generally in the traditional style, a turn-based map exploration game. The default graphics are done with tiles, but beneath them it even has the ASCII interface aficionados know and love.

As with many traditional roguelikes, there's a heavy emphasis on the items you find. In fact, the items are most of your character. Although you get the opportunity to upgrade the number of item slots in each of your bot's four major areas, Power, Propulsion, Utility and Weapons, slots are useless unless there's something in them. And those items are often taking damage or wearing out, frequently requiring improvisation on the part of the player.

This interview with Cogmind's creator, Josh Ge, is nearly two years in the making! The possibility arose back at Roguelike Celebration 2016, but various things kept coming up. We finally concluded it mid-October 2018. Because of this, some of the information in the first section is somewhat out-of-date. Most of this interview was conducted over Twitter, with some email. It has been edited for publication.

50.1 What Is Cogmind?

John Harris: First off, who the heck are you and what is Cogmind?

Josh Ge: I'm a roguelike developer relatively late to the party, having only discovered this great genre by way of DCSS in 2011. Roguelikes immediately took over my life and I began work on X-COM: UFO Defense-adaptation X@COM, followed by a 7DRL in 2013 and REXPaint, an ASCII art and roguelike development tool, that same year. Shortly afterwards I started developing Cogmind (originally that 7DRL) full time, having logged over 6,000 hours in the past few years.

With Cogmind I'm trying to innovate on the genre without losing that core roguelike experience, by drawing on methods and concepts more commonly found outside roguelike canon, like advanced particle effects, the broadest soundscape ever to appear in a roguelike, and a living world where not everyone and everything is out to kill the player.

JH: Ah, that's kinds of high-level and vague though. Let's get a little more concrete: what is your character in Cogmind, and what is it trying to do?

JG: In Cogmind you play a robot whose abilities are derived purely from what components you attach, hence there is no XP or grinding, and by necessity or choice your loadout might undergo significant

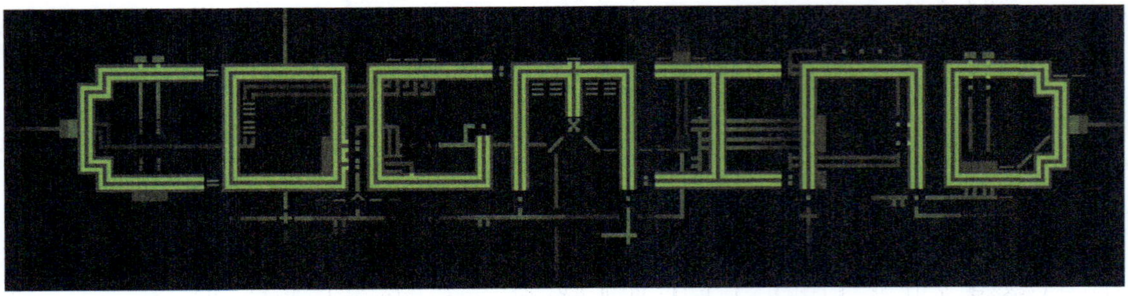

Figure 50.1

Cogmind title

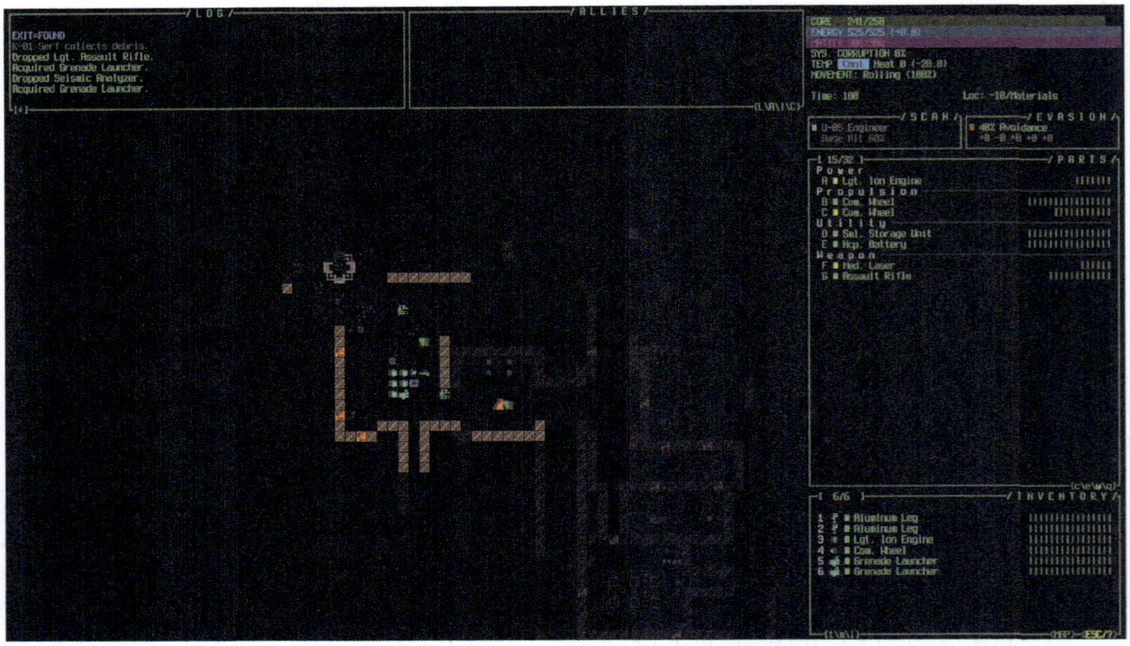

Figure 50.2

Cogmind

changes throughout a single run. I don't want to spoil the background or story, but strictly mechanically speaking you start deep underground and are trying to reach the surface of the world, usually via some nonlinear route. You can either fight your way out or rely more heavily on stealth and hacking, but in either case, understanding and adapting to how the world as a whole perceives and reacts to you are vital skills for survival. By the end you have over two dozen active components (you know, a-z) working together in a synergistic fashion, many of them possibly scavenged from fallen enemies.

JH: Ah okay. That's kind of outside the basic "lone human exploring a dungeon" structure that's traditional for roguelikes. What is character creation like?

JG: That's just it—there is zero character creation. You start out naked, and basically create your character on the fly by collecting and attaching parts, or taking those parts from other robots. Items are a lot more common than found in classic roguelikes, as destroyed enemy robots can each leave behind multiple parts to salvage, and there are hundreds of parts strewn throughout a single map (though maps are also quite large to accommodate the different space needs, usually ranging from 100x100 to 200x200). Equipment and inventory management naturally becomes a big part of the gameplay, and therefore the interface is designed to streamline a lot of it.

JH: So, do you generally always have the same parts available every game so you largely make whoever you want, or are some more common than others, forcing the player to adapt and make use of what he finds?

JG: Yes and no. There are currently about 900 different parts in all, and while many will be found randomly, a lot of them also come from salvaging the remains of other robots. Robots have static loadouts, therefore understanding which types of robots carry what is a way to work towards putting together a certain type of build. For example ambushing lone Sentries for their armor and treads to take a more combat-oriented approach; then maybe destroying Hunters for their targeting computers and kinetic weaponry. There is also a system for "fabricating" specific parts that you really want but cannot find. Still, players who can't adapt do not get very far! This is especially true because Cogmind includes item destruction—you can lose everything and anything you have attached. All parts are destructible, and that's a core part of the gameplay. But pretty much every player can describe runs where they've found themselves in one bad situation after another and are stripped naked, only to flee and rebuild into some new form not long after.

50.2 Basic Stuff

JH: Let's talk about the level generator next. One of the most interesting aspects of the game I've read about so far is that there are entities in the game that are responsible for digging passages and rooms. How generally does dungeon generation look? Are those entities I mentioned responsible for all the dungeons, or do they just mix things up a bit after the dungeon's already generated and in play?

JG: Map generation is actually handled in full before the player enters a given map. The in-game tunnelers and engineers sometimes seen building little new areas are purely for fluff/theme purposes, and are actually drawing on information the dungeon planner had already decided on beforehand.

They do represent one of the key AI features, though, that every entity in the game has one or more real functions that either generate changes in the world or react to changes caused by the player or other entities.

JH: That is interesting I think. So, if the player prevents those units from finishing their job, the level ends up half-finished? And could you give us some more examples of entities performing some side function other than being opponents? The analogy that comes to mind, BTW, are cells in a body, how they each have important roles to play in keeping it alive and healthy.

JG: Not by any means half, as it's just a small number of areas that work like that as a bit of fluff, but the analogy is overall very apt. Most of the robots you see in the world (by absolute number) aren't there to fight you, but carry out their own duties which have a real impact on the operation of the world. You can do your best to avoid disturbing the peace, and thereby stay out of trouble, or be a hostile presence that disrupts these operations for whatever purpose. Sometimes causing trouble is unavoidable, like trying to stop Recyclers from coming to take away the salvageable parts remaining after a confrontation. Those are probably valuable to you when trying to rebuild! There are Engineers which rebuild destroyed parts of the subterranean complex, Workers that clean machines and pick up debris, Mechanics that repair other robots, Haulers that move stockpiles of components, and more.

Hacking into these other robots, combat-capable or not, can also give you access to their abilities. That's not a heavy focus of the game, but it's there for players who want to toy with it. (Some can be quite useful, though!)

JH: What kinds of limits are there on just being able to get "one of everything?" Inventory size, equipment slots, power source?

JG: Items are divided into four types of slots: Power, Propulsion, Utilities, and Weapons. You start with 2 free slots for each (except 1 for power), and gradually gain more slots as you reach new areas—you choose the slots to "evolve." The base inventory size is 4 slots, but can be expanded by using storage utilities.

JH: You mention that most of the combat is with ranged weapons. One of the things about roguelikes is that missile weapons are always a bit more annoying to use than melee, because you typically have to enter a special aiming mode to attack. Does Cogmind have any ideas for remedying this?

JG: Cogmind's UI streamlines everything as logically as possible, so when it comes to attacking with ranged weapons, 'f' enters firing mode, and that automatically aims at the closest target in range, or the one you last attacked (if there was one). Then 'f' again fires, so ranged combat is often as easy as hitting 'f' twice. For combat with multiple hostiles there are also easy hotkeys such as Tab for cycling through all available targets using the same priority/preference system, and Shift-Tab to cycle in reverse. It's all pretty fast. Cogmind also offers full mouse support for everything, so naturally for mouse users it's as simple as clicking on things to shoot them.

JH: Let's talk for a bit about what's one of the most immediately striking aspects of Cogmind, the graphics. It uses graphic tiles for the game world, it seems, but ASCII for the interface and, amusingly, ASCII-art portraits for items. Is there anything you'd like to point out about the graphics? How long did it take to make all that art? Did using ASCII help, in the Dwarf Fortress style of taking less effort to construct a very large number of objects?

JG: Well, first of all Cogmind was actually designed purely in ASCII and for ASCII, even on the map, and about 25% of the current player base uses that mode. The tileset didn't even exist until more than two years into development, a few months before I released the first public version, so ASCII is very much at the core of the design, and even the tileset style I chose sticks pretty closely to that underlying aesthetic. That was important to me as both an attempt to keep the benefits of ASCII-styled tiles, while also helping the overall interface feel more cohesive.

There are currently over 800 pieces of ASCII art for items, and another couple hundred for both interactive and non-interactive machines. Altogether I've spent exactly 326 hours on just the ASCII art for Cogmind (yes, I keep track of stats like this :D). That comes down to an average 26 minutes per piece, which sounds about right. (I also have a bunch of failed/inappropriate/surplus art that got thrown out as part of that process, too.) So while individually I find each piece less difficult than I would pixel art, it's still fairly time-consuming to get it all just right, not to mention the significant multiplier when it comes to doing this for hundreds upon hundreds of objects!

JH: So, let's say I have just started a game of Cogmind. What does the general "shape" of the game look like? That is to say, are there major tasks to accomplish on the way up, like subgoals that must (or just could) be done, or is it mostly just a sort of a homogeneous journey? Like . . . the archetype that always comes to mind for me for this kind of thing is The Odyssey, where the nature of the journey changes several times as Odysseus returns home. In NetHack, after the initial period, there are some bits where the game changes in fundamental ways: the Mines, the Quest, the Castle, Gehennom, the ascension run and the Planes, each of which have major differences from the others. In other words, how varied is the trip up in Cogmind?

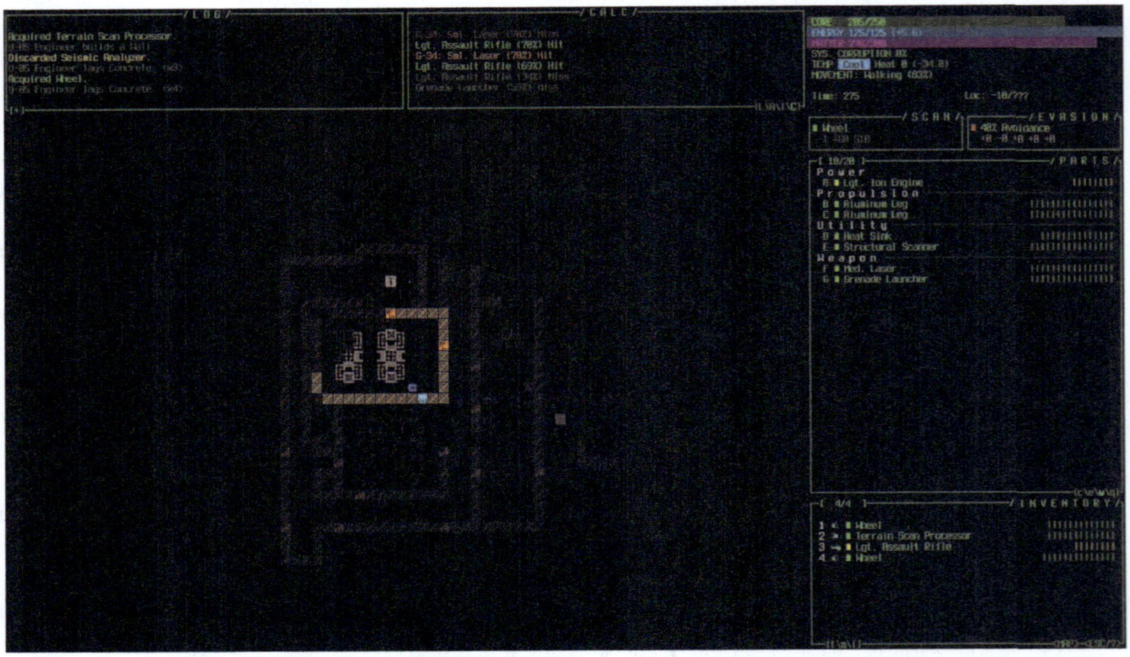

Figure 50.3

Cogmind

JG: There are several ways to look at this.

In terms of the world structure as a whole, I can't get into the details because spoilers, but while everyone starts from the same point there are a number of things you can do which have a significant impact at some point later on, or even throughout the rest of the game. Most of these elements don't come into play until the mid-game, but experienced players are able to leave the early-game areas within about 15 minutes (survival becomes increasingly challenging the further you get). None of these are absolutely required, but a player may decide to aim for a certain area to take advantage of whatever longer-term benefit it provides, be it a highly specific "doing this will later trigger something that I need" or a more general "this area is likely to have the kind of loot or intel I need right about now." The potential effects vary wildly, though they are not procedural; they're all features which were added very intentionally, designed to mesh with both the mechanics and lore.

On another level, each type of map will tend to have its own unique mechanical quirks, and require unique strategic approaches. So the world is by no means homogeneous.

And from an individual player character point of view, the aforementioned item destruction and potential heavy losses combined with the ability to eventually use 26 items at once mean that not only is one trip likely to vary from another, but even a single trip can include multiple unique phases. Compared to a class-based roguelike, for example, where at the beginning you choose to be a spellcaster and by the end you're likely just a better spellcaster, a single Cogmind might start out wanting to go at the enemy heavy combat style, but somewhere in the middle get crushed and have to flee, build back up into a guerilla-style hacker for a while, and then later find a sufficient cache of gear to once again transform into a fighter, likely with even deadlier firepower than before. Sometimes these are calculated shifts in strategy, and others they're just "going with the flow," where I believe Cogmind's design is at its strongest.

50.3 Project Progress (Circa 2016)

JH: Well, let's talk then about how it's progressing.

JG: It was first introduced at $30 in May 2015 on my site, and then half a year ago in May 2016 I lowered it to $25 for the anniversary. But it's gradually coming down and before long will be $20 by the Steam release. Regarding pricing I've been planning to write a blog post pretty soon to explain my decisions in more detail, but I prefer this model and it's working out quite well.*

Just a couple days ago I was planning out the final stretch before 1.0, and the more I look at it the more I'm thinking it's going to be a largely symbolic milestone. There are things I want to add to Cogmind, or improve further, for which it doesn't really make sense to continue calling the game "alpha" in its current state—even at Alpha 1 it's been a complete roguelike experience, and that was 18 months ago! So instead I'm going to consider 1.0 to represent "story complete," and continue developing for some time after that.**

Before long I'll also be looking to write a retrospective article examining Cogmind's evolution through alpha over the past year. As of today I've so far clocked 6,272 hours of Cogmind-related work since starting over three years ago.

JH: That is a lot of time, even if you don't consider it "finished" yet. There is still a lot of value in a solid 1.0 release though, psychologically and to the players. Especially if you get a lot of players from a solid major version release, some issues may only turn up only after you get a lot more eyes looking at it, I'd think.

JG: It's a labor of love. And the psychological meaning is certainly important to me. This is why I keep feeling tempted to postpone it while I make it "perfect" with all the other things I have planned. That said, there are already thousands of players. More than enough eyes, I think!

JH: So, the 1.0 release is planned soon then?

JG: Well, the main thing that bothers me is that even on my own long-term list of things to do, I'm aware of a near inexhaustible number of things that could be improved. This is without further input. And once I call it 1.0, newer players will certainly start to bring those things up, and dealing with that as a solo dev is a significant drag on development time, which is why I keep wanting to put off that release.

The story could be completed within as little as one more alpha release.

JH: So, that means you can play the game all the way through and reach a conclusion?

* Since then, Cogmind has been released on Steam, currently for $20.

** Josh's notes on Cogmind's development are published on the game's development blog, at www.gridsagegames.com/blog/.

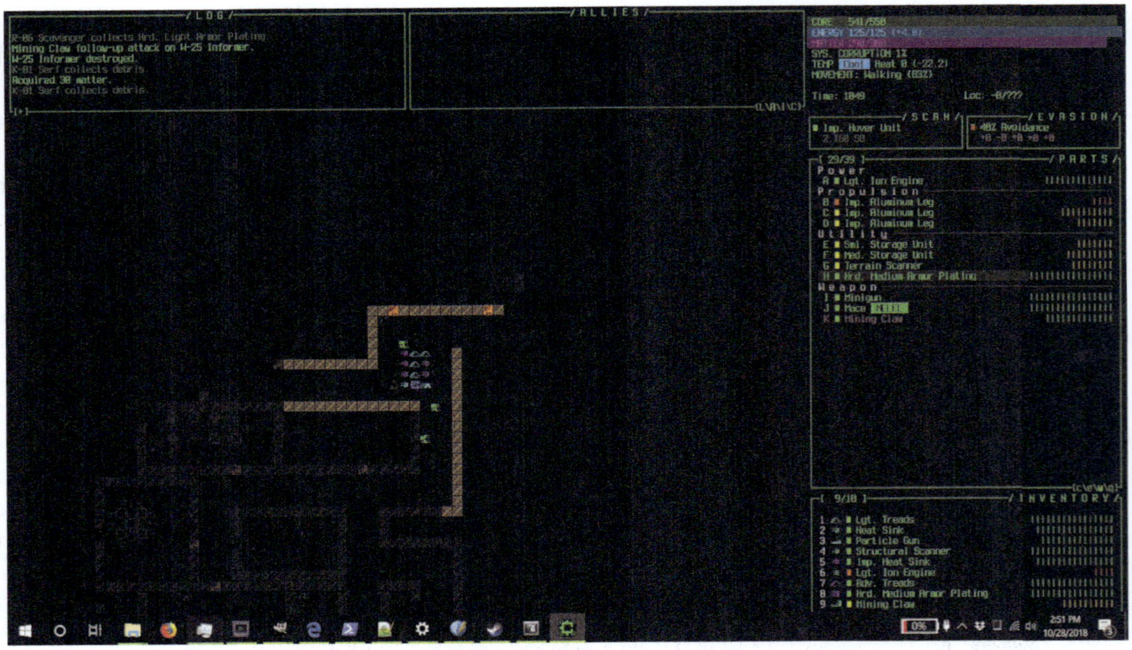

Figure 50.4

Cogmind

JG: I believe there are some more accessibility issues I should address before daring to say 1.0, namely key rebinding and an OSX wrapper, which altogether could be rather large stumbling blocks.

The game has had an end and conclusion since Alpha 1! What I'm doing now is adding all the outlying areas and alternative endings.

JH: Aaah. So outlying areas then are like dungeon branches? And alternative endings are like, say, the "ultra endings" in ADOM?

JG: What was missing for part of alpha was the ability to meet the NPCs that play major roles in shaping the world. Now there are only a couple of those left . . . Cogmind essentially has branches like DCSS, so yep, that's what I've been working on for the past year—adding more branches. All the branches are done now, except for a few little very special odds and ends to come soon. And yes there are multiple endings of varying difficulty, akin to ultra endings though probably not quite as involved.

50.4 Indie Business

JH: Literally just before I typed this, you sent out a tweet saying you had just reached 3,000 players, and expressing hopes that the game would one day be profitable. What do you suppose it would take, in terms of sales, for that to happen?

JG: Since this is my full-time job, I certainly keep a close eye on the financial side of things. As much as I dislike having to do that because my primary goal is to simply make a great roguelike, the only way Cogmind has been possible is through the community support that's kept development humming along for quite a while now. I could've pretty easily tapered off the roadmap and called it done last year, and by now it would've paid for itself, but what I decided to do instead is make the world and feature set much larger than initially planned. The thing is that means it's nearly impossible to break even for now because I continue to spend time/money on development while player growth maintains a pretty even pace, sustaining development without really accelerating to fully catch up to my progress.

That said, there have been good concentrated sales boosts like the times RPS/PC Gamer have written about Cogmind, and the initial launch which attracted support from a lot of long-time fans. So if I were to stop developing now, fewer than 3,500 players would be enough to break even. But as I mentioned before there's still more I want to do with Cogmind, even after declaring 1.0! And I'm cool with that plan for now, but I do also have to consider that at some point in the future I would like to have extra funding left over to create The Next Roguelike. Not to mention it's rough doing these ridiculous hours at minimum wage!

Note that my entire process is to be as open about as many aspects of development as I can, so in an article earlier this year I already shared revenue details (www.gamasutra.com/blogs/JoshGe/20160519/272832/Cogmind_Year_1_Sales_and_Dev_Time_Data_EA.php), though the full answer to questions of revenue is going to be another retrospective article I'll be writing down the line. It'll be interesting to see what kind of impact Steam has on the future of Cogmind and my work . . . (and by extension the potential exposure of mainstream audiences to traditional roguelikes, since Cogmind could reach players who are not yet aware of the likes of ADOM, ToME4, and CoQ).

50.5 The Game World

JH: Let's get back to the game itself . . . you talked a bit about how the other characters in the game have their own lives independent of their interactions with the player. What kinds of things go on in the game world when the player isn't around?

JG: Earlier I brought up some of the engineer, worker, mechanic, and hauler behaviors, and while there are more, discovering how the world works and what happens is a part of the experience I don't want to spoil. I do try to play it down, though—it's not as expansive as all that, i.e. they're not really "lives" in the sense of AAA RPGs and their AIs with unique routines and whatnot. That's on the generic side, while in the case of unique NPCs or those with dialogue, they're out there doing their own thing and the player is basically a side show to all of it. Sorry but I can't really talk about this stuff in detail.

JH: Is there anything in particular about your game that you think stands out, that you rarely get the chance to mention?

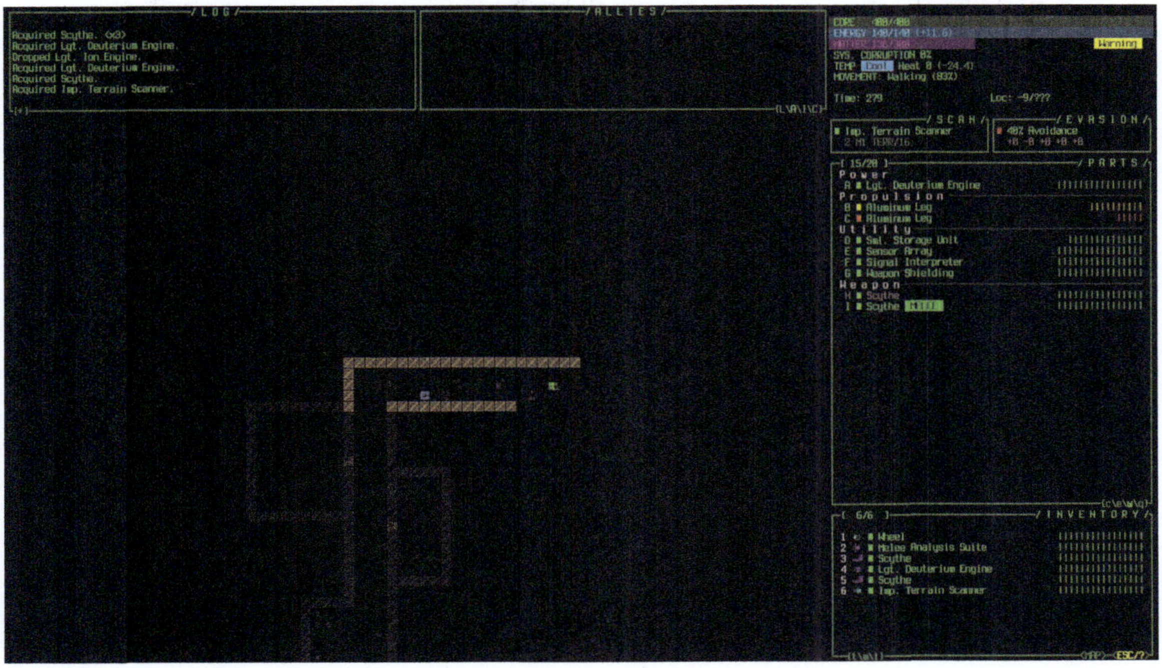

Figure 50.5

Cogmind

JG: Well I talk about Cogmind a lot, and write about almost everything I do in great detail on the dev blog, so not really :P. But because I've been working on it for quite a while and there is so much information out there already (easy to get lost in it all!), some time ago I put together a collection of images that summarize the types of things Cogmind is doing for the genre that have never been done before, or are rarely seen: www.gridsagegames.com/cogmind/innovation.html.

Though what individual elements stand out to each player are going to be different, probably the number one aspect that all other design decisions revolve around is immersion. It seems unusual to say that about a turn-based ASCII roguelike, but the sci-fi/robot/hacking theme combined with a vivid soundscape has worked out really well. I love fantasy games as well (before X@COM I spent five years creating a fantasy SRPG), but I feel that if I'd gone that route it would've been much more problematic to create such a believable world.

JH: Are you familiar with the Commodore game Paradroid, and was it an inspiration for Cogmind?*

JG: While I'd never heard of it before a few years ago, you can be sure I started hearing about it not long after Cogmind's release! About 5–6 times already I've had players mention that Cogmind reminds them of Paradroid. (I don't have any experience with Commodore, only Atari.)

As for my original inspirations, the 2012 7DRL idea came from a confluence of two sources. As a big fan of Battletech I wanted to make a roguelike version, but decided it wouldn't be right to do one without a hex-based tiling engine, which I didn't have. . . . So that idea was off the table—disappointing, but while browsing "game ideas" threads on random forums a few weeks later, I found a literal one-line post from someone who suggested a game where the player creates themselves from limbs and pieces of their enemies. It immediately hit me: What if I combined this idea with Battletech? And thus Cogmind was born . . .

Beyond that there are many other inspirations, mostly from outside video games, but that was the initial spark.

I've since searched for that post many times—I'd very much like to thank the poster and give them a gift, but it was already too long ago, and really was completely random forum browsing. What's even funnier is that I was doing the browsing in a hotel's internet cafe while on vacation, so it wasn't even my own computer :P

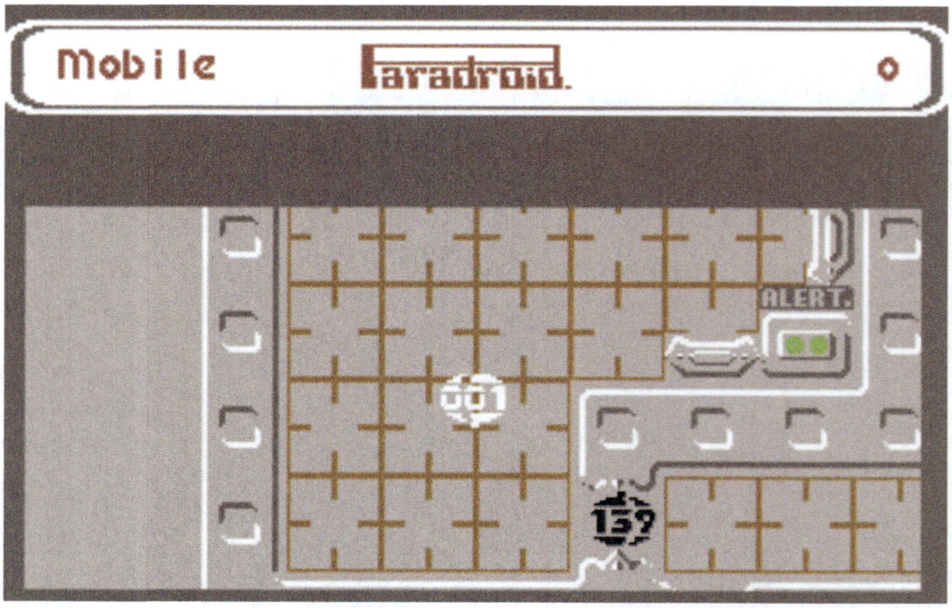

Figure 50.6

Paradroid

* There was a long lull in the interview around this point. We picked it back up again in July 2018.

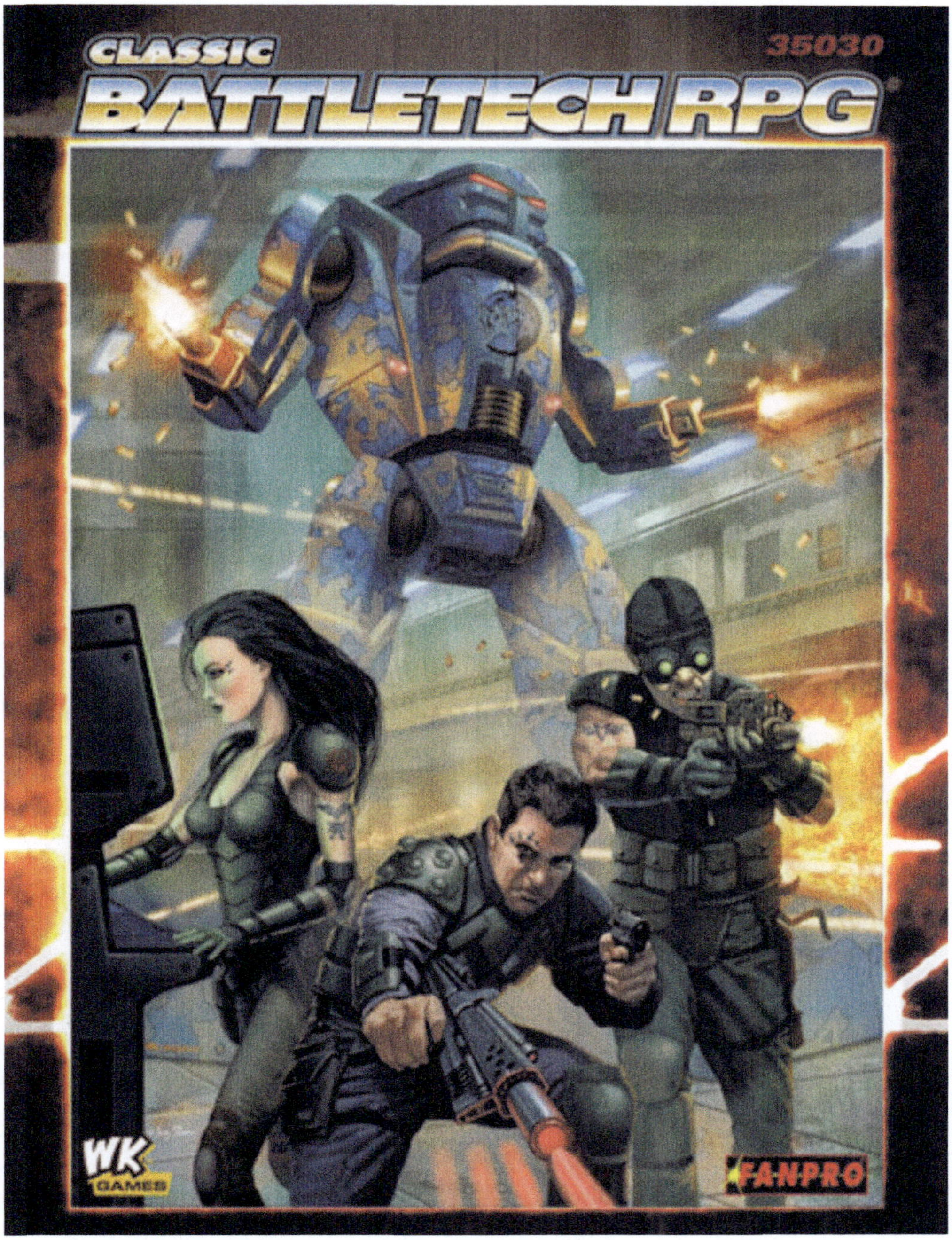

Figure 50.7

Battletech

50.6 ASCII Graphics, in Its Own Way

JH: In the 1 1/2 years since we last talked, you mentioned the ASCII effects. They've just gotten better in the time since then I think. How does the game display? Is it in a terminal window, or is it a graphics window with rendered ASCII? In the latter case, is there ever any temptation to "cheat?"

JG: It's an emulated terminal in the vein of libtcod, so yes it's essentially copying fonts from an image to display on the screen rather than using a regular font file. This allows the graphics to be pixel-perfect at every resolution, for which I've put together over 100 handcrafted bitmap fonts, and Kacper, the tileset artist, drew five separate sets of the same tiles for each primary tile dimension.

I've written about it, and many other technical and design aspects, in a FAQ for r/RoguelikeDev before. (www.reddit.com/r/roguelikedev/comments/3ee3pr/faq_friday_17_ui_implementation/.)

It's actually not possible to cheat, though, at least not without switching to a different engine, because all it can do is render ASCII onto grids and assign each a foreground and background color.

Technically it wouldn't be too hard to, say, add health bars for enemies using some sort of new overlay feature, but I'd rather find solutions that work within the terminal style itself. Once you've laid down a set of graphical rules and designed for those rules, breaking them later on inevitably leads to inconsistencies, and inconsistency is generally a bad thing in video games, especially where aesthetics and UX are concerned.

Having clear limitations set in stone early on is great, though. It's all about getting creative to maximize both the informational and aesthetic qualities of the interface.

50.7 Supporting Varied Gameplay

JH: If I read the notes right, there is a variety of ways to go about playing through the game, right? Like, combat, evasive, etc. Are there any specific kinds of playstyle that you aimed at supporting? Like, explicitly allowing the player to take on a D&D-ish role: an evasive rogue, a hard-hitting fighter, an area-effect wizard, a healer-mechanic, maybe a character with good diplomacy skills like a bard, etc?

JG: While there are a range of unique play styles, and hybrids in between, early on I had no explicit aims there. Cogmind's initial design came from the 7DRL, and the idea was to simply focus on implementing the core mechanic and making that interesting and fun. Although in building it I noticed right away that, coincidentally, three of the main categories of parts did to some degree conform to D&D tropes: propulsion is for your speedy/stealthy rogue, utilities are for jack-of-all-trades mages, and weapons are . . . yeah. So by evolving more of a given slot type, your build will naturally lean more towards that style.

In reality it's more complex than that, especially now with nearly 1,000 parts, and especially the utility category, which is the most versatile and can support any style—it's more about the individual parts.

Related to this topic, we did a r/RoguelikeDev FAQ on Character Archetypes, at www.reddit.com/r/roguelikedev/comments/659d61/faq_friday_62_character_archetypes/, in which I gave a rundown of Cogmind's more typical build styles as of last year.

It's interesting that you bring up this question now, though, because the very next release is specifically focused on adding a new play style, one which can also optionally be mixed with almost any other style in hybrid fashion for pretty good results, too.

The new robot hacking system (www.gridsagegames.com/blog/2018/07/robot-hacking-take-2/) doesn't have any direct analogs in fantasy, but could be seen as a sort of mix between rogue and mage, a strongly utility-focused "class" that operates outside the standard rules of combat and avoidance. Last year in talking about the concept of this class and the strategic space it could fill, players also referred to it as the "commando" build.

This is a major change from the older, simpler robot hacking system, which was focused on either disabling or befriending enemies, and when working on the older build style I very clearly had the idea to make it sort of the "summoner" of Cogmind. As I talk about in the blog post linked above, players eventually figured out how to take advantage of this system and I had to nerf it :P. Anyway, it'll be replaced by a much cooler and deeper system soon!

JH: The difficulty with designing for a variety of playstyles is allowing a character playing in unexpected ways to not encounter impassible roadblocks. Like, to go back to D&D as an example, a mage character encountering a must-defeat foe who is immune to magic and too strong for their meager fighting skills, or an enemy with perfect perception against a thief. One wants all trials to be passable with many different styles (or at least avoidable), without watering down the challenge. I imagine that must be tricky.

JG: Part of the way I got around the "impossible roadblocks" issue was by making almost everything optional, especially the most challenging areas. And of course running or circumventing danger is always an option. Many people who haven't played Cogmind don't realize that it's actually a stealth game. And most of Cogmind's world is optional, so players who aren't equipped to take on certain challenges can simply avoid them. But I do also explicitly design for multiple approaches to challenges in most cases. Personally I prefer the Shoot Everything approach to play, as do some, but then there's a large portion of players who enjoy the sneaking around and creatively overcoming obstacles rather than facing them head on.

JH: I wonder if you've given any consideration to a "pacifist" character, who eschews all weapons, maybe a peacemaker with high robo-charisma that only uses discarded parts? Well, it's an idea, heh. It's entertaining to think about but might not fit the game.

JG: Pacifist runs are already a thing in Cogmind. There's an official score bonus for it (which increases with every depth you don't kill anything) and people do that! Pacifist speedruns earn a lot of points and can get pretty high on the leaderboards to reasonably compete with combat runs.

JH: How easy is it to acquire new parts if you aren't making them yourself, so to speak?

JG: Easy, since all robots are made of parts.

JH: Do you have to race scavengers to them?

JG: Nah, you can just shoot at the Recyclers and they'll run away.

Although there is often a bit of drama there because they can arrive while you're still fighting, if it's a prolonged engagement. So you have to decide whether it's worth taking time out to shoo them. Battles can sometimes end with relatively clean surroundings, which can be dangerous if you aren't carrying enough spares for damaged gear!

JH: Reading through the interview from before, I like that the game feels like a world to itself, kind of almost like an ecosystem.

JG: It's very much an ecosystem, and I'm always adding new elements to that, making sure that any new system ties into multiple other aspects of the game, or even AI. Like the new robot hacking system, that'll introduce a couple new jobs for one of the common robot classes.

JH: That kind of reminds me of another thing Cogmind is sort of sideways-adjacent to, the obscure Gamecube game Cubivore. It's an action game where cubical animals tear parts off of other animals and eat them, and grow new parts that they've obtain.

JG: Oh wow that does sound interesting.

One of the big decisions very early in 7DRL dev, and again when I wanted to make Cogmind a commercial game, was whether to introduce biological parts. I imagined working a whole separate faction into the story which could be based on biology instead of machines.

JH: Biological parts seem to me like they'd be kind of less interesting, like thematic drift. Not that they couldn't be made to work, but it's like . . . . Cogmind is a game where you construct your robot as you go by taking parts from other robots. It feels like that's "enough." To go beyond that feels like it might be sequel territory.

JG: Yep, ultimately I decided it wouldn't work as well and cut all that out. I still might play with the idea for a 7DRL one day. I do have some plans. Too many plans . . .

Mixing bio-parts directly in with Cogmind would be worse though, especially considering the original point was to keep Cogmind "small." Look how that turned out xD. Was going to be a short project, then move onto the next, but here we are five years and over 9,000 hours of work later . . .

JH: How is it coming along, BTW? It has been like a year and a half since the first part of the interview. Is it still beta? Or alpha? Has it hit an "official release," whatever the heck that means these days. The animations look very polished.

JG: Beta 3 launched on Steam October 2017. The story is 100% complete as is all the primary content, I'm just adding lots of extra stuff for fun now, and do need to finish a few final required things before I'd call it 1.0. Currently it's Beta 6, and Beta 7 is in late dev. Already have solid plans for the next few Betas.

JH: Ah, you're still getting money from sales along the way, right? Is there a 1.0 scheduled eventually?

JG: Yeah, been on sale for . . . over three years now, and that's how I keep development going. No set schedule for 1.0 though. I'm happy to just keep improving it and adding more features if there's enough people who want to support the game. Earlier this year I showed a zoomed out image of my TODO/potential features list, which is twice as long as the changelog from five years of continuous full-time development, so . . . . :P

Cogmind 2 would be an alternative option in the long run, and allow us to explore more of the story and world that the first can't reach, so I like that idea as well.

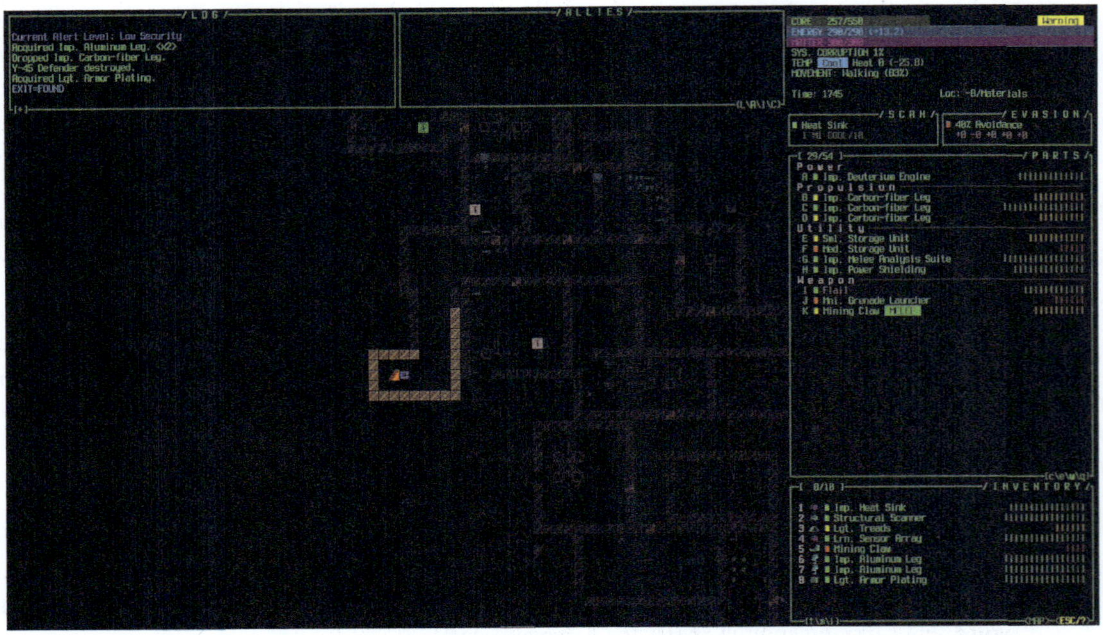

Figure 50.8

Cogmind

JH: Sounds like a Dwarf Fortress-style development schedule, heh. I'm glad it's working for you!

JG: Oh yeah it very much is—both DF-style and working for me.

JH: Is there anything about the game, the way it plays, it's "gameplay loop," you'd like to talk about?

JG: Well, the core gameplay loop is quite tight, but one of the things which Cogmind does differently than other roguelikes that can be a barrier for new players, even (sometimes especially!) those with a background in the genre, is that there are usually numerous loops going on at the same time.

It's not just about the enemies you're facing and parts and resources you have to manage, there's also the whole ecosystem to contend with. So coming up with a great plan for your current situation which only takes into account what you have and can see right now is almost certainly going to fall apart at some point, probably sooner rather than later.

You'll need to improvise a lot as enemies warn other nearby enemies, or call reinforcements, patrols and other squads actively circulate around the map, non-combat bots sometimes interfere with your own goals, the global alert level rises due to your actions and you attract more attention, and lots more (some of it contingent on what you've done elsewhere/before, plot-wise).

Also, the fact that item destruction applies to any item (armor or not the items are all protection for your core!), means that unless your build is perfectly balanced and unlikely to succumb to attrition, you're going to have to carefully consider what kinds of spare parts to carrk and plan ahead for how to acquire more parts when spares, or something vital from your build, is suddenly gone. So there's a lot to think about in terms of the "item churn loop."

Overall, high-level play is rather complicated and requires a decent amount of knowledge before you can be confident in survival, so it's not the kind of game you can keep throwing runs at and fooling around with in the hope of learning how to win. You'll have to really think about your decisions and their consequences to get further. Yes that describes a lot of roguelikes, but there usually aren't this many systems layered on top of one another, so it can be kinda overwhelming. It's also often difficult for new players to see exactly when they made the most important mistakes that ended up losing them a run, because death in Cogmind doesn't come swiftly and is usually a cumulative result of multiple mistakes made earlier on, but that's another tangent.

Playing without regard for all these other factors is fun (I often sorta play like this when streaming my runs), but that low-optimization approach won't cut it if you want to tackle the extended end game, alternate endings, or other difficult challenges.

50.8 Advice for New Players*

JH: What would be some advice you'd offer new players? What is a good strategy to make it out of the early game?

JG: All the best advice for that has been boiled down to a list of tips found in the dedicated Survival Tips section at the beginning of the manual (also found in game). It's really the only part of the manual that's recommended for new players to read, since the in-game tutorial messages and context help cover everything that's necessary in terms of mechanics. Though there is one other section at the beginning of the manual which talks about important differences between Cogmind and other roguelikes, specifically for those with experience. Knowing these in advance is a big help.

Probably among the most absolutely important notes from those tips: Never leave any equipment slots empty, and also keep a full inventory at all times, often with a storage unit for extra capacity and therefore more spare parts. Attach replacement parts even in the middle of battle! And when encountering early-game enemies, try not to confront them in the open, instead retreat to fight in bottlenecks at point blank range because you have so much "health" (integrity) that enemies plinking you for a few turns doesn't mean much in the grand scheme.

JH: After playing a couple of games, I notice a prominent early choice is whether to go for legs or wheels. From a beginner's standpoint, what are the advantages of each? How about when treads show up? How about projectile weapons vs. lasers?

JG: Technically you can find any type of propulsion even on the first floor (including by taking them from bots that use it), though airborne propulsion is not advisable until after a few floors. In a general sense, propulsion exists on a spectrum from low support/high speed to high support/low speed, from flight -> hover -> wheels -> legs -> treads, so wheels are in the middle there and may appear to be a pretty well-rounded option, but not recommended for new players because they'll tend to get shot off quickly without superior tactics (or good wheels :P). I always recommend legs for new players, because they're the beefiest propulsion which is also pretty common.

All types are valid, you just need to pair them complementary parts and suitable tactics. We just had the propulsion types question/discussion on the Cogmind subreddit: www.reddit.com/r/Cogmind/comments/9qg8hb/propulsion_proscons/. It can also be really effective to put together a hybrid build using multiple forms of propulsion.

Weapon categories are the same in that there's a wide variety and each has their own advantages and drawbacks, but all the strategic possibilities combined with all the mechanics you have access to right away are rather overwhelming for new players, so one of the Survival Tips is to simply go with whatever parts have the highest rating, to avoid decision paralysis when starting out. Smart players will always carry a spare launcher and melee weapon though (in inventory), the former for taking out groups of weak enemies and the latter for chopping through walls to make shortcuts, or to use as a last ditch weapon when resources or weapons are low.

In any case, it'd be hard to answer questions about weapon type without writing a lengthy guide, since there's such a variety and a lot of factors to consider in each decision. Just swapping out parts for those with a higher rating is the best way to ensure you'll come out ahead :D

JH: Things seem to get damaged easily, and weapons seem to degrade through use. Can you repair damaged systems, or is it something where you're usually switching things out?

JG: Repair is possible via several means, yes, but it's not all that common, and not something you'll do until maybe in the mid-/late-game, and even then only if it's something which is vital for your build strategy. It's more common for experienced players to get ahead of the attrition issue by avoiding much damage in the first place, either by avoiding combat, evading hits, using shields or resistances for mitigation, or "the best defense is a good offense—neutralize everything before it can mess you up!" And once you know how to give yourself strategic and tactical advantages in many different likely situations, you'll end up taking a lot less damage overall and usually be replacing damaged parts with even better parts before you lose the first ones.

For those who enjoy playing recklessly, however, or aren't yet skilled enough to avoid all that damage, having lots of spare parts in inventory like I mentioned earlier will often come in handy (read: allow you to not die xD). Like my Twitch streams are fairly suboptimal Cogmind play, but it's fun and I still often win, and carrying a variety of spares, basically having backups/alternates for everything, is as important as trying to theorize new ways out of sticky situations . . .

* The final portion of the interview took place in October 2018.

JH: If your energy core gets destroyed but you're not, is there anything you'd suggest a player try doing to get out of trouble?

JG: The best course of action depends a lot on the circumstances. You can escape almost any dire situation in Cogmind and come back to win, but in a very general sense one of the easiest ways to recover from a power loss scenario (certainly the easiest if you're not currently in battle!) is to just salvage a non-combat bot. The non-hostile green bots running around just doing their jobs can be great sources of vital emergency parts, like power and propulsion. That should be enough to tide you over to a better power source taken from a combat bot.

Also if there's already some nearby power source lying in the rubble from an ongoing battle, by all means head over and pick it up if that'll get your build back in working order! Don't worry too much about stray hits, I mean you're already less of a viable target when moving.

JH: It seems to me that Cogmind has "programmed" character development, by which I mean, experience-like advantages are gained not through in-level accomplishments, but as a result of progression (after specific levels). Is this accurate? What caused you to use this system? Are there any ways players could end up ahead of/behind the curve?

JG: Cogmind is very focused around what parts you use, so technically it doesn't have much in the way of stats at all. Only your core integrity increases with each depth closer to the surface, plus you get a tiny bit of "free" extra heat dissipation. That's it. All other capabilities and stats come from parts.

While there are a few special ways to get ahead of this curve, they don't really come into play until later in the game, and using this type of progression is an important part of the design because that means you are free to become anything at almost any time. Unlike most roguelikes you're not "locked into a class," and this allows a lot more freedom across a run—you can be tanky for one section of the world, then stealthy while exploring another. Sometimes you are even required to "respec" like this in order to get the most out of certain special areas, evolving your build for different capabilities in ways that would be unreasonable to expect in a class-based roguelike. This ties in very well to the fact that there are so many different parts out there, acquiring them is fairly easy, and item attrition means in some cases you're even forced to rebuild based on your environment.

I did play with a "modules that permanently upgrade your stats" approach for the Cogmind-like POLYBOT-7 this year for 7DRL, and it's fun, but results in a completely different experience built around that sort of thing. I wanted Cogmind to be entirely about your parts.

JH: What are "prototype" items? What are the advantages and/or dangers of using them?

JG: These are essentially Cogmind's version of the roguelike ID game and cursed items (at least that's where the idea originated), albeit not as nasty.

Stat-wise prototypes are always better than similarly rated parts, sometimes way better, and sometimes they come with unique properties or abilities. So if you can use prototypes you'll generally want to.

But sometimes they might be "faulty," in which case attaching them could cause your heat to spike, corrupt your system, temporarily disable other attached parts, meltdown and damage your other parts, or at worst permanently disable another part. Of course you can't tell which are faulty and which aren't, so attaching them blind carries that risk. As soon as you've identified one, however, all others of the same type are identified and you can distinguish which are faulty. Unlike cursed items in other roguelikes, you can remove them freely, so there's just that initial danger that they'll have some little side effect. There are many ways to ID unidentified parts before attaching them if necessary, or you can just attach them and hope for the best (they're not usually faulty).

Even more than the risk-reward aspect, though, I really like the idea of simply being unsure what this presumably good part is until you actually attach it. It's kinda like finding an unknown treasure, you know its general type so you're already interested, but it could be any specific prototype and you're eager to know what that is, and could be really happy with the results. That anticipation is a great feeling, perhaps multiplied when you find many at once, which is not uncommon.

JH: After playing a few games, I noticed the game started dispensing with the initial introduction, just plopping down my robot in a starting room with a variety of starting parts. I've also seen a message to the effect that the game tries to adjust itself to the player's skill. Is there a way to find out what the game's current difficulty is? Will it be possible for a player to turn that off eventually, say, in case he wants to test his skill, or participate in a tournament?

JG: I think you might've misunderstood one of the messages there, since there is no dynamic difficulty, just a message referring the player to the options menu to adjust the setting if they find the game too difficult. Mastering a game with relatively consistent, knowable difficulty is an important part of roguelikes for me, especially with Cogmind where any given run is already winnable, so it's more about improving one's own skill to meet and overcome the challenges balanced for the game, rather than hoping it provides a fun experience tailored specifically to you.*

As for the change to the starting area, yep after your third run it'll get rid of the four-room map and just plop you in that room full of parts. The four rooms were just built as a tutorial-by-layout where you'll encounter new elements in each room that coincide with the messages in the log as you interact with them, introducing concepts one by one, and by the time you've done those four little rooms you know . . . all the basic concepts you need to play!

So the "real" start just drops you in a room of items ("the Scrapyard," as per lore) and lets you go. In fact, there's now even a quick-start option for advanced players that literally just attaches everything in that room, puts the rest in your inventory, and places you next to the exit.

Technically Revision 17, that bot who welcomes you at the beginning, will occasionally appear at the start of a normal run just to remind you of the plot, since they play a role in it, just not every time since that could get annoying.

JH: We've established that, outside the player-settable difficulty setting, the game does not try to scale the challenge artificially. But, is there anything else, besides the tutorial, that can change about the game depending on concluded plays? Like Nethack's bones levels, or unlockable parts or dungeon branches?

JG: There are a number of meta activities that have only optional impact on the game, like the many achievements and the item gallery, where you can see your records of (and ASCII art for) every part you've ever used, but as for meta aspects that affect future runs, these are tied in to lore knowledge. There is a lore collection UI as well where you can review all your collected lore across every run.

There is a lot of lore, and within that lore are elements that give the player access to new content. For example there are a fair number of special machine hacks that can be learned from NPCs and other sources, and knowing how to do these hacks can change player strategies on that and future runs. On an even greater scale, though, because maps do not generally exist in isolation—there are multiple factions and major game-changing events waiting to happen, so as the player learns about intertwining plot threads and their related features and strategies, different runs might choose to hit different points specifically with the goal of triggering other effects down the line. Or in reading the lore they've already collected up to a certain point in their many runs, players might deduce that something interesting could result if they tried X, so that's something they can aim for and perhaps get some new results from.

50.9 Acknowledgments

Thanks again to Josh Ge for agreeing to talk with us. Cogmind can be purchased from its homepage and from Steam (https://www.gridsagegames.com/cogmind/).

* We tracked it down, in fact I did misread a message.

SECTION VIII
Roguelites and Related Games

51

Pixel Journeys: dnd for PLATO

December 2008 Subject: dnd, a.k.a. "The Game of Dungeons," a remarkably devious game that also happens to be one of the first computer RPGs made. It is not a roguelike, but it is of special interest to us here so I include it.

Welcome, class, if you'll be seated . . . .

Before we discuss the game of dnd, allow me to describe the old networked computer system known as PLATO. It's strange, really, how little-known it is today. While Unix systems, buoyed by the strength of its foremost ambassadors Linux and FreeBSD, are, numerically-speaking, more popular than they've ever been, its early contemporary PLATO lies mostly forgotten except by those who used the system in the day.

PLATO systems did many things in the 1970s that most PC users didn't get until 1993 or later. Online bulletin boards? Had them, in the form of notesfiles. Email? Personal notes. Chat? Talk-o-Matic. Instant messages? Term-Talk. MMORPGs? Surprisingly many, most of them older than MUD.

Our focus this month is not a MMORPG, but it is an RPG, one of the first computer RPGs ever created. It is called dnd, and if its title seems a little generic, it should be remembered that, at the latest, its first version was created in 1974, the same year Dungeons & Dragons itself saw publication.

51.1 Introduction

(*Note*: some of this information comes from the dnd history file, which its author Dirk Pellett states may be incorrect in places. I have not found anything to contradict the information stated here.)

dnd is not, to be clear, the first computer RPG. According to the creators of the game and the regulars on cyberl, an emulated PLATO system that accepts new users to this day, that game may well have been called "m199h." Its title was likely selected to be inconspicuous. Most PLATO systems were used for educational purposes in that day, so administrators frowned upon non-educational uses. A number of dungeon games were created, created by users with authoring access, and as soon as their existence became known to administrators they would be deleted. This is why we don't have a copy of m199h.

dnd's history file has it that soon after m199h's disappearance another game was written called pedit5. It, too, was deleted, but a copy was saved and eventually restored. I have personally discovered that it is often hazardous to make assertions, in gaming, about what came first. Recently it became known that Dungeons & Dragons itself may not have been the first "role-playing game," although that term probably didn't even find currency until a later printing of Basic D&D. But given the age of both computer gaming and D&D at the time, it seems safe to say that pedit5 is the oldest computer role-playing game which survives to this day.

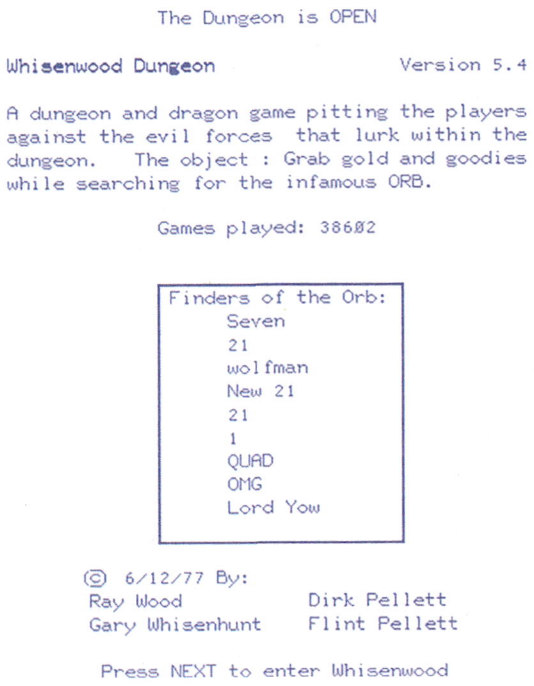

Figure 51.1

dnd

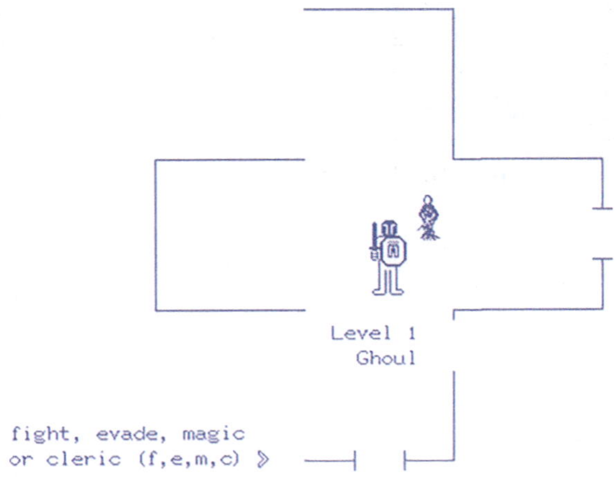

Figure 51.2

dnd

dnd also hails from that age. It was probably written in the same year as pedit5. The version described here is dnd5, which is not the most recent version. (That's the considerably more advanced dnd8, which is interesting for its own sake, but not the focus of this article.) It is the closest we have to the game's creation, however, so that's what I'm covering here.

51.2 Playing the Game

For starters, you have to create a character. This is a matter of sitting and watching a column of five numbers, pressing a key repeatedly until they meet your approval. Rerolling has been part of D&D since the beginning, and admittedly it kind of sucks. dnd's dungeon is an incredibly, ridiculously hazardous environment, so even a character with all 18s (the highest stat) will die very soon unless played carefully, but if the player knows what to do it'll make the dungeon more survivable in the long run.

The stats in the game are Strength, Intelligence, Wisdom, Dexterity and Hits. Hits is the easiest stat to raise (slight understatement there, you'll see), but Strength can be increased by drinking the right sort of potions. The only method for raising the others can also lower them, so it's for the best if they're as high as possible beforehand.

When a character enters the dungeon for the first time, he is immediately in grave danger. At this point, fighting a single monster will almost certainly leave him with so few hits that another fight will kill him. He also begins with one magic spell, and one cleric spell. (The player knows all spells at the start of the game, but only has one use of each type.)

Fighting in the game is a matter of choosing to evade, fight, cast magic or cast clerical. If magic or clerical is used, the player also gets to decide which spell is cast. That is the extent of player interaction; if the spell doesn't kill the opponent, then its remaining hits are put up against the player's in a simulated fight. This also happens if he fails in an evade attempt.

The player automatically takes damage relative to the monster's remaining strength, and if he isn't dead at this point, the monster is slain. It's a very quick system, which helps in maintaining the game's incredibly rapid flow, where fights end in seconds. No load times, no protracted engagements, no fuss. Not much strategy either, but the pacing, at least, is excellent.

Back to our starter character. With a few hits and his two spells, he has enough resources to handle three monsters, maybe four if he's lucky. Healing in the dungeon is extremely rare and not to be relied upon, and

```
    Shift-BACK for records
    LAB to reroll
    BACK for previous values
    NEXT to take these values

Strength      17
Intelligence  18
Wisdom        18
Dexterity     14
Hits          15
```

Figure 51.3

dnd

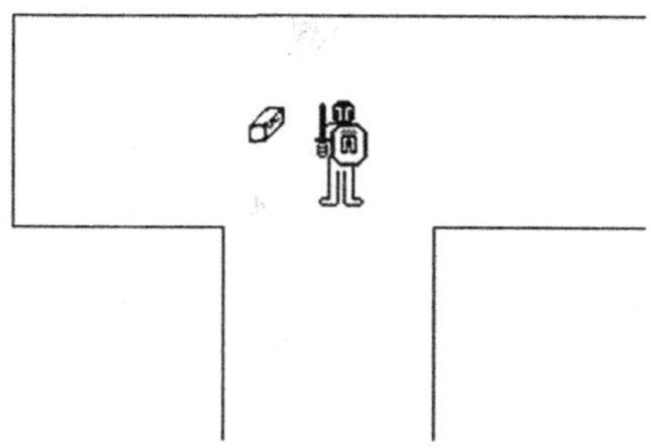

```
A Treasure Chest! Now:
leave it, Open,
Carefully open,
visually examine »
```

Figure 51.4

dnd

the torrent of monsters is unceasing. In the maze featured on cyber1 (different installations of the game had different maps, editable by the operator), there is an exit near the entrance although it must be searched for. Exiting the dungeon heals the player and restores his spells, a vital resource to the player in this phase of the game.

To say that characters tend to die a lot is an understatement. Probably more than 90% of dnd characters die in this phase. In order to become more survivable, the player has to do one of these things: find a magic item, collect 4,000 gold pieces or get 10,000 experience points. The first is rare, and is likely to be trapped and do far more damage to him than he has to spare at this stage. The other two, at the rate a new character is earning them, a few steps at a time, will take a while. Keep in mind, all this assumes that the player knows of the exit. The dungeon doesn't change between plays, but neither is it mapped out for him beforehand. It's usually a good dozen or so deaths, including a few inadvertent, fatal forays into level 2, before a good route is found.

There is a shortcut to character improvement. Once in a while on one of those jaunts the player will find a treasure chest. If it's trapped, opening it will probably kill the player, but if it's not then he'll be the recipient of a veritable windfall of loot, possibly over 20,000 gold pieces and a good amount of experience to boot. Two or three of these, and the player will nearly be able to tackle the whole first level without much danger.

Why are these things important? Gold isn't used to buy anything, it's basically just a score, a measure of achievement, but every 4,000 pieces harvested from the dungeon earns the player one additional maximum hit point. Also, every 10,000 pieces grants another max magic spell, and 16,000 is worth another cleric spell. So that 20,000-coin windfall is worth three more spells, and thus another three monsters that can be killed each trip. It also adds another five hits to the player's total, maybe enough to get in a second melee fight. The experience is useful too, in that it reduces fight damage and makes spells more powerful for every 10,000 earned, shortening the time before the player can explore deeper levels.

But it would be dishonest if I sugarcoated the fact that getting started in dnd is one of the hardest things I've ever seen in an RPG. Until that lucky chest is stumbled upon, only the slightest of trips through the dungeon can be risked. But the tremendous severity of the start makes the next phase incredibly gratifying. You see, that 4,000 gold price for a maximum hit point? That never increases. Throughout the entire game, every 4,000 gold taken through a dungeon exit is another maximum hit point, with no known limit.

On the first level of the dungeon, the player might find up to 60 gold in a single pile, and visiting every space may net around 900. On the second level, piles go up to around 260. On the third, they can be over a thousand. Gold values keep going up like that throughout the 20-level dungeon. On level 6, piles of over 10,000 are common, enough for two maximum hits all by itself, and there are many piles to be found.

After sweating through the game to get that first hit point, being able to find 120,000 or more in a single trip, and getting 30 hits from it, is a wonderful feeling. People remark upon Disgaea's powergaming design, but it has nothing at all on dnd, written way back in 1974. Winning characters often have tens of thousands of hit points. Spell costs similarly don't increase, but their capacities are limited at 25 each.

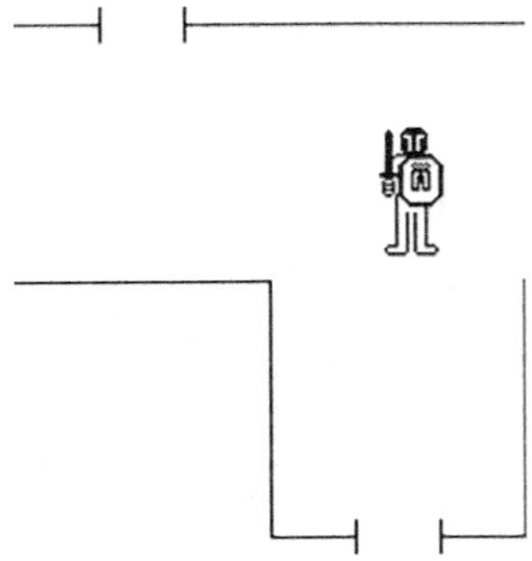

Figure 51.5

dnd

There is another interesting dynamic at work in this game, one that helps to rein in the ever-escalating rise in hit points: the monsters "know" how much gold the player is carrying on his trip through the dungeon. As the player begins to collect loot on a foray through the vaults, the monsters get harder. The more gold the player is carrying, the harder the monsters become.

Magic spells, if chosen well and the player's stats are good, can wipe out most monsters, but eventually opponent levels will rise so high that even spells won't destroy them outright. Exiting the dungeon resets both the gold carried total and the monster difficulty, but as the player delves deeper and finds even stronger monsters and bigger piles of gold, the onslaught becomes ever more perilous.

Part of this is the result of the player's own expectations. If you have 18 hits (the most you can roll up at the start) then even one additional is a good advantage, and the cost of a single additional hit point never rises. But when the player has 600 hits, gaining one more isn't so useful. The marginal utility of each additional hit point is less than the previous one.

In the same way, a player with 600 hits will find 30 more a good improvement, but a player with 6,000 not as much. The more impatient the player is with his growth, the sooner he'll wish to dive to the lower levels, but tougher monsters hang out there. Conversely, he can play it safe by lingering longer on the upper levels. The balance between the player's impatience with his character's advancement and the strength of the monsters he faces, the dive into danger and greater rewards vs. the frightened cower, this is at the core of dnd5.

51.3 Beneath the Surface

Also serving to limit the truckloads of loot the player can bring in are the hard spell caps (25 each), the fact that carrying lots of gold decreases the player's evasion ability and that he can't carry more than 100,000 times his strength at once. Although with a bag of holding that figure goes up a hundred-fold, allowing the exponential rise to continue a bit longer, it doesn't prolong it indefinitely.

In most cases, the most spells the player can ever have is 25 of each. They're good for more than safely killing monsters in one shot, too. One magic spell can be expended to cast a passwall spell. When one of those treacherous magic items is found, the player can get a chance to identify if it's dangerous or not at the cost of one cleric spell. (They should not be touched unless the player knows they're safe, for the damage done by booby-trapped items skyrockets deeper in the dungeon.)

At the cost of two magic spells and one cleric, the player can attempt to teleport one level up or down. This is the kind of thing that should only be used when the player is relatively safe, or in the direst of emergencies, since one time in ten it'll send him a level in the wrong direction instead.

At some point, the player will have to contend with the logistics of a dive to level 20. That's where the Orb is, guarded by the dragon. The instructions state that the dragon can do up to 100,000 hits to the player, but that he can choose to cast a "dragon" spell at it, killing it instantly but at the cost of most of his magic, leaving him to make a dangerous trek up the maze without most of his arsenal.

Plus, when the Orb is finally collected, the dungeon residents go into overdrive, meaning those spells will quickly become necessary. The player can choose to drop the Orb at any time, resetting the opposition to its base difficulty, but then the player will have to go back and fight the dragon again to get another one.

Does this sound to you like a game people would obsess over? How much play do you think such a game got back in the heady days immediately after Dungeons & Dragons hit the national scene?

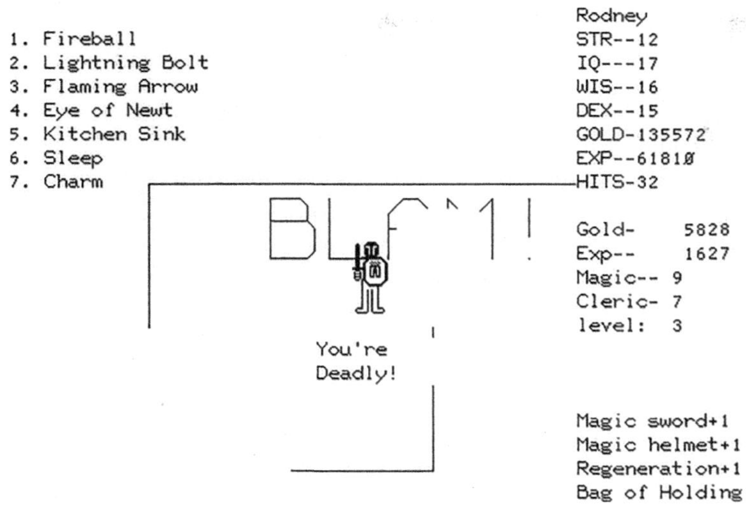

Figure 51.6

dnd

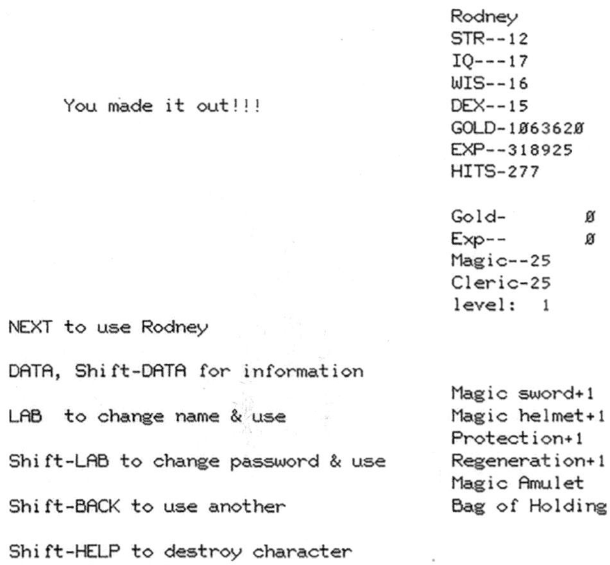

Figure 51.7

dnd

A groupnote from Dirk Pellett provides some perspective. The backup tape off of which dnd5 was scavenged also bore the game's record of how many times it had been played. Its counter listed over 2 million games since it was first made available on PLATO. Keep in mind, this only counts plays on that installation, and PLATO, although popular among those who knew about it, never had what one might call a wide release. And this backup was not the last; it's certain it rang up many additional games after the backup had been made.

Of course the great majority of those games ended before obtaining their first 4,000 gold pieces, but according to Pellett, over 150 characters were registered on the backup tape's victory board. The game on cyber1 now has been running since May 21, 2008, and at this moment has registered 40,200 games and seven victories. (I personally remember it being less than 40,000 last week; it's possible many of those games are mine.)

Nowadays, the bright luster has worn off of the bare concept of a dungeon exploration game, for the general gaming public at least. Adventurers no longer stalk dark corridors with no aim other than personal enrichment; they must always have some quest now, usually involving saving a world, which means it's never "just" a dungeon anymore, it's always some dire demonic place. The stakes have increased, all in honor of the dark god immersion.

Yet, to put it bluntly, most RPGs' attempts at immersion suck. Most (there are some exceptions) of what they have for stories would only make it into print as the worst trash fantasy, and their basic design shows less thought than games like dnd5 showed mere months after the release of D&D's original boxed set. There is sometimes a sense that they are chasing a false idol, abandoning strong design for flashy effects, and probably overuse of the word "corruption." Playing dnd5 may first seem like reaching one's hand into a box of snakes, but it is certainly an educational experience.

51.4 What Can We Learn from dnd5?

First, that an amazingly old game can still have the potential to be interesting. Computer games don't get much older than this, yet it's still possible to enjoy it. Back in its day, it was known to be extraordinarily addictive. Its graphics may have been lapped repeatedly in the race towards photo-realism, but gameplay does not go obsolete.

Second, it teaches us the joy of manual mapping. The ultimate fun of mapping, I believe, is that of personal creation. To use one's wits to produce a document with which to conquer a game, then getting use out of it. The rise of GameFAQs has done much to destroy this joy, but the mazes of the dnd games can be edited by the operator, which may help to keep the game interesting over longer periods.

Third, it has a deceptively elegant set of limits. When the player discovers that gold values increase exponentially and there is no limit to the maximum number of hit points, he gets the sense that the game is broken and sets about taking advantage of it. There are few joys in life greater than exploiting such an advantage.

But it's not broken at all. The spell caps, the carrying limits and especially the monster power increase in response to carried gold all serve to check the meteoric rise in power. The modern approach to this would be to just lower gold values or increase the amount needed to gain hit points, showing that, while the time developers spend on graphics has skyrocketed, they spend far less time in cooking up the rules.

Fourth, and the secret source of the entertainment it provides, is that old human failing: it rides heavily on the urge to gamble. That's what dnd5, and original Dungeons & Dragons, basically are all about. Every trip is a risk, every additional pile of gold raises the stakes and the chances that the next monster will be too strong to beat. Will the magic book increase a stat, or lower it, or even inflect Massive Damage? There is no way to know! (Actually it may be too much of a gamble. Later versions of dnd give the player more ways to detect if an object laying on the floor is useful or booby-trapped, and I can't say that's a bad thing.)

One of the most iconic D&D items is that potent slayer of PCs, the Deck of Many Things, which is simply a deck of cards, each with its own effect. There is no strategy to that; it's just a spin of the wheel, either amazing riches or sudden, permanent death. The rational approach to that situation is to not draw, for no possible

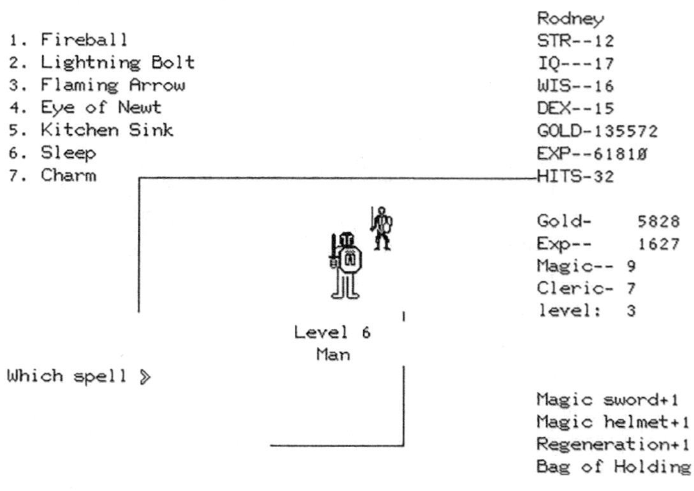

Figure 51.8

dnd

reward can make up for dying. But really, who in such a situation will fail to pull a card? Casinos exist on that margin, the irrationality of man. dnd rests there too, but no money is lost in its playing, just the life of an imaginary person.

51.5 Supplemental Information

If you'd like to try this game, or the rather more complex (and strategically interesting) later version, dnd8, up until May of 2008 you would have been out of luck. It was only on May 16th of that year that both games were rescued from oblivion.

Even so, the only known playable copy of these games is on the cyberl system, an emulated PLATO server which offers free accounts for the asking. There it is available for play, along with a number of other interesting games from the earliest days of computer gaming, including a few of those early MMORPGs. (The most popular of these is avatar, which still sees somewhat frequent play today.)

Registration for an account can be done at an address listed at the end of this chapter. Keep in mind that, the last time I checked, new registrations are processed on weekends, and since they're all handled manually it may be some days before yours is approved.

One might consider that it's not that strange how obscure PLATO is. Unix's current popularity can be tied, in large part, to the success of Linux and other free work-alikes. PLATO systems have no such work-alike. The only emulator of its hardware appears to be dtCyber, on which cyberl runs. I have heard it is open source but the extravagant licensing fees on its website speaks against that possibility.

51.6 Sources

Cyberl: www.cyberl.org/index.asp
Cyberl account application: www.cyberl.org/register.asp

52

ToeJam & Earl, the Roguelike That's Not an RPG

October 2006 Out in the distant reaches of interstellar space lies the appropriately named planet of Funkotron, a world somewhat allied with the philosophy of George Clinton. One day a teenage Funkotronian, the red, three-legged, besneakered, cap-and-medallion-wearing ToeJam, out on a space jaunt in his Righteous Rapmaster Rocketship, allowed his friend Earl to drive it through the asteroid belt of a certain backwater solar system. They crashed.

When everything came to rest they found their ship smashed into ten pieces, scattered throughout 25 regions of the most un-funky planet in the galaxy, with a wide variety of alien-hating natives out for their hides. The name of the planet: Earth.

This tale sets up one of the finest console games ever produced, Greg Johnson and Mark Voorsanger's ToeJam & Earl for the Sega Genesis. Although I consider it a roguelike (which is why we're covering it here), it's entertaining for other reasons than just that. It has an awesome sense of humor, music fully worthy of the game's premise, wildly imaginative enemies and terrific graphics considering the platform. And it is the best two-player co-operative game that exists anywhere. It's slated to be one of the early releases for Wii's Virtual Console feature, and I cannot recommend it highly enough.

52.1 That Evil Dentist Wouldn't Be Laughing If I Had a Sword

The game upsets many of the more commonly held notions of what a roguelike should be, and I'm not just talking about graphics here. Players are barely capable of attacking the enemies! Without a suitable present at hand there is no way to harm the Earthlings, and even with an offensive item (Tomatoes or Slingshot) most of the opposition is so dangerous to be around that unless the player has a lake or gap to stand behind it's wisest to just run. None of the traditional rewards for defeating an opponent are here either: points and experience levels (or "ranks" in this game) are instead earned through exploration and opening presents.

Presents are the game's random item class. A present that shares the same wrapping paper as another in the game will always contain the same effect. Many of them have excellent enemy evasion or distraction potential, with some (Super Hi-Tops) easier to use than others (Rosebushes), but again, getting real use out of them requires the player find out what they are first. There are fewer always-bad items in TJ&E than most roguelikes, but those there are are very bad. "Total Bummer!" causes a player to lose one life, regardless of

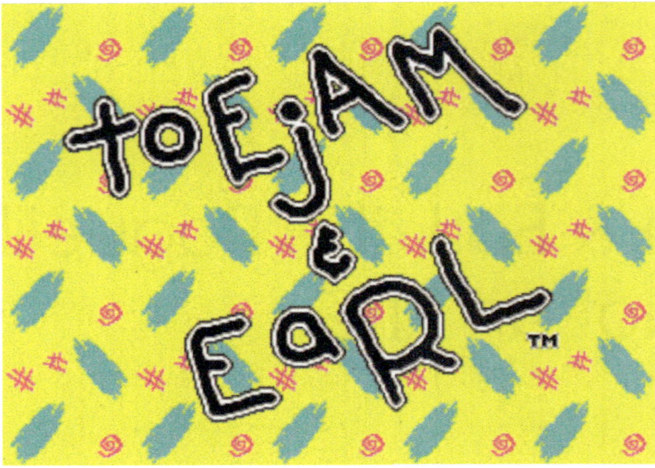

Figure 52.1

ToeJam & Earl

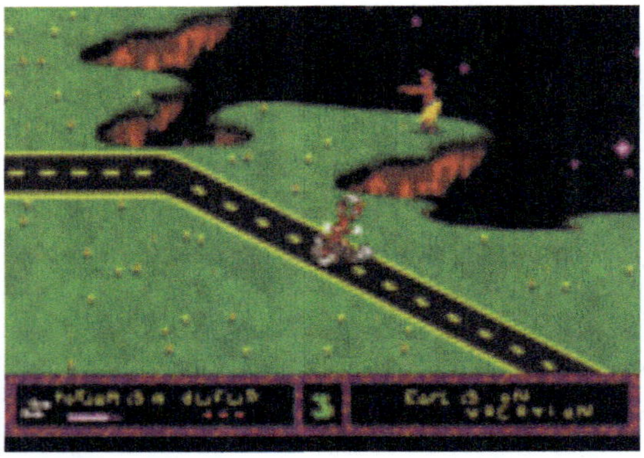

Figure 52.2

ToeJam & Earl

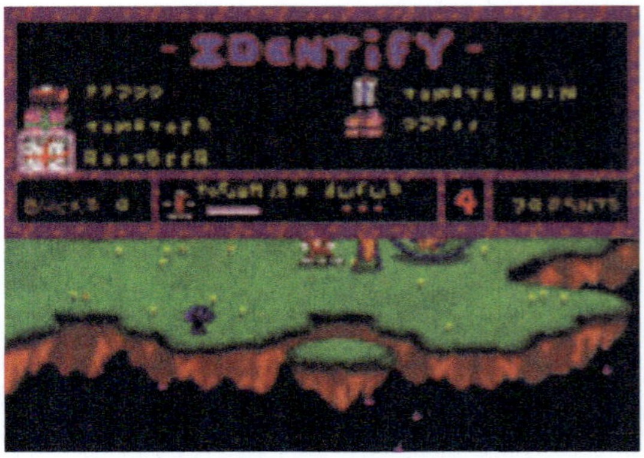

Figure 52.3

ToeJam & Earl

his health, yet it's not the worst of the lot. That distinction goes to the devious Randomizer, which scrambles the identity of all the presents.

The first game of ToeJam & Earl I almost won, on which I got to level 22 (of 25) and had more than enough resources to see me through the end, was ruined by a Randomizer. The implications it holds for the player's game make the tremendous "orchestra hit" noise that plays upon opening a Randomizer among the most dreaded sound effects in video games. The Randomizer even randomizes itself, so it's possible to recover from it, then hit it again, and again. The only way to find out what a Randomizer is ahead of time is to get it identified, or ID the other 25 types of present first and then guess its identity through elimination. This process is made more difficult due to the only source of identification in the game being the infrequently appearing Carrot Wise Men, who charge a lot for their services.

52.2 The Dual Gandhis of Funk

TJ&E is an unusually pacifist game for its class. Avoiding Earthling attack is the key skill of the game, and it's made more difficult due to the alien pair's slow walking speed. The trick to survival lies in realizing that many of the faster Earthlings tend to attack in straight lines, so they can often be avoided through a series of sidesteps. The consequences for failure are harsh though, and it's not uncommon to take multiple hits from a late-game enemy, like Lawnmower Guys, Boogie Men or (worst of all!) Phantom Ice Cream Trucks, and lose a life even if the player was at full health before. But even weak enemies can quickly slaughter the player if he is unwise in his movements near them. Successful ToeJam & Earl players have learned that hostiles should be given as wide a berth as possible.

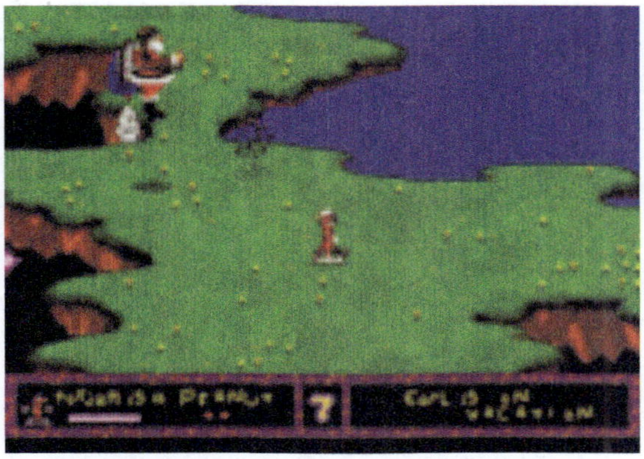

Figure 52.4

ToeJam & Earl

The most instructive thing about ToeJam & Earl's rogue-likeness, in the end, is the absence of almost all elements that trace back to Dungeons & Dragons. Most roguelikes have D&D accoutrements, equipment, attribute scores, spellcasting and so forth, sufficiently ingrained in their being that it seems almost nonsensical to think one need not be a roleplaying game at all, yet ToeJam & Earl has none of these things.

Other than money, presents are the only collectable in the game. The best advantages a player can get out of one are an instant promotion or an extra life, useful to be sure, but far from obtaining Grayswandir, or Ringil. There are no items (other than Randomizers) with the power to change the nature of the game. Because players cannot find armor or weapons that provide lasting bonuses, there is not a whole lot a player can do, over time, to improve his state other than collecting more presents and getting them identified, but the game's balance takes that into consideration. It would be just barely survivable with no items at all, so with presents added to the mix the game moves into a mortal realm of challenge.

52.3 But Is It a Roguelike? Point by Point

So with all those differences, what is it that even qualifies ToeJam & Earl as being a roguelike in the first place? The tremendous difficulty, randomized world, permanent death (players may have extra lives, but running out is easy and there is no way to continue so "lives" are more like a special kind of health), plentiful monsters with attacks that can mess up the player in ways other than damage, emphasis on survival in a hostile environment through canny use of limited resources, and above all that process of discovery, those are the things that make TJ&E more like Rogue than many games that define themselves by that quality.

What ToeJam & Earl is is an outlier case, a game that defines what it means to be roguelike, not through all the things it has, but from the things it doesn't:

It's not turn-based. But: you can always pause the game to think of your next move, and the action isn't all that fast paced, so in this case the action doesn't interfere with game in which some thought is required to progress.

It's not a one-player-only game. But: its two-player co-op mode is so well-integrated with the roguelike play structure that, should someone finally make a true multiplayer roguelike work, they'll probably do it after studying TJ&E. Players near each other both get the points and effects (good and bad) from presents, and can share health and lives too, but they can also mess each other up and race to get the good stuff on each level.

It's not a roleplaying game. Players gain points and ranks, but they don't really gain anything that could be called statistics. But: there is little in the way of combat either, and players do gain maximum health, and once in a while an extra life, as they earn promotions.

It does have unknown items and randomly generated player resources, but it does not, interestingly, have an item that identifies stuff. But: there is a character who identifies things, and he charges enough so that it is a serious decision whether to buy knowledge or risk Bummers and Randomizers to gain it through present-opening.

It's not ASCII. But: neither is Shiren the Wanderer.

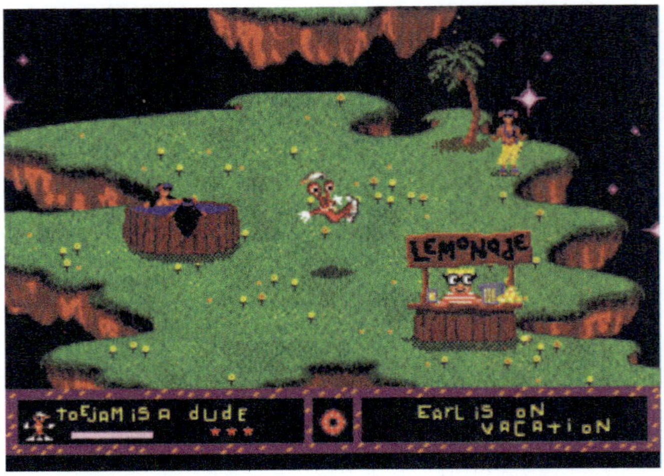

Figure 52.5

ToeJam & Earl

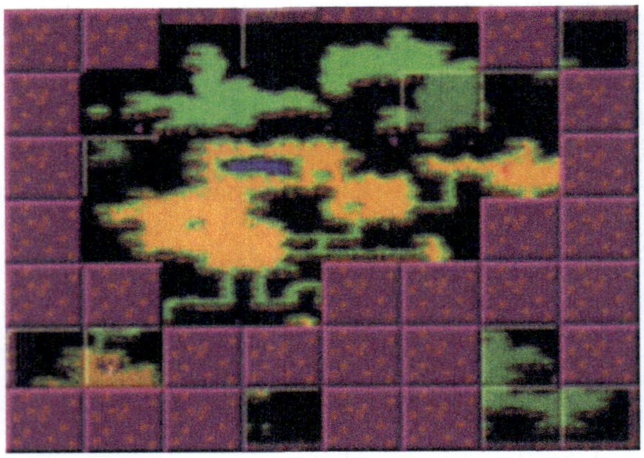

Figure 52.6

ToeJam & Earl

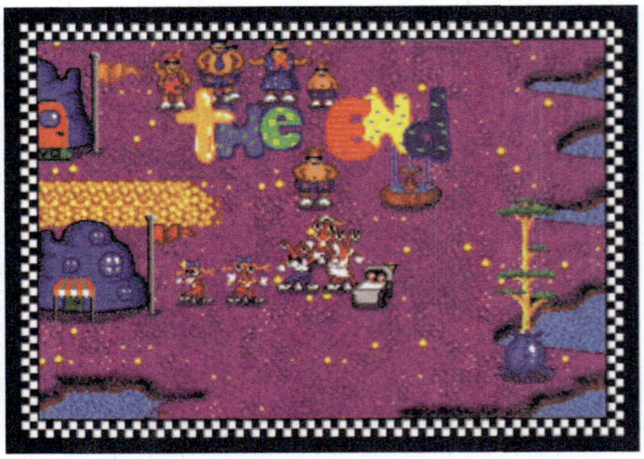

Figure 52.7

ToeJam & Earl

52.4 The Triumph of Sir Nose

ToeJam & Earl had two sequels, but neither game is quite the equal of the original, and in both cases it is due to the degree they stray from the roguelike formula. The second game, Panic on Funkotron, has incredibly vivid and imaginative artwork and ingenious platformer gameplay, and if it hadn't been the sequel to such an interesting game it would be remembered as one of the highlights of the Genesis. As for the third game, Mission to Earth for Xbox . . . while it does have some roguelike aspects, they are severely hampered by the fact that the game defaults to fixed worlds, and it starts out with all objects identified: item scrambling only occurs due to the attacks of a certain enemy. Both of these games have the original's sense of humor, but neither works the act of discovery into its gameplay nearly as well as the first did.

(*January 2016*: At that time, Greg Johnson had just announced a Kickstarter for a new ToeJam & Earl game.)

(*January 2020*: The new game, ToeJam & Earl: Back in the Groove, was released last year to moderate success. It's an entertaining and faithful update to the original, and available on a variety of platforms.)

53

Interview: Digital Eel on Infinite Space

(*March 2016*: Some of the best quasi-roguelike space games out there are Digital Eel's terrific Infinite Space games: Strange Adventures in Infinite Space, Weird Worlds: Return to Infinite Space and Sea of Stars: Infinite Space III. Quick-playing, always challenging and filled with secrets to discover. I spoke with the principals of Digital Eel, Rich Carlson and Iikka Keränen, about the long-lived series.)

John Harris: Tell me about your company—when was it founded, about the main people and your day jobs?

Iikka Keränen: Rich and I unofficially started Digital Eel in 1999 when we both worked at Looking Glass. That's when we bought the domain name and started working on the (never released) 4X strategy game we called Infinite Space. I have been working in the game industry since 1998 when I was hired by Ion Storm in Dallas TX. For the last fifteen years, I've been at Valve.

Rich Carlson: I was a musician in Minnesota for 20 years before deciding to try to make games for a living. I met Iikk at Ion. We ended up working at four game studios together! You may recall that Ion Storm, Rogue Entertainment, Looking Glass Studios were all closing, one by one, at the time. That was hard to watch, and hard be a part of but the games turned out well. Meantime, Iikka and I became friends and decided to make some games ourselves for fun. Later, when we came to Seattle for another game job, we met artist Bill Sears working at the same studio. He turned out to be as weird as we are, with a terrific sense of humor, and so we all became fast friends too. That's when Digital Eel was "officially" founded. Bill made the splash screen for Plasmaworm and we went on from there as a trio. Henry Kropf is the newest member of the Digital Eel nuclear family. He's been programming professionally for something like 20 years, starting at Vicarious Visions in 1996. (We all started in the game biz at about the same time.) He worked on PC and PS1 projects—the hardcore space-sim, Terminus, for example. Since then he's worked on a number of projects and ports, most recently for the latter Digital Eel games, as well as being the sole programmer of the fantasy word game SpellBounders.

JH: That's really interesting! The SAIS games have this outsider art feel, I think at least, like they're from some alternate universe where games evolved subtly differently. For some reason it's weird to think you're embedded in the traditional game development community! I find it difficult to believe you'd have the time or energy for this if you guys worked at, for instance, EA. Are you worried that the day job might interfere with the SAIS games?

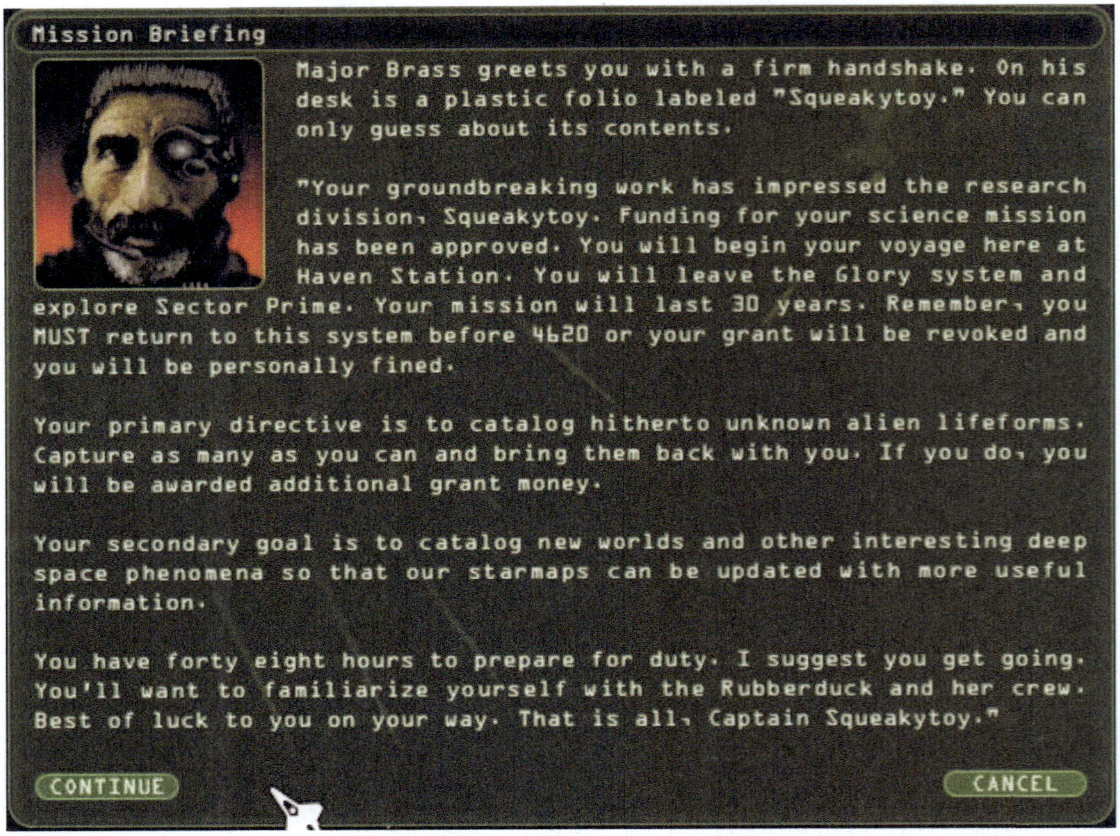

Figure 53.1

Weird Worlds: More Adventures in Infinite Space

RC: It is outsider art! Although Bill worked at game studios, he came from the era of Kustom Kars, underground comix and lowbrow surrealism. If you've read Juxtapoz or Zap Comix, that's the realm. That's what you see in Weird Worlds, and on the DE splash screens. 60's and 70's counterculture art (done only as Phosphorus can!)

IK: Sometimes it does interfere—Funny that you should mention EA, we actually worked on an EA-published game (American McGee's Alice) after we stopped working on the original Infinite Space "big game," and before we made Plasmaworm and SAIS. That was a time when we really didn't have the energy to do our own thing. Valve is much better at not interfering with life outside the office. I think it has to do with it being a more mature company—most people have families and can't be expected to work seven days a week, that sort of stuff.

RC: We have to work on our games slowly much of the time. But isn't that best if you can? Slow and steady wins the race. We plan carefully and go step by step. Looking back, 15 games in 14 years says we're finishers not flakes.

JH: How did Strange Adventures get started? What are its play inspirations? From whence came the series' unique backstory?

IK: We had run out of steam on the original 4X game, and I had realized I needed to learn proper Windows programming as my previous coding experience was DOS-based. As I taught myself DirectX, we made a simple arcade game called Plasmaworm in 2001 and then decided to make another small game using the content we had created for Infinite Space. This is what became Strange Adventures in Infinite Space. I was a big fan of Starflight, and we had also played a Star Trek boardgame that influenced the early design of Strange Adventures quite a bit. At the beginning, we were planning to have text-based mini adventures on each planet, that sort of stuff. But we soon realized that streamlining the game as much as possible was the way to go. We had written a lot of back story for the 1999 "big game" and had a very rich universe for you to explore—much more content than you'd ever see in a single session, and that kept the game lively and surprising.

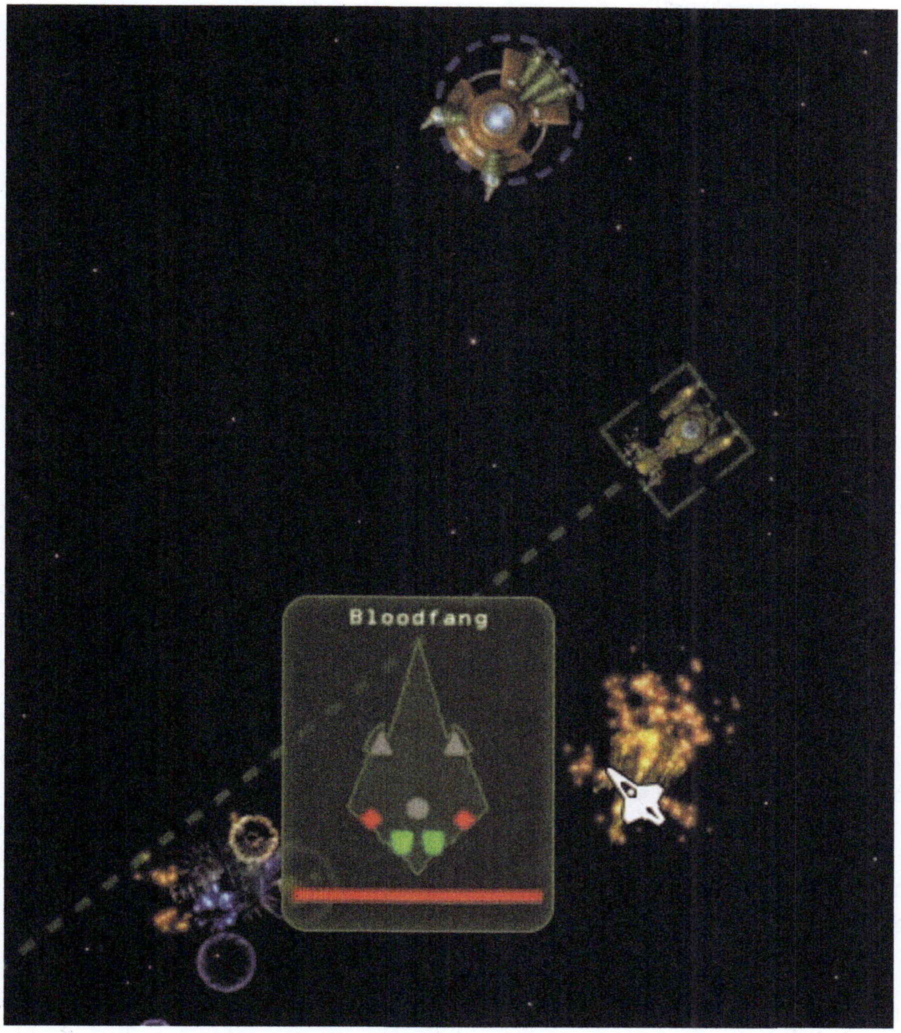

Figure 53.2

Weird Worlds: More Adventures in Infinite Space

RC: Other games we played that were inspiring were Frank Butterfield's Voyage of the BSM Pandora, which turned out to be a kind of proof-of-concept that a big game theme could be condensed into a small, short game yet still convey the feeling, not just the flavor, of a star spanning saga. Though the examples I'm mentioning are fantasy-themed, they played into the design concept directly. Proto-roguelike boardgames like Terrence Donelly's Sorcerer's Cave and Greg Costikyan's Deathmaze, were, like modern full-blown roguelikes like Henzell's Dungeon Crawl and NetHack, strong influences as well.

JH: Ah, you said the magic word! Starflight also came up in an interview I did some years back with Tarn Adams of Dwarf Fortress, who also cites it as an inspiration! And Starflight's lead designer Greg Johnson is also one-half of Johnson-Voorsanger, who made ToeJam & Earl, and the prime mover of the current TJ&E sequel/revision! It's starting to seem like Starflight is a secret nexus of inspiration for roguelike developers.

RC: Starflight was a big deal. I remember waiting and waiting, exasperated, for the C-64 port to be released. Seemed to take forever but it was worth it. Btw, Starflight's spiritual cousin, Star Control II, strongly influenced the way music is used in Strange Adventures and Weird Worlds.

JH: All of those games you mentioned before sound really interesting, especially Greg Costikyan's entry. He's a bit of a NetHack fan himself you know.

RC: I didn't. I know he was a hardcore Civ fan. Greg has a fantastic imagination. He's tackled quite a variety of subjects. His ludography is frighteningly impressive. ("A bibliography is a list of the books you've written; a discography is a list of the music you've recorded; and a ludography is a list of the games you've designed."—GC)

JH: I'm a bit interested in that 4X game you mentioned. Is that project entirely abandoned or might it reappear someday? Or alternatively, do you feel it's important to be able to abandon a project that's no longer working, or gone in uninteresting directions?

IK: We have abandoned a few projects for various reasons. The big 4X game was one—it was just too ambitious for us to finish, too similar to some other games, like Master of Orion, and I didn't really know how to do multi-player code at the time (plus the whole MS-DOS thing!). It was a good choice to switch to smaller projects.

RC: For us it's about being caught by something. Like when you get into Game of Thrones or Magic: The Gathering. Only the special, best things capture you. That's what we wait for and pounce on when it shows up!

IK: Even if we do decide to make a 4X style game in the Infinite Space universe, it will not be the old project resurrected. But it's interesting how much "stuff" from it appears in Sea of Stars—for example, the races and most of the items etc have a direct lineage to the old 4X project.

JH: You're calling the games "space roguelikes," could you explain, or even justify, that statement?

IK: Right, our games don't exactly look like the typical fantasy roguelike! But they do play like one in many ways. We have the procedurally generated maps, high level of randomness and the sense of being dropped in a world that's bigger than what you can experience in one play-through. There's no saving and reloading, so all your actions are permanent. There are tons of items and it's up to the player to figure out how to best use them. I'm a big fan of traditional roguelikes as well, so I know the dissimilarities too, of course. For a while, we used the moniker "Roguelike-like" but it's a bit clumsy.

RC: Strange Adventures and the rest of the series pass the test in most cases, yet they must be termed as hybrids. I've looked at the Berlin Interpretation and have thought a lot about this. We respect the pure roguelike form very much, for all of the good reasons. We do sometimes say these games are space roguelikes—but in the same way that FTL was termed that. The primary reason is that it is the best way to describe the Infinite Space gameplay, overall, with just one word. Describing SAIS as "space strategy" or "adventure strategy" or "strategy rpg" doesn't convey the gameplay experience at all!

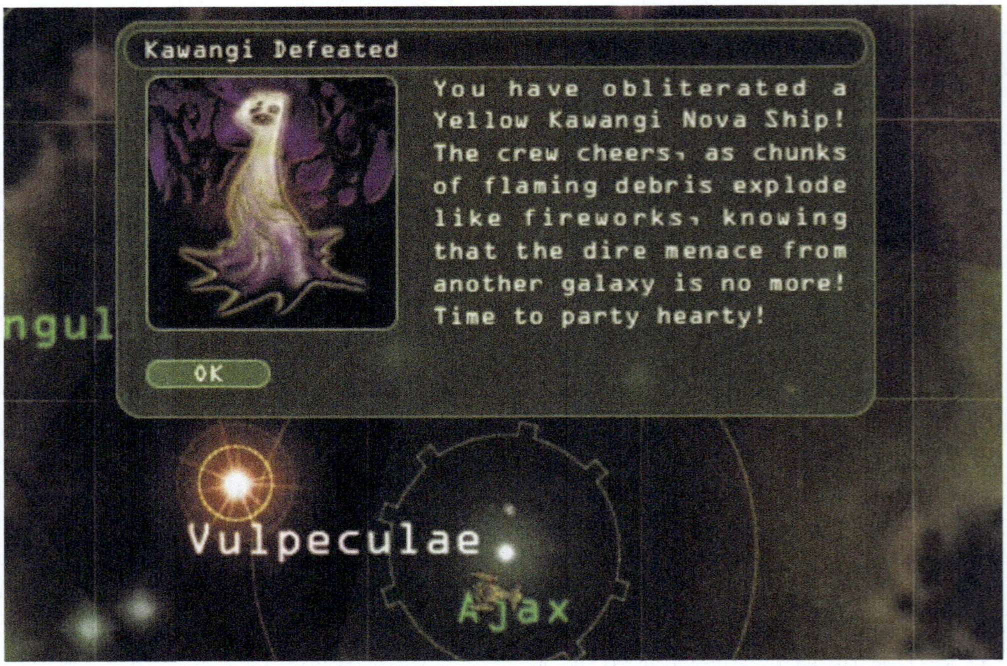

Figure 53.3

Weird Worlds: More Adventures in Infinite Space

JH: I didn't mean to imply that your games couldn't be roguelikes, we've certainly covered enough games that blur the lines! And I agree that "roguelike-like" is a bit clumsy, as you've probably witnessed, there's a bit of confusion on the proper way to identify games that are inspired by Rogue's randomness and replayable elements but aren't strictly top-down, tactical combat, dungeon exploration.

RC: We have to remember that the first makers of roguelikes didn't invent the Berlin list. Gary Gygax and Dave Arneson did. A roguelike is what it is (a randomized, turn-based D&D/Tolkien themed dungeon survival sim on a grid) because early roguelike creators were emulating the features of their favorite game. So, while the venerable roguelike form can number and claim these traits, it can't really own them.

JH: Describe the basic "explore a space in a limited time" gameplay.

RC: One roguelike aspect that isn't always mentioned—I don't think it's on the Berlin list—is clocks. Food clock. Radiation exposure clock. Spell duration clocks. Thirst clock. Poison damage clock. Etc. If one of these clocks time out, your character is in trouble, which adds more tension to the game. Awesome! I think clocks are an essential part of a roguelike game. Sea of Stars, Weird Worlds and Strange Adventures use clocks too. The primary one is to return to player character's homeworld within a set period of time or suffer a reward penalty. This victory condition mirrors somewhat the idea of Star Trek's "five year mission," or Darwin's voyage, or a pirate adventure for that matter.

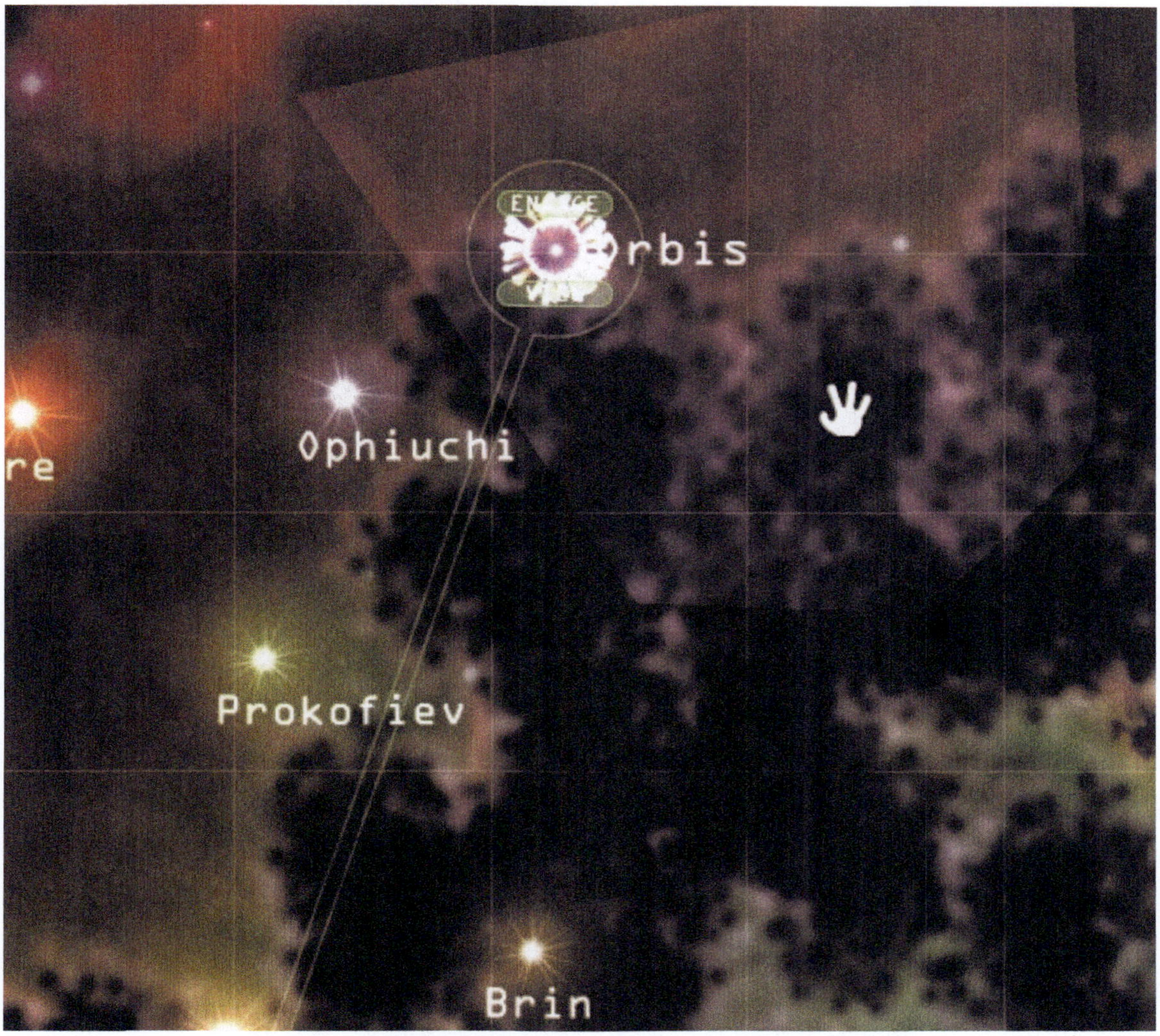

Figure 53.4

Weird Worlds: More Adventures in Infinite Space

JH: The alien races provide a good mix of beings to interact with, each of which presenting their own personality in behavior, text and combat. Any favorites?

RC: I really like one of the new species we added to Sea of Stars, the Calatians. They're mentioned in the previous games but actually make an appearance in IS3 as a full-fledged race. They boast of their mighty ships and fearsome weaponry that appear in combat as small and unthreatening. Are they bluffing? (Tip: If you're nice to them, you might even get rewarded with one to add to your flotilla.)

IK: The Tchorak have been my favorite for a long time, just because they are so . . . alien. Of course, I know much more about them than you'll see in any of our games, but I hope you'll get to know them better one of these days.

RC: I can't wait to explain the sex life of a Tchorak. Or maybe I can.

JH: Secret item features (Like "hypervision," or the Lookout Frogs & Toy Robot, or the Crystal Fish?) What inspired them? Why don't more items have these features? Is there a magic number?

IK: These items are a bit like a card that allows you to break one specific rule in a boardgame—they're limited by the number of rules that can be broken in a useful way. I do agree we should think of more, there are probably fun things that we've missed.

RC: What Iikka said. There is a sweet spot where it feels good and we sort of "call it." But it's also a matter of seeing a possible connection that might be interesting or entertaining or, more importantly, useful. If the designer puts a ship thief in the game, she should put one or two things in to help the player prevent theft as well.

JH: One-in-eight games in the original two Infinite Space games are "mission games," where the game rules change slightly and unexpectedly in the middle of play? What inspired them?

IK: I think it was at least partly inspired by some random events in 4X games, like Master of Orion where occasionally a "space amoeba" appears and starts to wreak havoc. In Strange Adventures we just had one, and we didn't want it to happen every time because that would have made the game very repetitive, so we made it fairly rare. Now, in Sea of Stars we have five different missions (and counting . . .) and we can just randomly pick one.

RC: These games are intended to be like instant space opera generators, so it stands to reason that every once in a while a chance to "save the galaxy," or save your character's homeworld, etc., should be included. It also breaks the game up from session to session, enhancing replayability, we hope, by helping to keep things fresh and surprising.

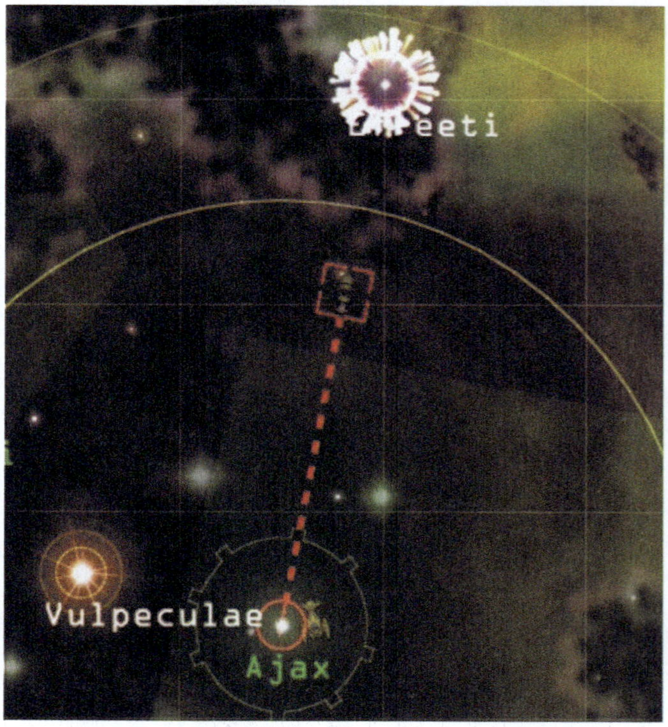

Figure 53.5

JH: One interesting thing about Weird Worlds in particular is how frequently one can come up non-combat, or what we might call "instant win" solutions to game problems, like [SPOILERS] Mirroring enemy fleets into black holes, Vacuum Collapsing the Yellow Kawangii or using the Chromium Gong on Primordius. These solutions seems to be deprecated somewhat in Sea of Stars in favor of more traditional combat. Is there a particular reason?

IK: With the exception of the mirror, these still work :) But we have tried to balance some items to make them less game-breaking—the gong no longer has unlimited uses, the hyperdrive is not always the best choice, and so on. This is mainly done to keep the game challenging even if you find the item.

JH: On the play changes with each version. Especially the substantial formula changes in Sea of Stars (Maj. Brass prologue dropped, set sector size, no need to return home at end, all mission games, removal of popular earlier items like Aetheric Mirror and Mantle of Babulon.) Was this to fix a perceived lack in the earlier games? Is the new game's 3D starmap related to them? Will we see any of these items return in later updates?

IK: We chose not to implement the mirror for various reasons—for example, we don't want you to accidentally move Haven Station or the Klakar Nest. If we made space stations non-mirrorable like the space hulk was in Weird Worlds, then you'd keep running into situations where you get a sensor blip but can't use the mirror, and that tells you it's a homeworld. If the mirror ever does appear, it will need to have some different kind of behavior. The Mantle would be easy enough to make, but as in Weird Worlds it would end up reducing your score so it's not a great item—also, combat is fun! It would perhaps be more interesting to come up with other ways to befriend specific races.

JH: Maybe describe a bit on the use of nebulas & black holes, their role in the design as an obstacle to exploration. (Nebulas usually slow the player down greatly upon entry; Black Holes may be hidden at the start of a map, and force the player to decide to turn back to forge ahead and possibly risk losing immediately.)

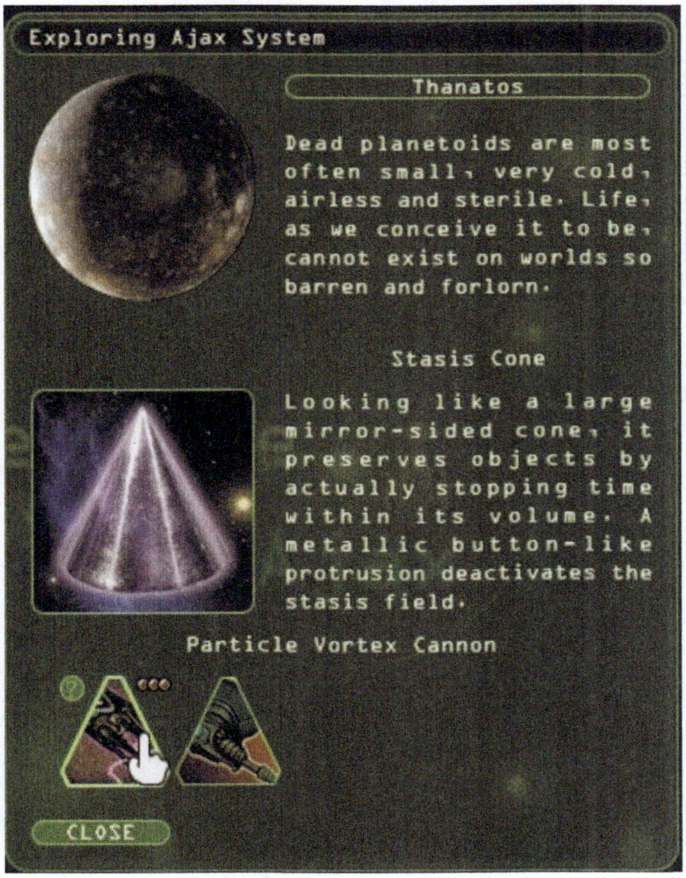

Figure 53.6

Weird Worlds: More Adventures in Infinite Space

IK: Since we're dealing with a time limit, adding "terrain" forces you to make plans around it and makes the game more interesting, and different each time. We originally had ideas for other kinds of obstacles, like asteroid fields, but just these two made the cut.

JH: Events—derelict ship, supernova, Esmeralda, alien rescues. Their appearance, and the timing with which they appear, has the potential to either profoundly change the game, or not really change it much at all, depending on when they turn up, it feels to me like an essential part of the Infinite Space experience. Do you agree?

IK: Oh yes, these are a big part of making each game session unique and giving you the sense that almost anything can happen in the Infinite Space universe, from the silly to the spectacular.

JH: The Infinite Space games have board and card game versions? What are they like?

RC: They're fun. Eat Electric Death! is an old school hex and turn-based tactical starship combat board-game based on the ships, ship system, items, and the way ships maneuver, in the computer game versions. Infinite Space: Explorers is essentially a starship combat card game that uses a "star-map" board to keep track of where fleets are, which stars have been explored and where card battles occur. The two Diceland Space sets based in the IS games use James Ernest's unique combat system with giant paper dice. Each die is a starship and you roll them on the table in combat. It's diceless and real time. Nobody makes games like Cheapass Games.

JH: How did James Ernst and Cheapass Games help the Strange Adventures series to get started?

RC: By generously providing a distribution point for the game. Indie game portals didn't exist then, so it was terrific to have his support. He also got CD's made of the first three or four games. Those are like collector's items now.

JH: On mods . . . Where did you get the idea to make the game moddable? How easy is it, would you say, to make a mod? What are your favorite mods?

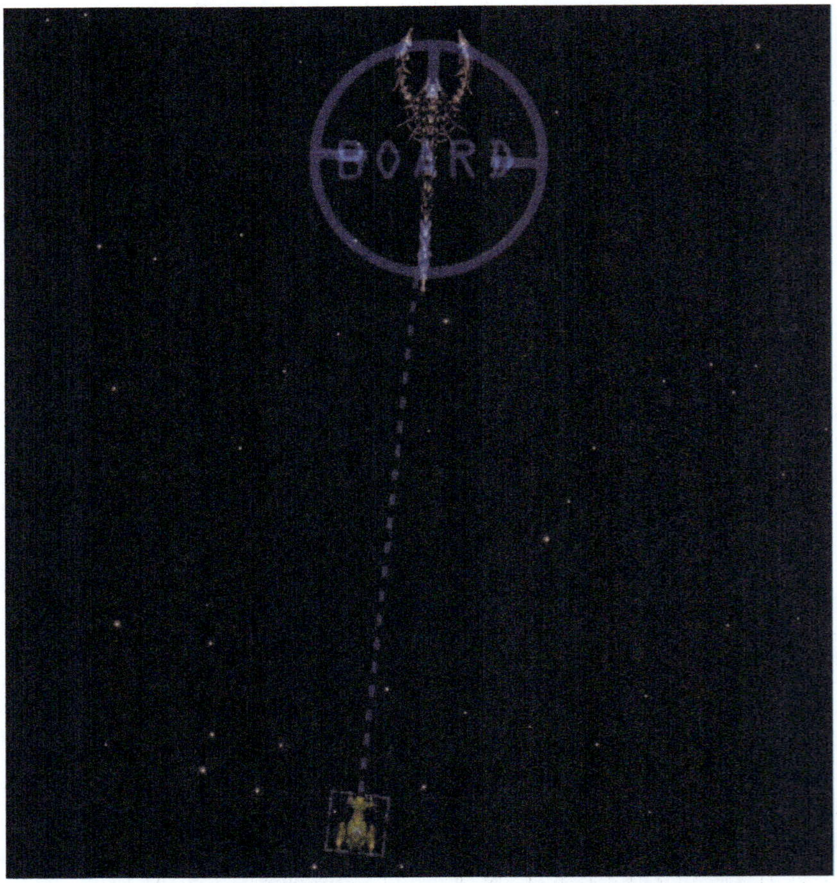

Figure 53.7

Weird Worlds: More Adventures in Infinite Space

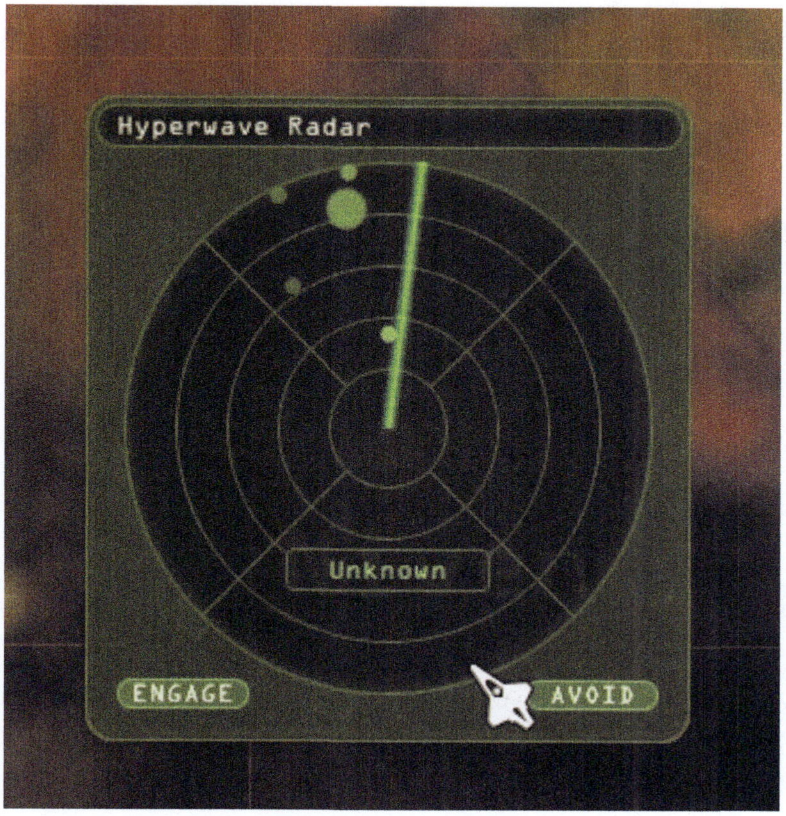

Figure 53.8

Weird Worlds: More Adventures in Infinite Space

IK: Rich and I both made mods before we started working in the game industry, so it was natural to us. I also think that the same things that make the game easy to modify, make it easier for us to create the content for it in the first place. There are a lot of cool mods, but the "Even Stranger" and "Even Weirder" series is a standout favorite for sure. Modding tends to get harder as games get more complex, but we try to make it as easy as possible. In Sea of Stars, we use standard text file format to store all the data in the game so it's possible to get started with just a text editor.

JH: Will we see the return of Major Brass?

IK: He's the face of the Terran Space Fleet :) Not sure if he's going to make a personal appearance, but anything's possible.

RC: New face; same Brass.

JH: Who was Phosphorous?

IK: Phosphorous, aka. Bill Sears was the third Eel and our main artist for over a decade. He made the splash screen art for half a dozen games, tons of Weird Worlds items and creatures, etc. We had some unforgettable times together, and multiple road trips down to IGF in California. He passed away after a heart attack in 2012. We really miss him.

RC: Bill was an amazing friend and contributor. And musician, as we later found out! But not in the traditional sense of guitars and trombones. His music was strange, handmade in his garage and surrealistic. Technically it would be called musique concrete and found sound music. You know how it is. Usually when you hear sound collages that are a bit avant garde, you say no! Turn it off! But it isn't that way at all with Bill's music. It is engrossing like falling into a mind adventure. Very special stuff.

JH: Is any of his music in the games? Do you think there might be a place for it, even if just one or two pieces, or are there rights or thematic issues? Is there a place where readers can find them on the internet?

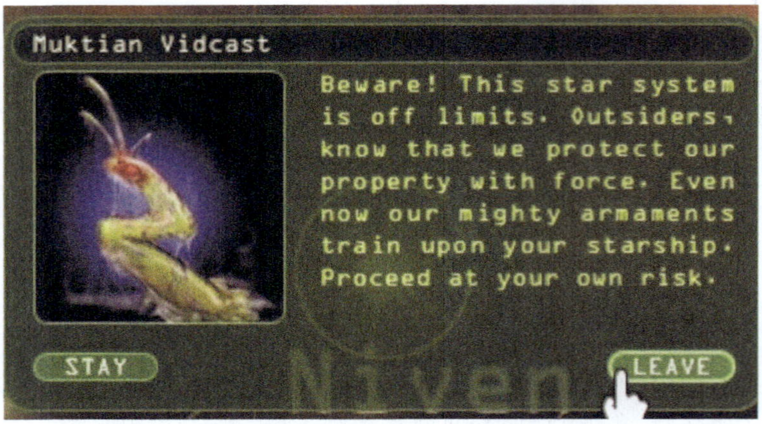

Figure 53.9

Weird Worlds: More Adventures in Infinite Space

IK: Bill created music for both Brainpipe and Data Jammers. We shared an Independent Games Festival audio award for Brainpipe. You can listen to some of Bill's music here: https://nightmareband.bandcamp.com/.

Thanks to Rich and Iikka for talking with me, and for putting up with my whimsical and makeshift interview process!

54

Interview: Rodain Joubert on Desktop Dungeons

April 2010 (*January 2016*: Since this was written, a commercial version of the game has been released on Steam for Windows, Mac and Linux, and for Android on the Google Play store and iOS devices on the Apple App Store.)

Desktop Dungeons is a quick-play freeware PC dungeon exploration game that has been enjoying tremendous popularity over the last few months. Each game involves a single screen of a dungeon, and is typically less than 30 minutes to complete. Yet it provides an abundance of races and classes to play as, and special dungeon types to explore, that endlessly remix its small number of basic elements into completely new challenges each time.

As comments in blog posts about it tend to point out, Desktop Dungeons is not technically a roguelike game. It doesn't have tactical combat, has no identification features, and its simulation of time is fairly simplistic. And yet, it has some fairly strong ties to roguelikes that definitely bring it into the purview of a roguelike column.

It is a game, ultimately, about gaining levels and making good use of limited resources; it's quite difficult and yet also has a strong sense of balance, where a decision made half the game ago can suddenly be what pushes you over the edge at the end. Also, live or die, each game is usually less than 30 minutes, so bad decisions don't drag you down. If it turns out you can't win, you just retire and try again. Really good players can tackle one of the challenge dungeons or even participate in ranked games the scores of which get uploaded to an online scoreboard.

The game seems to be pretty popular on the gaming blogs right now. In this April 2010 interview with South African creator Rodain Joubert, alias "Nandrew," we discuss the game's creation, its great, sudden popularity, its inspiration in Dungeon Crawl, and a little bit about goats and orcs.

(*Note*: I forgot I had Derek Yu's custom tileset for the game installed when I took a couple of the screenshots. I'm leaving them in, however, because his set is great. Not that the originals are a slouch mind you. And yes, it's the same Derek Yu who created Spelunky!)

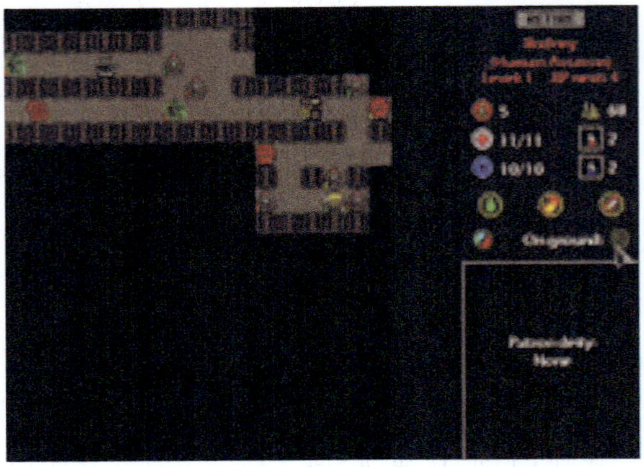

Figure 54.1

Desktop Dungeons

JH: First off, if you'd like to introduce yourself to our readers?

RJ: I'm Rodain "Nandrew" Joubert, a South African freelance journalist and indie game developer. I'm also a fedora wearer and proud of it.

JH: How long have you been developing games?

RJ: I've been developing games for at least ten years. Though a great chunk of that period would better be labelled as "screwing around and making stuff move on a screen." My game development career started gathering more steam when I joined up with South Africa's Game.Dev community and started enjoying the support and camaraderie of a local community :) I've been with that group for about four years now. They're awesome and stuff.

JH: Ah! A local community can help provide a lot of support, technically, morally, and with resources. Which, like, sounds like the most obvious thing in the world when I say it.

RJ: Definitely! I write frequent articles aimed at game development newbies, and one of the points I advocate is getting involved with a good community.*

54.1 Dungeon Crawl and Desktop Dungeons

JH: Let's talk a bit about Desktop Dungeons, then. How did you come up with the idea for the game?

RJ: In a sentence, I'd describe the idea as stemming from my love of Dungeon Crawl Stone Soup married with an inability to commit myself to long sessions of roguelike gaming. I'm a big fan of the idea that you can get a lot of gaming value out of much shorter sessions and "casual" experiences.

JH: It is true that most of the major roguelikes tend to be fairly long games.

RJ: I was also suitably inspired by Edmund McMillen's article on game development do's and don'ts at the time, and decided that I'd really just create the sort of game I'd love to play, using a lot of the lessons outlined in the DCSS philosophy.

Of course, it turned out to be barely anything like the game I claim inspiration from, but I reckon it's the thought that counts. :P

JH: The philosophy, correct me if I'm wrong as this is just an educated guess, would be to reduce or eliminate unnecessary variables, keep things as simple as possible without reducing complexity, and to eliminate grinding behavior?

It's both not like Crawl (in that it's not even a roguelike technically) and it is like Crawl (in that there are tradeoffs to a lot of player decisions). And Crawl is just generally inspiring too, its elements come together very well.

RJ: Yep. DCSS took EVERYTHING and made it a meaningful decision, and I wanted that to carry through to Desktop Dungeons. I ended up taking that idea to the extent that the very act of dungeon exploration became its own resource, and every monster encounter, movement, spell cast and

* Links at the end of the interview.

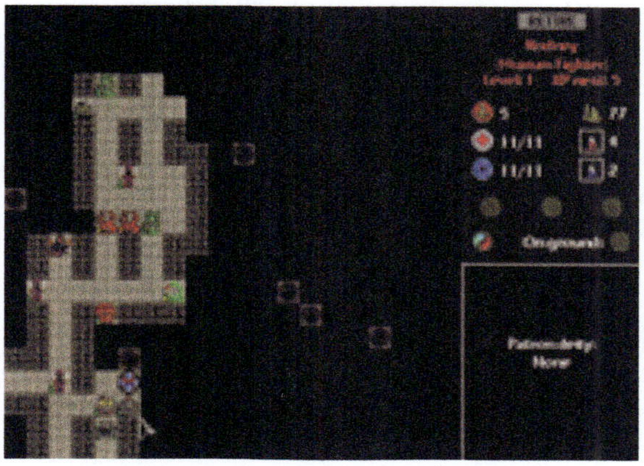

Figure 54.2

Desktop Dungeons

item pickup could tip the balance subtly, yet significantly. All of the game's elements did their best to interact with one another in as many ways as possible.

I reckon it's far from perfect in this sense, but I like to think that I gave it a jolly good shot. Crawl is astounding, not least because it wasn't afraid to knock convention. I mean, it takes real guts to develop a game to rival a dinosaur like NetHack while explicitly disagreeing with parts of its design.

JH: I think you did an excellent job at that. Probably Desktop Dungeons does it a little better, in fact, than Crawl, because it's a lot more, um, "elemental" is the word I think I'll use. Because there are fewer variables and it's a "simpler" game, the parts that are there take on greater import.

RJ: Elemental is a cool word. :P I was also inspired by researching and writing about game design minimalism, and the idea of distilling a genre as great and expansive as a Roguelike to its core—and almost puzzle-like—elements, was simultaneously daunting and . . . well, juicy!

JH: There are a few other games that Desktop Dungeons reminds me of, that take those limited elements and give them profound, and sometimes unexpected, uses. MULE is like that, and Rampart, and, not coincidentally, Rogue. It seems to have worked out very well, although I have to admit being a little intrigued with the idea of where you could go with it from here.

RJ: The original Rogue probably did it best in a lot of ways. It didn't need any fluff to justify its own existence.

54.2 Platforms and Implementation

RJ: With regards to where it goes from here:

I'm currently working for a South African indie studio, QCF Design, and the crew there have some pretty big plans lined up for a good and proper version of Desktop Dungeons with a nicer name, nicer graphics and more polished design in general. You know, the sort of stuff that people may actually be willing to pay for. We haven't decided on a final platform just yet, though we have some ideas. At the same time, I'll be looking to improve the freeware version that's currently being developed in Game Maker.

JH: I think if you took the game just as it is and put it on the iPhone you might find yourself with a hit. And it seems to me like the game is really made for the iPhone interface.

RJ: iPhone is one possibility! We're already keen to see how 100 Rogues does on release.

JH: (Nice plug for 100 Rogues. I'm sure Keith Burgun won't mind at all, heh.)

JH: Ah! I spot a segue opportunity! (Ahem.)

Would you like to tell us about how Desktop Dungeons is implemented? The language you use to develop? Or whatever the heck Game Maker is? Did you find it to be limiting?

RJ: Ahhh. well, a lot of people will probably know about Game Maker already. It's quite popular nowadays, and is the driving force behind some really great contemporary indie projects including Derek Yu's Spelunky (which, lo and behold, is also a tribute to roguelikes!). Basically, it's a rapid game creation framework which utilizes a drag-n-drop system backed up by code scripting and the

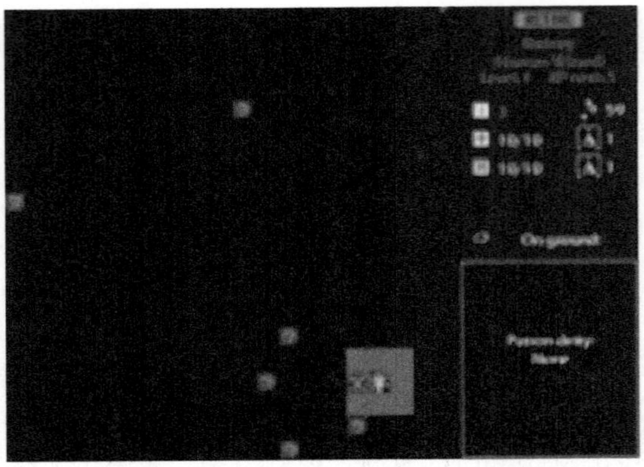

Figure 54.3

Desktop Dungeons

like. It's actually remarkably flexible for an "easy game creation" tool, especially since it follows good programming practice at its heart.

JH: It does seem to be used for more and more things lately.

RJ: It's an object-oriented, event-driven environment that anybody experienced with code should be able to recognize.

I've been using Game Maker almost exclusively for several years now: it allows me to focus on the design of a game instead of its technical implementation, which is a bit of a godsend after hacking through years of Pascal, Java and C++. In my opinion, a lot of developers focus on art and programming without recognizing good design as a skill of its own.

54.3 Design Process, Commercial Viability and Promotion

JH: Here's some more questions for you: How did you design it? All at once, or did it sort of accrue like a snowball over time? And do you have a final goal in sight, or at least in mind?

RJ: I have a personal rule that I like to follow, and encourage everybody I know to follow: if you sit down with a game design and fail to make something fun, engaging and relatively "complete" within a week, it's not an idea worth pursuing.

My original version of Desktop Dungeons was made in about six days, and it was a far cry from what it is even now (still at a tentative version 0.051), but it was something that could stand up on its own legs and provide people with some fun. I didn't have any plans beyond, say, another version or two before I moved on to another project, but people kinda got excited about it rather quickly. So I guess I just shrugged my shoulders and kept going :P

JH: So you have a pretty good idea where to go from here?

RJ: Definitely. I want to do more work on the freeware to incorporate all of the exciting ideas that began forming after the game started garnering some popularity. It sort of doubles as further service to the people who are enjoying it right now, and an excellent testing ground for concepts that could make its commercially worthy successor. As of the beginning of April, we'll also be starting work full-time on the main DD project.

JH: Although for various reasons I like open source and freeware games (after all, most roguelikes fall into that category), I think there is an opportunity to make a go of this one commercially. Good luck with it!

RJ: Thanks a bunch! I hope that people continue to enjoy the game. :)

JH: When you say "full time," then, you're still working on the freeware version "part time" so to speak, right?

RJ: Yeah, actually, when I mention "full time" on DD, I mean that we'll not be bogged down with the mobile advergame projects that QCF has been adopting to build up capital with. They're not the most inspiring jobs, but they put food on the proverbial table and allow us to start self-funding projects like DD for reasonable durations.

JH: It sounds like a good strategy for getting it off the ground.

RJ: It's solid, but we're still kinda poor in the bigger scheme of things :P Such is the lot of an indie, I'd reckon.

JH: Hey, the indie field is home to, by far, the most interesting game development AND game projects right now. Of course I may be a little biased, as most roguelikes would be considered to be "indie" by some measure.

RJ: Definitely interesting. But when I mention "poor," I'm talking about it in a very literal, financial sense. ;) QCF Design are small fish, even in the indie pond.

JH: If you have a company name, then you're already at least half up the ladder. Many indie developers are just one or two people. 2D Boy is two guys. Well, such is my opinion, heh.

RJ: A fair point. And that's not to say that QCF won't do its gosh-darn best and whatnot! I just think it's important to keep things in perspective.

JH: Let's talk for a moment about the fan community around the game, and the word-of-mouth publicity. When did Desktop Dungeons get its big "break" publicity-wise? Was it a mention on a specific blog? Or did it just sort of grow, spreading from person to person. I was a little surprised when two completely unrelated people mentioned the game to me within a couple of days of each other!

RJ: For quite a few of my recent projects (and other projects found within the Game.Dev community), I'd have to give credit to the IndieGames blog for that initial kick of popularity. That site is run by a pretty swell crew, and I tip my hat to those folks. Too many people treat gaming journalists with a certain degree of derision while forgetting just how important a role they play in the industry. It's what helps silly little people like me get their games out to a broader populace. It's what allows cool stuff like interviews to take place.

I can also give credit to some indie community folks I know, and in particular the tireless efforts of one DukeOFPrunes. He knows who he is, and he totally kicks ass. DukeOFPrunes is one of the Game.Dev community members. He's an all-round cool guy :P

JH: (The Management appreciates the compliment, regarding "cool stuff")

RJ: Funnily, though, I think that I was the weakest link in my own marketing chain. The word-of-mouth on this game really took a life of its own, and despite the fact that I've written about game marketing myself from time to time, I absolutely failed to take any action of my own on this thing. The fact that I've enjoyed this much attention is nothing short of amazing. I think it's the sort of story that would make the folks at Wolfire slap me.

JH: It is gratifying to see. A lot of indie developers sort of languish in obscurity, but every so often one goes nova.

RJ: But yeah, I really don't deserve this much attention for the game. I've broken every rule in the marketing book :P

54.4 Difficulty and Humor

JH: That's most of the general things. Would you like to take a few minutes now to discuss some elements of the design? Or would you consider that as being something of a spoiler?

RJ: There was a matter about the difficulty.*

JH: Ah, by all means go ahead.

RJ: The game is hard by necessity, yes, though I feel the difficulty helps make the experience more REWARDING rather than less challenging.

It boils down to the matter of meaningful decisions. One way of making a decision meaningful is to attach permanence, as most roguelikes would do. You make a choice, and you can't undo it, so make it a wise one.

JH: Right. This is related to permadeath.

RJ: However, a decision's impact is also affected by the impact of its consequences, and in a difficult game this can mean the difference between a narrow escape and said horrible permadeath. If roguelikes (and by loose extension, DD) were any easier, this impact would be lost, because there would be comparatively little consequence for your decisions. An easy game slaps you on the

* The original question was an aside halfway back in the interview and was edited out.

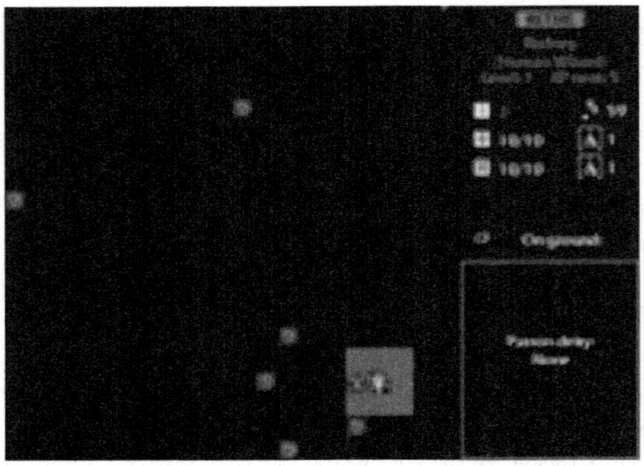

Figure 54.4

Desktop Dungeons

wrist and gives you a gold medal instead of a platinum one, so to speak. Not really something that can scare, motivate or involve a player. When there's more at stake, it's more emotionally engaging.

JH: It does seem that there are a lot of games out there that nearly fall over themselves to tell the player what a great job he's doing.

RJ: I doubt that anybody really likes steamrolling a game. Oh ho no. they like to win by that proverbial "one click" . . .

JH: A button marked "Win the game."

RJ: . . . and in the long term, that builds up a false sense of achievement.

It's great once in a while, and I have no problem with playing easy games. But I also know how satisfying overcoming a genuine challenge can be. In DD, the difference between a new player and a veteran becomes obvious. Although there's a reasonable element of luck involved, some parts of the game are highly deterministic and the average win rate of a vet is significantly higher than that of a beginner. It's all about the advanced tricks and tactics that emerge from creative application of the rules.

I'd like to stress that there's nothing wrong with easy games. They're pretty fun too. It's just that there's a time and a place for those, and not every game has to roll over and let you scratch its belly.

JH: One such trick is how, when you gain a level, your health and magic get refilled. That makes monsters themselves into a resource.

RJ: Exactly, it's a sneaky tactic whose value isn't immediately understood, but becomes an indispensable part of play once figured out.

JH: Everything in Desktop Dungeons is a resource in *some* way. Even, for one of the classes, those blood-stains left on the ground. I was rather surprised to see that.

RJ: Yep, that's DD's interpretation of Dungeon Crawl's idea that an enemy's dead body can be put to good use! There's actually a few nods to DCSS in DD which a savvy player may just pick up. Heck, I wanna find a way to throw Sigmund into the mix at some point. Sigmund would totally rock.

JH: Sigmund would be awesome. For the uninitiated, Sigmund is a deadly early unique opponent in Dungeon Crawl. He's sort of the game's mascot.

RJ: I also make a few cheeky indie references here and there related to other games.

JH: Some (boring) players may disagree with me, but I think joke monsters are generally awesome. I still get a kick out of Desktop Dungeons' Goo Balls. It had me looking around for a cameo by the Sign Painter.

RJ: The goo balls and the meat men are, in some ways, some of my favourite monsters, simply due to their presence being completely tongue-in-cheek. Funnily enough, a lot of people lose the goo reference. Because while the description suggests World of Goo, it's actually drawn like the Gish tarball. Dunno why I did that.

JH: The name of the Goo Ball boss makes the connection obvious though, as does the boss intro message. One of my favorite things about roguelikes (and Desktop Dungeons too, which I'm including here as a kind of honorary roguelike) is how they don't take themselves too seriously.

RJ: I truly appreciate that sentiment. :P Desktop Dungeons started out not taking itself seriously, and I want it to stay that way even if it starts making money and all that other boring stuff. Heck, our mascot is a damn goat! Goats are the antithesis of serious business.

JH: Goats are awesome. Goats are beyond awesome.

RJ: They also make for great fan art.

JH: Goat Bosses, however, are serious business. Ouch.

RJ: Very nasty for warriors to run into.

JH: Roguelike games could stand to have more goats in them.

RJ: If I recall correctly, actually, the goat was loosely inspired by Crawl's presence of those Yaks of bloody doom and death. Half of my characters wound up getting killed by yaks. It was rather embarrassing.

JH: The descriptions of yaks in that game are great. "The common dungeon yak."

RJ: Like that time my character starved to death while levitating over some food.

JH: The next adventure finds a skeleton floating in the air, upside down, its bony arm outstretched towards a food ration on the ground.

RJ: Those descriptions are great, but nothing beats the messages from your personal Orc army when worshipping Beogh.

JH: Never gonna give you up! Never gonna let you down!

RJ: That was the best part!

JH: It's like shepherding a horde of preschoolers through the dungeon!

RJ: Especially since some of them take the time to smile and wave at you when you're fighting off legions of monsters. Kinda like, "Hey! Hi! How goes it, buddy? :D"

JH: Eventually one of them graduates to First Grade and gains the ability to summon demons.

RJ: You know, that was the great thing about the orc army. You'd form attachments. Especially if you've carried one guy all the way from lowly orc to Warlord. Epic stuff.

JH: Yeah, it is a little saddening when one of your named guys kicks the bucket. Especially if it's a warlord. Then it's doubly sad.

54.5 Links Relating to the Developer

RJ: Oh, by the way, you wanted some links? I've got a small army of 'em.

JH: Was just about to ask about those.

RJ:
- www.devmag.org.za/: Dev.Mag, one of the places I write for.
- www.devmag.org.za/articles/249-MINIMISED-GAME-DESIGN-FOR-INDIES/: The article I wrote on minimalist design, referenced earlier.
- www.devmag.org.za/articles/78-ZERO-BUDGET-INDIE-MARKETING-GUIDE/: Another one on marketing which I totally didn't end up using.
- www.indiegames.com/blog/2009/12/opinion_indie_game_design_dos.html: Edmund McMillen's catalyzing piece about indie do's and don'ts, a great, inspiring read.
- http://nag.tidemedia.co.za/category/game-dev/: The lightweight beginner's articles that I write for NAG online. Not exactly heavy literature, but it's far more approachable for newbies. (*January 2016*: the series appears to have been taken over by someone else.)
- www.qcfdesign.com/: The QCF Design website.

JH: Hearing about all this writing makes me feel like a slacker.

RJ: I'm reluctant to give the Game.Dev and forum thread links, because the hard links for those will prolly break soon.

JH: Changing servers I hope, and not going under?

RJ: Yeah, changing domain name and everything, in fact. The links will break permanently.

JH: Ah! Let us know when it's all moved over then.

RJ: I encourage people to be linked here for the main "game info hub": www.qcfdesign.com/?cat=20 We'll keep this page updated with the forum thread location, and the wiki location.*

* Yes, Desktop Dungeons has a wiki. It's filled with lots of spoilers so read with caution.

55

Spelunky

February 2009 (*January 2020*: When this article was first written, the freeware prototype of Spelunky had just been released, and Derek Yu was best known for being one of the developers of early indie hit Aquaria. In the time since then, an extraordinarily popular commercial version was released, which has entertained and inspired players now for seven years. A sequel is in development. Please enjoy this early look at what would become a gaming sensation.)

> Probably the easiest way to describe Spelunky is that it's (kind of) like La-Mulana meets NetHack—every time you play the levels, items, monsters, and so forth, are all procedurally-generated. [. . .] My goal was to create a fast-paced platform game that had the kind of tension, re-playability, and variety of a roguelike. In roguelikes, the gameplay tells the story, and I wanted to give Spelunky that type of a feeling . . . but make the player rely on their reflexes rather than their brain (or knowledge of what 50 billion command keys do!). If there's a best of both worlds, that's what I was trying to go for.
>
> —Derek Yu, introducing Spelunky on TIGSource Forums

Spelunky has been talked about on a fairly substantial number of blogs in the short month of its public existence. Considering that its aim is to bring some of the unique characteristics of the roguelike games into a different genre, I figured it was fair game for examination here. The result is quite a clever little game, highly addictive and quick to play. Death is incredibly frequent, but that should come as no hindrance to us, right?

Right?

The object of Spelunky is to work through a series of cave levels, avoiding damage and sudden death while collecting treasure and working towards the mysterious goal. Every level begins with the player at the top, the exit somewhere at the bottom, and a lot of loot and pain to discover along the way. Yep, sounds like a roguelike all right.

But Spelunky is a platformer, an action game presented with a side view. Its controls are greatly simplified, and the emphasis is on finding clever ways around obstacles. Treasure is found in the form of money and jewels, as extra supplies, as carryable tools like teleporters and shotguns, and as special equipment ranging from climbing gloves to jetpacks.

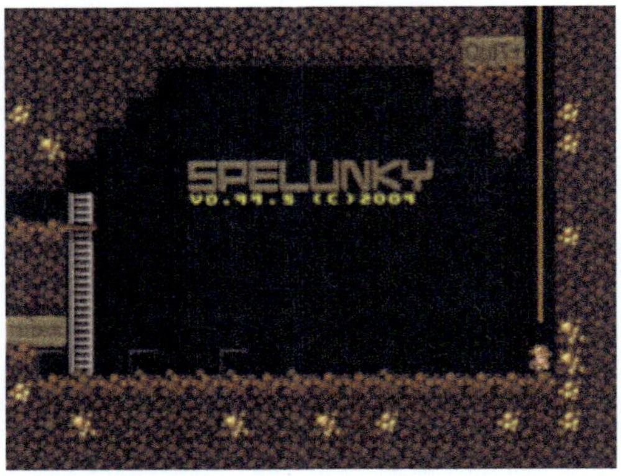

Figure 55.1

Spelunky (Freeware)

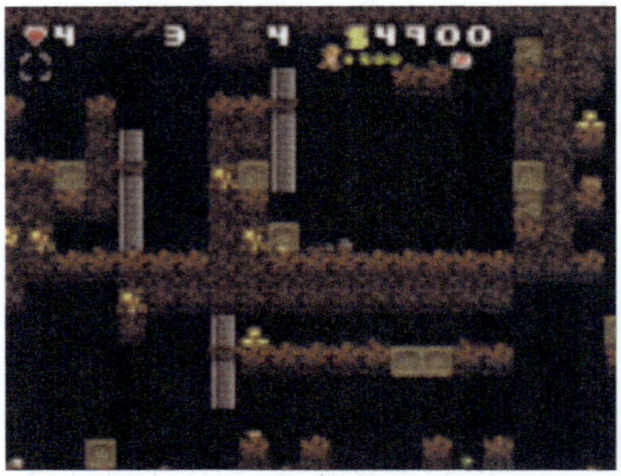

Figure 55.2

Spelunky (Freeware)

Making its array of dynamically created action puzzles possible is a fairly deep system of object interactions, which helps to push this borderline case back into our purview.

Nearly everything can be made use of in the right circumstances, including a lot of the enemies who are trying to eat our poor hero, who was unofficially dubbed "Indie" by the TIGSource Forums. Bats can be lured to set off arrow traps. Exploding frogs can break open sealed chambers. Falls from great heights can be survived by landing upon a hapless snake. One of the most impressive examples of these interactions has to do with the many ways of defeating arrow traps. Found in the first four levels, they are one of the game's most interesting obstacles, and they well illustrate the kind of situations the game's excellent random level algorithm can produce.

55.1 Avoiding the Point

One of the best ways to design traps, in other games as well as in roguelikes, is to give them an activating method, to simulate some operating mechanism. Not to just automatically harm the player when he enters the trigger area, but set some process in motion that harms him. It feels less arbitrary, and it potentially gives him a way of escaping the effect if he can come up with a way to avoid or subvert the process. In NetHack, for example, levitation means floor triggered traps or pits will not be set off, and if one can find and move the boulder-half of a rolling boulder trap, it is made harmless. This way it feels less like damage-by-fiat. It makes sense.

Spelunky's arrow traps are another good example. They operate by sensing motion. It doesn't matter what, of the game's many types of objects, is doing the moving. What follows, in the name of examining the kinds of design decisions that went into making Spelunky, is a fairly in-depth examination of them. It should go without saying that this is a spoiler, although in this game it's a relatively minor one.

In the following image (Figure 55.4), the trap is circled in white, and the extent of its sight range is represented by the red line. That's about six-and-a-half blocks in front of the statue. The orange line shows about the route the arrow will follow.

Now take note that, in Spelunky, objects in rapid motion may harm the player. A stationary or slow-moving arrow is harmless, yet if you throw a rock against a wall so it bounces back and strikes you at full speed it'll hurt you. So, when the arrow reaches the end of that orange line it'll be at rest on the ground and cease to be a problem. If there were a wall in the way, the arrow would bounce off, and possibly harm Indie on its rebound. If it hurts it hurts bad, for arrow hits in Spelunky do two points of damage. That's half the player's base total, and enough of a penalty this early in the game to warrant a restart unless some other advantage has been found.

One way to thwart an arrow trap is simply to fall straight down through its watch line. If the player is a full block away from the trap as he falls by the arrow will miss him, even with the arrow's high speed. So, falling from point 1 will set the trap off safely . . . but only if the player can bend his fall so he lands on the steps below; if he landed on the low portion of the ground, the fall might be enough distance to inflict a point of falling damage. (This, mind, could be avoided by doing a ledge-hang from the upper platform, a good technique to utilize if you're unsure if the fall is safe or not.)

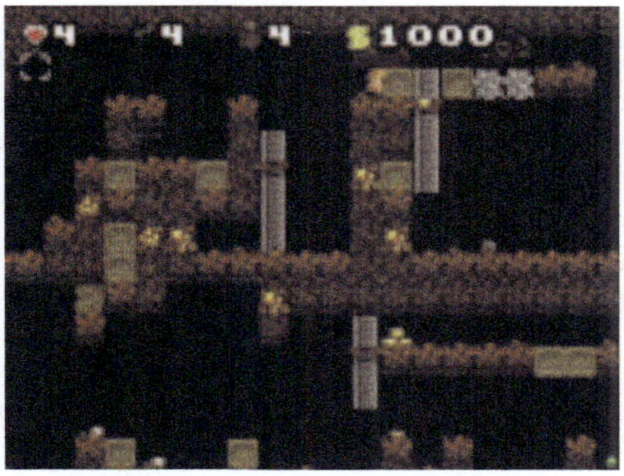

Figure 55.3

Spelunky (Freeware)

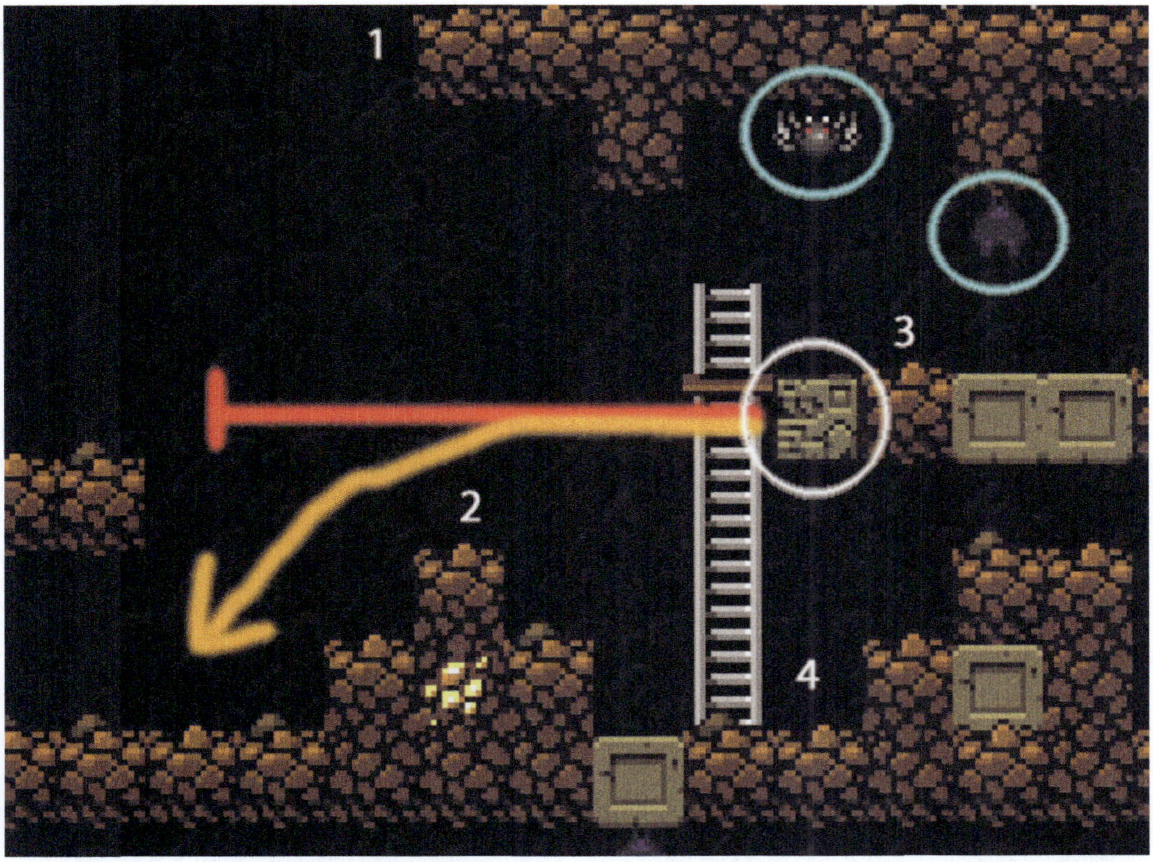

Figure 55.4

Spelunky (Freeware): The workings of arrow traps

If the player is approaching from ground level, then the situation is a little trickier. In many cases then it might be best to walk under the trap and let it be. But what if there were some prize on the upper route the player wanted to obtain, like a supply box or treasure chest? Standing on the upper-most step, at point 2, and jumping is a bad move. Indie would set off the trap at the apex of his jump, leaving him hanging for too long in the arrow's path, giving it plenty of time to strike and bleed off two pints.

But one of the enemies circled above is a bat. Bats trigger when the player enters a wide area beneath it, causing it to give chase. They're slow enemies, so in this case when it crosses the red line it'll trigger the trap and get killed instead of the player. Just standing at point 2, at the top of the stairs, should do the job. Triggering the spider would probably work too, though it activates only if Indie walks directly beneath, and it's more unpredictable in its attack than a bat.

What if the player is moving in from the right, and wants to pass the trap going left? It's a little expensive resource-wise, but he could drop a bomb above the trap at point 3 to outright destroy it. The player would have to be sure to get out of range of the blast; bomb hits are instant kills in this game. In a pinch he could also throw the bomb across from either point 3 or, in an upward arc, from point 4, and use its motion to set off the trap. Bombs are important equipment though, and it's best to look around for something else, like a rock, jar or skull to throw and set off the trap.

If none of these tools are available then it's really best to avoid setting it off at all, but if the player could find a way to enter the trap's sight at the very end and move slowly, he might be able to take advantage of the difference between its straight vision range and the arrow's curving path. This can be used to safely trigger arrow traps lying on flat ground; if the player slowly walks towards the trap, the arrow will actually hit the ground around the player's feet.

55.2 Spooky + Spelunky = Spelooky?

Roguelikes get their tension from the fact that the player, ideally, never has all the resources he might want. The tradeoff used in Rogue is food vs. experience; the player could stick around on the easy levels forever killing weak monsters to rise in level if he didn't have to keep moving to keep himself fed.

Spelunky's version of this takes the form of the Ghost. On all levels except the first and last, there is a two-minute timer on the level. After that the music turns spooky and a warning message is displayed. Thirty seconds after that and the Ghost enters the level, relentlessly chasing the player down and causing instant death on contact.

Some have complained about the timer, but I find that it's a brilliant addition, and the time limit seems quite well-tuned; if the player is working towards nothing other than reaching the exit then he has plenty of extra time; most levels can be beaten in less than a minute. But there are plenty of other rewards to find: damsels to increase health, idols worth a fortune if brought to the exit, and an abundance of gold and jewels.

There are also shops to buy from (or rob), supplies to collect and treasure to uncover. If the player is going along collecting these things as fast as he can, he might be able to get them all, but he'll have used up lots of his bombs and ropes getting them, and has probably taken a good amount of damage as well. The proper way to look at it is to look at an early exit, in the early levels at least, as a waste of resources. There's no benefit from having extra time at the end of a level (except for achieving a special trophy), so the player must strike a balance between efficient progress and loot collection.

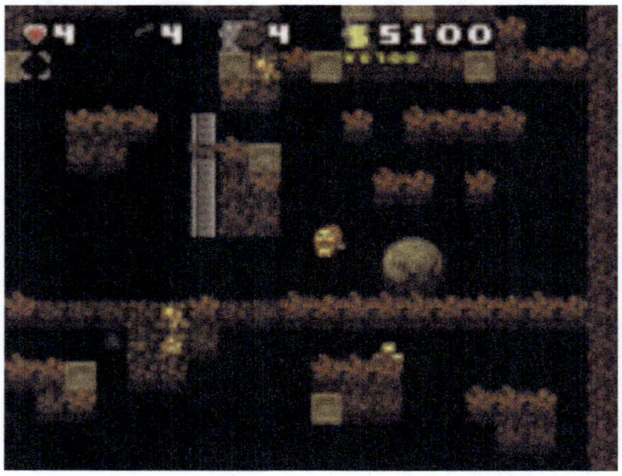

Figure 55.5

Spelunky (Freeware)

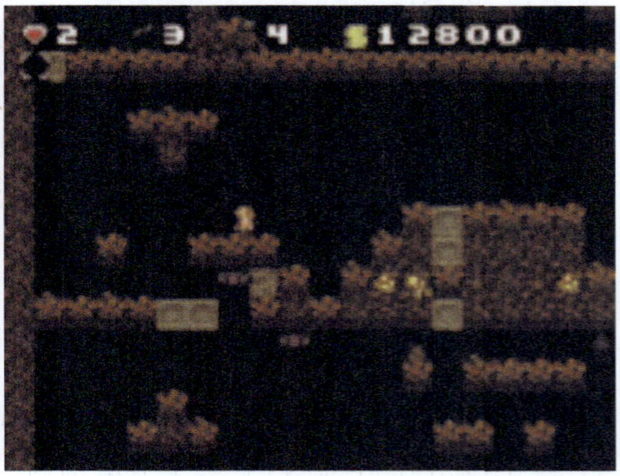

Figure 55.6

Spelunky (Freeware)

55.3 Somewhere, Izchak Miller Is Looking Down on Us, Smiling Maliciously

Of most interest to us roguelike fans, perhaps, is Spelunky's shops, which are lifted just about as completely as possible, given the completely different style of game it is, from NetHack. In NetHack a shop is a room with a shopkeeper at the door; the primary reason not to steal from the shop is that the owner will attempt to take out payment in flesh if you abscond with his merchandise. Spelunky's shopkeepers are similarly protective over their inventory; every one of them carries a shotgun, perhaps the game's most formidable weapon.

The following things will draw the wrath of a storekeeper: walking out of a shop carrying inventory without paying, damaging the walls, floor or ceiling of a shop, harming inventory or otherwise causing it to leave the premises, harming the shopkeeper either directly or indirectly, or sending an instakill object into a shop. (Throwing in a bomb is particularly entertaining, even if you are unlikely to survive the situation.)

Even if you escape the shopkeeper, or manage to kill him, all the remaining shopkeepers in the game will be out for blood. They'll also camp out by the exit waiting for you for a couple of levels. Of course, there are strategies to decrease the danger of robbery, but . . . but I don't think I'll be spoiling those kinds of things today, sorry.

55.4 Raising Real Estate Values in the Caves

For everything Spelunky does well, there are a couple of things that could perhaps use some work. (Well it is beta software after all.) What there is usually errs on the side of being just a little too difficult. There are a number of carryable items the player can use; firearms, exploration tools, flares, idols and damsels. But only one of these things can be carried in-hand at a time. The player can make do by running back and forth ferrying items along towards the exit, but this is somewhat annoying, and rapidly approaches unworkability as the player juggles more than two such items.

This could be seen as a limiting factor, to prevent people from being able to make full use of their inventory or to limit their usable possessions, but when the player encounters a dark level, carrying around a flare is essential unless the player wants to stumble into an arrow trap or jump down onto a bed of spikes. The result: dark levels tend to act as an effective barrier to carried items, making it difficult to keep even a single useful tool, like a shotgun, through them.

Even if the player manages to keep a flare all the way through a dark level, the odd way that light behaves in the game makes them less useful than you'd think. All light sources in a dark area display a very small portion of the (otherwise black) terrain around them. The player has a similar aura around him. If the player is physically close to a light source, however, his own circle expands, getting bigger the closer he is. The upshot is the technique of throwing a flare into a hole to see if there's spikes, monsters or arrow traps nearby is less useful than you'd expect, as the flare won't reveal anything beyond a block around where it

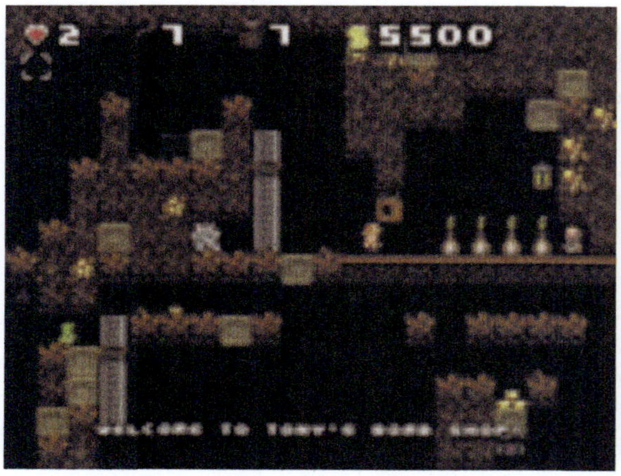

Figure 55.7

Spelunky (Freeware)

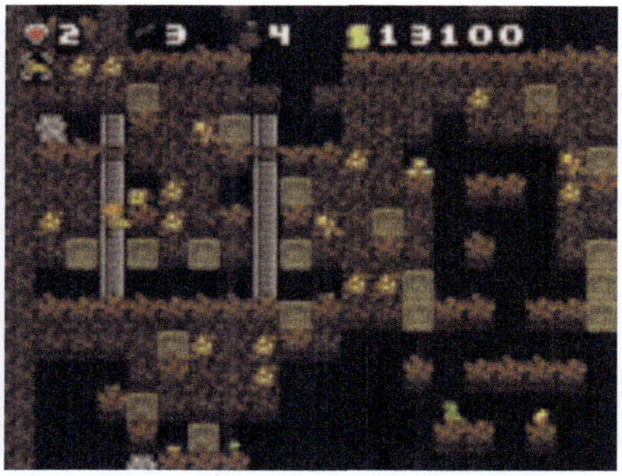

Figure 55.8

Spelunky (Freeware)

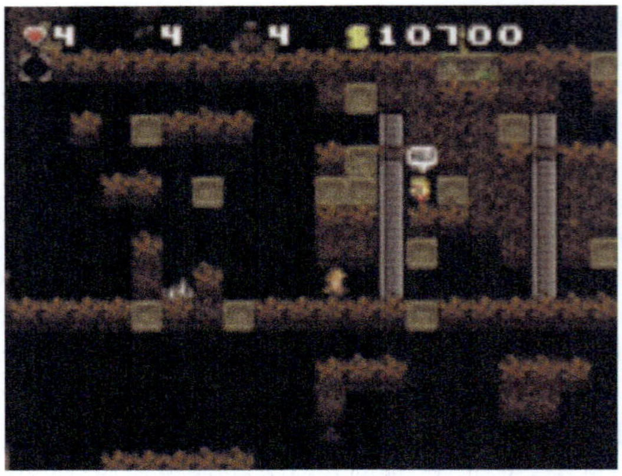

Figure 55.9

Spelunky (Freeware)

lands. (It may also find water, which kills the flare.) To see further, the player will have to jump down to be closer to the flare, but will then probably end up getting feasted upon by whatever lurks there unseen. This is potentially a big problem with the man-eating plants in some of the later levels.

Those arrow traps I mentioned before, for all their charming complexity, have a problem that makes them slightly too difficult in certain situations. Their sight range is 6 1/2 blocks, the play window 20 blocks wide. The player is typically in the middle of that, giving him 10 blocks of vision horizontally. The result is, when walking along level ground, the player tends to have little time to react to arrow traps lying on the ground in front of him, especially if he's using the run button to escape some other danger, like giant spiders or crushing boulders.

Some of the later areas are unusually demanding upon the player's supplies and equipment. He begins with four bombs and four ropes. Bombs can break through rock, generally one space horizontally and two spaces down; ropes allow the player to go upwards in a level without needing platforms to rest on. Extras can be found in the levels and bought in some stores, and while they're often common, they're just as often absent in the game. Not to spoil things unnecessarily, but the third area (levels 9–12) seems particularly bad in this regard. Making it through usually depends on loading up on ropes on the earlier levels, but sometimes there just aren't many ropes to be had.

All of these things come to matter a little more than it might in a traditional roguelike because Spelunky severely limits the number of hit points the player has. He has no maximum, but can only regain hits from damsels, and then only one at a time. Each level contains a huge variety of ways to get hurt for one or more hits, or get instantly killed, and our hero only has one life. As a result, everything that can harm the player effectively does so permanently; the player can never let himself just eat damage to get through a tiresome situation. This may be the hardest thing of all about Spelunky, and it's something that even roguelikes tend to offer more leeway towards; to regain health in most, the player need only find a monster-free room and rest a few dozen turns. I can't say if Spelunky's system really works; most games end far short of level 15, even for an experienced player, unless he gets a lucky break along the way. But then again, the action-oriented nature of the game, and relatively large number of empty spaces, means the player is abler to avoid damage than in Rogue or its kin. It seems to be another case where the game is only slightly too hard.

55.5 Spelunking Along, Singing a Song

Yet surprisingly, these issues don't detract from its addictiveness too much. Overall, difficulty is only a little high considering the mood of game; that is to say, the game is often brutal yet fair. It's only when the flipside of that "often" comes in that the player is screwed over, and then it's usually masked well enough that he's not sure if it was his fault or not. In a game where you're expected to die hundreds of times before you win, the fact that the game plays so quickly helps counter the frustration this might cause.

Spelunky's generation system seems to work by filling in map spaces with sections of pre-generated level templates and then "roughening" them up a bit before inserting extra blocks, monsters, traps and treasure. It's a mechanism not used often in true roguelikes, but it seems to work rather well for a platformer. And it's good that Spelunky doesn't tame its level design too much as it generates its randomized levels.

Lots of commercial games that make use of random generation do that. In their efforts to ensure all areas are fairly completable, they also restrict a lot of interesting generation results. Those interesting juxtapositions and finding ways to overcome them, or even utilize them, are most of the fun to be had in Spelunky, and it turns out to be rather a lot of fun after all. This makes me rather anxious about my complaints above: in a rush to fix them, it would be easy to go overboard and rob Spelunky of its delicious challenge. This, really, is the biggest challenge to roguelike design: making it hard but fair. To thrust the knife at the player's throat, but to never touch him, relying on his own actions to push it in.

The website tinysubversions has an illustrated demonstration of Spelunky Freeware's level generator: http://tinysubversions.com/spelunkyGen/.

Derek Yu has written an entire book about the making of Spelunky! It is available from Boss Fight Books.

55.6 Source

https://forums.tigsource.com/index.php?topic=4017.0

56

Exploring the Oasis

January 2016 Defense of the Oasis, a.k.a. just Oasis, is a thought-provoking game whose design has important implications towards maximizing the benefits of random content generation.

Oops, sorry, let me try that intro sentence again.

Defense of the Oasis shows designers how to squeeze the most effect out of simple random generation processes. . . .

No, that one's not great either. DotO is only questionably roguelike, but it has definite points of interest for both roguelike players and developers. It has some of the attributes of quasi-roguelike Desktop Dungeons, in how everything feels like a resource, but in different ways, and to succeed you have to both focus on those resources you need in the current board and tailor your strategy around what you've got. Some have described it as "Civilization meets Minesweeper," but in fact similarities to Civilization are mostly thematic. Really, Defense of the Oasis is its own game.

The game was originally called Oasis and sold by Mind Control Software, but their sales site appears to have gone down and it currently doesn't seem possible to purchase on PC. To explain why the game is interesting to us, it will be helpful to explain how to play it in some detail. It's a weird game, with a very strong and nuanced design, so please bear with me, because believe me, this is all important. . . .

(*January 2020*: Sadly, Apple has a policy of removing things from the App Store if they're not kept compatible with current hardware, or if they don't pay their yearly "privilege of developing for us" tax, or whatever reason. Because of this, Defense of the Oasis is no longer available on the App Store. The Windows version is also hard to come by. Until someone goes back and decides to republish this gem, it is doomed to be lost to the wilds of abandonware. The rest of this article presumes that you can find a copy. I understand that's a pretty tall assumption, but that's what writing about old software is like these days. Oasis is definitely worth your time in seeking it out; right now, old install disks can be had pretty cheaply on sites like eBay.)

56.1 Basics

Each board of Oasis is a small desert kingdom of ancient Egypt, a 10x10, single-screen board that starts out completely* obscured by "fog," except for one starting space* you get for free*.

* Many of the statements that follow are not true for certain exceptional boards, but they're generally true, for like 90% of boards. Exceptions are usually noted to the player before the board begins. I follow words that are only usually true with an asterisk.

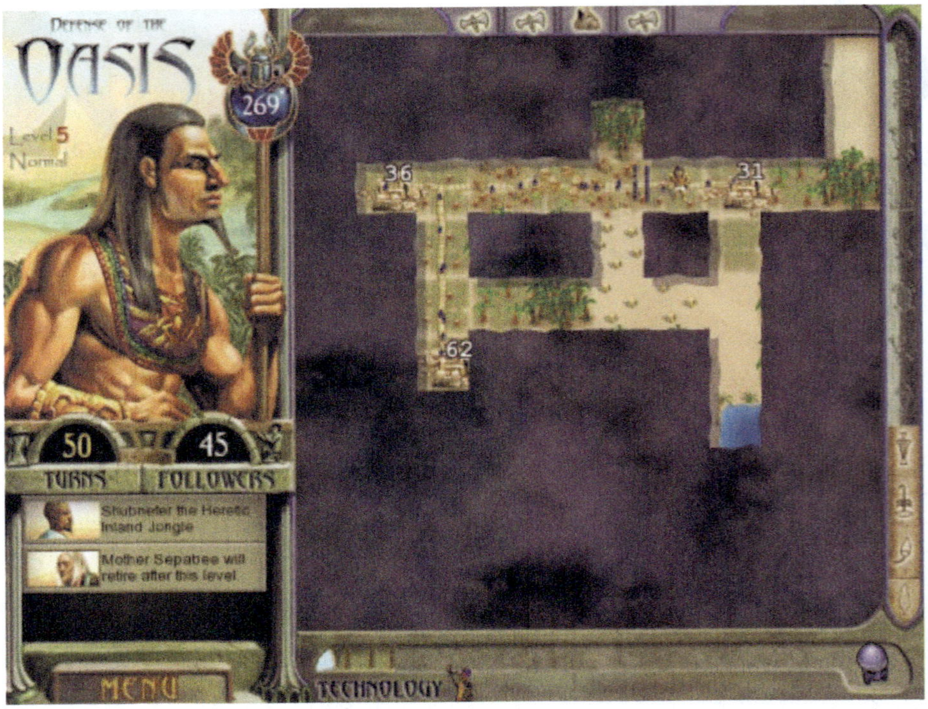

Figure 56.1

Early in a level, with most of the map still covered.

You start with 85* turns. You usually spend each turn uncovering one space of the board adjacent to a revealed spot. A 10x10 board has 100 spaces, so at the baseline for revealing the board, you'll end up leaving 14 spaces unseen—but this varies often. Revealed spaces can end up containing many different things. One of the most important things they might have is cities, each of which contains a small population of residents. When the turns run out, the revealed cities (only the revealed ones—if you don't find it, it's useless to you!) of your kingdom get attacked by one* horde of barbarian invaders. These fights are done as a series of many individual combat turns, the horde's population vs. that of the city tested over and over, but they happen very quickly and you have no direct control over them. If the barbarians wipe out the population of a city they torch it and move on to the next closest*. If all your cities are wiped out you lose the map, and possibly the game.

To help you in finding cities, they're all surrounded by farmland; plain farmland will always turn out to be adjacent to one city, and darker, dense farmland touches upon two or more. So, if you find farmland while uncovering spaces there must be cities nearby. But left alone, your cities are probably not going to survive the invasion, even if you find them all, so fortunately there are other things you can do, and find.

Most spaces you reveal (other than cities) grant you one or more followers when you reveal them, which is added to the five* you start the map with. At the end of the map, you can leave the followers you've collected in any one city by tapping on it, providing a useful supplement to those defenders, but even this might not be enough.

56.2 Followers, Roads and Mines

If you've found two or more cities, you can choose to connect them with roads. This is a costly operation: it takes one turn per space, so every turn you spend building roads is one less space you can reveal! Also, building a space's worth of road spends five* of your followers. But once two cities are connected, then for the rest of the map those cities will slowly increase in population through trade. The more turns that are left, the longer this goes on.

You can continue to connect more cities to this network. Each city connected to each other like this joins in the effect, and all the cities gain population faster too, for a geometrically increasing benefit. Since the effect only lasts as long as there are turns left, the earlier you start connecting cities, the greater the result.

* Many of the statements that follow are not true for certain exceptional boards, but they're generally true, for like 90% of boards. Exceptions are usually noted to the player before the board begins. I follow words that are only usually true with an asterisk.

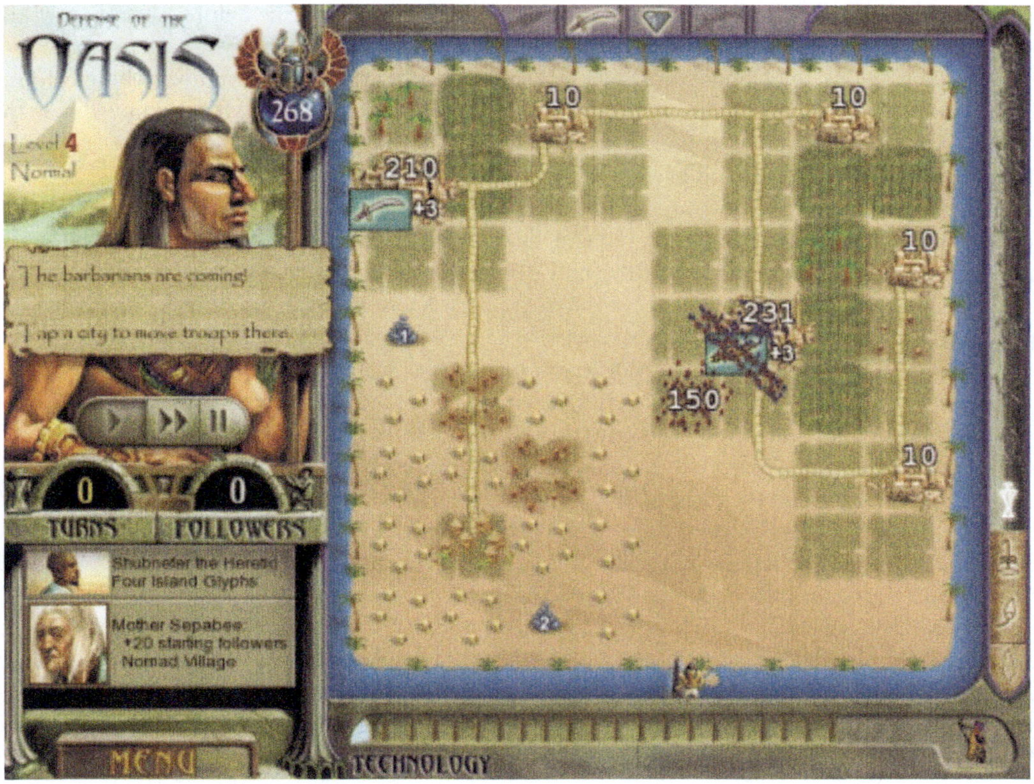

Figure 56.2

Battle against the barbarians.

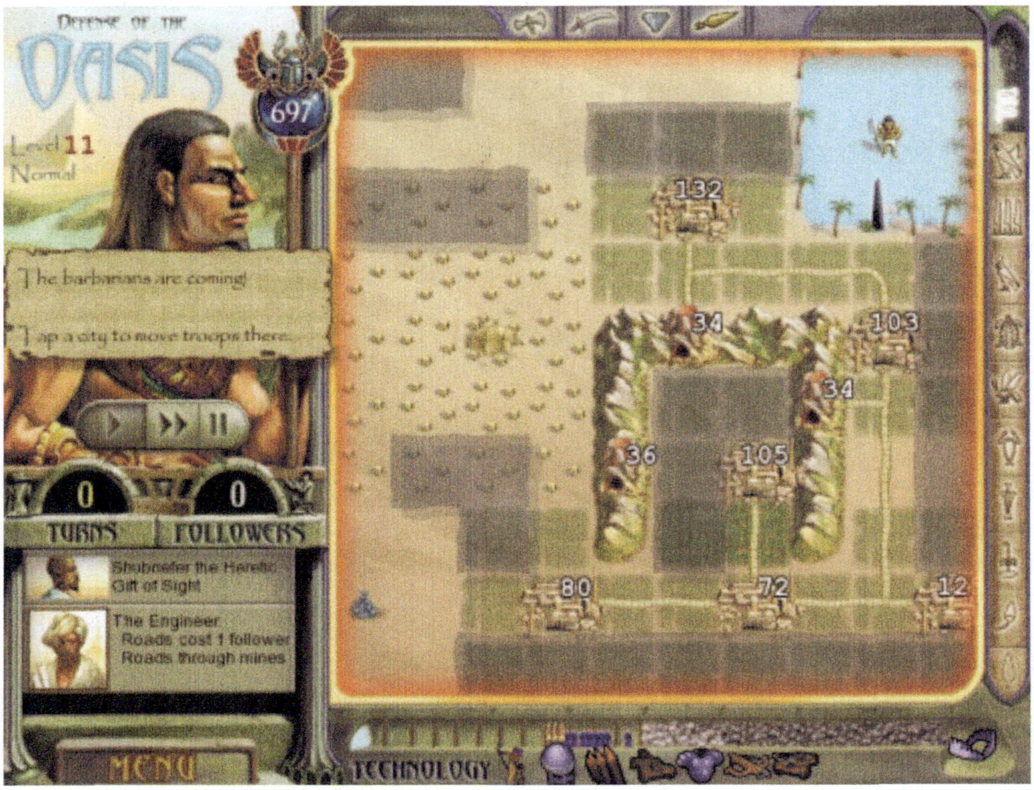

Figure 56.3

Mountains and mines—note the technologies at the bottom.

But since each road costs five followers, it usually takes a little bit of exploring before you can start building up. If you can start connecting early, though, and connect several cities quickly, you can double or more the total population you have to defend with. And what's more, during the final countdown phase before battle, you can tap on cities to move population from connecting cities to its location. If you know where the barbarians are going to attack from (because you found the Cairn; see later in this chapter), you can concentrate all your forces at the nearest city and overwhelm them, possibly scoring an easy victory.

Complicating matters, another thing you can find while exploring are mountains. Mountain spaces are revealed when you explore next to them, so in effect you reveal them for free! But you can't explore through mountains, and revealing mountains awards you no followers, which is a pretty big negative.

However, hidden in the mountains of each map are between one and three* mines. Once revealed, you can spend a turn adding workers to the mine. A single tap will permanently station up to ten of your followers at a mine. (You also get ten workers' worth of benefit from a given mine being manned at all, so even dropping a single guy in a mine has a big effect!) Once manned, the workers will hack away at the mine automatically throughout all the remaining turns, and even a little while (about five turns' worth) after.

Every so much mining done reveals a new technology. There are ten of these techs, which are graphically represented as being uncovered in the mine at the bottom of the screen. Most of them provide some extra combat bonus. Some examples: arrows (the first tech) may do extra damage each combat round against the barbarians; beartraps kill a set number of barbarians each time they reach a new city; catapults randomly kill a large number of barbarians in a round; armor randomly will completely negate the damage barbarians do in round. During battle, a little icon will flash when a tech's effect activates, but you still have no control over when that happens. Basically, each technology makes your troops a little more successful in one of a number of ways. Note that all your technologies help all your cities, not just one, and all the techs build on each other.

If you can get to the ninth tech, the cumulative effect of all those bonuses is so great that you frequently win the map even if you didn't manage to connect any cities, although it might be close. It helps if you managed to start your miners working early since, as with roads, effects are cumulative over time. That is the fundamental trade-off the game: spend workers and time building roads to increase population, or spend them developing technologies in the mines. Of course both at once is best, but you usually don't have enough workers to carry that far, and you still have to spend extra turns not exploring to develop them.

It's very hard to get to it, but the last technology on the track is Cartography, which reveals five unseen spaces on the map for free, without spending turns and granting you all the follower benefits. To get to the end of the track, however, requires a sizable investment in followers and invariably happens in the final turns of a map, so it's most useful for helping you fill out the oasis and track down the obelisk. . . .

56.3 The Obelisk, the Oasis and the Nomads

There is always one area of the map that doesn't grant you any followers or combat advantages for revealing it. That's the oasis, a rectangular* area of the map filled with water. The oasis would be completely useless except for two things. One, one of its spaces contains the obelisk, which you are required to defend; it is the last target the barbarians hit after they raze all the cities. If you don't find it they still have to attack it, so all is not lost. But if you find it, and the barbarians don't get that far, then you earn a glyph. Collecting glyphs is the ultimate goal of the game; you immediately win if you get 12 of them, saved up from map to map. If you don't get the glyph in a map you can continue on; there are an infinite number of glyphs out there, you only have to get 12 of them.

If the barbarians overwhelm all your cities (which happens fairly often on higher difficulties), you lose the glyph, and you have to expend magic power (which also builds from map to map) to defeat the remaining troops. That's your final line of defense; if you run out of that you lose.

If you manage to explore the whole oasis on a map, you earn a letter, pinball-style, in the word OASIS. If you manage to get all five letters through successive maps, you get to play a bonus game that's often worth a free glyph. In many ways though the oasis is a big distraction. You never get followers for exploring it, and it provides no advantages that grow as turns pass, so you nearly always want it to be the last thing you uncover on the board.

Another part of the map that seems useless at first is the nomad lands, a cluster of spaces that's always located in the part of the board furthest from any cities. The only advantage you get for exploring nomad spaces is extra followers. Instead of the two you get from exploring empty desert, you can get up to nine for finding the central camp. So, it's good to find it early, so you'll have more followers to spend on other things! But it's also good to find it late, because it does nothing but give you followers. Hmm.

* Many of the statements that follow are not true for certain exceptional boards, but they're generally true, for like 90% of boards. Exceptions are usually noted to the player before the board begins. I follow words that are only usually true with an asterisk.

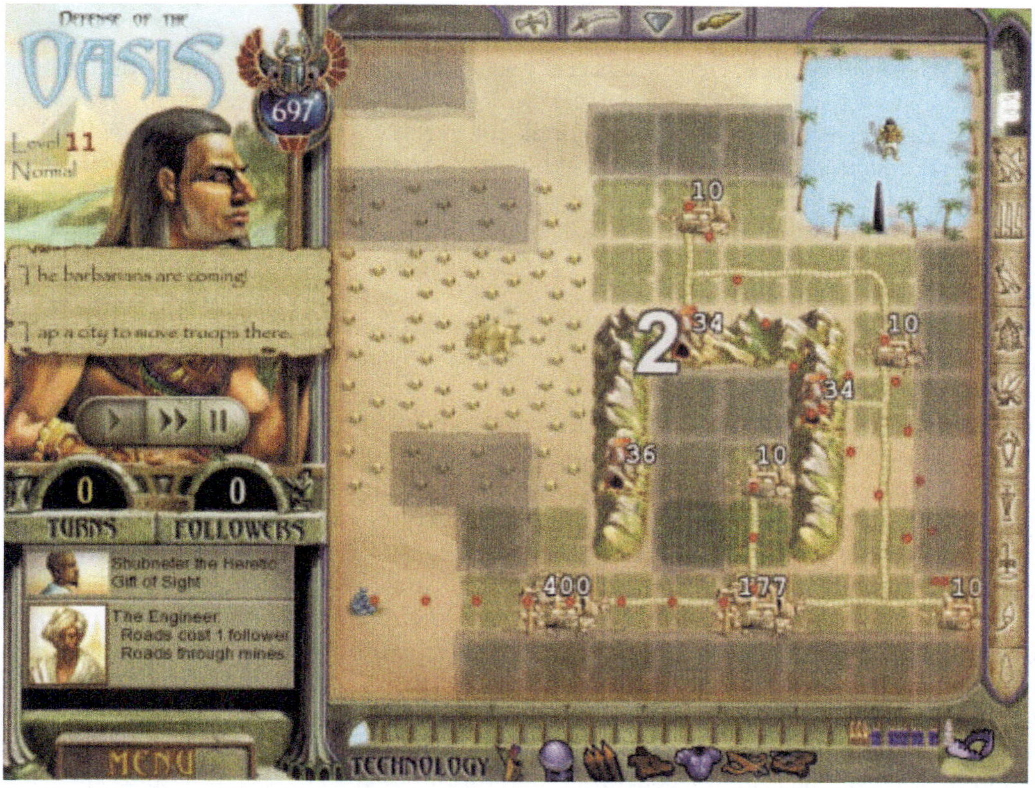

Figure 56.4

Countdown before battle.

There is one* last thing hidden on most maps, the Cairn*, a pile of rocks on the edge of the map* that marks where the barbarians will attack from. You don't have to find it to succeed at a map, but because it shows the point of entry of the barbarians, it's greatly useful in helping you focus on which cities to improve.

That's a lot to remember! And there's one more thing, too! You can also spend a turn searching a city for treasures that can help you! It's random which cities have treasures, and a city can even have more than one. All the treasures there are left to find are shown at the top of the window. Most of them provide a bonus in combat, extra damage that your troops can do each round if they hit, but this bonus only applies to the city it's found in.

Is that everything? Um . . . no! There one more thing. One of the "treasures" you can find is actually an advisor. Advisors do nothing on the current map except declare a number of cities to try to save on the current board. If you can protect at least that many, then they'll activate starting on the next map. Advisors provide a persistent bonus that follows you around for five maps, and are usually pretty great, like making roads costs only one follower each, improved mining power or starting a map off with 20 followers!

Whew, what a lot to remember. It is good that the game has an excellent tutorial campaign that teaches it all one map at a time. And you usually don't need to use all of this information to win each map until you reach the hardest difficulties, though you're rewarded if you can. Really, the hardest part about learning it all is that Defense of the Oasis is so different from everything else you've played. Minesweeper is a good comparison, but is really a much inferior game. It's kind of like Desktop Dungeons too.

Although Defense of the Oasis has similar space-revealing properties to Minesweeper, there are no "poison spaces" that mean instant defeat, and the great majority of maps are winnable. And yet, the game is still pretty hard later on, which is a neat trick in a board-uncovering game where you nearly always uncover more than 80% of the board.

That's a funny thing. You always get to see most of the board, but the game's still challenging! And yet, it's still fair! How does it do that?

Ah well you see, that's why we're talking about this game here. . . .

* Many of the statements that follow are not true for certain exceptional boards, but they're generally true, for like 90% of boards. Exceptions are usually noted to the player before the board begins. I follow words that are only usually true with an asterisk.

56.4 Why We're Talking about This Game Here

I've mentioned before that one interesting aspect of roguelike play is the *predictability* of the dungeon.

A map you explore that is entirely random, paradoxically, is less interesting to explore, is less fair to the player, than one that is biased in its generation. Think of it like this. If you're playing D&D with a DM who's made his own dungeon, and your character is walking down a hallway and given a choice of three routes, if there is no way to distinguish between them, no way to even guess what awaits down each, and if two lead to certain unavoidable death and one to vast riches, then what is the point? Roll a die and have that decide, you're probably doomed regardless. If you can use other means to figure it out though, then it can become an interesting challenge. The party cleric might expend a divination spell, or there might have been a rumor in town as to the right way (which might be false); or maybe you could only explore a route part way, get recon and go back, or maybe send a hireling ahead first, or look for other information like a map, or question monsters for clues, or just elect not to go.

All of these recourses, and others, can be thwarted by a motivated DM, but why would he want to? Thinking about problems like this is part of what the fun of dungeon exploration is about. Finding tells, figuring out what can be done about seemingly impossible problems, that is interesting. It is interesting in roguelikes too. It's why Rogue and NetHack's simple dungeon generation still works for those games, even though they are predictable (especially Rogue's) and make little attempt at realism.

Defense of the Oasis recognizes this and makes extensive use of it. It could be argued that figuring out the quirks of the map builder is the game! You can usually uncover nearly all the map, but the order in which you find things matters greatly to your success. So what you do is, use your early turns not just to find things but gather information that can help you gain an impression of how the hidden board is laid out.

This is a greatly interesting aspect of Defense of the Oasis, and it's something I'll be writing more about later, the role that intuition plays in the game, an aspect of gaming that is almost never discussed and even less examined. It's easy, when talking about this, to devolve into crazy Star Trek talk like McCoy would spout when arguing with Spock, about intuition and humanity and spirit and yada yada. I have a more rigorous definition of intuition in mind: the application of things learned unconsciously.

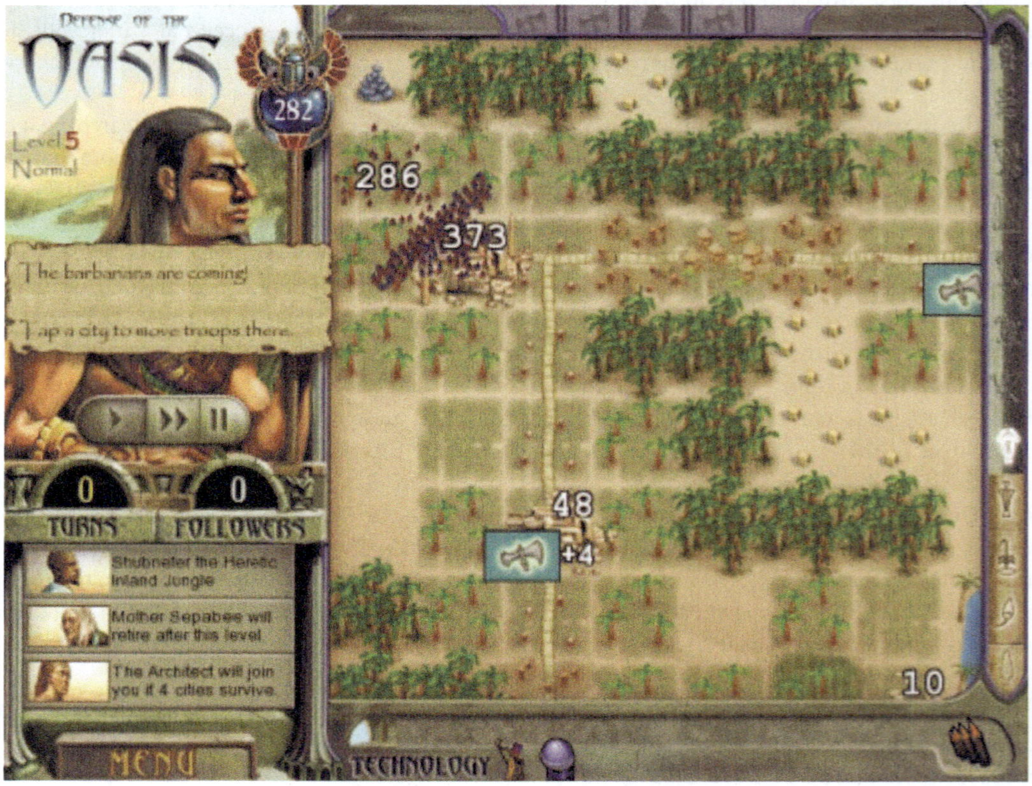

Figure 56.5

"Forests?? You didn't mention those!"

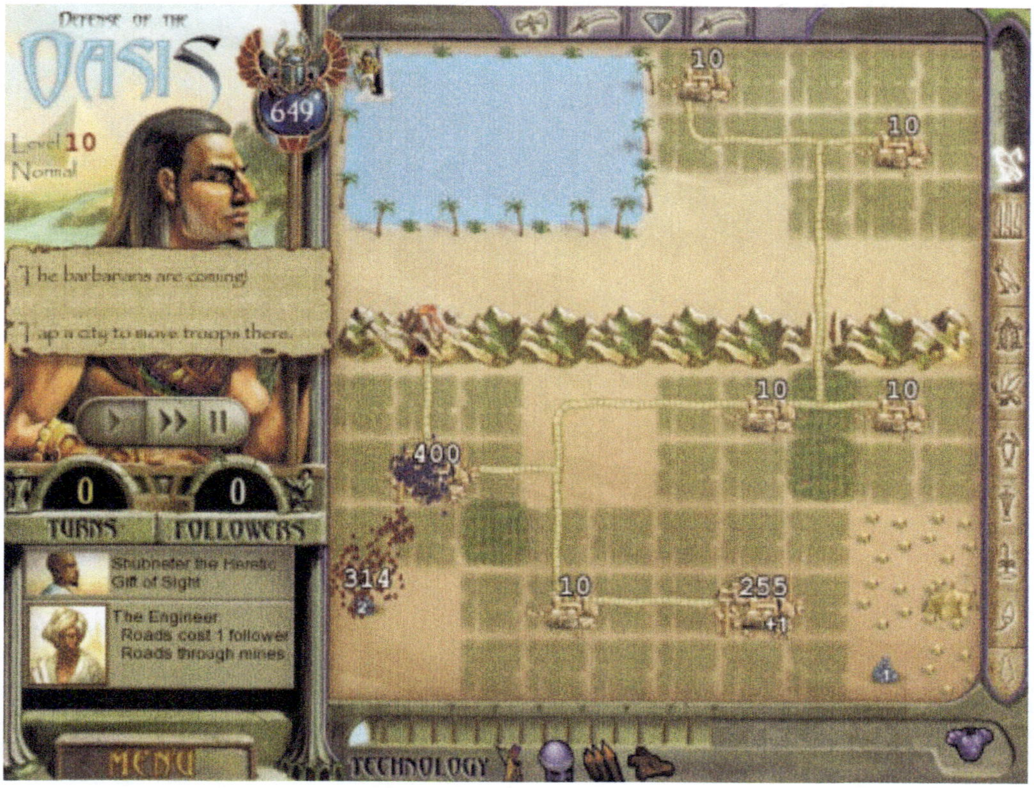

Figure 56.6

An exceptional map: mountains in a line!

Defense of the Oasis builds its levels according to an ordered set of procedures. Each step is partly random and partly algorithmic, just like how roguelike dungeons are built. Nowhere does the game explain in detail how it's done, but after every map it does supply you with a hint that might explain one of the secret truths of the game's generation. More likely, you'll just pick some things up while playing.

Eventually you'll notice that mountains tend to be arranged in C-shaped or zig-zagging ranges. That mines are never in a corner or end of one of these ranges. That the oasis is always in a corner of the map, and is rectangular. Eventually you learn that there are exceptions to some of these rules, if the board is a special type, but those types have their own rules.

Eventually, you're still never completely sure where everything is hidden, but you learn to play the odds. If there's a spot that two different useful things might be hidden behind, it's a better bet to pick than one that might only have one. When you get to the highest difficulty, the first few turns on a board often end up being the most important, so it's important that you find something useful quick. What Oasis, and some other games that hide a limited number of things to be discovered around a random board (especially Strange Adventures in Infinite Space and its sequels) do is make the order and timing of what you find matter. In DotO, you'll usually find it all, but what matters is what you find the most of and how early you find it.

There are certainly more advanced tricks than those I've mentioned (I have purposely left many I myself know out, because learning how to play is the real game of Defense of the Oasis), but they're things you just sort of have to pick up as you play. One aspect of intuition while playing is, the more you use it, the less intuitive it becomes. Eventually you realize what you're doing and it moves into the area of conscious knowledge. Eventually you might consciously know enough about the generator that you can write a FAQ about it. FAQs for games like this can be written, just like they can for non-random games. The subject is just raised a bit, to become knowledge about the generator, instead of the explicit steps of a walkthrough.

Is it possible to make a game that's entirely FAQ-proof? I am not sure. If you make a randomized game, you move the focus of the FAQ author a bit up the ladder to the details of that randomization, and while some of the possible items and dungeon elements that could be generated might not show up, the player

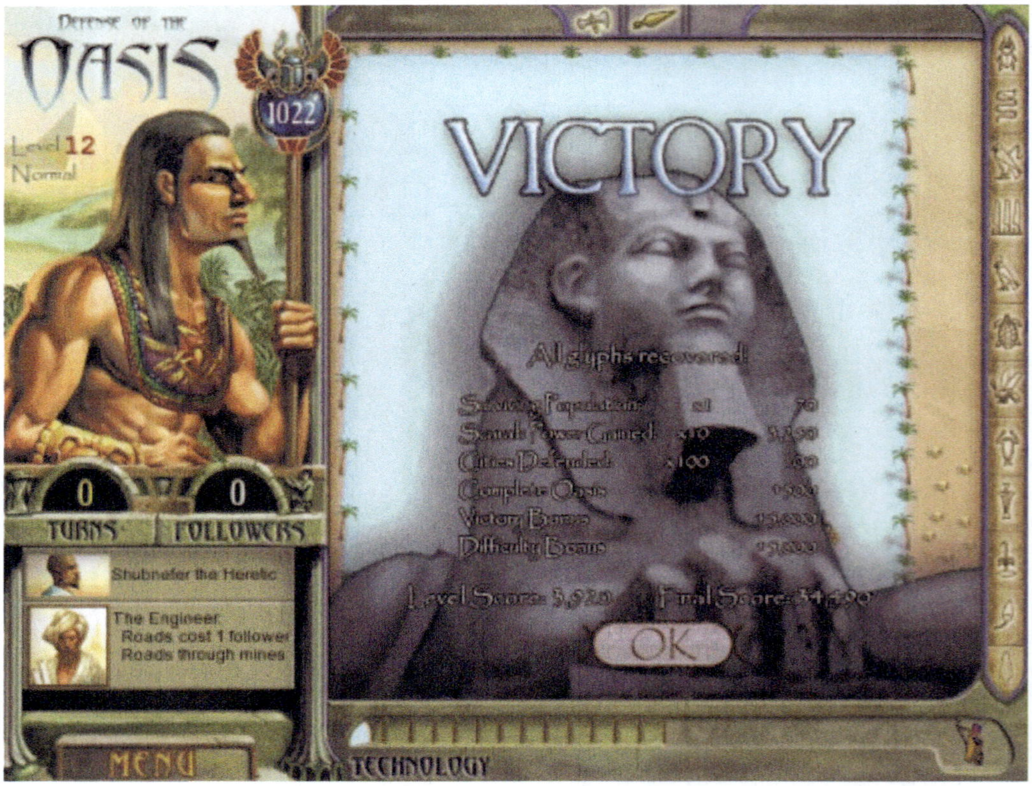

Figure 56.7

Campaign won! Try a hard one next time. . . .

can still be made aware of their existence and uses. If it's possible, the randomization will have to be more profound than that—almost along the lines of creating an AI that itself generated dungeon levels and items.

You could say the only way to make a FAQ-proof game is to have and raise a child who grows up to be a game designer. The details of implementing such a bold plan I leave it to you to discover.

57

The Rescue of Meta-Zelda

January 2016 So, what does it really mean to be a roguelike game? My contention, repeated often, is that turn-based tactical combat on a grid and basic randomization are not enough, and may not even be essential, that these things, while part of the basic definition of the term, don't get to the core of what makes the genre interesting from a play or design standpoint. My thesis is that some element of greater discovery, like item identification, is required, and that there needs to be some consequence to the player's explorations, some cost to searching.

By this measure, one of the most awesome roguelikes of recent memory? I'll tell you. It's called The Legend of Zelda.

(Zelda secret tune plays off-key)

Well, not just The Legend of Zelda. There is an important modification to it, or rather, a program that systematically makes modifications. That program is fcoughlin's Zelda Randomizer.

It was originally developed for speedrunners, who had to deal with an interesting problem. Speedrunning a known video game is not really the same thing as speedrunning a game you've never seen before. You learn where everything is, or refer to FAQs, for the first few plays, but after that it's all about optimizing a known world. Zelda is amazingly resistant to such optimization; the game seems almost designed around the idea that players should be able to use many different possible routes and approaches to completing it, to the degree that every enemy can be defeated by at least one weapon other than the player's sword until the very final boss of the game.

But despite this, and the fact that we're still not absolutely sure what the fastest way to complete Zelda is, the game is still a static thing. The use of randomization in the original Legend of Zelda is interesting (look up, some time, the algorithm used to determine what items enemies drop, that's a rabbit hole for you), but, ultimately, each room still contains the same enemies, the dungeons are all laid out the same, and the tough rooms and treasures are distributed the same way each game.

That is where Zelda Randomizer comes in. It is a fairly simple program, nothing more than a bunch of checkboxes really, that takes an unmodified ROM of The Legend of Zelda and, depending on what you check, scrambles it and basically makes a new quest for it.

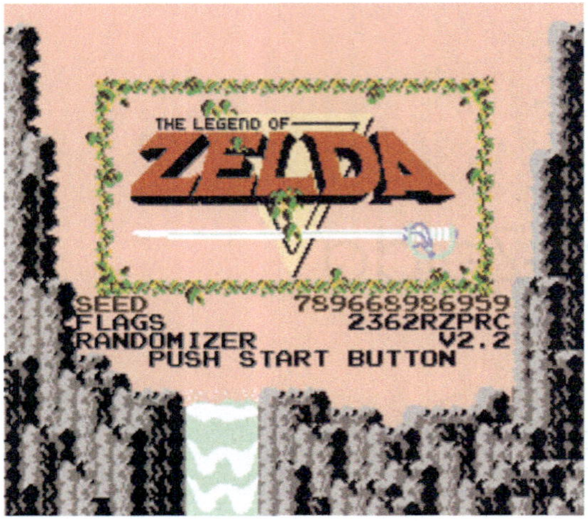

Figure 57.1

The Legend of Zelda

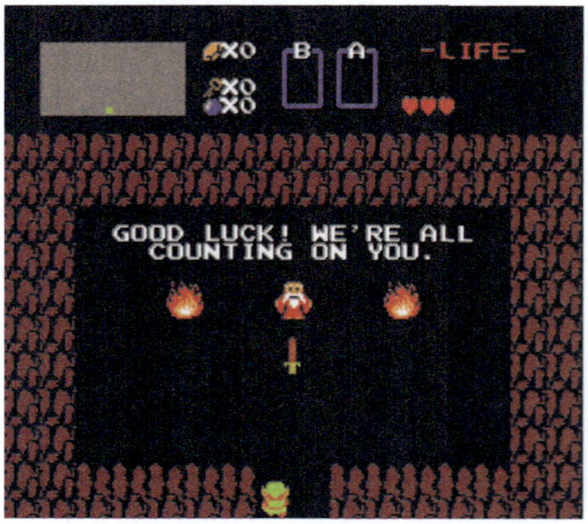

Figure 57.2

Starring Leslie Nielsen as the Helpful Old Man.

57.1 The Legend of Zelda (Famicom/NES), Described

While The Legend of Zelda is one of gaming's longest-running series, not as many people these days are that familiar with the game in its original form. A brief description follows.

The Legend of Zelda (1987) is fundamentally an exploration and combat game, somewhat like Metroid in that regard, although it's an overhead view game instead of a side-scroller, and exploration takes place across a wide and deep landscape instead of in a series of cross-sectioned tunnels like a huge art farm. The player guides an elf boy, Link, who gets his clothes by way of Pan of Neverland, through a large overworld, divided into 128 screens. Most of the screens have challenging monsters who try to kill Link. Scattered throughout this overworld are nine dungeons, also divided into screens, and containing even more challenging monsters. In each dungeon is at least one item, which allows Link to increase his combat ability and exploration power. Some important places in both the overworld and underworld cannot be reached until the necessary items have been obtained. Also in the overworld are shops, where some additional items can be bought. A very few items are just given to Link outright, though he may have to prove himself first.

Also in each dungeon is at least one boss, and one of the bosses in each guards a Triforce piece. The ultimate object of the game is to get eight Triforce pieces, which unlocks the way into the ninth and last dungeon. In there is Ganon, the hardest boss, who guards Princess Zelda, the aim of your quest. Defeating a dungeon's boss also awards Link a heart container, extending his maximum health by one unit. A few heart containers can also be found in secret places in the overworld. So, in a manner somewhat similar to Brogue, player character improvement comes from finding items instead of gaining experience points, and you don't always have to slaughter and slay to get them. But unlike roguelikes in general, Zelda is a real-time, action game. In fact, it's action is pretty sharp. There are enemies (especially the so-called Darknuts and Wizzrobes) that will kill Link pretty easily no matter how strong he's become if his player isn't skilled at attacking and dodging.

57.2 The Game That Defined Nintendo Hard

When The Legend of Zelda came out, it was kind of a sensation. Both Sega and Hudson Soft produced thinly veiled clones of it, for the Sega Master System (Golden Axe Warrior) and PC-Engine/Turbografx 16 (Neutopia), and Compile's Golvellius, also for the SMS, has some pretty strong similarities too. If you unfocus your eyes a bit a whole genre of Zelda-likes from around the time can be recognized, containing games ranging from Legend of Valkyrie, Crystalis, Faria, StarTropics, SoulBlazer and many more. And of course the Zelda series itself continues to this day.

The weird thing about a game this so copied, however, is how obscure it is. Not in the sense of being unknown, certainly not that, but in the sense of being unclear. To modern tastes it seems undirected. You spend a lot of time in the early going of The Legend of Zelda roaming around just looking for things. Most

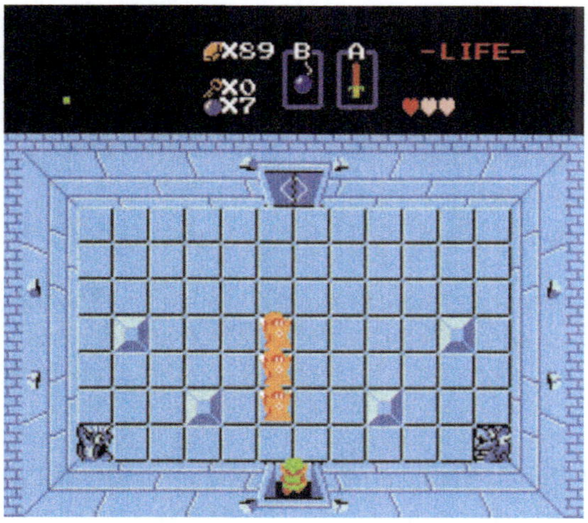

Figure 57.3

This is not a good room to find with three hearts.

of those clones I mentioned split the overworld up into smaller regions to help narrow down and direct your exploration, but The Legend of Zelda's land of Hyrule is one humongous, homogeneous world, and you can explore 98.5% of it from the start. Although the eight dungeons you have to find are numbered, they are not strongly ordered. Some can be done out of order, and the only clue besides the number that one dungeon follows the other is just that, a literal clue, a cryptic message in each dungeon giving a vague area to look in for the next. Players are just as likely to find dungeons by wandering around and looking than by going to a specified place.

And finding things just by roaming the map casually is difficult, because Zelda's enemies are not trivial to overcome. Even the weakest ones can do a number on poor Link at the start of the game, when it only takes six hits to kill him. The original LoZ doesn't use item-based gates to ward the player from advanced areas, but enemy difficulty: if you're in an area where the enemies make you sweat, you probably shouldn't be there yet. One class of enemy, called "Lynels" in the manual, very frequently shoots swords that do two-thirds of Link's starting health in damage in one hit, and the mountain areas that hide several later dungeons are infested with them. Large-scale sequence breaking in Zelda is possible but requires nerves of steel, and even advanced players often leave those areas for when they've gained some power.

There is a strong sense in Zelda of being dropped in a world and told to sink or swim. And many players sink, and sink often, and some eventually give up. There is a tendency, among some older players, to lament the weak spine of current players. Truthfully, I am kind of like that, but when I think about it I waver in my confidence. No one is naturally good at these kinds of games. Some skills can only be acquired through practice, and I've had lots of practice. Instead of pointing at a losing player, laughing and saying GIT GUD, I try to say: oh, you died. Ah well, try again?

The problem here is fear of failure, that is, thinking that lack of success at a game is a judgment on the player, and that dying just means you suck. These players don't suck. This happens to everyone. I'm better than most, but what skill I have comes from practice, and even so, still, sometimes I'm awful! And compared to roguelikes, LoZ is pretty darn forgiving: when you die you don't lose any items or money, and if you're in a dungeon you just get put back at its entrance. The worst that happens to the player is that he comes back without much health in his meter, which can be frustrating later on, but the game gives players ways to remedy even this.

57.3 Now, about This Randomizer Thingy

Some of the things that Zelda Randomizer can do:

- Move around the contents of caves in the overworld. The cave that contained a Heart Container may contain money, a shop, a text message or other things. It may even cost Link money. Since dungeons, where are hidden both essential items and the Triforce pieces that are the primary objects of your quest, are moved around too, you will have to do a lot of searching to find them. The Randomizer can even be set to leave its own cryptic hints as to the dungeon locations

- Move the enemies around in the overworld. The same general enemy groups are in the game, but their locations are mixed up among all the regions. The dangerous Lynels, the sword-throwing centaurs from the mountains, can make appearances in other places, and must be dealt with carefully if encountered early.
- Move the rooms around each dungeon. While each dungeon keeps its original shape, the rooms and internal layout of each dungeon are remixed.
- It can use the game's Second Quest (a long story) as a resource to take further dungeon layouts and enemy groups from.
- It can even be used to construct challenge games, which take the ubiquitous Wooden Sword you're ordinarily given at the start of the game and hide it somewhere randomly around the world map, or even put it in the room before the final boss (the only enemy in the game that requires a sword to defeat it).

Under some, most or all of these, and other, mixing operations, playing through Zelda regains some portion of the wonder that it had back when people first explored Hyrule, back in 1986. More recent gamers may not understand what playing a game like the original NES Legend of Zelda was like in the days of its original release. It was rather a deeper and more complex adventure than most were used to at that time, so hidden were its secrets. While nothing essential is hidden without some clue of its presence (usually an old man or woman to cryptically point you towards it), the games produced by Zelda Randomizer expect the player to know where all the secrets are already. Everything hidden by the Randomizer is where something had been hidden before, but when there's around 90 such places to look, that's not as much help as it might be.

So, Zelda Randomizer's output is mostly an additional challenge for diehards. Speedrunners are interested in this because it brings an aspect of the original game, the element of discovery and exploration, into play in a realm where those things are usually long vanished. People who play games over and over to improve their times come to know their prey very well. There is usually no aspect of them too obscure to be known. Randomization returns to play some of that aspect of mystery.

Zelda Randomizer was inspired by an earlier tool, a ROM randomizer for Super Metroid, which also was somewhat interesting. But Zelda is an unusually resilient game when scrambled. Since most enemies can be defeated in multiple ways, yet are still usually vulnerable to swords, the strategic implications of there being, say, the Bow, the Wand, the Red Candle or even just a lot of Bombs going forward from there are great. Also, one of the problems with randomizing a game like this is keys, which usually require a complex algorithm to make sure the player always has enough to open all the locked doors he finds. All later Zelda games would require such an algorithm. The original Zelda, however, contains more keys than are needed to win the game and has an item that eventually makes all other keys obsolete. Even when you're using normal keys, they aren't even dungeon-specific! They can be taken from site to site and used wherever. You can even buy keys in stores; they are expensive, but available to help the frustrated player.

That is not to say that Zelda Randomizer doesn't take steps to ensure the game is winnable. A number of items (specifically, the Bow, Ladder, Raft, Recorder and sometimes the Power Bracelet) must be found during play, and the program must ensure whatever result has a solution. It's just that not stressing out about the location of keys makes the job of randomization easier.

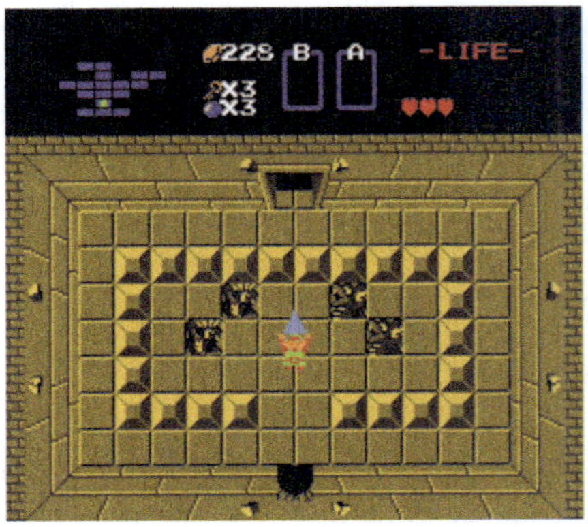

Figure 57.4

Random Zelda can be really random. I found a Triforce piece in the third room of this dungeon.

But this article isn't just about the joys of randomizing a beloved game into a new experience. Because strangely, The Legend of Zelda takes to being mixed up very well.

57.4 Random Zelda Is Hard, but Strangely Fair

Zelda's overworld was meant for getting lost in, and part of the strange joy of the game is getting lost and yet kind of getting rewarded for it anyway. The game's secrets are set up in such a way that the player will probably find one or two accidentally during the game. Bombs that break open secret caves are also one of the strongest weapons against monsters, the flames from candles both damage foes and burn trees, and once you discover you can push certain statues it's only a matter of time before every statue in the game has felt Link's sweaty grip.

In a properly randomized game, though, it's not just the secrets that have been moved around, but the monsters: you might have to spend this game tiptoeing around Lynels in central Hyrule! And also moved are the rooms in the dungeons, and the locked doors and the keys that go to them: since keys can be bought in shops in the original LoZ, the game doesn't need to make sure you can fully explore every dungeon without buying them. Or some of the required items, and the shops that sell some of those items.

Only seven or so of Zelda's many items absolutely must be found to win, but certain items make the process much easier. For instance, one of the game's many secret areas hides a guy who will give Link a letter that, if shown to the old women who hide in some of the caves, will cause them to offer to sell medicine to Link that will fill up all his health whenever he wants up to twice. Finding the letter is crucial to having a good game, but there is only one in the entire world, and the player may never find it. It's not needed, but it's greatly desired.

Another example. Only one of the shops in the game sells an item called the Blue Ring, which cuts all the damage Link takes in half. Again, you don't need it, but you'll be glad if you find it. Also, in five locations in the overworld there are hidden heart containers, permanent health extensions. You don't need any of them, but you'll want all of them. And there are enough of these really nice bonuses to find that you'll probably find a few of these helps regardless. They will likely not be found in the same order as the original game, but that just compounds how different the game feels when you find strange and useful things like the Recorder or the Wand in the first dungeon, or even outside of it.

The aspect here that connects this back to roguelikes is the tension between two opposed qualities, emphasizing the consequences of a player's decisions while keeping those consequences balanced.

Most rooms in the original Legend of Zelda are difficult, but not impossible, to clear with three hearts and a Wooden Sword. I've cleared rooms of Blue Darknuts, among the toughest monsters in the game, with that before. That is the outer edge of its difficulty; 99% of its rooms can be handled this way, but even skilled players would find such a run to be tiring, if they were able to do it at all. Because of that, even if a randomized game put the player into a situation where his starting location was surrounded by Lynels, he still has a

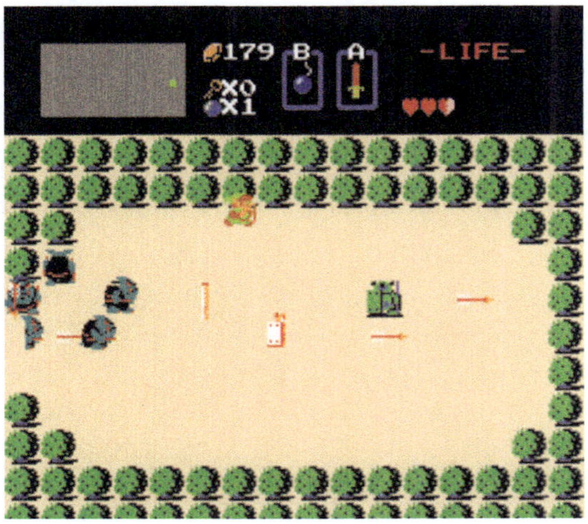

Figure 57.5

Well, well, what do we have here!

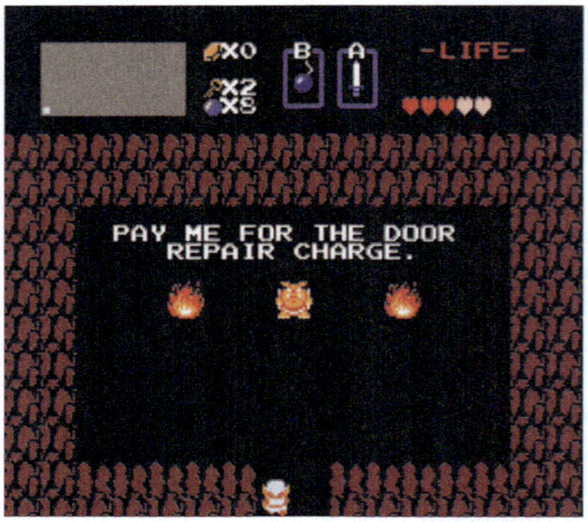

Figure 57.6

You will come to hate this guy.

chance of breaking out of it. The ultimate fairness of Zelda's gameplay is insurance, here, against malicious whims of the dice.

But the game also doesn't hand anything to the player on a plate. The player still must search for items and dungeons, some of which may be hidden in incredibly obscure places, and while it's possible for all a dungeon's best things to be placed close to the entrance of each labyrinth, practically, the law of averages limits the likelihood of that occurring too often. The possibility that a required mobility item (something that gives the player an ability that lets him cross formerly impassable routes) may be hidden behind a barrier that requires it is there, but that's where the Randomizer tool comes in, giving the resulting game a solvability check and regenerating the game world repeatedly until it passes.

The conceptual field of probability into which Zelda Randomizer casts its dice is rich enough that the situations produced are interesting even after many attempts, challenging but different, but generally not individually overwhelming so much that the player has no way to proceed.

It takes something like the Zelda Randomizer to demonstrate how meticulously the original game is constructed, really. You only need a scant few items to complete the game, but it's challenging enough that you still want everything you can get, and yet unlike in your more traditional games, skill and practice open the door to advanced play much more readily than grinding for money or experience points. If that doesn't feel essentially roguelike to you then I don't know what to tell you.

If this sounds more fun to watch than necessarily to play, you're in luck! The website Speed Runs Live hosts frequent races between players playing with the same seed and flags for your spectating enjoyment. Also somewhat along these lines is Speedrun Bingo, available for many games. Game randomization tools are an exciting frontier in the romhacking community—there also exist randomizers for Super Metroid, Zelda II and Dragon Quest.

(*January 2020*: In four years, randomizers have only grown in prominence. The Zelda II randomizer can create its own world maps, and there even exists a randomizer that will take the Super Nintendo Zelda and Metroid games and, not only randomize them, but *combine* them into one huge, mixed-up game.)

58

Space Peeing Out There

January 2016 What is it about space games that lends them to procedural generation? The classic space exploration games Elite and Starflight used such techniques to generate its starmaps and planet surfaces on the fly during the game, and all three Infinite Space games will create as many random sectors of space for you to explore as you like.

Out There (and its update Out There Omega) use randomized starmaps too. They are billed as space exploration roguelikes, set in a random universe, but in which there is no combat. While the player can meet aliens, outright fighting them is never provided as an option.

Your astronaut is stranded with his small spacecraft in a mysterious region of space an unknown distance away from Earth, and tries to find a way back home. Throughout his search, he finds new planets, encounters aliens, explores alien ruins and finds a whole periodic table's worth of elements to store on his ship. While events happen that give your character's adventures a direction and a narrative character, a surprising lot of the game consists of bumping around space and engaging in a process that I have come to call *space peeing*. But I'm getting ahead of myself.

58.1 Hovering Above the Drain

For starters, this isn't a traditional roguelike at all. There is no tactical combat, or indeed any fighting. How about we call it a rogue-ish game, instead? (Credit for the term goes out to Ian A.T. of Metafilter.)

Like in traditional roguelikes, there is permadeath, but the style of game makes its form unusual. Your ship has three statistics: Fuel, Oxygen and Hull, and running out of any one of them effectively ends your adventure unless you have the right materials on-hand to make up for it.

Fuel is consumed when traveling between stars and generally moving about in space. It's replenished by collecting Hydrogen and Helium, usually by scooping it up from Gas Giant planets. If you run out of fuel, you're pretty much stuck. You can keep an excess supply of these elements on board as cargo, but it takes up room.

Oxygen is consumed by just about everything. It's a general analogue for your ship's life support systems, and so is diminished by breathing and eating. You replenish it by landing on Garden Worlds, which

Figure 58.1

Out There Omega

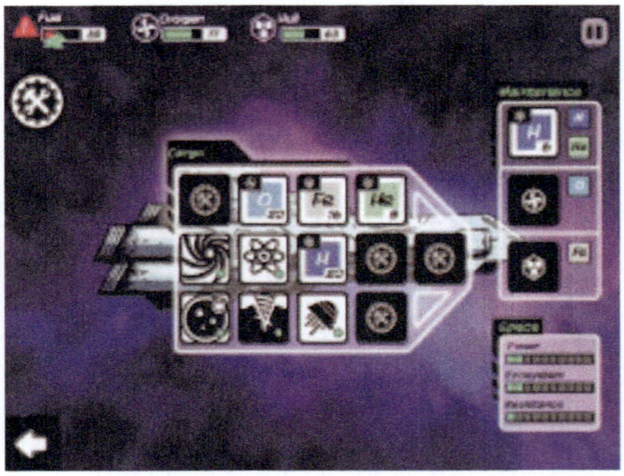

Figure 58.2

Your starting ship and cargo.

automatically boost it back up to 100%. You can keep spare Oxygen on-board ship (which you can find sometimes by drilling on Garden Worlds), but again, it takes up cargo room you might prefer to use for other things.

Hull is your ship's structural integrity. When your ship suffers damage from risky maneuvers (such as getting fuel from a Gas Giant), from hostile action by aliens or just random events, it comes out of your ship's Hull. Different ships require different elements to repair Hull, but most frequently you'll use Iron to replenish this.

So, those are your three gauges, your primary measures of health, the resources of Out There's resource management gameplay. The elements named above change depending on your ship and equipment, but there's always something you need, and those are the places you get it from. So, what else is in the game?

Well, from one perspective, that's it. You go places, you mine or scoop resources, and you refill tanks. Sometimes random events happen that add or decrease those gauges or damage equipment that also takes resources to refill. That's kind of it?

One way to look at Out There, instead of as a game, is as a kind of experiment in storytelling. There are these play systems you have to maintain in order to survive and move around, and if you can keep those going long enough, eventually, you'll obtain technologies and other systems that increase efficiency, and progress towards your destination star, and eventually reach the conclusion of the story. But if you fail to keep the resource management subgame up, then you'll die and have to start over.

And the resource management subgame is . . . well, I don't want to call it hard, really. What it is is insistent. You have to maintain all three of your gauges in order to survive, and each one puts pressure on the others. To get fuel for moving around, you have to visit Gas Giants. Visiting those is risky and usually takes a toll on your hull, in addition to costing a bit of fuel to reach orbit and operate the probe. To replenish your hull, you'll need Iron or other mineral elements that you get from drilling on Rocky Worlds, but it takes fuel both to get there and to operate the drill. All operations require Oxygen, so after looping those two needs a few times you'll have to set course for a Garden World, which of course also requires fuel.

Rocky Worlds and Gas Giants are common and you'll nearly always find both around any star, but Garden Worlds are pretty rare, so those keep you anchored. You switch back and forth for a while between getting minerals and fuel, and when the O_2 runs low you go load back up on that. Oddly, all worlds, except Oxygen from Garden Worlds, cannot be used for resource replenishment indefinitely. If you probe a Gas Giant for fuel repeatedly, you'll get roughly half as much fuel out of each successive time, and Rocky Worlds also turn up less minerals each time you mine them. You can "reset" these planets by warping to a different system, but of course, that takes fuel.

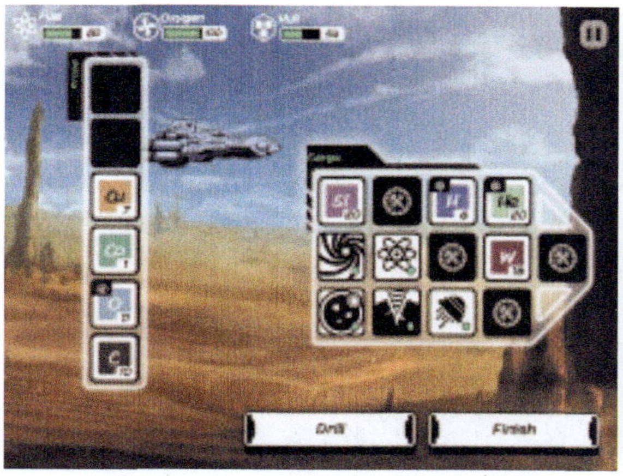

Figure 58.3

Drilling for minerals.

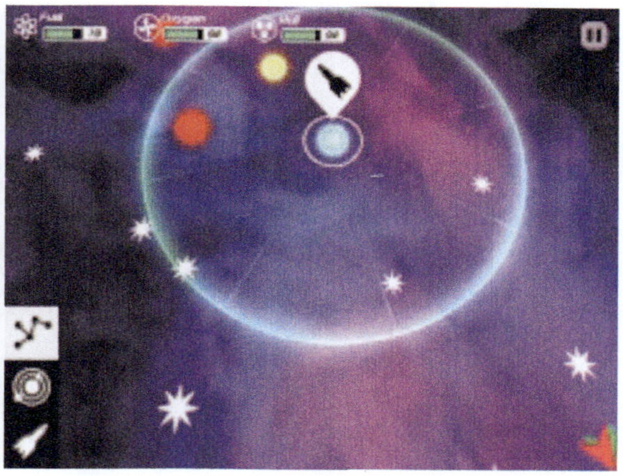

Figure 58.4

Selecting a destination from the starmap.

58.2 There's a Stuckies Ahead and They Have Helium

The use of Garden Worlds as Oxygen resupply bases gives your exploration efforts a leapfrogging character. Near the start of the game you are given a target planet to try to reach, on the other side of the star map, which (you guess) is the goal of your quest. Eventually you find four such planets, and what you do with them gives you one of a number of endings. What you end up doing is exploring around each Garden World, further and further, until you find the next Garden World, then transfer there.

The size of the costs, for travel, for repair, and for breathing, is designed so that the size of your cargo hold and the maximums of your gauges don't keep you very far insulated from the necessities of survival. Even once you've traded up your ship a couple of times (replacements are found randomly as you explore), many of the alternatives are deficient in certain major ways.

Several ships have limited cargo space. Many of them have extra equipment on-board that make your life easier in various ways, but each of these units takes up cargo room, and so also serves to require you to make more trips between planets just to keep yourself fueled. Eventually the demands of the story are that you'll have to get a good amount of such equipment, many of which increase efficiencies, but they also take up storage space for essentials. In terms of gameplay, a lot of the game is about juggling these elements. Eventually you come to realize that cargo space itself is your biggest resource, since you need it for so many things and having it greatly increases the time you can spend exploring instead of just subsisting.

It's admirable to try to make a rogue-ish game, especially one that's space-based, without having any means of combat. That is an extremely interesting design decision. There is a hostile alien race, but you never fight aliens ship-to-ship in this game, and there are no weapons systems. And all roguelikes, indeed all games, are fundamentally about managing resources in one way or another. Most of them try to obscure that essential function, though, with combat gameplay or strategy or something like that. Out There doesn't make much of an effort to hide that you're pretty much always trying to stay ahead of bare survival.

You never earn levels in this game. The basics never get easier, except in ways that reduce cargo space you need for other things. Increased efficiencies from new equipment help, but basically they mean you go one or two more systems until you have to relieve yourself again. Yeah, that's what refilling your gauges in Out There feels like: space peeing.

Ultimately, it seems, the only way there really is to die in Out There is to fail to space pee in a timely manner, when your astrobladder fills to the brim and there's nowhere to go. All the other events, at their

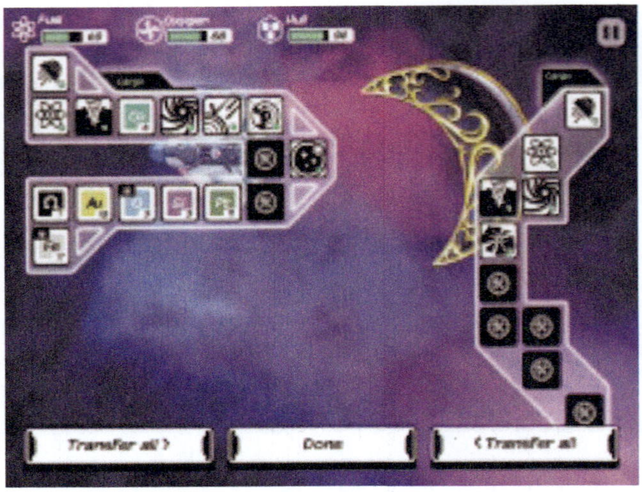

Figure 58.5

Transferring cargo between ships.

worst, will deplete your gauges. If you can get to the right kind of planet soon enough, the danger can be remedied.

58.3 Looking Beyond to the Real Game

The resource management serves as a kind of spacer, a basic game mechanic there to occupy the player and give weight to the rest of the game, which is thankfully loads more interesting, if you can put up with space peeing long enough to get into it. If it weren't for the resource management, the game would simply be a series of these events.

One good thing is that the basic process of refilling the gauges in new places, space peeing in different climes so to speak, is what ultimately drives both game advancement (the plans to build new systems and the materials to construct them) and advances the story. These events happen randomly when you travel to new systems and land on new planets, apparently just from chance. Some of these events deplete some of your health bars, although I've yet to see such a event directly put me at a deficit. (The Out There wiki confirms, the lowest a bar can get is 0.) Some events give you resources instead. Many give you one of the plans mentioned before.

There is a wide variety of these random events to find. Some ask you a question. None of the answers you give will outright kill you, although some might reduce a gauge, cause your ship to take damage or even cause you to forget technology.

Of special note are the "Encounter Life" events on Garden Worlds, which bring you in contact with alien races. Most of these speak in Space Language, which you don't know anything about at the start of the story. (My personal advice is, at the start of a game, if you're asked a question by aliens and have to agree or disagree, disagree. You seem to get good results more often that way.) After most alien encounters you'll pick up a word of Space Language, which persists with you throughout the rest of the play. All alien meetings and many random events make use of this Space Language, and learning it enables you to make sense of the choices you're offered.

In one sense, learning Space Language is the firmest sense of game progression you get. Ships can be damaged and switched, technologies forgotten and a full gauge greatly depleted from a roll of the dice, but nothing ever makes you forget a learned word except losing the game and starting over.

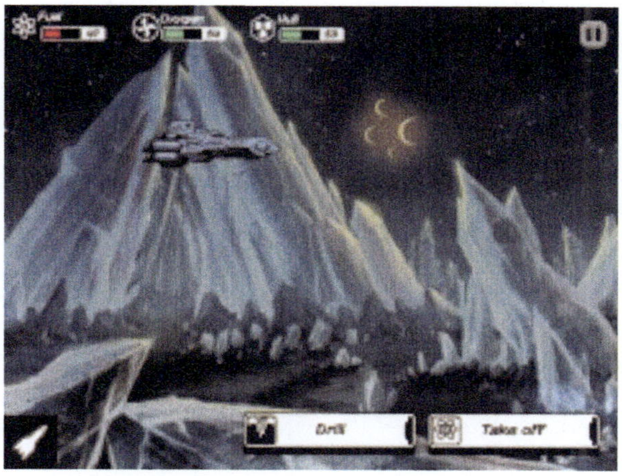

Figure 58.6

Arriving on a Mountain World.

58.4 Tips for Getting Started Out There

That should give you a good idea of what playing it is like. Most of the rest of Out There falls under the heading of story. If you can handle digging yourself out of the hole your small and inefficient starting ship puts you in, you might be able to get to the real game. Try to hang in there; there's some interesting things to discover ahead of you. Here's some advice to get you underway:

- Always keep tabs on your gauges. Failing to do so is how you lose.
- Try to visit new planets as much as possible. If you have a choice of landing on a rocky planet you've seen before or one you haven't, pick the new one. At least you have a chance of picking up new tech or words in the process.
- The deeper you drill or probe, the more likely your equipment will get damaged or even destroyed. The drill can be rebuilt with 4 Iron (FE). Rebuilding the scoop requires Platinum, but you get one unit of it back when the scoop is destroyed.
- Besides the harvesting equipment, the unluckiest things to get damaged are the Interplanetary Reactor (which lets you travel between planets) and the Space Folder (which lets you travel between stars).
- You start out with a pretty bad ship. The first sign that you're progressing in the game is finding a ship with more cargo space. Cargo space is the thing that helps you progress, more than anything else.
- When you change ships, the new one starts with all its gauges full, for free. Your old one remains where it was, with the same gauges. Nothing in the game will interfere with old ships, and all your old stuff will remain on them where you leave it. You can use old ships (or new ones you choose to pass up) as storage for rare elements.
- The most annoying thing about Out There is that there is no way to leave notes on the star map. You might want to use pen and paper to record important locations, like the sites of Garden Worlds, supply stations and other ships.
- Eventually you'll gain units of Omega, a special element. Omega has many uses (to tell you all of them would be a spoiler). In a pinch you can use it to fill 25% of any gauge, but there's some very important things you need to use Omega for. It's a good candidate for storage on those extra ships you find around the map, although it's important that you don't lose track of it.
- *Always* keep tabs on your gauges.

59

Doom, Doom, Doom, Doom

April 2007 DoomRL (now called DRL; see the end of this chapter) is a game I did not expect to like.

As you may have guessed by now, I have pretty strong ideas as to what constitutes "roguelike," one that is more in line with the term's original sense, as seen in games like Moria, Larn and especially Hack. These are all games with random areas and random items, where melee combat is the norm and distance attacks are fairly limited, where optimized exploration strategy is fairly important to survival. DoomRL has none of these things.

DoomRL is a roguelike game based on the classic first-person shooter Doom. Not based as in "inspired by." Based as in, if you ignore the overhead perspective and turn-based play, "pretty damn close to." It seems like it would be a quickie throwaway game, but the premise hides rather a lot of interesting play.

Is this gimmicky? Oh brother, of course it is. But so is that new-fangled "Wii" thing the youngsters are fussin' about. A good gimmick can get you pretty far, if it really is good. And DoomRL's gimmick is.

Fortunately, there's more to this than just a good gimmick. DoomRL's primary addition to the genre is that, while it still has walk-into-foes melee attacks if it should come to that, missile weapons are what players will use 99% of the time. Lots of monsters can also use missile weapons, changing the dynamic from the game from managing melee proximity to range and line-of-sight. Like in Doom itself, cover matters for a lot; facing down a small horde of soldiers will probably get you slaughtered, but if you retreat behind a wall, and put a bit of distance between you and them, you can keep yourself out of danger surprisingly long. It helps that most monsters are stupid enough to instantly forget about you the moment you leave their vision.

Also like Doom, it is important to learn the secret Art of the Reload: shotguns may be powerful, but it takes an extra turn to pop another shell into its chamber. More specialized shotguns can be found, like double-barreled, or combat shotguns. The combat ones have a limited automatic reload while you're fleeing, enabling a thoughtful player to use them nearly as effectively as a pistol.

One thing that DoomRL does not have, which I consider to be necessary for a true roguelike, is an item identification system, but where it lacks there it makes up for it with a rich tactical game and a limited, but well-designed, bestiary. All the monsters come directly from the original games, and their abilities line up pretty well with that much-admired spawn of Carmack and Romero. They're tough, tough in a way that brings to mind fond memories of running from Trolls and Griffins, which is to say, almost unreasonably tough. Just tough enough that there are times that fleeing for the stairs makes more sense than sucking down a tough monster's experience points. Tough enough that the high score list means something.

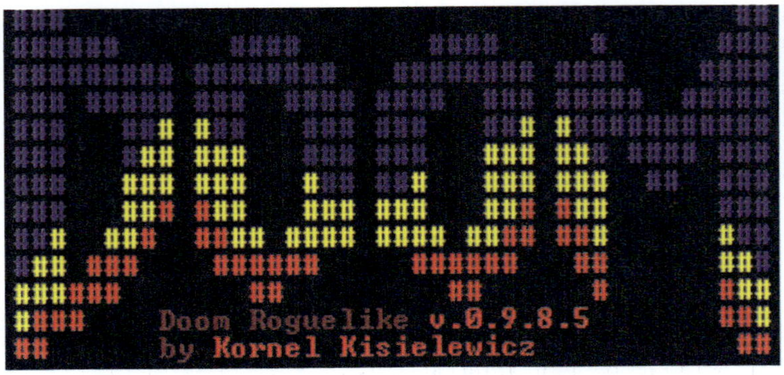

Figure 59.1

DoomRL (before it was DRL)

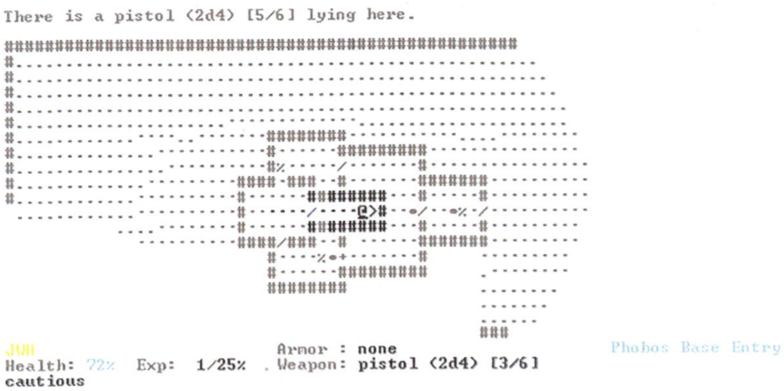

Figure 59.2

DoomRL

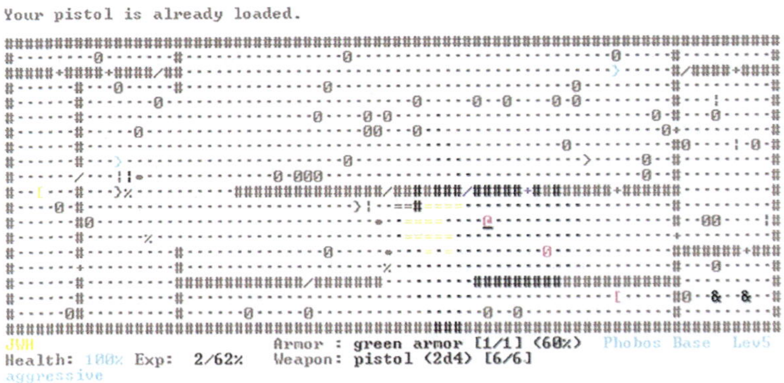

Figure 59.3

DoomRL

DoomRL's item system does have room for special equipment and multiple weapon types, which is more than Doom had, but it does suffer a bit for giving players many more pistols and shotguns than they'll ever need. They aren't strategically useless, but since their ammo cannot be salvaged, to gain proper use of them requires lugging about a lot of extra guns just to drop them when their bullets run out. DoomRL enforces a very strict inventory limit, even more strict than Rogue's, and it is easy to fill up much of that with stacks of pistol and shotgun ammo. There are also items that work like Doom's powerups, in that instead of entering inventory they activate the moment they are collected, which is a fairly significant innovation for a roguelike. And Doom's fairly clever health system, where players can supercharge their health over the normal maximum at the cost of it slowly draining until the surplus is gone, is copied unchanged.

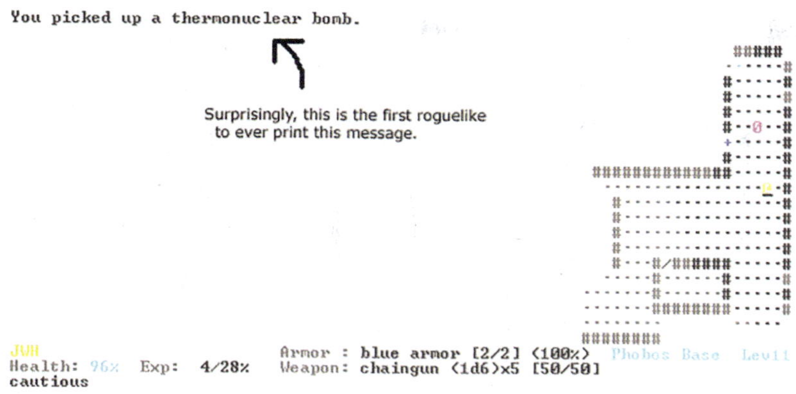

Figure 59.4

DoomRL

Probably the coolest thing about the game, though, is its approach to "user deformable terrain." Many roguelikes contain things like pickaxes and wands of digging, but in DoomRL changing level layouts like this becomes almost a first-class play mechanic. Most walls can be destroyed with a rocket launcher, or by pushing an explosive barrel up next to it and shooting it. Barrels, properly utilized, can greatly harm many monsters that would ordinarily outclass the player. Monsters can destroy walls too, and their explosive shots can set off barrels, providing a nice balance of risk to shoving those things around a level. One way to measure a roguelike is by noting how foes can be harmed through methods other than basic attacks, and those barrels make DoomRL very strong in this area.

One of the more entertaining things about the game is that, while the graphics are ASCII and the gameplay is turn-based, the sound comes directly from the original game. MIDI-based music that sounds pretty close to Doom's soundtrack plays throughout each screen-sized level, and it is difficult to avoid grinning when mowing down a horde of "h"s, and they make the same sounds as the original game. Especially interesting is that the sound effects are not only the same, but they serve the same purpose as Doom. While games like ADOM and NetHack play messages when something important happens out of sight on the level, DoomRL actually plays the sound, and adjusted in volume depending on how far the foe is from your angry little @-sign. The sounds only play after each move however, so it makes sense to play the game with the volume up.

While its lack of complex item play means the game will always lack in the greater scheme of roguelike strategy, it says a lot for the game that its inclusion would arguably dilute its play. DoomRL is, ultimately, an awesome little game that sets out to do one thing, and do it well. There is certainly room enough in the genre for something like that.

(*January 2020*: In the time since the first version of this was written, the whimsically named "Zenimax," current owners of the Doom IP, sent a cease-and-desist to the creators of DoomRL. Not ones to be easily dissuaded, they just changed the name of their game to "DRL." They have also created an expanded game with a similar theme, called Jupiter Hell, available on Steam.)

59.1 Sources

DRL: https://drl.chaosforge.org/

Jupiter Hell: https://store.steampowered.com/app/811320/Jupiter_Hell/

60

DreamForge's Dungeon Hack

November 2009 Roguelike games have been around for a good while, and from the very start many of them have cribbed system rules out of the Dungeons & Dragons books. Many of Rogue's items (especially equipment) come from that game, and NetHack goes so far as to retain the idea that armor class counts down, possibly the last game still in development to retain this convention; D&D dropped that back in its third edition.

But there is one roguelike, or close to it, that adheres to the Dungeons & Dragons rules out of necessity, because it is actually an official 2nd Edition AD&D computer game product! Dungeon Hack was created in 1993 by DreamForge Intertainment, a company that developed several other official D&D games for TSR back in the days when SSI still held the license.

I mentioned way back that Rogue's inspiration was likely the hack-and-slash play of old-school D&D mixed with the thinking (if not the actual geomorphs) behind the random dungeon generation tables in the 1st Edition AD&D Dungeon Master's Guide.

Perhaps partly due to these roots, Dungeon Hack is actually a fairly good game. It's not nearly as complex as NetHack, but that fact works in the game's favor as much as argues against it. However, some superficial aspects of the game may cause one to conclude that it does not deserve to be called by the term "roguelike."

60.1 "It Is Strong Magic That Can Point to Maps!"

The object of Dungeon Hack (explained in a pretty cool, for a DOS game, animated opening cutscene) is to obtain a mystic orb from the bottom of a large dungeon. Along the way are many monsters, traps, magic items (some of them cursed), tunnels to explore and map, and puzzles to solve. All of this is per roguelike normal. We'll come back to those shortly.

The first major departure from roguelike tradition a player will probably notice is the graphics. Not only does it have an opening cutscene and fancy title, but the game actually runs on the Eye of the Beholder 3 game engine. The play takes place in a Wizardry-style, discrete movement, first-person perspective maze. The game automatically maps out visible corridors for the player. A small version of the map is visible at the bottom of the screen, and it can be clicked on to reveal everything seen thus far.

Monsters roam the halls step-by-step, much like in the later classic Might & Magic games, although in this game they do so in real time. So long as the player has seen a square of the dungeon himself, any

Figure 60.1

Dungeon Hack

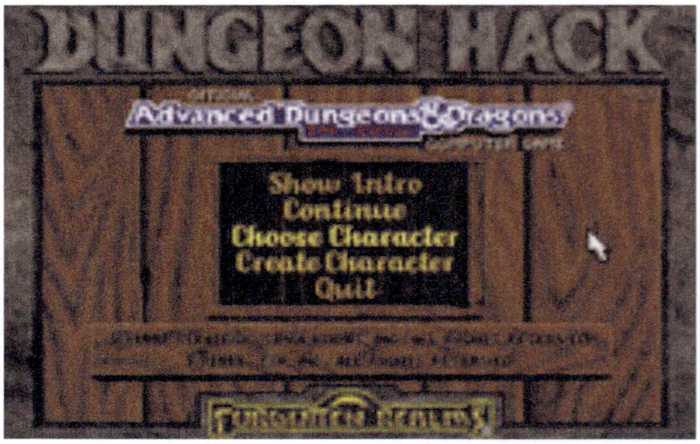

Figure 60.2

Dungeon Hack

monsters it contains will appear on the automap as a red dot, a feature which makes both exploring and avoiding trouble much easier.

Even though the main view window is a directional, first-person perspective, and combat relies on the player's facing, the useful automap, the turn-based (though still real-time) movement, the fact that combat does not take place in its own mode but in the same as exploration, and the variety of actions possible during that combat, helps to keep the game's roguelikeness intact.

Before the game even begins, however, a character must be selected. Roguelikes tend to favor quick starts, so as to allow players to get back into the game quickly after yet another death, but the AD&D rules encouraged lengthy, detailed character creation.

Dungeon Hack solves the problem nicely. It allows players to select from an extensive roster of pre-made characters that cover all the fantasy archetypes and then some. It also lets the player make a character using a well-developed creation interface, allowing for extensive rerolling and locking aspects like stats, class, race and alignment. When one of these things is locked, other items gray out to show incompatible options.

While Dungeon Hack doesn't support the entire, absurdly complicated extent of 2E AD&D character creation (probably the most involved character creation system the game has ever had), giving short-shrift to things like non-weapon proficiencies, it does let the player create multi-classed characters in the old-school style, available to non-human races only.

After character generation comes dungeon generation, which is even more detailed than character. Take a look at this (Figure 60.4)!

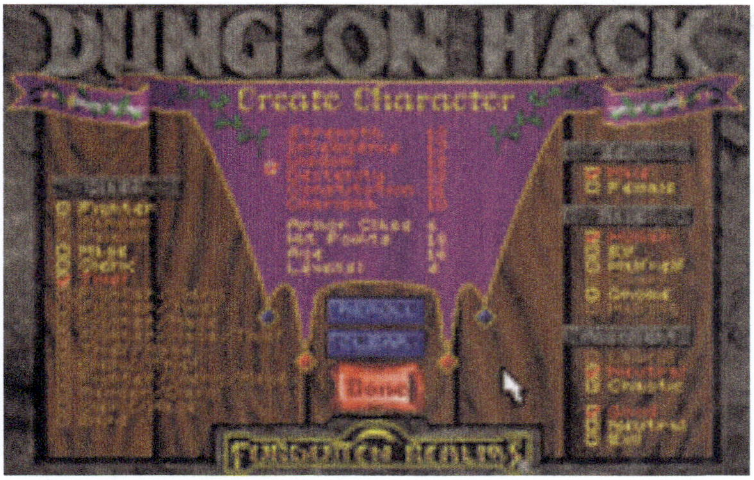

Figure 60.3

Dungeon Hack

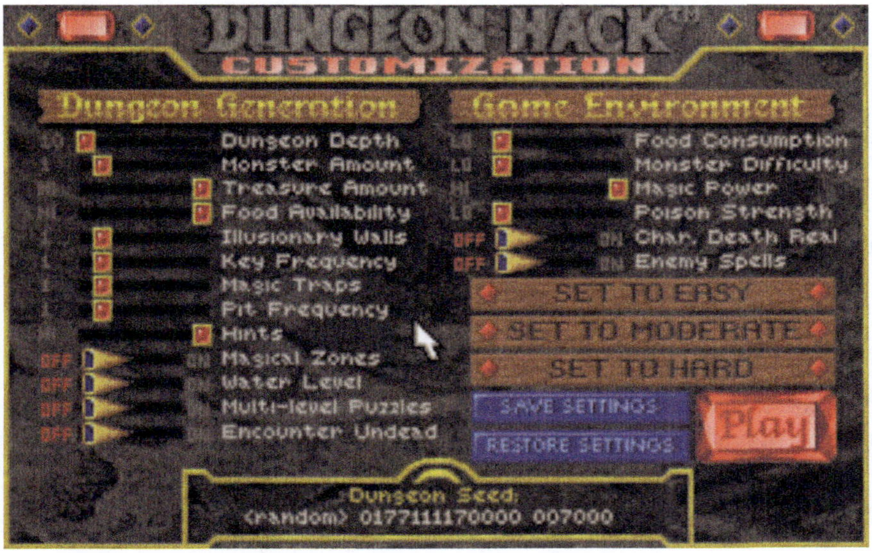

Figure 60.4

Dungeon Hack: Dungeon generation options

If this looks daunting to you, keep in mind this screen only appears if the player choses "custom" on a difficulty selection screen. Setting Easy either there or here automatically puts all the sliders to their easiest settings. Setting Medium puts them all in the middle, and Hard puts them all at maximum pain levels. Notice some of the setting names. "Water level" means a flooded dungeon level that may appear midway through the dungeon. On it, the player takes a small amount of damage each turn unless he has some means of water breathing, either by potion, Ioun stone or spell.

Magical zones are special regions of the dungeon that have unusual properties, such as anti-magic. Magical traps mean things like statues that periodically emit a burst of magic missiles, which must be evaded through good timing. Through this screen, many game features a player finds personally annoying can be disabled without changing the rest of the play experience.

Note the dungeon seed readout at the bottom. In this number is encoded both the complete set of options chosen by the player and a random number seed that can be used to recreate a dungeon at a later time. This system, combined with the permanent death option (which erases saves when the player's character dies), would actually make tournament play feasible.

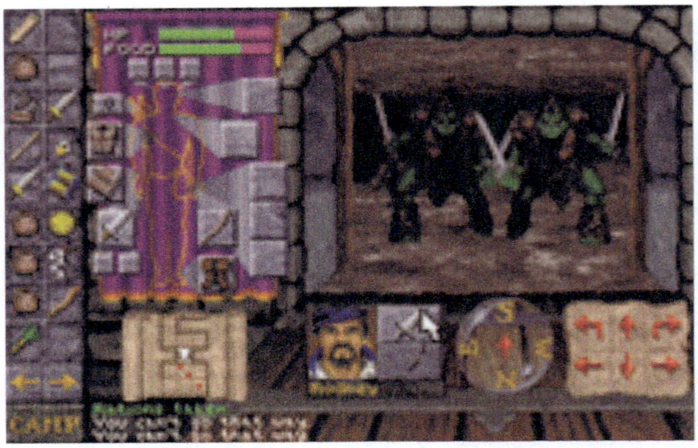

Figure 60.5

Dungeon Hack

The special powers of many roguelike monsters can be traced back to similar powers found in the D&D Monster Manuals, and some of them retain those powers in Dungeon Hack. One monster that has caused a lot of consternation among players is the Living Muck, a pudding-like beast that consumes weapons used against it. And level-draining undead monsters are so dangerous in this game that a special dungeon generation option exists to disable them. These powers are what make facing roguelike monsters more than simple bags of statistics, and their inclusion here, in a style of game where monsters are expected to have sharper teeth than in a traditional CRPG, is welcome.

It is sad that memory considerations greatly limit the number of different monsters that can appear on a floor. The most I've ever seen is three, two normal monsters that appear everywhere and one boss. A Living Muck's weapon destroying feature is an interesting challenge when you have to get through one of them, but when half the monsters on a floor know that odious trick it is an entirely different matter.

60.2 The 2nd Edition D&D Class Reunion

There are ways around that problem, yes, but many of them rely on the player being a specific character class. The differences between character classes is actually a good thing overall. You won't confuse a mage for a fighter in this game, they each have completely different gameplay options available to them, and they must rely upon them to succeed. But it is true that, since the fighter's advantage is mostly hits hard with lots of health, that they have problems in the more complicated dungeons.

Fighters must make use of magic items to get through all environmental obstacles, either that or just eat the damage. They can demolish most low-level monsters with a single hit, though, so it makes sense as a trade-off. I have yet to try to get one through a water level, however; it is possible that the class becomes unplayable at that point.

Of the basic classes, the fighter gets by with much better physical attack abilities and hit points, but the trade-off is that they have to rely on random magic items to get by obstacles and special monsters. Thieves are like fighters except they don't even get the physical attack abilities and hit points. They are able to use the thieves' picks they begin with on some of the door locks and thus explore levels with less backtracking, letting them get to more treasure on a level with less fighting.

They may also have a backstabbing ability, but I am not sure. They are a challenging class to play. As per the RPG archetype, mages are physically weak and have very few hit points but have magic spells with a wide array of combat and utility applications. Being a more-or-less by-the-book classic Dungeons & Dragons game, the magic system used in Dungeon Hack is strictly Vancian, that is, you set up camp, decide which spells to memorize, then click rest and they are regained.

None of these classes heal naturally as they roam the dungeon, healing being a primary function of the Cleric class. To regain hit points, others must either pay at a healing altar (those weird orb-like devices set into some of the walls; drag a silver coin over one to regain all hit points, or a gold coin to gain hit points and heal conditions like poison), use a magical means like a potion or, most commonly, rest until hit points are refilled.

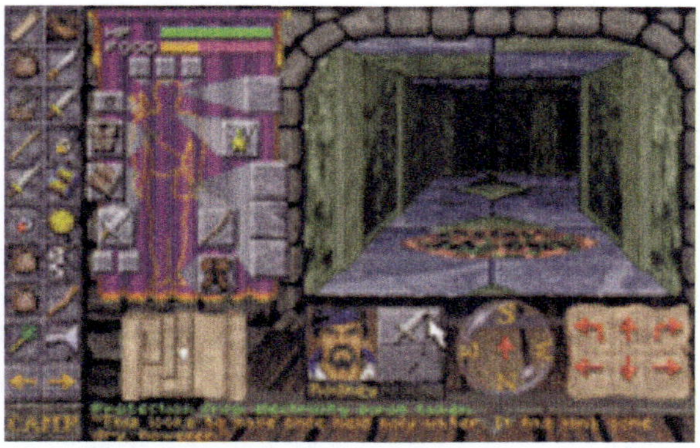

Figure 60.6

Dungeon Hack

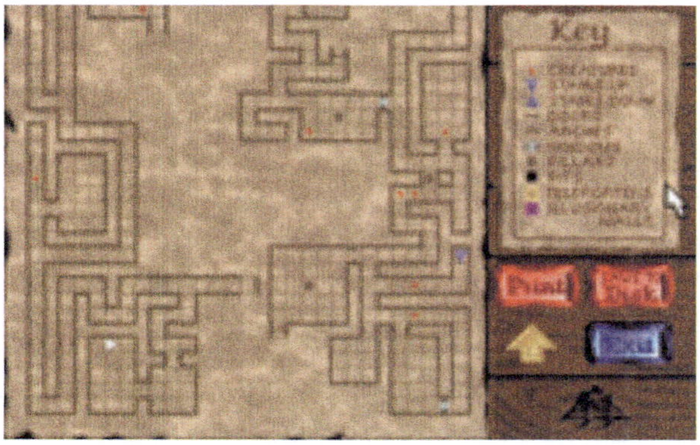

Figure 60.7

Dungeon Hack

Under the standard 2nd Edition D&D system, hit points regained through rest were quite low, requiring many days to heal a seriously wounded character. Dungeon Hack uses this system, and it is startling to see the game report "130 hours" as a typical time to get back to maximum health. That's over five days! But as a nod to playability, so long as the player doesn't rest too close to a presently active monster he will almost certainly be able to rest as long as he needs to heal.

Since monsters are not a credible limit on healing through rest, the game instead uses the traditional roguelike check on health regaining: a food requirement. New adventurers begin with two rations, and more are found in the dungeon. Food actually doesn't seem to decrease much (if at all) through mere exploration; it is almost entirely a check on spell replenishment and healing. Because of the food consumption needed to regain hit points the normal way, a popular creation choice is to multiclass Cleric.

60.3 The Environmental Persecution Agency

The environment is, truthfully, the most interesting thing about Dungeon Hack. The game's dungeon builder is one of the most interesting I've seen in any game, including more famous roguelikes. It doesn't just create a matrix of passages and rooms to explore, but it puts in key-and-door puzzles too, while ensuring that they are always solvable. Now, done wrong that could definitely be considered to be a minus, a superficial way to force the player to wander around levels back and forth repeatedly, and there is an aspect of that in the game. But locks can be picked by the thief class, or other classes if they have found gloves of dexterity, and there is also a magic item that can open those doors.

The algorithm by which locked doors always have keys available is, probably, one that works by digging outward from the entry stairs, placing locked doors along the way then depositing its key among one of the

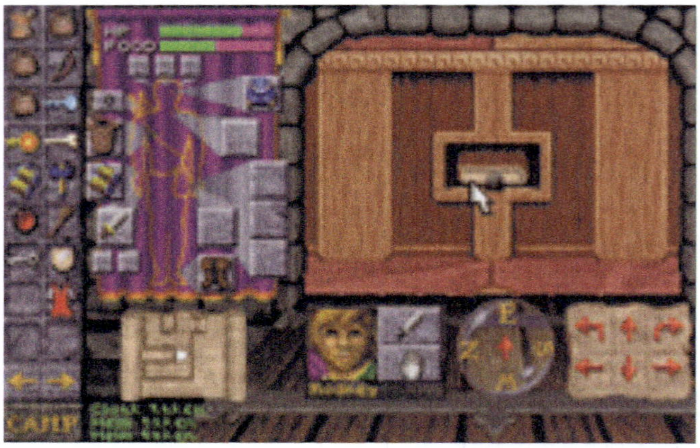

Figure 60.8

Dungeon Hack

already-dug areas. It is possible that this concept has implications for roguelike development beyond simply making sure doors have keys.

There are some other interesting things to find in the dungeons. Most items are found lying on the ground and are visible as tiny blue dots in the automap, but a few items are actually found in niches in walls, and those don't map. Illusion walls are just that, sections of wall that can actually be walked through. While it is possible for those to cause a long period of having to feel along walls to progress, it is just as likely that your character will notice them himself and say something in the message window indicating their presence. There are traps in the game that activate from stepping on them, but there are also objects on some of the walls that periodically emit a spell and that require timing to get by without harm. And there are a surprising number of little bits of "dungeon dressing" to be found that have no purpose except to add a bit of color to the surroundings.

60.4 Dudgeons and Drag-Ons

There are a few weirdnesses that should be addressed. It is possible to outrun your own thrown items simply by running rapidly down a corridor, and thus get hurt by them. It sucks to accidentally do this with a thrown potion with a damaging effect. (Hint: nearly anything can be thrown by dragging it to the view window.) Many magic items must be used by putting them in your hand and then clicking on the hand, which seems needlessly obtuse even though it does help to keep cursed items, which make it impossible to empty a hand, appropriately troublesome.

(So you know . . . the Scrying Mirror item, which identifies objects, is used by putting it in one hand, the item you want to identify in the other, then clicking on the hand with the mirror. Spells are cast by making sure that your spellbook is the only thing held—it works like a two-handed weapon—then the spell you want to use. And yet, thieves' picks are used by dragging them over the lock you want to pick.)

And the keypad controls make it easy to get mixed up a bit in the heat of a hurried escape, turning your character around when you mean to side-step or vice-versa. Movement and some actions can be performed easily with the keyboard, but attacks, equipping and item use require the use of the mouse, causing a bit of manual confusion that can be frustrating for a game that isn't actually trying to be an action game.

One thing that could be regarded as a problem to modern players more than older ones has to do, simply, with the nature of old-school D&D's experience system. That is to say, it is harsh. Most characters begin at around level 4. On the easiest monster difficulty level, killing one of the weakest monsters is worth just three experience points. Even at the hardest monster difficulty, they're only worth 24 XP each. For comparison's sake, earning even the earliest levels requires several thousand experience points. In short, this is not a game about fulfilling a player's empowerment fantasies. I tend to be in favor of slow character growth when it fits the game, and classic D&D tends to be a better game at low levels anyway. But still, if you decide to play Dungeon Hack, you should be aware of this.

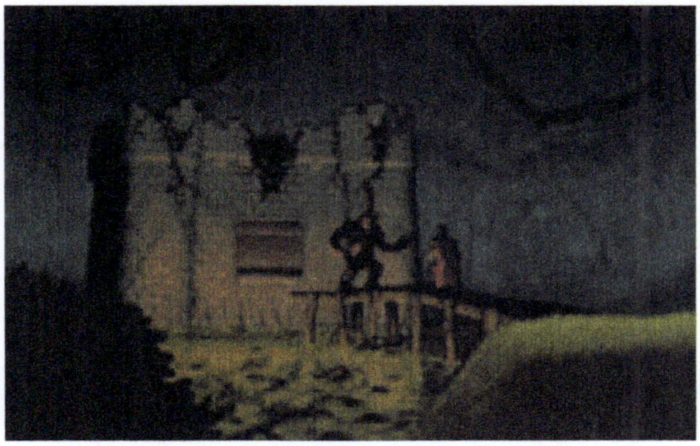

Figure 60.9

Dungeon Hack

But even so, I have to say that I enjoyed Dungeon Hack quite a lot, even more now, in fact, than when I played back after its original release. It is challenging, and different enough from the traditional roguelike that it feels fresh.

SECTION VIV
Design

61

The Eight Rules of Roguelike Design

January 2011 I call these rules for rhetorical purposes only. I don't think there are any inviolate laws of game design. But given we are talking about roguelikes, there are certain properties that have been important to the genre.

Maybe not to all roguelike games; some of these have to do with designing a good item identification system, for instance, and many of the more recent games do not use that. I'm fairly outspoken in my appreciation for item-ID systems, so please calibrate your wonk-o-meter appropriately.

I use the term "reasonable play" several times here. It refers to being in a neutral state in terms of danger. For example, almost any bad effect from using an item can prove fatal if the player uses it at the wrong time. Discovering the potion of confusion by quaffing when a troll is attacking you is dangerous—so don't do that!

If you're down to one hit point, even slight damage could kill you, and some games have items that do piddling damage, so don't play around with those. Most of the time in a roguelike the player is not in immediate danger. That is the fact on which the idea of reasonable play rests. Unknown items are possibly dangerous, so there must exist times of lesser danger in which to try them. A game built on the idea of literally constant peril would have different design demands. You are on your own in figuring those out.

Now, while a bad effect is active, it's possible for a previously out-of-sight monster to walk up and start hitting the player. That is a less obvious case, but the player could have test-ID'd the item while in a large, lit room, decreasing the chance that an unseen monster could reach him before the potion wore off. This helps to make it okay. In fact, the most effective roguelikes purposely make it difficult to always know when it's safe to perform dangerous actions. If there were a hard-and-fast rule about test-IDing potions of confusion, then an argument could be made that they shouldn't be in the game!

Of course game design is not a science. I tend to rebel whenever I hear someone tell me about features that "obviously" should never, or always, be present in a game. The following rules are no different. They are useful, however, when talking with respect to the default state of roguelike play and design, which I will define here as being that of Rogue itself. But they all apply, with different strictness, to all the other major roguelikes: NetHack, Angband, ADOM and Dungeon Crawl.

So here is a list of eight rules. Each leads with a name, in quotation marks, to facilitate discussion, followed by the rule itself in around a sentence, followed by discussion, and then finally followed by both examples of games using it well and "reverse examples" of games doing it badly. I apologize in advance for there being a lot of NetHack in these examples, but, well, it still has many features worthy of discussion.

1. **"No beheading rule." Provided reasonable play, the player's character should not be killed or harmed too greatly and permanently in one attack.**

Example: In NetHack, cockatrices can't themselves immediately kill the player through a single attack. They can initiate delayed stoning, but that gives the player a few turns to cure the condition.

Reverse example: In old versions of NetHack, Medusa was a random monster that appeared in a random room in the deeper dungeons. Since merely seeing Medusa kills the player, this breaks the rule unless the player had a way of knowing Medusa was there before stepping into sight, and the game was random enough that there was no reasonable chance of that happening. This was arguably bad design, which may explain why more recent versions of NetHack put Medusa on a special level, where at least experienced players will know where she lurks. Still, Medusa always appeared on a specific level of the dungeon, and it was always on the downstairs which were never generated in the same room as the upstairs, so a player could conceivably be prepared for her. It's still rather more reliance on spoilers than anything in Rogue requires.

There also are items that can be wielded by monsters that can kill with one hit, such as Vorpal Blade or the Tsurugi of Muramasa. But the chances of running into a monster wielding the first in the dungeon are vanishingly rare, and the second is in a specific location like Medusa, and only appears in the Samurai quest anyway. There are also other difficulties with monsters with wands of death, Touch of Death spells and disintegration beams and the like; after a certain point, the game requires that the player be proactive in protect himself from sudden instadeaths.

Reverse example: Shiren the Wanderer. Shiren is mostly really good at this, but its Skull Wraiths may be a little too strong. Their distance attacks can inflict amazingly dangerous status ailments that could conceivably result in Shiren dying before he gets to make another decision. With careful play this can be negated mostly, but there is still a chance on the last wide-open level that the player could face a situation he cannot escape.

2. **"No cyanide rule." No unidentified item should be immediately fatal upon use given reasonable circumstances, otherwise the player should never try to use-identify.**

Example: In Rogue, probably the worst item is the potion of blindness, which makes the game nearly unplayable. Not only does it give all spaces on the level a vision range even worse than that of dark passages, it is impossible to find secret doors while blind, which state has a good chance of stranding the player until the blindness wears off, or he drinks a potion of extra healing. But there is not ring of blindness, because for such an item to have bite it must be initially cursed, and if the player put on a cursed ring of blindness he might not have any means of curse lifting available, and if that were true and he was blocked from the exit by a secret passage he would be doomed to starve. The effect would be to make it unwise to try to test-identify rings because of the chance of death. One might qualify this by saying it'd be unwise to test-ID rings if no means of curse removal were available, but considering all curse-lifting in that game is from random sources it might be considered unreasonable.

Example: In NetHack, there is a random item that can kill in normal situations just from ordinary use: the amulet of strangulation. However, it is a delayed death, and prayer can get the player out of it. However, what if the player has recently prayed and his timeout hasn't expired? What if he's in Gehennom and can't effectively pray? What if his luck is negative, making it impossible to pray effectively? These aren't the more common states, though. In Gehennom, the player should know enough lore to know not to test amulets there.

Example: There are other items in NetHack that can kill instantly from use, but not by their most common uses. The wand of death, if zapped at self, kills instantly if the player isn't magic resistant. But players don't usually zap random wands at themselves, so one might consider this to be reasonable. Reverse example: Note that there *are* cases in NetHack where death might be considered unreasonable; every random egg has a chance of being a cockatrice egg, so eating eggs is an unexpectedly bad idea.

Reverse example: Dungeon Crawl has a potion of poison with a long-lived effect. This one plays carefully with the line, since it could well prove fatal to a very low-level character, but usually by resting during that time it has a chance to wear off before death ensues.

Rules 3 and 4 are about item identification. Many recent games don't include this feature. Here I give my reasons for suggesting such a system. While item identification in roguelikes does aid in presenting the world as a mysterious place to figure out, and in giving the dungeon itself a dangerous character as opposed to just the monsters, there is also a game design reason. It disassociates the player's progress from the random number generator: the player could find all of the best items in the game on the first level, but he'll still have challenge figuring that out without wasting the resources. The items found are not a gift to the player; he must still expend some effort to properly understand what he's found.

The identification game in roguelikes is one of the least considered by designers. Even to this day, it's probable that Rogue has the best ID game, although NetHack's isn't bad (though mostly irrelevant as soon as the mid-game). Rogue's is designed so that scrolls of identify cannot be relied upon, for players almost never find all the scrolls they want. Plus, since no random items are guaranteed, the player never knows if he'll find another item of a type. A few items are extremely good but easy to waste. The best of them all (scroll of scare monster) shows unusual care in its design. Using it in fact wastes it, but it is the only scroll that can be identified without even picking it up.

3. **"Item masquerade rule." Items should be difficult to identify even for spoiled players, due to similarities between items of the same type.**

It is best if this rule is not perfectly adhered to; giving observant players some benefit for their insight is in keeping with roguelike gameplay.

Example: Yes, another NetHack example. Both potions of see invisible and potions of fruit juice generally have the same messages upon use.

Example: In most games, the effects of most rings are vague and can only be deduced through close observation, if even then.

Example: NetHack and Shiren both take steps to obscure item identification through shop pricing by offering many items that sell for the same amount. Example: ADOM clearly marks the weights of items on the inventory screen, in "stones." A few random items and artifacts have distinctive weights, which an observant (or heavily spoiled) player can note and use to pick those things out.

4. **"Situational ID advantage rule." When unknown, item effects in a category should overlap in such a way that use in some situations would be good to discover, while others simultaneously would be bad.**

If no potions provide combat disadvantages, then it's in the player's best interest to test them out while fighting. If none do direct damage but one does heal, then the player should only test-ID when below maximum hit points. It is easy to go overboard in eliminating these kinds of situational ID advantages, but a good designer will still be cognizant of them and devote a little thought to lessening their influence on the game.

Example: Rogue has items that can be very useful when used in battle (extra healing) and very bad (confusion, blindness). When zapping wands at monsters, it's possible for a monster to be slowed (very good), hasted (bad), teleported away (generally good), teleported directly to the player's side (somewhat bad) or polymorphed (potentially game-ending at early levels, more beneficial as the game continues). Study of the items included in the game make it clear that some thought was put into providing a healthy amount of risk in most situations, to provide fewer "no brainer" situations to using unknown items.

5. **"Item enchantment rule." When known, items should as much as possible present interesting decisions.**

Example: All of the major roguelikes, to some extent, use scrolls of enchant weapon and enchant armor to do this to a degree. When you use a scroll, its enchantment bonus becomes a permanent fixture on the one item it's used on. If a better item comes along later that the player would rather use, maybe one that already has a high enchantment, it could be that the scroll was wasted. However, the longer the player waits to see if something better comes along, the less total use he gets out of it. All the major roguelikes feature this to a degree, but it's Rogue that makes the best use, since as stated previously, the player has no idea if he'll find a better weapon or any more enchantment scrolls.

Example: Also in Rogue, armor has an extra wrinkle. The weakest, leather armor, has the special property of being immune to the rust caused by rust traps and rust monsters/aquators. If the player uses all his enchant armor scrolls on leather, he can be sure of never losing those enchantments, but he probably won't be able to get the suit enchanted up to the heights of plate mail. The player can overcome this a bit by waiting until after the aquator floors before using his scrolls. All versions of Rogue offer rings of maintain armor which allow the player to not worry about having his armor weakened, though at a cost of food.

Reverse example: Later versions of Rogue also provide scrolls of maintain armor, which, if one appears (they are fairly common) make the decision pointless.

6. **"Two-sided coin rule." Given perfect knowledge of identifications and uses, items should never be completely useless.**

In fact, no roguelike that I know of does this perfectly, but many of them show a lot of effort has been expended towards reducing the prevalence of completely useless items. The reason for this is not just to reward player wit and knowledge; if no item is entirely bad, then the player is additionally insulated from the caprices of the random item generation.

This does not mean that all items need be great.

Example: In Rogue, even potions of blindness are useful when fighting medusas, which sometimes confuse on sight. Bad potions can also be thrown at monsters to possibly affect them.

Example: In Shiren the Wanderer, most of the bad items will affect enemies when thrown at them, making few things completely baneful. This can even be used to get a last use out of depleted wands.

Example: NetHack is pretty good about this and has shown special care in making sure many bad states have hidden upsides. Hallucination protects against "Touch of Death" magic. Confusion is sometimes very useful, providing most scrolls with alternate effects (which also make some bad scrolls into good ones). Thrown potions break and provide vapor effects (which are, sadly, usually negligible). "Bad" wands that help the monsters can be zapped at yourself to give you their benefits. Conversely, there are also good items, such as wands of cancellation, that can be very bad if used incorrectly.

7. **"Reducing grind rule." The mere act of spending time should deplete some finite resource, forcing players to keep those resources up, while also limiting the amount of "grinding" he can do.**

Example: Historically, this is done through a food timer. Rogue has the best of these: food only ever enters the game through item generation, which is tied to generating new levels. Technically food can be created by killing some monsters, but that's fairly rare, random and suitably dangerous.

Example: Dungeon Crawl's food timer, while not as strict as Rogue's, still serves its traditional function of forcing a hard limit to the player's activities. Dungeon Crawl is explicitly designed to reduce grinding, an admirable goal. (*January 2016*: Since this was written, some races have been introduced that play with the time limit in different ways, and food itself has become less of a hard limit.)

Example: ADOM does this okay for the most part. Although food is not limited as strictly as in Rogue or Crawl, its corruption timer serves much the same purpose. There are loopholes in its item scarcity, however, that can give particularly clever players a way out from under the weight of the clock. Look up "ADOM wish engine" on Google sometime. . . . (*January 2016*: ADOM's wish engines have been nerfed considerably.)

8. **"Race you can't win rule." The game's monster difficulty should increase slightly faster than the advancement of the player, given average stats and default equipment, so as to force him to rely upon items and tactics.**

The reasoning here is that if players don't have to rely on randomly found stuff then they become unimportant to play. However, if it's required to have specific items to be successful then many games will be outright unwinnable. The balance between these two poles is what makes random dungeon generation difficult, but it's also part of what makes random dungeon gameplay interesting.

Example: Rogue is, again, best at this. Even with excellent equipment, you can't just pound through all the monsters. Starting around the time you encounter trolls, you'll need to use some tactics or resources to survive more than one fight, and griffins up the ante even further, not to mention medusas, ur-viles and, of course, dragons. Shiren is also pretty good at it. More enemies in that game have special attributes, which in practice means you can get further on strategy.

62

Mapping the Infinite Cavern

January 2007 It is well known, among those who know of the genre at all (honestly if I see someone misidentify dungeon crawlers with roguelikes one more time I think I might break my tether and start trampling circus handlers—more on this below), that roguelike games have random dungeons, but it is not often that this is elaborated upon beyond just the statement. What does it mean to have a "random" dungeon? The meaning of this term is not as obvious as it first appears.

When people talk about a dungeon being "random," they rarely mean truly chaotic, but instead that the layout of rooms and passages, and their contents, are unpredictable enough between games that the player can be surprised to discover what lies in wait for him. This actually demands not pure, nonsensical randomness, but a well-honed generation algorithm that can turn the output of the random number generator into something consistent and explorable.

If we just set each cell of that grid to an equal probability of being a floor or a wall, what we would end up with would not be playable; we would not be assured of being able to explore the whole thing, or find the stairs to the next level (if we even thought to throw that in there). Random dungeon generation schemes must interpose an algorithm between the generator and the map, and of course that means it is not, strictly speaking, completely random.

Typically, for a dungeon exploration game, it is enough for the game's purposes that the player not be able to deduce the layout of the unexplored portions of the dungeon, but this is itself interesting because Rogue, the first game of the type, did not actually have all that random a dungeon.

Rogue generated its levels according to a fairly simple scheme by which the map was divided into a grid of nine sections connected by corridors, each being either a room, a longer corridor piece, an intersection, a dead-end or (rarely) a maze. See if you can pick them out from this screenshot. Almost every Rogue level follows this nine-sector pattern.

This is significant because, if the player was in a room that was in one corner of the screen, he could know for certain that there was no passage in the walls facing the screen edges. A major part of Rogue's strategy had to do with knowing when to search walls for secret doors and when to move on to check another room. If a room is near an edge of the screen, then that's one wall the player need not waste time checking. And if the player has found nine rooms or room-analogues on the level, he can be sure he's gotten all the treasure, and it's okay to head for the next level, and its nine fresh opportunities for more loot.

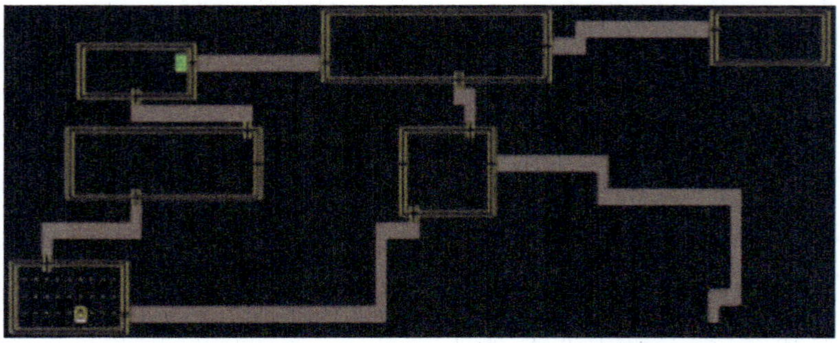

Figure 62.1

Rogue

Oddly, this doesn't make the game any easier for the designers took its predictability in account when balancing the game's food supply. Learning how to game the level generator became an essential skill for success.

Some mazes, too, present tactical advantages, such as doors that can be closed, or even locked, to discourage pursuers, and loops that wounded characters can travel indefinitely, slowly healing until they have regained enough hit points to make a stand. These things are important to realize because all these games place a high emphasis on coming up with an efficient exploration plan. In roguelikes, time is the greatest enemy. Every move wasted is one second closer to starvation, and that troll with your name on it could be halfway across the level or just about to walk through the door. The longer you live, here, the sooner you die; the only way to survive is to win.

More recent roguelikes may have more chaotic dungeon layouts than Rogue, but they, too, have design quirks and tendencies that can, indeed must, be exploited by a canny player. Sometimes the game chips in with hints to help the player decide whether to explore or not; Angband provides "level feelings" that can clue players into whether there is a good item on the level, and both NetHack and ADOM provide noises to alert the player when there are certain special rooms nearby. Canny use of knowledge of the game's dungeon generation algorithm, coupled with items like scrolls of magic mapping, often mean the difference between a dead adventurer and a live one.

Novice players think of the slaying of hundreds of monsters as being the primary element of roguelike play. Advanced players realize they should think beyond that, and learn to optimize their resources and figure out item identities. The first step towards mastery is to recognize the importance of this kind of exploration risk-management.

Here are screenshots of typical levels from some of the more prominent roguelikes, and what makes them unique:

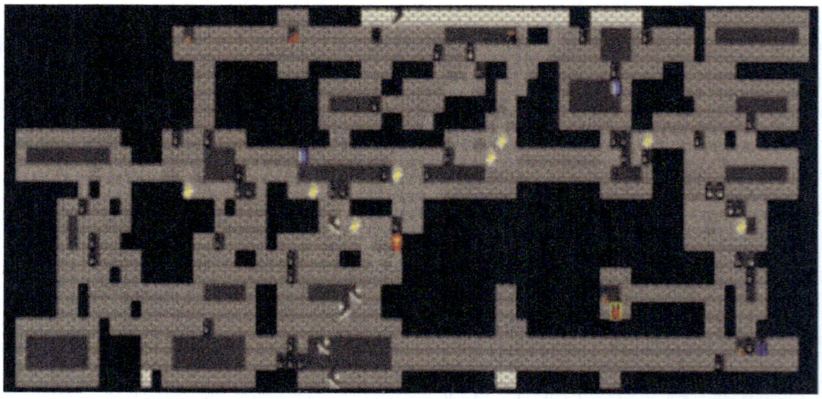

Figure 62.2

Angband level map

62.1 Angband

Size: Very large
Chaoticness: Low
Opportunity: Moderate

The image above is of the "compressed" map produced by the game's level overview command; each cell of the above represents several in the actual level, and it feels yet larger in play. On the other hand, while it has much bigger mazes, its level generator doesn't seem too much different from Rogues, just with more sectors and a greater reluctance to leave some empty. But those vast, scrolling levels make up for it, and the shape of its rooms are more varied than most other games as well, with a good number of variations upon the theme of rectangular box (one innovation NetHack has never adopted).

The most interesting thing about roguelike dungeons is the stuff contained within it, and Angband levels have lots of that. They also sometimes supply these incredibly horrible-wonderful things called vaults, which may well have the greatest challenge/reward ratio in the genre. Vaults are large rooms that contain many dozens of monsters, generated far out-of-depth (that is, much harder than the standard for that level), frequently with multiple uniques (think bosses) all in one room. But vaults are generated with treasure to match, frequently containing multiple artifacts. They are such over-the-top challenges that it is difficult to resist trying to clear them out as much for the fun of testing one's self as for the prime loot, but many games end in these places.

62.2 NetHack

Size: One screen
Chaoticness: Moderate
Opportunity: High

NetHack levels are minuscule in comparison, but they have a much greater variety of special rooms that can be found. The most common of these are its famous shops, which have more logic powering them than many games have at all, but there can also be found temples, swamp, throne rooms, army barracks and beehives to pick some of the more interesting types. Also, unlike Angband and ADOM, NetHack does not bias item generation based on how far the player has gotten in the game. He is as likely to find Grayswandir on the first floor as the 20th, which in the end helps ensure that every room is worth exploring.

In addition to a large number of non-random, special levels, NetHack is also known for having three other types of random levels besides standard dungeons. Cavern levels, which are wide-open and irregular in shape, are found in the Gnomish Mines and are best known to beginning players. Some way down is the rogue level, a single area that is built like Rogue's distinctive floors. (It has some subtle rule similarities as well, and uses Rogue's ASCII graphic scheme, even in graphic versions of the game!) But most important, and most annoying, are the mazes, which make up the full second half of the main dungeon. Since they take forever to explore and contain few special rooms, they are widely considered one of the game's greatest weaknesses.

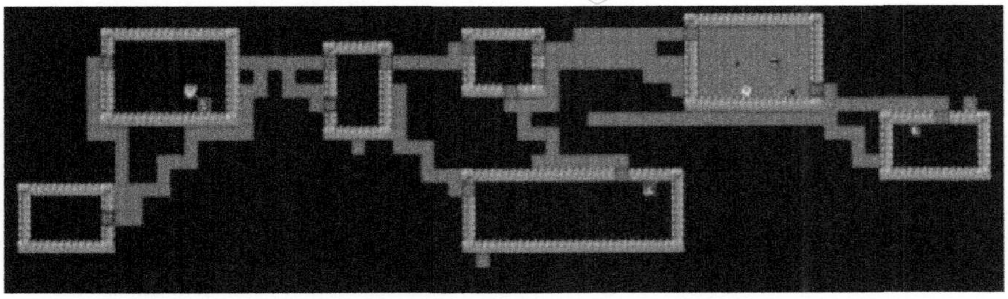

Figure 62.3

NetHack level map

Figure 62.4

NetHack maze level map

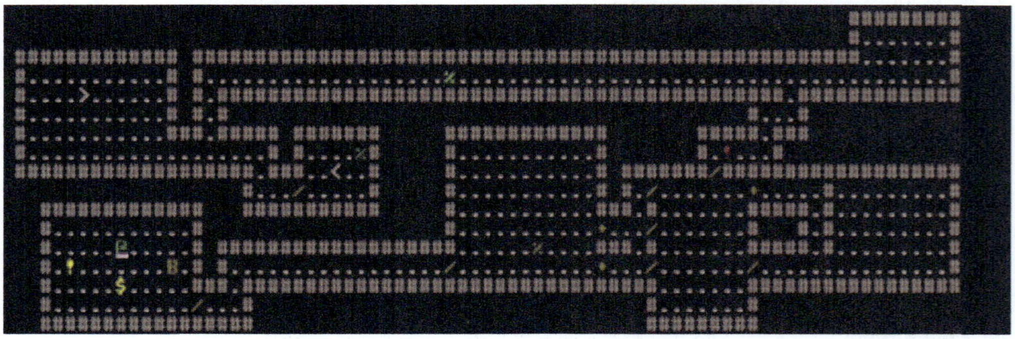

Figure 62.5

ADOM typical level map

62.3 ADOM

Size: One screen
Chaoticness: High
Opportunity: Moderate

ADOM has multiple dungeons connected by an "overworld" area, but many of them look suspiciously similar to each other. Players looking beneath first appearances will find lots of variety, however. One dungeon regenerates levels every time they are entered like Moria and Angband, and one level is unique in that the higher the player's level, the greater the danger he'll find, as it generates monsters of a level that is a multiple of the player's: if the player is very strong, then the monsters seen there will be very, very strong! Add in room-shops and a good selection of special levels, including several towns, and you have a game that looks a lot like alternate-universe NetHack. Yet, its random levels do not vary all that much, resulting in an impression of sameness at times.

62.4 Mystery Dungeon: Shiren the Wanderer

Size: Small (seems larger)
Chaoticness: Low
Opportunity: Moderate

Shiren's levels seem to be larger than they really are. Unlike the other games listed here, the size of one "space" is much larger than one character on a text screen, so less territory can be seen at once. Reduced in scale (as in the illustration, which is a copy of the game's translucent in-game map photoshopped to remove the background), the map is about the same size as a NetHack level.

Shiren doesn't have many special level types, Monster Houses (similar to Rogue's Zoos, a room with a lot of both enemies and random objects) are just about it, but this is made up for with its many level generation types. Depending on the player's progress through the game, there can be anywhere from four rooms to

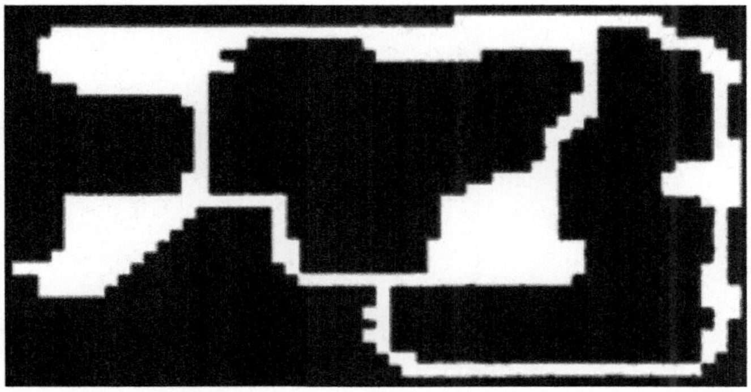

Figure 62.6

Shiren level layout

14 scattered around the board. It isn't too hard to recognize the level types after a couple of exposures, and some (especially the 14-room one) are as simple to exploit as Rogue's.

As promised, here is a word on the confusion, often seen of late, between dungeon crawlers and roguelikes:

Roguelikes are randomly generated, overhead-view games about tactics and strategy, with a strong emphasis on gaining information and resource management, and usually featuring some form of "permadeath."

Dungeon crawlers are, technically speaking, a large class of RPG that includes any that involves exploring a dungeon, and thus could be honestly considered to include Rogue and its ilk, but most precisely refers to a type of game that has its ultimate source in the likes of Wizardry and Akalabeth. They tend to provide a first-person interface, although one that may switch to overhead when not actually in a dungeon. The dungeon itself is pre-made, not random at all, and the player controls an entire party of adventures, but if one dies he can typically be revived in town, although usually for a fee.

Both game types were inspired by old-school Dungeons & Dragons, but each focuses on different aspects of that seminal game. Roguelikes focus on the specifics much more, and the idea of surviving general types of situations, such as those provided by the random dungeon, monster and treasure generation tables in the back of the first-edition AD&D DM's Guide, while dungeon crawlers are more like the experience of playing through a specific adventure, with monsters and treasure carefully placed to produce a challenging, but fair, experience and typically with much greater emphasis on following a story.

In other words, playing a roguelike is like playing an improvised game thrown together on the fly by an expert DM, while dungeon crawls have, as their hypothetical basis, the kind of world that a DM has spent days and weeks inventing, or got out of a guidebook. As far as play goes, crawls are about overcoming specific encounters cooked up by the designers, and thus favor linear thought and puzzle solving, while roguelikes are about dealing with whatever comes up, which is more non-linear thinking and problem solving.

63

Purposes for Randomization in Game Design

May 2010 Roguelikes are the genre of game most associated with randomization of game content. Some other games, especially classic games, feature substantial random elements, but most of them use them as an afterthought, or in an ineffective manner, or without fully realizing how they change the dynamics of their game.

As an example I offer a Gamecube game, Nintendo's Pikmin 2. One of the advertised features for the game is the randomized dungeons that players would enter during play. I consider the original Pikmin, which had little or no random elements, to be brilliantly designed.

It forced players to make wise use of their actions within a strict time limit (30 game days), and yet the limit was short enough that mistakes were duly punished and players had a disincentive to grind for additional troops. Yet, it wasn't really so difficult that it took players more than one or two attempts to win. And really dedicated players could win surprisingly quickly; the shortest possible time to win was nine game days out of the 30 allowed.

But some players, and more importantly game blogs, complained about the overall time limit, so it was removed in the sequel. Further, for the random dungeons which were advertised as the major addition to the game, the day timer is disabled. Each floor's layout is not actually randomly generated: instead, the maze layout, the treasures to be found, the resources provided and the enemy opposition are all static, predetermined for each floor. Without the timer, there is no pressure that might force players to move on without having found everything.

The only real randomness is in the locations of all these things. Scrambling the start location too helps a little, but not much. Thus, the only effect that the randomness has on the game is the order in which things are found and the relatively small variable tactical challenge that comes from fighting enemies under differing terrain conditions. For all the promise that randomization maps held, it made little sense to scramble object locations instead of keep them static.

When does it make sense to randomize? What benefits does this provide to a computer game? Here are a few . . .

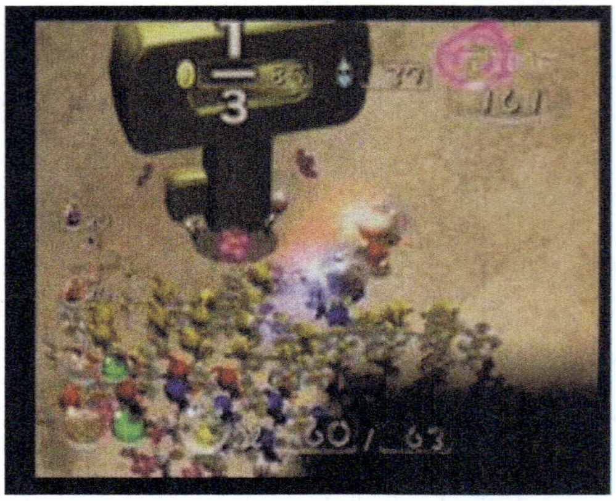

Figure 63.1

Pikmin 2

63.1 Preserves Player Interest across Multiple Playthroughs

This is the reason most given, and it is not a bad one if done well.

Most games will always have the same monsters in that corridor or the same item in that treasure box. Playing through it a second time provides little in the way of a new experience, since everything is as it was the first time through. It's not that a game cannot be played twice, it's just that the hidden knowledge of the game having all been revealed, a fundamental element of the experience is missing. The decisions the player makes in progressing through do not change.

He may optimize his playing style in order to best make use of the hidden events coming up, but this is a process substantively different from really playing the game. It is the difference between playing Super Mario Bros. to get through it and trying to speed run it; the game ceases to be about reacting to unknown events, an extremely complicated task requiring a human being to overcome, and becomes about planning and executing a trip through the game, which is difficult for entirely other reasons. It is the difficulty of forming a plan, and of exactingly following it, but not of reacting to unexpected events. Randomizing a game can provide this.

But allow me to pose you a question. What if you had a generic Dragon Quest-style JRPG in which every aspect was the same every playthrough except the layouts of the dungeons, but with the dungeon contents the same, just mixed up every game? Would that game, in truth, be any more replayable? A player may wander down dead-end hallways and thus fight a similar number of monsters to his first time through, but would a player really find that interesting enough to bother playing through a second time? A hypothetical roguelike of that type, which had everything static between plays except for dungeon layout, would be a little better off because the dungeon creates a tactical combat challenge which may vary between game. Even so, such a game would not be much more entertaining.

63.2 Provides Resistance to Spoilers

This is similar to the first point, but increasingly important with so many FAQ sites out there and so many players who are happy to steamroll through a game.

It is obvious that a game in which large portions are randomly generated is at least somewhat resistant to FAQs, but it is a difficult task to make a game that's spoiler-proof. It is impossible to write a walkthrough for Rogue, but on given floors certain monsters tend to show up, and there are learnable, and thus spoilable, strategies for how to deal with them. There are only a limited number of possible items that can be generated, and both learning what they are and using them are vulnerable to FAQs. NetHack takes this to extremes; it's very difficult to win without either spending years learning the game or reading a truckload of FAQs, but once you are sufficiently spoiled winning the game is much easier than you'd think. You might not be able to win every game like NetHack god marvin, but winning one in 12 is definitely within the reach of the average gamer, and more importantly once you get past a certain point early on winning can be almost assured. (In my opinion this is the point where you've gotten poison resistance, magic resistance and dragon scale mail.)

I doubt it is possible to take game randomization to a point where FAQs and other gameplay spoilers become useless, at least before the point where computers will be able to generate entire games whole cloth, which is several decades down the road at least. In the meantime, the only real resistance to spoilers there can be is to make the act of playing the game more fun than getting to the end. That would remove the incentive to cheat through the game.

A component of the urge to get through the game as quickly as possible and by any means necessary is the tendency of many developers to put in "unlockables," content that the player must earn the right to play. (That is ultimately an unhealthy development; for proof of this statement, I point to those lamentable games where the "unlocks" are actually DLC, a situation which would have made less intuitive sense to publishers if they hadn't been locking off features from players since the NES days.)

63.3 Challenges Player Deductive Skills

The combination of randomly generated and predetermined content, if planned right, can make possible an interesting kind of gameplay, one of the few that allows players to make use of deductive skills. Roguelikes generate random items from a list of possibilities, and identifying them requires making use of observable evidence in order to figure out item types while reducing or eliminating the risks of use.

NetHack makes the most use of this. The DevTeam went so far as to group items according to sale price, with most price tiers containing at least one bad item, to reduce the utility of "Price ID" as a means of item identification. (Observant players will note that the Shiren the Wanderer games group item prices in a similar manner, another proof that Shiren's Japanese developers must surely be aware of NetHack.) Overall, however, item identification is somewhat out of fashion as a means of adding challenge to a roguelike game; Dungeon Crawl's developers have outright stated that a design goal of theirs is to reduce the importance of the identification subgame, possibly because to make use of it the player must have a list of possible item types at hand, which to utilize demands either extensive note-taking over many games or spoilers.

It is possible, although uncommon, for a roguelike game to use this design concept in areas other than item identification. One of the few examples that comes to mind is NetHack's endgame, in which players must discover the proper altar, out of three possibilities, on which to complete his quest. Also in that game, it is possible to figure out what the reward is for finishing Sokoban before completing the puzzles leading up to it, which can aid an experienced player in deciding whether to go through with it.

63.4 Escapes the Limits of Conventional Narration

This one has only recently become solidly recognized. Yet it should not be underestimated; Dwarf Fortress has utilized it to become a darling of the internet. I should warn you, I'm going to display my under-utilized English Major powers here. If you are allergic to high-falutin' discussions on the nature of art, you may want to move to the next section heading.

The practice and technique of storytelling has evolved over thousands of years. Since Aristotle, all kinds of people have weighed in on what a story is, what it should be and what makes one good. When game developers decided they wanted it to become a storytelling medium, they adopted that advice and formulated their own rules, some unconsciously, as to what such a game should be. Rules like a three-act structure, rising action, a climactic moment, a paring away of irrelevant elements, a unity of theme and a certain purposefulness, sometimes going so far as to provide a distinct moral. These rules, in many ways, stand opposed to the ideals of game design.

Storytelling was devised to describe life, imposing a narrative pattern upon a series of real-world events. Fiction takes that pattern and seeks to synthesize a series of events to match it. Games also seek to emulate life, but whereas a story attempts to make sense of the randomness of life by suggesting a plan, games revel in that randomness.

You don't know how a (traditional) game will turn out, and that's the point. When you start a game of Monopoly, when you take to the field in a game of baseball, when you begin a hand of Bridge, the idea is to overcome a challenge set before you, one with inseparable random elements, through skill and wit.

That challenge may or may not conform easily to a narrative sequence. Sometimes a player heroically overcomes great odds in order to prevail, but usually the great odds win out. The odds-on favorite usually wins. The many times when the expected result occurs would be considered wasted to a storyteller, who instead of describing everyone the Cyclops ever devoured before Odysseus showed up wants to get right to the good stuff, but to a gamer they lend weight to those times when the expected results fail to occur. And

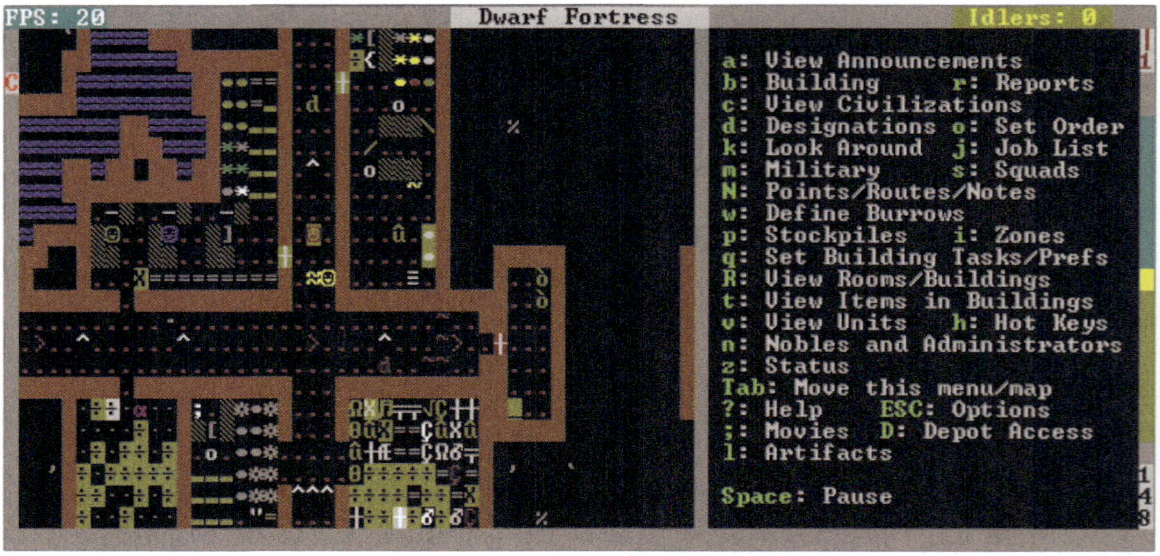

Figure 63.2

Dwarf Fortress

when the player can increase the chances of success through his actions, then he can feel good about himself because his skill really has won the day.

In games with pre-written stories, the favored result rarely happens. The evil forces with so much going for them rarely win out. Even when they do, it's not the fault of the player one way or another. Even if the player loses (or "gets a game over" in the parlance), he can return to a previous save and try again. Players subconsciously perceive this fact and it robs video game storytelling of weight.

Whether the ending to a God of War game has Kratos prevailing or not, it's already been determined which it is; the fact that the player must walk Kratos through the steps to get to that point doesn't affect his chances of success, they just slow down the story. Because of this, I say the narrative and the gameplay are not well-integrated. They are created following techniques for writing fiction: starting from the story and inventing the details to fill the mold. And anyone who has ever watched Scooby-Doo knows that this has certain drawbacks if the writer wants to keep the players in suspense.

Roguelike games have, for a long time, been one of the few types of computer games to go about writing the other way around. That is to say, few of them seek to write anything at all! They seek to emulate a realistic world, with enough tricks and traps thrown in to make it interesting, and ask the player to write a legend of his own. The legend means something because it was purchased with the player's skill and sweat; the story of the character becomes the player's own. Dwarf Fortress (the primary mode of which is not a roguelike, but it is kind of an honorary example of the breed all the same) makes this almost explicit, to the degree that there is a whole category of DF enthusiast: one who will never brave the UI or learn how to construct a moat, but loves to read the play reports, a.k.a. legends, of fortresses like Boatmurdered, Syrupleaf, Headshoots and Bronzemurders.

Why are video games worthy to be considered an important art form? What can we use to counter Roger Ebert when he claimed so certainly that they are not art? My answer to him has nothing to do with providing an experience to the player. No, ultimately the future of these games lies in their use as a creative tool, a way of exploring possibility, a method of aiding the player in creating his own narrative. In this, computer games have the potential to touch the divine in a way no other work can. It is *meta art*, art that aids in the production of other art. Every other art form limits the audience's involvement to interpretation; only interactivity can draw him in beyond that. In this area video games are unique, but the great majority of games squander this potential shamefully. The best roguelikes do not.

63.5 Provides Complex Play through Combining of Basic Elements

Let's end with a more solid use for randomized gameplay. It is also the one that is the most solidly roguelike: using it as a means of throwing together different features to provide unique adventure experiences.

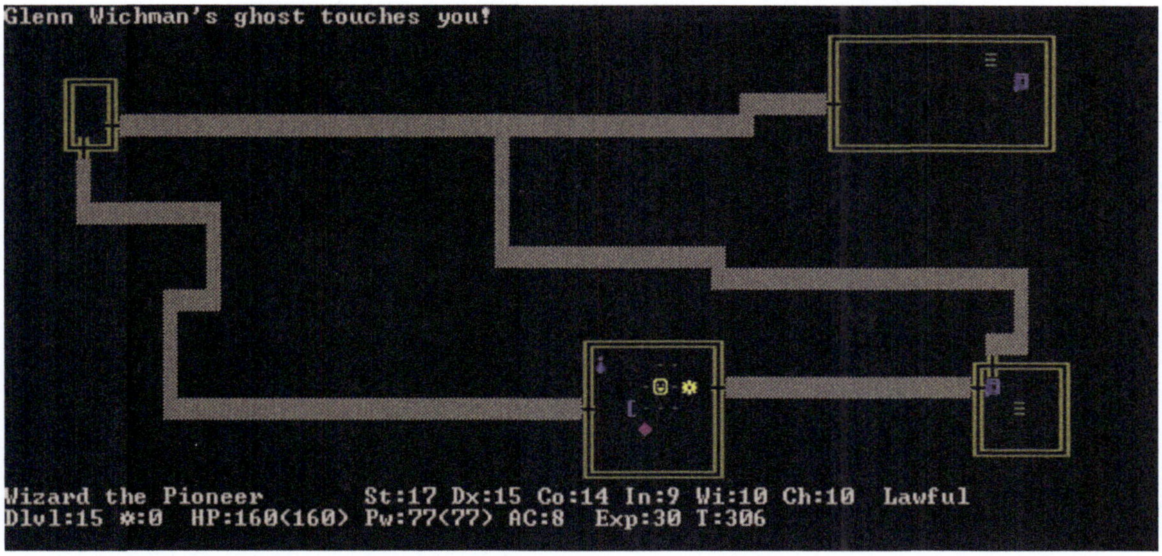

Figure 63.3

Rogue

For an example, let's take Rogue. There are no character classes in Rogue. You always begin with 12 hit points, 16 Strength, a +1, +1 mace, ring mail, a short bow and arrows and one food ration. At the moment of starting a game, your adventure always begins the same way.

Rogue is balanced, generally, against the player. At the start of the game the player is only a little stronger than the toughest type of monster he may face on level 1, the hobgoblin. He gains levels rapidly, but a new type of monster is introduced every floor until level 23. Given average rates of decent and combat, monster difficulty keeps pace with the player at first, and eventually surpasses him. And the hunger limitation forces him to keep exploring new dungeon levels instead of grinding out experience on the easier floors.

The only thing that gives him a chance of surviving, maybe even prevailing, is the random treasure generated along the way, and because the player is doomed without it he must make the best use of it he can. Many of these items give the player a minor advantage. Stronger armor reduces damage taken in combat; stronger weapons mean fewer successful strikes are needed to overcome a foe; wands provide a limited resource for overcoming the monstrous opposition; rings of maintain armor protect your armor from damage but consume food while wearing it; leather armor is weak but cannot rust and doesn't take up a ring slot; on the other hand rings of slow digestion push back the spiked wall of the food system a bit, letting the player level up a little, but in exchange for taking up a ring finger that might be used for something else.

Many of these items change the game significantly, even radically. Careful use of a wand of slow monster, for instance, can defeat most monsters, even if they greatly outpower the player. But a single magic item isn't nearly enough to get the player through the deeper levels; it is using them as a whole, and taking advantage of the ways that their powers overlap, that will see the player through.

If it wasn't for the various ways the treasure changes the game, Rogue would not be nearly as interesting to play. Merely having random dungeons and monsters is not enough to make it interesting; dungeons ultimately are just differently shaped spaces to explore and empty space isn't that involving. Monsters are more interesting, especially with all the special powers Rogue's set enjoys, but generally the same kinds of monsters are generated on each floor, so you end up facing everyone eventually, just in a slightly different order and proportion. If you can't handle trolls this game, you probably won't be able to handle them the next either.

But, what if you attacked a troll with a ring of increase damage +2? Or wearing plate mail? Or with a ring of regeneration, to match that of the troll? Or what if you have a scroll of scare monster? Or what if you use a potion of monster detection to see it from halfway across the map, and thus know where to avoid?

Collectible card games use a similar premise in the way played cards can modify the rules of the game. If the same cards, or items, could be drawn/generated when desired every game, then they would cancel out of the rules. Many games which allow for player choice at the beginning of a game to choose which options to take, when played by a sufficiently knowledgeable player, boil down to exactly this if he has determined that even one such choice is more powerful than the others. Then it becomes like those other choices aren't even available; why would a player choose a weak benefit if an obviously better one exists? Obvious choices are not really choices at all. In these cases, good design would demand that the designer just make them part of the main rules and not ask the player too much a trivial decision.

Making the player's advantages random forces him to make use of suboptimal equipment at times. Rogue does this excellently; you probably won't find every kind of item on a single playthrough, so you make do with what you get. NetHack is arguably worse designed than Rogue in this regard, since practically everything will be found on a given run-through, and if the most important stuff isn't by some chance, there are guaranteed items around to make up the slack, and a wand of wishing in the event of a hostile random number generator. These safeguards remove randomness from the game; you need never worry about a game in which no boots of levitation are ever generated, because there is a guaranteed pair in the game. NetHack does save most of its essential equipment for late in the game, but the general principle remains.

These failsafes make NetHack fairer, but at the cost of making it less interesting. That these two qualities exist, to some extent, in a mutually exclusive relationship, where reducing one increases the other, is strange, yet perhaps revelatory.

64

Interface Aids and the Strategy Window

January 2016 So you're playing NetHack, and you're wandering through a lit room, and you spy a blue "e" standing stock still in the center, and you think to yourself, "Hey I don't know what that is, but it's a monster so I think I'll go smack it," and then you get paralyzed in place and hundreds of turns pass and a newt walks up and eats all your skin, and a half-second later THE GRIM REAPER APPEARS, and to you he sings:

I'm sorry, I fear that's the end of your play.
I'm sorry, my dear, that it's my job to say,
You shouldn't have pummeled that darn floating eye,
You shouldn't have struck it, I'm not telling a lie,
If you hadn't I'd not now be telling you "fie!"
But you did, and so you've got to pay.

and then with solemn dignity he throws your ghost into a dumpster.

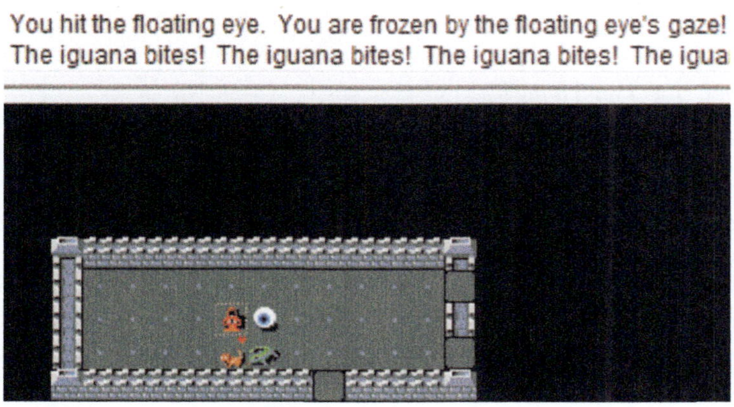

Figure 64.1

Situation 1

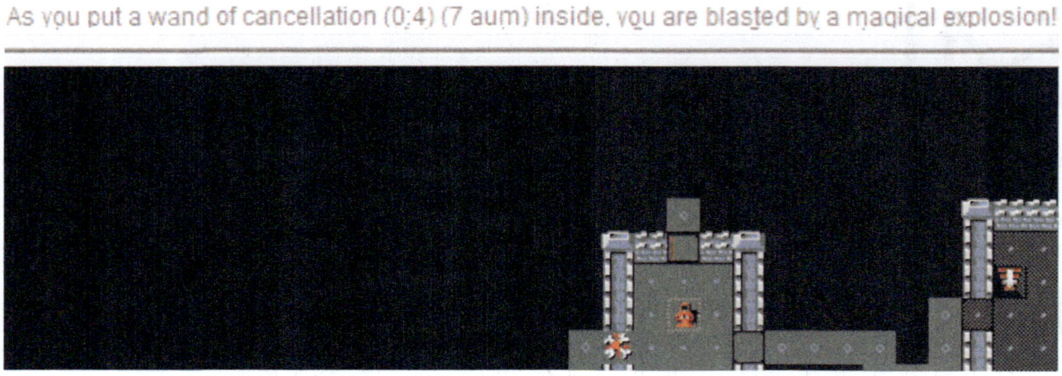

Figure 64.2

Situation 2

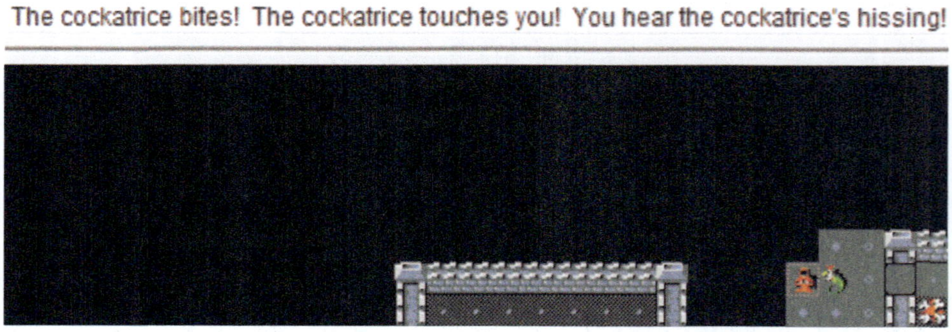

Figure 64.3

Situation 3

So you start a new game, and this time you get quite far, and you're feeling pretty smug, and you have a pack full of good stuff, and you've got [g] a wand of fire, and you've got [m] a wand of death, and you've got [x] a wand of cancellation, and you're carrying a lot so you're burdened, and it's not good to be burdened it slows you down and so monsters hit you a lot ouchy, so you 'a'pply your bag of holding, and you select item [g], and [m], and [x], and then there's a huge explosion, and you take up to 36 damage, and you had already been weakened by a minotaur, and your hit points go way into the negative, and oh here's THE GRIM REAPER AGAIN, he's playing the accordion this time, and says:

I know it must seem that I'm just an old nag,
You weren't careful enough when 'a'pplying that bag.
While a fire wand, of course, is a good choice to make,
Cancellation wand stashing's a foolish mistake,
Now your friends way back home are all planning your wake,
And in 'Hack you can't even blame lag!

and he flushes your soul down the toilet like a goldfish.

So this time you get down to the bottom of the mines, and the gnomes and dwarves aren't much of an obstacle for your Valk, and you're looking around for that luckstone so you can get your luck built up and enjoy that juicy to-hit bonus indefinitely, and you step on what you thought was an innocent square, but it wasn't so innocent no, and a big flash of light blinds you, and now there are monsters attacking you from all directions, but you keep cool and back your way to a doorway, and from there only one can hit you at a time, and you kill all the monsters on that spot, and you don't even know what you killed but there's gotta be some good loot there though, so you step on the space, and it says "Things that you feel here: a cockatrice corpse," and THE GRIM REAPER laughs a good long while about *that* one.

64.1 That's Funny, So I Assume, but What's This All About?

The three situations above have, in gameplay terms, one thing in common: they are all situations where a single action by the player directly resulted in death, when the game could have stopped him.

Once you know that hitting floating eyes results in long-lasting paralysis and likely death, why would you ever want to do that? The game could do something like: "That's a floating eye! Are you sure? (y/n)" It does that when you almost hit neutral monsters, after all.

There are only three types of items in the game that can cause explosions when put into bags of holding: other bags of holding, bags of tricks and wands of cancellation. If the items are identified, why not ask the player if he's sure that he wants to put the item in?

If you're blind, just walking around can be perilous if you've killed things unknowingly. Why not ask the player if he's sure he wants to feel objects at his feet until he can see again?

My contention is that, no matter what you may think at the moment, the answer to this question is not as clear-cut as you might think, that there are strong arguments to be made on both sides, and ultimately it is a judgment call on the part of the developer how far he wants to go in protecting the player from his own actions. So, let me go about explaining both sides . . .

64.2 Against: Testing Knowledge and Thematic Danger

Contrary to some people's opinion, NetHack's game world is not arbitrary for the most part. Most of its many gotchas have some basis, either cultural (either pop-cultural or sourced in myth), literary (coming from some work) or otherwise referential (homages to Rogue and other roguelike games, and Dungeons & Dragons), that gives players some indication of the danger that they're in. Floating eyes, wands of cancellation and bags of holding all come from 1st Edition Dungeons & Dragons, largely bearing the properties they had in that game (which in turn often originated in some published TSR adventure or other).

The specific interaction between wands of cancellation and bags of holding appears to originate with NetHack, but in context with the descriptions of those two items in the Dungeon Master's Guide (the touch of the first nullifies magic items, and the second is a magic item that holds things and ruptures space-time if it breaks), the behavior doesn't seem out of place. Cockatrices originate from English legend, where they were considered fearsome beasts that could kill with a glance, so from that angle their status as the NetHack monster that can kill you the most different ways is justified.

(By the way: in the 1E D&D Monster Manual, "Eye, floating" is actually a kind of fish, and would not generally be found out of water.)

An ordinary person encountering these things for the first time and getting killed may ask how he was supposed to know these things. Not everyone has memorized the D&D books or is familiar with English legend, after all. But that they have some outside source is part of the point of these games in the first place.

NetHack is an adventure game, adventure games are supposed to take place in strange and unusual worlds like Alice's Wonderland, and the literary point of a world following rules different from our own is that for every good thing you find in them there is at least one bad thing to match. In a dungeon you may find lamps that grant wishes and people who can heal you with a touch, but you might find furniture that tries to eat you. Similarly, explorers on alien worlds may find fountains of youth and gemstones of great worth, but there may also be caustic lakes and hostile monsters. To suppose that a different universe will be friendlier to the human condition than our own, which historically has been pretty darn hostile even though we're native to it, seems foolish.

From this perspective, the whole point of adventure stories, and adventure games, is unexpected danger, and the process of overcoming it. The danger, or at least its potential, is what makes the reward seem earned. Other matters come into it as well, of course, like the feeling you get from a work, suitability for play and perceptions of fairness. Without his ring of invisibility Frodo wouldn't have gotten out of half the scrapes he got into, but some amount of risk came out of its acquisition (and of course we find out later it carried its own perils), so we accept the successes he has through its use as his, instead of something that anyone could have done if they had a ring of invisibility.

This is a bit far afield from the original question, but it matters. Those choices that the game could, with just a bit of coding, protect the player from, they must still be offered in order to preserve that sense of danger in the fantastic, which the player himself may not yet be aware of. To ask the player if he really wants to put a specific object in a bag is, itself, a spoiler. Why that item? Why not a lizard corpse, or a potion of healing? To avoid giving the player information he should rightfully gain for himself, in whatever manner, the game would either have to ask for confirmation for all items (which is annoying and also basically useless), or randomly ask, which is pretty silly.

Action games never second-guess the player or offer advice. Neither do strategy or puzzle games. That said, there are other issues involved.

64.3 In Favor: Avoiding Unsatisfying Play and Maintaining Strategic Focus

It's one thing to talk about keeping a game faithful to its setting, but it's possible to take it too far and produce a game that's annoying, or outright frustrating, to play. And roguelikes, which usually have some form of permadeath, are a type where, if you make a grievous error, you cannot go back to an old save to salvage your play.

The example that comes to mind is, to get back to that floating eye, the case where the player hits one accidentally, say by leaning on a key when walking through a dark corridor or room. NetHack contains many such places, and in all of them, most characters can't see more than one space in any direction. Ninety-nine times out of 100, each space you traverse reveals more empty space ahead of you. It's not uncommon for even some experienced players, when progressing through these places, to hold down a key, or at least press it several times in a row, to save time when walking through yet another dark hallway. But this gives the player little time to react to the sudden presence of a floating eye, which may be revealed in a new space and then bumped against with no time to react between them. Such bumps are interpreted by NetHack as intent to attack, and without a confirmation prompt between keypress and execution, the result is frequently death via opportunistic predator. (This is just about the only way that newts kill anyone.)

Theoretically, it is the game's job to get out of the way and interpret the player's commands, whatever those may be. Practically, many games will intercede before deleting save files, or after quit commands. NetHack will ask, in standard play, in some other cases: often when eating while satiated, when trying to apply wands and level teleporting to 0. Beyond this, the game still sticks pretty closely to unquestioningly let the player make obviously bad choices.

64.4 Example: On the User Interface Helps of the Fire Emblem Series

Take, for instance, Nintendo's Fire Emblem games. These are person-level fantasy strategy war games, where you move your units around a map (although several moves at a time, instead of once space each turn as with classical roguelikes) and can have them attack opponents if they end their move adjacent to them.

Fire Emblem is an interesting series to roguelike fans, because it contains a form of permadeath. In most games in this series, if a character falls in battle, he is permanently out of the game unless he returns to a prior save. That is to say, there is almost never a way to revive dead allies except through reloading. And even reloading carries substantial penalties, in that the battle must be reset to the beginning. If the player finishes the fight and elects to move on, he must accept the loss of that character for the remainder of the game. (*Note*: some more recent Fire Emblem games, in an effort to be less frustrating to new players, default to not killing allies permanently.)

Fire Emblem generally doesn't offer y/n "are you sure" prompts except when asking if you want to end your turn. But it does aid the player in one important way. Even though a player's movement stat determines how far he or she can travel in a turn, and the game could be excused by leaving it at that and letting the player visualize the effects his or herself, the game additionally lets the player see, visually, the result of that movement range on screen, showing him not only every space a character can move to on its turn, but also every space it could attack. You can also call up this display for opponents. And, very interestingly, the Gamecube and Wii versions will even let you keep an enemy's attack range visible while you focus on your characters, and their ranges, which is of immense value in planning out your turn.

Although it takes a bit of thinking to see it, when it comes down to it this is basically a more advanced version of the y/n option. Opponents in Fire Emblem sometimes have deadly attacks, and if the wrong enemy hits an unusually vulnerable ally (like if an archer attacks one of your flying units) it could be wiped out in one hit. While it doesn't outright say, "Florina will probably become a kabob if you leave her here, are you SURE?" if you select the enemy archer, all the places that could be dangerous for her will be marked in blue or red. While the player has to apply more knowledge and insight to use the information well, it's still an interface aid, an option the program provides to the player to help him make good decisions.

What is key here, and what more clearly connects such battle range displays with lowly confirmation prompts, is the kind of play that the game wants to focus on. I am calling this, the body of choices that the developer chooses for the player to focus on, the game's strategy window. Choices beneath the strategy window, like guarding against obviously accidental actions and memorizing play data like enemy attack range, are considered too petty or trivial; choices above the strategy window are higher-ordered things, things that would optimize the game in ways that are against the desired nature of the play.

Fire Emblem could force the player to remember everyone's movement range, sure. Plenty of games do that. But the designers wanted not to focus on memory or visualization skills as necessary to success. FE isn't a memory puzzle but a wargame, and remembering statistics doesn't make the player feel like a strategist. Another way to think about it: a player of a game plays a role, necessarily, by his participation, and in a Fire Emblem game you'd expect such a person to maybe have aides on-hand to remind him of necessary battle information. From one perspective, you could say that the game showing ranges like that is depriving the player of the use of one of the skills he could use to excel at the game, but who really cares about whether a player can visualize overlapping ranges? The job of the developer is not just to implement the game, but to scale its tasks so that they fit within the desired range of a player's abilities, not demanding so much as to be overly burdensome, or so little as to be trivial.

To take it just a step further, there's really nothing saying that the Fire Emblem devs couldn't implement a borg autoplayer, which would automatically go through all the enemies, calculate their strengths and send your guys in to attack automatically. Indeed, they already did this to some extent, to run the enemy AI. But that would be moving the strategy window too high.

64.5 Back to Roguelikes: DCSS and Brogue's Autoexplore Features

In a sense, every key a player strikes in a roguelike game is an opportunity to make a wrong move. If the player never hits any keys, after all, he'll never die.

NetHack's few prompts are there to guard against catastrophic error due to pressing incorrect keys, something even experienced touch-typists do from time to time. It could do more, but it has to draw the line against protecting the player from bad moves somewhere, and it's found a good tradeoff between spoilers and implementation ease. NetHack does contain a "run" command, however, which will send a player running in a direction until it runs out of space or something interesting happens along the way. If you use the run command to explore a darkened corridor, then it will stop before hitting that floating eye. You can also repeat some keys, like searching, by typing a number first, and the game will cut you enough slack that your character will abort his task once a visitor arrives. Also, some versions of Rogue had a Quick Move option, which were good for getting those long, winding passages explored quickly and safely, without giving enemies found along the way more than one hit in.

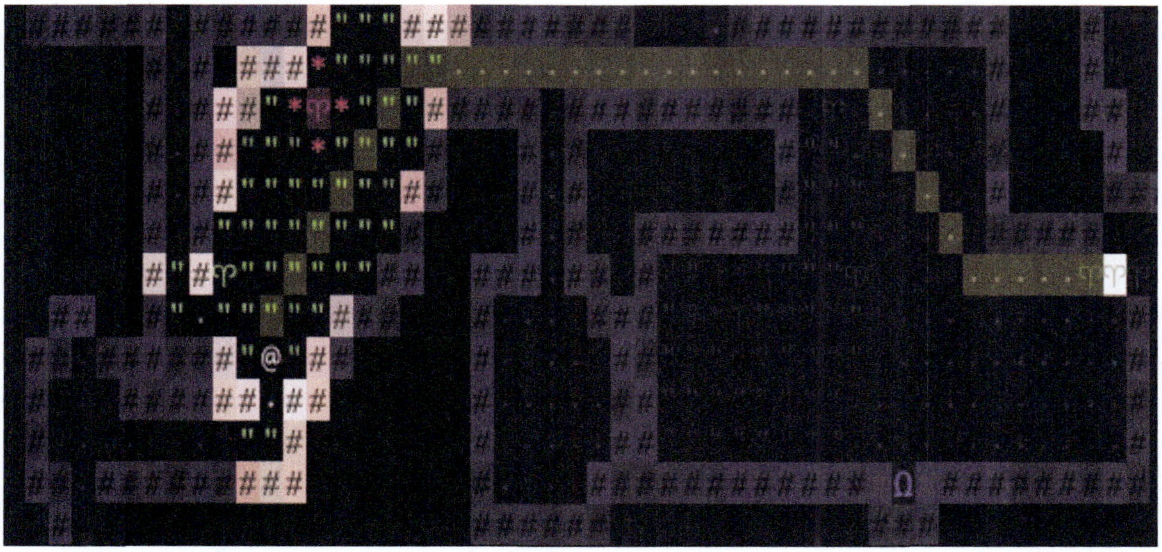

Figure 64.4

A Brogue autoexplore route

There are two particular games that do a lot more than this, in their way. Both Dungeon Crawl Stone Soup and Brogue have autoexplore commands, which act like a more advanced version of Rogue's Quick Move. Both games, once the command is given, will take it upon themselves to explore the dungeon automatically, not stopping at the end of corridors but going around corners, into rooms, and even backtracking if need be, stopping when an interesting enemy, object of feature comes into view, or when the level has been fully explored.

Here is the point where you'd expect me to say, "They're not perfect, but . . ." But actually, these features are not all that far from optimal. There are not many reasons not to use it all the time, other than maybe the fact that, in DCSS, frequent use interferes with picturing how the level fits together. You can't use it for everything; both games will not search for hidden doors while auto-exploring, and DCSS won't autoexplore places by default if they're suspected to be dangerous (such as when near an Oklob).

These kinds of features border on being computer-assisted play aids, almost like invoking a limited version of a borg to help you explore empty dungeon areas. Crawl has large dungeon levels, so autoexplore greatly helps minimize boredom there, boredom and the resultant lack of attention being major contributors to death in turn-based roguelikes. It does carry the cost of making it seem almost like a quasi-random situation generator, though.

That these autoexplore features draw the line at activities like searching or combat reveal the design goals of the developers. These kinds of situations appear to be judged too risky/unusual/interesting for automation. Note that, while they try to limit their actions to the domain of the extremely safe, it's still possible for the player to hit a trap while exploring, or spend autoexploring in a less-than-optimally-efficient manner and thus incur a greater food cost.

65

Modeling Motion on a Dungeon Grid

August 2008 Here's a bit of hopefully useful insight into a topic that every roguelike designer has to cover eventually: how to simulate variable rates of movement on the game's essentially integral, Cartesian grid.

One of the most distinctive aspects of a roguelike game is time-equivalency of actions. Moving a step, picking up an item, dropping an item, hitting an opponent, drinking a potion, reading a scroll, wielding a weapon, putting on or removing armor or a ring, and zapping with a wand: all of these things take the same amount of time, that is to say, one turn.

This is a subtly powerful concept. If the player swings at an adjacent monster, it uses up the player's turn so the enemy can get a hit in. If he's adjacent to an armor-degrader, taking off his armor to protect it still takes a turn in which the monster can get a swing in first. If he's wielding a weapon ill-suited to a foe, like a bow when fighting an adjacent monster, it'll take him a turn to change it, again giving the monster a free opportunity to hit.

And significantly, so long as a player and monster are the same speed and adjacent to each other, the monster is impossible to shake. The player must use some special item or ability to get away, because no matter what direction he steps, the monster will be able to match it. Since the player can't get away, once a same-speed monster gets adjacent melee combat will, barring special effects on either side, always be tit-for-tat, attack-trading affairs. The player can run in order to pass time, hopefully regenerating hit points, but that gives other monsters the chance to join in pursuit.

All the actions that change the player's state consume a turn. There are a few commands, particularly Inventory, that never take up a move. It should be noted that this is not realistic. A real person rummaging through his pack for a particular item will probably spend more time unslinging it, setting it down, opening the flap and getting out the needed item than it would take him to walk across one space's worth of dungeon floor. Giving him this action for free is a concession to playability. If there were a game penalty for looking to see what you're carrying, then it would be advantageous to keep notes on paper of your inventory instead of relying on the command, and a game that pedantic would probably scare away even the most devoted of @-signs.

But concerning those actions that consume time, there are two major types of speed systems for handling them in roguelike games: player-centered and world-centered.

65.1 The World Revolves Around Me

Player-centered is the simplest and oldest system. Rogue used it, the Mystery Dungeon games and Izuna use it, and some other popular roguelikes used it early in their history. Hack probably used it, but its descendant NetHack dropped it some versions back.

Example player-centered game loop:

```
# Code is object-oriented pseudo-Python
# NOTE: doesn't take slowing into account
while !done:
        Player.domove() # Normal turn
        for monster in monsterlist: # Fast monster's first turn
                monster.domove()
        if player.speed == fast: # Fast players second turn
                player.domove()
        for monster in monsterlist: # Monster's turn/fast monster's 2nd turn
                if monster.speed == fast:
                monster.domove()
```

Under this system, the player's moves are organizing moments of game time. All the monster turns are scheduled relative to the turns the player gets. Most roguelike monsters have "average speed," one turn per turn of a normal player, and such monsters behave identically under either system. The player acts, then all the monsters act, then repeat. It's when either the player or monster is faster this situation changes. Greater speed in roguelikes is handled by handing out more turns. If the player is faster (drank Rogue's potion of haste self, zapped the monster with a wand of slow monster, is wearing SuperRogue's ring of speed, et cetera) then he gets two consecutive turns before the monsters can act. If a monster is faster, it gets two actions after each of the player's one.

Just because this system is simple doesn't mean it doesn't work well for many games. In particular Japanese roguelikes, which tend to latch onto roguelike play systems more for being like a special kind of puzzle game rather than a simulation of dungeon exploration, benefit from making turn ordering predictable to the player. (This is part of the general tendency of JRPGs to abstract role-playing game rule systems away from being a simulation towards general gameishness.)

Being faster than an opponent, in a roguelike world, is a tremendous benefit. Your options are greatly expanded by being faster than a foe, more than nearly any other single advantage. You can either get twice as many attacks, or you can attack and use magic items, or you can successfully run away from melee-only monsters, or, by using your extra moves wisely, you can change your equipment without danger. Most significantly, so long as you have running room, you can always kill arbitrary melee foes by using your extra moves to hit and running on the others, allowing the player to both get in his damage while himself escaping any attacks.

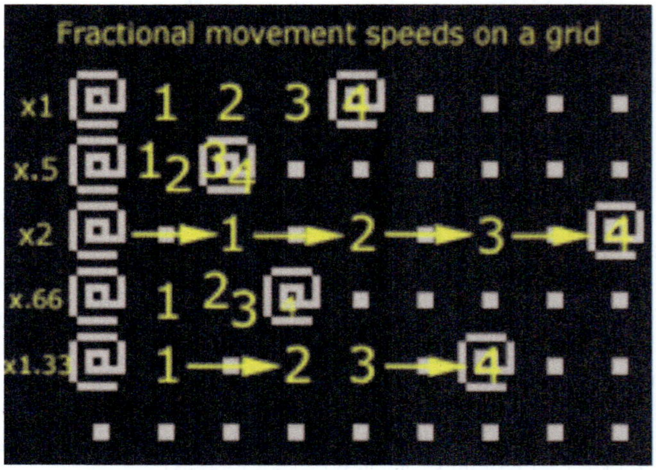

Figure 65.1

Fractional speeds on a dungeon grid

(By the way, being slower than a monster, while painful, is not usually as bad for the player as a fast player is for the monster. This is because very few roguelike monsters seem to have the presence of mind to adopt hit-and-run tactics as players can. In fact, only one comes to mind: not only will NetHack's unicorns occasionally hit then step away, they'll even attempt to remain at least a knight's move away at the end of a turn so they can't be hit by missiles or wands.)

But player-centered timing is a fairly limited system. There are only three "speeds" under the basic scheme: half-speed, normal and double-speed, and each level is much more than twice as good as the one below. If the programmer is cagey, he might make an effort to simulate fractional speeds. If the player is fast by half a turn, then he gets an extra move every other time, and if monsters are faster they get extra turns at the same rate. But due to the nature of roguelike world simulation, this is actually only slightly worse than if the player were faster by a full turn. All a 1/2-turn speed advantage player has to do is to run on the two regular turns and attack on the one extra. It'll take longer, and he'll end up running farther, but the monster still doesn't get any licks in.

Also, the case where both the player and monster have extra speed must be considered. If not handled specially, the game could run into a case where the player gets two turns, then the monster gets two turns, over and over, which is nonsensical; in such a case, each side should get one turn.

To counter these problems, a programmer may choose to randomize the awarding of turns, either giving the player or the monsters an extra half the time (which sometimes gives him strings of lucky, or unlucky, extras) or dividing the player's moves into pairs, and randomly deciding which will be followed by the extra. This works, but by this point most of the benefits, in terms of simplicity, of using a player-centered turn scheduling system are lost.

65.2 Wait . . . Do You Hear Ticking?

A world-centered system is rather more complicated to implement, and it loses the abstract purity of integral turn scheduling schemes. Although it loses that simplicity, it's a method of scheduling turns that's much more amenable to fractional speeds. The idea is that both the player and monsters get scheduled turns according to a world clock. There's an internal game timer that counts what we might call time atoms, instants of time that pass for every actor in memory simultaneously.

Example world-centered game loop:

```
# Code is object-oriented pseudo-Python
# Assumes player is in the creature list
turnlength = (some sufficiently large number)
while !done:
        for creature in creaturelist:
                creature.energy -= turnlength - creature.speed
                if creature.energy <= 0:
                        creature.domove() # Either player or monster
                        creature.energy += turnlength # Go to back of line
```

One way to implement such a system, similar to NetHack's current scheme, goes as follows. Each monster, and the player too, keeps track of its place in the global queue. The creature's readiness-to-act is measured in energy. After acting, the creature's energy is set to zero. As each atom of time passes, the creature's speed rating is added to its energy, and when it exceeds some value the creature gets a turn. Or alternatively, 1 could be added to energy when a time atom passes, and when the value exceeds (maximum speed—monster's speed) the turn occurs.

Under this system, the greater the energy threshold (or maximum speed), the more flexibility is available in timings. It's best to pick a number that's evenly divisible by many other numbers, like 24, 36, or 72, since the programmer will probably want most monsters to act in a manner similar to Rogue's integral system: a monster with a speed of 12, compared to a player with a speed of 24, will behave as if it was a half-speed monster in Rogue. If the player were to obtain a slight speed increase, say a +1 to speed, then he'd get an extra turn only once every 12 moves, still an exploitable advantage, but one that's a bit trickier to take advantage of. And it even allows for different actions to consume different amounts of game time; a quick action could result in less energy being depleted.

I've used the words turn and move pretty much interchangeably here, but more recent versions of NetHack make a distinction between these terms. There, a move is when the player makes a decision, essentially a unit of volition, and a "turn" is an objective measure of game time equal to one old-style move. If the player is faster than normal, then there will be times when he gets two moves in the same tick of the game's turn counter, which can be observed by watching the turn counter.

65.3 Special Cases

Two games in particular, one of each style, take advantage of the flexibility of their respective speed systems in interesting ways.

The Mystery Dungeon series, which either use player-centered timing or a system so close to it that it makes no difference, have extra, in-between levels of monster speed. One of them is two moves per turn, but only one attack. Mecharoid-family, Baby Tanks, Death Reapers and Guard Dogs have this type of movement. Effectively, the monsters can move twice, but if it attacks on the first move it loses its second turn. The other system is single-move-multiple-action, and higher-level Sabergator monsters have it: a single move per turn, but if adjacent to the player they get multiple attacks (more for higher-level monsters).

Among games with world-centered speed there's ADOM, which uses a neat system whereby there's no real maximum to the player's speed, but the higher it gets the less frequent are the additional extra turns granted to the player. Greater speed increases player hunger at a linear rate, but additional turns increase at a declining rate as speed gets higher. Eventually a point is reached where further increases in speed are not worth the greater food consumption. While ADOM's source code is closed so we really have no idea how turn scheduling in that game is implemented, to work this kind of system in a game with player-centered timing would be quite annoying.

66

Rogue's Item ID in Too Much Detail

April 2015 Last time I said that the least-copied feature of Rogue is its item identification system. Of the horde of "roguelike" and "roguelite" games now flooding Steam, very few think to adopt this aspect. Darren Gray, who I'll have you know is pretty sharp on roguelike ideas generally, suggested that people participating in the Seven-Day Roguelike Challenge don't bother implementing an item ID system.

Well, I'm here to make an attempt to argue against all that. Rogue is probably the most tightly designed computer game I know of (and I know of over a thousand), and every aspect refers, in some way, to another aspect, no part of it can be considered in complete isolation from the others, and that includes item identification. I think not only does item identification add something interesting and substantive to it, but that it ties the rest of the game together, that it's really a part of a whole with the other things that make Rogue fascinating, and that the things it adds are not easily replaced with other features. But, as with everything else in your design (if you aren't a designer then bear with me), you shouldn't include item ID thoughtlessly: instead, you have to work carefully to make it fit in with the rest of the game, in order to get the greatest benefit from it in terms of depth of player choices. But this is just like everything else in your game, so really it's not any different from deciding what powers your monsters should have or whether you should have a food clock or not.

The core idea is that items in an identification system, the things you collect in the dungeon that go under the increasingly overused name loot, can have hidden properties. You don't know everything about the objects you're carrying at first sight. Some things about them are known from casual observation, like what general type it is (Sword? Armor? Potion? Ring?), but for some things there's an additional descriptor, like a color (pink potion) or material (lapis lazuli ring) that extends across a hidden class of items. Many items have individual properties themselves that have to be discovered uniquely for each one, like plus or curse status, but for this discussion we're concerned about the descriptive classes of items, not miscellaneous aspects.

66.1 Item ID, Fantasy Literature and AD&D

The idea that magic items may not be known to the player immediately on finding is something that dates back to the roots of fantasy role-playing gaming: fantasy literature.

Sainted Gary Gygax drew from many sources when inventing (with Dave Arneson) Dungeons & Dragons. But a common thread running through a lot of it, something that if you asked me isn't played up nearly as

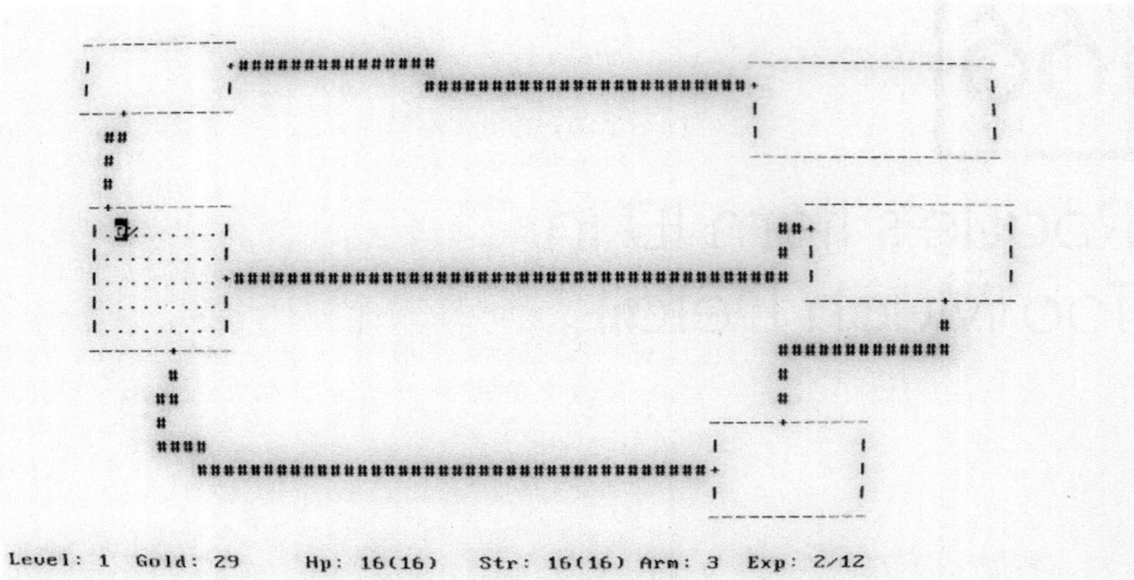

Figure 66.1

Rogue

much these days as it should, is that magic is mysterious. Even to a wizard, spells are dangerous business, not always working as you expect. It doesn't make sense that a level 1 Rogue Muggle would be able to recognize a Sword of Casual Dismemberment on first glance, or even 30th.

This is of course another intrusion of that persistent game designer bugaboo, realism. Making appeals to reality is doubly damned these days, first for being inconvenient to play, second for being outright ludicrous in a genre where people throw around fireballs, monsters breathe fire, and gold never seems to lose its value despite the hundreds of thousands of pieces PCs exchange for their diamond swords. And yet, you can never wholly discard realism. After all, we meet Harry Potter properly first, not as a wizard himself, but as a dejected adoptee of non-magical caretakers. Bilbo Baggins is a relatable character, not because he's a Hobbit, or he might have a distant fairy ancestor, or he has a sword named Sting or a ring of invisibility, but because we meet him in a hole in the ground, surrounded by comfortable, normal furnishings. If you're going to author fantasy—and make no mistake, fantasy game designers are authors whether they want to be or not—your work will be more understandable if you have some realistic basis behind it, or at least a logical basis.

(*Note:* I mention elsewhere the list of Gygax's inspirations for D&D, the famous 1st Edition DMG Appendix N. I was inordinately pleased to see that it has returned to the game, with additions, in the form of D&D 5th edition's Appendix D.)

This isn't to say that magic shouldn't be strange and exotic, no, just the opposite. Part of the job of the magic system designer is to interface the realism needed to be understandable, to be relatable, with the wonder of magic, to which it is fundamentally opposed. Reconciling these things is (and should be!) a hard problem, and how you go about it reveals a lot of what you're about as a designer. I could name names here, revealing examples of games that I don't think do it well. There are lots of them. But I prefer here to show by example, showing off a game that does it right. And hey, that game is Rogue itself, and its magic system basically is its item system.

Speaking of Gygax's Dungeon Master's Guide . . . have you ever read the magic item descriptions in the back of it? That whole book is amazing. Whatever you think about it in terms of playability as a game (there's plenty good and bad if you can sift through it all), you have to admit that it's brimming with joy and full of ideas, hundreds of ideas. Its magic item lists are terrific. Of course all the editions of D&D provide a certain amount of fun just to flip through, to read about dozens of strange, bizarre and enchanting gizmos, but the 1st Edition book is unquestionably the best, in terms of both ambition and

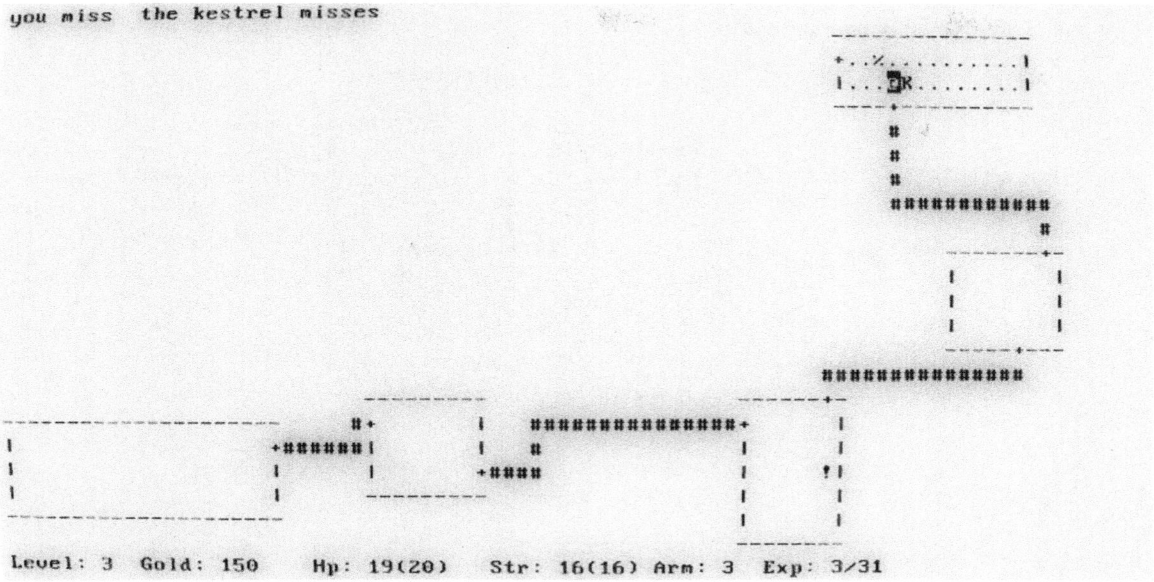

Figure 66.2

Rogue

range. (*Note:* each subsequent edition bled a little more of that joy out of it. Don't look for it in the 4th Edition.)

Anyway, I bring the list up because of a special kind of item that's spread through the magic item listings, intermingling with the more useful devices, and those are the bad items.

Alongside listings for things like sword +1, +2 vs. magic-using and enchanted creatures (I like to imagine it like a long, sharpened spork) is sword +1, cursed. Although it's a +1 sword, and thus "one better," in a Spinal Tap sense, than an ordinary weapon, the sword magically compels the wielder to fight to the death in all battles, which isn't a recipe for long survival against dungeon monsters. It's an item you're really better off without. Then there's the plate mail of vulnerability, which "appears to every test to be magical +1, +2, or +3 armor," but is actually cursed, carries a protection penalty and immediately falls apart when struck on a natural roll of 20. Then there's the shield −1, missile attractor, the talisman of yearning (which tries to make the wielder drown himself), the vacuous grimoire (which permanently sucks some of the reader's Intelligence and/or Wisdom scores into it), the stone of weight that NetHack players will recognize as like a lodestone, the potion of delusion, the rug of smothering, the scarab of death and so on. All of this is just from a casual scan; there's plenty more. Pretty much every baneful object in the 1E DMG mentions what other, helpful magic object it's indistinguishable from.

The origins of CRPGs were recreations of pen-and-paper RPGs. And we've covered before that Rogue's closest analogue was to the random dungeon generation tables in another of 1st edition AD&D's marvelous appendices. But most computer fantasy games, for one reason or other, didn't try to simulate this aspect of the game, the presence of bad items. Part of the reason was likely technical, for a bad item can only have a chance of inflicting its badness if a player decides to use it, and that depends on disguising it, which is an extra layer of complexity to add to a game running on limited hardware.

But it should be noted . . . "because that's how D&D did it" isn't always a good justification for including something in your own game. Rogue's random item system is arguably better than 1E D&D's! Effectively, cursed items in D&D are impossible to tell apart from their helpful lookalikes until triggered, even if one has been seen before. They are basically an elaborate screwing-over mechanism, provided by Gygax to the DM, to help keep metagaming players in line. ("A magic bowl? I've seen one of those before, dibs!") Such items have no good purpose in a roguelike game.

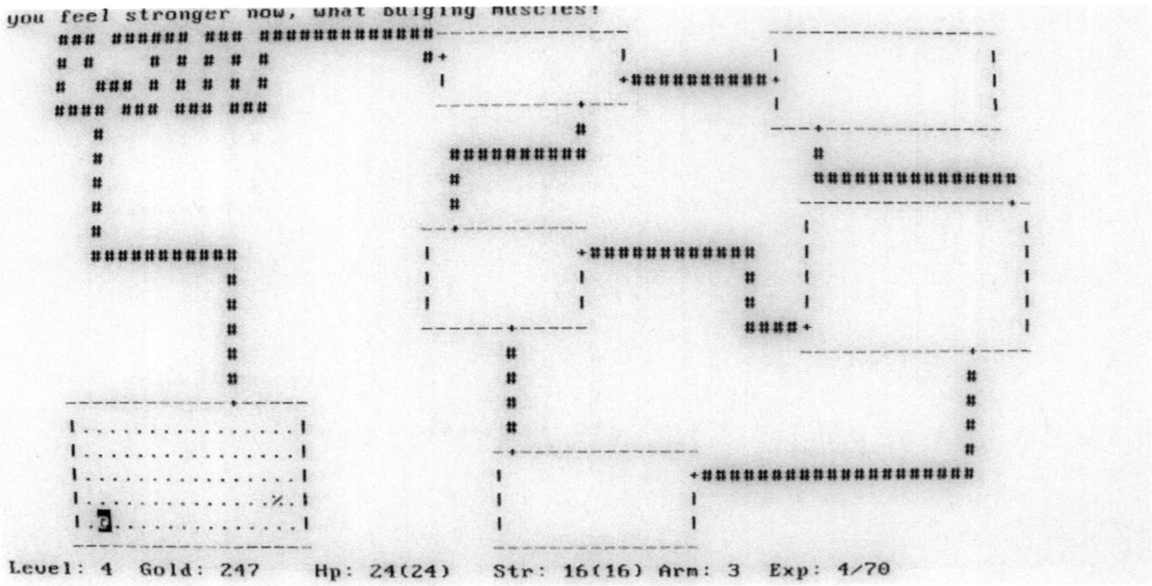

Figure 66.3

Rogue

66.2 Item ID in Action

If you don't have substantial experience with Rogue this article might seem a bit esoteric. The following narrative is intended to give you some idea of how random items work during play. Our hero Rodney the Rogue enters the dungeon at the top level and begins exploring . . .

LEVEL 1: He finds one unknown potion and two unknown scrolls of different types. He doesn't do anything with them yet. Not much to say yet.

LEVEL 2: The monster opposition is still fairly light. A ring, a wand and a longsword are found. The player switches from his starting +1, +1 mace to the longsword; it's +0, +0, but not cursed. On the average, this a slight improvement. If it had been cursed, he would be stuck with the sword until he found an enchantment scroll, or one of remove curse.

LEVEL 3: This is the first level with giant ants (in some versions called rattlesnakes). These can drain Strength (the sole attribute score) on a successful hit. Two more potions are found here, and two more scrolls, and a food ration. One of the potions is of the same type as the one found on level 1 (they're both "plaid," however that works), and he also now has two of one type of scroll (they have the same title, something like "swerr mep"). Rodney makes the decision to test-ID one of the scrolls, hoping it might be identify (the most common scroll). It is! He wisely uses it on the ring (the hardest kinds of item to figure out) and finds out it's a ring of teleportation. These are cursed and annoying, but potentially a lifesaver. He keeps it in his pack, but mentally notes when he runs out of room it's high priority for trashing.

He also tries one of the duplicate potions, which provides the message "you feel much better." The potion is of extra healing; even though he was fully healed when he drank it, extra healing potions raise your maximum hit points by two in such a case. That's a nice bonus, but he decides it's better to keep the remaining potion in reserve for emergencies. Later on, when monster attacks do more damage than an extra healing potion restores, he'll drink it for further maximum HP. Healing potions also curse confusion, blindness and hallucination. Blindness is the big one there, one usually wants to see that ended as soon as possible, so it's worth hanging on to one until the potion of blindness is discovered.

LEVEL 4: The new monster here is orcs, which aren't too much trouble. Rodney finds another ring, two more potions and one more scroll. He's now carrying 18 items, and maximum is 26; not tight yet, but it's getting there. The potion is a duplicate of one he's carrying so he drinks it. "you feel very sick," and he loses three points of Strength! It was Poison. This puts his Strength down from its starting 16 to 13. This isn't a huge problem yet, but with giant ants around the Strength loss may continue. A Strength of 6 is the trouble zone, that's where penalties begin to accrue. (He did lose some combat potency though, because Strength 16 provides a +1 bonus.)

He drops the duplicate potion of poison and tries his last unknown potion, and it turns out to be Raise Strength. That was a mixed blessing. It puts his Strength back up to 14, but if he had drunk it before drinking the poison his Strength would have gone up to 17. But what's more, his "natural" strength (that is, the highest your Strength has ever been in the current game) would also have gone up to 17. The difference is what happens when a potion of restore strength is drunk; it restores up to natural Strength. When he does find a restore strength potion now, he'll end up with 16 instead of 17. It was bad luck that he drank the poison before the raise strength.

In Rogue these things happen all the time. One cannot let himself get worked up about what could have been if there had been no way to know. Of course, he could have spent his spare scroll of identify on one of the potions. But now thinking about it Rodney is reminded he has an unknown ring, and tries the identify scroll on it to discover to his delight that it's a ring of slow digestion, one of the most valuable rings. Once put on this cuts food consumption by 50%, significantly reducing the pressure of the food clock. It's a good thing, actually much better than having a Strength of 17. Having good identification priorities tends to work in a player's favor in the long run.

LEVEL 5: The new monster is zombie, still not a huge problem. Treasure found on this floor is two new scrolls and a suit of chain mail. That's probably going to be better than the +1 ring mail Rodney began with, but when he tries it on he finds to his dismay that it's cursed and –2! His best option now, Rodney reasons, is to test-ID the new scrolls.

Three possibilities will free him of the armor. A scroll of remove curse will lift the curse and let him switch back to his ring mail, which is one point better than the –2 chain mail. Or a scroll could be enchant armor, which would raise the chain mail to –1, the same power as the +1 ring mail, and also lift the curse. And it could be protect armor, which wouldn't change the plus or power, but would lift the curse, and also protect the chain mail from erosion from rust traps and rust monsters, who will begin appearing on level 9. He reads them both: the first produces the message "you hear a high-pitched humming noise." It was aggravate monster, a bad scroll, but all it does is wake up all the beasties on the current level and make them want

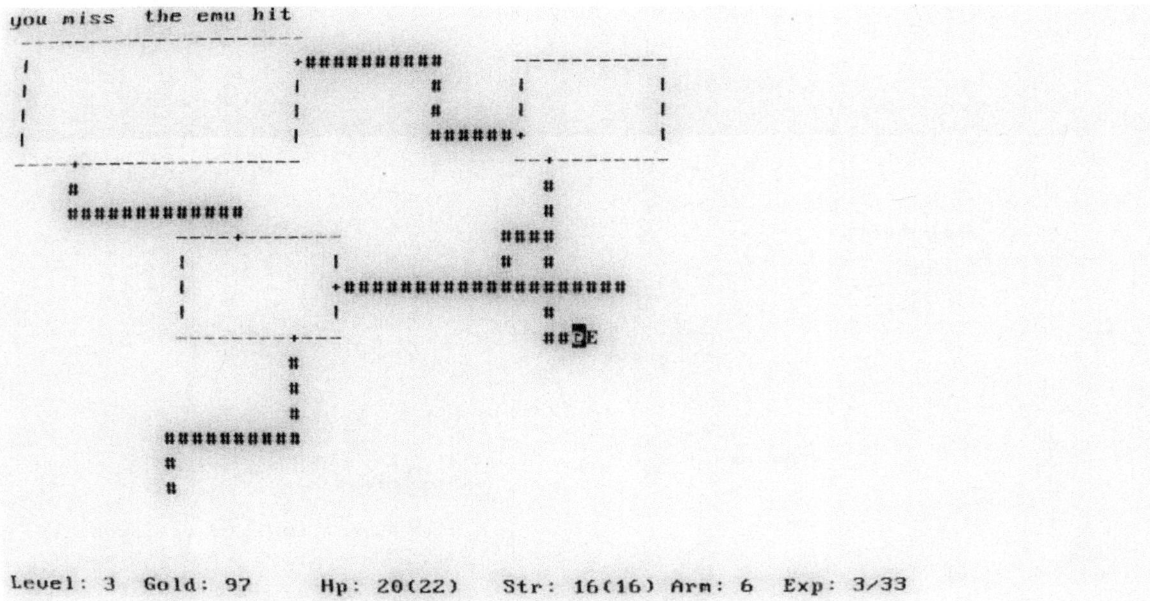

Figure 66.4

Rogue

to attack the player, which is not a bad thing on such an easy level. Really, it's a blessing that it was discovered among such innocent surroundings. The other is an enchant scroll—but it's enchant weapon. Rodney's Longsword is now +0, +1. Not bad, but he's still stuck with the armor for the time being . . .

And so the game continues. Rodney is an experienced player, so as he decides whether to use-test items he keeps in mind all the things that haven't been discovered yet, in order to minimize risk. The worst of them all is the potion of blindness, which at best means drinking a healing potion to immediately cure, and at worst makes the game unplayable for several hundred turns, causing the player to get beat up by monsters he can't effectively run from because he can't see them while also taking a big hit to hunger, because you can't effectively explore what you can't see. The beginning of the tough monsters is level 13, home of the trolls (although centaurs can hurt before then). A blind player will probably die if he meets a troll, so it's best either to discover blindness before then or to abandon use-testing potions there. If they aren't known by that point, he'll probably try to use identify schools on potions from then on, until blindness becomes known.

He's conflicted about that wand in his inventory. It's usually pretty easy to identify wands, but the problem is, if it's polymorph it could be a game ender if the dice don't roll just right. On the other hand, if Rodney stood on a scroll of scare monster and created an extremely hard enemy with a wand of polymorph, he could gain a huge windfall of experience points without much trouble. This is still risky (if the monster's new form is dragon then Rodney will get fried), but the prospect of getting free experience quickly is enticing enough that some people will throw caution to the wind. Maybe the danger could be minimized if the player were standing near the stairs? And so on.

66.3 What They Did, and Didn't

This is the system I described last time: each kind of magical item has an obvious specific description that is randomized each game. Potions come with colors, patterns and other descriptions, for instance, and even without using them, if you find two blue potions you know they're at least the same kind. Scrolls, wands and rings work similarly. You can find out what items do conclusively with a scroll of identify, or sometimes just from using them, or sometimes speculatively, where the game will ask you what you want to call that type of item. If definitely identified that class of item will be permanently named for the rest of the game; if known speculatively it can be renamed later, although if it's later conclusively identified the definite name will overwrite the guess.

The most interesting thing about the system, to my eyes, is its originality. No idea emerges from whole cloth, and every thought a human being has ever had has had antecedents, inspirations, foundations. But

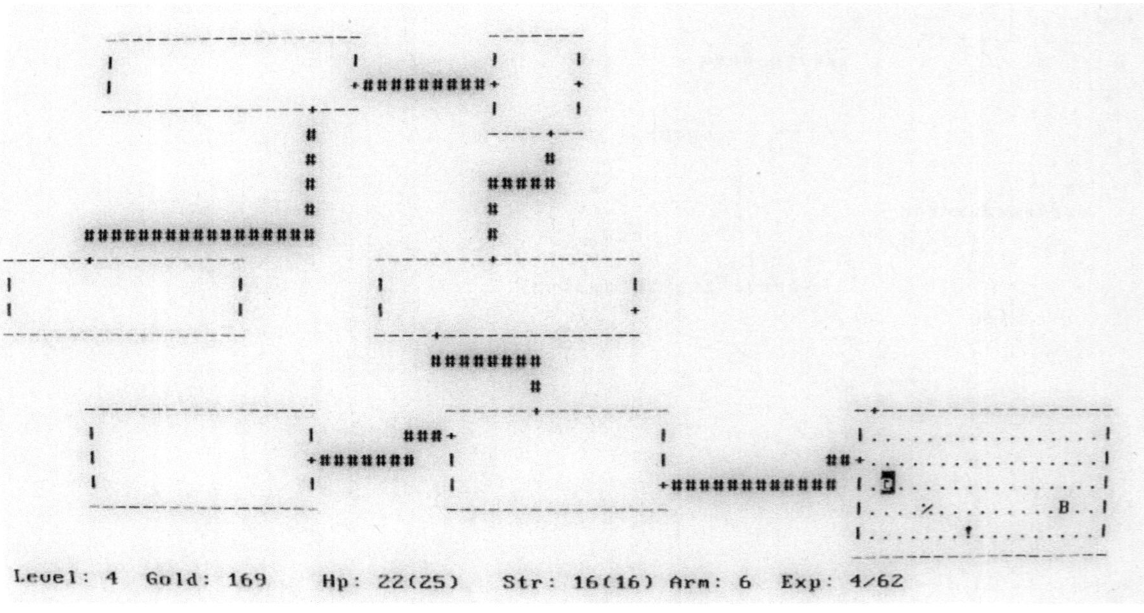

Figure 66.5

Rogue

it didn't originate in AD&D, whose bad items, the Dungeon Master's Guide says, are indistinguishable from the good ones, even by magical means. According to the descriptions given there, no amount of examination will be enough to distinguish a bowl of commanding water elementals from a bowl of watery death. If divination could do the job the DMG doesn't say, effectively leaving it up to the tender mercies of the DM.

The way Rogue does it makes for interesting situations, of the type demonstrated in the play example above. It gives the player an additional way to demonstrate skill, and thematically it makes a point about the nature of magic. But a lot of games don't do this; they don't bother to offer item identification as a subgame, and it's often not bad that they don't!

If you implement item ID badly, what you end up with can be distracting, or annoying, or even frustrating. If all items are identified immediately on the point of use (Mystery Dungeon games sometimes do this in bonus dungeons), then you effectively make the first item of each type the player finds a waste ("Oh, so that's what that did. If only I had another one."), and if it's a bad item, the effect is not that different from a trap that the player merely has leeway towards when it goes off, unless he decides simply to never use-ID anything.

This isn't to steer you away from making games with it, but instead to suggest caution. If you're going to put randomized item definitions in your game, here are some important questions to ask yourself:

- Can you use the item without identifying it first? If not, then why require item identification at all? In principle it just makes players wait until town to get the thing identified, or to just throw away such items. You should be trying to increase the number of interesting decisions the player has to make. In Rogue, all items can be used, whether you know what they are or not, although the consequences might be dire. Make the player decide: use it and maybe get hit with a bad effect, or save it and maybe get killed when the right thing could have saved your life.
- Are there any bad items that the player might find? If not, then there's not much reason not to wait for a tight spot before testing, on the off chance that it'll be a helpful thing. In Rogue, every item type has bad versions mixed in with the good ones.
- Are sources of identification scarce and uncertain enough that the player may be seriously inconvenienced should he decide to wait until using instead of using right away? If not, then best play demands that the player always wait, and the purpose of identification is lost. In Rogue, the only means of definite identification besides use is identify scrolls, which are the most common scroll, but still random.

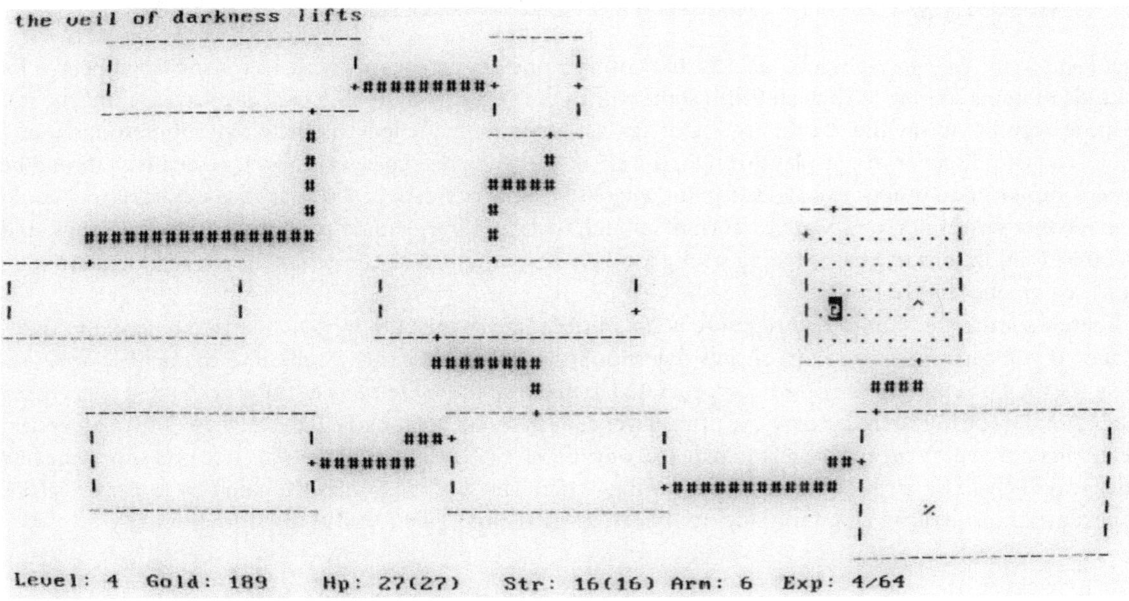

Figure 66.6

Rogue

Enough yet? We're just getting started!

- Is the game hard enough that the player has to use unknown items once in a while? If not, then he'd be foolish to take risks, and the items might as well not even be in the game. Some games are so easy that a skilled player might not have to use any items at all, unknown or known. In Rogue . . . well, the game is of legendary difficulty.
- Are items sometimes not identified after use? If not, then it only takes finding a single example of each item to learn what it is. In Rogue, frequently items are not ID'd on use. Particularly rings are only ever identified with scrolls or careful observation, but other items that sometimes appear to do nothing on use might not be ID'd.
- Does it matter much what order items are used in, or do item effects mean different things situationally? If not, then item effects start to look like a sequence of unrelated events, rather than something that builds on the rest of the game. We saw how Rogue does it in the play example: if you drink raise strength then poison, the effect is different than if you drank poison then raise strength. Same items, but different consequences depending on how the player uses them. Healing potions can provide either a large immediate benefit or a small permanent benefit, depending on how many hit points the player has then drank, and can also cure blindness, making them incredibly valuable before blindness potions are known.

Still a bit left . . .

- Can bad items sometimes be put to positive use? If not, then it starts to look again like the random number generator is directly determining how well the player will do, as opposed to giving him an opportunity to use his skill to make the most of a situation. In Rogue: actually, most bad items don't have much in the way of alternative uses, although bad potions can be thrown at monsters to affect them sometimes.
- Is it possible to identify things in ways other than use and identify scrolls? If not, well it's not a huge thing; there aren't many items in Rogue that can be figured out without use or identification. (There is one though, and it's important!) But this is one of the best aspects of NetHack's item ID: serious thought has obviously gone into making many items discoverable without identification, and even if it seems a bit easy in some cases (wands are pretty easy once you know how), it's still pretty interesting, without requiring a player resort to such means, if he happens to be unspoiled or doesn't want to bother.
- Are there enough items in the game, relative to the length of the game and item generation rate, that the player is reasonably sure not to find everything in one game? If not, then at the point where the player knows what all the items are, item ID becomes moot. This is particularly bad in NetHack, where most stuff is known by midgame. In Rogue: players will typically find around 60% of possible item types in a winning game. *, **

That last bit, by the way, goes a bit against prevailing game design dogma, which says you don't need a lot of kinds of items so long as they all fulfill some role in the game. Well, that does make sense . . . maybe it'd be more accurate to say that it's an argument against excessive game length. The greater the proportion of things you can discover in one playthrough, the easier the game becomes. Of course, some items should be more common than others, even to the point where they're very likely to show up. A good argument could be made that scrolls of identify are important enough that the player should probably always find a few, and of course food rations in a game with a strong food clock are important enough that even Rogue guarantees they turn up one level in three.

There's another reason for having more items in the game than could be generated each play, and that's variety. If you can't find, say, rings of slow digestion in your current game, you'll have to make do without, using the magic items that are otherwise generated to make up for it. One way to think about it: if everything can reasonably be found in one play, then the player can use whatever tools he likes the best, which gives him greater agency, which means he gets to play the way he wants, true, but also means once he's won once he's much less likely to want to play again after winning—there's little scope to vary the game on successive plays. If the player must instead adapt his playing style to the situation, then replayability is increased.

* NetHack's DevTeam actually took some controversial steps, according to some fans, to remedy this, by introducing the possibility for some items and monster attacks to unidentify items.

** ToeJam & Earl's Randomizer item, mentioned previously, is one way around this, by giving players the possibility of accidentally scrambling the item definitions.

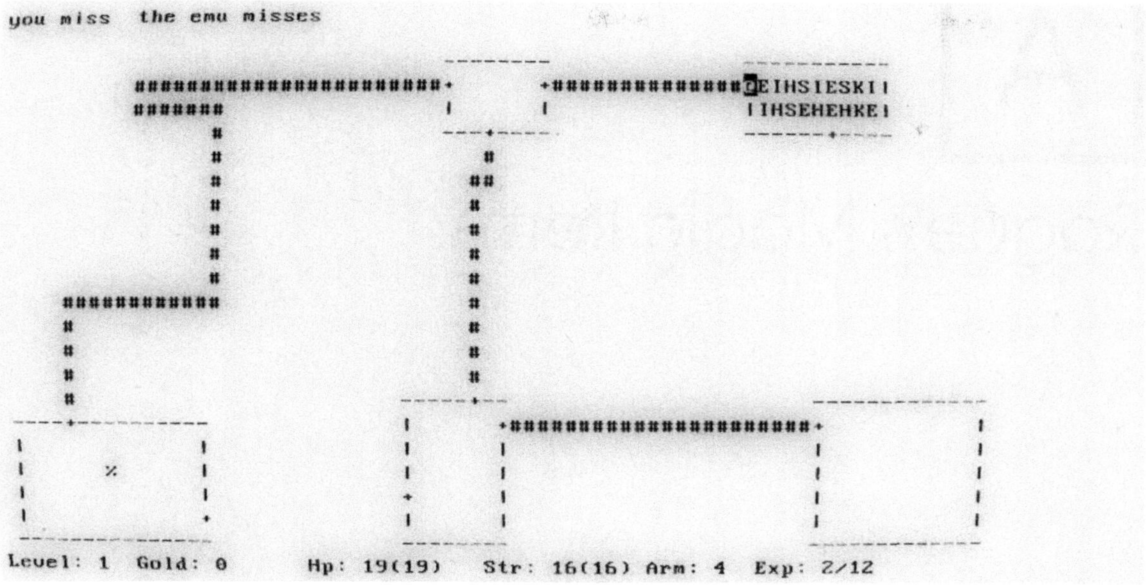

Figure 66.7

Rogue

This has all been a huge infodump, and I'm sorry if it's been fairly obscure for casual readers. And yet there's still a lot left to say! But that I'll save for some other time.

Rogue's random items are carefully selected so that each has a specific gameplay purpose, some way in which it either lessens the weight of difficulty or (for bad or obfuscatory items) increases it. NetHack's items show similar attention to detail, each item with a specific play purpose. And there's still the topic of the identifications system of the future: Rogue's ID system is based on descriptions, but what would a game be like in which you had to, say, discover the specific gravities of potions to identify them, or apply something like the Mohs hardness scale to gemstones, or figure out a magic language to read the titles of scrolls? Maybe item types should be harder to differentiate from each other, or more vaguely typed. Don't be too quick to decry these ideas! It's not as easy to tell what ideas are good or not except in hindsight, and even then, execution is everything.

A game in which item identification takes center stage would be harder compared to Rogue, all other things being equal. So, what if we relaxed the difficulty in some other way? Maybe make the food clock is a little more generous or give the monsters a bit less variety. Maybe such a game should provide players a list of all the possible items in the game, in order to reduce the usefulness of spoilers and FAQs?

An idea that I personally quite like is including a lot more kinds of items than could possibly appear in a single playthrough, reducing the availability percentage from Rogue's 60% to something more like 35–40%. What would the consequences of this be on the game? Individual items would have to have less subtle effects, perhaps, to make up for the fact that the player probably won't be able to find more than one. Or maybe the possible items could be selected randomly from a list before the game starts, and those items would be the only ones generated; that way, whatever you do find, you have a good chance of finding more than one of, but other things won't show up at all.

Some of these items seem interesting, but they all also have their negative aspects. This is because Rogue's item ID system is exceptionally well-balanced. It's difficult to usefully change it in a way that could unequivocally be seen as better. To me, that indicates genius game design. But it also makes Rogue ID system a tough act to follow . . . which may explain, ultimately, why so few other games have tried to follow it.

A

Rogue's Magic Items

These items are those found in common versions of Rogue. Some versions may differ, like by splitting up identify scrolls among different item types or not offering scrolls of vorpalize weapon, so this should not be taken as definitive.

- Scrolls: Monster Confusion, Magic Mapping, Hold Monster, Enchant Armor, Identify, Scare Monster, Food Detection, Teleportation, Enchant Weapon, Remove Curse, Protect Armor, Vorpalize Weapon, Light, Gold Detection, Genocide, Create Monster (bad), Aggravate Monster (bad), Sleep (bad), Blank Paper (useless)
- Potions: Healing, Extra Healing, Gain Strength, Restore Strength, Haste Self, Magic Detection, Monster Detection, Raise Level, See Invisible, Levitation, Blindness (bad), Confusion (bad), Paralysis (bad), Poison (bad), Hallucination (bad), Thirst Quenching (useless)
- Rings: Add Strength, Dexterity, Increase Damage, Maintain Armor, Protection, Regeneration, Searching, Slow Digestion, Stealth, Sustain Strength, Teleportation, Aggravate Monster (bad), Adornment (useless)
- Wands/Staves: Light, Striking, Lightning, Fire, Cold, Magic Missile, Slow Monster, Teleport Away, Cancellation, Drain Life (often bad), Polymorph (often bad), Haste Monster (bad), Invisibility (bad), Teleport To (bad), Nothing (useless)

67

Item Design: Potions and Scrolls

October 2009 This chapter is an in-depth examination of some of the most popular items within the two most common categories: potions and scrolls, both of which we might term "one use" items for the fact that utilizing them consumes them.

Exploring a monster-filled dungeon is not what we might consider a healthy activity. If the game were just about looking around, mapping territory and killing monsters until the player's inevitable demise, the game might be interesting in a simplistic kind of way, but it wouldn't have that roguelike spark. No, the player must get something out of the exploration. That something is treasure.

Treasure is the carrot held in front of the player's face, leading him on into ever-more dangerous situations. The majority of treasure in most roguelikes is found lying around the dungeon. Some of the treasure is food, and the need to find more is what prevents the player from building levels indefinitely on the easier levels, but the good stuff is what pushes him downward. Unlike the trend in most RPGs these days, equipment is often a larger component of player power than experience level in roguelikes, and it is randomly generated.

67.1 The Justification for Treasure

Why is it so satisfying to find treasure? It cannot be denied that, without it, many roguelikes would be a lot less interesting. I suggest the reason that the expectation is that players will find treasure, or other things and opportunities of value, in those dangerous places they explore is related to the exploration urge evolved out of humankind's tribal pre-history. But I digress.

The random treasure generation is the biggest scrambling factor in a roguelike. Monsters are random but still appear in the same proportions on each level. Dungeons are random but even with traps most of the time the maps are not themselves very interesting. But a single item of treasure, in a good roguelike, can have the power to change the game significantly, and the variety of powers they grant, intersecting with each other and the monsters and dungeons, is what allows different plays of a single roguelike to seem different from each other.

The biggest problem with giving players lots of treasure to find is determining how powerful it should be. If it's not powerful enough players may consider, why bother? If it's too powerful then it's unbalancing, and it is more the treasure that is the reason for success than the player's skill. It might be useful to examine the basis for treasure in the source from which RPGs arose: fantasy literature. Bilbo's ring, for instance, enables him to overcome many of the dangers in the latter half of *The Hobbit*. Setting aside the ultimate identity of that ring revealed in *The Lord of the Rings*, a lot of the characters in that book kind of equate the ring's powers with Bilbo himself. They say that there is something more to him than meets the eye. That thing is, literally, the ring. But he found the ring through his own wit and guile, so it does make a kind of sense to say that. And even with the ring, Bilbo is in danger and must use it wisely to escape from dungeons, dragons and wars. In other words, Bilbo's possession of the ring is a manifestation of his ingenuity. So the treasure found in a roguelike, since it is gained by the player's own wit and guile, is a manifestation of it, and it is the job of the designer, as creator and custodian of that world, to have it be fitting.

It is interesting that, although Rogue is over 20 years old now, the major item types provided by that game remain the major types used in nearly all roguelikes.

67.2 Disposable Magic: One-Use Items

The primary one-use item types, other than food (usually a simple case), are potions and scrolls. Some games also provide for random food items like berries and mushrooms. Shiren provides herbs, which are good for a small amount of food value when eaten, but generally function more like potions. This can be seen in the way that a good number of herbs provide special effects when thrown. ADOM has herbs which are unique in that their functions are not randomly scrambled, but are the same from game to game.

(ADOM's herbs have other unique and interesting properties, however. They are one of my favorite things about that game, but they are a special case that doesn't fit in with the general roguelike categories.)

Scrambled one-use items are often challenging to identify items in a standard roguelike. The biggest problem with identifying one-use items is that, once the item is gone, it isn't there anymore. You only get one use with which to discover its purpose. And a few of these items are situationally useful, to the degree that the player may be helped considerably by using the item effectively, at the proper time or with specific preparation. And a few one-use items can cause a great deal of trouble; Rogue's potion of blindness can be a game-ender if used at an inopportune moment.

Many games auto-ID potions and scrolls upon use, but Rogue and the Hacks do not. These games require that the item's visible effect be detectable by the player, and are obviously the purpose of the item, before they'll auto-identify. Some items have effects that are so obscure that they never auto-ID this way, forcing the player to either name it themselves from experience or expend an Identify scroll on it. Others only identify sometimes (like detection scrolls when there is something to detect), and some will prompt the player for a temporary name in some situations.

The one-use-only property of potions is one area where roguelikes differ from classic Dungeons & Dragons. By-the-book OD&D and 1st edition AD&D state that found magic items are unknown, but potions may be tasted and thus given a chance of identification without consuming the thing. In those games some potions have multiple uses, and others have functions that require the liquid not be drunk at all, but instead applied to an object or the skin, or in some cases the bottle merely unstopped. The classic roguelike play style is directly inspired by these versions of D&D, and both Rogue and the Hack-like games provide for item uses beyond the basic "quaff." In Rogue and NetHack throwing potions at monsters is an option for getting effective use even out of "bad" items. In Rogue, this may cause the item to affect the monster; in NetHack, a thrown potion breaks and may subject nearby creatures to a reduced "vapor effect." NetHack also allows for dipping items into potions, and even mixing them together, each option of some strategic worth. But even so, most potions are still meant to be drunk. Both games also contain scrolls of scare monster, which are wasted when read. Their true value appears only while they're resting on the floor.

There are usually many one-use items to discover in the game, and unlike random wearables (such as rings and amulets) the player usually will get a fairly substantial hint for what it does upon use, so, scrolls of identify are generally best used for other things. Significantly, identify scrolls themselves are random one-use items in most games. In many games, before any items can be identified by using identify scrolls, the player must use trial-and-error to discover them. Games that support selling items to shops often provide identification hints by offering items to shopkeepers, a tactic I refer to as "price ID." It's based on the idea that more powerful items cost more. The usefulness of this strategy ranges from slightly unbalanced in NetHack to nearly essential in Shiren's Final Puzzle dungeon. Because this trick provides one of the few ways to narrow down object functions that doesn't use the thing up or require knowledge of Identify scrolls, it is particularly useful when applied to one-use items.

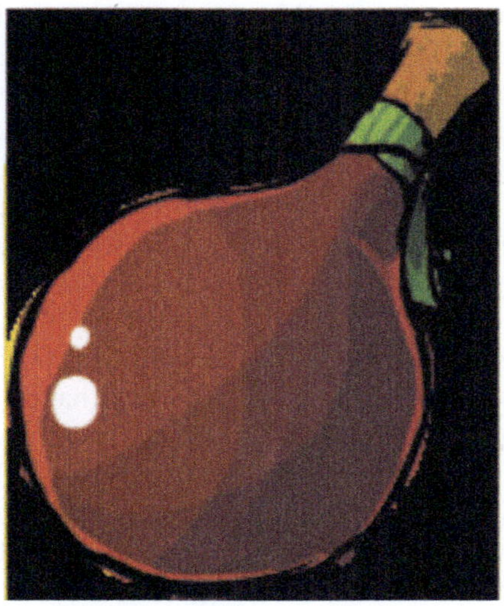

Figure 67.1

Potion

67.3 What Is the Functional Difference between Potions and Scrolls?

- Potions are much more likely to have an effect when thrown. The only roguelike (or roguelike series) I know that provides thrown item effects for scrolls is Shiren the Wanderer.
- Potions are, basically, chemicals, and the avenues for useful non-magical potions are much greater than those for scrolls. For some games this is a significant difference: should a potion of magic detection locate a flask of oil? In NetHack, the most useful potion is water. It is similarly useful in ADOM.
- Potions may also be more versatile in their uses than scrolls. In addition to being thrown, it may be possible to dip items into them, or to mix then together. NetHack uses hard-coded potion mix results according to type. The Color Alchemy patch randomizes potion results, making them mix according to potion color and subtractive color mixing. ADOM puts a lot of work into its alchemy system, defining a number of mixture "recipes" randomly at the start of the game, and granting the player knowledge of them as they advance in the Alchemy skill.
- While scrolls may have many varied effects, potions usually work on the subject's physical form. Note, however, that this is not always the case; some detection effects may be implemented as scrolls, and others potions, in the same game. (D&D did this too sometimes; there is a line of potions for controlling various types of creatures. These potions work by the user drinking them; their influence then extends outward from the drinker, apparently.)
- If the effect requires any further input from the player, particularly selecting an item to work on, the item will almost certainly be a scroll.

Here's a list of some of the most notable potions and scrolls, from various games, and their interesting properties.

67.4 Potions

67.4.1 . . . *of Healing* (and Extra/Full Healing, Cure Light/Moderate/ Serious Wounds, and so on)

Other than weapons, potions of healing may be the most common item among all roguelike games. While most roguelike characters heal quickly, usually returning to maximum hit points after at most a hundred turns of rest, the danger presented from facing multiple opponents at once, or surviving an encounter with a single powerful monster, sometimes necessitates a way to restore hits rapidly.

One of the most interesting gameplay choices in these games is the traditional max-HP-boosting trick of healing potions. If you drink one when you're at full health, many games will let you push against the ceiling, giving you a tiny, permanent maximum HP increase. This seems like the better use of these potions at first, since the main method of gaining maximum hits in most games is gaining an experience level and those are rather harder to achieve, but the best move depends on your situation. Weaker healing potions are probably best quaffed for max health, especially later in the game, but the stronger ones can be so effective that they may come in handy when escaping from a superior foe, which the restrictive vision rules of Rogue make essential. Another obscure use of these potions is to instantly alleviate status effects like confusion and poisoning. Stronger types generally cure more types of these ailments. This use is of great importance in NetHack when facing certain rare, but very dangerous situations, such as facing down the fearsome Demogorgon.

One thing about healing potions is that giving the player an abundance of them can be less damaging to the design than you'd think. They require a turn to use, and a foe that really outclasses the player will probably put him right into trouble again with the next hit. Shiren the Wanderer has an item, the Chiropractic Jar, that instantly heals the player completely and restores most status ailments. These items have multiple charges and are not usually rare, and yet the game still has a reputation for lethality. This happens because the player must have both time to use the item, and the presence of mind to use it, and also because for their commonness they are still a limited resource, so the player tries to conserve uses. This often proves to be deadly.

67.4.2 . . . of Restore Ability

The only one of D&D's six attributes to make it into Rogue is strength, which influences bonus damage done to monsters. The game begins players with a score of 16, and it also tracks "maximum strength," which also starts at 16. There are monsters, traps and items in the game that can lower strength. All of these effects leave maximum strength alone. But unlike hit points, strength does not regenerate naturally over time. In Rogue, only the potion of restore ability, which resets strength to its maximum score, can undo damage done to it.

Like the danger of losing armor value, the danger of strength loss is mostly specific to a limited region of the dungeon, that which plays host to rattlesnakes, which by far cause most of its attribute damage. One consequence of Rogue's sight rules (only one space around the player is visible in corridors and dark rooms) is that there are certain times when it is impossible to avoid taking a hit from a monster, which means sometimes strength loss is unavoidable. This makes restore ability potions fairly important.

When I say "maximum" strength, what I mean is the player's current maximum capacity for it, which is considered to be its value when all attribute damage has been restored. Most other roguelikes provide more stats, with different functions, but they usually expand Rogue's ability restoration potions to work on all of them.

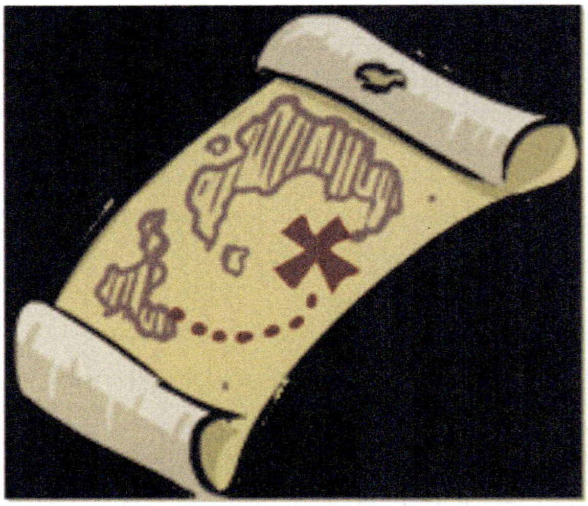

Figure 67.2

Scroll

67.4.3 . . . *of Gain Strength* (and Other Stats, and Ability)

In Rogue, a potion of gain strength increases the player's strength score by one. If it was already equal to maximum, then both strength and maximum strength increase by a point. If the player has taken some strength damage, though, then the result is that only one point is restored.

This means that, if strength is later lowered, drinking a restore ability potion will return strength to the new maximum. Having high strength is a subtle, yet significant, advantage, so it's fairly important to save these for when the player is at max strength.

The trick to these two items lies in the inescapability of strength loss. Most characters will take at least a point of strength damage during the game, and often more. Both types of potions are generated randomly; it is possible that none of one type will appear in the game. If your strength starts getting dangerously low and you haven't found a restore ability potion yet, is it a good idea to increase your damage done by one point by drinking a gain strength potion, or is it better to continue waiting, hoping to find a restorer to drink first? Keep in mind that the player doesn't even know which potion is which at first, and often one potion type, poison, will drain strength. At their best, roguelike games are full of these kinds of choices.

ADOM has probably the best-developed statistic system of the major roguelikes. Whereas most games satisfy themselves with, or something like, D&D's six stat system, ADOM has nine, and provides individual potions for improving all of them . . . and potions for temporarily boosting them, and potions solely for raising their maximum. (It also has the diabolical potion of exchange, which swaps them around. This can easily ruin your game if drank carelessly.) Additionally, it has potions of Gain Attributes, which are more general but do not raise maximums. Of particularly awesome note: ADOM's system has no hard limit on how high stats can rise, although it becomes much tougher to increase them as they go up. Interested readers are directed to the Stats chapter of the ADOM Guidebook.

67.4.4 . . . of Gain Level

Another example of a difficult choice is deciding just when to drink a potion of gain level.

As is normal for D&D-inspired role-playing games, each experience level requires a rapidly increasing number of experience points to earn in order to achieve it. Some games, following from old-school D&D, even use a doubling progression. Harder monsters are worth more experience points, it is true, but in many roguelikes they don't quite keep pace with the higher point totals needed, meaning levels gainscome more and more slowly. Rogue, particularly, is infamous for monsters that generally get harder faster than the player gains ability. Rogue characters thus get put into ever increasing amounts of danger as they delve down, and every experience level counts.

As a consequence, the longer the player waits before drinking a potion of gain level, the more value he'll get from it. If it's used early, the experience points gained won't be significantly greater by the amount received for killing a few monsters. On the other hand, the longer you wait the less the portion of the game you'll have made use of it, and if you get killed the advantage is lost entirely.

67.4.5 . . . of Poison (and Sickness)

This is an example of a bad item, one that has no good primary purpose. Nearly all classic roguelike item systems have a good secondary purpose for it: bad potions can be thrown at enemies. And even the worst item can be useful if a nymph happens to steal it instead of something better. But the "usual" method of using potions, drinking them, will cause you grief if you try it with poison.

Take note, poison is not, in itself, fatal. That is a no-no in games where the player is expected to identify things through use. If the player must rely on using unknown things, then none of those things can be immediately deadly! This doesn't mean using the item cannot be deadly if the player's state is bad (low on strength when drinking a potion of poison), or if used in a non-standard way (zapping one's self with a wand of death), or if a member of a very limited class of items (wearing NetHack's amulet of strangulation, and even that can often be survived if the player prays). Items also cannot make the game as good as lost. Rogue's worst one-use item is the potion of blindness, a long-lasting potion that removes even the game's slight one-space vision range, but it does wear off after a few hundred turns.

67.4.6 . . . of (Something) Detection

While not obviously useful to new players, detection objects are potentially among the most useful objects in roguelikes. Monster detection allows you to choose your fights, item detection enables you to direct your exploration, and map detection points out useful escape routes. Note that detection items are in a gray area between potions and scrolls; different games allocate this power to these item classes differently. Rogue has types of both: food detection is a scroll, while magic detection and monster detection are potions.

67.4.7 . . . of Confusion, Blindness, Paralysis

These items are bad when drank, but sometimes good if thrown at monsters. Saying "bad" is relative to the situation; in Rogue, a potion of blindness can be useful when entering the Medusa floors.

They primarily exist as an identification foil, to add danger to identifying things by use and to make random potion drinking in moments of danger an inviable strategy. These particular one-use items are fairly easy to identify.

67.4.8 . . . of Thirst Quenching (and Water, Holy Water and Unholy Water)

Each of Rogue's item classes has a do-nothing item, to throw off people who think all items must have some function. For scrolls it's blank paper, and for potions it's thirst quenching. The others are the wand of nothing and the ring of adornment. It is notable that NetHack still has all of these items, but with special uses for three of them.

67.5 Scrolls

67.5.1 . . . of Identify

The scroll of identify is, after healing, the most common of roguelike items. In many games they are also the most-often generated item.

Here is something I find very interesting. Scrolls of Identify are very common, but I am aware of no roguelike game that will purposely misidentify something. NetHack's cursed scrolls of Identify identify fewer items; they don't lie to the player about what things are. D&D has dangerous objects that purposely resemble useful things, and the diabolical potion of delusion that, depending on a group's play style, could cause the DM to lie to the player about what is happening to his character. Roguelike games, while tricky in the knowledge games they play, do not tend to go that far.

67.5.2 . . . of Enchant Weapon/Armor

These items are the scroll versions of the potion of gain strength. That potion increases the player's damage-dealing ability by increasing his physical attack bonus. The scrolls increase weapon attack bonus and decrease enemy hitting chances, while the player is using a specific piece of equipment.

All of these items improve the player's state indefinitely. They do not expire naturally, but must be undone by enemy attack, unfortunate item use or trap. That makes these items extremely useful. Although a single point of bonus is a rather subtle effect in a single encounter, over time the benefits are profound. If the player is lucky enough to find several of these the game will become much easier, maybe even too easy. Most games guard against this possibility by limiting how high strength can be raised, or how far an item can be enchanted. It is kind of a cheap way around the problem, since it means a whole class of item suddenly becomes useless just because the game designer thinks the player is getting too powerful, but it is frequently used.

A particular note . . . in Rogue, scrolls of enchant weapon are unusual in that they increase one of a weapon's two different kinds of pluses. That game distinguishes between pluses to-hit and to-damage, and the scroll decides randomly which of the two values is increased. Some Rogue variants split enchant weapon into two separate items. And some go the other way, and combine the weapon and armor scrolls into a single "enchantment" scroll, which asks the player which item will be subject to the item's power upon reading.

In most roguelikes, these scrolls function immediately on a relevant item in use at the time. If no weapon or armor is in use, the scroll's effect is wasted. NetHack uses this as the basis of a subtle trap; one of its bad scrolls is that of destroy armor. If you're reading unknown scrolls, you might want to wear armor in order to take advantage of an unknown enchant armor scroll. But what if that scroll should be destroy armor instead? Another possible trap, used by other games, is the scroll that asks you for an item to operate on, but that doesn't tell you what for.

As an extra ability, these scrolls also lift curses from the item they operate on.

67.5.3 . . . of Vorpalize Weapon

What does it mean, to "vorpalize" something? No matter what one might have gleaned from its use in video gaming, vorpal is actually a nonsense word. It can be traced back to Lewis Carroll's "Jabberwocky," where it is applied to a sword and can be assumed by context to mean powerful. Role-playing games have adopted it, although there is no consensus about what it should mean.

Rogue contains a scroll called "vorpalize weapon." When read, it makes the player's weapon flash violently for a moment. It applies a pretty good enchantment to the weapon, and additionally chooses one of the monsters in the game to be the weapon's target foe. The next monster the player attacks of that type will die instantly. There is a drawback, however. If the player tries to use a second vorpalize weapon scroll on the same weapon, it is destroyed!

The idea here is to punish the player for being too greedy. Of course, the player doesn't know how greedy is too greedy until he loses his weapon. In practice, this becomes another of those little things players must learn as they play, another fact that must be acquired in order to eventually win. If this seems rather a harsh way of teaching the lesson . . . well, Rogue really isn't that long a game. If you lose, just try again.

NetHack doesn't have vorpalize weapon scrolls, but will destroy a weapon or a piece of armor if it is over-enchanted. When a weapon is enchanted beyond its safe limit, it vibrates warningly. A further enchantment has a very high (but not for certain) chance of destroying the weapon.

67.5.4 . . . of Confuse Monster

To a new player, this is one of the more enigmatic items in Rogue. Upon reading the only immediate effect is that the player's hands begin to glow red. This causes the next monster the player strikes to become confused for a short while. That is all. In principle this is a powerful item, although reading it in advance of combat usually creates a risk of it being wasted on a weak monster.

67.5.5 . . . of Scare Monster

One of the most mysterious items in the game if the player doesn't know its secret. It is also the only one that can be identified without picking it up. In fact, especially in Rogue, it is best not to pick it up until you've gotten at least some use out of it.

67.5.6 . . . of Genocide

Ah, that word again. The scroll of genocide, often thought of as a Hack item, got its start in one of the later versions of Rogue. When read, it wipes out one entire type of monster from the game.

Items that powerful, in a good roguelike, will have a tradeoff, and in Rogue it is that other types of monsters become more common, to fill the generation hole left by the eliminated species. Plus, according to a website called the Rogue Vede-Mecum at least, there is only one of these generated in a game, preventing the player from wiping out too many monsters.

67.5.7 . . . of Maintain Armor

This scroll, which prevents armor pluses from being reduced, is one of the most useful items in the game. Seriously, it is almost overpowered! It is a late addition to Rogue's item list, appearing in V5, and it is one of the rarest items. There is a good reason that many later roguelikes do not include it.

Armor can be harmed both from enemy attack (by rust monsters or aquators, depending on the version of Rogue) and from traps. One of the many little devious facts about Rogue is that even permanent advantages can usually be undone due to unwise play, or even bad luck. Getting your strength up can be undone from a single unlucky encounter with a rattlesnake, for example. The balance between the possibility of the player getting super strong armor, from finding a suit of plate mail and a number of enchant armor scrolls, is that Aquators will easily weaken armor, and rust traps become progressively more common in the deeper dungeon.

These armor ruiners can be overcome by working on building an emergency set of armor (which is balanced due to the fact that it costs two turns to switch to it, and the possibility of putting in cursed armor which cannot be removed easily), using unrustable leather armor (balanced by its being the weakest in the game), putting on a ring of Maintain Armor (balanced by increased food consumption) and reading a scroll of Maintain Armor, which . . . has no drawbacks.

It has no drawbacks! Except perhaps due to it only affecting a single suit, which is nowhere near as bad a drawback as the other things. If you put this on plate mail, you have just made one of the few unequivocally good decisions you can make in Rogue.

NetHack's analogue for this is reading a scroll of enchant armor while confused, which provides rust-proofing, and is similarly powerful (although possible to remove in rare cases). Shiren has Plating scrolls, the effect of which can be removed by a certain monster (which nearly never happens). Both are, in my opinion, subtle failures of design.

67.6 Sources

Thanks to Keith Burgun for the artwork in this chapter! These images were created by Keith Burgun for the article and are used with permission.

68

Towards Building a Better Dungeon

June 2008 I've beaten the drums pretty loudly for roguelikes here, I suppose. They are a style of roleplaying game that has much to teach game designers, in its tactical depths, its subtle incorporation of logical puzzles, its open-endedness and the sheer variety in them. As said last time, nothing in computer roleplaying games so preserves the spirit of 1974-vintage, Original Dungeons & Dragons as roguelike games do. I've cheered for roguelikes so much, in fact, that I believe I'm allowed a bit of pessimistic contemplation here. Roguelikes are great, yes, yes, but they are not perfect. There are some things lacking with them.

In this, I'm not talking about the kinds of things dredged up by many game reviewers when they're forced to comprehend a roguelike for the first time. Like the absences of: a central narrative; scripted events; clumsy metaphor; and amnesiac 14-year-olds somehow seeking absolution for their dark pasts while saving their generic fantasy world from empires fueled by the corrupting forces of Chaos with the aid of a dozen anime stereotypes.

But if viewed in the light of classic Dungeons & Dragons, of a semi-adversarial game between players and a referee set in an ancient dungeon filled with all manner of tricks, traps and treasure, there remain some important things that roguelike games lack.

These lacks, nearly without exception, come from their following of Rogue. The ways that Rogue fails to measure up to the spirit of OD&D are also the ways that they fail. If one makes a study of the evolution of game design, one finds that this is common throughout the game industry. The first game of a genre gets its inspiration from some outside source; other people or companies, seeking to duplicate its success, make games that seek to improve upon the original by addressing its faults, but lacking the knowledge of the source material that the first game had; still other companies build upon those; and so on, until Strat-O-Matic sports has mutated into Madden 'XX.

But to return to the subject, these are all things that are not necessarily problems with roguelikes, but for some reason continue to be. These are things present in D&D that are not typically followed by roguelikes, and could conceivably gain by adopting. Well, I think so anyway:

68.1 D&D Has Much More Interesting Traps than Roguelike Games

D&D traps can be nearly anything imaginable; pressure plates, tripwires, magical detectors, monster cages, flame shooters, etc., but roguelike traps are uniform in comparison. The only way roguelikes can get away with this is because nearly every other CRPG has even less interesting traps, if they have them at all.

Rogue's trap model is very simple, and every roguelike I can name adopts it unquestioningly. Some of the spaces in the dungeon contain traps. The player is not shown those spaces at first glance, but if he steps into one it is revealed, and the player might be harmed by the trap.

Searching while on a space adjacent to the trap may reveal it, but searching every space takes too long and will likely cause the player to run out of food or die to wandering monster attacks, so in practice the player must forge on despite them.

In roguelike design theory, traps exist to provide a cost for careless exploration. It is impossible to entirely negate the danger from traps, so the player must instead reduce this risk by not stepping on unnecessary spaces, and retracing his footsteps whenever possible. This is a useful idea, but the game already includes the food requirement pushing the player towards move conservation.

In classic D&D on the other hand, traps are everywhere, and an integral part of the game. Often, especially in older modules, they can be deadly all by themselves. Traps are not placed willy-nilly but tend to guard things, like treasure or important rooms. And while surviving or defeating a trap is worth little or no experience points, any treasure guarded by the trap is worth experience in versions up to and including 1st Edition AD&D.

Exceptions: NetHack's rolling boulder traps are multi-part, and its bear traps and land mines can be disarmed, carried around and even reset. These are recent additions, however. The game still mostly follows Rogue in its trap model.

68.2 All Monsters Are, in Tactical Terms, the Same Size

In roguelike games, a pixie tends to be the same size, in terms of the game, as a dragon. Gnomes and giants take up the same space on the grid. They can all fit through the same doors and down the same narrow passages.

Again, NetHack has an exception to this. It expended a good amount of code in making its long worm monster, which can extend for many spaces through the dungeon, and be split in two like an earthworm. Mystery Dungeon: Shiren the Wanderer, and some of the other Mystery Dungeon games, have some boss monsters that take up 2x2 spaces. Although those games aren't against conveniently forgetting this at times: their size doesn't seem to deny them access to narrow passages.

Possibly more roguelikes have not tried to simulate monsters more than one dungeon space in size because doors and passages tend to be one space wide, and it would limit their mobility. A monster bigger than that won't be able to leave the room it was generated in. In OD&D, it should be noted, passages are usually 10 feet wide, equivalent to two game "spaces," and nothing says the dungeon designer has to use standard doors for all rooms.

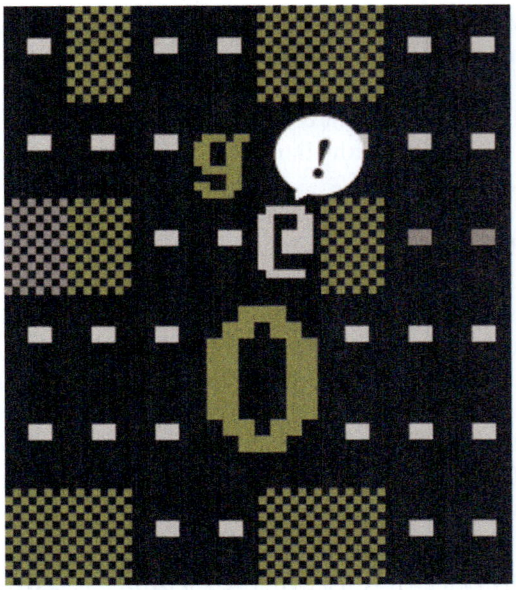

Figure 68.1

Giant ogre

68.3 Hidden Doors Are All Identical

OD&D had only three character classes: "fighting Man," magic user and cleric. The final core archetype, Thieves, didn't enter the game until the first supplement. Before then, traps were detected and handled in what we might call "narrative space." The referee explains the surroundings to the player, and that description contains the clues that might lead the player to examine the trap's hiding place by investigating and asking about it, perhaps then disabling the trap by taking explicit action like pulling a lever or cutting a wire. (If this sounds a bit like playing a text adventure game, it's no accident. Colossal Cave was likely inspired by this style of Dungeons & Dragons, and Dungeon/Zork definitely was.)

When thieves entered the game, they could find traps simply by succeeding on a die roll. This is the beginning of the game's trend towards including rules abstracting everything out. Finding secret doors, one of D&D's most thrilling discoveries, also comes down to a die roll. Instead of pressing a loose brick or finding a hidden lever, the player simply must search. Roguelike searching works the same way.

68.4 Stairs Not Matching X and Y Positions between Levels

A fact I find interesting: no roguelike game I've seen even attempts to have stairs and other ways of going between levels be logically consistent with each other. Unlike D&D dungeons, stairs on one level almost never match up with the same location on the floor below. In other words: if you find two stairs next to each other in a game with multiple stairs (like Angband or Dungeon Crawl), if you were to go down each of them, you would probably end up in spots far removed from each other on the next level. Stairs don't preserve X and Y location when taken; they instead come out anywhere on the next level. And pit traps lead to a random location on the next floor that changes every time they're fallen down.

This may seem minor, but it prevents the level generator designer from including intra-level mazes, like places where the player must travel back and forth between two levels to ultimately find the way down to still deeper areas, or secret rooms that are intended to be found by finding stairs from the prior level that can be found by paying attention to the level.

There are solid technical reasons that roguelike games do this. Rogue was created at a time when computers had very little memory, so levels are generated when entered instead of at the start of the game. Later games aren't so restricted in memory, and some games like ADOM, Crawl and the 'Hacks either save levels not being explored to disk or keep them in an alternate memory buffer, but they still generate the levels on a need-to-see basis.

While the initial entrance to the level could be guaranteed to be a suitable location for stairs (that is, not in a wall), if the levels were to get generated in a non-linear manner, inconsistencies could arise. If levels 15 and 17 get generated before level 16, then whichever entrance to 16 is used first could be guaranteed to get a consistent staircase, but the stairs to the other level might not. Forcing staircase locations before the map is created means that level must be built around them, and random map generation is still enough of a black art that this might be regarded as being too difficult.

Now of course, this is only the case if the whole dungeon isn't created at the start, when these matters could be resolved simply. And even if the game doesn't keep the whole dungeon in memory at once, a sufficiently advanced generation algorithm certainly could ensure logically consistent stairs. That no roguelike to my knowledge, and certainly no major game in the genre, has done so yet is strange.

68.5 Item Identification Is Much Easier Than Classic D&D

One of the most interesting things about roguelikes is how item descriptions and types match up. All items of a given type share a description. Bubbly, yellow, milky and purple potions are different types, types that might not be known at the start of the game but persist during it. All types of one description are the same, so once one is known, they're all known.

For Rogue the item system is well-balanced, for there are practical limits on the number of items that can be generated on each level, there were no guarantees that any specific item would be found, and even if the player managed to explore down to Amulet level, chances were high that some items would never make an appearance. The result is that, even at the deepest levels, players continue to find unknown objects, good or bad, whose types must be discovered through expending resources, insight, process of elimination or risky usage. And since no item is really essential to win and there are tricky uses for some bad things, even an exceptionally unlucky player who only finds bad stuff still has a chance.

This balance has changed as roguelike games have become more complex, and dungeons have increased in size. In a game of NetHack, nearly all random items will be generated, either randomly or from guaranteed creation, before the player reaches Gehennom, halfway through the dungeon. Those items which are certain to show up do so because a few kinds of items are necessary to win: a means of crossing water, for example, will probably be needed on either the Medusa, Castle, Juiblex or Plane of Water levels. On the other hand, successful Angband players spend lots of time farming levels in order to find the stuff they need. Angband changes item generation probabilities as the player gets deeper into the dungeon, so not only must he know what he needs, he must know the levels it's found on.

The roguelike identification system was inspired by Original Dungeons & Dragons, in which items were much harder to figure out. Many items had secret switches or command words that activated their powers, and did nothing until those were found. Cursed items had much more variety and were much more diabolical. There were a number of extremely bad items which looked exactly like more valuable stuff, like potions of delusion. A bowl commanding water elementals is a very useful object, but it looks exactly the same as a bowl of watery death, which can kill a character so dead that even a wish won't bring him back. These items seem to exist only to punish players who might try to figure things out through observation! Enough referees must have seen this as unfair that most recent versions of D&D de-emphasize the identification of treasure. In an OD&D game he ran in 2005, Gary Gygax is known to have himself told his players what most of the stuff they found was, although there were some exceptions to this.

Whether this aspect of Dungeons & Dragons, that even with experience there are items that are fatally indistinguishable from each other, is good or not I don't think I can say. I recognize why it's there, but I lean against it. Item identification has become a uniquely distinguishing characteristic of roguelike gaming. And yet, the identification game of roguelikes other than Rogue tends to get easier later on to the point of meaninglessness. Especially in NetHack: most of its items will be discovered before halfway through the dungeon, and this is unquestionably one of the sources of that game's declining difficulty midway through. Fixing this problem would require design innovation, but there's no reason to believe it's impossible.

68.6 Lack of Multiplayer

Adding multiplayer to (insert roguelike name here) is one of those features that seems so obvious but makes their programmers weep openly. The NetHack DevTeam has a whole item on their FAQ devoted to rejecting this idea. The problem is that roguelikes are turn-based. If you're in the same room as another player, and he nips off to the bathroom for a while, what do you do in the meantime? Twiddle your thumbs?

The reason multiplayer would be important to roguelike games is that it is a feature of pen-and-paper roleplaying that is lacking in CRPGs: the participation of other players in the game making it into a social experience.

It is the one aspect of old-school roleplaying gaming that another genre arguably does better than roguelikes: MMORPGs may have plexiglass-coated designs that reduce player classes to a surprisingly limited set of archetypes, prevent characters from ever dying or even suffering any serious losses and typically have designs that center around combat as the be-and-end-all of RPG play, but by gum, they do let you cooperate with your friends.

To their credit, MMORPGs actually solve it fairly well. The biggest change they seem to suggest is that a multiplayer roguelike should be mostly real time. But in addition to the fact that this would completely change the way a roguelike game is implemented, it'd mean that players would no longer be able to sit and

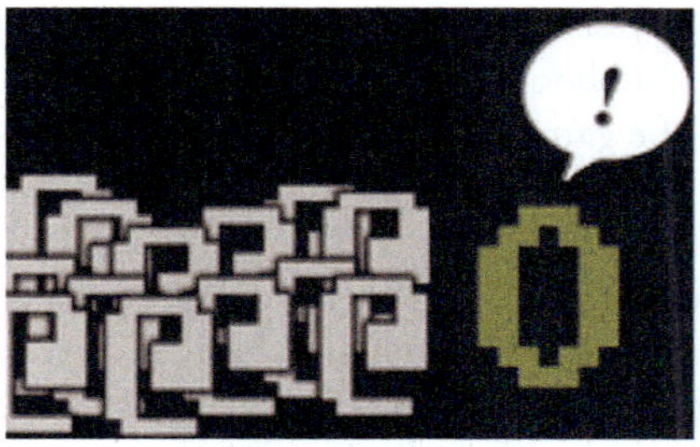

Figure 68.2

Ogre outnumbered

fully think through the ramifications of their moves before making them. These unexpected ramifications are a major part of the appeal of many roguelikes.

So fixing this problem is not a trivial matter. But it could well be solvable. In fact, it may have already been solved: MAngband is a full, internet-enabled, real-time variation of Angband. I haven't looked into it much yet, but it's been around for years and is still undergoing active development. It seems to have an active player community too.

Many years ago there was a project called Interhack, which purported to be a multiplayer recreation of NetHack. Its developer claimed to have devised a system he called "surreal time," which shifted between completely turn-based and real-time play depending on how close players were to each other. Alas, it seems its developer became disenchanted with the project along the way, or became involved in an altercation with some of the NetHack player community, and removed all traces of the project from the internet. But undoubtedly, there are important lessons there for roguelike developers contemplating allowing more than a single player into their dungeon at once.

SECTION VV
Miscellaneous

69

A Coward Dies a Thousand Deaths, but My Computer, Several Thousand

December 2006 I ask you to halt your busy day for a moment and consider the challenges inherent in getting a computer to play a game. Not to sponsor a game for human beings, but actually play the game, itself. To manipulate virtual controls in order to successfully maneuver through a game made for human play.

There is at least one computer game made specifically for the computer itself to play, although it is really more of a joke. (That game is Progress Quest.) And there are ways to get the machine to play through the game itself and display the results. Some action games that have an ability to record demos, in fact, work by "playing" the game. When the user plays, the game software records the sequences of control inputs, in the order and timing in which they are made, and stores them in a file. When the demo is played back, the opponents and level structure are handled as if it were a real game, and the program substitutes the recorded control stream for a player. It's the same principle, these days, as in tool-assisted speedruns.

One may object to this, saying that this is not really playing, but it is, from the computer's standpoint. If the game is the same every time, if there is no randomness, then the process of a human playing it is actually the process of discovering the essential control inputs needed to win, and once that sequence is discovered one need only feed that sequence into the world simulation, like stimulating a brain in a jar, to cause the computer to play itself.

But the process of discovering that sequence, that is really where the game lies, isn't it? Getting a computer to play back a recorded set of inputs is easy, but designing a program to examine what a human being would see, then send the game process the discovered control stimuli to play with no prior knowledge of the game world, that is much harder. In the roguelike genre of computer games, in which all dungeons are created randomly each time and even the identities of the items shift from game to game, it is much harder to create a computer program that can play well. So hard as to be impossible, one might think.

It is so impossible, it has been done at least twice.

69.1 Rog-O-Matic: It Dies Over and Over So You Don't Have To

The first automatic roguelike player, or "borg" as they have come to be known, was written for Rogue itself. Rog-O-Matic is a program that, if you have the fairly specific, ancient Unix hardware it runs under, plays Rogue 3.6, and plays it extremely well. It runs as another task on the machine that intercepts the output coming from the game process and supplies it with its algorithmically determined input, and thus cannot "cheat" with inside knowledge of the hidden portions of the game's state. It has exactly the same information that a human player would have in a game.

(*June 2020*: Some good news! An open-source compilation of Rogue versions called Rogue Collection, available at https://github.com/mikeyk730/Rogue-Collection, includes an updated and usable version of Rog-O-Matic that you can run yourself on Windows and Linux machines!)

Very few people have the means to run Rog-O-Matic anymore. In fact, although the source was available from Boudewijn Waijers' Rogue page (his site was, for a long while, just about the only notable roguelike game resource on the Web) that link seems to be broken now. Like many of the earlier roguelikes themselves, the program is sliding into obscurity and may already be permanently lost. But we do have the paper they presented at the Conference of the Canadian Society for Computational Studies of Intelligence, and it makes for an interesting read, from standpoints both of player and programmer.

Rogue, like NetHack but unlike some other roguelikes like Angband, places as heavy emphasis on the item discovery aspects of the game as combat tactics, so an automatic player will have to actually figure out aspects of the game world instead of merely exploring it. Since it begins every game with no knowledge of the identities of potions, scrolls, wands or rings, and information on these things is difficult to come by during play, there is a large component of luck in any player's progress, whether it is soft- or wet-ware.

Rog-O-Matic does not cheat, in that it has no knowledge of the game a human player could not obtain, say by reading the memory of the game process or examining the executable, but it does use what amounts to spoilers. It begins with a hard-coded list of all the possible items in the game, and it has some built-in tricks for figuring out what they do, which is important for such items like scrolls of scare monster which are not used in the normal way. This information would be hard-won to a person playing, so the game begins with what amounts to a fairly significant spoiler. This kind of cunning, the ability to figure out non-typical item uses, is something that a programmer would indeed find it difficult with which to imbue an algorithm, so Rog-O-Matic gets around it by granting that knowledge to the borg. However, it does seek to learn the abilities of monsters honestly, keeping notes in a monster memory file between runs, in which it records whatever data it has been able to acquire about monster statistics and abilities. (It is rumored that this feature was added to universalize the algorithm, to make it less vulnerable to changes made by Rogue's developers specifically to counter Rog-O-Matic's effectiveness.)

So then, how well does it play? According to the paper, very well, as well as the best human players. It cannot win every game, neither can anyone, for Rogue is random enough so that victory is never absolutely certain even given perfect knowledge, so this is about as well as can be expected. The skill with which Rog-O-Matic plays makes sense when one considers that Rogue is, ultimately, a logic game married to a tactical combat simulation.

The procedure for identifying items is a puzzle with many special cases that need to be accounted for in order to obtain the most information from each test. Potions of object detection do not identify from use if there is nothing on the level to locate, scrolls of scare monster can be conclusively identified without touching the object, and rings of regeneration are obvious when worn if the player thinks to watch what his hit points do after taking damage. Once all these special rules are built into the system, what is left are the true challenges of writing an automatic roguelike player: optimizing player actions to minimize the resources consumed during the player's trip through the dungeon and creating an excellent tactical combatant.

(Trivia! One of the authors of Rog-O-Matic, Michael L. Mauldin, went on to found Lycos. More trivia! There was once a big information company called *Lycos,* they made a popular search engine before Google obliterated them.)

69.2 Did Three of Eight Just Tell Sauron Resistance Is Futile?

The other significant automatic roguelike player was created by Ben Harrison during his run as maintainer of Angband, and although it has the advantage of being a branch of the Angband source tree, which means it doesn't have to decipher a terminal data stream to figure out what is going on (it is said not to utilize any secret knowledge), it has a much more difficult task to accomplish. Rogue had a strong item discovery focus, but Angband's play concerns itself more with defeating ever-stronger opponents than simple survival.

Angband's item discovery game is much more shallow than Rogue's, but that game has shops from which scrolls can be purchased, and levels can be regenerated indefinitely to generate more scrolls of identify if need be, so piecing together such knowledge requires a lot less effort from the machine. On the other hand, Angband has many, many more kinds of foes than Rogue, and they can do many more kinds of things to the player (like summon in large numbers of additional foes), so the Angband Borg doesn't make an attempt to learn what the monsters can do, it just uses its built-in knowledge of the bestiary. There are also monsters that can kill even a perfectly equipped player in just a few turns, and from a distance, meaning that a successful borg must prepare for and be alert to such problems so they can be dealt with at a moment's notice. Angband's tactical depth is a bit deeper than Rogue's as well: players can dig their own tunnels, block off spaces from monsters with glyphs, or randomly warp a region of the dungeon around the player, and all of these options may have to be considered, weighted by their costs and risks.

The original Borg is no longer being actively worked on, with Harrison having passed the Angband torch off to others. Currently (as of this essay's writing), the primary fork of the Borg in development is the APWBorg (link deceased). Watching it play can be either a humbling or inspiring experience, depending on what one thinks about the potential of computers. The Borg has been known to win at Angband on occasion, but unlike Rog-O-Matic it tends to not be as good as an experienced human player. Watching it in action (and saving and reloading often to get around an annoying crash bug) shows it has an inordinate fondness for level 1, spending much of its time there even after it has achieved experience level 19. (The Angband dungeon is 100 levels deep, and maximum character level is 50.)

Unless the program is slowed down by adjusting a configuration file the game passes by much too fast to be able to tell what's happening, but once slowed down watching the Borg in action can be a useful way to gain ideas for how to play. Or, and here we're moving from the realm of simply cool to full-fledged awesome, there is a version of the APWBorg that works as a Windows screen saver! It you are unable to see the coolness inherent in having your computer play a game on itself at spare moments then I sincerely suggest that you turn in your geek badge, as it clearly must be a forgery.

(*January 2020*: Automatic players, whether you call them borgs or something else, have become more prevalent. Some MMORPGs consider them a scourge. I have heard that someone has successfully written one for NetHack.)

70

Running Atari ST Rogue in 2016

January 2016 Way back in 1980 there was a computer game called Rogue, originally written for Unix systems, that for a time was the toast of student computer rooms in universities. Inspired by its ingenious gameplay, a number of people made clones and play-alikes. Some of these would be forgotten, such as the "lost roguelikes." Some, like Moria and Hack, focused on specific elements of Rogue and developed them, and ultimately inspired their own progeny.

A few years after Rogue's release, its creators themselves decided to try to earn some money off of their creation. They developed versions for various microcomputers of the day and licensed it to game company Epyx, publishers of legendary early RPGs the Temple of Apshai series, among others, and the history of which could fill a book by itself. (Epyx also had a hand in the development of the Atari Lynx portable console, and several of that system's best games were produced by Epyx programmers.)

Several of these versions were developed and released in 1985. They didn't do hugely well, but a number of these versions escaped, through software piracy, and they're pretty much all playable today. British company Mastertronic also developed a few versions of Rogue for other systems, including the Commodore 64.

Of all of these versions, I single out a few of particular of interest.

One I refer to frequently as "PC Rogue," a small executable 98KB in size that is a complete implementation of the game. It is quite hard as Rogue versions go. At one point a fairly popular version, these days it's probably been eclipsed by versions like the bsdgames-nonfree compilation of the original game for various Linux distributions, and Rogue Clone IV. It was my own introduction to Rogue, and thus the reason I started writing this book to begin with.

Two other interesting versions are the Amiga and Atari ST versions, which are versions with actual graphics! The DOS versions just use a text mode window. Of the two, the one I tell you about here is the Atari ST version, notably because it's the one that Glenn Wichman implemented.

I and some of the fine folk responsible for Roguelike Radio interviewed Glenn Wichman about the game for Roguelike Radio episode 31. It was in that interview where Glenn revealed that Atari ST Rogue has a few features not found in other versions of the game. Huh, it does, does it? Let's have a look . . .

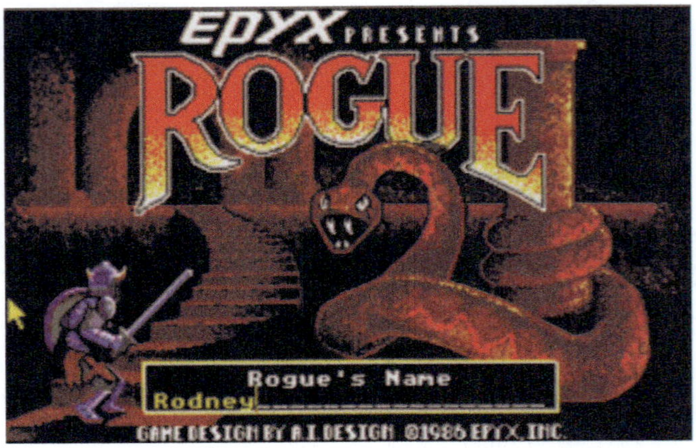

Figure 70.1

Atari ST Rogue, title screen.

70.1 Running Atari ST Rogue

70.1.1 Step 1: Download and Unpack the Atari ST Emulator STeem SSE

(Current as of January 2020)

STeem SSE (no relation to Valve's Steam software store and maintenance service) is one of several emulators that can allow you to run Atari ST software on your PC. This is, by itself, entirely legal, but requires the use of software that is, strictly speaking, probably still under copyright by someone, out there, somewhere.

The OS and assorted basic runnables of the ST's competitor, the Amiga home computer, are still claimed under copyright by an outfit called Amiga Forever. The state of the IP of the basic ST software is of more uncertain nature, and it is less likely, in any event, that anyone is left that cares. Still though, this has been your essential notice about copyright and IP and copying old software and yadda yadda.

Windows users should note that STeem has no installer and should be unzipped to its own folder before running. You will also need to obtain a copy of the TOS operating system that the Atari ST ran on. You will have to find that yourself; Google might be of some help.

A previous version of this chapter recommended that users seek out a version called "STeem Engine," but in the years since that has been replaced with a cryptocurrency miner. Please ensure that you find the correct version; I was able to find it on Sourceforge.

70.1.2 Step 2: Obtain the Atari ST Rogue Disk Image

As of this writing, you can obtain it from a number of places. You are looking for a file named A_079.st. At least one source I've found had insufficiently cracked copy protection, and will end games early around level 2.

70.1.3 Step 3: Running the Game

After you have unzipped STeem and the TOS files to the same folder, and put your disk image A_079.st into it, you may then run (by double-clicking) the Steem.exe file within its folder. It will ask you a number of questions about setting up your virtual Atari ST. It is okay to use the program directory as your storage for disk files (you can change this folder later if you decide that general Atari ST emulation is something you'd like to pursue). There is no need to set up a folder as a hard drive. Beyond that, the defaults should be fine.

After the system boots you will face a green desktop screen. The Atari ST was one of the earliest computers to adopt a desktop metaphor for its OS, originally popularized commercially with the initial releases of the Apple Lisa and Macintosh computers, so you should be able to get around fairly easily.

Note that you can freely resize the emulated ST's window to get a better look at it. You should probably do that, as it's quite difficult to use at normal resolution.

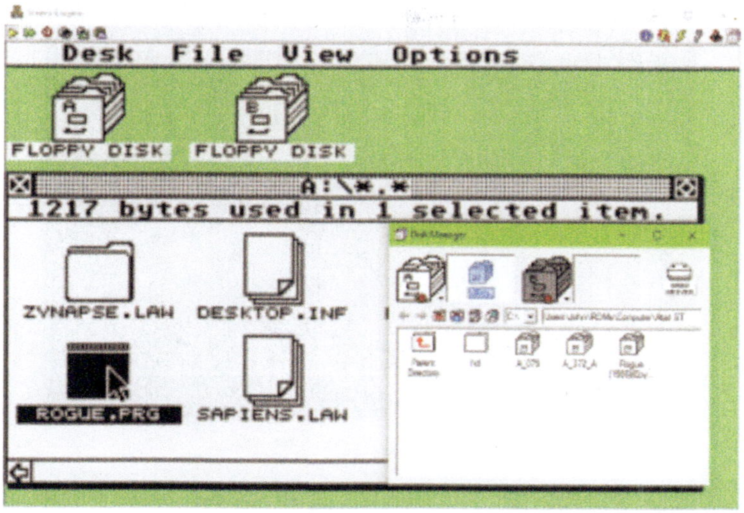

Figure 70.2

STeem showing the ST's desktop interface, with disk inserted in Disk Manager.

It's best if you don't have the disk image in the virtual drive when you boot the emulated ST. Instead, after you're already on its desktop screen, click the Disk Manager icon (the one furthest to the left), navigate to the folder where A_079.ST is saved, and then drag its icon to the box besides the A: file cabinet image. If you need to get your cursor back to do this, you can Alt-Tab away from STeem and back.

Then back on the desktop screen, double-click the Disk A icon, then from within it, the file labeled ROGUE.PRG. The game will spend a little time loading, then it'll show a colorful title screen on which you can enter your character's name. The default is "Rodney."

70.2 Getting Started with ST Rogue

As I said before, unlike most other versions of Rogue, this one has graphics. More than that, it actually has a graphical interface! For people allergic to the standard Rogue control scheme (see Chapter 2, What the Hell Does Q Do Again?), this is possibly the best way to play the game.

The main window contains a view of the dungeon around you. Your carried items appear in a window to the right. Double-clicking an item uses it in the most appropriate way: equipping, reading, drinking, etc. Clicking once on an item brings up a list of things you can do and also lets you rename the item.

You can move around using the arrow keys, although that disallows diagonals of course. You can use a number pad too, but note that some emulators may have trouble with it. (In another ST emulator I tested, Hatari, they worked strangely. STeem works great with it. This is one reason I focus on that emulator.) The vi-like keys used by NetHack, hjkl/yubn, work for movement too but are most useful to people already used to vi.

One fairly friendly solution is to use your mouse to move. If you click on a space adjacent to your rogue, you'll move or attack there. If you click further away, it'll fast-move you generally in that direction. Note that this form of travel doesn't make any attempt to pathfind. If you click up and to the right of your rogue, then he'll try to go diagonally up and right, even if that leads him into a wall.

Note that, other than the movement keys, the usual Rogue keys do not work. You don't 'r'ead scrolls or 'q'uaff potion, generally. The game doesn't even show you numbers for your hit points, strength or level, just green bars representing these things. Some keys that do work: Shift-Q offers to quit the game. Note especially that the period key searches—not "s"! If it doesn't say "Hmmmm" in the message window, you aren't searching.

By default, you have a "zoomed-in" view that shows the dungeon around you. You can get an overview of the whole level by clicking the diamond widget in the upper-left corner of the map window (the one that seems like it should close the window). You can also switch views with the Enter key. Experienced players may prefer to play the whole game zoomed out. While zoomed out, monsters are depicted using their

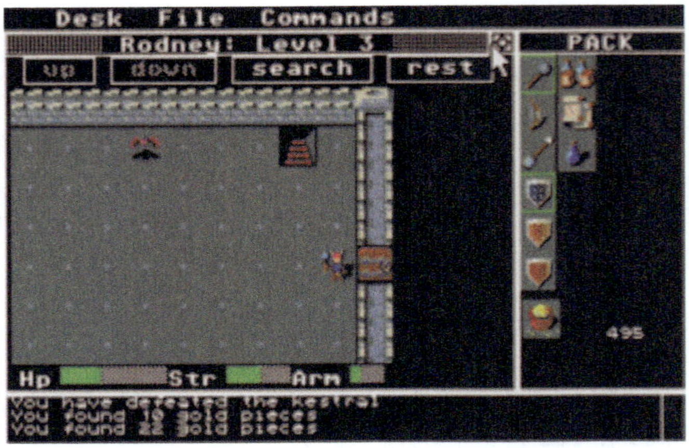

Figure 70.3

Level 1, exploring the dungeon.

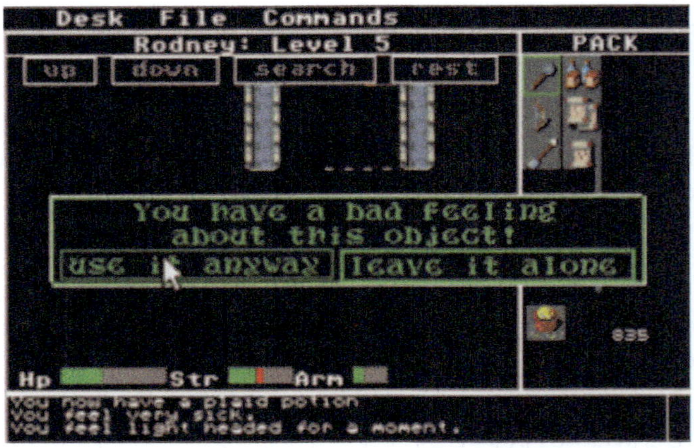

Figure 70.4

The results of a potion of discernment.

traditional letters; while zoomed in, they have graphics. If you click your inventory window it will make a corner-diamond appear; clicking on it will give more information on your possessions. To find out what something is from a distance, hold Alt and click on it. To move onto something without picking it up, hold Shift while moving.

70.3 Reasons to Play Atari ST Rogue

The primary reason to run this version of the game is that it is the one that Glenn Wichman himself wrote, and it contains a few extra features not in other versions. Additionally, as anyone who has played NetHack will discover, the images used for its graphical versions are basically swiped from the dungeon and much of the character and item artwork from ST Rogue.

In my own playing I discovered these differences. Maybe you can find more?

A new item is the "potion of discernment." When quaffed it produces the message "You feel light headed for a moment." It's an extremely useful object: it warns you if an object you're about to use is bad by producing a message like "You have a bad feeling about this object!" The effect doesn't diminish with a single warning either! I don't know how long it lasts, but it doesn't seem to be forever. Once you get the warning about an object, you might want to click on it in your inventory and name it something like "bad feeling." And note that many bad items in Rogue are actually good items if you find the right use for them . . .

Item: "Scroll of wild magic." Weirdly, using this identifies it, then gives you a confirmation prompt of whether you really want to use it, reading something like "There is something uncontrollable about this

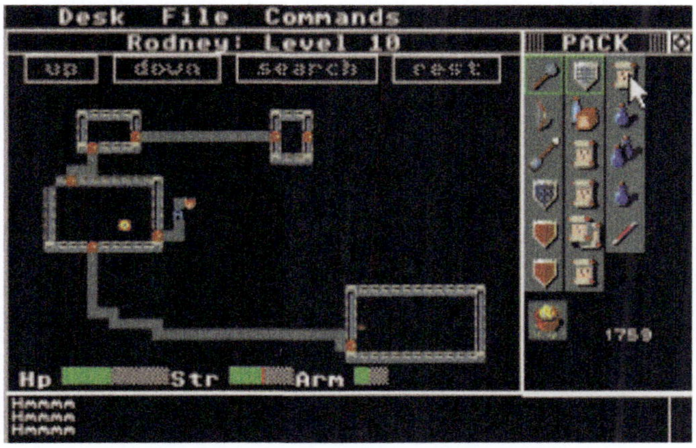

Figure 70.5

Dungeon overview.

object." I have tried using it once, and then I got the message "There is a commotion in the distance." Apparently it aggravated monsters; I was soon swarmed by foes around the level. I don't know if that's what it always does, or if it has random effects.

Scrolls of identify have been notably changed. Instead of prompting you to ID something immediately, you are instead granted "the power of identification," which manifests as an extra button on the action dialog box of items. Clicking that Identify button then identifies the object. Usually then the power goes away, but I think I caught it once offering a second ID . . .

There is a monster called the "Slime," replacing the Snake. When hit it has a chance of splitting in two. These can appear fairly early in the dungeon. It seems to be best to fight these guys in a corridor, which limits how overwhelmed you can get by them.

I vaguely remember Glenn saying something's changed about the behavior of centaurs. Myself, I've only noticed them killing me a lot, which is standard centaur protocol.

One quirk of Epyx's versions of Rogue is that, instead of a numeric "level," they assign the player a rank that amounts to the same thing, just not as clearly stated. Here are the first ranks of Epyx Rogue; see if you can get beyond them yourself. 1. No rank, 2: Guild Novice, 3: Apprentice, 4: Journeyman, 5: Adventurer, 6: Fighter, 7: Warrior, 8: Rogue, 9: Champion.

70.4 Acknowledgments

Thanks to the man himself, Glenn Wichman, and Matt Barton for help in setting up my emulation of ST Rogue!

70.5 Further Reading

Glenn Wichman's A Brief History of Rogue. As of this moment, it's preserved at www.digital-eel.com/deep/A_Brief_History_of_Rogue.htm

For more of all versions of rogue, coredumpcentral.org has a big page of versions. Roguelikedevelopment.org also has a list.

71

Rogue and Its Inspiration

September 2006 I could offer that Rogue was the second roguelike game.

I say it's the second, yes. The first one wasn't a computer game at all. It was the random dungeon rules published as Appendix A in the back of the Dungeon Master's Guide, way back in the 1st edition of Dungeons & Dragons. Ultimately, the play experience that roguelikes seek to duplicate is that of a hack-and-slash role-playing game, like those improvised sessions of D&D, and most of them are steeped in it. Hack-and-slash has come under a lot of criticism as lacking in story and character development, but a well-designed game of the type brings much more to the table than just the killing of monsters.

71.1 Foundations of the Dungeon

The 1st edition D&D books contained, within their poorly organized pages, all the information a sharp DM with a dozen bookmarks needed to improvise such a game. What room is behind this door? Roll dice to find out. Is there a trap inside? Roll for it, and which trap it is. Are there monsters, and if so what are they? Roll on the appropriate level tables. What treasure is found? Tumble those bones. There are even tables that can be used, if the DM decides, to determine what kind of decoration is on the walls.

The book admits that random determination is not usually the best way to play the game, but there is still a certain charm to those chaotic games. What made this interesting to players is that there are so many strange obstacles, and so many magic items with which to overcome them, that each game will have a wildly different character, and with good players and a better DM, many items can be put to use in such ingenious ways that there are actually not a lot of situations that cannot be overcome in some way. At its core, roguelike games seek to replicate that kind of play.

Since player ingenuity matters for so much, the developer must not shirk from the challenge of taking into account the unusual uses players might find for things. NetHack's infamous DevTeam is so good at this that rec.games.roguelike.nethack has an abbreviation for it: TDTTOE, which stands for The DevTeam Thinks Of Everything. Even the more combat-oriented roguelikes, such as Angband, tend to have some element of this.

But I'm getting off the subject. It's time to settle some misconceptions, and of the many there are in the mainstream gaming press about roguelikes, the most serious have to do with Rogue itself.

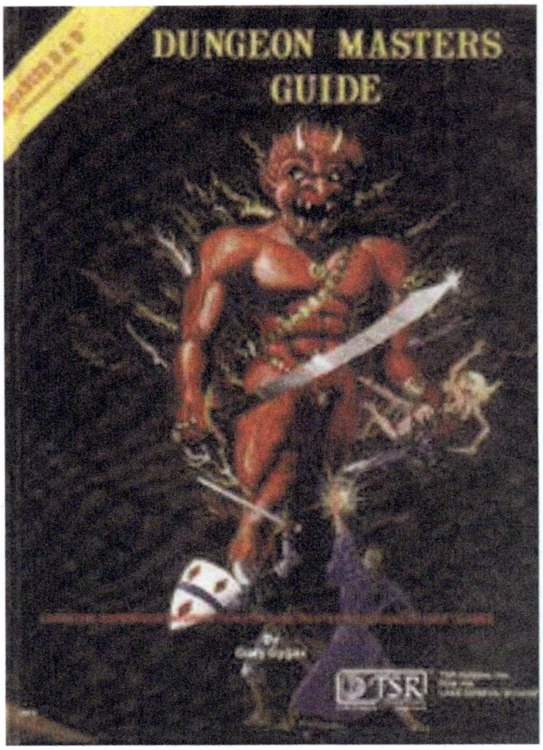

Figure 71.1

Cover of the 1st Edition (or "1E") D&D Dungeon Master's Guide.

71.2 But It's So Hard

There are still things that Rogue does better than any other game, even its descendants. Although its days of ruling the computer lab are long over, people will likely still be playing Rogue 20 years from now. While it has been around for well over two decades, there are still many interesting things about it—even when compared to other roguelikes.

Unlike many other random games that grant the player some static benefits to make up for the capriciousness of the Fates, Rogue doesn't do much to blunt the spiked edges of its random number generator. In a game of indefinite length, it's just a matter of time before there occurs a situation the player is ill-prepared to survive. The longer you live, the more likely you will die. Because of this, a properly played game of Rogue is always a search for treasure carried out at break-neck speed, where every move counts, where both ruthless monsters and the player's limited food supply drive a continual thirst for more loot. A game of Rogue that is not won as rapidly as possible is probably lost. (Well, games are probably lost in any case . . .)

The primary reasons players must be loot-happy are the 26 monsters from A to Z, the bloodthirsty residents of the Dungeons of Doom. Many of them are quite unwise to face in melee combat, no matter what level you may be. Most RPGs are balanced so that the player grows in power, through level gains and equipment, at roughly the same rate as the monsters' stats improve, so that he faces a constant level of challenge throughout. In a few games the player actually grows in power faster, especially if he's been building up his experience level and doing subquests for better equipment, so that at times final bosses seem easier than ordinary monsters faced early on.

71.3 The Subterranean Arms Race: MAD (Mutually Assured Dragons)

Distinguishing Rogue from these games, including other roguelikes, is that its monsters increase in power faster than the player improves. The player begins the game stronger than most of his opponents, but the average experience and equipment gain of the player on a given level is not enough to keep up with the increase in monster power. As the game continues this difference builds up, until near the end many monsters can wipe out a player in three, or even two, turns. Even if you were to take your time to build experience (and your food supply means you can't for long), you'll still be unlikely to survive fights deeper in the dungeon by merely pounding away at foes. Many RPGs almost seem like you could progress by taping down the "A" button, but it is impossible to win at Rogue by playing in a mindless manner. The high strength of monsters late in the game demands that players must learn to flee, or perish.

Even the weaker monsters pose serious dangers, some of them draining strength, armor and even maximum hit points when they strike. To an experienced Rogueist, it is priceless to behold the look on the face of a console RPG fan playing and discovering that, when a rattlesnake drains the player's strength, or an Aquator strikes and lowers his defense by one, that those penalties do not go away after the fight, but accumulate until a means is found to overcome them, if one is found.

In addition to the controls, this is another reason Rogue is quite formidable to new players. As with random 1st edition D&D sessions, the game is not impossible only because of the great usefulness of some of its treasure. A single scroll of scare monster, properly utilized, can allow a player to safely destroy any number of foes. A single zap from a wand of slow monster can allow even weak characters to destroy a Troll without risk. A scroll of genocide eliminates one entire species of the player's choice from the world, potentially taking care of all dragons without even having to see one. So useful are some of the things that may be found just lying on the dungeon floor that in other games they would seem unbalanced. Here, they're just right.

These factors contribute to place Rogue, even after all the years since its creation, among the most difficult roleplaying games ever made. Although most other random games take greater steps to decrease the sharp-edged chaos of their dungeons, at their core they all deal with the same issues: how much loot to give out, how fast do the monsters get tougher, and how rapidly must the player explore? Rogue's answers to these questions are a lot less conservative than players are used to.

Some versions of Rogue rank among the hardest winnable computer games ever made, so hard that many play for score, with no expectation of victory. The following statement is astounding enough to risk a descent into boldface type: *Rogue is more difficult than its successor, NetHack*. NetHack has a reputation as a player killer, but it also contains great helps if you know how to use them. Once one is aware of the true dangers, risks and resources in both games, it is obvious that Rogue is harder. In NetHack almost every game can be won, but in Rogue possible victory is never guaranteed.

Unavoidably this means Rogue is a less fair game, as a percentage of games ultimately cannot be won even with perfect play . . . but that fact doesn't dissuade people from playing Solitaire, either.

72

The Rights to Rogue

May 2009 Perhaps no genre of computer game has as close a tie to the open source community as the roguelikes. Eric S. Raymond, noted open source booster, both wrote the guidebook to an earlier version of NetHack and the oft-cited argument for open software, The Cathedral and the Bazaar, in which NetHack is mentioned.

Angband's source is so open that it's become one of the most-permuted computer games of all time. Linley's Dungeon Crawl picked up new life when the Stone Soup guys started developing their variant, which is now recognized as pretty much the premier version of the game. And nearly all of the 7DRLs are open source.

An interested observer could be forgiven for assuming all roguelikes must be open, but they aren't. None of the Japanese commercial roguelikes are. The source code of one of the big ones, ADOM, remains closed.

But the first closed source roguelike is the first of all of them.

A recent article over at Gamasutra, "The History of Rogue: Have @ You, Deadly Zs" (which, despite the hokey title, I did not write) attracted a fair number of comments from people involved with the development of the original game, including Ken Arnold and Glenn Wichman, two out of the three original Rogue guys.

The information in the article's comments, which are fascinating, go as follows:

1. Rogue was, and is, copyrighted by the Regents of the University of California, with the justification that the game was developed on their computers. Whether that rationale would suffice to day I don't know; most commercial software these days is owned by the developing studio under, if I remember correctly, the principle of work-for-hire.

   But the developers were not concerned with it. The game continues to be distributed with BSD Unix, but unlike most of the other parts of the system, the source code is not shipped with it. The reason they gave for keeping it secret was to prevent people from source-diving to discover the game's secrets. Such diving is the main reason NetHack's so thoroughly spoiled now, and Rogue, being a much simpler game, would be more easily harmed by this inspection. (Although the game is also more resistant to spoiling, since it has fewer tricks.)

   It also hindered player efforts to hack save files, high score lists and the wizard's password. To continue the comparison with NetHack: it contains considerable save file tamper protection, it doesn't bother protecting its score list, and access to its wizard mode can be compiled out of the game.

Ken Arnold notes that at the time of the height of Rogue's popularity, Richard Stallman had yet to start the GNU project, upon which Linux and most of the current open source movement is based. Open source was just a vague notion floating around, not a legitimate movement yet.

This probably explains why Linux distributions make it available in a special extra non-free supplement to the bsdgames package (called bsdgames-nonfree, natch), although to produce that package they probably have the source code form somewhere. BSD's license was eventually opened, according to Andrew Grillet, since U.S. taxpayers ultimately funded it.

David Dingwall notes that Rogue's source, once escaped into the wild, quickly suffused the user communities for both BSD and AT&T versions of Unix, and that it was even backported to older versions of BSD running on PDP11s. He also notes the spread of Rog-O-Matic, the first roguelike "bot" and predecessor of Ben Harrison's Angband Borg.

2. The source code then escaped. Several possible incidents are reported in the comments about when this occurred. A student used an open terminal logged into the games account, and the source was accidentally left world-readable one day. They were then spread around between systems.

   These inadvertent source releases could also be the origins of some of the code in the "lost roguelikes" (Advanced Rogue, XRogue, Super-Rogue and others) which are all fairly close to Rogue in many of their features, but many of them could also just be reimplementations.

3. When the developers of Rogue reimplemented it and attempted to sell it for home computers, first under the name A.I. Design, then when they granted a distribution license to fondly remembered classic games company Epyx, they had another reason to horde the code: to preserve their commercial rights to the game.

   The game didn't do well in the market, perhaps because of a high piracy rate, although the authors of the article doubt it. (And so do I, for that matter.) Ken Arnold states that if he wrote it now, he'd go ahead and publish the source. (He does have the source of the most recent version of the game up at Sourceforge.)

   Mastertronic also released some versions for various computers, including the Commodore 64. I have no information on how they obtained the rights.

   That's from the Gamasutra comments. Here is more information, gathered from other sources:

4. There is a game called "Rogue Clone" out there that is definitely open source. It's an independent close reimplementation of Rogue and pretty much the same in most ways I've noticed. It may be a little easier; I've had multiple wins at Rogue Clone IV, but I've never won PC Rogue without cheating.
5. The "lost roguelikes," Advanced Rogue, Super-Rogue, UltraRogue and XRogue, as well as versions of the original game's source, are available from the online/offline Roguelike Restoration Project. They were also closed source for a long time, and have only recently been recovered and made working again.

   Advanced Rogue's copyright notice states that AT&T is one of the copyright holders. This may be due to confusion over who owned the rights to Rogue; BSD Unix contained some AT&T code, and so BSD carried an AT&T copyright notice in addition to one held by the Regents of the University of California.

6. The game Hexrogue is a recreation of Rogue in Java using a hexagonal grid instead of a rectangular one. It also supplies two modes that are more like the original game, Newer Rogue and Old Rogue. These are also open.
7. There was also a Japanese version of the game, for early computers over there. The developer of that version seems to have authorized the Japan-only PS2 remake Rogue Hearts Dungeon. I suspect that these versions are not authorized by Rogue's creators. In any case, they do not seem to be open.

72.1 Other Facts of Possible Interest

- The wizard's password for the original versions of Rogue, according to Ken Arnold, is "cute, huh."
- The article shows a close-up image of the graphics from Glenn Wichman's Atari ST port of Rogue that makes it plain that NetHack's dungeon graphics are taken more-or-less directly from it, or at least greatly inspired by it.

72.2 Sources

Gamasutra: Have At You, Deadly Zs: www.gamasutra.com/view/feature/4013/the_history_of_rogue_have__you_.php

Hexrogue: www.hexatron.com/hexrogue/index.html

The 7DRL page at RogueBasin: www.roguebasin.com/index.php?title=Seven_Day_Roguelike_Challenge

The Cathedral and the Bazaar: www.catb.org/esr/writings/cathedral-bazaar/

The files of the Roguelike Restoration Project: https://sourceforge.net/projects/roguelike/

The source code to Rogue: https://sourceforge.net/projects/rogue/

73

Some Recent Information

January 2020 The chapters in this book were begun way back in 2006, and the roguelike genre moves at a strange mix of rapid and slow. Thus, much information among these chapters is still good, but some may be a bit outdated. While I have attempted to update the chapters, this chapter is here to update the book a bit more explicitly for the start of a new decade.

When the NetHack chapters were originally written, the newest version of the vanilla game was 3.4.3, a venerable version that was current longer than any other, including 3.1.3, the previous champion. 3.4.3 was the current version for so long that many observers had assumed the game was no longer being worked on; one variant released this time was even named by its author NetHack 4.

Then, on December 7, 2015, the DevTeam broke their 12-year silence and finally released NetHack 3.6.0. (Version 3.5.0, an incomplete version of 3.6.0, was leaked before its release, so the DevTeam skipped that number to avoid confusion with it.) It is another incremental improvement, along the line of previous minor version improvements, of the same general version of the game as 3.1.0, the dawn of "modern" NetHack. The most recent of these, as of this writing, is 3.6.4, released on December 18, 2019. More information on versions can be gained from the Game History page of the NetHack Wiki.

A lot of the code was cleaned up in 3.6.0 to make later improvements easier to create. The news that the game was still being worked on, plus the codebase cleanup, may explain the plethora of new variants that came about around this time. Older variants like UnNetHack, GruntHack and SporkHack were joined by SLASH'EM Extended, xNetHack, SpliceHack, EvilHack and more, of varying levels of challenge and ludicrousness. An overview of such variants is available on the NetHack Wiki. Many of these versions address what were considered long-standing problems with the game, such as it becoming too easy later on for experienced players and the monotony of the mazes of Gehennom.

Popular public NetHack server alt.org increased further in prominence and was joined by Hardfought (www.hardfought.org/), which hosts many of the variants listed above, including, new as of this writing, a preview version of official NetHack 3.7.0.

Of important note. Sometimes in the past I may have been heard complaining that, while the DevTeam obeys the letter of open source, through their secretiveness they may have been missing a bit of its spirit, often spending many years between releases, grabbing features from and maintainers of popular variants, both of which would then vanish in a cloud of obscurity, and generally not saying much in public except through occasional Usenet posts and rare releases. This has certainly changed; the DevTeam is a bit more communicative these days, and even maintains a public github repository (https://github.com/NetHack/NetHack).

Popular yearly NetHack tournament dev/null, considered by some the oldest still-running continual yearly game tournament on the internet (the one referred to in an interview in this book), finally shut down in 2016 after 18 years. It continues in memory on Hardfought as their November NetHack Tournament. Another popular yearly tournament, Junethack, which focuses on variants, continues.

Angband isn't as prominent a game as before, but continues bearing a sizable fanbase. ADOM developer Thomas Biskup has debuted his game for sale on Steam, where it has cool graphics! Also on Steam are two new and highly interesting games, Caves of Qud and Cogmind. And Bay 12 Games' incredible Dwarf Fortress continues getting sporadic updates, with the word being that it's preparing for its own release on Steam.

Speaking of Steam. Since the years most of these chapters were written, there has been an explosion of games calling themselves *roguelikes*. I've already mentioned them and how many probably should be instead called roguelites, but that doesn't mean that many of them aren't extremely interesting. Spelunky, possibly the best known of them all, was a sensation to many and a revelation to some. A bit after its original freeware release came The Binding of Isaac, and after that The Binding of Isaac Rebirth, inaugurating the subgenre of the roguelite dual-stick shooter. Particular prominent examples of this include the terrific games Nuclear Throne and Enter the Gungeon, among many others. On the very edges of the genre are randomly generated platformers like Rogue Legacy and, more recently, A Robot Called Fight. There's also Tumbleseed, which is difficult to classify, but is kind of like a roguelite variant of the classic mechanical arcade game Ice Cold Beer.

The rise of gamejams as a means of novice and amateur developers to test the waters of new game concepts, both developmentally and popularly, has helped to fuel a boom of indie game development that has helped to carry aloft the roguelike banner. One of the earliest of these was the Seven Day RogueLike, or 7DRL, Challenge, which right now has been going for 14 years. Throughout its history it has produced over a thousand games, many of which are great, such as the consistently awesome works of Jeff Lait. If you go through the new creations each year, you will invariably find a handful of games of which you've never seen anything the like.

These days, many people who can't, or won't, play video games still manage to enjoy them by watching the efforts of streamers, on Twitch, YouTube and other places, and Let's Players, often on YouTube. Some very good players have come to prominence this way, such as legendary Spelunky player Bananasaurus Rex. Roguelikes and roguelites are a popular fuel for these streamers, considering that they are random and seek to provide new experiences on each play.

I know of two prominent roguelike development conferences. From 2008 to 2017 there was the IRDC, the International Roguelike Development Conference; I myself managed to attend the one in 2015. The first of these gave birth to the popular Berlin Interpretation yardstick for determining roguelikeness. For the past four years (2016–2019) there has been Roguelike Celebration in San Francisco, and a new one due this year in 2020. In its halls have been seen Tarn Adams of Dwarf Fortress, Thomas Biskup of ADOM, and even some less likely attendees and presenters such as Kingdom of Loathing's Zach Johnson.

That brings us to the end of this book, but by no means the end of the genre. Now, even more than in its humble origins in a university computer room, the shadow of Rogue casts further and darker than ever before. In its inky depths spawn dangerous monsters, true, but also wondrous treasure. Take up shield and sword, daring adventurer, and go explore!

Index

B

C

D

E

F

G

H

M

P

Q

R

S

T

X

Y

Z

9780367482596